Treat this book with care and

*It should become part of your personal
and professional library. It will
serve you well at any number
of points during your
professional career.*

INFORMATION SYSTEMS FOR OPERATIONS AND MANAGEMENT

Dan Voich, Jr.
Professor of Management
Florida State University

Homer J. Mottice
Professor of Accounting
Florida State University

William A. Shrode
Professor of Management
Florida State University

Published by

G33   **SOUTH-WESTERN PUBLISHING CO.**

CINCINNATI   WEST CHICAGO, ILL.   DALLAS   PELHAM MANOR, N.Y.
PALO ALTO, CALIF.   BRIGHTON, ENGLAND

ISBN: 0-538-07330-6

Library of Congress Catalog Card Number: 74-79992

3 4 5 Ki 9 8 7

Printed in the United States of America

PREFACE

Information is a fundamental resource of an organization. Managers need information to define goals and to guide the operations of the organization so as to bring about the achievement of goals effectively and harmoniously. Managers use information to make plans, to communicate plans to subordinates, to coordinate their execution, and to insure that plans are executed properly. Managers also need information about their customers, suppliers, and the environment to redefine goals and alter plans.

To provide this information, parallel developments in decision making and information processing have occurred. Organizations now invest considerable resources in staff specialists who are responsible for providing top management with better and more timely information flows and for developing more effective planning and control. One major feature of these planning and control concepts is that they attempt to analyze and evaluate operations and management within a general framework of systems theory; the organization is viewed as a set of interrelated decisions, functions, activities, tasks, and resource flows. A second feature of these planning and control concepts is that they require comprehensive yet flexible types of information about the organization's operations and management within a changing environment.

While information provides a means for the organization to survive, grow, and prosper in an uncertain future environment, the design, implementation, and monitoring of large-scale information systems suggested by more advanced planning and control concepts are becoming major capital investment decisions. Because of this, there is a need to manage the information function in a large organization, just as the organization manages its materials, personnel, financial, distribution, and other major functions.

Within this environment of increasing needs for and costs of information, the authors' purpose in this book is to present basic concepts for the effective management of the information function in an organization. Important concepts of systems theory and analysis are explained and illustrated in a context that enables the reader to understand and apply them in the design, implementation, and monitoring of an information system for operations and management. The analytical framework used in this book views information both as a process of transforming data into information and as a facilitator for the performance of the basic functions of the management process. Basic information needs to facilitate planning, operational control, and managerial/financial control are defined through the analysis of a series of operational decisions, functions, activities, work, and resource flows that take place in an organization. These basic types of information provide the basis for designing the transformation processes needed to produce reports for operations and management.

A major feature of the analytical framework used in this book is its objective-user orientation in defining information needs. In order to effectively serve a large variety of users of information, the information system must be able to generate a large variety of information that can be interrelated in a number of ways, for example, by management function, by product, by resource, by organizational responsibility center, and for special analyses. The information system's purpose is thus to provide operations and management with information for multiple needs, information that directly supports internal operations yet that can also be used for external reporting requirements.

A second major feature of the analytical framework used in this book is its capability of assembling, interrelating, and transforming a large variety of input data from many basic source documents. With the aid of a comprehensive data coding system, data base, and computerized data processor as described in this book, many of the data inputs can be used to build the multiple data flows required without developing an excessive number of special purpose feeder reports or separate information systems.

A third major feature of the analytical framework is the provision for an emphasis on management of the information function and its information processing activities and responsibilities. This involves centralized design, monitoring, and control of proposed and existing information flows at the top management level because of the importance of the information function to the organization in terms of its potential benefits and the large investment it requires.

These three features, objective-user orientation, integration of information processes, and management of the information function, are explained and illustrated in the first four parts of the book. Part 5 presents and illustrates a number of more advanced planning and control informational concepts and techniques needed by larger and more complex organizations.

The treatment of all topics is at a basic introductory level, suitable for the first course of information systems at the undergraduate level. End of chapter review questions and student exercises provide opportunities for students to apply the concepts presented in each chapter. The advanced information concepts for planning and control presented in Part 5, coupled with the comprehensive cases included at the end of the book, can be utilized in those classes which want to emphasize case analysis to a greater extent. With the use of supplementary readings, and placing more emphasis on application of concepts presented in the text to the design of information systems for larger and more complex organizations, the book is suitable for an introductory course in information systems at the graduate level.

We wish to acknowledge the many individuals who have reviewed the manuscript and provided valuable suggestions and comments. We especially acknowledge the valuable comments, insights, and case materials provided by Raymond Thompson, Sharon Johnson, and Robert Sharp.

CONTENTS

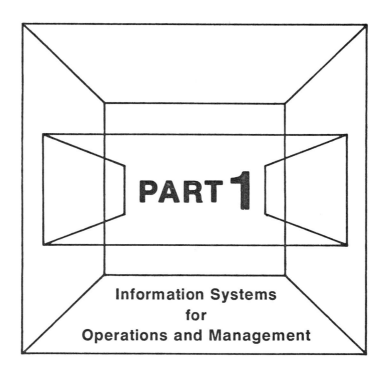

PART 1

**Information Systems
for
Operations and Management**

1 INTRODUCTION TO INFORMATION FOR MANAGEMENT

Information is a fundamental resource of an organization. It is so essential to the operations and management of an organization that it is often justifiably referred to as the "life blood of the organization," the "fabric of an organization," or the "agent for sustaining organizational viability." Managers need information to define goals and to guide the operations of the organization so as to bring about the effective and harmonious achievement of these goals. Managers use information to formulate plans, to communicate the plans to subordinates, to coordinate the eventual execution of plans, and to establish whether the execution is proceeding satisfactorily. Managers also need continual flow of information about their customers, their suppliers, and the environment in order to redefine goals and alter plans when a shift in the environment makes such action necessary.

For example, the manager of a clothing store assembles the following information: sales and inventories of his various clothing lines, next season's fashions, population growth, and income level shifts in his market area. He uses this information in defining sales goals for the next clothing season. Additionally, his decisions on purchases of fashions and price lines are based on this market information. Subsequently, suppliers of clothing are contacted in order to determine their ability to provide the fashions and price lines appropriate to the volume and delivery requirements of the store. Advertising and sales promotion programs are developed to reflect the goals, fashions, price lines, and time of arrival of merchandise. Specific sales quotas, policies, procedures, and merchandise information are communicated to salesmen to serve as guidelines for their contacts with customers. During and after the clothing season, information is compiled on sales volumes by fashion and price lines, performance of salesmen, and profitability of the sales program. This information is used in the development of goals and plans for the next clothing season when the cycle begins again.

This book is about *processing* and *using* information for the operation and management of organizations. Information must be systematically processed in order for it to be effective for managing an organization. An information system capable of doing such processing and developed specifically to assist in managing is called a *management information system* (MIS). The MIS should provide the *necessary* information at the proper *time* and *place* so as to enable the effective management of all facets of an organization. The complete MIS comprises special-purpose information systems integrated into a single unified framework. This means that the individual information systems, such as payroll, manpower, inventory, sales-receivables, purchases-payables, and forecasting are combined. Since each is a system, the resulting MIS is a system of systems.

The first two chapters of this book introduce its two major topics: *how information is used* and *how it is processed*. In this chapter, the general nature of information and its uses for facilitating management are described. In addition, the changing nature of organizations, their management, and the impact of developments in information technology on organizations are considered in relation to how the information needs of management are changing. Chapter 2 describes the nature, scope, and purpose of an integrated MIS.

THE NATURE OF INFORMATION

Although information is a commonly used term, it is, as we shall see, a relatively complex subject. *Webster's* defines information as: (1) the "act or process of informing." and (2) "that which is received or obtained through the information process." In other words, information can be regarded both as a process and as the output of that process. In an organizational setting, the former definition refers to the "information processing function," while the latter definition refers to the use of information in facilitating operations and management, i.e., a "facilitating function" which is related but parallel to the information processing function. Both ideas are more fully explained in the following sections.

Information as a Process

The information process can be viewed as the transformation of raw data into information. Viewing information as a process highlights two basic concepts: data and transformation of data into information. *Data* is generally interpreted as unstructured facts that have been acquired from direct observation, experimentation, or historical review. Data represents potential information. Only when data has been transformed and restructured via the information process does it become information.

The *transformation* of data into information can be a mental, manual, or automated process. In the first case, the process is referred to as reasoning, and the output of this is usually called knowledge rather than information. The reasoning process is excluded from further consideration in this book because it is not yet applicable to computerization in a practical sense, and because this book is limited to information processing as it directly supports the formal functions of management.[1]

In the case of manual and automated processing of data, the transformation process actually consists of a set of activities. These include:

---

[1] Research is presently being conducted in the area of *artificial intelligence*; i.e., thinking and reasoning by a computer. This may eventually be commercially practical. For example, see Julius S. Aronofsky (ed.), *Progress in Operations Research* (New York: John Wiley & Sons, 1969), III, 50-51.

1. *Recording*—Identifying and transcribing data about events or transactions; e.g., sale of a product, purchase of a material, payment of a bill, and production of a product.
2. *Classifying*—Encoding data on events or transactions by major types, e.g., sales by salesman and material purchases by type of material.
3. *Sorting*—Screening, segmenting, and compiling encoded data on events and transactions into categories; e.g., identifying and compiling sales made by each salesman and purchases by type of material.
4. *Calculating*—Adding, subtracting, multiplying, dividing, comparing, arranging, etc., transaction data; e.g., computing total sales volume for each salesman during the month or total purchases of types of materials each month.
5. *Summarizing*—Arranging transaction data and related calculations into report format; e.g., developing a sales performance report for each salesman or a material status report for each type of material.
6. *Storing*—Holding transaction data or summarized data temporarily or permanently, as needed; e.g., as a matter of official record or for use in later reporting periods.
7. *Retrieving*—File searching or scanning of stored data to perform additional calculations or to update data on file; e.g., identification of all sales transactions recorded during a period.
8. *Reproducing*—Printing or developing reports; e.g., sales performance reports or materials status reports.
9. *Distributing*—Moving reports to users of information; e.g., to sales manager or procurement manager.

Any information processing situation involves at least one and usually more of the above activities. For example, consider the preparation of a university catalog prepared to provide information to applicants. The information process that might typically be employed is:

INPUT	INFORMATION PROCESS	OUTPUT
Facts about the academic programs, services, and facilities of the university	Sorting Summarizing Reproducing Distributing	A university catalog containing information on degree options, courses offered, tuition, living accommodations, etc.

Other examples of the information process appear at the top of page 5.

It is useful to view information as a process when analyzing and evaluating its outputs. Data that is used to produce a report should be evaluated to determine whether it is relevant, accurate, and complete in terms of the purpose of the report. For example, a complete course grade should include all relevant measures of a student's performance which indicate how much he has learned in the course. This may require more than just exam scores. Analysis may also reveal that a measure used in determining the course grade is not significantly related to the amount of

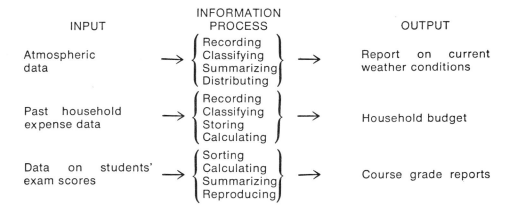

INPUT	INFORMATION PROCESS	OUTPUT
Atmospheric data	→ { Recording, Classifying, Summarizing, Distributing } →	Report on current weather conditions
Past household expense data	→ { Recording, Classifying, Storing, Calculating } →	Household budget
Data on students' exam scores	→ { Sorting, Calculating, Summarizing, Reproducing } →	Course grade reports

knowledge acquired in the course and hence should not be used. Also, it is necessary that the systems analyst clearly define and specify what processing activities are required to transform particular raw data into information which has the desired reliability and timeliness.

Information as the Output of the Information Process

There are numerous definitions of information pertaining to it as the output of a process, such as:

1. The raw material for thinking, decisioning, problem-solving, and all the specifically human activities that concern us about our own psychological functioning and the behavior of people.[2]
2. *Evaluated data* in a specific situation.[3]
3. Knowledge derived from the organization and analysis of data . . . data that are useful in achieving the objectives of the business.[4]

Viewing information as the output of the information process highlights the "purpose" of the information, rather than its "processing" aspects. In a general sense the reason for acquiring information is to reduce uncertainty. The following quotations illustrate this idea:

The (amount of) information I obtain when you say something to me corresponds to the amount of uncertainty I had previous to your speaking, of what you were going to say. If I was certain of what you were going to say, I obtained no information from your saying it.[5]

---

[2] Lee Thayer, *Communication and Communication Systems: In Organization, Management, and Interpersonal Relations* (Homewood, Ill.: Richard D. Irwin, 1968), pp. 18-19.

[3] Adrian M. McDonough, *Information Economics and Management Systems* (New York: McGraw-Hill Book Co., 1963), p. 71.

[4] Howard S. Levin, *Office Work and Automation* (New York: John Wiley & Sons 1956), p. 122.

[5] Claude E. Shannon and Warren Weaver (eds.), *The Mathematical Theory of Communication* (Urbana: University of Illinois Press, 1949), p. 7.

As information about a system increases, uncertainty about it decreases, and so information is the negative of uncertainty. When uncertainty about it is zero, no further information about it can be received.[6]

A more precise definition and model of information can be constructed from all the foregoing ideas about the nature of information. Information can be defined as *data which after transformation via the information process reduces uncertainty related to the outcome of a particular problem, event, or activity*. This definition is reflected in the following schematic model:

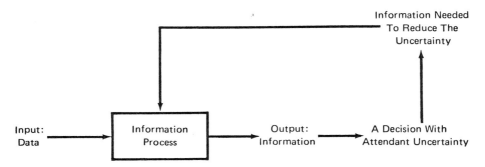

The need for information to reduce an uncertainty activates the information process as it provides the basis for defining what information must be produced and consequently what data must be input. For example, consider the case of an individual faced with the decision regarding which university to attend. This and other situations are illustrated in Exhibit 1-1.

The examples in Exhibit 1-1 illustrate the point that as information is produced relating to a problem, event, or activity, decisions can be made on the basis of some reduced levels of uncertainty about the future. As more information is produced concerning a problem, event, or activity, additional uncertainty reduction occurs. For example, the problem of whether or not to buy a new car may have been decided differently if additional information had been obtained which indicated a high probability of receiving a salary increase during the year. Also, additional information on expected changes in state tuition rates may have altered the selection of a university.

THE FUNCTIONS OF INFORMATION FOR MANAGEMENT

Thus far, information has been viewed broadly as (1) a processing function, and (2) a facilitating function parallel to the processing function. Generally the purpose of these functions of information has been considered to be the reducing of some uncertainty related to a problem, event, or activity. This section describes the facilitating function of *organizational information* as it serves to reduce the uncertainty encountered in the performance of the various functions which comprise the process of management.

---

[6] Gordon Pask, *An Approach to Cybernetics* (London: Hutchinson & Co., 1961), pp. 26-27

Exhibit 1-1

INFORMATION USED TO REDUCE UNCERTAINTY

INPUT DATA	INFORMATION PROCESS	OUTPUT INFORMATION	NATURE OF THE DECISION UNCERTAINTY	NEW STATE OF REDUCED UNCERTAINTY
Facts about university programs, faculty, and productivity of graduates		University catalog →	Uncertainty over which university to attend →	Of all candidates, "State University" seems best suited.
Atmospheric data	Appropriate combinations of information processing activities	Report on weather conditions →	Uncertainty over whether a trip to the beach will be worthwhile →	Yes, indications are that weather will be favorable.
Household expense data		Household budget →	Uncertainty over whether the family should buy a new car this year. →	No, indications are that all uncommitted funds will be needed for home maintenance.
Students' exam scores		Course grade reports →	Uncertainty over whether all students passed the course →	Yes, all score averages are above the cutoff.

There are a number of ways to classify the functions that make up the management process. One group of management functions deals with planning in general and is oriented to the future. Basic management texts traditionally list planning, budgeting, designing of work systems, organizing, and staffing as the constituents of this group. A second group of functions deals with the implementation of plans, designs, and decisions concerning the commitment of resources in a current and ongoing situation. Directing, coordinating, commanding, actuating, and leading are some of the functions traditionally specified. A third group of functions involves analysis of financial and managerial performance and is ex post oriented. Controlling, reporting, and replanning are commonly identified as of this type.

This book utilizes a classification of management functions that is closely related to the above major groupings. They are: *planning, operational control,* and *managerial/financial control.* This classification has considerable similarity to the Anthony classification of the three types of major problems organizations regularly face:[7]

1. *Strategic Planning* is the process of deciding on objectives of the organization, on changes in these objectives, on the resources used to attain these objectives, on the policies used to attain these objectives, and on the policies that are to govern the acquisition, use, and disposition of these resources.

2. *Management Control* is the process by which managers assure that resources are obtained and used effectively and efficiently in the accomplishment of the organization's objectives.

3. *Operational Control* is the process of assuring that specific tasks are carried out efficiently and effectively.

In our framework the planning function encompasses both strategic and operational planning. Operational control is somewhat analogous to Anthony's definition of this function. Managerial/financial control encompasses the control and evaluation of managerial performance, and it also includes the financial evaluation of organizational performance for interested external parties. Specifically, then, information is required in an organization in order to facilitate and even make possible the fundamental functions of planning, operational control, and managerial/financial control.

Information for Planning

Information for planning supports problem solving and decision making concerning the design of the organization's future structure, facilities, and operations on a periodic basis. The planning function involves a preoperating analysis which deals with defining objectives, forecasting demand, committing resources, and budgeting funds. In this context information is required to define and to evaluate these alternative objectives, resource allocation

---

[7] Robert N. Anthony, *Planning and Control Systems: A Framework for Analysis* (Boston: Harvard Business School, 1965), pp. 16-18.

patterns, and policies. Only information can provide the means for comparing the expected relative costs and benefits of various operating alternatives and can serve as the basis for optimal selection.

For example, various pieces of demand information such as population size, consumer income, and consumer propensity to spend are compiled and evaluated. From this, a projection of product demand is made. This projection of demand is compared with the organization's production capability as determined by analysis of information on available resources, technical ability, and managerial competence. By merging the results of these analyses, decisions are made concerning the specific operational objectives, sales forecasts, budgets, work statements, schedules of performance, and quality standards for future operating periods. Thus the future direction of the organization is defined and the supporting structure, facilities, and operations are designed, none of which could have been accomplished without the basic planning information.

Information for Operational Control

The use of information for operational control is communicative in nature. Information is the means for conveying objectives, plans, policies, and procedures to all segments of the organization. Such information directly supports the coordination of operating performance in a current day-to-day ongoing process. Operational control involves a continual insuring that the operations of the organization are being carried out as planned. It includes coordination of the individual efforts of those involved in group tasks and the regulation of resource and work flows among the different work groups. n its operational control context, information serves both as a *process activator* by communicating requirements to each group and as a *feedback mechanism* by providing a basis upon which to determine whether requirements were received, understood, and carried out.

Examples of information as a process activator are: a work statement as a guide for performing a job; a material specification as the basis for a purchasing agent to buy a certain material; a budget as an authorization to use specific resource quantities; and a quality standard as the basis to make a decision to accept or reject a shipment of material. Examples of feedback information include budget variance reports, schedule slippage reports, consumer complaints, and employee grievances.

Information also links the organization with its environment. Consumers' use and performance requirements for the organization's products must be defined, translated, and communicated to the organization's internal segments responsible for design and production. For example, a customer order for an automobile, a blue convertible with full power and air conditioning, must be translated into engineering and production specifications in order for it to be produced by the assembly line. As another example, an organization may acquire information about consumer apprehension concerning the use of phosphates in detergents. This will be interpreted and decisions may be made to change the ingredients used in its detergent products.

Similarly, organizational resource requirements must be communicated to appropriate sources of supply. For example, material specifications for new or changed product lines are developed into purchase requisitions, and this information is conveyed to suppliers in the form of requests for bids. As another example, information about a new direct-mail advertising brochure must be prepared and clearly arranged so that printing firms can bid on and produce the advertising materials in the form, number, and time desired by the organization.

Information for Managerial/Financial Control

Information used for managerial/financial control supports the analysis of past operations and performance on a periodic rather than a continuous basis. Managerial/financial control involves postoperating analysis and evaluation of performance. In this context information is used to measure and evaluate financial results of operations, management, and the organization in relation to its goals, plans, budgets, and standards of performance. This type of information may result in corrective action and replanning, i.e., revising goals, plans, budgets, and standards for the next operating period.

Managerial/financial control information provides feedback to various levels of management about the performance of responsibility center directors. For example, the actual versus projected volume of sales for each sales region is a type of information used by the national sales manager to evaluate the performances of his regional sales managers. Also, the actual versus projected labor costs per unit of product produced during an operating period is information useful to the vice-president of production who must evaluate the effectiveness of his production superintendent.

Income statements, balance sheets, and other financial reports dealing with profitability and liquidity of the total organization are information produced because certain external parties, e.g., investors, stockholders, and money lenders, must have such information in order to evaluate the propriety of their relationships with the organization. Legal-financial reports such as tax reports, employee witholding statements, and information for the Securities and Exchange Commission are part of the information set associated with the managerial/financial control function.

To summarize, the general facilitating function of organizational information reduces the uncertainty inherent in the performance of the planning, operational control, and managerial/financial control functions of management. The types of information discussed here may be seen to have design, communicative, and analytical purposes within a preoperating, operating, and postoperating framework. This is illustrated schematically in Exhibit 1-2.

The functions of management are interrelated and cyclic in nature, i.e., planning leads to operations which require control, which initiates replanning, and the cycle begins again. Similarly, the types of information utilized

Exhibit 1-2

INFORMATION AND THE MANAGEMENT CYCLE

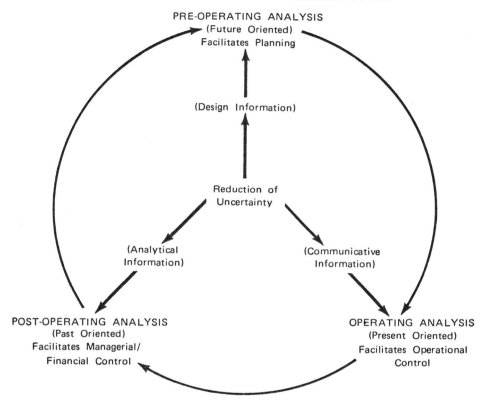

in design, communications, and analysis are interrelated and cyclic as they facilitate the performance of planning, operational control, and managerial/financial control. These types of interrelationships are the essence of management in a viable organization.

THE EXPANDING ROLE OF ORGANIZATIONAL INFORMATION

The basic need for information in an organization is certainly nothing new. However, during the last 25 years the role of organizational information and the formalized use and processing of information have expanded at a phenomenal rate. The reasons for such growth include: (1) the rapid growth in size and complexity of organizations and their environments, (2) proliferation of staff groups within large organizations, (3) improvements in planning and control techniques, and (4) improvements in information technology.

Growth in Organizational Size and Complexity

Business, educational, and governmental organizations have been increasing in size over the past several decades at an extremely rapid rate. This growth has resulted from, among other things, population growth and technological innovation.

Population growth has had perhaps the greatest impact in the field of education. There are now more than 2,000 four-year colleges and universities in the United States with an enrollment of about 10 million students. Some of the larger universities have over 100,000 students. Even if the current trends in population growth and emphasis on higher education do not continue to accelerate as they have in the last several years, large and complex educational organizations seem to be here to stay.

Population growth and technological innovation have also had a marked impact upon the size of business organizations. Increased demand for new products and services, together with the technological capability and financial means to produce and purchase them, have resulted in the establishment of a multitude of corporate giants. For instance, General Motors now has over 775,000 employees using materials and parts from over 40,000 suppliers for a variety of products sold by thousands of independent businesses. Although there are antitrust laws which limit such growth and enhance competition, most industries in the United States today include large multibillion dollar corporations.

The growth in size of governmental organizations has been beyond most expectations. The federal government alone now employs approximately three million people. State and local governments collectively employ approximately 10 million people. In contrast, 50 years ago the federal government employed just a half million people and state and local governments employed only 2.5 million people. This represents a six-fold increase in the number of federal government employees and a four-fold increase in state and local government employees over the past five decades. Although growth in the federal government has occurred for the most part in existing departments and agencies, it encompasses the birth of some new organizations as well, such as the National Aeronautics and Space Administration and the Environmental Protection Agency.

In addition to size, organizations also have grown in complexity. As they have expanded, many business organizations have diversified their product lines and decentralized their production and distribution operation geographically. To be more responsive to the educational needs of a growing society, most colleges and universities now offer a variety of academic programs at different levels, and many of the larger state universities have regional or branch campuses. With growth and diversification typically come added specialization and differentiation, conditions which require more effective cooperation among individuals and closer coordination of activities. Unfortunately, cooperative effort is seldom complete and is usually sprinkled with conflict, which leads to inefficiency and makes the tasks of management considerably more difficult.

The greater complexity and size of organizations have had pronounced effects on management's need for information, both internal-based and external-based types. Large-scale operations, conducted by a huge organized work force, demand a great deal of internally generated information. The vast decentralization of operations requires much additional internal information so as to allow for overall control of the organization from the centralized headquarters. External information also plays a more important role. Growing public concern over the social responsibility of business firms, the relevance of academic programs, and the costs of governmental programs and services has increased the flows of information into and out of organizations. In the main, the flows have dealt with society's informative and regulative demands. More rigorous tax laws and new legislation on ecology and consumer protection are examples of such increasing demands upon organizations to provide a richer stream of information to the government and to society in general.

Proliferation of Staff

Organizations are traditionally made up of line units that carry out the organization's primary purpose and staff units that advise and assist the line units. In manufacturing organizations, production and sales are examples of line units, while personnel and accounting are examples of staff units. In universities, the academic departments and schools, such as chemistry or business, are line units, while the library and the computer center are staff units. The management structure of an organization is likewise made up of line and staff managers.

As an organization grows and becomes more complex, the responsibilities of each line manager tend to increase, and a larger portion of his time is devoted to directing and coordinating the activities of his subordinates. Consequently, he usually comes to depend more upon staff units to assist him in providing the information needed in carrying out his primary managerial functions such as planning and control. The result of this increased dependence is almost invariably a proliferation of staff units and activities. Some examples of the many different types of staff groups which may be created for the purpose of generating planning and control information needed by management are:

Controller	Operations Research
Internal Audit	Personnel
Management Audit	Materials Planning and Control
Forms and Records Control	Long-range Planning
Market Research	Facilities Planning

As staff groups grow in number, size, and influence, competition among their managers for authority over specific staff functions often occurs. Thus, it becomes difficult to differentiate among staff groups and to determine which group should perform which functions. Duplication of staff effort results, indicating that coordination among staff groups is breaking down.

The impact of staff proliferation upon the demand for information in an organization is very significant. Staff groups typically utilize information as primary input for the services they perform and the advice they offer to line managers regarding planning and control matters. In order to carry out their functions, staff groups must obtain basic information about the operations of the organization from its line units and from other staff groups. Consequently, the number and size of staff groups have a direct bearing on the amount of information demanded in an organization. Further, these staff groups affect how the information will be used to facilitate management.

Often the demand by staff groups for information from line units becomes excessive, especially when staff effort is duplicated. As a result, much redundant information is produced. Such a state is undesirable because the line units becomes overburdened in supplying information which is partially unnecessary, thereby increasing processing costs unnecessarily.

Improvements in Planning and Control Techniques

The proliferation of staffs has brought about changes in the procedures used for planning and controlling the operations of organizations. Prior to 1900 managers used relatively simple budgeting and bookkeeping practices for planning and control. During the early 1900's time and motion studies and other work measurement techniques were pioneered by industrial engineers to improve the efficiency of routine operations. These studies resulted in the development and use of more precise budgeting, charting, and cost accounting procedures, and the collection of more detailed information about the operations of the organization.

As organizations expanded, each major department or division began keeping records for its own use. Eventually several bookkeeping-type information processing centers and activities were created within organizations. Because of these multiple centers, duplication of information became common. Often information was inaccurate and untimely due to the overburdening of operating personnel who were merely assigned the additional responsibilities for collecting the data. Consequently, these early information processing activities were only marginally effective in serving the planning and control information needs.

The techniques developed by these early staff experts were the forerunners of the sophisticated procedures and techniques employed today by staff specialists for planning and control. For example, operations research specialists use mathematical models for inventory control, and long-range planning specialists are able to employ computer simulation techniques in the evaluation of new proposals and programs. Virtually all large organizations, and many lesser sized ones as well, make regular use of such techniques to facilitate the planning and control functions of management. Even the once simple process of budgeting can now involve the use of complex linear programming models for budgeting and allocating resources. Such models are capable of dealing effectively with the vast number and variety of products or services produced in highly diversified organizations.

More sophisticated techniques require additional internal and external information in an organization. Increased requirements for internal information spring from the need to collect and use much more accurate and timely information than in the past in order to implement the day-to-day scheduling and control techniques. For example, maintaining inventory control over the thousands of parts needed to manufacture an automobile requires the use of literally millions of pieces of information. The development and use of long-range planning models to evaluate new opportunities and to forecast future needs for resources require myriad types of external information. These external needs for information are much more pervasive than the internal needs because they have to do with the entire environment, including its political, economic, and social forces. For example, facilities planning techniques for a large state university involve the collection and use of information on population growth, program demand, program costs, student attitudes toward programs, public interest in higher education, status of existing facilities, maintenance requirements, and even the political climate in the legislature and governing bodies, just to name a few. Information on all these factors must be available rapidly in order to make enrollment projections as a basis for facilities planning decisions. These and other similar planning and control techniques now used by management have expanded considerably the needs for and role of organizational information.

Improved Information Processing Technology

Perhaps the greatest impact on the role of information in organizations in recent years has been that of the electronic digital computer. Prior to 1950 virtually all information processing was done manually or with semiautomated office machines. First generation digital computers, such as the IBM 650, were introduced in the early 1950's. These computers were relatively small and very limited in application. Although they were used successfully to carry out certain basic accounting operations such as payroll processing, they were mainly used in scientific applications, mostly as high-speed calculators.

In the late 1950's, second generation computers, such as the IBM 1401, became available. These computers were designed primarily for business applications. They are capable of handling a large volume of data input and information output. These computers use high-speed printers for producing large quantities of printed information, facilitating the production of standardized reports and documents. It became possible for an organization to produce almost an unlimited amount of information output using one or more of these second generation computers.

In the mid-1960's, third generation computers, such as the IBM 360, were introduced and quickly became the nucleus of modern computerized information systems. In addition to being considerably larger and faster than earlier machines, these computers provide a time-sharing capability. Time-sharing involves the simultaneous sharing of time on a single computer by different users, usually from remote locations. Whereas second generation computers process batches of information one at a time, third generation computers are able to process information for several users more or less simultaneously and continuously. This capability enables an organization to receive, process, and distribute more timely information to users throughout the organization. The effect of third generation computers has been to stimulate the use of computer processing of information for almost all facets of management.

So-called fourth generation computer technology is now becoming available.[8] Fourth generation computers are differentiated from third generation in that they are generally faster, more compact, and less expensive. Such improvements will undoubtedly continue to add to the expanding role of organizational information, as has earlier technology.

The introduction of computers in organizations has not been without problems, however. Some clerical workers, afraid of being displaced in their jobs by computers, have viewed computers with apprehension. Resistance to the use of computers has resulted. Competition may arise among managers to have authority over the computer facilities in their organization. In extreme cases individual factions of an organization have acquired their own computer in order to set up an information processing center for their own purposes. This usually leads to duplication of effort and overall inefficiency in information processing for the organization. Another problem stems from the ease with which computers enable massive quantities of information to be produced. As a result much unnecessary information is generated, sometimes at the expense of some critically needed items.

In sum, the greater size and complexity of organizations, the proliferation of staff groups, and the improvements in planning and control techniques have generally brought about greater demands for and wider use of information. Also, the development of high-speed computers has established a much larger and more significant role for information processing in all organizations. In addition to the individual impact of these factors, they tend to reinforce each other, as shown below:

Organizational growth requires staff additions that in turn require better information processing technology. As this becomes available, improved planning and control techniques are possible which permit further organizational growth.

---

[8] There is no real consensus yet on what constitutes a fourth generation computer. Although IBM does not claim that its System 370 is the fourth generation, many in industry see it in this light.

The role of management information has become very important because information represents a sizeable percentage of the total dollar budget of the organization. It is also important because of such factors as resistance to change, inflexibility in terms of sunk costs of information, and the great potential of computer technology. The increasing costs of information processing contrasted with increasing operational needs for information are the two basic issues to be resolved in modern organizations. The combined effects of these two issues in the context of the changing nature of operations and management have truly created an "age of management information" for organizations in the 1970's.

REVIEW QUESTIONS

1. Define and discuss the nature of information as a process and as the output of the information process. Provide several examples for each classification.
2. What relationship does uncertainty have to the management process and the function of information for management?
3. How are the design, communicative, and analytical dimensions of information related to the management process?
4. Describe the characteristics of information needs for planning, operational control, and managerial/financial control.
5. Describe the emerging environment of organizational information systems and its impact on the need for and design of information systems in an organization.
6. The dichotomy of increasing needs versus increasing costs of information requires a greater emphasis on the information function of an organization. Discuss the meaning and implications of this development for the design of information systems.
7. Why has proliferation of staff emerged in large organizations? Give examples of proliferation of staff as it relates to the information function in an organization.
8. Explain how recent improvements in information processing technology have impacted the use and provision of information for management.
9. Discuss the interrelationships between the increasing size and complexity of organizations and the development of specialized staffs utilizing improved techniques of planning and control.
10. Of the four factors cited in this chapter, which have had the most significant impacts on the design and use of information systems? Which do you feel will pose the greatest problems in the future?

EXERCISE 1-1: Information for Management

Select an organization with which you are familiar. The organization may be profit-making (business), nonprofit (government or educational), or social (fraternity or sorority). For the organization selected, give several examples of the following:

1. Types of information that are used to facilitate the *planning* of operations, activities, or events for this organization. General categories of this type of information may include: projections of demand, available resources, important constraints, and value criteria.
2. Types of information that are used to facilitate *operational control* for the effective implementation of plans. Examples of this type of information may include those items you feel are important for providing insights into the volume or quality of work accomplished and the budget status of the organization.
3. Types of information that are used to facilitate *managerial/financial control* of operations, activities, and events. Examples may include evaluating performance of the organization and its people if you were in charge and evaluating the financial status of the organization.

EXERCISE 1-2: The Marnox Company (Part A): 1969 Staff Meeting

President: The first item on the agenda is Project Able. Production, what is the status of Project Able?

Production: We have had a few minor problems concerning availability of materials, but in general we are proceeding satisfactorily.

President: Procurement, why the delay in materials acquisition?

Procurement: According to my records I did not receive the requisition from Stores until seven days before the date the materials were required.

Stores: According to the Inventory Status Report, seven days is the lead time specified for the materials in question, and my job is to keep inventory storage costs down.

Procurement: I appreciate that, but I need time to do my job to satisfy production, who after all is the user. Besides, the seven days lead time only refers to buying and delivery functions, and does not include the time required for receiving, inspection, movement of materials into stores, and issuance to production.

Production: This bothers me since we have had similar problems in the past. I furnished Stores our material requirements three weeks ago and I assumed the materials would be here when I needed them. It seems to me that if I am responsible for completion of work by a certain date I should be assured of material availability by Procurement. If I can't have this assurance, let me do my own buying of materials.

Stores: I would like to clarify the record if I may. In this particular case you did give us advance notice of your needs and we

	did follow procurements guidelines for lead times. However, concerning several of these "past problems" you refer to, we did not receive advance notice of your needs.
Procurement:	I can substantiate that.
Production:	If you dig out your records, you will see that the reasons for short notices of needs were due to late specifications from Engineering.
Engineering:	Don't blame me. I did not have a final statement of customer specifications from the Marketing Contracting Officer in time. Besides, the R&D personnel needed for Project Able that I requisitioned from Personnel were not assigned to me until recently, which further delayed development of specifications.
Personnel:	The budget authorization from the Controller for the hiring of additional R&D personnel was delayed.
Controller:	The company's current policy on additions to the work force requires the personal approval of the President. This was obtained immediately upon his return from Washington; however, it amounted to a few days delay.
Engineering:	Didn't the original proposal which the President approved for the undertaking of Project Able include these additional personnel in the cost estimates?
Controller:	Yes they did; however, my understanding was that the President wanted to OK each personnel action request.
Quality Control:	Pardon me for changing the topic of conversation for a moment, but when can I expect the completed prototype from Production? I have set aside manpower and time, based on the original production schedule, for testing the prototype. Can we meet this schedule or should I lay off some of my personnel?
Marketing:	What do I tell the customer about delivery?
Finance:	Are we going to meet our original profit objectives on Project Able?

1. Describe the organizational problems or complexities that are reflected in this organization, and comment on how these problems or complexities may have resulted because of inadequate information.

2. Identify problems caused by inefficient information processing and ineffective information outputs.

3. Discuss the general importance of information for facilitating the management of the organization described and of Project Able specifically.

4. Provide several examples of the types of information needed to facilitate the planning, operational control, and managerial/financial control within this organization.

EXERCISE 1-3: Farm Products Corporation (Part A): The Function of Information for Management [9]

Farm Products Corporation (FPC) was established in Memphis, Tennessee in 1947 as a manufacturer of farm implements. FPC products were marketed through retail tractor and farm equipment dealers located in Arkansas, Missouri, Mississippi, Kentucky, and Tennessee. In 1954, plant size was doubled to add a line of garden tools and to meet the increased sales demand for farm implements. Alabama and Indiana were added to the market area. The garden tools were distributed primarily through hardware and garden supply stores.

The Foundry formed smaller parts by melting iron ingots and pouring the molten metal into sand castings. Other parts were manufactured from sheet and bar steel in the Machine Shop. Parts such as screws, bearings, and wooden handles were provided according to FPC specifications by outside suppliers. The final stage of manufacturing took place in the Assembly Shop.

By 1960, there were 600 people on the payroll and the FPC brand was well known throughout the Southeastern and Midwestern United States. The Personnel Office had tripled in size and was reorganized under a Vice-President for Industrial Relations when the work force was organized by the United Metal Workers in 1959. The Sales Division included an Advertising Department and a Customer Service Department. The Controller's staff had been expanded to include a Factory Accountant and an Internal Auditor.

1. Give several examples of the types of information which would be useful to FPC managers for decision making for each of the three basic functions of management.
2. Do you think FPC management had a significantly greater need for information in 1960 than it had when the company was founded? Explain why.

EXERCISE 1-4: The Nature of Information

Using the framework presented in Exhibit 1-1, provide examples of information as a process and as an output of the information process for several of the following decisions:

1. The decision as to whether to join a sorority or fraternity.
2. The selection of the sorority or fraternity (assuming you decide to join).
3. The selection of a major program of studies in a university.
4. The selection of elective courses.
5. The selection of a church to join.

---

[9] Much of the material for the Farm Products Corporation cases presented throughout the book were compiled by Robert Sharp, a graduate student at Florida State University.

6. The decision to study at regular and frequent intervals rather than cramming for exams.
7. The decision to buy or not to buy season football tickets.
8. The decision to run for a position in student government.
9. The selection of a career.
10. The evaluation of your performance in a course.

2 THE MANAGEMENT INFORMATION SYSTEM

Tremendous growth in size and complexity of organizations has made possible and necessary the use of more advanced planning and control techniques. Advances in information processing technology have made available increasing amounts of information to staff groups and to other managers in the organization, in order to facilitate the performance of management functions. The use of staff groups to utilize these advanced techniques more effectively has grown steadily, and in fact there is often a danger of proliferation of staff efforts. As operational and management needs for information increase, costs of processing information increase correspondingly. Because of increasing needs and costs, greater attention must be given to the management of the information function in the organization.

Many organizations have developed management information systems (MIS) using advanced information technology to satisfy increasing demands for information and to reduce the costs of information processing. To date, MIS development is relatively crude and segmented. What is needed is a better understanding of the nature, characteristics, and uses of the MIS by managers, along with a more systemic approach to the design of the MIS.

This chapter presents an overview of the nature of a system and specifically an information system. Criticisms of information systems are described, followed by an overview of several approaches to the design of information systems. Finally, the MIS concept as used in this book is defined.

THE NATURE OF SYSTEMS

A *system* may be defined as an organized combination of parts forming a complex, unitary whole. Numerous examples fit this definition. For example, an automobile is a mechanical system composed of valves, wheels, wiring, electrical motors, metal frames, pipes, and tubes arranged into a system of transportation. The human body is composed of cells, nerves, blood vessels, hair, skin, and organs combined into an animal system. An organizational system, such as a university, is composed of students, faculty, and staff, as individuals and groups arranged in a logical set of interrelationships and responsibilities.

In view of our definition of a system, almost anything having identifiable parts can be considered a system. Hence it is necessary to look further for a more discriminating concept. An alternative view of a system which focuses closer on its activity holds that it is "made up of sets of components that work together for the overall objective of the whole." [1] A still more precise definition is given by Optner: [2]

> A system is defined as some on-going process of a set of elements, each of which are functionally and operationally united in the achievement of an objective.

This definition emphasizes the most important features of a system. First, the achievement of an objective or purpose is fundamental to a system. The major purpose of the automobile is to provide transportation. The human body exists to perform work, play, service, etc., while the university exists to provide education and research.

A second important feature of a system is its interconnected and interrelated elements. A system can be viewed as a "system of systems" which work together within an overall ongoing process. In addition to viewing the automobile as a combination of valves, wheels, and wiring, it is useful to view it as a system of systems. For example, the power system and fuel system combine to produce energy which is used to produce motion, which in turn is directed by the steering system; and all these systems are integrated by the electrical system. Each of these systems and others have a specific and distinctive purpose as systems, yet they combine to form a larger system of systems, the automobile. Similiarly, the digestive, circulatory, muscular, skeletal, and nervous systems serve distinctive purposes, yet they are interrelated functionally within a larger system called the human body. The university is composed of schools, colleges, programs, and departments as systems within a larger system.

The concept of hierarchical levels of systems is an important characteristic of the system relationship. Boulding describes the levels of systems in the universe ranging from an atom as the basic micro system to the universe as the most macro system.[3] The parts of a system have vertical as well as horizontal interrelationships. A state university is related to and affected by higher level educational agencies such as the board of regents, department of education, and legislature; these are vertical relationships. In addition, the university has horizontal relationships with other universities in its state system.

A third feature of a system is that it exhibits integration and cohesiveness of its parts and subsystems. This means that a system and its subsystems must be regulated, evaluated, and adjusted as it operates, or else the entire system ceases to function effectively. The fuel, electrical, heat, and oil guages are examples of mechanical devices for insuring that the automobile is operating effectively. The driver of the automobile, of course, interprets

---

[1] C. West Churchman, *The Systems Approach* (New York: Dell Publishing Co., 1968), p. 11.

[2] Stanford L. Optner, *Systems Analysis for Business Management* (2d ed.; Englewood Cliffs, N.J.: Prentice-Hall, 1968), p. 3.

[3] For a complete discussion of general systems and a description of the levels, see Kenneth E. Boulding, "General Systems Theory—The Skeleton of a Science," *Management Science* (April, 1956), pp. 200-202.

the information and makes adjustments accordingly. In the human body the nervous system and the brain combine to regulate the subsystems of the body, to evaluate its vital signs, and to generate various symptoms which the individual (or his doctor) can interpret as a basis for the use of remedies. In the university information is compiled and evaluated about the activities, responsibilities, and performances of its people, schools, colleges, departments, and programs in order to make adjustments.

In summary, a system contains several important features: achievement of an objective, interconnected and interrelated parts, and coordination and integration of functions and operations. An *information system* has these same features. To be effective, the information system must accomplish the following:

1. *Serve the objectives of the organization.* The information to be produced by the information system must be user oriented. The reports produced must be useful and timely in order to facilitate the management process.

2. *Develop and operate a set of interconnected and interrelated information processing activities.* Individual information systems in an organization, such as payroll, inventory, purchases-payables, sales-receivables, and general ledgers, should be formally tied together into a system of systems in order to produce the information required by operations and management.

3. *Provide for management of the information system.* The definition, evaluation, and design of reports should be regulated, reviewed, and adjusted by management to insure that reports reflect the needs of both operations and management and to insure that the costs of information processing are minimized.

The objectives of an effective information system are not easily attained, as evidenced by some of the more common criticisms of information systems.

CRITICISMS OF INFORMATION SYSTEMS

Several criticisms are commonly made regarding information systems. These criticisms reflect the problems associated with the types of information produced, the cost of information processing, and the management of the information system.

Useless Information

Useless information results from inadequate evaluation of information needs in operating activities and decisions. The systems analyst must not assume that he knows what types of information are needed for operations and management, but must investigate the nature of these activities and decisions. The production of useless information is more likely when the selection of information provided for operations and management is influenced by availability of data rather than by real needs for information. In other instances, the information system may provide adequately the information needed by a particular function, such as purchasing or sales, while the information produced concerning multifunctional activities and decisions may be inadequate. For example, information about the status of a customer order requires data about production schedules, purchasing, inventory status, and shipping schedules. Also, an organization may overemphasize top management's information needs for long-range planning, and thereby neglect day-to-day operating needs of lower level managers.

Another reason for poor quality of information is that the information processes are designed inadequately or they are operating ineffectively. The design of information processes may not take into account the formats of the reports that are needed by managers and hence may render the information in a faulty or even unusable format. Also, controls for the collection, storage, retrieval, and distribution of information may not be adequate, thereby allowing system effectiveness to fall far below design potential. An accurate definition of needs and uses of information and an effective information processing system are needed so that users can build confidence in the system.

Excessive Information

"Too much paperwork" is a common criticism of computerized information systems. This criticism is closely related to that of poor quality of information, and the reasons for an excessive volume of information are also similar. First, the analysis and evaluation of needs and uses of information may not have been accomplished effectively. The concepts of "need to know" and "exception reporting" may not have been considered. Second, the design of the information processing system may not be effective. Selectivity is needed in collecting, processing, storing, retrieving, and distributing information to serve specific needs.

Untimely Information

"Reports are too late to be of use" is another commonly encountered criticism of information system performance. Often the reason for this inadequacy is seen by systems analysts and data processing personnel as a lack of sufficient computer hardware capacity. Another view, likely a more appropriate one, is that the design of the information processing system is inadequate. The design does not take into account the specific needs for information and its uses by management in terms of frequency as well as quality and volume. Problems of late information may also be due to technical malfunctions in information processing operations or to human malfunctions in data acquisition and coding. Again, the proper definition of needs and uses of information and proper design of information processes are issues central to this criticism.

Excessive Processing Costs

High costs of information processing result from improper definition of information needs and inefficient design and operation of information processing systems. Problems develop because precise estimates of costs of the information system are not made or because analyses of real needs for information in terms of cost are lacking. Also, the value of changes in frequency, volume, or quality of information for improving operations and management is difficult to estimate. Such factors cause information processing costs to seem excessive in many information systems.

Disruption of the Organization

A new information system or a change in the present system often results in organizational disruption. One type of change is the centralization of some functions or activities related to information processing. Many managers fear centralization of information processing. It seems natural for a manager to feel more secure if he controls the information he needs for his own operations. When control of information is taken away from a manager, he may become apprehensive about getting accurate and timely information. Managers also tend to be apprehensive about providing information about their operations to a central office for compilation and distribution because they feel that dissemination of information about their department's performance would be damaging.

Another type of disruption in an organization is job insecurity due to the automation of information processing activities. Also, competition for authority and control over the information system may be disruptive to the organization's operations and management. Because of these concerns by members of the organization, there may be a tendency to resist or to criticize the information system, even though it is ultimately beneficial for operations and management.

In summary, the criticisms of information systems can be related generally to the three features of an effective information system described earlier. First, information which is not useful, or which is not provided in the volume or time required by management, means that the information system is not user oriented or supportive of the objectives of the organization. Second, if the costs of the information system are excessive, the design, operation, and monitoring of information processing activities are inefficient. Also, the various information subsystems and processes may not be interrelated effectively into an overall information system. Third, disruption of the organization, coupled with the problems of inadequate information and information processing, means that the management of the information function is not effective Specifically, this means that the information is in fact not a system since it does not exhibit a unified purpose or its subsystems are not integrated effectively.

Problems often stem from the approach used to design an information system. The next section discusses several approaches to the design of information systems and how each approach contributes to the solution of problems.

APPROACHES TO DESIGN OF INFORMATION SYSTEMS

There are a number of views on design of an information system. For discussion and comparison the terminology used by Blumenthal will be used in this section. Blumenthal has categorized the approaches to information system design in the following manner:[4]

1. The organization chart approach
2. The data-collection approach
3. The management survey (or top-down) approach
4. The data bank approach
5. The integrate-later approach
6. The integrate-now (or total systems) approach

The first five approaches are based on a traditional rather than a systems perspective of an organization. The sixth approach is a systems approach, and one that will be adapted with some modification for use in this book.

Traditional Approaches

The *organization chart* approach relies on formal organization boundaries in designing information systems. An information system is designed for each functional area of the organization as the need arises. For example, the accounting function is often the first department for which an information system is developed. Financial reports, such as income statements, balance sheets, payroll lists, purchases-payables reports, and sales-receivables reports, are the usual information produced. The next functional unit for which an information system is developed might be the purchasing department. Purchase order status, inventory status, receiving, and inspection reports are examples of the types of information produced. Examples of other functions for which separate information systems may be developed include marketing (demand analyses), production (planning and control reports), and personnel (manpower analyses). Each of these separate information systems serves one particular function, and the processing of information for each system does not relate to other systems. In fact, each generally is a separate, mutually exclusive, parallel system that can cause great duplication of the information compiled, stored, and processed.

The *data-collection* approach gathers all possible relevant data as the first step in designing the information system. Data is compiled and converted into special reports for managers as needed. Obviously, potential exists for collecting large amounts of data that will never be used, creating inefficiency in the processing of data. Also, the method of classification of data may be inadequate for producing the reports needed by managers.

The *management survey* or *top-down* approach defines top, middle, and lower level management's needs for information. The information needs of each higher management level are assumed to satisfy the needs of lower levels. Under this approach the first priority is top management's strategic information needs, rather than the operational needs of lower level managers. This approach generally results in less interest in and support for the information system by lower level operating managers. In addition, often other information

---

[4] Sherman S. Blumenthal, *Management Information Systems: A Framework for Planning and Development* (Englewood Cliffs, N.J.: Prentice-Hall, 1969), p. 20.

systems may be required for operational control. Duplication of information processing occurs, and several separate rather than interconnected information systems are developed.

The *data bank* approach is related to the data collection approach, but it involves the development of a more formal and larger collection of data, or data bank. Its central feature is the collection, establishment, storage, and maintenance of this data bank. The data bank contains every type of data that could possibly be used for operations and management. The data bank approach has problems similar to those of the data collection approach. Without a definition of specific needs for information, the data bank may include data that is not needed or exclude data that is needed. This is a basic disadvantage of "data input-oriented" rather than "information output-oriented" approaches to designing an information system. As a result, the costs of data processing generally are much greater.

The *integrate-later* approach incorporates some of the features of the organization chart approach. Essentially it is a piecemeal approach to information system design based on the premise that a completely integrated system can not be designed in advance. However, as opposed to the organization chart approach, there is an intent eventually to integrate the smaller systems. This requires conceptualization of the integrated system and the combination of the smaller systems into a unified framework. Sooner or later the integrate-later approach requires a major systems revision to realize the full potential of information technology and to meet the information needs of management.

The integrate-later approach provides small information systems which may be more useful in the short run. However, managers are often reluctant to change these smaller systems into a larger interconnected information system that has greater potential for the total organization in the long run.

In conclusion, each of these five traditional approaches to design of information systems contains features that contribute to the problems of information systems described earlier. First, none of the five approaches formally considers the information needs of all managers in the organization as the basis for the design of the system. There is an inadequate evaluation of how various reports are interrelated among functions, levels of management, and external users of information. Instead, a segmented approach to design results in several nonconnected reporting systems and the full potential of information technology is not realized. The data input-oriented approaches consider management's needs for information primarily as a function of available data. In contrast, the organization chart, management survey, and integrate-later approaches are more user or information output-oriented, although they are designed and operated on a segmented basis.

Second, advanced information technology should lead to lower costs of producing information for operations and management. Just as introduction of automated techniques in manufacturing is based on the goal of reducing production costs and improving quality, advanced information technology has a goal of minimizing the costs of information processing and improving the usefulness of information. These five approaches, because they result in segmented and duplicative information systems, do not lead to optimum reports or an efficient set of information processing activities.

Third, these segmented approaches and their failure to reduce cost make the management of the information function in the organization ineffective. Greater attention must be given by top management to the increasing uses of information in the organization and to the increasing costs of producing information. A more effective approach to managing the data resource must be developed. The objectives of the information function should be specifically stated and plans developed for carrying out these objectives. Programs relating to the information function should be designed, implemented, and reviewed with a goal of gaining the active support of all managers. The keys to gaining this support are to provide managers with information that is useful to them and to minimize the costs the managers incur for information (i.e., compared with other resource costs). Most importantly, each manager within the organization must view his operating activity and needs for information as a subsystem of the larger organizational system.

The Total Systems Approach

The limitations of the five approaches described can be reduced considerably under the *integrate-now* or *total systems* approach. This approach is based on the premise that all information needs and uses can be defined and organized before the system is implemented. Information collection, storage, and retrieval activities are designed and operated within one all-encompassing framework.

Critics of this approach say that it is difficult to define all information needs of operations and management, or what "total" means.[5] Also, even if "total" can be defined, it may not be necessary or feasible to include all types of information needs in a formalized, integrated information system. Operational information used for functions such as materials management, financial accounting, and production control exhibit routine operating features which can be interrelated and brought together within a total operational information system. However, it may not be possible or even desirable to include certain types of nonoperational or strategic information in the total system. Information on the changing attitudes of consumers, the impact of new technology, or impending legislation which may affect the firm in the future are indistinct information which may not be formally included in the information system. In general, information for future nonroutine events is difficult to define or anticipate and hence may be excluded from consideration in the design phase.

---

[5] See Charles A. Myers, ed., *The Impact of Computers on Management* (Cambridge, Mass.. M.I.T. Press, 1967), p. 13; John Dearden and F. W. McFarlan, *Management Information Systems* (Homewood, Ill.: Richard D. Irwin, 1966), p. 46; and Hershner Cross, "A General Management View of Computers," *Computers and Management-The Leatherbee Lectures* (Boston: Harvard University, 1967), p. 16, for more detailed discussions and arguments concerning the difficulty and inappropriateness of the total systems approach.

Some General Design Considerations

In practice, the development of most information systems has followed some combination of the traditional design approaches. Some designers emphasize the notion of total systems in their design, while others are more concerned with specialized operating information systems. No approach deserves criticism until the organization involved has been considered. Factors such as the following have an important bearing on the approach selected:

1. *Size of operations.* Larger organizations need more and different types of information. The use of advanced information technology in large-scale businesses can be justified and utilized more effectively than in small businesses. In small businesses, payroll, inventory control, purchasing, and financial accounting are the major types of information needed. In large businesses, these types of information are needed in much greater volume. In addition, there may be a need for cost accounting reports, market analyses, manpower analyses, and complex budgets which require a greater investment in information technology and manpower.

2. *Current state of computer usage in the organization.* An organization that is not currently using a computer may wish to move into computerized information systems development at a much slower pace than an organization that has had some experience in the use of computers.

3. *Personnel capabilities and knowledge of computerized information systems.* If the organization has had experience in computer usage, it is likely to have some expertise in the design of information systems. Also, if an organization has computer manpower capability and experience, it is likely that managers in the organization have been exposed to some degree of computerization of information. If existing information systems are operating satisfactorily, these managers will tend to support an extension or enlargement of the information system.

4. *Kinds and frequency of operational and managerial problems.* This is related to the size factor described in 1, above. Those organizations that have a large number of routine and more programmatic decisions and activities, such as a manufacturing firm, are more likely to make extensive use of computerized information systems. On the other hand, a service type organization, such as a legal firm, does not have as many routine or programmatic problems and activities, and the use of computerized information systems is not as widespread.

5. *Availability of resources.* Information technology and manpower are costly and organizations have varying needs for information. The investment in information systems should be evaluated by top management in relation to other investment alternatives.

The above factors imply that all organizations do not need nor can they create the same specific kind of information system. The final definition of information needs and the design of the information system may vary considerably among organizations and still be effective for each. Of course, all criticisms of information systems discussed earlier probably can never be eliminated entirely.

The fact that it may not be possible to design a perfect information system does not mean that a system designer should not strive for perfection. Because of the shortcomings of most information systems, there is a need to improve greatly the management of the information function in the organization. A central issue facing most organizations is how best to realize the full potential of information in facilitating operations and management. And it is important to emphasize that there may be several paths to the same end.

Providing information has become a major function in organizations, comparable to such other important functions as purchasing and personnel. The commitment of resources to the information function is also quite large and is increasing rapidly. The output of the information system influences all levels of management and all aspects of operations. It is not a question of whether or not to have an information system but of what kind it should be. Regardless of the path selected, there are a number of guidelines that should result in an optimum design of an information system. These guidelines incorporate a central perspective of the information system as a system. This systems perspective is the essence of the MIS as described in this book.

THE MIS CONCEPT

In spite of the difficulties involved in defining total and in incorporating all possible information in an information system, the integrate-now or total systems approach to MIS design has more overall advantages than do other approaches. The central feature of the MIS concept is its systems perspective; that is, design, operation, and monitoring of information processing are integrated into a comprehensive system. The MIS as a system deals with all information subsystems in combination rather than with several individually. The need for integration and coordination of segments of an information system is aptly presented by McDonough:[6]

> It is clear that after more than twenty years of experience with computer applications in business, the major problem remains one of coordination. . . . We should look ahead by moving out beyond the analysis of single or isolated systems and attack some of the problems of coordination among the variety of systems and among the varied content of positions in the organization. . . . To provide for coordination of these situations is no easy matter. The starting point, however, is the recognition that neither systems content nor job content can be designed separately. The search for better management must bring jobs and systems together in an integrated framework.

Within the integrative framework as suggested by McDonough, a management information system is defined as *a group of information systems that are interconnected in their design, operation, and management to serve operations and facilitate the performance of the management process.* The MIS thus requires clustering the information needs of the various operating segments or functional systems into an integrated data base which is flexible enough to provide all types of information. This view is quite similar to the total systems view; it involves integration of most of the basic operational needs for

---

[6] Adrian M. McDonough, *Centralized Systems–Planning and Control* (Wayne, Pa.: Thompson Book Co., 1969), p. i-ii.

information into a unified information system. It differs from a strict total systems approach in that all possible types of information may not be included because of certain special characteristics of each organization as described earlier. However, if the MIS is designed properly, major types of nonoperational or strategic information can be included, especially if they are by-products of operational information.

The systems approach to MIS design, operation, and management used in this book encompasses the advantages of the total systems concept. Specifically, the MIS emphasizes: (1) an objective-user orientation in the design of information needs, (2) the design of individual information processes so that they are interconnected through an integrated data base, and (3) the need for management of the design, operations, and review of all aspects of the MIS. These three properties of the MIS are described in the remainder of this chapter.

Objective-User Orientation

In the design of reports to be produced by the MIS, an organization is faced with a problem of determining information priorities. The approach advocated in this book is to provide for operational information first. *Operational information* needs are those of line managers. The information is used for short-run purposes to develop, implement, and review yearly forecasts of demand, resource capacity, operating budgets, work schedules, and logistics plans. Operational information facilitates the planning, operational control, and managerial/financial control functions of line management, plus middle and upper level management needs for coordination and evaluation of operations. This is a feasible and realistic approach to MIS design, as noted by Hanold:[7]

> The key to MIS is an integrated data base, not a universal genius omniscient in everything. . . .
> It follows if our functional information systems cover the operations of the firm with reasonable sufficiency, there is information in the data base to support an executive management information system. Some further data will be needed, of course, because executive management considers a different opportunity horizon and a different time span than does operating management. But with this modest qualification the material is at hand to do the job.
> And the job is no more complex—indeed it is less so—than the problem of creating the several operating systems. . . .

Executive management or strategic information needs are those of top management, including high level staff groups, to analyze the costs and benefits of long-run objectives, programs, and resource utilization patterns of the entire organization or major segments of it. Examples of strategic information needs include demographic trends to develop product line strategies and programs, industry analyses to develop competitive strategies, and facilities utilization analyses to develop capital acquisition programs.

---

[7] Terrance Hanold, "An Executive View of MIS," *Datamation* (November, 1972), p. 71. Mr. Hanold is president of the Pillsbury Company, a firm which is extensively involved in developing its own MIS.

Emphasis on operational rather than strategic needs for information is important for several reasons:

1. Most information needs reflect the activities of the operating areas. Top management's strategic information is derived from historical operating information and from special purpose analysis.
2. Acceptance of a new information system by operating managers is greatly facilitated if their needs are given a high priority.
3. By focusing initial attention on improving operational performance, the payback period for the investment in an information system is generally shorter. Direct benefits are aimed at short-run needs.

In designing information systems, there are four criteria with which the effectiveness of reports can be measured. The first is the *quality* of information. Quality relates to the effectiveness of information in reducing the uncertainty surrounding a particular decision. Improving the relevancy and reliability of information are ways of reducing uncertainty. A decision to purchase a material for inventory can be made more effectively if future materials cost levels, production and shipping schedules, and level of customer demand are known than if these variables are not considered or if only estimates are made.

Second, the *quantity* or *volume* of information may influence the effectiveness of performance of operations and management. Too many reports or too much information on a report may discourage their use completely. Consider a large computerized report received daily which may require several hours for a manager to read and understand, versus a summary report of the same information which highlights only key variables and which can be read and understood in ten minutes or less. The summary report is certainly superior. On the other hand, too little information, which often reflects insufficient analysis, may be equally ineffective. A summary report, for example, should contain enough information to make a decision effectively. In the previous decision relating to purchasing a material for inventory, a ten-year projection of costs, schedules, and customer demand is not needed to make a yearly decision about materials purchases. On the other hand, a one-week projection of these variables is not enough information.

Third, the *timeliness* of information processing and distribution affects performance. Information that is sent to the wrong place or is received too late to affect a decision has no value to a manager. Need-to-know and exception reporting are ways to improve the timeliness of information and to eliminate any unneeded information. For example, rather than reporting all events and transactions, such as the time spent by each laborer in a manufacturing process, a production control report only needs to include information on favorable and unfavorable deviations from schedules.

Fourth, the effectiveness of systems has a *cost dimension*. The reports designed for the MIS have a value in terms of their use and a cost in terms of processing. The relationship between the costs of the MIS process and the benefits derived from the uses of information in operations and management determines the cost effectiveness of the MIS. For example, the cost of producing a report about projections of costs and materials, schedules, and customer demand should be compared with the savings generated in reducing unit cost of materials, production down-time, and loss of customer orders. Improvement of the cost effectiveness of the MIS may result from better definition and design of information outputs or better design and operation of MIS processes.

Part 3 describes the approach used for defining needs of information for operations and management. Specific types of information are identified within a system of interrelated reports. Also, Part 3 describes how these types of information are interrelated in working toward the accomplishment of the objectives of the organization. Part 4 contains a discussion of how the dimensions of quality, quantity, timeliness, and cost are utilized to design and evaluate MIS reports and the processes needed to produce them.

Integration of Information Processes

The information process can be viewed conceptually as an input-output transformation unit, as shown below:

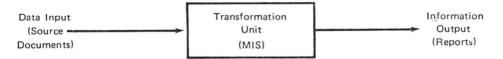

Viewed in this way, the information processes link data input with information output.

For purposes of design and analysis, the information processes must be broken down into meaningful parts. In Chapter 1, the information process was defined as consisting of a number of detailed activities such as recording, classifying, sorting, and calculating. This breakdown is especially necessary for the computer programming of these activities and for developing related documentation procedures.

Basic processing activities are often classified in other ways for analytical purposes. For example, a commonly used classification for cost analysis of information processing is data verification, data storage, data transmission, information retrieval, conversion into usable format, report preparation, and report distribution. Under this classification scheme, individual cost estimates are compiled and evaluated for each activity and these estimates are combined to develop a total cost of information processing.

A third breakdown of information processing for design purposes, and the one used in this book, is a classification of the information processing system into three components: data base, data coding scheme, and data processor. This classification of the information processing system considers detailed processing activities only in a general way, but then this book is not involved with computer programming and the detailed analyses which it requires. The data base connects information subsystems through a data coding scheme. The data processor, which is usually computer based, physically acquires, moves, processes, stores, and delivers data and information as required for the production of reports for operations and management.

According to the MIS concept, the design of the data base, data coding scheme, and data processor must be comprehensive yet flexible enough to service a variety of needs using a minimum of data input. Information generated by one subsystem should be usable as data to produce additional information in other subsystems. For example, time card data can be used in payroll reports, tax reports, financial statements, and indirectly in budget preparation. Time card data, material cost data, and overhead cost data can be combined to produce production cost variance reports, payroll reports, and inventory status reports.

To achieve this flexibility of data use, the data base and data coding scheme must be designed to permit recording, classifying, sorting, calculating, and summarizing data for multiple uses in reports. If this can be accomplished through the design of MIS processes, duplication of information processing equipment and operations can be reduced. Any reduction in recording and classifying data reduces the amount of data processing and data storage equipment required.

Design of the MIS processes to accomplish the foregoing requires a high degree of integration of information needs and data sources. Specific information elements on reports must be defined as the basis for determining the data needed to process the information for the reports. For example, a production cost variance report requires data on labor costs, materials costs, and overhead costs. Time cards, job control cards, and special purpose labor utilization reports may be used as sources of labor cost data. Similarly, purchase orders, material issue slips, and material usage reports can be used to acquire material cost data. The designer of the data acquisition procedures, data base, and data processing steps must decide which documents to use as the official sources of data for each MIS report.

Part 4 describes the approach for designing, implementing, and controlling the MIS processes needed to produce the desired reports. These processes are discussed within the systems perspective of an interrelated set of processes and with a view toward assessing the costs of processing versus the benefits produced. Details concerning the integration of information needs with sources of data also are described.

Management of the MIS

The management of the MIS directly involves the design and monitoring of information uses and the MIS processes required. Once users' requirements for information are determined and the reports and MIS processes are designed and implemented, monitoring of information processing insures performance according to plan. Of course, needs change and improvements in information technology become available from time to time. The MIS must cope with its changing environment. To adapt to change, the MIS relies on a process of feedback, evaluation, and adjustment as illustrated at the top of page 36.

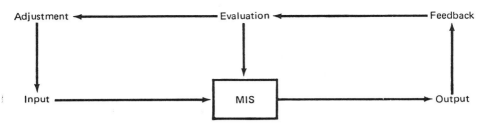

Feedback from users of information is used to adjust data input and to evaluate and regulate information processes.

For example, a production cost variance report may not be useful for evaluating the performance of a production manager if it includes noncontrollable costs such as overhead cost allocations. The variance report should show only controllable costs, such as labor and materials usage. In addition, if the variance report is received too late by the production manager to make adjustments correcting unfavorable cost overruns, the frequency of the report must be changed. The cost of producing the variance report may also be excessive in relation to its usefulness, suggesting a need for change in report or system design.

It is important to establish specific criteria for evaluating the performance of MIS processes and the usefulness of reports. The cost of producing each category of report should be compiled and reviewed periodically. Costs should be compared with the costs of similar reporting systems in other organizations if possible and with the costs of subcontracting the reporting system out to a computer service bureau. Improvements or reductions in the operating efficiencies of managers should be measured and evaluated periodically. A new report may be justified on the basis of its improvement of operational efficiency. The designer of a report must specify measurable variables which can be reviewed to determine if savings did in fact occur. A production cost variance report may be planned to reduce unit product cost of production. Once the report has been implemented, the change in unit product cost of production should be evaluated to determine if efficiency improved.

In addition to the design and monitoring functions, the concept of *wholism* or *synergy*, the unification of parts into a complex whole, is a most important aspect of MIS management. Synergy centers on the notion that the whole is greater than the sum of its parts, for example:

> A brick wall is more than a pile of bricks.
> A sentence is more than a collection of words.
> A team is more than a group of people.
> An organism is more than a mass of cells.
> An information system is more than a group of reports.

The MIS has value if it produces information that is more useful or less costly than information produced by each single, specialized information system. As mentioned earlier, the greater value may be due to providing information processing activities more efficiently with no change in information output or services.

The concept of synergy implies that the members of the organization, especially its managers as information users, acknowledge and support the MIS concept. Top management must communicate to managers how the MIS facilitates the accomplishment of functional and organizational goals and reduces the costs of information processing. Convincing managers to accept and support the MIS concept is no easy task. Often this involves a departure from the traditional emphasis on individual operating entities and the development of an awareness of how operating entities interact in achieving the objectives of the organization.

Other interest groups in the organization besides managers may pose special problems for achieving acceptance of the MIS concept. For example, systems analysts, computer programmers, machine operators and technicians, and other data processing personnel may be more interested in information processing efficiency than in the ultimate usefulness of reports to managers. Or data processing personnel may be interested in building a larger and more advanced computerized information system than is feasible or useful to the organization.

Part 2 deals with the systems approach to MIS design, describes organization for MIS and the systems methodology of MIS design, and presents a basic organizational systems model.

SUMMARY

The major criticisms of information systems are related to three factors: (1) the information that is produced often is not useful, (2) the costs of information processing generally are excessive, and (3) introduction of information systems is often disruptive to the organization. These criticisms often stem from the approach used to design the information system. Traditionally, segmented approaches have been used to design information systems. This has resulted in the generation of reports geared to individual functional needs for information, rather than reports that also provide information on multifunctional operations. In addition, duplication of information processing activities has occurred, leading to excessive costs of acquisition, storage, processing, and distribution of information.

REVIEW QUESTIONS

1. Define "system." Discuss three features of a system important for designing an information system.
2. Describe several major criticisms of information systems. Which do you feel are the most significant?
3. Describe several approaches to the design of information systems, and the advantages and limitations of each approach.
4. How are the approaches to the design of information systems related to the general criticisms of information systems?
5. Discuss several general considerations that may influence the approach used for designing an information system.

6. Discuss the MIS concept as a systems approach to the analysis and design of information systems.

7. Differentiate between operational versus strategic information and discuss how they impact the approach used for designing an information system.

8. Describe four dimensions with which the effectiveness or value of reports can be measured and give examples of each.

9. A central feature of the MIS concept is the integration of information processes. Discuss the meaning and significance of this feature and provide a general example of how integration can be achieved.

10. Identify several categories of people in an organization whose attitudes influence the successful design, implementation, and operation of the MIS.

EXERCISE 2-1: The Marnox Company (Part B): 1970-1973—Design and Implementation of an Information System[8]

As a result of serious problems relating to planning and controlling its operations, the Marnox Company in 1970 embarked on an extensive commitment to the development of a computerized information system. This case summarizes the events that have transpired since then. In the main these events relate to the design and implementation of the information system.

In addition to the problems relating to planning and controlling its operations, the Marnox Company made its initial decision to embark on an extensive commitment to a computerized information system for the following reasons:

1. Competitors in the industry had already acquired computers.
2. The company had a highly favorable cash position, and considered computers a sound investment.
3. The company wanted to expand its operations to include the sale of computer services and computer time.
4. The Controller believed that the computer had a lot to offer in the more efficient processing of accounting information.

An influential engineer in the company with widespread computer experience was given the responsibility for the overall planning, design, and implementation of the computerized information system. At the time of the initial decision, the president made a substantial commitment for acquiring the most sophisticated computer equipment available. Also, there was a commitment to acquire an on-line, real-time system as soon as they could be proved operational. As the computer hardware was being installed, the data processing manager (the engineer assigned this position) began to acquire the needed support personnel and facilities for the new operation. Within a year the hardware was in place and operable, and by that time a sizeable data processing staff had been acquired.

---

[8] This is an extension of Exercise 1-2; however, these two exercises can be treated separately.

From the time in 1970 when the decision had been made to invest in the computer, the company scheduled quarterly meetings of its key managers so that they could keep up with developments and to resolve any problems regarding the changeover to a computerized system. At the end of the first two years, there still had been only limited success in converting from manual to automatic systems. In 1973, there was growing skepticism among management about the utility and practicality of a computerized system for this company. The following is a summary of the most recent quarterly staff meeting. It is indicative of the emerging organizational climate.

Summary of Quarterly Staff Meeting, April, 1973

President:	The major item on the agenda concerns the progress we are making with the new "centralized, third-generation, random-access, on-line, real-time, fully integrated, computer information system." Substantial investments in equipment and personnel have been made, and I have not seen any appreciable improvement in operations. In fact, it appears we may have created another layer of problems and frictions. Where do we stand in terms of applications and problems?
Data Processing:	We are currently testing the payroll and inventory control systems, and we are beginning the design of applications in other areas such as production control, purchases-payables, and sales-receivables.
President:	Are there any problems in Data Processing, or between Data Processing and using areas?
Data Processing:	There tends to be lack of agreement between various users concerning the types and frequency of information needs.
President:	What is Data Processing's role in this effort?
Data Processing:	Basically, we take the input and output flows as specified by the users and program them.
Controller:	First let me say that the computer has great potential for accounting. As you will recall, I advocated the investment in the computer. Our basic problem is not one of knowing what information we need for accounting, but one of lack of technical knowledge in systems design and the capabilities of equipment.
Production:	Right now we do not have much on the computer, but what we have seems OK. To be frank with you, we have been so busy I haven't been interested in another system.
Procurement:	There is no question in my mind that there are computer applications for procurement. The basic question is can my budget afford it?

Controller and Production:	Amen!
Data Processing:	OK, I admit costs are high, but this is due to the fact that we are operating at considerably less than full data processing capacity; therefore, higher rates are charged to present users. It is important that we generate more applications so a lower rate can be used and fixed costs spread over a greater number of users.
President:	What has been the general reaction of your employees to computer applications?
All Using Areas:	Initially, skepticism, fear, or apprehension. Now, skepticism plus an "I told you so" attitude.
President:	How do we stand concerning our original estimates of applications, schedules, and costs?
Data Processing:	We are four to six months behind, but much of this is because we have changed our original plans for applications. Naturally, as our applications increase, costs estimates must be revised.
President:	In other words, the feasibility study isn't feasible anymore. Does anyone have a clear conception of what our information needs are now and in the future; or do we even have a framework that can be used to analyze our requirements?

1. Identify how each individual described in the case perceives his role as it relates to the computerized information system, and his specific criticisms of the information system.
2. For the developments described in the case, identify examples of the following:
   a. Lack of objective-user orientation in the design of information needs.
   b. Need for integration of information processes.
   c. Need for management of information systems design and operation.
3. Consider the decision to invest in the computerized information system. Comment on the positive and negative aspects of decision. What would you have done differently?
4. Consider the present state of affairs (April, 1973). What should the company do now?

EXERCISE 2-2: Farm Products Corporation (Part B): The MIS Concept

The objectives of this exercise are to understand information systems design approaches, and to become aware of major criticisms of past information systems and to learn how these problems can be minimized.

Each organizational unit at FPC is responsible for preparing periodic reports of its activities. The Sales Order Section prepares a weekly report for the Sales Vice-President which shows the quantities and dollar amounts of each product item sold according to the orders processed during that week. Each Branch Sales Manager receives a weekly report from his Branch Accountant which shows sales volume for each salesman. Each salesman gets a monthly report of his sales, by customer, from the Branch Accountant.

Material Control, Scheduling, and the Plant Supervisor all need to have certain information, on a daily or weekly basis, about the status of raw materials on hand. The Stores Custodian prepares a daily total of items received, items issued, and balance on hand for Material Control. In order to reduce the amount of labor required for preparing reports, a copy of this report is made for Scheduling and the Plant Supervisor, from which they can extract the information they need.

As the volume of manufacturing and sales have increased, more time has been required to prepare reports for the individual managers. Although the number of clerical personnel has increased considerably in all offices, many reports were being prepared late and mistakes were becoming more numerous. The use of electronic computers for data processing seemed to offer a solution to at least some of these problems. It was decided to rent a third generation IBM computer and to convert to computer those processes causing the most serious difficulties.

The most obvious and serious problem involved getting the paychecks issued on time each week. The Payroll and Cash Disbursement sections were each required to work overtime at least one night a week, although three extra clerks had been hired in the past year. Even so, some paychecks were not always ready on time and mistakes were often made because of the additional pressure of meeting the deadline. Along with acquiring the computer and associated hardware, FPC hired a programmer to operate the EDP system and train personnel of the Payroll Section on how to convert employee timecard data into punched cards for computer processing. These punched cards were batch fed into the computer which produced the weekly payroll summary sheet and made out the paychecks. The Controller was authorized by the President to proceed with this implementation and to apply computer techniques to other accounting procedures as soon as the payroll processing was running smoothly.

1. Before acquiring the computer, what type of information system did FPC have? What are your criticisms of this system?
2. Do you think FPC's approach in applying computer techniques will solve the problems you have mentioned above? Would you have used a different approach? Why?

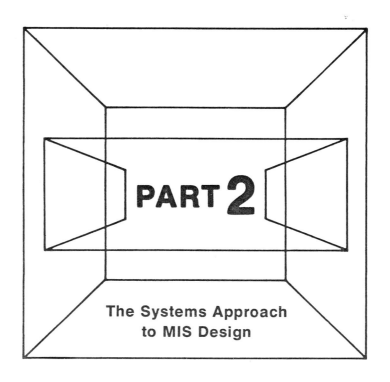

PART 2

The Systems Approach
to MIS Design

3 ORGANIZATION FOR MIS

The introduction of computer technology in an organization often necessitates structural changes. The design, operation, and monitoring of a computerized MIS usually requires realignments in staff groups. The structure of the line organization and the types of information developed for planning, operational control, and managerial/financial control may also require alteration. This chapter identifies and discusses the organizational implications of computerized information systems, especially the MIS. The objectives of this chapter are to:

1. Review a number of predictions, research findings, and basic issues concerning the impact of computerized information systems on organization design.
2. Describe the nature and purpose of the MIS staff and discuss its major functions in the design, operation, and monitoring of the MIS.
3. Discuss a number of important factors concerning the assignment of responsibility for the performance of the MIS functions.

Management of the MIS is a vital concern of the organization because of the increasing needs for information and the increasing costs of information processing. The proper assignment of responsibilities for designing, operating, and monitoring the MIS is critical. The impact of this decision on the organization generally results in a realignment of organizational responsibilities; this realignment often is accompanied by resistance to change or competition for responsibility by manager groups in areas such as accounting, data processing, and systems analysis. Proper organization for MIS can improve the probability of its success in implementation and operation.

IMPACT OF COMPUTERS ON ORGANIZATION DESIGN

With the advent of large-scale computers, the amount and types of information used in organizations has increased greatly over the past two decades. A number of these changes were described in Chapter 1. They include the whole array of quantitative techniques for planning and control, such as simulation, linear programming, queuing, inventory, and PERT models. In addition, increased external reporting requirements have changed financial accounting and analysis in the form of additional reports to governmental agencies such as the Internal Revenue Service, Securities and Exchange Commission, Environmental Protection Agency, Federal Trade Commission, and Department of Commerce. The improvement in techniques for planning and control and the increase in information used to operationalize these techniques, plus the increase in external reporting requirements, have led to the introduction of new staff groups in the organization, such as systems analysis, operations research, market research, and information systems. These staff groups not only utilize the information produced by the computer, but they inadvertently compete for authority to control the computer itself. In addition, the line units such as production, marketing, and procurement, along with the traditional staff groups such as personnel and accounting, are uncertain as to how the computer should be used and who should control its use. Thus an aura of confusion over utilization expectations and control develops among staff and line groups.

Concurrent with these developments are a lack of understanding and subsequent speculation about the impact of computers and information systems upon organization structure and processes. Traditionally, this speculation has centered around the potential impact on such structural characteristics as task specialization, task coordination, span of control, and the size of functional elements, as well as the impact on the planning, operational control, and managerial/financial control processes. It is informative to review pertinent research findings to date concerning the impact of the computer upon internal structure and processes, in light of the predicted impact of information technology and computerization on modern organizations.

Some Early Predictions

As early as 1958, Slater made the following predictions about the impact of the computer upon company operations and management:[1]

- More operations will be shifted to the electronic data processing (EDP) department.
- Fewer departments and fewer managerial levels will exist in the firm.
- More emphasis will be placed upon defining objectives as the primary job for top management.
- More influence will be exerted by EDP managers in organizational decisions.

Predictions made by Leavitt and Whisler included the following:[2]

- There will be an increase in organizational centralization.
- There will be fewer middle managers, with more routinization of the middle management job.
- Top management will place added emphasis on goal setting.

---

[1] Robert E. Slater, "Thinking Ahead: How Near Is The Automatic Office?" *Harvard Business Review*, Vol. 36, No. 2 (March-April, 1958).

[2] Harold J. Leavitt and Thomas L. Whisler, "Management In The 1980's" *Harvard Business Review*, Vol. 36, No. 6 (November-December, 1958), pp. 41-48.

In 1960, Simon predicted the impact of the computer upon the organization:[3]

- There will be fewer manual and clerical jobs of the sort which center about routine operations.
- Maintenance-type jobs (i.e., monitoring and updating systems that perform programmed operations such as production scheduling and inventory control) will increase.
- Well-structured managerial decision problems will be computerized.
- Certain middle management activities will be automated (i.e., production scheduling, inventory control, and payroll processing).

These predictions stimulated a controversy which persists today over the impact of computers upon organizational structure, namely the *centralization-decentralization controversy*.

In 1960, Anshen the following predictions:[4]

- Computer technology will not replace middle management; rather it will offer opportunity for enlarging middle management capabilities and performance.
- Middle management tasks will become more like those of top management.
- The trend toward decentralization of decision making will decline.

Burlingame concurred in general with Anshen in the following predictions:[5]

- If a company's philosophy is one of centralization, the likely evolution will be that of increasing centralization.
- If a company's activities are centralized because of difficulties in unifying individual creativity and initiative, the computer will enable increasing decentralization to resolve these difficulties.
- If a company's philosophy is one of decentralization, then the computer should strengthen decentralization of operations, and middle management should grow and flourish rather than the reverse.

In a series of articles, Dearden added a slightly different dimension to the controversy with the following predictions:[6]

- The computer will have no impact on top and divisional management organization.
- It will have very little impact on top management's ability to control profit centers.

---

[3] Herbert A. Simon, "The Corporation: Will It Be Managed by Machines?" *Management and the Corporations, 1985*, edited by M. L. Anshen and G. L. Bach (New York: McGraw-Hill Book Co., 1960), pp. 17-55.

[4] Melvin Anshen, "The Manager and the Black Box," *Harvard Business Review* (November-December, 1960), p. 85.

[5] John F. Burlingame, "Information Technology and Decentralization," *Harvard Business Review* (November-December, 1961), p. 121.

[6] John Dearden, "Can Management Information Be Automated?," *Harvard Business Review* (March-April, 1964), p. 128; "Myth of Real-Time Management Information," *Harvard Business Review* (May-June, 1966), p. 123; and "Computers: No Impact on Divisional Control," *Harvard Business Review* (January-February, 1967), p. 99.

- It will have limited impact on management levels below the divisional manager level, though there may be some centralization of data processing systems.
- Except for certain routine operating control problems in areas such as logistics, production scheduling, and inventory control, it will not be practical to operate a real-time information system; and even if it were practical, this would not solve any top management problems.

Recent Research Findings

To shed some light on the centralization-decentralization controversy and to obtain a better understanding of the impact of computers and information technology on organization structure and processes, a number of research studies have been conducted over the past decade. The findings from four such studies are summarized in Exhibit 3-1.

Exhibit 3-1
SUMMARY OF RECENT RESEARCH FINDINGS ON THE IMPACT OF COMPUTERS ON ORGANIZATION

Study A[1]

- Computers led to drastic changes at the middle management level, where many jobs were either combined or eliminated.
- As more operations are computerized, the power and status of computer personnel expanded, while the functions of other department eroded.
- EDP stimulates recentralization, causing integration of specific functions and regrouping.

Study B[2]

- While EDP eliminated a vast amount of routinized administrative work, there was no accompanying reduction in need for middle managers; actually, EDP made the typical middle manager's job more complex.
- The centralization of activities was not accompanied by a reduction of managerial positions; rather, EDP and the new activities resulted in the addition of over 50 middle management positions in the firms studied.

Study C[3]

- The nature and size of EDP impact was governed by the management attitude toward use of computer technology.
- Centralization of decision making and reduction in middle management jobs have not occured to date in the companies studied during their early experience with EDP.

Study D[4]

- Top management did not appear to make direct use of the computer for decision making.
- The use of the computer by middle management enabled top management to do the following:
  - Make earlier decisions.
  - Gain advanced time.
  - Review problems more thoroughly.
  - Consider alternatives and their potential impact in more detail.
  - Obtain additional information from middle managers prior to making decisions.

---

[1] Ida R. Hoos, "When the Computer Takes Over the Office," *Harvard Business Review* (November-December, 1960), p. 102.

[2] Donald Shaul, "What's Really Ahead for Middle Management?" *Personnel* (November-December, 1964), p. 8.

[3] Hak Chong Lee, *The Impact of Electronic Data Processing Upon Patterns of Business Organization and Administration* (Albany: State University Of New York at Albany, 1965).

[4] Rodney H. Brady, "Computers in Top Level Decision Making," *Harvard Business Review* (July-August, 1967), p. 67.

Unfortunately, each of these studies supports some one of the predictions given earlier, so that the controversy and disagreement on computer impact still has not been resolved. In 1967, a conference involving a number of leading experts on organization and information technology examined forecasts and research findings about the impact of the computer on management. At that time, the findings from various studies concerning the impact of computerized information systems on organization control were summarized by Whisler, as follows:[7]

- The current impact of information technology is to centralize the control structure in organizations or their parts to which it has been applied.
- Information technology tends to alter the power structure among the various functional departments in a manner consistent with the centralization thesis.
- As a result of the closer integration of activities made possible by computer-based systems, the individual manager has less discretion in the use of his time. This means that a greater amount of the manager's time will be devoted to providing data inputs to the information system, and to analyzing company-wide reports.
- The manager also has less discretion in the methods and procedures he uses to carry out his job as new information technology is used in the organization. (For example, top management will impose policies and procedures for MIS use, how a manager can originate new reports, the review of new and existing management reports, and the general evaluation of costs of reports.)
- Computers are beginning to perform the function of control.

And in an in-depth study of two manufacturing firms, Hofer reported that the effects of the computers were:[8]

- The same for both companies, even though one was 25 times larger than the other.
- Greater on organizational processes (planning, budgeting, and evaluating) and delegation of authority than on the characteristics of formal structure (task specialization, coordination, span of control, and element size). In other words, the computer was used more to facilitate planning and control functions through the development of models for resource allocation and evaluation of resource utilization for various organizational functions and programs, and less to design organization structure.
- Greater at the operations level than at the middle management level, and greater at the middle management level than at the general (top) management level. This indicates that computers were used for more programmatic, routine, and recurring operations, such as inventory control, production scheduling, payroll processing, and financial accounting than for strategic and nonstructured decisions.
- Greater on the organizational components whose main tasks involved processing large amounts of quantitative data than on components whose tasks did not (e.g., accounting, payroll, and production planning and control rather than personal, maintenance, and customer services).

[7] Thomas L. Whisler, "The Impact of Information Technology on Organizational Control," *The Impact of Computers on Management* (Cambridge: M.I.T. Press, 1968), pp. 16-48.

[8] Charles W. Hofer, "Emerging EDP Pattern," *Harvard Business Review* (March-April, 1970), pp. 160-170.

Summary of Basic Issues

The major themes underlying the predictions and research concerning the impact of the computer are: (1) how the organization structure is affected, and (2) how the computer is used to facilitate operations and management

The *structural issues* involve the centralization-decentralization controversy and the related effects of the computer on the scope of middle management. Both of these issues are somewhat unresolved. The cumulative and permanent effects of computerized information systems on middle management are unclear and incomplete. To the extent that a high degree of integration of MIS design and monitoring occurs, centralization of the organization is more likely to be the rule rather than the exception and the role of middle management will be correspondingly subordinated. In other words, the creation of a high level MIS staff often results in the generation of more information about plans, operations, and performance at all levels of management which leads to centralization of the planning and control functions.

As more information about company-wide operations is compiled, analyzed, and evaluated by top management, there is a tendency toward greater centralization of policy making and decision making. High level planning and control staffs often are set up in larger organizations to utilize more fully the great quantity of information produced by the MIS. These staffs advise top management on alternatives for the future direction the organization should take, and they provide analyses of the pattern and efficiency of resource utilization that have occurred in the past. In the long run, the utilization of these high level staffs by top management often result in a high degree of centralization of planning and control in the organization.

The extent of this tendency toward centralization depends in part on top management's philosophy about *how the computer will be used in the organization.* Two uses of the computer are for data processing and problem solving. The introduction of the computer in an organization traditionally has been for the purpose of substituting mechanized data processing for manual processing of data, rather than for more advanced problem solving. Research findings reveal that the computer is used extensively for programmable (routine and recurring) tasks and decision making, such as inventory control, payroll processing, production scheduling, and financial accounting. These tasks and decisions often involve large amounts of data compilation and processing, and for the most part use the computer as a substitute for manual processing of data.

The use of the computer in *problem solving* is increasing with the greater use of quantitative decision models such as simulation, linear programming, queuing, more advanced inventory control, and production planning and control systems; PERT; and planning, programming, and budgeting systems (PPBS). As this trend continues, specialized operations research activities by high level planning and control staffs tend to emerge, and these developments contribute to greater centralization, as discussed previously

The foregoing predictions and research must be analyzed and evaluated in terms of how the computer is used (for data processing and problem solving), and what changes in manpower requirements will result. A third important factor concerning the impact of the computer is who will have the authority and responsibility for its design, operation, and monitoring. This factor also involves structural and usage issues similar to those discussed earlier in this section concerning organization and management generally. In other words, organization for the management of the MIS has an important bearing on how effectively the computer will be used and the severity of structural problems that may occur. The remaining sections of this chapter discuss these issues in more detail as related to the nature of the MIS staff and responsibility for its management.

THE NATURE OF THE MIS STAFF

The predictions and research findings reported in the previous section are concerned with the impact of large rather than small scale computerized information systems. Therefore, in addition to the impact of large scale uses of the computer on organization structure, operations, and management, the factor of large size involves a corollary problem of who should manage the MIS. In other words, large investment in computer technology and manpower requires top management planning and control of the information function, generally accomplished with the assistance of a high level MIS staff. This section discusses the nature of the MIS staff and its impact on the overall management structure of an organization.

Purpose and Functions

The general purpose of the MIS staff is to design, coordinate, and monitor the MIS in an organization. The MIS staff provides various information services for operating line managers in the organization and for middle and upper levels of management. The specific services provided by the MIS staff include:

1. Design and monitoring of an integrated set of data-information flows and reports.
2. Design and monitoring of an integrated set of MIS processes: a data base, data coding scheme, and data processor.
3. Review and evaluation of the effectiveness of MIS reports and of the MIS processes in providing these reports.
4. Review and coordination of changes in information needs and MIS processes.
5. Development of procedures for prospective users to obtain access to the MIS.
6. Formulation of policies regarding priorities and criteria for processing and evaluating reports.

These responsibilities primarily involve systems design and monitoring, rather than actual operation of the MIS processes, that is rather than the actual acquisition, coding, processing, retrieval, and distribution of data or the operation of the computer facilities.

Systems Design

Systems design provides a center where requests for MIS reports can be brought together for analysis and design from a total organizational perspective. Systems design includes the investigation, analysis, and evaluation of all operations to define information needs and the combination of these needs into an integrated set of reports. The MIS processes needed to generate reports are designed and cost estimates for these processes are developed. Finally, the expected benefits of these reports are estimated and evaluated against the costs of producing them.

The staff will also specify procedures for processing requests for new reports, how these reports will be reviewed by the MIS staff, and which criteria will be applied to the evaluation of reports. Specifications for information processing hardware and software are developed and feasibility analyses are made. Ideally, policies and procedures relating to the operation of the MIS are made explicit to other parts of the organization so that all are aware of how the MIS is intended to operate.

Systems Monitoring

Systems monitoring provides a center for the review and evaluation of the MIS from a total organizational perspective. The MIS staff is responsible for insuring that the MIS processes operate in the intended manner. This involves the continual review of policies and internal control procedures for the distribution and use of reports, the operation of MIS processes, and data acquisition and coding.

The usefulness of reports and the efficiency of MIS processes should be evaluated on a regular and continuing basis. Specific performance measures are required for MIS processes and reports. Performance measurement reports should be included in the set of MIS reports developed for the entire organization. The MIS itself should be treated as any operating system in the organization, and it should be evaluated in a similar way.

Data Processing

Data processing[9] is concerned with the physical acquisition and processing of data to produce reports. Data processing is not a major responsibility of the MIS staff, but it is highly interrelated with systems design and monitoring. The data processing department (usually computerized), rather than the MIS staff, collects and codes data and transforms computerized data for use throughout the organization. Physical centralization of data processing facilities, equipment, and personnel are not required for an effective MIS. The

---

[9] The term data processing, rather than information processing, is used to coincide with the common designation of a data processing department, personnel, or staff. Data processing is analogous to information as a process as described in Chapter 1.

data processing activities of the MIS can be, and usually are, decentralized. All segments of the organization are involved in data processing since each originates source documents, codes events or transactions, and may even convert data into information. For example, the production department prepares timecards, the sales department codes sales transactions, and the personnel office prepares payroll forms. These timecards, transaction documents, payroll forms, and other data are accumulated by the data processing department to be processed into reports designed by the MIS staff.

The design and monitoring of the data processing system normally are the responsibility of the MIS staff group which is separate from those involved in the physical processing of data. The separation of data processing from systems design and monitoring is analogous to separation of responsibilities within the production division of a firm. The manufacturing department of the production division is concerned with the physical processing of resources to produce a product. The design and monitoring of the manufacturing operations normally are the responsibility of a staff group (production planning and control), which is separate from those persons involved in the physical processing of resources into products. In either system, MIS or production, the three types of responsibilities (design or planning, data processing or manufacturing, and monitoring or control) are highly interrelated. Even though there is a separation of responsibilities between staff units and line units, there must be very close liaison between them to achieve optimum productivity.

Summary of the Operation of the MIS

Exhibit 3-2 shows the organization of the MIS staff and the data processing staff. Requests for information are made to the MIS staff. These requests are reviewed and analyzed in terms of need related to existing reports, possible duplication of reports, frequency requirements, formats, and the impact on existing data acquisition, coding, storage, processing, and retrieval. In this analysis, the intended uses of reports and the costs of producing them are evaluated. The MIS staff recommends changes to reports based on their analyses, and coordinates these changes with the areas of the organization that are affected. Final designs of reports are then approved by the appropriate managers. The design of MIS processes (if required) is coordinated through top management if additional resources are required for data processing, facilities, or manpower. If additional resources are not required, new report requirements are communicated to data processing for programming. The MIS staff serves in a coordinating capacity between data processing and users of reports until the data processing operations are performing effectively. The MIS staff monitors the flow of data and reports between the data processing department and users. It reviews and evaluates the effectiveness of these reports and the efficiency of the data processing activities. Review and evaluation is made by the MIS staff relating to the usefulness of reports in terms of the information they contain, format, accuracy of information, timing, and distribution. The actual costs of data processing are calculated and compared with the cost estimates made at

Exhibit 3-2

ORGANIZATION OF THE MIS STAFF

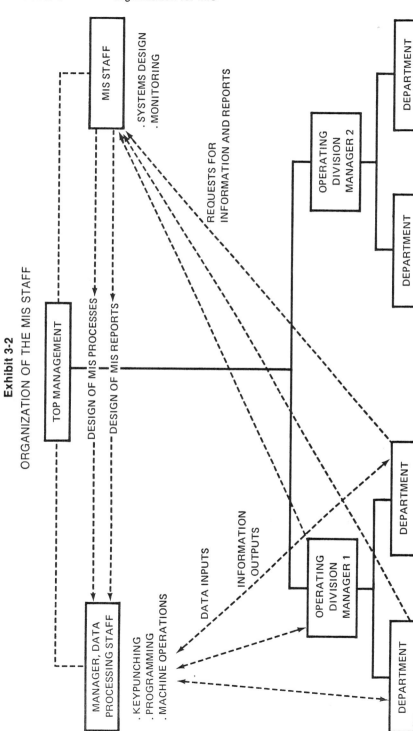

NOTE: THE MIS STAFF AND DATA PROCESSING STAFF ARE SHOWN SEPARATELY HERE TO EMPHASIZE THE SEPARATION OF THEIR RESPONSIBILITIES. IN PRACTICE THEY ARE OFTEN PLACED UNDER A COMMON MANAGER, SUCH AS THE DIRECTOR OF INFORMATION SERVICES, WHO REPORTS TO TOP MANAGEMENT.

the time the reports were designed. Based on this type of review and analysis, the MIS staff initiates, coordinates, and recommends changes to the reports and to the data processing operations.

Levels of MIS Staff

The MIS staff is generally a high level staff. Their formal authority must be at a level high enough to accomplish the coordination and integration of information needs, MIS processes, and information flows throughout the organization. In order to accomplish this coordination and integration in large organizations, subordinate MIS staffs may exist at lower organizational levels. Exhibit 3-3 illustrates multiple levels of information systems design and monitoring. It reflects a level of information systems similar to what has occured in the organization of other staff units such as personnel and controller. When organizations are small, operating departments typically perform their own accounting and personnel functions. As organizations grow and become more complex, these activities are centralized under top management staffs to take advantage of economies of scale and to better coordinate and integrate policies and procedures. For example, a decentralized accounting or personnel staff which reports to a top management staff is common in large organizations.

Hierarchical staff arrangment for the MIS facilitates considerably the coordination and review of information needs in each respective lower level operating area. This is because the high level staff is able to interface with a staff who are not only information experts but are extremely well versed on operating area needs and capabilities. The hierarchical arrangement insures that operating area needs will be met most effectively. This means that the MIS staff and its lower level counterparts can develop a solid understanding of operational problems and the information needs to solve these problems, while being able to interrelate these needs within the MIS for the total organization. If The MIS staff can interface only with operating personnel, some degree of effectiveness would be lost.

In summary, the essential features of the MIS staff concept are:

1. A staff unit provides advice to top management and to line managers, and as such it is user-oriented. That is, the MIS staff is set up to serve managers by designing reports that are useful to them in the performance of their responsibilities and by designing the most efficient MIS processes to produce the reports.

2. The MIS staff is primarily involved in information systems design and monitoring, not data processing.

3. The staff coordinates and centralizes the dispersed design and monitoring efforts throughout the organization.

4. Data processing activities (including data collection, coding, conversion, storage, and retrieval) are carried out throughout the entire organization.

Exhibit 3-3

AN INTEGRATED SYSTEMS DESIGN AND MONITORING STAFF

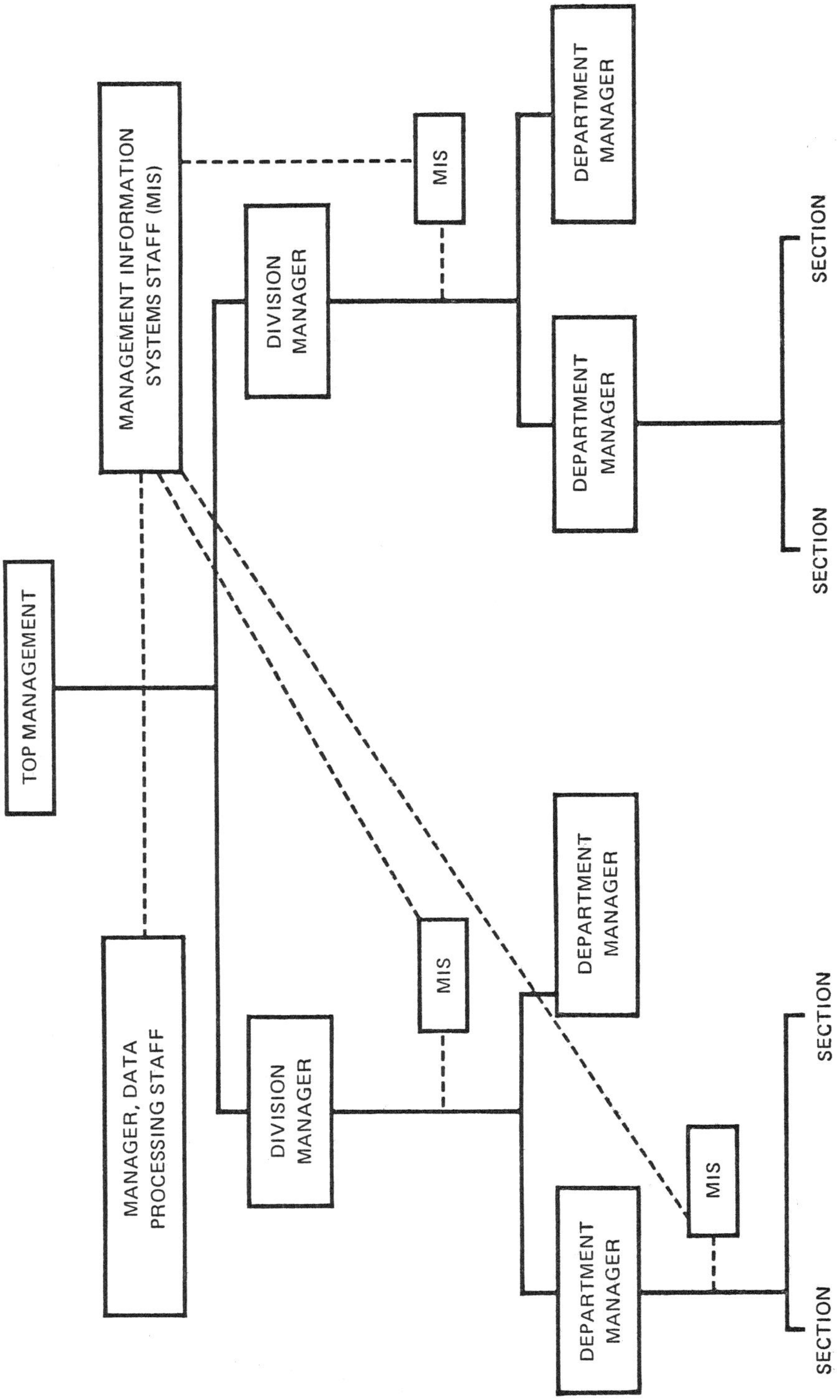

RESPONSIBILITY FOR MIS: SELECTED ISSUES

Systems design and systems monitoring responsibilities should be closely coordinated. Ideally, these responsibilities should rest with one staff group. Whether or not a firm assigns the responsibility for systems design and monitoring to one manager, it ought to consider the following issues when attempting to determine the appropriate organizational placement of the MIS staff:

1. Ability to provide organization-wide service.
2. Acceptability by operating segments.
3. Simplicity of organizational structure.
4. Capabilities of existing personnel.

Organization-Wide Service

The optimal organizational placement of the MIS staff insures that all segments of the organization have the opportunity to be served. This can be accomplished more readily if the users of information and the providers of information services are separated. Besides insuring that all users are served with equal effort, separation of users and providers leads to a more objective and independent analysis of information needs. Thus, crossing departmental lines becomes less of an obstacle, and more emphasis can be given to attaining organization-wide objectives.

Acceptability by Operating Segments

Before the MIS staff and its services can have any real utility, the MIS staff must achieve widespread acceptance within the organization. Their acceptability is substantially enhanced when they provide a truly organization-wide service. This becomes especially important when systems design involves an appreciable amount of change. MIS design may require changing many existing technical, organization, and procedural aspects of a firm's operations. For instance, the design of a new set of reports dealing with production planning and control may require changes in the production organization, such as the formulation of a new production staff unit responsible for scheduling, cost analyses, and control operations. This new staff unit may be instrumental in changing some of the technical aspects of production dealing with work and material flows, plant layout, and facilities utilization as new information is analyzed and evaluated. To support these technical and organizational changes and to explain the new reports to production personnel, new policies and procedures may be required. Frequently if not always, this involves crossing departmental lines. The new production planning and control reports may require information about sales forecasts, availability of materials, status of purchase orders, shipping schedules, and availability of funds. Since information items must be furnished by areas other than production, procedures having direct relevance to nonproduction areas must in effect be instituted by a production staff.

Generating organizational support for changes of this type is always difficult; hence there is a definite need to ease the situation by attaching the systems design group directly to top management, perhaps even to the president. The importance of top management's direct support has been demonstrated in the findings of various studies comparing the characteristics of successful and unsuccessful information systems.

A 1963 McKinsey survey, "Getting the Most Out of Your Computer," showed that the active support and involvement of top management was the primary ingredient for achieving above average results in designing and implementing a computerized information system.[10] A later McKinsey study identified five responsibilities that should not be delegated by top management if maximum results from the organization's computer effort are to be obtained:[11]

1. Top management must approve objectives, criteria, and priorities for the corporate computer effort, with special attention to the development program.
2. They must decide on the organizational rearrangements required to carry out policies and achieve objectives.
3. They must assign responsibility for results to the line and functional executives served by the computer systems, and see to it that executives exercise this responsibility.
4. They must insist that detailed computer systems plans are made an integral part of operating plans and budgets.
5. They must follow through to see that the planned results are actually achieved.

There are two other important reasons supporting top management's involvement: they are needed to overcome the resistance of people in the organization to the computerized information system, and they will evaluate the investment in computer hardware, facilities, and manpower. The commitment of top management to the computerized information system is vital for developing its acceptance by people in the organization.[12]

Simplicity of Organization Structure

Additional staff units or special project groups to utilize computer technology and sophisticated managerial techniques for planning and control often severely complicate the organization structure. Effective management may become difficult. Administrative elements (staff units) of an organization may outnumber or overshadow operating elements (line units), and the resulting excessive number of clarification policies and procedures may actually diminish operating efficiency. Consider the dilemma of a production

---

[10] See Joseph A. Orlicky, *The Successful Computer System* (New York: McGraw-Hill Book Co., 1969), pp. 207-209, for a summary of this survey.

[11] See *The McKinsey Quarterly* (Fall, 1968), pp. 17-31, reprinted in Donald H. Sanders, *Computers and Management* (New York: McGraw-Hill Book Co., 1970), pp. 167-168.

[12] See Thomas L. Whisler, *Information Technology and Organizational Change* (Belmont, Calif.: Brooks/Cole Publishing Co., 1970), pp. 7-9, for a discussion of the problems of resistance to change as related to information technology.

manager who must frequently furnish large amounts of data to accounting, data processing, personnel, payroll, inventory control, operations research, systems analysis, corporate planning, and MIS staff units. As more of the production manager's time is devoted to providing data to staff units, much of which data is not used in reports and analyses for the production department, the production manager's operating performance may deteriorate. He will soon become disenchanted with the demands of the MIS and will resist its implementation and use.

Capabilities of Existing Personnel

Since the organizational placement of the MIS staff is a potentially sensitive issue, the capabilities of existing personnel in the organization are significant. In the short-run, especially as the firm begins to formalize and centralize its MIS staff responsibilities, the knowledge of computer technology held by its existing personnel has considerable influence on where the MIS staff is placed within the organization. This means that MIS staff responsibilities tend to be assigned to persons in the organization who are specialists in computer technology. These individuals may have limited understanding of other concepts that are important for providing effective MIS staff management and for providing organization-wide information services. For example, the following types of knowledge and expertise are important requisites for the MIS staff if it is to function effectively:[13]

1. *Managerial and Financial Accounting Concepts.* The measurement and communication of relevant economic and financial information is a major segment of any formalized information system. Knowledge in this area is needed in order to assist each manager in formulating information needs and reports for performance measurement. Also, knowledge of accounting is necessary because such information constitutes a large segment of the MIS.

2. *Behavioral Science Concepts.* Effective motivation of personnel is an essential ingredient in every aspect of MIS functions. Understanding of concepts in psychology, sociology and anthropology relevant to individual and group motivation is important.

3. *Industrial Engineering Concepts.* Flowcharting and work methods and analyses are useful in analyzing the interrelationships between operating work systems, resource flows, and related data-information flows.

4. *Computer Concepts.* Most MIS's incorporate the use of automatic data processing equipment. A knowledge of hardware and software capabilities, limitations, and economics is essential.

5. *Quantitative Concepts.* Quantitative concepts provide a more precise and logical means for optimizing the allocation and control of resources for MIS functions. An understanding of the use, limitations, and economics of mathematical and statistical methods for problem solving and decision making is necessary.

---

[13] See Richard G. Canning, "Needed: A Planning Training Program," *EDP Analyses,* Vol. 5, pp. 4-6 and 10-11 (August, 1967), reprinted in Donald H. Sanders, *Computers and Management* (New York: McGraw-Hill Book Co., 1970), pp. 343-349, for a similar discussion of knowledge required.

These types of knowledge by MIS staff personnel are necessary for better understanding of how operating managers can use these concepts more effectively.

Organizational Placement of MIS: The Role of the Accountant

The foregoing issues concerning organizational placement of the MIS staff have not addressed the question of which organization unit should have major responsibility for performance of the MIS functions. The following discussion assumes that systems design and systems monitoring are to be placed under a common manager.

Currently, the basic issue is whether to assign the responsibility for the MIS to the accounting area, which traditionally has been the major provider and user of information in the organization. Exhibits 3-4 and 3-5 illustrate the possible organizational impact of placing the MIS in alternative positions.

In Exhibit 3-4 the controller-accountant is the head of the MIS. In this case the controller-accountant is the provider of information throughout the entire company. In Exhibit 3-5 the MIS is the responsibility of a vice-president for administrative services. The controller-accountant is responsible only for the traditional areas of general accounting, tax, and auditing, and he is a user of information generated from the MIS just like the vice-presidents of marketing, production, and finance.

How effective can the accounting manager be in directing the MIS? Experience indicates that an accountant can be effective as the manager of the MIS if two conditions prevail. First, his frame of reference must consider internal, as well as external, information needs. If the accountant is preoccupied with accumulating information for stockholders, creditors, and governmental agencies, he is likely to be insensitive to the operating manager's information needs.

Second, the accountant must be reasonably knowledgeable in the use and limitations of certain techniques from industrial engineering, computer science,

Exhibit 3-4

PARTIAL ORGANIZATION CHART: ACCOUNTANT HEADS MIS

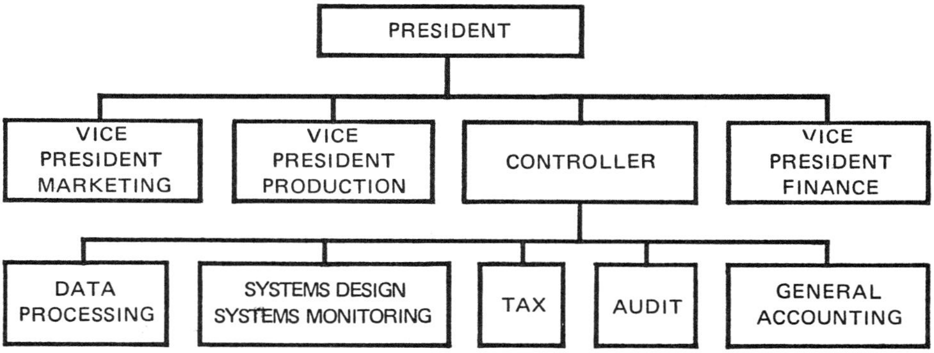

Exhibit 3-5

PARTIAL ORGANIZATION CHART: ACCOUNTANT DOES NOT HEAD MIS

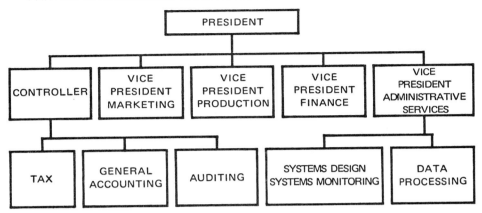

quantitative methods, and behavioral science. As manager of the MIS, his knowledge must enable him to incorporate these techniques in systems design where appropriate.

Organization-wide service is easily attained with the accountant as head of the MIS. In performing traditional accounting functions, the accountant is already a provider of an organization-wide service by supplying external users with information pertaining to the entire firm. Retaining his overall scope, he need only become service oriented regarding internal users of information.

Simplicity of organizational structure may actually be enhanced with an accountant as head of the MIS. He is already the central source of a great deal of economic and financial data; placing the MIS under his jurisdiction will lead to a more complete central information source and will eliminate the need for creation of a new organizational staff unit.

Acceptability of the accountant as the head of the MIS is dependent on: (1) a user-oriented frame of reference on the part of the accountant and (2) broader education and training of the accountant. As this is attained, the desire for "capability of personnel" will also be satisfied. The acceptance of the accountant as the head of the MIS by the other functional managers or other staff areas have been varied. Initially, the computerized information system was concerned almost exclusively with processing financial accounting data. Therefore, other areas of the organization were not concerned with the fact that the accountant was responsible for its design and processing. As computerized information systems were developed for nonfinancial accounting applications, such as inventory control, production scheduling, managerial accounting, market research, and sales forecasting, nonaccounting areas of the organization such as production, sales, and purchasing suggested moving the responsibility for the MIS away from the accountant. In addition, as centralized systems analysis, operations research, and corporate planning staffs were set up in the organization to facilitate top management planning and control, a need developed for a considerable amount of company-wide information, in addition to the financial accounting information.

These developments led to the view that a high level autonomous department should be created to assume the responsibility for the MIS.

The MIS Staff as an Autonomous Unit

The MIS staff as an autonomous unit is analogous to the vice-president for administrative services shown in Exhibit 3-5 or a vice-president for information services. This type of organizational arrangement reflects a corporate-wide scope of information, provides for an interdepartmental view of data-information flows, and facilitates the integration of information subsystems.

In addition to the issues of organization-wide service, acceptability, simplicity of organization structure, and capabilities of existing personnel, there are other important factors which may influence the decision about the proper organizational placement of MIS responsibilities. For smaller organizations the creation of a separate autonomous department may not be feasible. Smaller organizations usually do not require extensive use of computerized information, and coordination of data-information flows is not a serious problem. A separate autonomous department often requires additional facilities and manpower; these additional costs should be evaluated in relation to the benefits from other investment alternatives.

The organization should determine whether there are serious problems in providing information services with its existing organizational arrangement. If there is a spirit of cooperation among managers and staff, the organizational placement of MIS responsibilities is not a primary issue. In fact, the McKinsey survey concluded that the selection of an MIS manager who commands respect and confidence throughout the organization by virtue of his personal nature and professional skills can minimize the importance of where the MIS staff is located organizationally.[14] In the final analysis, the placement of the MIS staff must be based on multiple variables as described in the foregoing section, and each organization has different operating characteristics, personnel capabilities, and spirit of cooperation. Therefore, the organizational placement of the MIS staff may vary among organizations, and yet be optimal for the organization.

SUMMARY

Predictions and research findings concerning the impact of computerized information systems deal with (1) the impact on organization structure, the centralization-decentralization controversy, and the related effects on middle management; (2) the uses of the computer for operations and management, especially as related to data processing versus problem solving applications;

---

[14] See *The McKinsey Quarterly* (Fall, 1968), pp. 17-31, reprinted in Donald H. Sanders, *Computers and Management* (New York: McGraw-Hill Book Co., 1970), pp. 167-168.

and (3) assignment of authority for the design, operation, and monitoring of the computerized information system.

The nature and purpose of the MIS staff and its major responsibilities are described as they relate to systems design and systems monitoring. Also, the interrelatedness of these staff responsibilities to data processing operations dealing with the physical collection, coding, storage, processing, and retrieval of data throughout the organization is discussed. The need to separate systems design and monitoring responsibilities from data processing responsibilities also is discussed. An overview of the operation of the MIS is presented and usefulness of levels of MIS staffs are described.

Finally, important issues concerning the responsibility for MIS are presented, dealing with organization-wide service, acceptability by operating segments, simplicity of organization structure, capabilities of existing personnel, and cost. The organizational placement of the MIS staff and the role of the accountant versus a separate and autonomous staff are discussed.

REVIEW QUESTIONS

1. Summarize and discuss the major issues identified in the research findings concerning the impact of information technology on organizations. What are several important organizational implications that you feel the MIS will have in the future?

2. What are your views concerning the impact of the computer on centralization versus decentralization and on changes in middle management? Give your views on the feasibility of using the computer for data processing vs. problem solving.

3. Discuss the nature of the MIS staff as a provider of information services.

4. Explain the meaning of the systems design responsibility of the MIS and its organizational implications.

5. Describe the systems monitoring responsibility of the MIS and some of the important issues concerning its performance by the MIS staff.

6. Discuss the nature of data processing in relation to systems design and monitoring. What activities are involved in data processing and who generally performs these activities?

7. Describe the concept of levels of MIS staff. How is this concept analogous to other major staff functions in the organization such as controller and personnel departments? What is the usefulness of this concept?

8. Identify and discuss four major issues for assigning responsibility for the MIS staff. Which of these are most important?

9. Describe the role of the accountant as it relates to MIS functions and responsibilities, versus using a separate and autonomous staff unit.

10. What do you visualize as important types of knowledge or expertise that the manager of the MIS staff should possess? The MIS staff personnel should possess?

EXERCISE 3-1: Organization for MIS: Safeway Airlines, Inc.
                          (Part A)[15]

In 1958, Safeway Airlines assigned certain data processing functions to the Tabulating Section of the company's Treasury Department, which operated a small punched card installation. The office methods and procedures installed during the 1960's were well conceived in view of the existing informational needs for the airline. By 1969, however, the growth of the company had burdened the system beyond the complexity and activity for which it had originally been designed. The improvement of office methods and procedures had been afforded only slight managerial attention and the development of systems clearly had not paralleled the growth of the airline, with the possible exception of the maintenance and supply areas.

During the early months of 1969, the Tabulating Section experienced major difficulties in the preparation of certain important reports. Several regulatory and governmental reports were late and the routine accounting activities of the company were seriously slowed. At that point the tabulating supervisor resigned and Safeway hired George Lewis as a replacement. Mr. Lewis had considerable data processing experience, mainly with a local utility company. His initial assignment was to improve the company's tabulating operations. In March, 1969, Safeway also retained a national accounting firm for overall assistance in defining and resolving the data processing problems which now loomed as formidable.

DEVELOPMENT OF A PROJECT GROUP

The task of upgrading the systems and procedures was begun with the formation of a project group. The group membership consisted of one individual from each department of the company. The project group's purpose was: (1) to provide a vehicle for documenting the existing procedures, and (2) to serve as an interim clearinghouse for coordinating the development and installation of new or revised methods. Some of the project group's specific functions were to:

1. Evaluate the management information and reporting needs of the various departments throughout the company.
2. Analyze the company's existing procedures—from the preparation of source documents to the end use of information by management.
3. Relate the individual reporting and control requirements and redesign the procedures to expand the use of exception reporting techniques, to shorten total processing times, and to minimize duplication of effort.

By early summer, several improvements already had been made in the Tabulating Section. The workload was current and interim operating instructions were being prepared. Punched card procedures for the areas of expense

---

[15] Part A of a two-part case describes the formation of a systems project group, performance of a study, and the development of a systems organization. Part B, presented in Chapter 10, describes a computer feasibility study. This case was developed from materials compiled by Raymond L. Thompson, of Hoskins and Sells, Certified Public Accountants, and Dr. Homer J. Mottice, of Florida State University.

distribution and payroll were being revised and expanded. Furthermore, several reports had been eliminated; those remaining were made simpler, more timely, and more accurate.

It was becoming apparent to top management that a considerable potential existed for the improvement of information systems, especially in terms of reduced clerical costs. The project group, therefore, was charged with the additional responsibility of projecting the company's future information and data needs, taking into account potential route awards, plans for re-equipping the fleet, and various new facility programs. The project group arrived at the following conclusions regarding Safeway's data processing efforts:

1. The principal cause of the difficulties with Safeway's punched card methods was the condition of source data. The project group observed that the source data frequently had been late, inaccurate, or incomplete. If the input data was not reliable, it followed that the output could not be reliable—the GIGO principle. It was apparent that correction of this problem would involve several factors—improved procedures, a new training program, establishment of a data control function within the Tabulating Section, and a data processing schedule which would reduce the extreme peaks in workload.

2. A definite need existed for more management information throughout the company. The Sales Department and the Research Department urgently required additional statistical information in order to meet the regulatory reporting requirements as well as to achieve better planning and control. The Maintenance and Engineering Department needed additional labor utilization and operating statistics. The project group expected—correctly, as it turned out—that those existing needs would not diminish, but would grow at a pace with the company.

3. It was evident that the combination of an expanded group of tabulating applications and the expected growth of the company would cause the unit record equipment rentals to double in a comparatively short time. At that point the rental for the punched card installation would have been just under the rental for a small computer and its peripheral devices. It was also evident to the project group that a computer would provide greater processing speeds, more flexibility, and greater accuracy. A computer would allow more complex calculations to be made; it would permit certain routine decision making to be performed electronically; and its capacity could be increased in modules without the addition of a corresponding number of people.

The national accounting firm recommended that a complete computer feasibility and evaluation study be made. The project group agreed with this recommendation.

FORMATION OF THE ADMINISTRATIVE SERVICES DEPARTMENT

The project group had served a most worthwhile purpose in launching and coordinating the data processing upgrading project during its early days. As the work progressed, the project began to require considerably more time than the group members could provide and still attend to their normal duties. The accounting firm recommended that a permanent systems organization be established to perform not only the systems and procedures functions for which the project group had been responsible but also such other company-wide service activities as research, forms control, programming, and data processing. Accordingly, an Administrative Services Department was formed. J. K. Atlas was assigned responsibility for the new department and was appointed Vice-President—Administrative Services.

Prior to 1969, more than three fourths of the workload of the Tabulating Section had been generated by the Treasury Department. The project group's early planning showed that this figure would be reduced to approximately one third of the section's output as the new data processing system was revised and expanded. This resulting redistribution eliminated the requirement for keeping the Tabulating Section administratively within the Treasury Department. Thus, tabulating became the first function to be transferred to the newly formed Administrative Services Department.

As soon as Administrative Services became an official entity, the functions of the project group were realigned so that the group was empowered to serve only in an advisory capacity. As systems development and installation work was being carried out in each department, project group representatives and personnel from the Administrative Services Department worked as a team under the guidance of the national accounting firm.

CONDUCTING THE SYSTEMS STUDY

The Administrative Services Department had started work on the preliminary phases of the following responsibilities assigned to them by the president:

1. Balance the need for rapid, accurate information processing against the costs of operating a management reporting and control system.
2. Develop specifications for the data processing equipment necessary to support a management control system appropriate for Safeway's needs.
3. Prepare a detailed project plan and train Safeway's personnel to install and operate the new system effectively.

In October, 1969, the accounting firm's role was enlarged to include providing Safeway's systems and data processing personnel with additional technical training, project organization, managerial assistance, and procedural review. The accounting firm's specific task was to guide Safeway in:

1. Reviewing the individual information requirements and further improving the existing procedures on an interim basis.
2. Defining a systems and data processing approach which would yield an appropriate focus of effort on the dual goals of better managment information and clerical expense reduction.
3. Evaluating the data processing equipment requirements.
4. Evaluating the cost justifications for more sophisticated data processing equipment.
5. Planning and implementing the new systems utilizing the selected equipment.

During the next 18 months (1969-1971), The Administrative Services Department helped Safeway chalk up the following accomplishments, relating principally to the interim improvement of existing systems:

1. Approximately 60 forms were eliminated.
2. All existing systems and procedures were flowcharted.
3. Improved training records were installed.
4. The preparation and updating of the Stores Material Catalog were mechanized.
5. A new mechanized cross-reference guide for vendor and company part numbers was installed.
6. Exception reporting of promotional fare sales was instituted.
7. The company's teletype system, which then covered eight states, was utilized for the transmittal of flight information to the main base in Atlanta.
8. A daily flight and load factor statistical report was developed to be distributed the following morning—in contrast to a much less complete monthly version which required about 90 days for processing.

As a result of the interim modifications, better management information was made available. A considerable reduction of clerical effort also resulted.

As the existing systems were flowcharted, information needs evaluated, and interim improvements instituted, the new department was engaged in conducting a company-wide systems study. A distinction was made among mandatory, high priority, and desirable information requirements and data handling applications. For example, the daily, weekly, and monthly processing of certain accounting transactions is mandatory from a survival standpoint. Certain other processing applications, such as those arising from an inventory control project, were initially classified as "desirable," with an escalation of the priority rating to "mandatory" based upon anticipated company needs at specified future times.

1. Discuss several potential impacts on the Safeway organization and management by the creation of the Administrative Services Department and by the introduction of information technology (especially computer hardware and manpower).
2. Describe the emergence of the Administrative Services Department and comment on:
   a. Why it was needed and its advantages and limitations.
   b. Its short run and long run purposes, and the specific functions it performs relating to systems design, systems monitoring, and data processing.
   c. What capabilities are required of the personnel in the Administrative Services Department?
3. Evaluate the assignment of responsibilities for systems design, systems monitoring, and data processing.

EXERCISE 3-2: The Clark Company

The Clark Company is a multi-division manufacturer of office equipment and furniture. Bill Miller is the Controller of the Clark Company. Over the years he has been regarded as the troubleshooter for a wide variety of problems for the company. In addition, he has had experience with computers and is probably the most capable person in Clark Company in this area. In May, he attended a meeting of sales representatives of computer manufacturers who were attempting to sell the company on the benefits of the computer for their operations. Costs and savings were the principal themes of the presentations made by the sales representatives, and were also the topics emphasized in the questions asked by those managers who attended from the Clark Company.

The president of the company, Ray Clark, was deeply inpressed with the potential of high-speed data processing equipment. After the sales representatives meeting, this topic was of primary concern during the weekly staff meetings. The key managers of the company generally supported the presidents' views in this area, and encouraged the immediate investment in a computer operation. Based on this enthusiasm, the president set up a committee to come up with a concrete plan of action. Bill Miller was appointed chairman, and the other members consisted of top management; vice-presidents of marketing, production, and finance; and the directors of personnel and procurement.

The committee met weekly and it was soon obvious that none of the committee (with the exception of Bill Miller) knew anything about computer technology or how it could be used in the Clark Company. The Vice-President of Production suggested setting up a project group with the necessary expertise to develop the "nuts and bolts" of the computer applications potential (cost-benefit analysis). This project group would report to Bill Miller's committee, which would take on a top management advisory function. While the project group performed its function, the advisory committee would continue to meet (monthly, instead of weekly) to learn about and discuss progress of the project group. Since the company did not have the necessary expertise, the advisory committee suggested using an outside consultant. The following types of consultants were considered:

1. Independent management consulting firm
2. Public accounting firm
3. Two or three computer manufacturers (to study the problem with the objective of offering a bid for equipment, software, and systems analysis).

The advisory committee decided on contracting with a management consulting firm. The president approved the decision, but stipulated that several operating company personnel should be assigned full time to the consulting firm team in order to develop the statement of information needs of the company. Representatives from production, marketing, and the controllers' operations were designated. The consulting firm was to define the types of information needed by the company that could be included in a computerized information system, and show costs benefits of a computerized information system. Implicit in this task were recommendations for hardware, software, manpower, and operating policies and procedures. The company agreed to pay the consultants $100,000, with the proposed system to be submitted to the advisory committee within six months.

1. Evaluate the general approach of the Clark Company in organizating for a systems study to design a computerized information system. Consider in your comments:

   a. The responsibilities and organizational arrangements.
   b. Use of outside personnel.
   c. The charge to the management consulting firm.
   d. The utilization of company personnel with the consulting firm.

2. Developing a set of criteria that you feel would be appropriate for organizing for a systems study, to include design, monitoring, and processing responsibilities.

EXERCISE 3-3: Study of Organizations

1. Read and critique several articles on the variations in organizational and staff structures for management information systems.

2. Based on an actual organization, describe the impact of the computer on its organizational design. Include in your discussion alternatives for organization design that were considered, the rationale or criteria that were the most important for selecting the organization design, and a comparison of these points with the concepts described in Chapter 3.

EXERCISE 3-4: Farm Products Corporation (Part C)

The objectives of this exercise are to become aware of the structural and behavioral impact of computers on an organization, to demonstrate the problems to be overcome and the skills required to design and implement a computerized information system, and to understand the purpose and responsibility of an effective management information system.

FPC's new payroll processing system was not an instant success. Although the actual printing of paychecks was performed faster, it required almost as much time to convert the data to a form suitable for computer processing as it had previously required to prepare the payroll sheet manually. The conversion process increased the possibility of introducing new errors, and some unusual paychecks were issued during the first month (one assembly worker received $1,188.00 for a week's work). This problem was later corrected by using employee clock cards which were machine readable. After four months, paychecks were being issued accurately and on time, but the total costs of computer processing were nearly double previous manual costs. Because of the reduced need for manual processing, the three clerks who had been hired during the previous year had to be laid off. The Payroll Section, under Jim Peyton, was still operating considerably over budget, and the computer was only in use two days per week.

Peyton was anxious to add new computer applications which would be charged to other responsibility centers, thereby reducing his overhead costs. After conferring with his programmer, he recommended to the Controller that they begin working with Ed Coster, manager of the Cost Distribution section, to set up computer processing for the distribution of direct labor costs, as this process had previously been judged to be having serious problems in meeting report deadlines. News of this caused an uproar in the Factory Accountant's department. Coster, after seeing the mistakes which occurred during the initial application, was afraid that computerization of cost distribution (especially under someone else's control) would result in even more errors, which would be his responsibility to correct. Coster's clerks were aware of the layoffs in Payroll and Cash Disbursement, and were extremely worried that the same thing would happen to them.

The Controller was confronted with several problems in making his decision. Converting labor cost distribution to computer processing would require more EDP personnel and fewer clerical personnel. He believed the processing would be more accurate and timely, but costs would still be high and the computer would still be idle half the time. Peyton and Coster both wanted to retain control of their functions, but the Controller felt that neither of them was fully capable of handling both functions. They both lacked knowledge of computer techniques, and the programmer was not familiar with either financial or cost accounting.

The Controller decided to hire Joe Sisco, who was trained as a systems analyst and had a degree in accounting, as Systems Manager. Peyton was informed that Sisco would take over the responsibility for all computer processing and EDP personnel. Coster was instructed to cooperate with Sisco in setting up a procedure for computer processing of direct labor distribution. The Billing Section was informed that customer billing would be converted to computer processing on completion of the labor distribution changeover, within six months. It was estimated that six clerical jobs could be eliminated, while only two or more computer operators would be needed. A clerical hiring moratorium was put into effect, and it was felt that normal attrition would eliminate the excess personnel problem by the time all three procedures had been computerized.

With only a few minor problems, the cost distribution changeover was completed in four months, and computer billing was completed three months later. No personnel had been laid off, and the computer was being used at 75 percent of capacity, based on a seven-day week.

1. Consider the implications of the introduction of computer processing at FPC. What new structural and behavioral problems were created?
2. Evaluate the method of implementation decided by the Controller. What important aspects were considered in making his decision? What would you have done differently?

4 SYSTEMS METHODOLOGY FOR MIS DESIGN

Chapter 3 described the MIS staff as having primary responsibility for the design and monitoring of the MIS. This chapter examines in more detail the methodology of MIS design, implementation, and control. This methodology incorporates the systems approach to the design of information systems as discussed in Chapter 2. You will recall that the essential features of the systems approach are: (1) an objective-user orientation in the definition of information needs, (2) the design of individual information processes and subsystems so that they are connected through an integrated data base, and (3) the need for continual management of the design, operation, and review of all aspects of the MIS.

This chapter, which describes in detail the systems methodology for designing the MIS, has these specific objectives:

1. To describe which important steps are involved in the organization of the MIS design study.
2. To describe the methodology for defining the information needed by operations and management in the most effective manner.
3. To describe the methodology for designing and implementing the MIS processes that will produce the information needed by operations and management in the most efficient manner.
4. To describe the process of internal control and evaluation of the MIS.

The foregoing objectives reflect four major phases of systems methodology for designing, implementing, and controlling the MIS which will be used as a general framework for discussion in this chapter:

Phase 1—Origination of the MIS Study
Phase 2—Definition of Information Needs and Uses
Phase 3—Design and Implementation of MIS Processes
Phase 4—Internal Control and Evaluation of the MIS

Keeping the features of the systems approach to the design of information systems and the role of the MIS staff in mind, let us look at the process and steps involved in the organization of the MIS design study.

ORIGINATION OF THE MIS DESIGN STUDY

The origination of the MIS design study involves: (1) determination of the need for developing a new, or making changes to the existing, information system, (2) definition of the specific objectives to be accomplished by the study, (3) determination of how the study will be accomplished, and (4) development of top management support for the study.

/ Determine Need for Study

Often the need for the MIS design study originates because of unfavorable performance by the organization or one of its divisions. For example, an excessive number of customer complaints regarding the quality of merchandise may trigger a need for a study to design a quality control system. Frequent cost overruns may require a study to design a more effective budgeting and cost control system. A study to design a demand forecast and production scheduling system may be undertaken because of frequent and costly delays in the delivery of products to customers.

In other cases, an MIS design study may be undertaken to improve the efficiency of data processing or to expand the MIS to achieve fuller utilization of available computer hardware and manpower capacity. Growth of the organization, changes in its objectives and products, departmental reorganization, and changes in key managerial positions are factors which can lead to a study to design an information system which can cope with these changes or which will satisfy the information needs of new managers.

Suggestions for the need for an MIS design study may originate from several sources. Operating line managers, such as production, sales, procurement, and traffic, may request a redesign of reports they currently receive or may indicate they need information not currently provided to them. Staff units, such as personnel, accounting, or the MIS staff itself, may point out the need for changes to the information system. Top management is another major source of suggestions for a need for an MIS design study.

In many cases these managerial segments, line, staff, and top management, may recommend a study based on feedback incorporated in existing reports. For example, existing budget variance reports may reveal severe and frequent cost overruns in manufacturing, or an existing shipping report may show a significant number of late deliveries to customers. These types of feedback may result in a decision to develop a better budgeting or cost control reporting system or a better schedule control system.

In other cases, a special ad hoc study may be conducted to determine if the information system should be changed because of negative feedback on its performance. For example, the production cost overrun or the schedule slippage problems revealed by existing budget variance and shipping reports may not reveal the causes of these problems. Before changing the budgeting and cost control or the schedule control reports, an investigation should be made to determine if the poor performance was due to inefficient work processes, procedures, and operating personnel in manufacturing and traffic, rather than because of inadequate information about these operations. Instead of a redesign of the information system, the ad hoc study group may recommend a redesign of work processes and organization.

2 Define Study Objectives

Once a need for change to the existing information system has been identified, the specific objectives to be accomplished by the MIS design study must be formulated. Often the need for a change in the information system may be stated in very general terms, such as "a more effective schedule control system is needed to improve the timing of product delivery to our customers." Before a design for change is proposed, more specific features of the problem should be identified and the scope of the study specified. For example, exactly what is to be included in the schedule control system? Will the study be concerned only with the analysis of traffic and shipping information needs, or will it also include complete analysis of schedule control, involving the sales forecast, procurement, production, and quality control schedules?

The expected accomplishments of the study also should be defined. The objectives of the study usually are stated in terms of the general types of recommendations, designs, and documentation to be generated from the study. When possible, it is more useful to be specific as to what the design is intended to accomplish for operations and management. As an example, an objective of a study to design a schedule control system may be to reduce the number of late deliveries of products to customers to less than one percent within two years after it is implemented. An objective of a new budget and cost control system may be to reduce the dollar cost overruns to less than five percent within two years. An objective of a new quality control system may be to reduce the number of sales returns because of poor quality of products to less than one percent within two years. An objective of a study to achieve more efficient utilization of the computer facilities, hardware, and manpower may be to increase the actual use of the computer to at least 95 per cent of its operating capacity, or to reduce the dollar cost per reports processed.

The objectives of the MIS design study, when stated in specific and measurable terms, provide a sounder basis for approving the study and for subsequently evaluating the information system in terms of its benefits to operations and management. A clear-cut decision relating to the scope and objectives of the study is necessary for it to be effective.

3 Decide on Method

Based on the objectives and scope of the study, a statement of how the MIS design study will be accomplished should specify: what is to be done, who is going to do it, what time is required, and what resources are required.

An outline of *what work is to be performed* to accomplish the study should include a definition of the data collection effort and the types of documentation to be developed. Proposed questionnaires or interviews with key personnel, existing reports and documents to be reviewed, and flowcharts describing present and proposed work, resource, document, and report flows that will be developed should be specified. Also, the operating areas to be evaluated should be specified so that these areas can be informed of the need and purpose of the study and so that their cooperation with the study group can be solicited.

The individuals *who will perform the study* may include both full-time and part-time or advisory personnel. The MIS study team usually includes the following types of personnel:

Full-Time Personnel
- MIS staff personnel or outside consultants
- Personnel from major areas to be affected

Part-Time/Advisory Personnel
- Accounting personnel
- Data processing personnel
- Other key managers of operating areas
- Top management
- Outside consultants

Personnel who devote full time to the study generally include MIS staff personnel and representatives from the areas most affected by the study. This is necessary to insure a continual involvement of those personnel in the major areas to be affected so that their information needs are correctly evaluated, defined, and communicated to the MIS staff.

The managers of the affected operating areas and top management should regularly receive information regarding the status of the study, and should have the opportunity to provide suggestions as the study proceeds. Similarly, the accounting and data processing areas continually advise the study team on the feasibility of preliminary proposals since these two areas generally are affected by the design of the MIS. Outside consultants also may provide advice and guidance to the study team. In summary, the key factors to be considered in selecting personnel for the MIS study team are: (1) involvement of areas to be affected by the study, (2) top management involvement through the MIS staff, and (3) inclusion of the necessary specialized skills needed for the study, e.g., accounting, data processing, quantitative, and systems analysis techniques.

It is important to specify the *time span for completion of the study*. This will require formal and detailed planning of what is to be done and who will be involved. This does not imply that slippages in schedules will not occur; however, the schedule of performance is a mechanism for reviewing and evaluating the performance of the study team. For more complex studies, sequential scheduling techniques such as PERT may be used as aids for planning and controlling time and cost performance.[1] The schedule of performance also indicates when progress reports are due and who is to be informed of the status of the study.

Supporting resource needs for the study often include:

- Working space for the study team.
- Clerical assistance.
- Travel funds (if needed to review similar problems in other firms).
- Computer time for testing information designs.

---

[1] See Richard I. Levin and Charles A. Kirkpatrick, *Planning and Control with PERT/CPM* (New York: McGraw-Hill Book Co., 1966), or Harry F. Evarts, *Introduction to PERT* (Boston: Allyn & Bacon, 1965) for a basic treatement of PERT, its mechanics, and applications.

Working space is often a neglected item, but it is essential because there is a need for the individuals assigned to the study to be physically removed from their parent organizational surroundings during the course of the study. Otherwise, frequent interruptions of their concentration on the study may occur. Also, the study may call for the collection and display of a large amount of documentation, such as proposed alternatives for changes to the information system or to the organization.

A useful practice concerning resource needs is to set up a separate account number against which all the expenses of the study are charged in order to determine the total cost of the study. This often is useful for evaluating benefits of the study and for estimating the cost of future studies.

Obtain Top Management Approval

A final important step in originating the MIS design study is to obtain the approval of top management for the objectives and scope of the study, the resources required, projected time span, and procedures for accomplishing the study. This approval is communicated in writing directly to the affected areas of the organization and to the study team members. A kick-off meeting for top management and personnel from the affected areas and the study team can clear the air about what is going to happen, why it is needed, who is involved, and the time span involved. This type of meeting is typically helpful for generating operating level support for the study.

In summary, statements of need, objectives, and methodology and the commitment of top management support for its accomplishment are the major issues to be resolved during the origination of the study phase of MIS design. The more thorough the analysis of these issues, the more likely the study will be accomplished efficiently and produce the desired results.

DEFINITION OF INFORMATION NEEDS AND USES

The definition of information needs and uses involves (1) an analysis of operations, and (2) a classification of information needs and uses into major subsystems to be included in the MIS. Both of these are discussed in detail in this section.

Analysis of Operations

An analysis of operations is an examination of the nature of decisions, work, and activities of each major operation within the organization. From a formal or traditional viewpoint, the organization's operations can be viewed as a combination of functions such as shown in Exhibit 4-1. Each function such as production, marketing, and procurement is the responsibility of a manager and is designated as a *responsibility center*. Each manager of a responsibility center needs certain types of information peculiar to his internal operations. The marketing manager requires information regarding his consumer's demographic characteristics, income level, and inclination to buy. These pieces of information are usually not required by other managers, such as production or

Exhibit 4-1
A SIMPLE TRADITIONAL ORGANIZATION

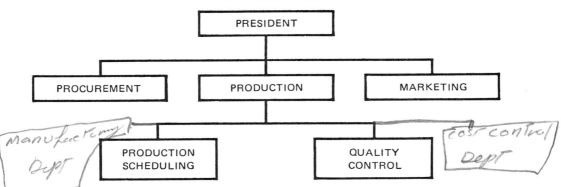

personnel. The procurement manager requires information regarding material prices and a vendor's ability to perform; this is not likely to be required by marketing or quality control.

The classification of responsibility centers by function may be extended to any level of detail and in fact must be extended to the level needed for defining information needs. The production division normally consists of a production scheduling, cost control, quality control, and manufacturing department. A manufacturing department may be broken down further into fabrication, assembly, and finishing sections.

Classification of responsibility centers by function is useful for analyzing information needs because:

1. The responsibility center is a logical and convenient way to enter a system for analysis and design, since it relates directly to the formal organization structure.
2. Responsibility centers reflect the nature of the work, decisions, and resources about which data is compiled and reports are produced.
3. Past performance levels of responsibility centers may in fact be the indicators of the need to act on the information system. Then future performance levels can be reviewed to provide a useful measure of the effectiveness of gain.
4. Responsibility centers represent the sources of most of the data inputs to the information system.

To be an effective unit of analysis for information system design, each functional responsibility center should be:

1. Defined as to its organizational purpose, responsibilities, and activities.
2. Appropriately placed in the formal organization structure.

When either of these conditions do not exist, responsibility may not coincide with intrinsic organizational functions or split responsibility over a single function may occur. Where unclear delegations of authority and responsibility exist, clarification and perhaps realignment by top management are made before defining information needs. Thus, using the functional responsibility center as a unit of analysis for designing an information system also helps make adjustments within the operating subsystems of the organization.

The Responsibility Center As An Input-Output System. For analytical purposes, the responsibility center can be viewed as an input-output system. A basic input-output model for viewing the organization and its responsibility centers as systems has been suggested by Optner.[2] This model is relatively simple and it can be conveniently used to analyze any form of organized human endeavor, whether business, governmental, or education. Using the input-output idea, Exhibit 4-2 presents the major components of a basic systems model and several examples of its application for analyzing the evaluating operations and management. The major components of the input-output model are:

> *Managers As The Control Unit.* This is the individual responsible for the input-output system's operation.
> *Users of Outputs.* This component reflects the purpose of the system. Satisfaction of the user is a primary goal of the system.
> *Outputs.* These reflect the value added by the system, determined in large part by the users of outputs.
> *Processor or Transformation Unit.* The processor is comprised of a mix of money, human, physical, and data resources under the responsibility of the control unit. This is where resource utilization and creation of value (outputs) occur through the performance of functions, activities, and work.
> *Inputs.* These are resources (money, human, physical, and data) required by the processor to create value or produce outputs.
> *Sources of Inputs.* These are the sources of the resources (money, human, physical, and data) needed by the processor.

System model components may vary in size, purpose, or operating characteristics; however, they are common to all organizations in that they involve resource utilization to create value. Examples of variations of major components for an entire firm, a personnel department, and an information system are shown in Exhibit 4-2.

Variations primarily involve the purpose of the organization (i.e., goods versus services) and the processing functions involved. Resources generally include a mix of money, human, physical, and data, although the actual mix and specific subcategories may vary. It is important to note from these examples that the basic input-output model can be conveniently applied to virtually all organized activity, regardless of type, size, or complexity. When a high degree of aggregation is desired in modeling a system, such as that for an entire organization, the basic model components can be generalized, as shown by the firm example in Exhibit 4-2. When less aggregation and more detail is desired, the organization can be divided into individual input-output subsystems, such as that for the personnel department shown in Exhibit 4-2. The input-output model also can be used to reflect other formal functional entities of the

---

[2] Stanford L. Optner, *Systems Analysis For Business Management* (2d ed.; Englewood Cliffs, N.J.: Prentice-Hall, 1968).

Exhibit 4-2

MAJOR COMPONENTS FOR A FIRM, A PERSONNEL DEPARTMENT,
AND AN INFORMATION SYSTEM

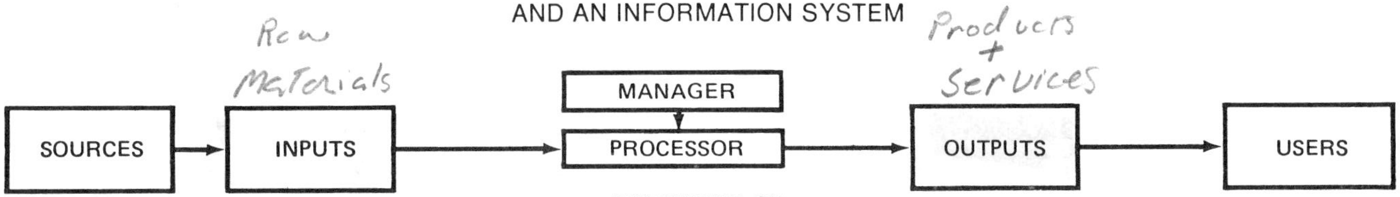

SOURCES → INPUTS → [MANAGER / PROCESSOR] → OUTPUTS → USERS

(handwritten annotations: "Raw Materials" near INPUTS; "Products + Services" near OUTPUTS)

	SOURCES	INPUTS	FUNCTIONS OF:	OUTPUTS	USERS
FIRM:	VENDORS LABOR MARKET DEBT, EQUITY, SALES	MONEY FACILITIES EQUIPMENT PERSONNEL MATERIALS SUPPLIES	MARKETING PRODUCTION PROCUREMENT FINANCE PERSONNEL DATA PROCESSING	FINISHED GOODS WORK–IN–PROCESS SERVICES INFORMATION	CUSTOMERS OTHER FIRMS INTERNAL MANAGERS
PERSONNEL DEPT.	VENDORS LABOR MARKET DEBT, EQUITY, SALES	MONEY FACILITIES EQUIPMENT PERSONNEL MATERIALS SUPPLIES	RECRUITING JOB ANALYSIS TRAINING UNION NEGOTIATION GRIEVANCE HANDLING MANPOWER PLANNING	INTERVIEWS JOB DESCRIPTIONS UNION CONTRACTS MANPOWER TABLES & BUDGETS TRAINING MANUALS	INTERNAL MANAGERS EMPLOYEES UNIONS
INFORMATION SYSTEM:	VENDORS LABOR MARKET DEBT, EQUITY, SALES	MONEY FACILITIES EQUIPMENT PERSONNEL MATERIALS SUPPLIES	ACQUISITION CLASSIFICATION STORAGE RETRIEVAL COMPUTATION DISTRIBUTION	INFORMATION (RECURRING & SPECIAL REPORTS)	INTERNAL MANAGERS EMPLOYEES EXTERNAL AGENCIES

organization such as personnel, production, and marketing. Its universality of application makes the systems model extremely useful for analytical purposes.

Linking of Input-Output Subsystems. The major components of the input-output systems model do not by themselves reflect the interrelatedness of subsystems within the organization. Exhibit 4-3 shows how the input-output framework can also be used for analyzing the interrelationships that exist between subsystems. The *output* of one phase of processing (materials shipment) is the *input* of the next (procurement); the *processor* of one phase (procurement) is the *source* of the next (production); and the *user* of a phase (traffic) is the *processor* of the next (customer). Thus, the organization can be viewed in terms of how its parts are interrelated through a series of processes and flows.

Exhibit 4-4 provides a more detailed example. A sales forecast is generated as an output from the sales manager. The forecast becomes an input for the production manager as a basis for production budgeting, scheduling, and requisitioning of materials.

The horizontal analytical emphasis provided by the input-output framework does not preclude a formal organization analysis in a traditional functional sense. Consider the business firm shown in Exhibit 4-3. Horizontal flows take place through a number of functional entities or departments (procurement, production, and traffic). The output of one department is the input of another, and the using department is the processing department in the next subsystem, the source in the next, etc. This type of analytical structure clearly focuses on the interfaces between processes and identifies how formal functional entities are interrelated. Thus, viewing the organization and its responsibility centers as interrelated input-output systems is a useful framework for defining information needs.

Resource and performance information is needed to provide more effective coordination of functional performance and to insure that end products and services are produced in the optimum quality, quantity, time, and cost. Each manager of a responsibility center is concerned with making decisions regarding quality, quantity, cost, and timing of physical, human, and data resource flows from the standpoint of internal operations and the relation of his operations with other operations of the firm.

The coordinating element in this decision-making process is the objectives of the entire organization as the major responsibility center. Information is required by upper levels of management regarding the operations of each responsibility center in relation to its objectives and to overall objectives. Exhibit 4-5 depicts the traditional organization as an interrelated set of input-output functions that are tied together by common objectives relating to quality, quantity, time, and cost. Customers' requirements for products are interpreted by the marketing department, and the ability and desire of the organization to fulfill these requirements are determined by such factors as production capacity, material availability, and financial capacity. The requirements flow cuts across several functional areas of the organization, and

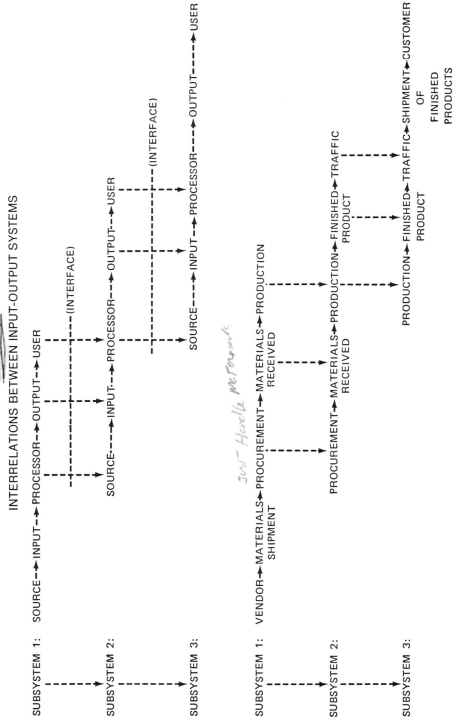

Exhibit 4-3

INTERRELATIONS BETWEEN INPUT-OUTPUT SYSTEMS

SUBSYSTEM 1: SOURCE—▸INPUT—▸PROCESSOR—▸OUTPUT—▸USER

SUBSYSTEM 2: SOURCE----▸INPUT---▸PROCESSOR---▸OUTPUT---▸USER

SUBSYSTEM 3: SOURCE----▸INPUT---▸PROCESSOR----▸OUTPUT----▸USER

(INTERFACE)

SUBSYSTEM 1: VENDOR—▸MATERIALS—▸PROCUREMENT—▸MATERIALS—▸PRODUCTION
SHIPMENT RECEIVED

SUBSYSTEM 2: PROCUREMENT—▸MATERIALS—▸PRODUCTION—▸FINISHED—▸TRAFFIC
RECEIVED PRODUCT

SUBSYSTEM 3: PRODUCTION—▸FINISHED—▸TRAFFIC—▸SHIPMENT—▸CUSTOMER
PRODUCT OF
FINISHED
PRODUCTS

Just Have me forward

Flows Backward

Exhibit 4-4

INTERRELATED OPERATIONAL AND INFORMATIONAL
ACTIVITIES AND FLOWS

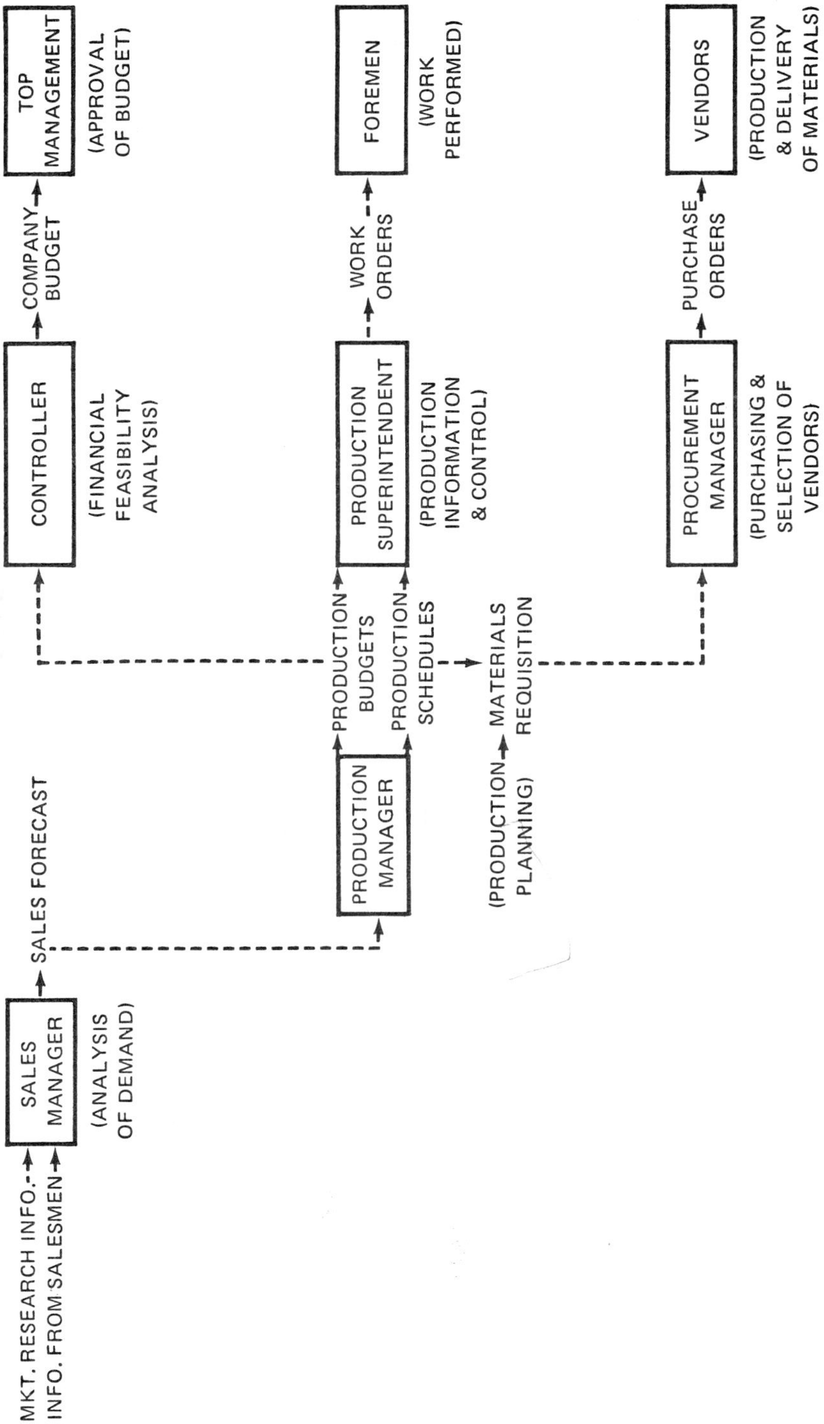

SALES MANAGER
(ANALYSIS OF DEMAND)
· MKT. RESEARCH INFO.
· INFO. FROM SALESMEN

SALES FORECAST

CONTROLLER
(FINANCIAL FEASIBILITY ANALYSIS)

COMPANY BUDGET

TOP MANAGEMENT
(APPROVAL OF BUDGET)

PRODUCTION MANAGER
(PRODUCTION PLANNING)

PRODUCTION BUDGETS

PRODUCTION SCHEDULES

MATERIALS REQUISITION

PRODUCTION SUPERINTENDENT
(PRODUCTION INFORMATION & CONTROL)

WORK ORDERS

FOREMEN
(WORK PERFORMED)

PROCUREMENT MANAGER
(PURCHASING & SELECTION OF VENDORS)

PURCHASE ORDERS

VENDORS
(PRODUCTION & DELIVERY OF MATERIALS)

Exhibit 4-5

TRADITIONAL ORGANIZATION AS A SET OF INTERRELATED FUNCTIONS

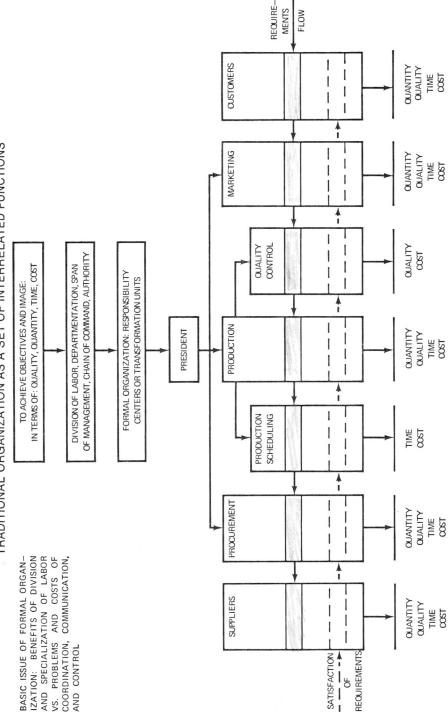

the final decision concerning which customer product requirements to meet is made by top management from a total organizational perspective.

Once a decision is made by top management concerning the quality, quantity, time, and cost of products to produce, the satisfaction or fulfillment of customer requirements is accomplished through the performance of several functions. For example, procurement acquires materials for production, work orders are scheduled, production takes place, inspection of the qualtiy of products occurs, and shipments are made to customers. Standards relating to the quality, quantity, time, and cost of performance are used as coordinating devices as products are processed. The notations at the bottom of Exhibit 4-5 emphasize that all functional areas are concerned with customer requirements relating to some aspects of quality, quantity, time, and cost of products.

Describing the organization and its responsibility centers as interrelated input-output systems also provides an analytical framework for investigating interaction between subsystems (e.g., between procurement and production and between production and traffic). These points of interaction normally are where breakdowns in performance or serious problems of coordination may occur. For example, a late delivery of materials means production delays, and late production means late delivery of products to customers. They also represent areas of potential needs for better information, such as more reliable information regarding procurement lead times, capacity of vendors to deliver on time, or status of materials inventory reserves.

As each manager develops a better understanding of the purpose, operation, and nature of resources used by his responsibility center and how his responsibility center is interrelated with others to achieve the organizational objectives, decisions made in one center are recognized as directly related to decisions made in others. As the level of understanding of organizational goals, problems, and information by managers is improved, managerial attitudes toward designing the MIS become much more favorable. This is because managers finally come to form a complete organizational picture without which they will not be supportive of many aspects of the MIS.

Classification of Information Needs and Uses

The nature of the interdependencies of the operations of responsibility centers influences the design of the MIS. Besides the interdependencies between formal or functional responsibility centers, other interdepartmental classifications of information needs must be employed to complete the definition of information needs and uses. Alternative classification schemes include programs or projects, product lines, and resource categories. Such classifications tend to cut across formal organizational lines, and consequently require information of various types. For example:

- An *advertising program* decision requires information regarding production capacity, cost, consumer demand, and materials availability.
- A *product line* analysis requires information regarding all costs, revenues, and projected demands for the entire product line

- A *manpower resource* analysis requires information regarding the manpower availability, capabilities, and needs for each functional area in the organization.

Responsibility centers can be defined in different ways, e.g., according to responsibility for function, program or project, product line, or resource category. Multiple classifications of responsibility centers can identify different perspectives of information needs which often are not revealed by a functional classification alone. A multiple classification perspective is important for facilitating the integration of MIS processes. The MIS should be capable of providing the following types of information which actually comprise the four major subsystems of the MIS:

- *Product/service related* information needed for analyzing, evaluating, and determining the appropriate outputs to produce. This is *output*-oriented information.
- *Resource related* information needed for decisions concerning requisition, acquisition, and utilization of each major type of resource used. This is *input*-oriented information.
- *Organizational function related* information needed by production, marketing, personnel, etc., for planning, operational control, and managerial/financial control of their respective functions. This is *processor*-oriented information.
- *Management related* information which is needed for planning, operational control, and managerial/financial control of the total organization. This is *management process*-oriented information.

This classification permits detailed analysis of relationships between information needs and uses. It also facilitates the design of meaningful reports. For example, reports are needed by management to evaluate customer acceptance and profitability of existing and proposed product lines. These demand analysis reports facilitate product strategy and promotion decisions. Design of a set of demand analysis reports requires data from a number of interrelated source documents. Sales forecasts, market research reports, customer complaint reports, and product cost and revenue reports are compiled, coded, stored, processed, and retrieved.

Similarly, another set of reports is needed by management to analyze and evaluate resource utilization patterns in order to develop budgets by resource categories. Data on a number of interrelated source documents such as purchase orders, receiving reports, vendor invoices, issue slips, and inventory reports are combined and processed to produce resource utilization and budgetary reports.

The four classifications of information subsystems overlap and are further interrelated as they combine to produce other types of reports that are combinations of the four basic classifications of information. For example, reports dealing with the performance of the production division include both product and resource information (e.g., labor cost per product produced, or materials cost per product produced). Product analysis reports may include costs as well as demand factors such as revenues.

Since different managers need different types of information, the design of the MIS must consider these different needs. By classifying information needs into the four subsystems described in this section and designing the MIS so these four subsystems are connected through a data base and data coding scheme, the MIS can provide reports about interrelationships between subsystems as well as specialized reports within each subsystem. Exhibit 4-6 provides a systems view of how these four subsystems are connected through the data base and data processor components of the MIS.

The central thrust used in this book for defining information needs is management process related, or specifically the definition of information needs for planning, operational control, and managerial/financial control. Within this framework, product, resource, and function related information also can be provided by coding of data on source documents according to the resource, product, and function classification. For example, the sales forecast is a planning source document which contains data on the expected volume of products to be sold. The production budget is a functional source document which contains data on expected resource needs or costs of producing products. The data on these two documents can be coded and processed through the data base with the aid of a data processor to produce demand analysis, resource capacity and utilization, and functional reports that are useful for planning, operational control, and managerial/financial control.

Data Collection Methods

The analysis of operations involves a considerable amount of data collection. Block diagramming and flowcharting analytical techniques typically are used to define and document the type of interrelated network shown in Exhibit 4-4.[3] In addition, extensive communications and interviews with users of information, providers of data, data processing personnel, and perhaps external parties such as customers and suppliers are required. The objectives, constraints, and interrelationships of existing information flows and operational activities are defined and documented. A preliminary compilation of important needs for information is accomplished during the data collection task. These information needs are incorporated into proposed alternatives for MIS design later in the study. The complete analysis of the organization's operations in this manner provides the basis for grouping or classifying information needs and uses for operations and management.

DESIGN AND IMPLEMENTATION OF MIS PROCESSES

The definition of information needs constitutes the basis for identifying and designing the necessary source documents which will provide the data inputs to

---

[3] The appendix provides examples of flowcharting and block diagramming concepts and techniques. For a thorough treatment of these techniques, see Clarence B. Randall and Sally Weimer Burgly, *Systems and Procedures For Business Data Processing* (Cincinnati: South-Western Publishing Co., 1968), Part III, or *Business Systems* (Cleveland: Systems and Procedures Association, 1966), Chapter 4 for a basic introduction and review of flowcharting symbols, techniques, and applications.

Exhibit 4-6

SYSTEMS VIEW OF THE MIS

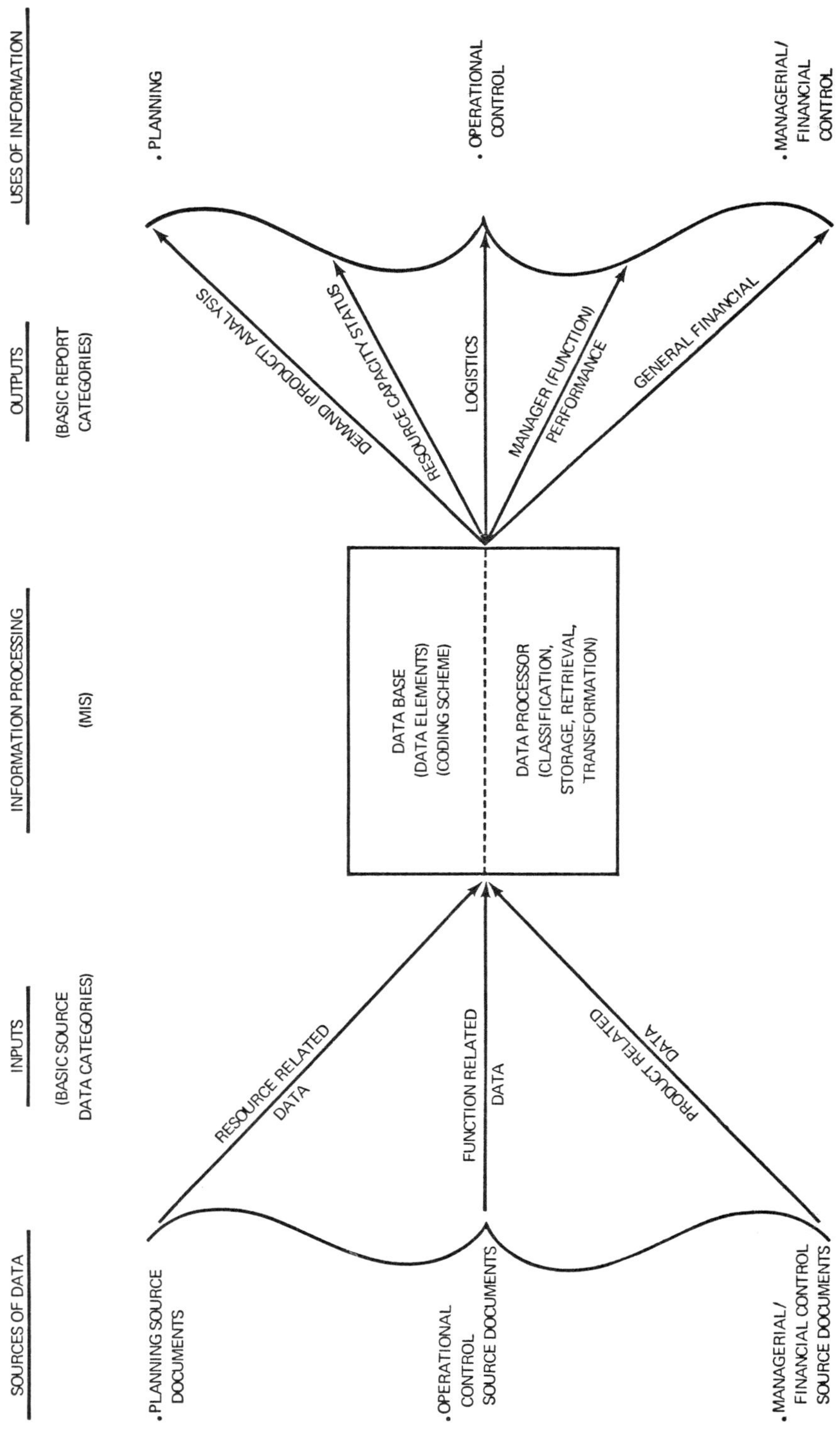

SOURCES OF DATA	INPUTS (BASIC SOURCE DATA CATEGORIES)	INFORMATION PROCESSING (MIS)	OUTPUTS (BASIC REPORT CATEGORIES)	USES OF INFORMATION

- PLANNING SOURCE DOCUMENTS

- OPERATIONAL CONTROL SOURCE DOCUMENTS

- MANAGERIAL/ FINANCIAL CONTROL SOURCE DOCUMENTS

RESOURCE RELATED DATA

FUNCTION RELATED DATA

PRODUCT RELATED DATA

DATA BASE (DATA ELEMENTS) (CODING SCHEME)

DATA PROCESSOR (CLASSIFICATION, STORAGE, RETRIEVAL, TRANSFORMATION)

DEMAND (PRODUCT) ANALYSIS

RESOURCE CAPACITY STATUS

LOGISTICS

MANAGER (FUNCTION) PERFORMANCE

GENERAL FINANCIAL

- PLANNING

- OPERATIONAL CONTROL

- MANAGERIAL/ FINANCIAL CONTROL

the MIS. Also, the design of MIS processing components (the data base, coding scheme, and data processor) is based on the definition of information needs.

Design of MIS Processes

The design of source documents and MIS processes involves four tasks. First, _design criteria_ relating to quality, volume, and timing of reports are specified within the cost limitations set by top management. Design criteria insure that the source documents developed contain the appropriate quality, volume, and timing inputs, and that the data base, coding scheme, and data processor can satisfy processing needs. For example, a daily budget variance report showing budgeted versus actual costs by products requires the submission and processing of production work orders completed, labor time cards, and materials issue slips on a daily basis. If the costs of producing these reports on a daily basis are excessive, or if the information on the reports is of poor quality (i.e., incomplete or inaccurate because of the difficulty in regularly obtaining the data), the design criteria specifying the timing of the reports may require alteration. Weekly or monthly budget variance reports may be designed so that more complete or more accurate information is produced within the established cost limitations.

Having resolved the report quality, volume, and timing requirements, a second task is to _identify the specific data and information elements_ to appear on the source documents and reports. The formats of the documents and reports must be designed in terms of exactly how the data and information will be arranged. This is necessary for the subsequent design of procedures for data acquisition and processing, and for developing computer programs relating to collecting, sorting, storing, and retrieving data and printing reports.

The third task involves the _design of a data base and coding scheme_ to accomodate the data and information elements specified and to produce MIS reports in accord with the quality, volume, timing, and cost criteria. The data base and coding scheme facilitates the movement of data from source documents through the computer, which processes the data into the information to be distributed on the reports.

Data collection, sorting, processing, storage, and retrieval activities are designed to minimize the data processing costs associated with the production of multiple reports. The same data inputs should be used as the basis for multiple reports to minimize duplication of data processing systems. In order to accomplish this, the data base must be capable of providing multiple uses of data in different types of reports through the use of a data coding scheme that can classify events and transactions according to their relationship to function, product, program, and resource categories. A computerized data processor can produce many reports without creating a separate data base for each type of report. Thus, the data processing activities, as well as the reports they produce, are integrated.

The first three design tasks form the basis for the fourth task which is the _design of a computerized data processor_. This task involves the design and selection of computer hardware and software to accommodate the flow of data and information through the data base in the manner specified, and within the quality, volume, timing, and cost limitations agreed upon by operating managers and top management.

All four design tasks require accurate definition and analysis of operational activities and information flows. Analyses of design alternatives are made within the set of objectives and constraints concerning the purpose and scope of the MIS. The final design often may require changes in organizational structure, techniques of work processing and decision making, and personnel, and these changes should be examined as part of the feasibility evaluation process.

Testing the MIS Design

Pilot testing of selected parts of the MIS design may be possible using one department of the organization as a test area. Although this type of test may be disruptive to normal operations, it is usually invaluable for correcting design problems before full implementation. For example, problems relating to data recording, acquisition, or processing may be readily uncovered during a trial run in a specific department. Often there is considerable uncertainty over which code numbers to use to classify transactions properly because of the new data base and coding scheme. These problems will surface and allow for correction during the trial run. An analysis of the type and frequency of problems encountered during the test period provides useful information to refine the MIS before its implementation throughout the organization. Suggestions for revisions to report formats or information on the reports may be made by the pilot test department as it uses the sample reports in operational decisions.

Testing of the software or programming design of the MIS often is possible with the existing hardware. Computer program testing is essential to insure that the data base, coding system, and supporting procedures for data acquisition, storage, and processing have been designed properly. Existing hardware in the organization may not be capable of performing tests of software if the MIS design includes a large extension or major upgrading of the hardware. In these instances, experimental modeling techniques, such as computer simulation, should be investigated as a means for testing the new MIS design. This would involve using computer simulation experiments to build a test model of segments of the MIS software for evaluation of the design. The procedures to be included in the data storage and retrieval software packages could be modeled and tested with the existing hardware to insure that they will work properly in the scaled-up system.

Implementation of Changes

In a well-performed study, the MIS design takes into account users' needs and cost benefits of alternatives for serving these needs. Regardless of the thoroughness of the systems design effort, the environment for implementation may be different from that visualized during the design effort. This may be due to changes in user personnel, changes in or inaccurate estimates of attitudes toward the new design issues, omission of key design requirements, changes in resource availability, and other related occurrences. Because of this uncertainty over the implementation environment, the design effort may in reality be a continuous process.

To optimize the implementation of the MIS design, five key considerations should be taken into account:

1. Timing of implementation.
2. Gaining acceptance.
3. Documenting system design specifications.
4. Providing support requirements.
5. Designating implementation responsibilities.

These are discussed in the following sections.

Timing of Implementation. In developing a schedule of implementation there is a tendency to be optimistic about what needs to be done and how long it will take. It is common to overlook or miscalculate possible absences or turnover of key personnel, need for time-consuming meetings and approvals on key issues, availability and efficiency of computer programmers, and the importance of the MIS project related to other projects or operational matters. If the MIS design group develops the attitude that theirs is the only important activity in the organization, the design effort may never get off the ground.

The timetable for implementation should reflect the management environment. Changes must be timed to take into account the available capabilities of personnel and resources and the prevailing attitudes of personnel to be affected by the MIS (i.e., possible resistance to change). In many cases, a change in the information system involves changes in responsibilities in the operational areas. These organizational changes often involve retraining, orientation, and recruitment of new personnel. Since implementation of the MIS is effected through people, organizational changes must be realistically scheduled. In some cases, implementation of a part of the design may be postponed because of personnel considerations.

To optimize the timing of implementation and the performance of personnel, manpower inventory status information should be maintained by the organization's personnel staff. Personal data, qualifications in terms of education and experience, estimates of potential, and other related data are normally included in the manpower inventory file. Every organization has some personnel whose accomplishments cause them to be considered leaders or crisis solvers. Others, representing the largest percentage of personnel, are content to follow and carry out programs, yet these personnel are important to the organization. A third group, hopefully the smallest percentage, are those who have become obsolete relative to the MIS needs of the organization. It behooves top management to categorize its management personnel in order to properly assign to them responsibilities for the implementation program, as well as for their ongoing organizational functions. An up-to-date inventory of personnel capabilities is essential for developing a realistic schedule of implementation.

In the design of the MIS, budget data generally represents a major part of the information system, and changes in information flows are often scheduled to coincide with the beginning of the yearly budget cycle. New requirements for budgeting can be included with the budget materials that generally go out to organizational segments. New coding schemes and procedures are also explained at this time. Special teams normally assist operating managers in the preparation of their budgets. It is useful and convenient to utilize these special teams to familiarize operating managers with new information system requirements, such as new reports, changes to the source documents, revised coding schemes, and the overall purpose of the MIS. When the timing of implementation centers around the budget cycle, timetables for the completion of other significant activities should fall into place. Exhibit 4-7 shows a typical example.

Gaining Acceptance. In the design of the MIS one generally has better results in gaining acceptance of the proposed changes to the information system by beginning at the lower levels and working upward. A description of the proposed MIS as a provider of more useful information in forming a basis for justifying additional resources places the design issues within a framework

Exhibit 4-7

IMPLEMENTATION SCHEDULE TIED TO BUDGET CYCLE

Activities	*Milestones*
Hardware changes completed and tested (beginning depends on availability and procurement lead times and definition of needs) ↓	June 1
Organizational realignments completed (beginning depends on complexity of reorganization and availability of personnel) ↓	June 1
Budget packet designed (including training of persons to orient operating managers and persons responsible for coding) ↓	June 1-July 31
Budget packet reproduced ↓	Aug. 1-Sept. 15
Budget packet distributed (materials, forms, procedures, coding) ↓	Sept. 15
Budget prepared ↓	Oct. 1-Oct. 30
Computer programming completed and tested (depends on size and complexity of designs and when designs completed) ↓	Nov. 1
Budget reviewed ↓	Nov. 1-Nov. 30
Final budget approved ↓	Dec. 1
Final budget reproduced & distributed ↓	Dec. 1-15
Budget takes effect	Jan 1

which lower level managers understand and appreciate. As lower level managers participate in the design effort and have an opportunity to see and understand what is being developed, they tend to relate to and support the new design. Lower level managers represent the fundamental responsibility units about which information is collected, processed, and evaluated. Therefore, convincing these managers of the need for and validity of the new information is essential. In an extensive empirical study of an organization's information system, it was found that managers who participated in the design of the information system placed a significantly *greater value* on it in terms of its usefulness for operating decisions and activities than those managers who were not involved in the design.[4]

In obtaining the approval for changes in the information system from managers at higher levels in the organization, it is useful to include lower level operating managers at meetings when their superiors will be discussing the new design. Lower level managers can then justify the new design to their superiors. This approval process tends to be cumulative as it moves toward higher organizational levels. The extent of informal communications between superiors and subordinates that precedes the formal meetings to gain approval of the MIS is usually substantial, and the new design can actually sell itself to top management. Such an approval and implementation process provides for not only initial but continual involvement of operating managers.

The changes in an organization's structure that may accompany a new MIS design are considerably more sensitive issues than the changes in information. Individual jobs, prestige, and influence are involved. There is often a degree of fear present that something might happen, generally reinforced because of the uncertainty about the type and timing of organizational change. Because of the extreme sensitivity and the long-run implications, gaining acceptance of organizational changes should be initially resolved and supported by top management, rather than lower level managers. This represents a logical continuation of the approval process relating to MIS design. When top management reviews the information design proposal in terms of its cost benefits, the impact on the organization structure will be one of the major issues.

Reorganization involves a structural decision and a staffing decision. The structural decision deals with the ideal classification and alignment of functions and responsibilities, that is, division of labor, chain of command, span of management, and authority relationships. The staffing decision generally involves modification of the ideal structure to fit the capabilities and personalities of available personnel, at least in the short run. It would be a mistake to force structure on a staff not capable of comprehending it or having the talents to make it work. As indicated in the section on timing of implementation, it is sometimes necessary to deviate from the ideal structure in the short run, but the ideal will be kept in mind as the long-run goal.

---

[4] Charles A. Gallagher, "Measurement and Analysis of Managers' Perceptions of the Value of Selected Management Information" (Doctoral dissertation, Florida State University, 1971).

Structural changes, availability of personnel, and sensitive reassignments are issues to be evaluated by top management. Once the approval by top management of the informational and organizational changes has been obtained, middle management is brought into the implementation process. Middle management is involved in selecting the key managers needed under the new organization structure. These key managers then identify and select those personnel they feel have the talents and personalities needed to make their organization function. Personality is significant in the reorganization process; therefore, each manager needs to have some voice in the selection of key personnel.

Gaining acceptance of informational and organizational changes is a cyclical process as shown in Exhibit 4-8. The information review process focuses on gaining acceptance for the need for the new information system and its makeup. The feasibility review takes place at the top management level. At this point the issue of organizational change is formally reviewed if the information needs are considered to be valid and feasible.

Introducing or considering the issue of organizational change too early may provide a convenient scapegoat for sabotaging the information needs issue. Delaying its consideration postpones the sensitivity and fear problems until the

Exhibit 4-8
GAINING ACCEPTANCE FOR CHANGES IN INFORMATION
AND ORGANIZATION

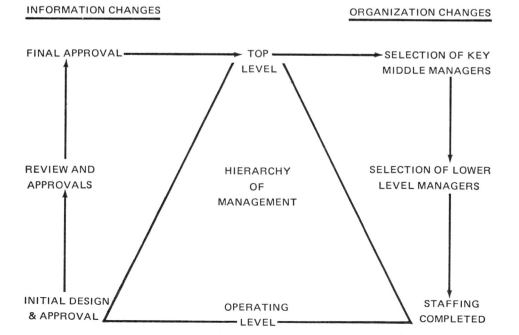

INFORMATION CHANGES   ORGANIZATION CHANGES

FINAL APPROVAL ────────────→ TOP ────────────→ SELECTION OF KEY
                              LEVEL   MIDDLE MANAGERS

REVIEW AND   HIERARCHY   SELECTION OF LOWER
APPROVALS   OF   LEVEL MANAGERS
                           MANAGEMENT

INITIAL DESIGN   OPERATING   STAFFING
& APPROVAL   ─ LEVEL ─   COMPLETED

decision is made to proceed with the information system design. The feasibility of organizational changes is a top management decision and should not be introduced at lower levels until it is a certainty.

This does not mean that desirable organizational changes are not considered by systems designers throughout the MIS design effort. However, there is a tendency by line or operating managers to be reluctant to recommend changes in their respective organizations for fear of the impact on themselves and their subordinate managers. Views of operating managers on organizational matters are certainly solicited by systems design personnel who then provide top management with recommendations for organizational realignments based on a company-wide, integrated perspective.

The design and implementation efforts are highly interdependent. In fact, in a broad sense the design process is a continuous one, and quite often modifications are suggested to both the informational and organizational designs during the gaining-acceptance cycle. Modifications suggested by operating managers may be accepted so long as they do not alter the basic philosophy and purpose of the information system. The systems design group should be especially alert to suggestions made during the implementation phase that might contribute to a better information system or organization structure.

Documenting System Design Specifications. Documentation of the specifications of the MIS design includes report formats, coding schemes, data base structure, source document formats, and timing of data flows and report processing. Documentation is essential for several reasons:

1. To communicate program requirements to programmer-analysts.
2. To insure that programs for new reports are compatible with existing reports.
3. To facilitate the review of programming status relative to the schedule of implementation.
4. To permit outside contracting of programming if necessary.

The development of effective and complete documentation of design specifications minimizes problems associated with the transition from user language to machine language. Documentation is even more important to organizations that are involved in facilities management arrangements in which programming and computing services are performed outside the organization or by centralized data processing centers servicing a number and variety of information systems. Facilities management arrangements are becoming increasingly common and pose problems different from those of strictly internal system development efforts.

Providing Support. Computer programming is probably the most significant support needed to achieve effective implementation of the information system design. Major changes to design should be minimized after programming has begun. A design change often results in a need to reprogram a large segment of work; therefore, the programming effort should not begin until the acceptance cycle shown in Exhibit 4-8 has been completed. This may squeeze the implementation schedule, and there may be a resulting need for outside programming, but the expected benefits, namely the more timely implementation of the MIS, normally outweigh the higher costs of subcontracted programming. It may also be better to postpone implementation rather than program a less than optimum design, since later updates in programming may never occur, and if they do the operating managers must undergo two changes in the information system instead of one.

The admirable tendency for programmers to work toward program efficiency and simplicity can have a serious impact on the usefulness of reports. The format of a report may be changed to facilitate programming; however, the new location of information may be inconvenient for its user. The timing of a report may be changed to coincide with the processing of related data for other reports; however, the programmers may unknowingly decrease the report's timeliness to the user. To minimize this sort of occurrence, it is essential to select a member of the design group with solid programming knowledge to serve as a continual liaison with the programming staff. The programming staff then has access to design personnel as questions arise, and the design group is able to keep abreast of programming progress and problems.

Conversion of forms is often required as a result of a new information system design. Part of the implementation process involves the design and ordering of forms. Consideration should be given to the inventory of existing forms and the possibility of modifying them. This might be accomplished by the use of rubber stamps to provide spaces for the additional data required for the new information system. For example, the data on an issue slip showing units and costs of materials used by each operating department could be stamped and coded to reflect the product for which the material is being used in order to produce a product cost or departmental cost report. The lead times involved for conversion of forms must be incorporated in the schedule of implementation.

Another important support requirement is the documentation required to announce and explain the new information system to operating managers and those personnel in the organization who will be responsible for coding source data. This documentation normally includes policies and procedures, training aids, charts of accounts or coding schemes, and other similar materials. Careful design is required since this documentation is a major bridge between the design and implementation phases. Acceptability and effectiveness of the design are influenced by this documentation.

Designating Implementation Responsibilities. The design group performs a staff or advisory function to the line or operational managers. It recommends an information systems design and participates in the approval process. After top management has approved the information system design and any organizational changes, coordinating and monitoring the implementation activities may continue to be the responsibility of the design group. The same is true for forms conversion, documentation development and explanation, and general coordination of the activities required for implementation. The design group continues to be involved in the critical areas of the study recommendations.

The responsibilities for implementation involve coordination of the total effort. The coordination responsibility should belong to the design group because of this group's familiarity with all aspects of the new design. Responsibilities for some specialized activities, such as computer programming, development of the budget packet, and hardware acquisition, can be assigned to non-design-group personnel; however, coordination and monitoring of their performance by the design group are essential. The design group must also be available to answer questions of operational managers as implementation progresses.

INTERNAL CONTROL AND EVALUATION OF THE MIS

A periodic review of changes made and implemented must be formally incorporated in the information system of the organization. Cost benefit estimates used to justify changes should be evaluated against future performance. Review of the status of the new system should occur after a reasonable period has been allowed for implementation (generally at least a year). For continuity, a member of the original design group should appear in the review group.

On a permanent basis, internal control and evaluation of the MIS are necessary. The flow of transaction documents related to decisions, work, and resources used must be controlled to insure validity. In a formal accounting or auditing sense, internal control involves procedures relating to the authorization, execution, and recording of transactions, and the accountability for assets or resources.[5]

Internal control procedures insure that only authorized transactions occur, that they are executed in the prescribed manner, that they are recorded correctly on the appropriate doccumentation, and that they are processed through the MIS data base in a timely and accurate manner. For example, a purchase transaction in a firm can not occur without the authorization of the procurement manager, and it must be executed through a prescribed bidding process. Purchase requisitions, requests for bids, vendor appraisal forms, purchase orders, and receiving reports are documents commonly required for recording the purchase transaction in order to insure internal control. Similarly, accountability for the acquisition, storage, and use of the materials acquired must be verified through inventory records, reconciliation procedures, and physical inventory inspections.

The purpose of internal control is to provide procedures which will insure reliable data inputs to the data base, to safeguard assets, to promote efficiency of operations, and to assure adherence to company policy. Without internal control procedures, reports on the status of the organization's operations, its resource use and levels, and its performance levels may not reflect the true state of operations. Internal control procedures also facilitate the auditing of operational and financial transactions and they operate to purify the data inputs to the MIS, as well as to safeguard and report on the use and status of the organization's assets and resources in a financial accounting sense.

---

[5] Based on *Statement of Auditing Standards*, AICPA, 1973.

In a similar way, internal control procedures are important for the operation and management of the MIS itself. Procedures must insure that only authorized documents and data elements are processed and that the process is executed by the authorized persons. Also, a procedure for accounting and auditing the assets and resources acquired and used by the MIS, such as hardware, materials, facilities, and manpower, is necessary to safeguard these assets and to insure that they are utilized efficiently.

SUMMARY

This chapter describes the procedure for designing the MIS, using the systems approach as the analytical framework. The systems approach emphasizes the interaction and interdependency of decisions, work, and resource flows.

Four major phases make up the MIS design study. The first is origination of the study, involving defining study objectives, method, and the need to obtain top management support for the study. The second phase deals with the definition of information needs and uses. The responsibility center as an input-output system is the analytical framework for examining information needs. Within this framework, product-, resource-, and function-related information can be provided.

The third phase of the MIS design study is the design and implementation of MIS processes, the data base, coding scheme, and data processor. This design effort includes four major tasks: establishing design criteria relating to the quality, volume, timing, and cost of the MIS; identifying the specific data and information elements to appear on source documents and reports; design of a data base and data coding scheme; and design of a computerized data processor. Optimum implementation of the MIS involves five key issues: timing, gaining acceptance, documentation, support, and responsibilities for implementation.

The need for formal internal control and evaluation of the MIS after implementation is the fourth phase of study methodology. Internal control procedures are needed for insuring the proper authorization, execution, and recording of transactions and the accountability for assets and resources.

Exhibit 4-9 summarizes the systems methodology for MIS design as it is used in Parts 3 and 4.

REVIEW QUESTIONS

1. Discuss the characteristics of the systems approach. How does the systems approach methodology facilitate the design of the MIS? What are four major phases of the systems approach methodology?

2. Describe the issues and factors that need to be resolved in the origination phase of the MIS design study.

3. Discuss the importance of analysis of operations for defining information needs and uses. Describe several ways of viewing the operations of an organization.

Exhibit 4-9

SYSTEMS METHODOLOGY FOR MIS DESIGN

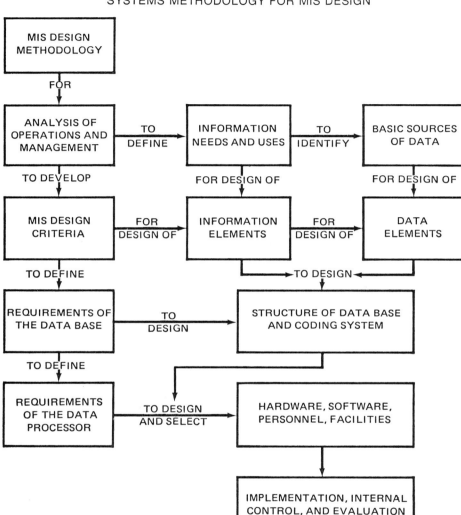

4. Describe and contrast the traditional functional view of organization versus the systems view of an organization as an input-output system. Identify the major components of the input-output model, and contrast the operational and informational subsystems of the basic systems model. What is the nature and purpose of each?

5. Describe how the responsibility center can be used for the MIS design. Give examples of types of responsibility centers and indicate their information needs. What are the advantages for using the responsibility center as a basic unit of analysis for MIS design?

6. Describe how information needs and uses can be classified for the design of the MIS, and give examples of each classification. Indicate how these classifications are interrelated.

7. Describe the four major tasks involved in the design of MIS processes. How are these tasks interrelated?

8. Gaining acceptance of the results or recommendations of a systems study generally involves approvals for information flow changes and organizational changes. Discuss these two categories of change. Discuss the importance of designating responsibilities for implementation of the MIS. What people are involved? What problems need to be resolved?

9. "The timing of implementation should consider the budget cycle." Discuss why this is important and describe some of the steps that need to be provided for.

10. Discuss the importance of systems documentation for effective MIS implementation. How does systems documentation facilitate internal control and evaluation of the MIS?

EXERCISE 4-1: Discount, Inc. (Part A)

Discount, Inc. Store Number 18 is one of 30 in a national chain. It is a large department store located in a city of 800,000 population. The sales volume of the store has been increasing slowly each year with the population of the city, and last year it reached a new high of $1,000,000. The store carries a variety of hardline and softline merchandise, many items being brand name items sold at a discount. The store greatly relies on price competition to attract customers and generate sales. Only recently it began to emphasize services such as credit, free packaging, and servicing of appliances.

The major categories of operating expenses (as a percent of sales) incurred by the store last year include merchandise cost of goods sold (65.9), salaries and wages (18.4), occupancy (2.6), advertising (2.2), and all other expenses (9.6). Gross margin was 34.1 percent of sales and net profit before taxes was 1.3 percent of sales. The total assets of the store were $350,000, of which $200,000 was in merchandise inventory. Inventory turnover averaged 5.0 during the last five years. Current assets to current liabilities averaged 3.0, and fixed assets to total assets averaged 28 percent during the last five years.

The manager of the store is concerned about the unfavorable trend in operating costs, especially those related to the other expense category, which includes merchandise loss, excessive discounts due to product obsolescence, and excess inventory carrying costs. The following paragraphs describe the major operations relating to the acquisition, promotion, display, and sale of merchandise.

MERCHANDISE SOURCES

The Discount, Inc. chain purchases merchandise from over 100 vendors and importers. It buys in large quantities at special prices. In order for it to be economical to buy in large quantities, Discount, Inc. must be able to turn over the merchandise rapidly. On basic items in the hardline departments, orders are made up from a list of items available from inventory maintained in the chain's regional warehouse. This ordering is done on a weekly basis: orders are placed on Tuesdays and the merchandise is delivered on Saturdays. Fifty percent of all hardline merchandise including major appliances is ordered in the above fashion; the remaining 50 percent is ordered directly from the vendor by the chain buyer located in New York.

The hardline department supervisor must take a physical count of all merchandise listed on the order copy, enter this figure in the "on-hand" column, and then decide how many he needs for a six-week period. He must then check the open file in the stockroom to see if there are any on order. If none are on order he submits an order to the assistant store manager for approval and expediting. Approval of the order is dependent upon the amount of money the store is permitted to spend for merchandise over a four-week period. If insufficient funds are available, the order is not passed at that time.

Ninety percent of all softline merchandise is ordered through the chain's buyers in New York who deal directly with vendors. All software items are marked with a four-digit code on the price ticket. This code is punched into the cash register when the item is sold. The detailed cash register tapes are periodically sent to a data processing center for item tabulations. The tabulation results are sent to the New York buyers. This information gives the buyer a good idea of the turnover rates for various items. Reorder decisions are based largely upon turnover rates. The remaining 10 percent of the softlines, which includes men's underwear, some ladies' lingerie, socks, gloves, and other basic items, are ordered on a regular basis, usually quarterly.

All merchandise ordered through the chain buyers in New York takes from four to six weeks to arrive in the store, depending on the vendor. (This excludes hardline merchandise available in regional warehouses.) All orders which have not arrived two weeks past the shipping date are cancelled, and the store manager has an option to keep or return merchandise which has been delivered late (however, the majority is kept with the exception of seasonal merchandise). The major fault of this system for ordering merchandise is the lack of a feedback link from the store to the buyer, in that there is no procedure for determining possible late deliveries or failures to deliver. This results in duplication of merchandise ordered and an overstock condition in the hardline areas. A recommendation for alleviating this problem has been made which would involve sending all orders for basic merchandise directly to the New York office, where the buyer would have a record of what is ordered and could take advantage of quantity discounts.

MERCHANDISE INPUTS

All merchandise received at Store Number 18 comes through the receiving department, at which time a key-rec[6] is prepared for the merchandise. A

---

[6] A key-rec is the record produced by a special system of receiving merchandise which encodes the quantity, vendor, date received, freight company, and whether shipment was prepaid or collect. It also shows damages, overages, and shortages.

key-rec number is stamped on the cartons, along with the number of cartons in the shipment, and then the key-rec is filed in numerical order. The receiver and a helper, if necessary, place the merchandise on one of two conveyors (one for hardlines and one for softlines). For hardlines, the packages are opened and checked in and the following information is placed on each carton of every shipment: vendor, department number, and order number.

The bundle opener checks the shipment to see that all cartons shown as received are present. He then goes to the open order file which is a file according to department number, in numerical order, and removes the correct order. He circles the amount on the order copy if it is correct or notes any discrepancies in quantity. He leaves one copy of the order with the merchandise and attaches the corresponding key-rec to the other copies. The bundle opener also inserts the key-rec number date with his initials on the order.

At this time the merchandise is ready to be marked. In most cases, hardline merchandise is marked by the bundle opener who checked it in. He spot-checks the order for accuracy and then makes up the appropriate tickets showing period code, merchandise and department numbers, and price. He attaches the tickets and the merchandise goes to the sales floor or stays in the stockroom to await a sale date.

Softline merchandise is handled in much the same way. The conveyor is approximately 80 feet long. The softline bundle opener pulls the corresponding order and fills it in the same way as his hardline counterpart. The softline merchandise is removed from the shipping carton and placed on masonite pallets which are then conveyed to the pin ticket machine where the merchandise is marked. The softline marker checks the order for accuracy and marks the merchandise with a pin ticket. At this time, regular merchandise is placed in a rolling bin and sent to the selling floor. At the end of each working day, all sale merchandise is placed on top of bins (approximately 10 feet tall). All merchandise which cannot be used is pushed down an aisle in the stockroom and left there

MERCHANDISE CONVERSION

Merchandise conversion consists of the advertising and merchandising efforts. At least once a month and occasionally twice, the store inserts a 12-page circular in the local newspaper.

These circulars are developed by the buyers in the New York office. Half of the circulars are printed by the newspaper for home delivery, and the other half are printed by a New York printing company and mailed directly to store customers. Approximately 90 percent of the advertising is directly controlled by the New York office. The rest are clearance ads which are made up in the store, usually by the assistant store manager. Many times merchandise which is selected by New York to be advertised is not even in the store; in these cases a rapid item substitution is made.

The store has difficulty in reducing its inventory of items with which it is overstocked. In fact the overstock condition is compounded in many instances in that merchandise in an ad is received even when the store already has more than enough to cover the sales generated by the ad.

The paperwork relating to sales consists of recapitulation sheets, arranged by department number, which are preprinted with the item and sale price. The hardline and softline department supervisors fill in the quantity on hand and turn it in to the assistant store manager. After the ad, the department supervisors record on the recap sheet the amount on hand and they compute the quantity sold. This information is forwarded to the buyers in New York.

The display and sale of merchandise are the direct responsibility of the hardline and softline department supervisors. The departments are in a constant state of change because of new items being brought in. It is not common to reset a whole display counter in order to display a new item properly. This causes what the supervisors and their workers regard as unnecessary work. To overcome this problem, a plan to map out locations of sale merchandise was put into effect, but it failed due to lack of cooperation between the assistant store manager and the supervisors.

Widespread changes are made seasonally and when store managers change. When the store manager is transferred or replaced, his replacement usually rearranges the store layout. This change entails the moving of approximately 150 display features. Fortunately, managers usually change only every three or four years. Seasonal changes are necessary to emphasize popular merchandise.

MERCHANDISE OUTPUT

Merchandise output consists of sales, the amount of which depends largely on customer satisfaction. Discount, Inc. Store Number 18, being the first discount store in the city, learned its merchandising by trial and error, and unfortunately they are still paying for some of their initial errors. For example, the people of this city were accustomed to being catered to and waited on in the stores where they had previously shopped. Because of the low pay scale (federal minimum), the clerks were not of the highest competence and consequently the store bears a poor image for service.

Another sore spot with the people of the city was the company return policy which specified that no merchandise was to be returned without a receipt or more than ten days after purchase. One year ago this practice was changed so that merchandise could be returned at any time without proof of purchase and with very little difficulty.

One other practice that still works a hardship on the store's image is its check cashing policy, which states that all persons cashing a check must be photographed. Most people of the city regard this as an insult. However, the store has held as much as $2,500 in worthless checks at one time and has found that photography discourages professional check passers. Another system for check cashing convenience involves a courtesy card. Customers can fill out a form which is then sent to the customer's bank, which is requested to provide information on the person. Some banks refuse to provide information. When a card is not issued, the store bears the brunt of customer dissatisfaction, not the bank. Even if a customer possesses a courtesy card, the check must still be verified by a supervisor, and customers take this as an affront to their dignity, even though the purpose is to double check for common errors (date, amounts, signature).

MERCHANDISE USERS

A great variety of people shop in Store Number 18, varying from the governor's wife to those in very low income brackets. Generally the customers are understanding and easy to get along with. A small amount of courtesy on the part of the employees appears to be all that is required to maintain cordial relationships. For the most part, even those few people who do get aggravated and leave muttering under their breath that they will never return actually do.

The present store manager has an open door policy and is quite willing to listen to any complaints customers have about personnel or the store in general. Furthermore, he takes the necessary steps to alleviate problems and to soothe irate customers.

One significant problem involving customers is shoplifting. One store detective is on the floor at all times; however, only part of the problem is to catch thieves. The other is determining what to do after they are caught. The shoplifting laws are weak and those prosecuted often receive only a modest fine. The majority of offenders are not prosecuted, due to proof problems or potential adverse publicity, but they are dismissed with the admonition never to enter the store again. Three percent of inventory is considered by the industry to be the maximum amount tolerable for shrinkage from pilferage and paperwork errors. The store has a shrinkage of about three percent.

CONTROL UNIT

The store is controlled by a store manager with an assistant manager directly under him. The next level of management are four supervisors: hardline, softline, receiving, and customer services. Each supervisor controls from one to ten people, the average being five.

1. Draw a traditional organization chart of Discount, Inc. Store Number 18, based on the information in the exercise.

2. Develop an organizational systems model (source-input-processor-output-user) from the description of the operations of Discount, Inc. Store Number 18 (similar to Exhibit 4-2).

3. Prepare a summary flowchart of the operational flows of Discount, Inc. Store Number 18 pertaining to merchandise decisions and work flows (similar to examples shown in Exhibits 4-3 and 4-4).

4. Identify several examples of various types of information needed to facilitate planning, operational control, and managerial/financial control of the merchandising function.

EXERCISE 4-2: The Organization Chart

Select an organization with which you are familiar. The organization may be profit-making (business), nonprofit (government or educational), or social (fraternity or sorority). For the organization selected:

1. Prepare an organization chart showing its major functions and departments.
2. Recast the organization chart into the input-output systems model, examples of which are shown in Exhibit 4-2.
3. Prepare a summary of the major decisions or work activities performed and identify major types of information needed for each decision or work activity within the general context of the operational subsystem (refer to Exhibits 4-3 and 4-4) and use the appropriate flowcharting symbols presented in the Appendix.

EXERCISE 4-3: The Marnox Company (Part C)

Review Part B of the Marnox Company in Chapter 2. Using the specific outline of the steps included in Exhibit 4-9, develop a critique of the positive and negative factors that are evident at each step of the methodology relating to the company's design and implementation of their information system.

EXERCISE 4-4: Farm Products Corporation (Part D)

The objectives of this exercise are to provide practice in analyzing informational problems of an organization and in defining specific objectives to be achieved by the MIS study group; to stress the importance of top management approval and learn effective means of insuring that it is obtained prior to performing the study; and to achieve a feeling for the actual methodology which should be used in analyzing the operations and designing the MIS processes.

Assume that you are the managing partner for the Management Services Division of a national accounting firm. Since Farm Products was founded, it has employed your firm, primarily for auditing its financial statements. The President of FPC has indicated that they have been experiencing serious problems with internal communications lately. He referred to a "paperwork explosion" and said they were considering a major expansion of their computer facilities as a possible solution of their problems. The President has requested assistance from your division, and has invited you to attend the next FPC Executive Committee meeting to get a better idea about their problems.

During the course of the meeting, you took note of the following comments:

Sales: Our biggest complaint is that deliveries are too slow. We've always been able to promise delivery in a week to ten days. Lately, it's taken twelve days on the average, and often as long as three weeks. We've already lost some good accounts, and I'm afraid we'll lose a lot more if we can't deliver the goods when they need them.

Shipping:

I've noticed that orders are getting out slower, of course, but there's nothing we can do about it in Shipping. The orders are six to eight days old when we get them. It usually takes a couple of days to schedule shipments at the best rates. Then the orders have to be packed and loaded, and they can't always be delivered over night. Besides, we get orders nearly every day for items that aren't even in the warehouse. We can't do anything then but wait until it comes out of Assembly.

Production
Supervisor:

Our work schedule is dictated by Production Control. We make what they say, when the materials are available. You can't make a bush hog blade without the right grade of steel, though, and a garden rake is no good without a handle. When this happens, we sit around and polish machinery for a day or two, and then have to go on overtime for a week to catch up. There's no way I can meet my budget with that going on.

Material
Control:

Some of that is our fault, but lately Purchasing has been getting about 15 percent of the orders mixed up. We've been getting the wrong grade of bar steel and the wrong widths of sheet steel. I admit there are problems in my department, but it's mainly because we stay covered up with paperwork. Production is up 30 percent in the past two years, but I'm still operating with the same people as before. When we're this short-handed, mistakes are bound to happen and some things are going to get done late.

1. What are some of FPC's problems which might be remedied by an effective MIS? What specific objectives should be assigned to the MIS design staff?
2. What personnel should be assigned full time to the study, either from FPC or from your firm? Is it necessary to have a part time advisory committee also?
3. The approval of top management is essential prior to performing the study. Write a preliminary report to the President, stating what is to be accomplished, the resources you will need and any assistance you would request in getting the study started on the right track.
4. How will you conduct the study? What methods will you use during the first few weeks of the study? Be as specific as possible within the limitations of the known facts. If it is necessary to make additional assumptions, be sure they are reasonable and state them clearly.

EXERCISE 4-5: State University Information Systems Project

The following paragraphs describe the general methodology used in the analysis and design of a university information system. The description is followed by a PERT chart (Exhibit 4-10) and a tabular presentation of the methodology and activity involved in the study showing schedules and responsibilities (Exhibit 4-11).

ORIGINATION OF THE PROJECT

During the summer of 1970, a committee was organized to investigate and evaluate a state university's communications problems, especially as they related to the university's information system. The purpose of the investigation was to define an area which could be formally studied and organize a project group to perform the study. The preliminary investigation and evaluation of the current university information system began on September 2, 1970, and continued for four weeks. The four-week evaluation period included a series of concurrent activities broken down as follows:

Systems committee meetings
Discussions with university personnel
Review of literature relating to development by other universities
Review of comments from board of regents and governmental agencies relative to information needs
Miscellaneous feedback

The review of the materials and information obtained from the evaluation phase led to a formal statement of need for a study. This review period to develop the statement of need for a study lasted two weeks, until October 14, 1970.

The need for a study being defined, the statement of project objectives was formulated. The initial task was to define the scope of the study which was expected to take seven weeks. Two other concurrent tasks followed, with each expected to take about two weeks.

Obtain approval and secure authority for the study to proceed.
Determine the expected completion date.

After the statement of project objectives was completed and accepted, the organization of the project team would follow. This involved the determination of the types of personnel needed (.5 week).

Approval of the project organization and budget and securing space for the project team took 2.0 weeks (completed by January 4, 1971) and were performed concurrently. Following these steps, the establishment of working procedures and work schedules took about .5 week. The organization of the project team was complete.

A preliminary statement of the methodology for the study took about .5 week for completion, or until January 8, 1971.

PERFORMANCE OF THE STUDY

The performance of the study included three major phases: analysis, design, and testing. The *analysis phase* included two major tasks to be undertaken concurrently. These tasks related to data collection and are listed with expected completion times:

A. Inventory of current information used. The inventory of current information includes two subtasks to be performed concurrently:
   1. Preparation of a memo requesting copies of existing reports used (1.0 week or by January 15, 1971).
   2. Development of a cataloging scheme for the types of information (1.0 week or by January 15, 1971).
   Based on these subtasks, four additional subtasks followed:
   3. Definition of source and format of input documents to update master files (5.0 weeks or by February 19, 1971).
   4. Determination of current studies being done concerning university information systems by the study group or by offices in the university and provision of a means for coordinating all of these studies (3.0 weeks or by February 5, 1971).
   5. Interviews with affected areas to insure full identification of the information used and needed (5.0 weeks or by February 19, 1971).
   6. Cataloging of information used (5.0 weeks or by February 19, 1971).
B. Inventory of current information coding schemes (5.0 weeks or by February 19, 1971).

After data relating to information used was collected, current information uses and needs were analyzed (3.0 weeks or by March 12, 1971). Concurrently, current coding schemes used and needed were analyzed (3.0 weeks or by March 12, 1971). The conceptualization of segments of the information system began after these two activities were completed (2.0 weeks or by March 26, 1971).

The *design phase* included two major subphases:

A. Definition and design of the recommended information system. Three sequential activities initiated the design phase:
   1. Definition and design of the long-range total system to be developed (5.0 weeks or by April 30, 1971).
   2. Definition and design of the selective segments of the total system to be implemented in the fall of 1971 (2.0 weeks or by May 14, 1971).
   3. Approval of the selective system for the fall of 1971, i.e., the segments of the total system to be implemented in the fall (2.0 weeks or by May 28, 1971).
B. Programming of the segments of the system for the fall of 1971. The programming phase included the design of programs, source documents, and materials needed for implementation. The effort involved began with three concurrent tasks:
   1. Development of specifications for computer programs (2.0 weeks or by June 11, 1971).
   2. Design of source documents (8.0 weeks or by July 23, 1971).

3. Design of procedures and manuals for implementation (8.0 weeks or by July 23, 1971).

Based upon completion of computer program specifications, computer programs were written and documented (8.0 weeks or by August 6, 1971).

The *test phase* followed the completion of development of computer programs and their documentation. It primarily involved testing and debugging of computer programs for the selective information system (3.0 weeks or by August 27, 1971).

IMPLEMENTATION AND MANAGEMENT OF THE SELECTIVE INFORMATION SYSTEM

Initial tasks for the implementation and management of the selective information system were performed concurrently:

A. Ordering of new forms (5.0 weeks or by August 27, 1971).

B. Training of key areas (5.0 weeks or by August 27, 1971).

Three concurrent activities followed these tasks:

C. Collection of data for new system operation (16.0 weeks or by December 17, 1971).

D. Development of information retrieval programs for selective information system (16.0 weeks or by December 17, 1971).

E. Continual review and evaluation of the system during implementation (16.0 weeks, through December 17, 1971).

Modification and testing of all aspects of the selective information system followed the valuation of the system (3.0 weeks or by January 28, 1972).

REVIEW OF SYSTEM

Continual review, evaluation, and updating of the system occurred after implementation.

1. Contrast the methodology used in this case with that described in Chapter 4, and comment on:
   a. How the study was originated.
   b. The sequencing and scheduling of activities.
   c. The types of personnel used.
2. Discuss the usefulness and limitations of the tabular presentation of the methodology as a device for planning and controlling the study (as shown in Exhibit 4-11).

Exhibit 4-10

PERT CHART OF STATE UNIVERSITY INFORMATION SYSTEM PROJECT

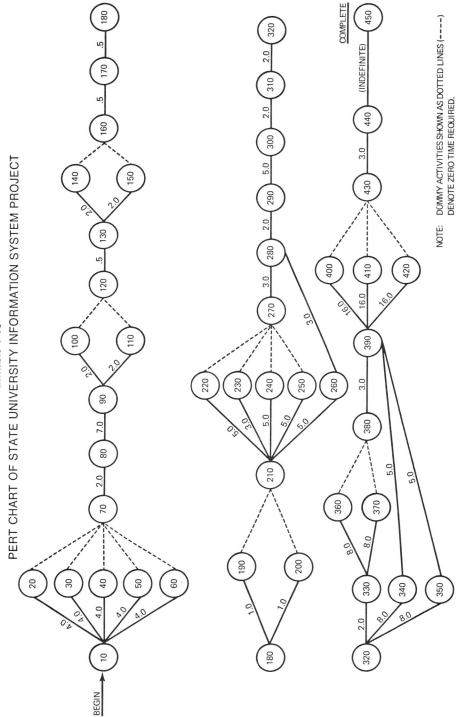

NOTE: DUMMY ACTIVITIES SHOWN AS DOTTED LINES (----) DENOTE ZERO TIME REQUIRED.

Exhibit 4-11

STATE UNIVERSITY INFORMATION SYSTEM
PROPOSED METHODOLOGY AND ACTIVITY IDENTIFICATION
August 16, 1970

Activity Number	Activity Description	Weeks to Complete	Expected Dates	Job Assignment
	I. Origination of the Project			
	1. *Evaluation of performance of current university systems*			
10-20	a. Systems committee meetings	4.0	9/2—9/30, 70	
10-30	b. Discussions with university personnel	4.0	9/2—9/30, 70	
10-40	c. Review of literature relating to development by other universities	4.0	9/2—9/30, 70	
10-50	d. Review comments from Board of Regents and governmental agencies	4.0	9/2—9/30, 70	
10-60	e. Miscellaneous feedback	4.0	9/2—9/30, 70	
70-80	2. *Statement of need for study* (Evaluation of 1 above)	2.0	9/30—10/14, 70	
	3. *Statement of Project Objectives*			
80-90	a. Scope	7.0	10/14—12/2, 70	
90-100	b. Obtain authority for study	2.0	12/2—12/16, 70	
	(1) Primary—Vice-President for Academic Affairs & Vice-President for Administration			
	(2) Facilitation—Board of Regents and Legislature			
90-110	c. Determine expected completion date	2.0	12/2—12/16, 70	
	(1) Need historical data by May 1971, for period of Sept. 1970—March 1971			
	4. *Organization of project team*			
120-130	a. Determine types of personnel needed	.5	12/16—12/18, 70	
	(1) Project Director (1 full-time)			
	(2) Project team members (2 half-time graduate students)			
	(3) Programmers (selection later)			
	(4) Primary advisory personnel (2 part-time)			
	(5) Facilitating advisory personnel (affected areas, such as administration, computer center, comptroller, personnel, registrar, academic deans)			
130-140	b. Obtain approval of project organization and budget	2.0	12/18—1/4, 71	
130-150	c. Secure space for project team	2.0	12/18—1/4, 71	
160-170	d. Establish team working procedures and schedules	.5	1/2—1/6, 71	
170-180	5. *Develop Statement of Methodology*	.5	1/6—1/8, 71	
	II. Performance of the Study			
	1. *Analysis of existing information requirements*			
180-190	a. Inventory of current information used	1.0	1/8—1/15, 71	
	(1) Memo requesting data gathering documents			

Code	Activity		Dates
180-200	(2) Develop cataloging scheme for all types of information used	1.0	1/8—1/15, 71
210-220	(3) Define source and format of input documents to update master files	5.0	1/15—2/19, 71
210-230	(4) Determine existence of systems work currently being done on university information systems	3.0	1/15—2/5, 71
210-240	(5) Interviews with affected areas to ensure full identification of information collected, used, and needed	5.0	1/15—2/19, 71
210-250	(6) Cataloging of information used	5.0	1/15—2/19, 71
210-260	b. Inventory of current information coding schemes used	5.0	1/15—2/19, 71
270-280	c. Analysis of current information used and needed	3.0	2/19—3/12, 71
260-280	d. Analysis of current coding schemes used and needed	3.0	2/19—3/12, 71
280-290	e. Begin conceptualization of segments of university information system	2.0	3/12—3/26, 71
	2. Design of new University Information System		
290-300	a. Definition of recommended Information System (input documents, master files, reports, and coding schemes)	5.0	3/26—4/30, 71
300-310	(1) Define and design the long-range total system that will be developed	2.0	4/30—5/14, 71
310-320	(2) Define and design the segments of the system to be implemented September, 1971	2.0	5/14—5/28, 71
	(3) Obtain approval of selective information system for September, 1971		
	b. Programming of selected segments for September, 1971		
320-330	(1) Specifications for computer programming	2.0	5/28—6/11, 71
320-340	(2) Design/redesign of source documents	8.0	5/28—7/23, 71
320-350	(3) Design of procedures & manuals for implementation	8.0	5/28—7/23, 71
330-360	(4) Computer programming	8.0	6/11—8/6, 71
330-370	(5) Documentation of computer programs	8.0	6/11—8/6, 71
380-390	*3. Test Information System—Test and debug computer programs for selected system*	3.0	8/6—8/27, 71
	III. Implementation & Management of the Selective System		
	1. Implementation of Selective System for September, 1971		
340-390	a. Order new forms	5.0	7/23—8/27, 71
350-390	b. Conduct training sessions for key areas	5.0	7/23—8/27, 71
390-400	c. Collect data for new system operation	16.0	8/27—12/17, 71
390-410	d. Develop selective retrieval programs	16.0	8/27—12/17, 71
390-420	e. Review and evaluation of system	16.0	8/27—12/17, 71
430-440	*2. Test and modify all aspects of Selective Information System*	3.0	1/7—1/28, 72
	IV. Review of System		
440-450	Continual review, evaluation, and updating of system		Indefinite (Begin 1/28, 72)

NOTE: The job assignment column can be used to show which members of the project team are responsible for each activity.

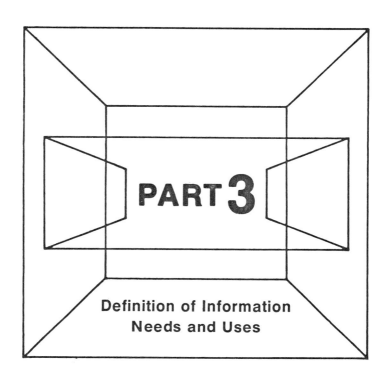

PART 3

Definition of Information Needs and Uses

5 INFORMATION FOR PLANNING

The general function of information was described in Chapter 1 as facilitating the performance of various functions which comprise the process of management, namely, planning, operational control, and managerial/financial control. In this chapter, the basic types of information needed for effective planning are discussed, while the next two chapters deal with the information needed for operational control and managerial/financial control, respectively.

The systems methodology for defining information needs described in Chapter 4 emphasizes the analysis of operations (i.e., the operational subsystem of the organization) as the basis for determining information needs. The nature of the work, activities, and decisions associated with each major function of management must be defined and evaluated in order to define the types of information that are needed by management. Management functions array themselves along a time dimension in the manner shown below:

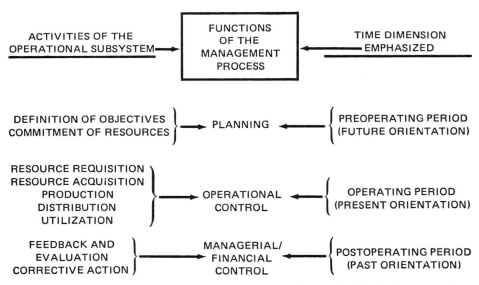

These relationships provide the framework for analysis of the operations and definitions of information needed for the performance of the various management functions. An analysis of the operational subsystem activities would in practice require an extremely detailed description of the management functions. On the other hand, the analysis of the management functions in terms of a time perspective results in a more general frame of reference suitable for analyzing the operational activities relating to the functions of management.

Both types of analyses (operational subsystem activities and time dimensions) are useful for defining management information needs. The more detailed analysis of activities is useful for insuring that operating managers' information needs are well identified and provided for, and for identifying and evaluating the information currently used in the organization. The summary of the detailed analyses of activities within the time dimensions related to the functions of management is useful for interrelating information needs into an information system which serves the general functions of management.

In Part 3, this general framework for defining information needs for planning, operational control, and managerial/financial control is used as shown in Exhibit 5-1. Examples of detailed and summary analyses are described. This chapter, which discusses the basic types of information needed for effective planning, has these specific objectives:

1. To describe what is involved in planning and to provide examples of analyses that are involved in defining information needed for effective planning.
2. To describe in detail several demand analysis reports that are useful for defining objectives and evaluating demand for products and services.
3. To describe in detail several resource capacity status analysis reports that are useful for commiting resources to specific objectives and operations.
4. To describe budgeting as a mechanism for evaluating demand versus capacity to perform and for communicating to managers decisions relating to objectives and resource commitments.

Before examining the types of information and reports required for planning, the meaning of planning must be firmly established.

PLANNING

As a major function of management, planning is concerned primarily with projecting the future operations of the organization. Planning is predictive in nature; it attempts to reduce the level of uncertainty regarding the future performance of the organization. Reduction of uncertainty is accomplished by examining the consequences and their likelihoods associated with the various future alternative courses of action which the organization can pursue based on its capacity to perform. The overall purpose of planning is to achieve the optimum balance between *demand* for products or services of an organization and its *capacity* to produce them efficiently. The decisions relating to this optimum balance between demand and capacity are reflected in the *operating budgets* for the organization.

The effective execution of the planning function involves definition of objectives and commitment of resources. Exhibit 5-2 provides a conceptual framework for analyzing activities for the purpose of defining types of information needed to facilitate planning. In order to support decisions relating

Exhibit 5-1

SUMMARY OF PART 3: DEFINITION OF INFORMATION NEEDS AND USES

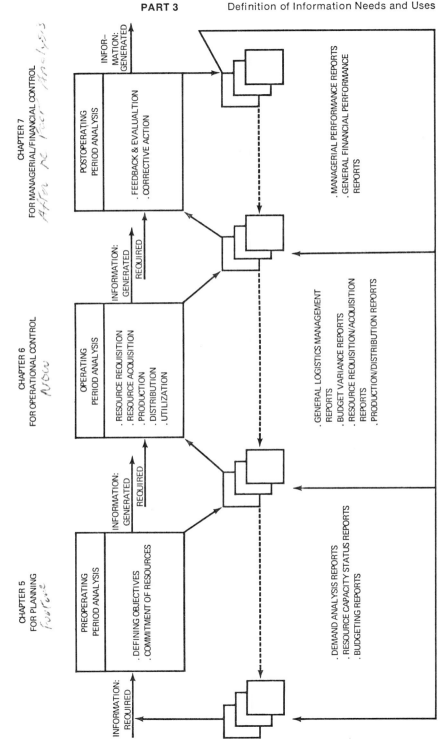

Exhibit 5-2

THE PLANNING FUNCTION (PREOPERATING PERIOD ANALYSIS)

OPERATIONAL SUBSYSTEM   INFORMATIONAL SUBSYSTEM

(0100) DEFINITION OF OBJECTIVES Goals
(DEMAND ANALYSIS)

(0110) ANALYSIS OF CONSTRAINTS
AND DECISION CRITERIA- - - - -► PRELIMINARY STATEMENTS
OF OBJECTIVES   (0111)
(0120) ANALYSIS OF DEMAND
DETERMINANTS AND PRODUCT/
SERVICE POTENTIAL- - - - - -► PRELIMINARY FORECASTS
OF DEMAND   (0121)

(0200) COMMITMENT OF RESOURCES
(RESOURCE CAPACITY STATUS
ANALYSIS)

(0210) DEFINE RESOURCE REQUIREMENTS
FOR PRODUCTS/SERVICES- - -► RESOURCE SPECIFICATION
LISTS   (0211)
(0220) CONVERT RESOURCE
REQUIREMENTS INTO
PRELIMINARY BUDGETS- - - - -► PRELIMINARY BUDGETS   (0221)

(0230) ANALYS   OF PRELIMINARY
BUDGETS, FORECASTS, AND
OBJECTIVES TO FINALIZE
COMMITMENT OF RESOURCES
TO PRODUCTS/SERVICES,
FUNCTIONS, AND PROGRAMS- -► REVISED OBJECTIVES   (0231)
►REVISED DEMAND
FORECASTS   (0232)
►REVISED BUDGETS   (0233)
►WORK STATEMENTS
AND SCHEDULES   (0234)
►QUALITY SPECIFICATIONS   (0235)
►RESOURCE REQUISITIONS   (0236)

(0300)(0700) OPERATIONAL CONTROL FUNCTION
(0800)(0900) MANAGERIAL/FINANCIAL CONTROL FUNCTION

NOTES:
1. THE NUMBERING SYSTEM SHOWN IS ALSO USED IN EXHIBITS 6-1 AND 7-1
FOR OPERATIONAL CONTROL AND MANAGERIAL/FINANCIAL CONTROL,
RESPECTIVELY. THIS NUMBERING SYSTEM AND THESE EXHIBITS WILL BE
USED IN PART 4 TO SHOW HOW AN INTEGRATED MIS MAY BE DEVELOPED.

2. THE ANALYSES AND DECISIONS SHOWN IN THE OPERATIONAL SUBSYS-
TEM ARE MAJOR EXAMPLES FOR ILLUSTRATIVE PURPOSES AND ARE
NOT INTENDED TO BE COMPLETE. ALSO, THEY ARE ONLY SEQUENTIAL
GENERALLY; IN ACTUAL PRACTICE THEY ARE HIGHLY INTERRELATED
AND EXTENSIVE AND CONTINUAL RECYCLING OCCURS.

3. THE DOCUMENTS GENERATED (0111 THROUGH 0236) ARE EXAMPLES OF
THE MAJOR TYPES OF DOCUMENTS THAT NORMALLY ARE PROCESSED AS
INPUTS TO THE MIS FOR OPERATIONAL CONTROL AND MANAGERIAL/FI-
NANCIAL CONTROL ANALYSES AND DECISIONS.

to defining objectives (0100), analyses are undertaken which should provide answers to the following two general questions:

1. What are the major *constraints* and *decision criteria* which impact the organization's operations and the image the organization is attempting to maintain or achieve (0110)?
2. What are the major *demand determinants or factors* which impact the organization's *product or service potential,* and how will these factors impact future demand for the organization's products or services (0120)?

Answers to these two general questions should lead to decisions concerning organizational objectives (0111) and estimates or forecasts of demand (0121), respectively. These types of analyses and decisions provide information for the commitment of resources to future operations of the organization (0200).

In order to support decisions relating to the commitment of resources, analyses are undertaken which should provide answers to a third general question:

3. What are the *resource requirements* of the projected demand for products or services (0210, 0220) and what is the *resource capacity* of the organization to service the projected demand (0230)?

Answers to this third question should lead to decisions concerning revised objectives, forecasts, and budgets (0231-0233), and decisions concerning work statements and schedules, quality specifications, and resource requisitions (0234-0236).

The three general questions to be answered through demand and resource capacity status analysis are not intended to be universal. Yet they do include the most important types of analyses which are needed for effective planning. For example, without extensive analyses relating to organizational objectives and forecasts of demand, the organization cannot develop optimum decisions for future operations. Nor can it make optimum decisions concerning the commitment of resources to these operations through a set of operating budgets.

The following sections provide example answers to these three general questions for an office furniture manufacturer and a state university. These examples reflect the types of analyses and information involved in planning for each type of organization, and they are patterned generally around the framework provided in Exhibit 5-2.

Constraints and Decision Criteria

Constraints are factors which limit what the organization can do (such as a law prohibiting the sale of specific products to minors) or requirements (such as a minimum wage law or tax law). For an office furniture manufacturer, constraints may include legal requirements concerning pollutants, minimum wage laws, fair trade regulations, union agreements, and availability of financing. For a state university, typical constraints are accreditation standards (such as faculty-student ratios, library facilities, and qualifications of faculty), size of legislative budget for higher education, maximum state enrollment quotas, and state tuition limits.

Existing constraints are evaluated in terms of their impact on the future objectives and operations of the organization. Assumptions and projections of new constraints or possible changes in existing ones are also made. The overall purpose of this analysis and evaluation is to reduce the uncertainty associated with the impact of the organization's environment on its operations. If the organization can develop a clear picture of what its environment will be, it can better plan its future operations. If an office furniture manufacturer can accurately project the outcome of future collective bargaining agreements, it is better able to estimate future wage rates and fringe costs. Good estimates of these figures enable an assessment of their potential impact on the prices of office furniture. Knowledge of expected changes in state enrollment quotas enables a state university to make better estimates of its space, faculty, staff, and other resource requirements.

Decision criteria reflect the goals of the organization in ways that also reflect the image the organization is attempting to maintain or achieve. For example, the office furniture manufacturer may wish to produce and sell low priced furniture, thereby emphasizing volume production, fast delivery (production for inventory), and small profit margins. The combination of these goals leads to a company image which emphasizes economy to the consumer. This means that if the company wishes to maintain this image, its product, price, promotion, and distribution decisions will be reflected in a mass production, low cost, mass distribution, low price type of operation. If the company wishes to develop the opposite type of image, it would change its goals to reflect quality products, higher costs of production, production for order versus for large inventories, higher prices, lower sales volume, and higher profit margins. These two cases are extremes along a continuum; however, they illustrate the importance of decision criteria for the objectives and operations of the company.

Similarly, for a state university, decision criteria may include high quality degree programs, specialized degree options (e.g., accounting, finance, management, and marketing versus a single degree in business administration), major emphasis on instruction versus research, and regional versus national visibility of programs. Decision criteria may also be defined in ways other than the product or service related examples described above. For example, a business firm may develop an image as the industry leader in terms of the average wage and fringe benefits paid to its employees. Also, it may develop an image of "customer satisfaction guaranteed," "antipollution," and "equal opportunity for minorities" through its decisions, policies, and operations over a number of years.

The overall purpose of defining and evaluating decision criteria is to formulate long-range objectives and strategies for developing the desired image the organization wishes to achieve. These long-range objectives and strategies provide the basis for developing operational objectives and policies. For example, the furniture company's long-range objective of developing an image of a high-quality producer of office furniture is the basis for setting higher prices for its furniture and developing higher production specifications and tighter controls, together with promotion programs and distribution channels which will ensure the production and sale of high quality furniture. A university that has as a long-range objective to be recognized as a leading institution of higher education in a region in both instruction and research must develop appropriate operational objectives and policies. These may take the form of increasing faculty compensation and fringe benefits to attract better faculty, reducing student-faculty ratios in classes, allocating resources to faculty research positions, and improving instruction and research facilities and equipment.

In summary, the analysis and evaluation of constraints and decision criteria should lead to decisions concerning organizational objectives. These statements of objectives are tentative; an analysis and evaluation of demand determinants and product service potential must be accomplished to determine their feasibility.

Demand Determinants and Product/Service Potential

Demand determinants are factors which influence demand for the products/services of the organization. For the office furniture manufacturer, they include the number and size of organizations using office furniture; general economic conditions affecting growth of business, educational, and governmental organizations; competitive factors relating to products and firms; price elasticities for office furniture; and customer preferences. For a state university, important demand factors include projections of population size and age levels, number of high school graduates, growth in size and number of state higher education institutions, and industry-government demand for college graduates by discipline and level of degree.

The overall purpose of analysis and evaluation of demand determinants is to identify feasible product/service objectives for the organization to pursue. Demand determinants are analyzed and evaluated in terms of how they will impact the organization's objectives. The assumptions made concerning constraints and decision criteria are reviewed and evaluated to develop feasible product objectives. The office furniture company may wish to expand its product line to include a low-quality and low-priced line of office desks. However, through an analysis of demand for this type of product and because of the existing number of firms producing economy-line office desks, the firm may discover that this is not a feasible objective to pursue at this time.

Evaluation of the demand determinants which affect the organization's products/services potential provides the basis for developing forecasts of demand. For a business firm, forecasts of demand are sales forecasts by products, customers, sales regions, salesmen, and major divisions of a company. The sales forecasts may be in terms of units of products/services or dollar revenues. For a university, forecasts of expected enrollment for each college, school, and program type and level, and by sources of students (e.g., in-state, out-of-state, and international) are made.

The development of more accurate forecasts of demand often requires an analysis of historical information relating to the products/services produced. The office furniture company can analyze past sales volume for each line of furniture by customer and sales region. Information may also be compiled relating to past customers' levels of satisfaction with the office furniture products. The number of back orders for office furniture also is an important type of information to evaluate in forecasting demand because it reflects the level of unfilled demand. For a university, past enrollment statistics for each type and level of degree program should be analyzed to ascertain the relative demand for particular programs in the university. Feedback from industry, governmental, and educational organizations that have hired graduates of the university should be compiled to determine if changes to programs are needed.

The definition of objectives and the development of forecasts of demand is an interactive and cyclical process because objectives cannot be finalized until demand potential is determined. From the foregoing examples of information required for analyses leading to decisions concerning objectives and forecasts of demand, it is evident that a large number of variables must be evaluated. Some information is required for developing long-run strategies, while other information is needed for operational planning. Also, the assumptions the organization makes concerning constraints and decision criteria play a major role in the definition of its objectives since these assumptions are the best estimates of the organization concerning its future operating environment. As such, they must be reviewed and reevaluated continually to verify their existence and impact on the organization's operations.

Resource Requirements and Resource Capacity

Decisions concerning the commitment of resources requires an analysis of *resource requirements* based on forecasts of demand for the organization's products/services. This analysis is necessary to determine what types and amounts of resources are needed to produce each unit of product/service. For example, the office furniture company's forecast of wooden office desk demand is used to estimate the types and amounts of wood, materials, component parts, varnish, and labor that will be required to produce the forecasted unit volume. Added to these direct production costs are items such as administrative, overhead, selling, and distribution costs. These costs are combined and shown on a resource specification list for wooden office desks.

For a university, costs of production are not as variable. For example, faculty salaries and costs of classroom, research, and administrative facilities make up the greater part of the total costs needed to generate a student credit hour. Because the levels of these types of costs are determined on a yearly basis, and are therefore somewhat fixed, a separate resource specification analysis is not required before each class or credit hour can be taught. Yet on a yearly, semester, or quarter basis, an analysis of actual cost per class or credit hour taught may be developed in order to evaluate instructional cost performance.

As information is compiled on actual historical costs per unit of product/service, better estimates or standard costs can be developed for planning resource needs. This is true for either a university or a business firm that produces a similar type of product/service each year. When a new product/service is planned for possible production, more detailed materials requirements and engineering analyses may be required to estimate resource requirements with satisfactory certainty.

The overall purpose of analysis and evaluation of resource requirements is to determine the types and amounts (units as well as costs) of resources needed to produce each type of product/service which has been forecast as potential demand. This information is necessary for pricing of products/services. Also, the definition of resource requirements provides important information for analyzing and evaluating the *resource capacity* of the organization to produce the products/services. This involves a comparison and evaluation of demand for products/services and related resource requirements versus the future capability of the organization to acquire and use resources efficiently.

The office furniture company must analyze current versus projected production capacity in the fabrication, assembly, and finishing departments to determine if the forecasted demand for wooden desks can be accommodated. Similar analyses for labor and materials availability and costs are necessary. Also, the analysis of the availability and sources of funds for expansion of facilities, equipment, and manpower (if forecasts of demand indicate large growth potential) must be undertaken before long-range sales goals can be finalized. For a university, projections of the number and qualifications of faculty for each discipline in the university must be developed in relation to expected enrollments. Concurrently, projections of available classroom space, research facilities, and support facilities such as the library and computing center must be developed in order to compile a university budget.

The purpose of resource capacity analysis is to convert resource requirements (which have been developed from forecasts of demand) into preliminary operating budgets. These preliminary operating budgets are evaluated along with the organization's objectives, forecasts of demand, and resource requirements in order to finalize plans, policies, and budgets for the next operating period. From this type of evaluation, decisions are made concerning revised objectives and forecasts of demand for each product/service. Also, operating budgets are developed in terms of dollars, quality standards, quantity expectations, and schedules of performance.

The following are examples of the types of areas wherein decisions would be finalized for the next operating period, for the office furniture manufacturer and the state university. (The figures used in the examples are for illustrative purposes only, and the items shown are not intended to be exhaustive.)

For the Office Furniture Manufacturer

    1. *Objectives*

- A 15% return on investment on each furniture line
- A 20% market share in each sales region

- An annual dividend of $2.50 per share
- A 10% annual growth in sales volume for the total company

2. *Forecast of Sales*
   - Units of sales volume for each product line
   - Sales revenues for each product line
   - Volume of sales by sales region and salesmen

3. *Budgets to be Prepared for.*
   - The total firm
   - Organizational responsibility centers (e.g., sales, production, procurement, and personnel)
   - Each product line (e.g., desks, chairs, and tables)
   - Capital acquisitions (plant and equipment)

4. *Quality Standards*
   - 15% rejection rate for finished goods (sales returns)
   - 10% rejection rate for raw materials inspection (materials rejects)
   - Engineering specifications for quality grades of materials

5. *Quantity Expectations*
   - Quantity budgets for each production center (e.g., fabrication, assembly, and finishing)
   - Monthly or quarterly quantity budgets (as well as annual)

6. *Schedules of Performance*
   - For each product line or customer order
   - For each organizational responsibility center

For the University:
1. *Objectives*
   - Regional recognition of quality of programs (e.g., one of top three schools in the region)
   - Variety of program offerings (e.g., liberal arts, professional schools, law school, medical school, and undergraduate, masters, and doctoral programs)
   - Equal blend of teaching, research, and service to community

2. *Forecast of Enrollment (Students and Credit Hours)*
   - For each college, school, and program
   - By source of student (e.g., county, state, out-of-state, and international)
   - For level of program (lower, upper, masters, doctoral)

3. *Budgets to Be Prepared for*
   - Total university
   - Organizational responsibility centers (e.g., administrative offices, deans, program chairmen, and department heads)
   - Type of degree program (discipline and level)
   - Type of function (instruction, research, service, student services, and administration)
   - Type of facilities (instruction, research, and administration)

4. *Quality Standards*
   - Student-faculty ratios (average class size; varies by level of course, e.g., lower, upper, masters, doctoral)
   - Faculty positions for instruction per research position (e.g., 12 to 1)
   - Square feet of facilities per student enrolled (varies by classroom, research, support)
   - Average number of faculty classroom hours taught per week (varies by discipline and level)

5. *Quantity Expectations (Students and Credit Hours)*
   - Enrollment expectations per academic period (e.g. quarter, semester, trimester; varies by program)
   - For course offerings

6. *Schedules of Performance*
   - Class schedules by faculty and courses
   - Course sequencing by programs

The foregoing examples reflect large numbers of variables and different types of information involved in planning. In addition to requiring comprehensive information as summarized in the foregoing sections of this chapter, planning analyses and decisions generate a large amount of important information (several examples are shown in Exhibit 5-2). Some of this information is a major input to the MIS, which processes it into reports for operational control and managerial/financial control as well as for planning. For example, budgets and work schedules provide information on the projected cost and time schedule of expected work. These projections serve in operational control as standards of performance against which actual levels of costs and times of performance are evaluated. Also, budget information is used to prepare financial control reports such as pro forma income statements for stockholders and investors.

The MIS must provide information for planning in the areas of demand analysis, resource capacity analysis, and budgeting if the organization is to achieve the optimum balance between *demand* for the products/services it produces and its *capacity* to produce them. The remainder of this chapter describes demand analysis, resource capacity analysis, and budgeting information and reports. The timing, quality, and quantity of these reports are discussed.

DEMAND ANALYSIS REPORTS

Demand analysis reports provide information about the future demand for the products/services offered by the organization. These reports are used to make decisions concerning resource requirements and capacity for future operating periods. Demand forecasts may involve two classes of outputs: products and services. Some common examples of demand projected for various types of outputs are listed on the following page.

For Products:
- Tons of steel to be used by manufacturers
- Number of automobiles purchased by consumers
- Number of washing machines purchased by consumers

For Services:
- Number of medical patients requiring hospitalization
- Number of travelers going to Europe
- Number of students enrolled in the college of business

These examples demonstrate that it is possible to project either the quantity of output demanded or the number of instances in which output is demanded. The choice depends upon the nature of the product or service. As a general rule, forecasting the potential number of users is more useful for services because of the intangible nature of services.

Exhibit 5-3 shows a general format that is useful for constructing demand analysis reports. Columns 1, 2, and 3 provide identification information, while columns 4 through 12 show forecasts or estimates.

Although the exact format and level of detail included in a demand analysis report varies according to the specific product/service being forecast and the needs of the organization, the format generally contains a comparison of most likely versus optimistic and pessimistic estimates of demand for current and future periods. Exhibit 5-3 shows a forecast of demand for 2,000 office desks (most likely) versus 1,500 (pessimistic) and 2,500 (optimistic) in year 1; compared to 3,500 (most likely), 2,500 (pessimistic), and 4,500 (optimistic) in year 2.

The types of information shown in Exhibit 5-3 are considered the minimum needed for effective demand analysis. Without this information an organization cannot determine the type, level, and direction of demand for its products/services (i.e., undergraduate instruction for business majors is likely to reach a level of 15,400 credit hours in year 2, and is expected to increase further in year 3). This type of information is essential for planning future resource requirements and for allocating classroom facilities and manpower to the undergraduate instruction program.

In addition to forecasting units of demand for products/services, the revenues to be derived from this demand must be projected. Such projections are necessary to develop revenue budgets for each product/service so that cost of production can be evaluated in terms of expected revenues. Exhibit 5-4 shows an example of a revenue forecast report that is useful for evaluating projected revenues. For example, the projected revenues from office desks is increasing steadily over the three-year period ($600,000 to $1,280,000), while the projected revenues from office chairs is projected to increase moderately ($500,000 to $550,000). Based on this type of information, analyses should concern such factors as the feasibility of increasing prices of office chairs and why demand for chairs is expected to decrease drastically from year 1 to year 2. In the university example, graduate enrollments are expected to increase 33

Exhibit 5-3

FORMAT FOR A DEMAND ANALYSIS REPORT
FOR A BUSINESS FIRM AND A UNIVERSITY

(1) Output Code	(2) Units of Measurement	(3) User Code	Year 1			Year 2			Year 3		
			(4) P	(5) ML	(6) O	(7) P	(8) ML	(9) O	(10) P	(11) ML	(12) O
Products:											
*Office desks	Hundreds	*Industry	15	20	25	25	35	45	30	40	50
*Office chairs	Hundreds	*Government	40	50	60	60	70	90	30	50	60
Services:											
*Under-graduate instruction	Credit hours (Students)	*Business Majors	12,000 (1,000)	14,400 (1,200)	16,400 (1,360)	13,000 (1,080)	15,400 (1,280)	17,400 (1,450)	14,000 (1,110)	16,400 (1,360)	18,400 (1,530)
*Graduate instruction	Credit hours (Students)	*Business Majors	10,000 (830)	12,000 (1,000)	14,000 (1,200)	11,000 (910)	14,000 (1,200)	17,000 (1,410)	13,000 (1,080)	16,000 (1,330)	20,000 (1,660)

NOTES: 1. The individual outputs (desks, chairs, etc.) would be shown on separate reports. This exhibit shows only two items in each output category for illustrative purposes; actual reports may contain more output items.

          2. P, ML, and O stand for pessimistic, most likely, and optimistic.

          3. For a university, forecasts of credit hours and number of students are useful because both are used for budgeting and for generating revenues or funds.

          * Code numbers need to be assigned from coding system or chart of accounts for items in columns 1 and 3. These will be developed for this example in Chapter 9.

Exhibit 5-4

REVENUE FORECAST REPORT
FOR A BUSINESS FIRM AND A UNIVERSITY

	Year 1			Year 2			Year 3			Years 1-3
	Units Forecast	Unit Price	Revenues	Units Forecast	Unit Price	Revenues	Units Forecast	Unit Price	Revenues	Total Revenues
Products										
1. Office Desks	2,000	$ 300	$ 600,000	3,500	$ 310	$1,085,000	4,000	$ 320	$1,280,000	$2,965,000
2. Office Chairs	5,000	$ 100	$ 500,000	7,000	$ 105	$ 735,000	5,000	$ 110	$ 550,000	$1,785,000
			$1,100,000			$1,820,000			$1,830,000	$4,750,000
Services										
1. Under-graduate Students	1,200	$ 600	$ 720,000	1,280	$ 600	$ 768,000	1,360	$ 600	$ 816,000	$2,304,000
2. Graduate Students	1,000	$1,000	$1,000,000	1,200	$1,000	$1,200,000	1,330	$1,000	$1,330,000	$3,530,000
			$1,720,000			$1,968,000			$2,146,000	$5,834,000

NOTES:
1. The units forecast figures for periods 1-3 are taken from Exhibit 5-3 (most likely estimates).
2. The unit price for services is the tuition fee per student enrolled.
3. The number of products/services and periods on this type of report can vary. Also, the periods may reflect years, quarters, or months.
4. Unit forecasts represent net unit sales. Sales returns have in effect been deducted.

percent (1,000 to 1,330), while undergraduate enrollments only about 13 percent (1,200 to 1,360) during the three-year period. This development, plus the higher tuition fees for graduate enrollments ($1,000 versus $600), may lead the university to evaluate the feasibility of further expanding the already growing graduate programs and stabilizing undergraduate enrollment.

In summary, the demand forecast and revenue forecast reports described in this section are intended to provide information needed for making decisions concerning demand for outputs, namely for analyzing resource requirements and capacity constraints and the preparation of budgets. Reports such as those shown in Exhibits 5-3 and 5-4 are typically prepared for major divisions of the organization as well as the total organization. A university normally prepares a series of reports for each program, school, college, and discipline. A business firm prepares reports for regions, divisions, and perhaps salesmen.

The *timing* of demand analysis reports is normally geared to coincide with the regular budget cycle because the information provided is used as a basis for budget preparation. When new products or services are contemplated and potential demand information is needed in the new product evaluation, special demand analysis reports are prepared to serve this need. The *quality or accuracy* of information in demand analysis reports generally is shown in probabilistic terms, e.g. pessimistic, optimistic, most likely. More specific statistical probability measures also can be included. The *quantity or volume* of information in these reports varies depending upon the forecasting period used and the time span of the forecasting periods. Also, when both pessimistic and optimistic estimates are used to supplement most likely forecasts of demand, the amount of information required is substantially increased.

RESOURCE CAPACITY STATUS REPORTS

Resource capacity status reports provide information on the capability of the organization to meet the demand for its products/services. The definition of objectives and the commitment of resources require information on current and future needs for resources. A number of resource capacity status reports that are common to most organizations are:

For Fixed Resources:
- Plant Accounting Reports (facilities and property)
- Plant Construction Reports (facilities)

For Current Resources:
- Material Status Reports (on hand and on order)
- Work In Process Reports
- Finished Goods/Services Reports

For Human Resources:
- Personnel/Manpower Status Reports
- Manpower Training Status Reports

For Financial Resources:
- Cash/Funds Flow Reports
- Accounts Receivable Status Reports

The examples are not intended to be all inclusive; similarly, it is often necessary to supplement the reports shown with subsidiary reports. While the titles of reports vary somewhat, the types of reports listed and their purposes have become fairly standard.

Exhibit 5-5 shows a general format that is useful in constructing resource capacity status reports. Columns 1, 2, and 3 provide identification information relating to the resource capacity information in columns 4, 5, and 6. This identification information includes the description of the resource, the unit of measurement used, and the source of supply. Columns 4, 5, and 6 show amounts of resources on hand and in process of being acquired and the total that will be available during the forecast period. Columns 11 and 12 provide identification information relating to the resource demand information shown in columns 7 through 10. This identification information includes the description of the product/service for which the resources will be used and the projected customer or user of the products/services. Columns 7 through 10 show the amounts of resources that are required to produce the current and future demand for products/services. In addition, information on reserves and total demand are shown.

The format of a resource capacity status report also generally includes a comparison of capacity (columns 4 through 6) versus demand (columns 7 through 10), since the purpose of analyzing resource capacity is to determine the capacity of the organization to produce the products/services that are in demand. Reports designed within the general format shown provide important insights to a manager about the capacity of his organization to satisfy demand for its products/services. For example, Exhibit 5-5 shows that the demand for fixed and current resources (column 10) is equal to the current and planned acquisition of these resources (column 6). A question may be raised as to whether the size of the facilities reserve (90,000 square feet) is too large based on more detailed analyses of demand forecasts. On the other hand, the demand for labor resources (103,000 hours) exceeds the planned resource availability (93,000 hours). Also, a large amount of the labor resource demand is for temporary labor (30,000 hours of the 103,000 hours needed), which may indicate a growing level of inefficiency of part of the organization's labor resource.

The types of information shown in resource capacity status reports are considered minimum needs for effective planning because without this information an organization could not determine its capability for satisfying the demand for its products/services. Exhibit 5-6 provides additional examples of resource capacity status reports for a business firm and a university. Based on the selected information shown in Exhibit 5-6, it is evident that expected demand for office desks by industrial firms will exceed the availability of wood, labor, and equipment needed to service that demand. Hence, the firm must at least consider one or all of the following:

1. Reevaluate its sales forecasts, particularly their accuracy.
2. Consider adding resource capacity.
3. Shift capacity from other product lines, if possible.

Exhibit 5-5

GENERAL FORMAT FOR A
RESOURCE CAPACITY STATUS REPORT

		(1) Resource Code	(2) Units	(3) Source	(4) (5) (6) Resource Capacity → Information → On Hand + In Process = Total		
Fixed Resource		20 Facility 20 Facility	(K) sq. ft. (K) sq. ft.	Construct. Contract	150 300 450	100 200 300	250 500 750
Current Resource		10 Paper 10 Paper	Reams Reams	Buy Buy	100 300 400	300 600 900	400 900 1300
Labor Resource		40 Labor 40 Labor 40 Labor	(K) Hrs. (K) Hrs. (K) Hrs.	Temporary Permanent Permanent	10 30 30 70	10 10 3 23	20 40 33 93

NOTES: 1. The individual resources (20, 10, 40) would be shown on separate reports. If the analysis is by user code (40, 50) or output code (10, 50), all resources would be summarized on a single series of reports as shown in this exhibit. The extent of summarization would also be conditioned by the number of items (i.e., level of detail) included. This exhibit shows only a few items in each resource category for illustrative purposes, and actual reports generally contain more items.

4. Review operations to determine whether greater efficiency and productivity can be generated with existing resource capacity.

The firm's final decisions concerning its operating objectives, budgets, and schedules cannot be made effectively without first performing the type of analysis described above.

A similar situation exists in the university example, and a similar analysis should be made. Additional undergraduate instructional capacity must be secured to meet the demand shown in Exhibit 5-6. A simple alternative would be to require the faculty to teach an average of 14.4 credit hours versus its budgeted standard of 12.0 credit hours. In implementing this type of solution, however, the possible impact on quality standards must be determined to ascertain whether the decision is the optimum.

In summary, the resource capacity status reports described in this section provide information for making decisions concerning the allocation of the resources necessary to produce the firm's products/services. The demand for resources (based on the demand for products/services) is compared to the supply of resources, and from this comparison decisions can be made concerning the feasibility of forecasted demand and the need to shift resources from one product to another, alter delivery schedules, authorize overtime, and expand production facilities. These types of decisions will not be made without a thorough analysis of demand information in conjunction with resource capacity information since demand and capacity are highly interrelated.

(7)	(8)	(9)	(10)	(11)	(12)		
	Resource Demand → Information			Output	User		
Current +	Future +	Reserve =	Total	Code	Code		
130	80	40	250	10 Product	10 Manufac.	Fixed	Resource
300	150	50	500	50 Service	40 Procur.		
430	230	90	750				
90	210	100	400	n/a	40 Procur	Current	Resource
250	600	50	900	n/a	50 Actg.		
340	810	150	1300				
10	20	0	30	n/a	40 Procur.	Labor	Resource
30	9	1	40	n/a	40 Procur.		
30	3	0	33	n/a	50 Actg.		
70	32	1	103				

2. It may be also necessary to record units of output similar to column 2 for units of input.
3. Code numbers (as well as descriptions) generally are shown for columns 1, 3, 11, and 12 (and perhaps column 2).

The *timing* of resource capacity status reports generally is based on the yearly budget cycle, with perhaps monthly reviews for selected resources, because the information provided also is used to develop budgets. The resource capacity status report for current resources is needed most frequently because this resource is consumed, or turned over, more rapidly than the others. A high level of *quality or accuracy* of information in resource capacity status reports is important because this information provides the primary basis for making decisions concerning budgeting for specific products/services, functions, organizational components, and programs. The *quantity or volume* of information included in resource capacity reports may be quite large because of the many different types of resources an organization uses. The level of detail included in resource capacity status reports varies according to the individual organization's needs. For example, unit cost or price data may be included when an analysis of dollar (as well as unit) consumption of resources is appropriate, such as for the labor resource. Other variations suggested in Exhibit 5-5 are units of measurement for outputs and code numbers for source of supply of the resource. Also, the level of detail included on a specific report may vary with the 'evel of the organization for which it is prepared. For example, the materials analyst analyzes resource demand and supply in considerable detail (i.e., by each type of material), however, the manager of procurement or the vice-president of production is concerned with summary analysis by major categories of resources.

Exhibit 5-6

RESOURCE CAPACITY STATUS REPORTS FOR
A BUSINESS FIRM AND A UNIVERSITY

(1) Resource Code	(2) Units	(3) Source Code	(4) Capacity Information On Hand	(5) In Process	(6) Total	(7) Demand Information Current	(8) Future	(9) Reserve	(10) Total	(11) Output Code	(12) User Code
BUSINESS FIRM:											
*Wood-Lumber	Thou. Sq. ft.	*ABC Lumber Co.	90	10	100	80	60	10	150	*Office Desks	*Industry
*Carpentry Labor	Hundred Man Hr.	n/a	600	20	620	600	100	10	710	*Office Desks	*Industry
*Fabricating Equipment	No. of Desks	*XYZ Equip. Co.	3,000	0	3,000	2,700	2,000	300	5,000	*Office Desks	*Industry
UNIVERSITY:											
*Faculty	Number	n/a	100	0	100	100	20	0	120	*Undergraduate Instruction	*Business Majors
*Faculty Instruction	Credit Hours	n/a	12,000	0	12,000	12,000	2,400	0	14,400	*Undergraduate Instruction	*Business Majors

* Code numbers need to be assigned from coding system or chart of accounts. These will be developed for this example in Chapter 9.

The resource capacity status and demand analysis reports are used to summarize and highlight the important variables for planning. By themselves, these reports are incomplete, and in fact require a large amount of supporting analyses and information. An organization may benefit from an analysis of patterns of resource used by type of resource in order to determine which resources are the most frequently used, which are most costly, and which have caused production problems because of unavailability, excessive waste, or poor quality. In order to perform this type of analysis, each resource type must be coded and information about the resource must be compiled, stored, and analyzed periodically and on a continual basis. Similarly, an analysis of vendor or supplier performance requires that the source of resources be coded and information be compiled about each vendor's and supplier's past performance in terms of delivery, price, quality, and volume capability. A customer information file can be developed to analyze which customers are the most important in terms of size and frequency of purchases, and other related information such as quality and price preferences.

Also, information regarding exogenous factors and their impact on the capability of the organization to adapt to new demands and to changes in environment is useful for developing long-run strategies and objectives for the organization. These long-run strategies and objectives are used to develop more specific short-run objectives and budgets. Strategic or long-range planning information is required by top management and their staff in order to evaluate the costs, benefits, and general feasibility of long-run objectives, programs, and resource utilization patterns of the entire organization. While simulation approaches, such as industrial (system) dynamics and planning-program-budgeting systems (which are described in Chapter 12), provide useful concepts for the evaluation of objectives and policies, their application is still rather limited and often rather expensive. Generally, only larger organizations have used simulation extensively; its widespread application is still in the future.

BUDGETING REPORTS

The actual translation of objectives and demand forecasts into operational terms normally is accomplished by developing a set of budgets for the organization. Budgeting, which is an essential part of organized economic activity, ensures that sufficient financial and other resources are available to carry out stated objectives in an efficient and timely manner. Information and decisions made from the comparison of demand and resource capacity serve as the basis for preparing budgets which adequately reflect resource requirements. A budget also serves as means of communicating objectives and operating plans to managers and as a standard for evaluating performance. For example, the production budget informs the production manager of the volume of production, its timing, and cost expectations. The measurement and comparison of the actual versus budgeted performance of production in terms of volume, timing, and cost utilizes budget information as the standard for evaluating the production manager's performance.

The types of information and the level of detail included in budget reports may vary, as well as the report format itself. Most organizations include: (1) dollar, (2) quantity, (3) quality, and (4) time related information within their total set of budgets. All four of these factors must be controlled in the production of products/services if the organization is to achieve its objectives and satisfy demand efficiently.

Dollar-Related Budget Information

Dollar-related budget information includes revenue, cost, profit, and cash flow projections. Expanding on the information shown in Exhibit 5-4 (Revenue Forecast Report), Exhibit 5-7 shows an example of a summary *revenue budget* for a business firm (using year 1 projected revenues from Exhibit 5-4). Normally, as shown on Exhibit 5-7 projected revenues are shown for each product type, as well as for any other expected source of revenues. The schedule of projected receipt of revenues (shown by quarters in Exhibit 5-7) may be monthly, quarterly, or semiannual. This information is important to determine future cash inflows, and to determine if there are any significant sales fluctuations during the year. For example, the fourth quarter projected revenues from the sale of products is down significantly for the business firm shown in Exhibit 5-7.

A format similar to that shown in Exhibit 5-7 can be used for a university. Instead of products, tuition fees would be shown. Also, legislative appropriations, contracts and grants, and endowments are examples of the other types of revenues that would be shown on a university revenue budget.

Cost budgets may be developed to show unit costs of production for each product/service produced. This type of analysis provides useful information for pricing of products/services, and for evaluating resource capacity and operational efficiency. Exhibit 5-8 shows a cost budget for a business firm. The major unit cost items are included in Exhibit 5-8, such as materials, labor, burden, and selling, to show their relationship to projected unit selling price of each product. Projected gross and net profit margins are shown. In the preparation of this type of cost budget, standard costs can often be developed for cost categories such as labor, burden, and materials.

For a university, cost budgets take the form of itemized and projected unit costs involved in the production of a student credit hour. For example, projected costs of faculty salaries, teaching materials, classroom facilities, and administrative support are prorated and allocated to each class section taught in a department. The number of students (25 students) and the course credit hours (4 hours) are computed for each class to determine the total student credit hours produced (100 hours), which are divided into the total costs of each class section taught to determine the unit cost per credit hour. This type of cost information is useful to a university for setting tuition fees and making funding decisions, and for evaluating the efficiency (but not the quality) of the teaching process.

Profit budgets relate revenue to costs in the form of projected income statements for the entire business firm, product lines, or geographic sales areas.

Exhibit 5-7

YEARLY REVENUE BUDGET FOR A BUSINESS FIRM

Source of Revenue	1st Quarter	2nd Quarter	3rd Quarter	4th Quarter	Total
1. *Gross Revenue from Products*					
Office Desks					
Units	330	550	770	550	2,200
Revenues	$ 99,000	$165,000	$231,000	$165,000	$660,000
Office Chairs					
Units	880	1,320	1,980	1,320	5,500
Revenues	$ 88,000	$132,000	$198,000	$132,000	$ 550,000
Gross Revenues	$187,000	$297,000	$429,000	$297,000	$1,210,000
2. *Less:* Sales Returns					
(about 9.1%)	(17,000)	(27,000)	(39,000)	(27,000)	(110,000)
Net Revenue					
from Products:	$170,000	$270,000	$390,000	$270,000	$1,100,000
3. *Plus:* Investment Income	40,000	50,000	60,000	50,000	200,000
Miscellaneous Income	10,000	15,000	15,000	10,000	50,000
Net Revenues	$220,000	$335,000	$465,000	$330,000	$1,350,000

Exhibit 5-8

COST BUDGET FOR A BUSINESS FIRM

	Office Desks		Office Chairs	
1. Unit Selling Price	$300	100%	$100	100%
2. *Unit Production Costs of Goods Sold*:				
Materials	$ 50		$ 15	
Direct Labor:				
Fabricating	30		8	
Assembly	20		6	
Finishing	20		6	
Total Direct Labor	$ 70		$ 20	
Burden (Overhead)	$ 30		$ 10	
Total Unit Costs of Goods Sold	$150	50%	$ 45	45%
3. Gross Margin	$150	50%	$ 55	55%
4. Selling Expense	30		10	
5. Administrative Expense	15		5	
6. Miscellaneous Expense	15		5	
7. *Net Profit Before Taxes*:	$ 90	30%	$ 35	35%

Exhibit 5-9 shows an example of a summary profit budget for a business firm. The profit budget is compiled from the information on the revenue forecast and the unit cost budget to show the overall projected revenues and costs of operations for a year, quarter, or month. It provides useful information for projecting cash inflows (revenues) and outflows (costs) and for estimating the profitability from operations.

While a university or other educational or governmental organization does not sell a product for revenue, it does incur costs for operating various programs. These costs are related to units of services produced by the programs. For example, in lieu of revenue, the units of services produced by a university are in the form of credit hours of instruction, degrees granted, or students enrolled. The total costs required to produce educational programs are analyzed and compared with sources of funds, such as tuition fees, legislative appropriations, and contracts and grants.

Cash budgets project the cash receipts and disbursements for an operating period such as a year, quarter, or month. Exhibit 5-10 shows an example of a summary cash budget for a business firm. The receipts section of the cash budget shows the schedule of projected cash receipts, rather than when sales or accounts receivables will occur (the example in Exhibit 5-10 assumes cash receipts and sales will occur at the same time). Disbursements show actual cash outflows that will occur for operating expenses such as wages, salaries, materials purchases, and advertising. Noncash expenses such as depreciation are not shown. Projected disbursements such as dividend payments and facilities renovations are shown if they involve cash disbursements during the operating period.

Income Statement

Exhibit 5-9

SUMMARY PROFIT BUDGET FOR A BUSINESS FIRM

	Office Desks	Office Chairs	Total
1. Gross Sales Revenues	$660,000	$550,000	$1,210,000
2. *Less:* Sales Returns	(60,000)	(50,000)	110,000
Net Revenues	$600,000 (100%)	$500,000 (100%)	$1,100,000 (100%)
3. Production Costs of Goods Sold:	(2,000 units)	(5,000 units)	
a. Materials	$100,000	$ 75,000	$ 175,000
b. Direct Labor:			
Fabricating	60,000	40,000	100,000
Assembling	40,000	30,000	70,000
Finishing	40,000	30,000	70,000
Total Direct Labor	$140,000	$100,000	$ 240,000
c. Burden (Overhead)	60,000	50,000	110,000
Total Costs of Goods Sold	$300,000 (50%)	$225,000 (45%)	$ 525,000 (48%)
4. Gross Margin	$300,000 (50%)	$275,000 (55%)	$ 575,000 (52%)
5. Selling Expenses	60,000	50,000	$ 110,000
6. Administratve Expenses	30,000	25,000	55,000
7. Miscellaneous Expenses	30,000	25,000	55,000
8. Net Profit from Operations Before Taxes	$180,000 (30%)	$175,000 (35%)	$ 355,000 (32%)
9. *Plus:* Investment Income			$ 200,000
Miscellaneous Income			50,000
10. Total Before Taxes			$ 605,000

NOTES: 1. Revenue figures are taken from Exhibit 5-7 and cost figures have been developed from unit cost information in Exhibit 5-8.
2. Number of units projected (2,000 desks and 5,000 chairs) are based on $300 price per desk and $100 price per chair, assuming 200 unit sales returns of desks and 500 unit sales returns of chairs.

The purpose of the cash budget is to analyze the liquidity of the firm in terms of its ability to pay its bills. The information on a cash budget shows when additional financing may be needed (i.e., first quarter in Exhibit 5-10), and when excess cash may be available to pay off some bills or for investment (e.g., third and fourth quarters in Exhibit 5-10). Cash budgets also are useful for educational and governmental organizations. A university's funds are received throughout the entire academic year rather than only at the beginning. Similarly, cash disbursements for wages, salaries, materials, supplies, and other operating services and resources are made on a periodic and continuous basis. The levels and rates of cash receipts and disbursements vary, and often there may be a need to invest idle cash.

Exhibit 5-10

SUMMARY CASH BUDGET FOR A BUSINESS FIRM

	1st Quarter	2nd Quarter	3rd Quarter	4th Quarter	Total
1. *Receipts:*					
a. Net Revenues from Products	$170,000	$270,000	$390,000	$270,000	$1,100,000
b. Investment Income	40,000	50,000	60,000	50,000	200,000
c. Miscellaneous Income	10,000	15,000	15,000	10,000	50,000
Total Receipts	$220,000	$335,000	$465,000	$330,000	$1,350,000
2. *Disbursements:*					
a. Materials	$ 27,000	$ 43,000	$ 62,000	$ 43,000	$ 175,000
b. Labor	37,000	59,000	85,000	59,000	240,000
c. Total Other Cash Expenses	37,000	59,000	85,000	59,000	240,000
d. Renovation of Facilities	100,000	50,000	50,000	50,000	250,000
e. Dividends				100,000	100,000
f. Payment of Principal on Bank Loan	100,000	50,000	50,000	50,000	250,000
Total Disbursements	$301,000	$261,000	$332,000	$361,000	$1,255,000
3. Beginning Cash Balance	50,000	50,000	124,000	257,000	
4. Excess or (Deficit) of Receipts plus Cash Balance Over Disbursements	(31,000)	124,000	257,000	226,000	
5. Minimum Cash Balance Required	50,000	50,000	50,000	50,000	
6. (Deficit) to be Financed, or Excess over Minimum Cash Balance Required	($81,000)	$ 74,000	$207,000	$176,000	

NOTE: Items 1a-c (Receipts) and 2a-d (Disbursements for material and labor) are based on Exhibits 5-7 and 5-8. Other items are for illustrative purposes and are not related to previous exhibits.

Quantity-Related Budget Information

In addition to dollar-related budget information, *quantity-related budget information* is useful for effective planning. For example, budgets in terms of units of sales or demand and units of resources are shown in Exhibits 5-3 (demand analysis report) and Exhibits 5-5 and 5-6 (resource capacity status reports), and their usefulness was described in performing analyses of demand and resource capacity status. Sales forecasts normally are developed in terms of units of products or services, as well as their dollar value. This is necessary to develop production schedules and resource requirements. Exhibit 5-11 shows examples of a production schedule and a labor hours budget for a business firm. The types of information shown in Exhibit 5-11 are useful for scheduling production operations and for estimating resource utilization requirements in order to meet production schedules. Exhibit 5-11 shows that 400 chairs are scheduled for production in January. Assuming four hours as the average direct labor required to produce a chair, 1,600 hours of direct labor is budgeted for January.

For a university, the expected number of students to be enrolled must be determined in order to allocate dollar appropriations. Estimates or budgets of units of materials, equipment, and faculty teaching of classroom hours are common examples of resource quantity related budgets which are useful to project how the university will operate during the academic year, semester, or quarter.

Time-Related Budget Information

Time-related budget information is useful for planning performance of work during the operating period. Exhibit 5-11 shows two examples of time-related budget information. Schedules of performance are essential for the effective accomplishment of objectives and plans. Normally, schedules are developed for the acquisition of resources, production or work performance, and delivery of finished goods. In a university, schedules of course offerings and sequencing of curriculum must be defined in order to provide a logical developmental process and to enable students to schedule courses consistent with their graduation date objectives.

Quality-Related Budget Information

The entire budgeting process includes, at least implicitly, *quality-related budget information*. Quantity related budgets generally are supported by quality specifications in that the quality level of products or services to be produced by an organization are specified, and the units of resources to be used are defined in terms of quality specifications or grades. Grades of materials, models of equipment, and training or education of manpower must be defined prior to the acquisition of resources. In many cases, dollar, quantity, time, and quality information may be consolidated in a single budget report. For example, a sales budget often includes *units* of sales forecasted, type or *quality* grade of

Exhibit 5-11

PRODUCTION SCHEDULE AND LABOR UTILIZATION BUDGET
FOR A BUSINESS FIRM

Production Schedule (Units):

Product	Beginning Inventory	Jan	Feb	Mar	Apr	May	Jun	Jul	Aug	Sep	Oct	Nov	Dec	Total Production	Projected Sales	Projected Ending Inventory
Office Desks	100	150	150	200	200	200	200	200	150	150	150	150	100	2000	2000	100
Office Chairs	200	400	400	500	500	500	500	400	400	400	400	300	300	5000	5000	200

Labor Utilization Budget (Hours):

Product	Jan	Feb	Mar	Apr	May	Jun	Jul	Aug	Sep	Oct	Nov	Dec	Total Labor Hours	Average Unit Direct Labor Rate	Projected Direct Labor Costs
Office Desks	2100	2100	2800	2800	2800	2800	2800	2100	2100	2100	2100	1400	28,000	$5.00 hour	$140,000
Office Chairs	1600	1600	2000	2000	2000	2000	1600	1600	1600	1600	1200	1200	20,000	$5.00 hour	$100,000

NOTES: 1. Types of use of direct labor also could be shown (e.g., fabricating, assembly, finishing).

2. The information for these two examples is based on the information shown in Exhibit 5-7 (Projected Net Sales) and Exhibit 5-9 (Projected Direct Labor Costs). Other figures are for illustrative purposes.

3. Assuming a $5.00 per hour rate, it takes 14 hours ($70 ÷ $5) to produce a desk and 4 hours ($20 ÷ $5) to produce a chair using the unit cost information in Exhibit 5-8. These figures are not intended to be true rates or hours, but are used to show how budgets are interrelated.

product, *dollar value* of these units, and an estimate of the schedule or *timing* of sales of these units. In a university, student credit hour projections, dollars required for instruction, and schedules of instruction may be shown on a single report.

SUMMARY

The purpose of planning information is to facilitate the definition of objectives and the commitment of resources to operations which are designed to achieve the objectives of the organization. Analyses are undertaken concerning constraints and decision criteria, demand determinants, and resource requirements and capacity which provide information inputs for three major components of the MIS data base: demand analysis information, resource capacity status analysis information, and budgeting information.

Information relating to these three components of the MIS are merged, stored, analyzed, evaluated, and processed by the MIS to produce a series of reports such as those listed in Exhibit 5-12. These reports are: (1) *future* oriented, (2) aimed at matching *demand* for products/services with the organization's *capacity* to produce them efficiently, and (3) *periodic,* rather than continuous, and timed to the budget cycle (since they culminate in a set of operating budgets).

In respect to more traditional types of information systems, the planning information subsystem is similar to a sales or marketing information subsystem, except that it also includes information relating to the commitment of resources through the budgeting process. Under the traditional approach to the design of information systems, sales or marketing is treated as a separate system, apart from resource capacity and budgeting information systems. However, in treating the planning function as an interrelationship between demand and capacity analysis, the design of the MIS emphasizes the interconnection of these information subsystems (demand, capacity, and budgeting) through a comprehensive data base.

REVIEW QUESTIONS

1. What are the significant characteristics of planning? What types of analyses are involved in defining information needed for effective planning? Are the types of analyses that are involved in planning universal to all managers? To all types of organizations?
2. Discuss the importance of constraints and decision criteria for effective planning, and give examples of each.
3. Discuss the meaning and importance of demand determinants for determining product/service potential, and give examples of demand determinants.
4. List the interrelationship between forecasts of demand and decisions concerning resource capacity, and give several examples of this interrelationship.

Exhibit 5-12

PLANNING INFORMATION SUBSYSTEM

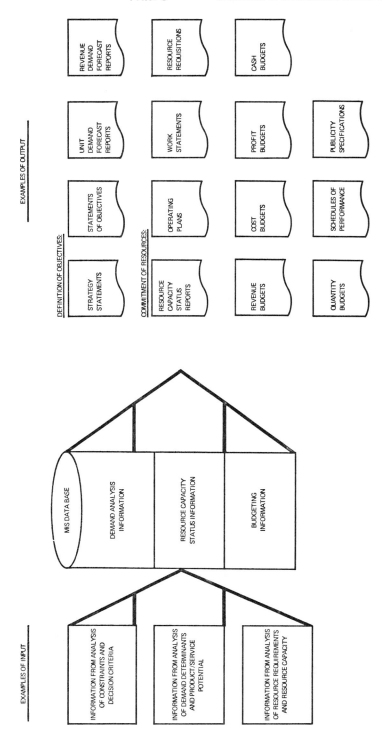

NOTE: THE EXAMPLES PROVIDED IN THIS EXHIBIT SHOW THE MAJOR TYPES OF ANALYSES AND INFORMATION THAT ARE REQUIRED FOR EFFECTIVE PLANNING; THEY ARE NOT INTENDED TO BE A COMPLETE STATEMENT OF ALL INFORMATION INVOLVED IN PLANNING.

5. Give several examples of demand analysis reports and resource capacity status reports. What functions do these reports perform for management? What are the quality, timing, and volume dimensions of these reports?

6. What is the relationship between the timing of demand analysis and resource capacity status reports with the budget cycle?

7. What are several important types of budgets that are useful for the effective commitment of resources to the organization's operations?

8. Differentiate between dollar-related, quantity-related, quality-related, and time-related budget information. Give an example of each. What is the purpose of each type of information?

9. Contrast and discuss the use of budgeting as a process for evaluating demand and capacity to perform versus budgeting as a mechanism for communicating planning decisions to managers in the organization.

10. Summarize the planning information subsystem in terms of its (a) major types of information inputs, (b) major components of its data base, (c) and major types and purposes of reports produced.

EXERCISE 5-1: Custom Machine Tool Company (Part A) [1]

The Custom Machine Tool Company is a manufacturer of custom high quality machine tools and special equipment. Their headquarters and production facilities are located in Atlanta, Georgia. The company is medium sized, has an annual sales revenue of $4 million, and has 200 employees. It sells its products mainly in the Southeast. The facilities of the company are modern, with 80,000 square feet of manufacturing space and 10,000 square feet of office space.

ORGANIZATION

Exhibit 5-13 is an organization chart of the company. The board of directors, which is responsible for the overall management of the company, has the authority to hire the officers of the company who will manage the day-to-day operations of the business. The board of directors is accountable to the owners for maximizing long-run profits.

The president is responsible for the implementation of the long-run profit-maximization objective. He has the authority to make all decisions relating to the daily business operations. The president has appointed three vice-presidents, accountable to him, who are responsible for production, marketing, and finance and administration. The vice-presidents have the authority to hire and fire all subordinates under their jurisdictions.

---

[1] Part A (of a three-part case) deals with the definition of information needs for planning and resource allocation. Parts B and C (Chapters 6 and 7) build on this case.

Exhibit 5-13

ORGANIZATION CHART OF CUSTOM MACHINE TOOL COMPANY

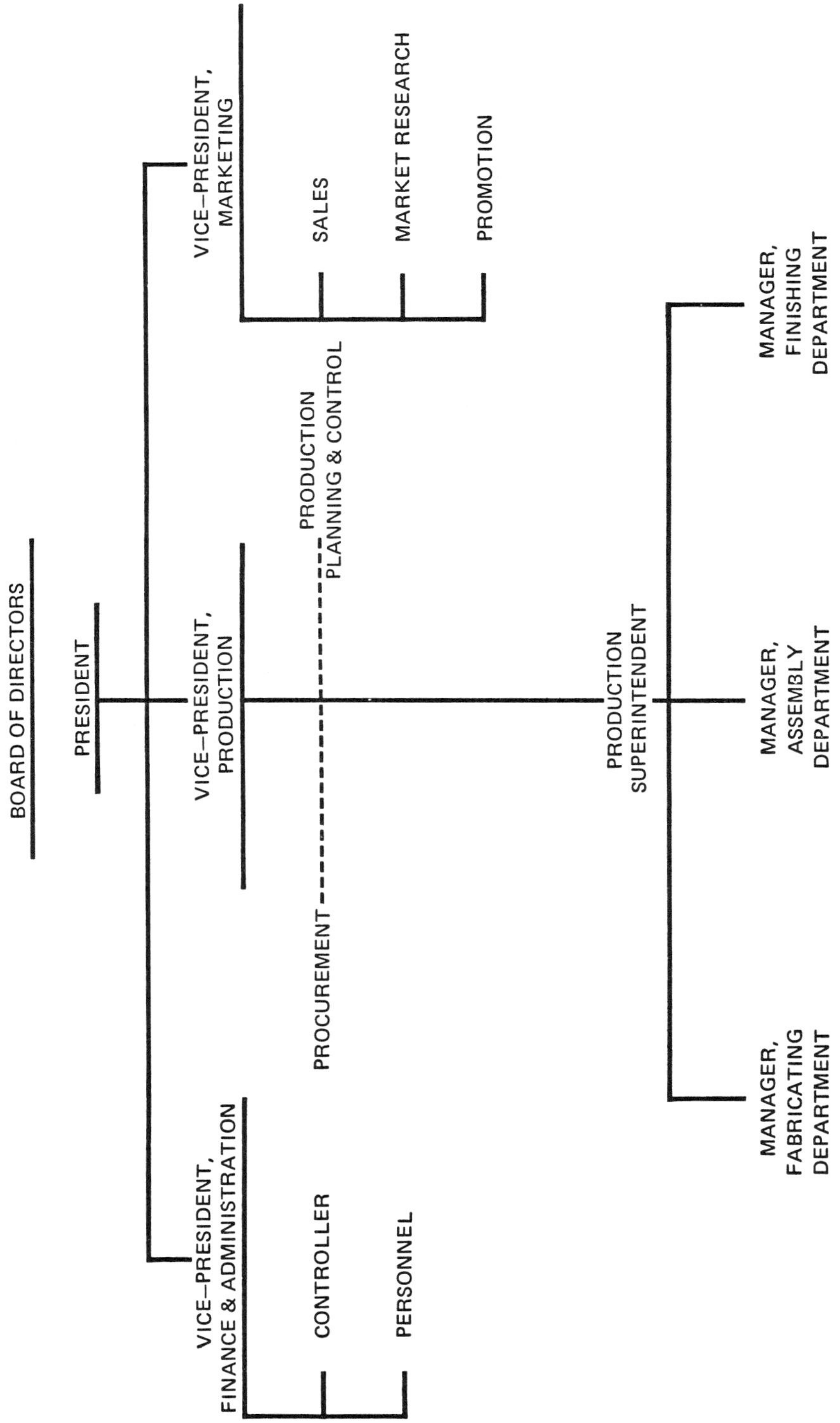

Production

The vice-president of production supervises three department heads: the production planning and control manager, the procurement manager, and the production superintendent.

The production planning and control manager has the authority to initiate all production orders. He is accountable to the production vice-president for scheduling production with a minimum amount of overtime and idle time charges and for controlling costs of production.

The procurement manager is responsible for having the required materials on hand to meet the scheduled production. The production planning and control manager maintains perpetual inventory records for all raw materials, work in process, and finished-goods inventory. When the production planning and control manager receives a production request, he checks the bill of materials (a listing of materials necessary to fill the request) against the perpetual inventory records. He immediately reports shortages to the procurement manager, who then orders the materials required to meet scheduled production. The procurement manager is accountable to the production vice-president for providing the materials required for production at the desired quality and at the best price.

The production superintendent has responsibility for the three production departments (fabricating, assembly, and finishing). The managers of the fabricating, assembly, and finishing departments are responsible for the construction, assembly, and finishing of the machine tool products, respectively. Each manager has the authority to hire and fire all department employees and is accountable to the factory superintendent for the accomplishment of his responsibilities within predetermined operating standards (schedule, quality, quantity, and cost).

The production system is primarily a job-lot process. For example, an order for machine tools would normally proceed through a series of processing points such as cutting, shaping, assembly, and finishing. Quality inspection is performed at each processing point. However, a particular job-lot may include several customer orders for the same type of machine tool; thus information is needed on the status of customer orders as well as status of work at each of these processing points. Since the company deals in high-quality custom products, the size of an order from a single customer is generally small, yet the number of orders to be filled may be quite large at a given time.

The daily production capacity (units processed) for each of the production processing points is not equal because of the customized nature of the products. Backlogs of work are sometimes created at several of the processing points (e.g., the number of units fabricated may exceed the capacity of assembly or finishing for a particular machine tool). When this occurs, the vice-president of production coordinates with the other vice-presidents to determine how these backlogs should be reduced or eliminated (by overtime, rescheduling, reduction of new orders, etc.).

Marketing

The marketing vice-president is responsible for all aspects of selling, including market research, selling, profit margins on sales estimates, and advertising and promotion. He has complete authority over his employees, including 12 salesmen who are each responsible for a geographical region in the Southeast. The salesmen are accountable to the marketing vice-president for the fulfillment of predetermined sales quotas.

The procedure for processing sales orders is as follows: The salesmen accept orders from customers, quoting a contract price that is subject to the approval of the marketing vice-president. A clerk on the sales staff in the home office checks the order, verifying the completeness and accuracy of the salesman's estimated cost of production. The marketing vice-president reviews the order and approves it by signing the original copy of the order, which is then sent to the customer as confirmation of the sale. Copies of the order are sent to the production planning and control manager and the controller for customer billing and cost analysis.

The company's sales tend to vary with the gross national product (GNP) and level of manufacturing employment. Since the product objective is a high-quality custom line of machine tools, promotion efforts emphasize durability, appearance, delivery, and service. The service aspect includes advice on particular customer problems that may be resolved with special purpose tools or equipment. Business manufacturing firms account for 90 percent of the sales volume, while other commercial enterprises account for about 10 percent of sales. Products are primarily sold on special orders from customers; however, the company produces a number of general purpose machine tools for inventory.

Promotion is primarily of two types: advertising in trade (business, government, and education) journals, and personal selling by salesmen. Major competitors consist of three small firms located in the Southeast and several large national firms. The company has about one-third of the market in the Southeast and is considering expanding its operation to include the Southwest, either by expanding its sales force and advertising efforts or by setting up a complete division (production, marketing, and finance) in Dallas. If the company decides not to expand into the Southwest, it plans to increase its selling and advertising effort in the Southeast with the objective of obtaining 50 percent of the market.

Finance and Administration

The vice-president of finance and administration is responsible for securing adequate funds as needed to enable the company to fulfill its objectives. The vice-president uses a cash budget to forecast the company's cash position. He also supervises the controller, who assists top management in controlling the operations of the business by the preparation of financial and statistical reports.

The controller is assisted by the accounting staff. This staff sends sales invoices to customers after merchandise has been shipped and handles all company bookkeeping—recording, classifying, and summarizing daily business transactions such as sales, purchases, and the receiving and disbursing of cash. The information about these transactions is used by the accounting staff to prepare reports for management. First, it prepares earnings statements that measure performance in dollars of the company as a whole. Second, it prepares performance reports for use in cost control in evaluating production foremen and other line managers. Since these individuals are not responsible for deciding how much to produce or what their operating framework should be, they are judged primarily by whether they keep costs at a minimum. One way to evaluate this is to compare actual costs of completed production orders with their estimated costs. The president then reviews these reports with the marketing vice-president to determine what corrective action, if any, should be taken on estimates for new sales contracts. The accounting staff also prepares financial statements for nonmanagers—stockholders, investors, and the government. Statements of earnings, retained earnings, and financial position are prepared for investors; federal, state, and local tax reports are prepared for the government.

The vice-president of finance also has the responsibility for personnel activities, which he delegates to the personnel staff. It hires and fires employees on the recommendations of supervisors throughout the company. The personnel staff also maintains a personnel file for each employee. Exhibits 5-14 through 5-17 provide examples of financial data compiled in the company.

Exhibit 5-14

UNIT COST REPORT FOR A MACHINE TOOL

	Estimated	Actual
Production Costs:		
Fabrication		
Materials	$278	$300
Labor	214	227
Supplies	18	20
Subtotal	$510	$547
Assembly		
Materials	$ 13	$ 12
Labor	30	30
Subtotal	$ 43	$ 42
Finishing:		
Materials	$ 10	$ 10
Labor	24	24
Subtotal	$ 34	$ 34
Salesman's Commission	$114	$114
Total	$701	$737

Exhibit 5-15

SALES ORDER FOR A MACHINE TOOL

Sales Price Per Unit		$1,140
Production Costs Per Unit:		
Fabricating	$510 (Estimated)	
Assembly	43 (Estimated)	
Finishing	34 (Estimated)	
Total	587	
Salesman's Commission (10%) per Unit	114	
Total Production & Selling Costs per Unit		701
Excess of Sales Price over Production & Selling Costs per Unit		439 (Estimated)

Exhibit 5-16

MONTHLY SALESMAN PERFORMANCE EVALUATION

	Salesman		
	1	2	3
Total Sales	$15,000	$20,000	$18,000
Excess of Sales Price Over Production & Selling Costs	5,000	6,000	5,500
Miles Traveled	1,000	800	1,200
Customers Visited:			
New Customers	6	10	12
Repeat Customers	20	30	25

Exhibit 5-17

OTHER SELECTED TYPES OF INFORMATION COMPILED BY
THE CUSTOM MACHINE TOOL COMPANY

Demand Information

Sales revenue by customer type, size, location
Sales revenue by salesman
Gross national product levels
Level of manufacturing employment
New manufacturing business statistics
Competitors market performances
Customer complaints and rejects; nature and number

Production Information

Product cost-revenue analyses by products
Job order status; budget, schedule, quality, quantity
Overtime statistics
Machine downtime
Operating capacity versus operating levels; fabricating assembly, finishing
Inventory status; materials, supplies, work-in-process, finished goods

Financial Information

Balance sheet summaries
Profit and loss summaries
Cash flow summaries
Payroll summaries

1. Identify and discuss the major constraints and decision criteria that you feel are important for the operation of the company. Based on the information in the case, how would you describe the company image? The company's objectives?
2. Identify the major demand determinants that impact the product potential of the company.
   a. Describe the types of demand analysis information that would be useful in developing sales forecasts.
   b. Prepare a simplified demand analysis report for the company.
3. Identify and describe several major types of resource capacity analyses and information that would be useful to the company in commiting resources to products and organizational functions.
   a. Prepare a simplified resource capacity status report for the company.
   b. Describe the important interrelationships between demand information and the development of resource capacity reports.
4. Provide several examples of types of budget information that would be useful to the company, and explain why you feel they would be useful.
   a. Identify dollar, quantity, time, and quality related budget information; provide an example of each type.
   b. Consider how demand, capacity, and budget information are interdependent, and provide several examples of this interdependency for this company.
   c. Contrast budgeting as a process for evaluating demand and capacity to perform, and as a mechanism for communicating planning decisions to managers. Provide an example of each.
5. Summarize the planning information subsystem for the company in terms of:
   a. Major type of information inputs
   b. Major components of its data base
   c. Major types and purposes of reports produced

EXERCISE 5-2: Discount, Inc. (Part B)

Refer to the description of Discount, Inc. (Part A) in Exercise 4-1. Also, consider the following general description of the activities and operations of Discount, Inc. as shown in Exhibit 5-18. Some of the major problems of the company were described in Exercise 4-1. They include:

1. The method of ordering does not balance supply of and demand for merchandise, thereby resulting in excessive overstocks of merchandise.
2. There is inadequate demand analysis of merchandise needs for Discount, Inc.
3. Poor timing and coordination of advertising exists, including lack of timely information about merchandise items featured. This results in last minute replacement of ads, requires rapid replacement of merchandise, and results in inadequate notification of impending advertising to Discount, Inc.
4. Merchandise display and movement are cumbersome and not effective.

Exhibit 5-18

SUMMARY OF THE OPERATIONAL SUBSYSTEM OF DISCOUNT, INC.

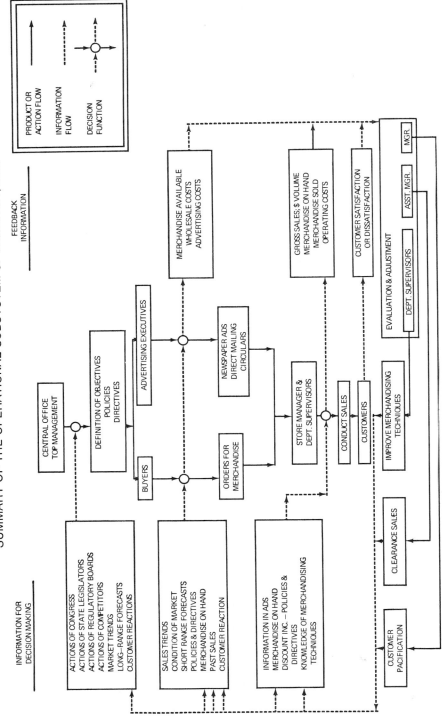

5. There is inadequate analysis of Discount's capacity (e.g. facilities, merchandise, and manpower) in relation to potential demand for products and services.

Using the framework for analysis in Exhibit 5-2, perform the following:

1. Identify and discuss several major constraints that you feel are important for the operation of the company. Based on the information about the company's operation in the case, how would you describe the company image? The company's objective?

2. Identify the major demand determinants that impact the product potential of the company.
   a. Describe the types of demand analysis information that would be useful in developing sales forecasts.
   b. Prepare a simplified demand analysis report for the company.

3. Identify and describe several major types of resource capacity information that would be useful to the company in committing resources to product lines.
   a. Prepare a simplified resource capacity status report for the company.
   b. Describe the important interrelationships between demand information and the development of resource capacity reports.

4. Provide several examples of types of budget information that would be useful to the company, and explain why you feel they would be useful.
   a. Identify dollar, quantity, time, and quality related budget information; and provide an example of each type.
   b. Consider how demand, capacity, and budget information are interdependent, and provide several examples of this interdependency for this company.

5. Summarize the planning information subsystem for the company in terms of:
   a. Major type of information inputs
   b. Major components of its data base
   c. Major types and purposes of reports produced

6

INFORMATION
FOR OPERATIONAL
CONTROL

Operational control involves essentially the implementation of the planning decisions made during the preoperating period. It includes the continual coordination of the efforts of individuals performing group tasks and the regulation of the resource flows. As decisions concerning objectives, demand forecasts, and resource commitments become operational, the MIS is depended upon to provide information relating to performance status. In broad terms, this information facilitates the continuous comparison of budgeted or projected versus actual performance.

This chapter discusses the basic types of information needed to facilitate operational control. Specific objectives are:

1. To describe operational control and to provide examples of analyses that are involved in defining information needed to facilitate operational control.
2. To identify and describe in detail a number of general or summary logistics management reports that are useful for achieving operational control.
3. To describe several specialized logistics management reports that are useful for controlling resource acquisition and production and distribution activities.

Before examining the information and examples of reports required for operational control, the meaning of operational control must be firmly established.

OPERATIONAL CONTROL

Operational control, as a major managerial function, is concerned with insuring that day-to-day operating activities are accomplished according to the projections and decisions made during planning. Operational control is performance oriented; it attempts to minimize the unfavorable deviations of the organization's actual performance or at least some aspect of the organization's operations from planned performance. Minimization of unfavorable deviations is facilitated by measuring and evaluating actual performance on a continuous basis and making appropriate adjustments to operations as unfavorable operating events occur. A slippage in the production schedule is a type of unfavorable deviation from planned operation that requires measurement and evaluation to determine its seriousness and to determine feasible remedial adjustments to the production operations capable of compensating for the slippage and generating of output in time for shipment as scheduled. A possible adjustment would be to authorize the production department to work overtime to meet the original production schedule.

The emphasis of operational control lies in the comparison and analysis of *actual* versus *projected* performance of activities. The effective execution of operational control involves the following activities of the operational subsystem: resource requisition, resource acquisition, resource transformation, distribution of output, and utilization of output. Exhibit 6-1 provides a conceptual framework for analyzing these activities for the purpose of defining types of information needed to facilitate operational control. For example, in order to support decisions relating to the requisition (0300) and acquisition (0400) of resources, analyses are undertaken which should provide answers to the following two general questions:

1. What is the *availability of resources* and their *potential sources of supply* in relation to projected needs for resources by the organization (0310)?
2. What is the *actual versus projected receipt, inspection, and processing of resources* in relation to projected needs for resources by the organization (0410)?

Answers to these two general questions should lead to decisions concerning selection of supply or source of each type of resource (reflected in 0311 to 0313), and should provide information relating to the status of processing of resources that have been acquired (reflected in 0411 to 0416), respectively. These types of analyses and decisions provide information for production (0500) which produces products/services for distribution (0600) and subsequent utilization by users or customers (0700).

In order to support decisions relating to production and distribution of products/services, analyses are undertaken which should provide answers to three additional general questions:

3. What is the *actual versus projected resource usage, performance of work,* and *production of products/services* (0510)?
4. What is the *actual versus projected delivery of products/services* to users or customers (0610)?
5. What is the *status of receipt of and level of satisfaction* relating to products/services received by users or customers (0700)?

Answers to these three general questions should produce information relating to the status of production (reflected in 0511 to 0516) and distribution (0611 to 0613) and feedback from users of customers (0711 to 0715), respectively.

The five general questions to be answered are not intended to be universal, yet they include the most important types of analyses which are needed for effective operational control. For example, without extensive analyses and information relating to the availability, sources, and processing of resources, production of products can not be controlled effectively, nor can shipments of products be scheduled and accomplished when required by customers.

Exhibit 6-1

THE OPERATIONAL CONTROL FUNCTION (OPERATING PERIOD ANALYSIS)

OPERATIONAL SUBSYSTEM   INFORMATIONAL SUBSYSTEM
                                         ──RESOURCE REQUISITIONS (0236)

(0300) REQUISITION OF RESOURCES (SOURCE ANALYSIS)
       (0310) ANALYSIS OF AVAILABILITY
               OF RESOURCES AND POTEN──
               TIAL SOURCES OF SUPPLY─►PURCHASE ORDERS   (0311)►
                                     ─►EMPLOYMENT CONTRACTS   (0312)►
                                     ─►FINANCIAL INSTRUMENTS   (0313)►

(0400) ACQUISITION OF RESOURCES (RESOURCE INPUT
                                 PROCESSING)
       (0410) RECEIPT, INSPECTION, AND
               PROCESSING OF RESOURCES─►RECEIVING REPORTS   (0411)►
                                      ─►INSPECTION REPORTS   (0412)►
                                      ─►PURCHASE INVOICES   (0413)►
                                      ─►STOCK RECEIPT SLIPS   (0414)►
                                      ─►PERSONNEL ACTION FORMS   (0415)►
                                      ─►CASH/FUNDS RECEIPTS SLIPS (0416)►
                                        BUDGETS   (0233)
                                        WORK STATEMENTS AND
                                          SCHEDULES   (0234)
                                        QUALITY SPECIFICATIONS   (0235)

(0500) PRODUCTION (RESOURCE TRANSFORMATION)
       (0510) RESOURCE UTILIZATION,
               PERFORMANCE OF WORK, AND
               PRODUCTION OF PRODUCTS/
               SERVICES──────────────►WORK COMPLETED REPORTS (0511)►
                                     ─►INSPECTION REPORTS   (0512)►
                                     ─►TIME REPORTS   (0513)►
                                     ─►MATERIALS USAGE REPORTS (0514)►
                                     ─►FACILITIES UTILIZATION
                                         REPORTS   (0515)►
                                     ─►COST REPORTS   (0516)►

(0600) DISTRIBUTION (PROCESSING OF OUTPUTS)
       (0610) ASSIGNMENT AND DELIVERY
               OF OUTPUTS TO INVENTORY OR
               USERS/CUSTOMERS────────►STOCK RECEIPT SLIPS   (0611)►
                                     ─►SHIPPING/ISSUE SLIPS   (0612)►
                                     ─►SALES INVOICE/CHARGE OR
                                         TRANSFER SLIPS   (0613)►

(0700) UTILIZATION (CONSUMPTION OF OUTPUTS)
       (0710) RECEIPT, INSPECTION,
               PROCESSING, AND USE OF
               PRODUCTS/SERVICES──────►USER RECEIVING REPORTS   (0711)►
                                     ─►VOUCHER RECEIVABLES   (0712)►
                                     ─►CREDIT MEMOS   (0713)►
                                     ─►CASH RECEIPT SLIPS   (0714)►
                                     ─►SALES RETURN SLIPS   (0715)►

(0800)(0900) MANAGERIAL AND FINANCIAL CONTROL FUNCTION (CHAPTER 7)

NOTE:
  1. THE NUMBERING SYSTEM SHOWN IS AN EXTENSION OF THE ONE USED IN
     EXHIBIT 5-2.
  2. SEE NOTES 2 AND 3 OF EXHIBIT 5-2 CONCERNING LIMITATIONS AND
     CHARACTERISTICS OF THE FLOWS, ACTIVITIES, AND DOCUMENTS DE-
     SCRIBED IN THIS EXHIBIT.

The following sections provide example answers to these five general questions for (1) an office furniture manufacturer, and (2) a state university. These examples reflect the types of analyses and information involved in operational control for each type of organization, and they are patterned generally around the framework provided in Exhibit 6-1. The five questions and related analyses have been grouped into two broad topics for discussion purposes: analysis of resource requisition and acquisition activities; and analysis of production and distribution activities and user/customer feedback concerning products/services received.

Resource Requisition and Acquisition Activities

The *requisition activity* includes the traditional procurement, recruiting, and financing functions of an organization. Procurement relates to purchasing physical resources or services such as materials, supplies, equipment, and contractual services such as custodial and security. The personnel division of the organization recruits the needed manpower for its operating and staff functions, while the finance division is responsible for locating and acquiring funds. The requisition activity involves an analysis of the availability of resource types and quantities on hand and on order (or in process of being recruited, developed, or acquired) versus their projected need in the organization. For example, an office furniture manufacturer surveys its supply of wood, screws, varnish, carpentry labor, fabricating equipment such as saws and drills, and finishing materials on hand and on order. These are all needed to produce the projected demand for office desks and chairs.

If the resources required to meet the projected demand for office desks and chairs exceeds the amounts of resources on hand and on order, the company must acquire additional resources during the operating period. For example, potential sources of supply of raw materials for desks and chairs are analyzed in terms of their ability to provide the needed quantity and quality of materials within the required time and at the lowest possible cost. Additional carpentry labor that may be required might be obtained through the addition of carpenters to the labor force. However, if the need for carpentry labor is thought to be temporary, the hiring of part-time carpentry labor or authorization of overtime for the present carpenters may be feasible solutions. If additional cash or funds in excess of that expected to be generated from sales are temporarily required to finance production of desks and chairs, the company will be required to seek a loan, line of credit, or additional credit from its suppliers.

For a state university, the analysis is similar to that required for the office furniture company in that the types and amounts of resources on hand and in process of being acquired are analyzed in terms of availability versus projected need. However, the types of resources required are quite different, especially in terms of the type of manpower the university uses. Also, university production requires faculty manpower and instruction and research facilities as primary resources, rather than raw materials and carpentry labor for desks and chairs. Although the university's major concern relating to resource availability centers on more permanent types of resources (faculty and educational facilities), it also utilizes office supplies and clerical and administrative manpower. Most of the cash or funds needed to finance the operations of the university are authorized at the beginning of each fiscal year. Thus, the university does not have as much flexibility in financing decisions as a business firm, but instead must operate within funding allocations provided to it each year.

The analysis of availability of resources and decisions concerning sources of supply require information relating to the quality, quantity, and cost of resources that are required, and when they can be acquired by the organization. The decision to select a source of supply for desk lumber requires an evaluation of the supplier's capacity to furnish the types and grades of wood desired, in the amounts and times required, and at a cost that is acceptable to the company. Information relating to these factors is included on a purchase order which serves as a contract between the company and the supplier. Similarly, employment contracts and finance instruments reflect agreements the company makes with employees and financial institutions in acquiring manpower and funds. Purchase orders, employment contracts, and financial instruments are documents which reflect the decisions made in the requisitioning of resources and which provide information needed for the acquisition of resources by the organization.

The *acquisition of resources* involves the processing of resources that have been procured, recruited, or financed. The acquisition activity involves the receipt, inspection, and processing of resources and making them available for use by the organization and its components. For example, the receiving department of the office furniture company verifies the types and amounts of lumber received, inspects it in terms of grades or quality specifications, and notes the times the shipments are received. This information is recorded on receiving and inspection reports which are compared with information on purchase orders to determine whether the supplier has performed according to the contract. Also, this information is used to determine whether there will be any serious production delays owing to late shipments or receipt of incorrect grades of wood. The information on the vendor's purchase invoice for wood also is compared with cost information on the purchase order to verify correct billing by the supplier. For a state university, the acquisition activity is quite similar, except for the types of materials purchased. Stock receipt slips show the types, amounts, and costs of materials that have been placed in inventory and the dates of receipt.

The processing of manpower involves an orientation and perhaps a training program. New employees, whether for a business firm or a university, are furnished a variety of information, such as the nature of the organization, its policies, their jobs and responsibilities, and their compensation. The personnel action form shows the job assignments, responsibilities, compensation, and related appointment information.

The procedures involved in processing the receipt of cash or funds are similar for a business firm and a university. The receipt of cash or funds is reflected in cash/funds receipt slips which include information sucn as the amounts, sources, and dates the cash/funds were received.

The analyses involved in performing resource requisition and acquisition activities produce information that is useful for the production of products/services, such as that which is contained in documents 0411 to 0416 in Exhibit 6-1. In addition, budgets, work statements and schedules, and quality specifications (0233 to 0235 of Exhibit 5-2) which have been produced during planning provide important types of information for the production activity, which is described in the following section.

Production and Distribution Activities and User/Customer Feedback

The *production activity* involves the transformation of resources into products/services which have been specified in operating budgets, work statements and schedules, and quality specifications. As production activity occurs, resources are consumed in the performance of work. Fabrication, assembly, and finishing are major activities involved in the production of office furniture. Resources such as wood, screws, glue, and varnish are transformed into office desks and chairs. Also, fabricating, assembly, and finishing equipment and facilities are used by carpenters and other types of manpower to facilitate this transformation process. Information on the status of work performance is shown on work-completed, inspection, time, materials usage, facilities usage, and cost reports.

A university produces services such as credit hours and degrees, research studies, and advice to students concerning career objectives through the performance of teaching, research, and counseling production activities, respectively. The transformation of resources into these types of services is accomplished primarily by faculty using educational and research equipment and facilities. The status of work performance is shown on grade, student-attendance, faculty workload, space utilization, and cost reports.

The *distribution activity* involves the processing and delivery of products/services to users or customers. For the office furniture manufacturer, this means that desks and chairs are shipped directly to customers or are transferred to finished goods inventory to await shipment to customers. Information on the completion of distribution activities is shown on shipping slips and stock receipt slips (transfers to inventory). Sales invoices show the types, amounts, and costs of products shipped to customers and they are the basis for payment of products received.

For a university, the distribution of services occurs when teaching, research, and counseling activities are performed, and as such there are no shipping or stock receipt slips, as in the case of shipment of products by a business firm. Instead, reports are produced which show such information as the number of credit hours and degrees produced and the number of students counseled. Research produced is reflected in articles, books, and reports on special studies completed.

In order to analyze the effectiveness of production and distribution activities, information must be obtained from users/customers of products/services. This type of information relating to *utilization* or consumption of outputs is received in a number of documents such as user/customer receiving reports. For example, a customer indicates the types, amounts, and dates of receipt of desks and chairs on a receiving report to acknowledge receipt from the office furniture manufacturer. This report triggers a voucher/account receivable or a credit memo which eventually leads to a payment from the customer and the generation of a cash receipt slip by the company. The furniture company also analyses the types, quantity, and frequency of sales returns and customer complaints to determine what adjustments need to be made in the production and distribution activities.

Information relating to user satisfaction with university services includes such factors as student demand for classes, programs, degrees, and instructors, and public attitudes toward higher education which are eventually reflected in legislative appropriations. Verification of receipt of instruction is shown on class rosters and student grade reports. The level of satisfaction with the quality of research produced by a university is reflected in the number and dollar value of research grants received and the national reputation of journals in which research articles by the faculty appear.

In summary, the overall purpose of operational control is to insure that the operations of the organization are carried out or performed as planned. From the foregoing description and examples of the operational control activities, it is evident that these activities are highly interrelated and that their performance involves a large number of variables requiring many different types of information. Also, as in the case of the planning function of management, operational control analyses and decisions generate a sizeable amount of important information (a number of examples are shown in Exhibit 6-1). Some of this information is a major source of data for the MIS, which processes it into reports for managerial/financial control and planning, as well as for operational control. For example, materials usage and time reports provide information on actual costs of resources used for the production process. This information is used in the preparation of financial reports (such as income statements) and for establishing production cost budgets for the next operating period.

The primary purpose of operational control information is to facilitate the implementation of plans and budgets, and to control the commitment and utilization of resources. Such information is often referred to as logistics management information. Managerial control, on the other hand, is accomplished by means of analyzing information about the performance of managerial responsibility centers. This type of information is basic to the evaluation of the performance of organizational segments and their managers. Finally, general financial control involves evaluation of overall organizational performance and compliance with the external reporting requirements of stockholders or the federal government. Managerial/financial control reports are discussed in Chapter 7, while the remainder of this chapter describes logistics management reports.

LOGISTICS MANAGEMENT REPORTS

Logistics management reports provide information to facilitate the control of cost, quality, quantity, and time (or schedule) of work performance and the flow of resources that are involved in the production of products/services. The following are examples of types of information needed to control the performance of work for the office furniture manufacturer and the state university. (These examples are for illustrative purposes; the items listed are not intended to be exhaustive or universal.)

For the Office Furniture Manufacturer:

1. *Cost Control Information:* Materials, labor, and total costs per desk or chair; fabricating, assembly, and finishing costs per desk or chair.
2. *Quality Performance Information:* Number and types of inspection rejects of raw materials; amount of waste from raw materials used; number and types of inspection rejects of desks and chairs produced.
3. *Quantity Performance Information:* Units of raw materials used per desk or chair produced; labor hours used per desk or chair produced, and for each phase of production, such as fabrication and assembly.
4. *Schedule Performance Information*: Dates of completion of fabrication, assembly, and finishing operations to produce customer orders for desks or chairs; dates raw materials are received, processed, and made available for production.

For the State University

1. *Cost Control Information:* Costs per credit hour and degree produced; costs per student counseled; costs of library and computer support facilities; administrative costs per student credit hour or student enrolled.
2. *Quality Performance Information:* Student-faculty ratios; number of graduate-student or part-time instructors; number of faculty with terminal degrees; number of student withdrawals.
3. *Quantity Performance Information:* Enrollment levels per instructor, course, program, and college per semester; number of degrees granted; number of credit hours generated.
4. *Schedule Performance Information:* Average length of time to complete program or acquire degree; frequency of course offerings in relation to demand for courses; frequency and availability of student counseling.

These four types of information provide a useful framework for defining information needs for logistics control since they are patterned after the four broad types of budgets (discussed in Chapter 5) dealing with dollar, quality, quantity, and time related information. This facilitates the comparison of actual versus projected performance of operations in terms of these four types of information.

General Logistics Management Information

An essential feature of a logistics report is that it should relate the status of performance to future impact on objectives, budgets, and schedules. A logistics

report should be viewed as containing a number of basic information elements
such as:

1. Output (products/services) or input (resource) identification.
2. Unit of measurement (for information contained in 5-8 below).
3. Identification of the responsibility center or processor producing the
   output or using the input.
4. Identification of user of output.
5. Normal or projected level of performance.
6. Actual level of performance.
7. Variance from normal or projected level of performance.
8. Revised projected performance level.
9. Comments regarding action taken to correct unfavorable variance.

These information elements are used in Exhibits 6-2 and 6-3, which are
examples of logistic management reports for an office furniture manufacturer
and a state university.

Each of these exhibits present these information elements in the context of
cost, quantity, schedule, and quality control. Although the exact format and
level of detail included in a logistics report may vary depending on the
organization, the format generally contains a comparison of projected versus
actual levels of cost, quantity, time, and quality of performance. For example,
Exhibit 6-2 shows that the company's actual costs of production of desks (Item
A) exceeds projected costs ($160 versus $150), and this cost overrun is due to
an increase in the cost of fabrication (Item B, $40 versus $30). This increase in
production costs has been caused in part by a deterioration in the *quality* of
production (Item F, 5 percent actual defect rate, versus the projection of 1
percent), which is due initially to poor quality of wood. Also, the total *quantity*
of carpentry labor (Item C) has increased because of inefficiency due to poor
quality of wood, as well as higher actual quantity of desks produced (Item D,
250 versus 200 desks).

Another type of useful quantity information not shown in Exhibit 6-2 is the
number of labor hours per desk produced. This type of quantity information is
useful for analyzing the cause of the variance. For example, using the
information provided in Exhibit 6-2 (Items C and D), the labor hours per desk
produced has increased from 4 hours (projected) to 5 hours (actual), and the
revised projection of labor hours for the next operating period reverts back to 4
hours per desk.

Item E is an example of information which is useful for controlling
schedule or time of performance, and shows that wood for desks has been
acquired about two weeks in advance of production needs. This has the
advantage of reducing the purchase cost of wood, which may be offset in part
by the increase in inventory costs for stockpiling wood. The production
information (Item D) also can be used for controlling time of performance. The
projected schedule of production, which calls for 200 desks to be produced in
the current operating period, has been exceeded; as a result, the production
schedule has been modified for the next operating period.

Exhibit 6-2

LOGISTICS MANAGEMENT REPORT FOR AN OFFICE FURNITURE MANUFACTURER

(1) Ouput/Input Code*	(2) Unit of Measure	(3) Responsibility Center/Processor Code*	(4) Output User Code*	(5) Normal Projection	(6) Actual	(7) Variance	(8) Revised Projection	(9) Explanatory Comments
A. Office Desks	Cost Per Desk	Production Division	ABC Company	$150	$160	+$10	$155	Unfavorable increase in costs due to excessive waste from wood used in fabrication of desks. Higher quality wood will be used next period.
B. Office Desks	Cost Per Desk	Fabrication Department	Assembly Department	$ 30	$ 40	+$10	$ 35	Unfavorable increase in costs due to excessive waste from wood. Projected unit costs per desk will be $35 due to higher quality of wood to be used next period.
C. Carpentry Labor	No. of Hours	Fabrication Department	Fabrication	800	1250	+450	600	The increase in total labor hours is due to the increase in quantity of production, plus the increase in labor (4 to 5 hours) required to produce a desk because of poor quality of wood. In the next period, labor used will decrease to normal rate of 4 hours per desk due to higher quality of wood to be used.
D. Office Desks	No. of Desks	Fabrication Department	Assembly Department	200	250	+50	150	The excess desks produced anticipates an overhaul to production equipment next period.
E. Wood for Desks	Date Needed	Procurement Division	Production Division	1st of mo. i.e., July 1	Jun 16	−15 days	Aug 1	The shipment of wood was received early because of favorable prices for wood in June. Normal delivery schedule is expected next period.
F. Office Desks	Percent Defects	Fabrication Department	Assembly Department	1%	5%	+4%	1%	Increase in number of defects due to poor quality of wood used. Procurement has agreed to purchase higher quality of wood for next period.

NOTES: 1. The information in columns 1, 3, and 4 (denoted by *) need to be assigned code numbers from a coding system or chart of accounts. A coding system is developed for this example in Chapter 9.
2. The examples shown in this exhibit normally would be shown on separate reports (e.g., cost information such as items A and B; quantity information such as items C and D; schedule information such as item E; and quality information such as item F). These types of information are combined here for illustrative purposes, and they are not intended to be exhaustive or universal.

Exhibit 6-3

GENERAL LOGISTICS MANAGEMENT REPORT FOR A STATE UNIVERSITY

(1) Ouput/Input Code*	(2) Unit of Measure	(3) Responsibility Center/ Processor Code*	(4) Output User Code*	(5) Normal Projection	(6) Actual	(7) Variance	(8) Revised Projection	(9) Explanatory Comments
A. Under- graduate Instruction	Cost Per Credit Hour	School of Business	Under- graduate Students	$ 63	$70	+$11	$59	Unfavorable increase in costs due to offering too many small class sections. Larger sections will be offered next semester.
B. Graduate Instruction	Cost Per Credit Hour	School of Business	Graduate Students	$100	$86	−$14	$86	Increase in enrollment without comparable increase in the number of faculty members.
C. Under- graduate Instruction	No. of Credit Hours	School of Business	Under- graduate Students	14,400	2,000	−240	12,000	Decrease in credit hours due to decrease in enrollment. No increase in enrollment is expected next semester.
D. Faculty Instruction	No. of Class Hours	School of Business	All Students	12	14	+2	12	The increase in the number of class hours taught per faculty, due to too many small class sections, will be reduced next semester by offering larger class sections.
E. Classroom Space	Sq. Ft. Per Student	School of Business	Faculty and Students	30	36	+6	30	The increase in space per student, caused by the loss of undergraduate enrollment, will be offset by a comparable increase in graduate enrollment next semester.
F. Research Project	Percent Complete	School of Business	Ford Founda- tion	70%	80%	+10%	No Change	Research is proceeding ahead of schedule, and no major problems are foreseen for completing the project on time.
G. All Instruction	Students Per Faculty	School of Business	All Students	20 (standard)	18	−2	20	The decrease in undergraduate enrollment will be offset by additional increase in graduate enrollment next semester.

NOTES: 1. The information in columns 1, 3, and 4 (denoted by *) need to be as-signed code numbers from a coding system or chart of accounts. A coding system is developed for this example in Chapter 9.

2. The examples shown in this exhibit normally would be shown on sepa-rate reports (e.g., *cost* information such as items A and B; *quantity* information such as items C, D, and E; *schedule* information such as item F; and *quality* information such as item G). These types of informa-tion are combined here for illustrative purposes, and they are not in-tended to be exhaustive or universal.

For the university (Exhibit 6-3) similar types of cost quantity, schedule or time, and quantity control information are shown. For example, the *cost* of undergraduate instruction (Item A) has exceeded projections (70 versus 63 dollars per credit hour) while the cost of graduate instruction (Item B) has decreased (100 to 86 per credit hour). These changes in cost can be explained by the decrease in the *quantity* of undergraduate enrollment as reflected in student credit hours (Item C), coupled with a comparable increase in graduate enrollment, and with no increase in faculty members (Item B). Items D and E also are an example of quantity-related control information relating to the average number of classroom hours per faculty member and the average amount of classroom space available per student enrolled, respectively.

Item F is an example of information which is useful for controlling *schedule or time* of performance of a research project funded through a research grant, and shows that the project is ahead of schedule. Information which is useful for controlling the *quality* of instruction is shown as Item G, which indicates that the university is staying within the projected student-faculty ratio of 20 to 1.

From the foregoing examples, it is evident that logistics information is highly interrelated, and several types of information must be analyzed concurrently before adjustments to operations can take place. For example, part of the increase in carpentry labor can be explained by the increased quantity of desks produced. Also, the increase in production costs of desks is due to a comparable increase in fabrication costs, which in turn is due to waste caused from poor quality of wood.

General logistics management reports, as described in the foregoing sections, assist operating managers in making day-to-day operating decisions. As such, they are *real-time* reports in that the frequency of reporting unfavorable deviations from projections is concordant with the time requirements for instituting corrective action by operating managers. For example, in the production of office desks, the hour that fabricating equipment becomes inoperative, immediate decisions can and must be made concerning repairs and utilization of excess labor. In this case the deviation information would be directed to operating management within minutes of the breakdown. However, for the university enrollment case, actions concerning course offering changes do not take place until the following semester, and changes in budget projections are made only during the latter part of the academic year. Hence the deviation information in these areas is furnished with less frequency and urgency.

The *content or quality* of information on logistics reports does not normally have the precision or exactness that is found in financial reports for external agencies (e.g., financial statements to stockholders or the Internal Revenue Service). This is because the essence of operational control involves timely variance reporting and subsequent operational adjustments. A reasonably accurate estimate of the variances in the quantity of desks to be produced at the end of the day, week, or month provides more usable information than a report prepared after the close of the reporting period which shows the exact number of desks completed during the previous day, week, or month. By estimating actual performance levels, plans for adjusting operations to compensate for the expected unfavorable variances can begin much earlier. Because it is geared to short-run operating performance, the *quantity or volume* of information on logistics reports is best handled by adhering to the exception principle. Operating managers should be presented with only pertinent and action-oriented information. Managers might postpone report examination if it appears to require much analysis and reflection. Such postponements undermine the utility of logistics reports. The use of standards of performance in logistics reports as the normal or projected level of performance also is essential for clarity in exception reporting. Ideally these standards are developed during the planning period.

General logistics management reports tend to highlight and summarize important developments occurring during the operating period. These reports serve as a channel for integrating a large, complex variety of operational activities and decisions, which often require supporting analyses and summaries. While the reports described in the foregoing sections should be viewed as minimum types of information needed for effective operational control, the supporting analyses and summaries should be designed within the general framework of variance reporting. One important type of summary logistics or variance information is budget variance information, examples of which are provided and discussed in the following section.

Budget Variance Information

Major types of budget variance information show projections of revenue, cost, profit, and cash flow made during planning, compared with actual performance by the organization in each of these areas. As such, these types of budget variance information link operational control with planning, since budget variance information provides the basis for adjusting projections of revenues, levels of production, and cash requirements. Exhibit 6-4 shows a revenue variance report using first quarter projections of revenue made during planning (Exhibit 5-6). A revenue variance report provides periodic (usually weekly, monthly, and quarterly) information on actual versus projected revenues. The business firm shown in Exhibit 6-4 is exceeding its first quarter projection of net revenues by about 6.8 percent ($15,000). This has occurred even though the percentage of sales returns has increased from the projection of 9.1 percent of gross revenues. Returns were actually running at a rate of 10.6. percent of gross revenues. This type of information is useful for adjusting revenue budgets and production levels for the remainder of the year. An increase in both is indicated for the business firm in Exhibit 6-4.

A cost variance report is shown in Exhibit 6-5 using first quarter projections of costs made during planning (Exhibit 5-7) for office desks. This type of information is useful for identifying changes in unit cost patterns and profit levels. Although the company has increased its revenues over projections, its percentage gross margin and percentage net profit before taxes have both

Exhibit 6-4

REVENUE VARIANCE REPORT FOR A BUSINESS FIRM

Source of Revenue	1st Quarter Projection	1st Quarter Actual	Variance
1. *Gross Revenue from Products:*			
a. *Office Desks:*			
(1) Units	330	380	+50
(2) Revenues	$ 99,000	$114,000	+$15,000
b. *Office Chairs:*			
(1) Units	880	930	+50
(2) Revenues	$ 88,000	$ 93,000	+$ 5,000
Gross Revenues:	$187,000	$207,000	+$20,000
2. *Less:* Sales Returns	($ 17,000)	($ 22,000)	(+$5,000)
Net Revenue from Products:	$170,000	$185,000	+$15,000
3. *Plus:* Investment Income	40,000	45,000	+ 5,000
Miscellaneous Income	10,000	5,000	− 5,000
Net Revenues:	$220,000	$235,000	+ $15,000

Note: The first quarter projections are taken from the revenue budget shown in Exhibit 5-6.

dropped under projections (50 to 47 and 30 to 26 percent, respectively). These unfavorable results have been caused by a rise in unit materials cost ($50 to $55) and unit costs of fabricating labor ($30 to $35). However, administrative expenses and miscellaneous expenses, owing to their fixed nature, have fallen on a per unit basis.

    Using some of the information shown in Exhibits 6-4 and 6-5 and the first quarter projections of profit information made during planning (Exhibit 5-6), an example of a profit variance report for office desks is shown in Exhibit 6-6. The profit variance report shows information similar to that included on the unit cost variance report, but total instead of unit revenues, costs, and profits are shown. This type of information is useful for evaluating projected versus actual total profit levels. The actual percentage gross margin is 47 percent versus 50 percent projected because of the increases in unit materials and fabricating labor costs ($50 to $55, and $30 to $35, respectively). These increases in actual production costs, plus the increases in selling expense ($2,900), have resulted in a decrease in the actual total net profit from the first quarter projection ($27,000 to $26,700), even though actual net sales revenues exceeded the estimate of $90,000 by $12,000.

    The profit information also is used for estimating variances in cash flows. Exhibit 6-7 shows a cash flow variance report using the first quarter projections made during planning (Exhibit 5-9). The cash flow information shows a sizeable increase in receipts ($15,000) versus a small increase in disbursements ($2,500),

Exhibit 6-5

COST VARIANCE REPORT FOR OFFICE DESKS

Cost	1st Quarter Projection		1st Quarter Actual		Variance
1. Unit Selling Price	$300.00	100%	$300.00	100%	
2. *Unit Production Costs of Goods Sold:*					
a. Materials	$ 50.00		$ 55.00		$ 5.00
b. Direct Labor:					
(1) Fabricating	30.00		35.00		5.00
(2) Assembly	20.00		20.00		————
(3) Finishing	20.00		20.00		————
Total Direct Labor	$ 70.00		$ 75.00		$ 5.00
c. Burden (Overhead)	30.00		30.00		————
Total Unit Costs of Goods Sold	$150.00	50%	$160.00	53%	+$10.00
3. Gross Margin	$150.00	50%	$140.00	47%	−$10.00
4. Selling Expense	$ 30.00		$ 35.00		+$ 5.00
5. Administrative Expense	$ 15.00		$ 13.23		−$ 1.77
6. Miscellaneous Expense	$ 15.00		$ 13.23		−$ 1.77
7. *Net Profit Before Taxes*	$ 90.00	30%	$ 78.54	26%	−$11.46

NOTE: The first quarter projections are taken from the cost budget shown in Exhibit 5-7.

which reduces the amount of financing required ($12,500). The sizeable increases in cash required for materials, labor, and other expenses ($12,500) have been mostly offset by the reduction of cash disbursements for facilities renovation ($10,000).

In addition to budget variance information, logistics information is needed for controlling specific operating segments of the organization. The following sections describe two broad operating segments for which specialized logistics information is required: resource requisition/acquisition and production/distribution.

Resource Requisition/Acquisition Information

The purpose of a resource acquisition report is to facilitate the control of procurement, acquisition, and receipt of resources by providing information on the status of resources. A number of commonly used resource acquisition reports are those relating to current, fixed, human, and financial resources.

In order to facilitate the control of *current resources,* a purchase order status journal provides useful information for keeping track of the status of materials on order. It shows such items as the date order was dispatched,

Exhibit 6-6

PROFIT VARIANCE REPORT FOR OFFICE DESKS

Profit	1st Quarter Projection	1st Quarter Actual	Variance
1. Gross Sales Revenues	$99,000	$114,000	+$15,000
2. Less: Sales Returns	(9,000)	(12,000)	+(3,000)
3. Net Revenues	$90,000 100%	102,000 100%	+12,000
4. *Production Costs of Goods Sold:*	(300 units)	(340 units)	
a. Materials	$15,000	$ 18,700	+$3,700
b. Direct Labor			
(1) Fabricating	9,000	11,900	+2,900
(2) Assembly	6,000	6,800	+$800
(3) Finishing	6,000	6,800	+$800
Total Direct Labor	$21,000	$ 25,500	+$4,500
c. Burden (Overhead)	$ 9,000	$ 10,200	+$1,200
Total Costs of Goods Sold	$45,000 50%	$ 54,400 53%	+$9,400
5. Gross Margin	$45,000 50%	$ 47,600 47%	+$2,600
6. Selling Expense	9,000	$ 11,900	+$2,900
7. Administrative Expense	4,500	4,500	————
8. Miscellaneous Expense	4,500	4,500	————
9. Net Profit Before Taxes	$27,000 30%	$ 26,700 26%	-$300

NOTES: 1. The first quarter projections are taken from the profit budget shown in Exhibit 5-8.

2. The first quarter actual revenue figures are taken from Exhibit 6-4 and the cost figures have been developed from unit cost information in Exhibit 6-5.

3. Number of units projected (300) and actual (340) are based on $300 price per unit, and reflect projected sales returns of 30 units and actual returns of 40 units.

expected delivery date, vendor identification, and whether the order is overdue or may be received late. As such, the purchase order journal provides information that is used for expediting late purchases of materials. A vendor appraisal report shows the rating of the vendor's past performance in terms of quality of materials received (i.e., inspection reject rate), delivery according to schedules, and unit prices of materials purchased. This type of information is useful for selecting sources of supply. The purchases/payables schedule provides information on the status of payment for materials purchased and insures that purchase discounts are taken. Receiving and inspection reports

Exhibit 6-7

CASH FLOW VARIANCE REPORT FOR A BUSINESS FIRM

Cash	1st Quarter Projection	1st Quarter Actual	Variance
1. *Receipts:*			
a. Net Revenues from Products	$170,000	$185,000	+$15,000
b. Investment Income	40,000	45,000	+ 5,000
c. Miscellaneous Income	10,000	5,000	(−$ 5,000)
Total Receipts	$220,000	$235,000	+$15,000
2. *Disbursements:*			
a. Materials	27,000	31,250	+$ 4,250
b. Labor	37,000	42,250	+$ 5,250
c. Total Other Cash Expenses	37,000	40,000	+$ 3,000
d. Renovation of Facilities	100,000	90,000	−$10,000
e. Dividends	———	———	———
f. Payment of Principal on Bank Loan	100,000	100,000	———
Total Disbursements	$301,000	$303,500	+$ 2,500
3. Beginning Cash Balance	50,000	50,000	———
4. Excess or (Deficit) of Receipts plus Cash Balance Over Disbursements	($ 31,000)	($ 18,500)	(−$12,500)
5. Minimum Cash Balance Required	50,000	50,000	———
6. (Deficit) to be Financed or Excess over Minimum Cash Balance Required	($ 81,000)	($ 68,500)	(−$12,500)

NOTE: The first quarter projections are taken from the cash budget shown in Exhibit 5-9.

show the timing and condition of materials received, and with the information provided by purchase order journals, the complete status of materials on order and in process of being received is provided. The materials inventory status report (discussed in Chapter 5 as a resource capacity status report) also shows the availability of current production resources after they have been acquired and processed.

In addition to the procurement-related information discussed above, several types of information are useful for facilitating the control of *fixed resources*. For example, a construction status report provides information relating to such factors as projected versus actual costs and completion times of facilities under construction. With these reports cost overruns or schedule slippages can be detected quickly and necessary adjustments made in the construction program. Equipment utilization reports show the current and planned operating capacity of the organization's production equipment, so that reallocation of work can optimize equipment utilization by minimizing production downtime. For example, the scheduling of production for office desks and office chairs must take into account the availability of fabricating, assembly, and finishing equipment as an interconnected system, rather than as independent activities. This is necessary to achieve optimum use of equipment and labor in each phase of production.

Information relating to *human resource* acquisition generally serves the personnel division of the organization. Recruiting status, manpower status, and labor usage status are types of information needed to facilitate the acquisition of human resources. A recruiting status report provides information on the future acquisition of manpower, similar to the purchase order journal relating to current resources discussed previously. The information provided by a manpower status report is similar to that in a resource capacity status report, but it often shows other types of information such as promotion status, education and training, and need and plans for further training. These types of information are useful for long-range planning of manpower needs as well as providing the basis for short-run recruiting programs.

Cash flow information is needed to acquire and control *financial resources* required by the organization. The cash flow status report, discussed previously (and in Chapter 5), provides fundamental information for effective cash control. In addition, a schedule of sales/receivables provides useful information relating to the timing of sales and the timing of conversion of sales into cash, through the accounts receivable mechanism. Normally, there is a substantial lag between a sale and the actual cash receipt which ties up cash needed for operations. A cash discounts earned/lost report shows whether the organization has taken advantage of discounts offered for payment within a specified period, but it also reflects additional needs for cash because of more rapid payment for materials and supplies. These types of information are important for materials cost analysis and for cash flow analysis.

The primary purpose of resource requisition/acquisition reports is to provide information on the status of resources on order and in process of being acquired versus operational needs. The types of reports described above are highly interrelated as they directly serve the procurement, engineering, personnel, and finance functions in providing information for controlling the acquisition and use of resources.

Production/Distribution Information

The purpose of production/distribution reports is to facilitate the control of production and distribution of products/services, by providing information on the status of work performance. A number of commonly used reports are those relating to work completed, schedule performance, utilization of capacity, and feedback from users/customers.

For example, work-in-process and finished goods reports are typical *work completion* reports which are useful for scheduling deliveries or shipments of products. Order backlog reports provide useful information for future scheduling of production and decisions relating to adding to production capacity. Also, a schedule of shipments provides useful information for the shipping department in scheduling labor and transportation equipment to insure that products are delivered when scheduled to customers, and to achieve efficient utilization of these resources.

Equipment downtime reports and overtime reports provide useful information on the status of *utilization of production capacity*. Downtime information may indicate that production facilities are not being used efficiently, while overtime information may indicate that additional production capacity is required to meet the demand for products.

Feedback from customers often is reflected in a sales returns and allowances report, which indicates the type and degree of customer non-acceptance of products. In many cases, this report is accompanied by a detailed description of the customer's complaint about the product, which the company analyzes to determine the alterations needed to minimize sales returns. Inspection reports of products produced should also reduce sales returns.

The reports described above may also be applicable to segments of the production activity, such as sections, departments, shops, or production processes. Production/distribution reports are highly interrelated as they serve the production division and shipping department by providing information on the status of production/distribution performance.

SUMMARY

The purpose of operational control information is to facilitate the activities involved in the requisition and acquisition of resources and the production and distribution of products/services. Analyses are undertaken concerning the activities of the operational subsystem which provides the information inputs for the four major components of the MIS data base: general logistics management information, budget variance information, resource requisition and acquisition information, and production and distribution information.

Information relating to these four components of the MIS are merged, stored, analyzed, evaluated, and processed by the MIS to produce a series of reports such as those listed in Exhibit 6-8. The key features of these reports are: the reports emphasize *current* operating performance; the reports match and compare *projected* versus *actual* performance of work, resource flows, and consumption; and the reports are *continuous* in that exception reporting is used to provide management with information relating to unfavorable variances from projections when they occur.

The operational control information subsystem, as described above, encompasses the more traditional procurement, personnel, finance, and production information subsystems, and interconnects these subsystems through the development of an interrelated set of reports that are produced from the MIS data base. In contrast, under the traditional approach to the

Exhibit 6-8

OPERATIONAL CONTROL INFORMATION SUBSYSTEM

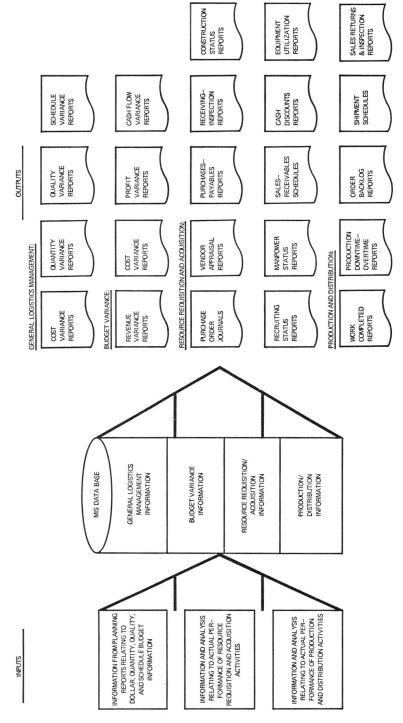

design of information systems, these functional subsystems are treated as separate systems not usually linked to a common data base. The linking feature of the operational control information subsystem of the MIS offers a definite advantage for achieving overall organizational efficiency.

REVIEW QUESTIONS

1. What are the significant characteristics of operational control?
2. What types of analyses are involved in defining information needed·for effective operational control?
3. Give several examples of general logistics management reports. What are the quality, timing, and volume dimensions of these reports? What functions do these reports perform for management?
4. Identify and describe several budget variance reports and their purpose.
5. Identify and describe several resource acquisition and requisition control reports and their purpose.
6. Identify and describe several production and distribution control reports and their purpose.
7. What is the relationship between the timing of logistics reports and the budget cycle?
8. Describe the importance and relationship of planning information to operational control information.
9. Describe the interrelationships of logistics management reports, and give several examples of these interrelationships.
10. Summarize the operational control information subsystem in terms of its (a) major types of information inputs, (b) major components of its data base, and (c) major types and purposes of reports produced.

EXERCISE 6-1: Custom Machine Tool Company (Part B)

Refer to the description of the Custom Machine Tool Company in Exercise 5-1. Also, consider the following description of the general flow of steps in the processing of work and of decisions relating to processing of customers' orders for tools:

1. Sales receives customers' orders for tools and projects demand for tools for the coming year.
2. Engineering develops design specifications for materials, labor, and costs.
3. Controller and Finance evaluate costs of tools and feasible prices for tools, and recommend to the President which tools should be produced.
4. Production schedules manufacturing of tools and requisitions materials from Stores.
5. Stores furnishes materials to Production or, if out of stock, prepares purchase requisitions for Procurement.
6. Procurement selects vendor and issues purchase orders for materials.

7. Procurement receives, inspects, and delivers materials to Stores as they are received.
8. Stores records receipt of materials in inventory and issues materials to Production.
9. Production manufacturers custom tools according to engineering specifications.
10. Quality Control inspects manufactureed tools prior to delivery to customers.
11. Shipping delivers tools to customers.
12. Payment for tools received by Controller.
13. Controller evaluates financial performance of each order.
14. Finance periodically assesses the need for financing future production of tools.

Using the framework for analysis of Exhibit 6-1, perform the following:

1. Identify and discuss the types of resource requisition and acquisition activities of the company and provide several examples of types of analyses and information that are involved in performing these activities.

2. Identify and discuss the types of production and distribution activities of the company and provide several examples of types of analyses and information that are involved in performing these activities.

3. Identify and describe several major types of general logistics information that would be useful to the organization to facilitate operational control.
   a. Identify cost, quality, quantity, and schedule performance information; and provide an example of each type of information.
   b. Identify several types of budget variance information which would be useful for operational control; and provide an example of each type of information.
   c. Describe how operational control information is dependent on planning information; and provide several examples of this interdependency.

4. Identify and describe several major types of resource requisition/acquisition and production/distribution information that would be useful to the organization to facilitate operational control. Describe how resource requisition/acquisition activities are interdependent with production/distribution activities; and provide several examples of this interdependency for this company.

5. Summarize the operational control information subsystem of the company in terms of:
   a. Major types of information inputs
   b. Major components of its data base
   c. Major types and purposes of reports produced

EXERCISE 6-2: Discount, Inc. (Part C)

Refer to the description of Discount, Inc. in Exercises 4-1 and 5-2. Also, consider the following general descriptions of activities and operations of Discount, Inc. as shown in Exhibits 6-9, 6-10, and 6-11. Exhibit 6-9 shows Discount, Inc. as a general input-output system with three major interrelated subsystems: buying, receiving, and selling. Exhibits 6-10 and 6-11 describe generally the merchandise flow decisions and work flows involved.

There are four ways to order merchandise:

1. Hardlines, direct order (see 1 in Exhibit 6-10)
2. Hardlines, preprinted (see 2 in Exhibit 6-10)
3. Softlines, 90 percent are ordered by New York buyers who use the information generated through the key-recs and register tapes (see 3 in Exhibit 6-10)
4. General order items are ordered by New York to cover sale adds (see 4 in Exhibit 6-10)

Dotted lines in Exhibit 6-10 indicate desirable information feedback loops that are missing from the existing system.

Work flows for hardlines and softlines are shown in Exhibit 6-11. In order to sell merchandise, four main steps are necessary:

1. Unbundling
2. Inventory adjustment (verify order accuracy, adjust quantity on hand)
3. Marketing (pricing)
4. Final routing

Using the framework for analysis provided in Exhibit 6-1, perform the following:

1. Identify and discuss the types of resource requisition and acquisition activities of the company and provide several examples of types of analyses and information that are involved in performing them.
2. Identify and describe several major types of general logistics information that would be useful to the organization to facilitate operational control.
   a. Identify cost, quality, quantity, and schedule performance information; and provide an example of each type of information.
   b. Identify several types of budget variance information which would be useful for operational control; and provide an example of each type of information.
   c. Describe how operational control information is dependent on planning information; and provide several examples.
3. Summarize the operational control information subsystem of the company in terms of:
   a. Major types of information inputs
   b. Major components of its data base
   c. Major types and purposes of reports produced

Exhibit 6-9

DISCOUNT, INC. AS A GENERAL INPUT-OUTPUT SYSTEM

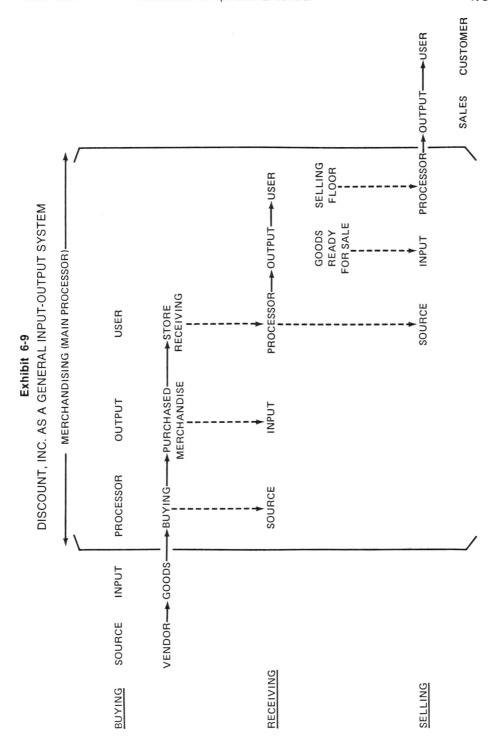

Exhibit 6-10
DISCOUNT, INC. MERCHANDISE FLOW DECISIONS

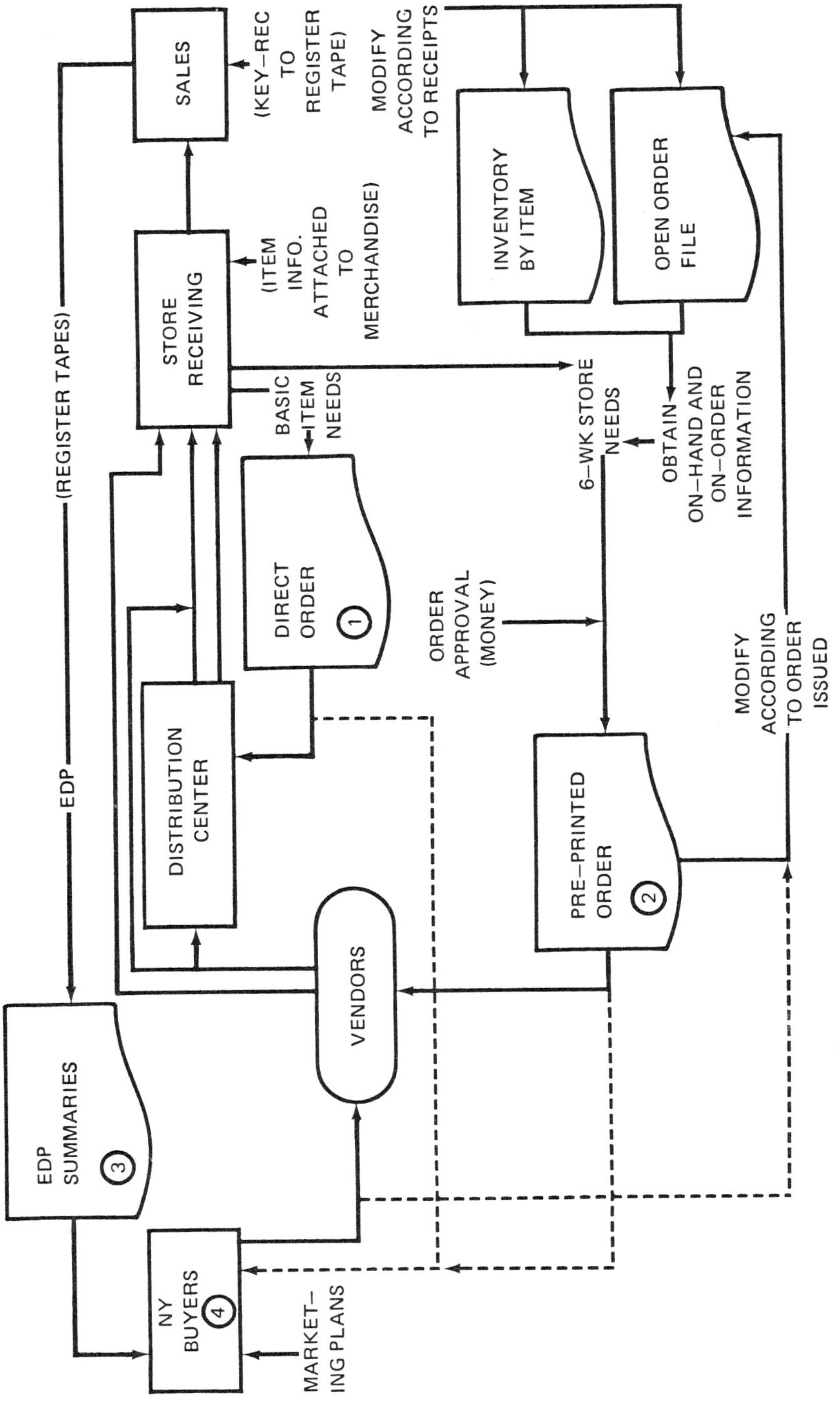

Exhibit 6-11
DISCOUNT, INC. WORK FLOWS

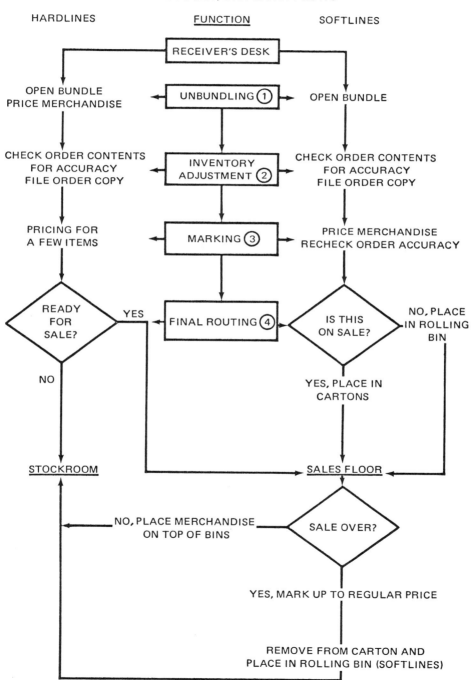

EXERCISE 6-3: Admissions and Registration Division of State University (Part A)

State University is a large multidiscipline university located in the southeast. It has Colleges of Arts and Sciences, Business, Education, and Law, and Schools of Nursing, Home Economics, Theater, Social Welfare, Library Science, and Recreation. Enrollment in the total university has reached 15,000 students, with undergraduate, masters, and doctoral programs in most of its colleges and schools. The university has experienced a very rapid growth in students, faculty, and staff, as well as its overall budget. Recently, the university was required by the legislature to use a state-wide budgeting system which was based primarily on the number of "student credit hours generated" in each disipline or program in the university. These "student credit hours generated" produced faculty positions, which in turn generated expense, capital outlay, and other operating budget needs.

As part of the budgeting process, the university developed projected enrollments for each of ten disciplines or programs for the coming year. These projections of enrollment were converted into faculty and staff position budgets, and support resource budgets (expense, capital outlay, and other resources) by the university administration. A critical feature of this process for State University was the need to develop accurate projections of enrollments. Also, there was a need for information relating to current enrollments during each quarter in order to compare the accuracy of projections with actual enrollments in order to permit timely adjustments to budgets.

The Admissions and Registration Division of the university has the responsibility for making projections of enrollments and for providing timely and accurate information regarding current enrollments. In addition, the Admissions and Registration Division has a variety of responsibilities relating to admitting and registering students each quarter. Because of the rapid growth in enrollments, these responsibilities have been performed in less than an optimum manner. For example, students have had considerable difficulty in finding courses they can take, and as a result considerable dropping and adding of courses take place after the regular registration. This makes it difficult to produce accurate information on current enrollments in each quarter. Also, accurate information on previous years' enrollments is difficult to obtain because of the lack of a good student information system. In the admissions area, the procedures for processing of applications to the university have become very cumbersome because of inadequate procedures and systems for keeping track of requests and applications. This further complicates the job of developing accurate forecasts of enrollments for the coming years, as well as discourages students from attending the university.

In addition to the above problems, the admission and registration process requires an excessive amount of paperwork to be completed by both faculty and students. Much of the process consists of manual operations, and there is considerable redundancy in the forms and reports prepared by students and faculty. In spite of the considerable amount of paperwork required, there is little control over what courses the student can select each quarter. Also, processing of grade or class rosters and final grade reports is quite complex and usually late.

Because of these problems relating to the admissions and registration process and because of the need to develop more reliable enrollment projections and information, the President of the university set up a study group to recommend a restructuring of the admissions and registration process, its organization, responsibilities, and information needs. The main features of this study effort were to: (1) provide more effective procedures and systems for keeping track of the student from the time he first contacts the university about admission until he graduates, (2) develop the means to acquire, process, store, and retrieve information about student applicants, current students, and past students in an accurate and timely manner, (3) minimize the number of drops and adds students process each quarter, and (4) simplify and minimize the requirements laid on faculty and students during the registration period each quarter. The remaining sections describe the recommended functions of the admissions and registration process, and the organization structure and job descriptions of key personnel in the division, as developed and proposed by the study group convened to improve the Admissions and Registration Division.

RECOMMENDED FUNCTIONS, RESPONSIBILITIES, AND CONTROL CONSIDERATIONS

Exhibit 6-12 presents a summary of major functions and work flows pertaining to the Admissions and Registration Division of State University. These are summarized in the following sections.

Development of Supply

The supply development function refers to the development of curriculum and programs, the acquisition of resources such as faculty, housing, space, and financial aid to students, and the presentation of these kinds of information in the university catalog. These factors limit what the university can offer to present and future students in terms of quality, quantity, timing, and cost of programs. The following sections describe the involvement of the Admissions and Registration Division in the supply development functions.

Catalog Development and Maintenance. The development and maintenance of the catalog is the responsibility of the Admissions and Registration Division. The catalog provides information to prospective and current faculty and students regarding academic programs and curricula, admissions and retention criteria, regulations and procedures, and general topics of interest concerning the university. The responsibility of the admissions and registration process is to maintain and coordinate changes to the catalog, while the academic colleges and schools and the university central administration are concerned with policy making regarding academic programs, curriculum, and academic standards.

Exhibit 6-12

ADMISSIONS AND REGISTRATION FUNCTIONS

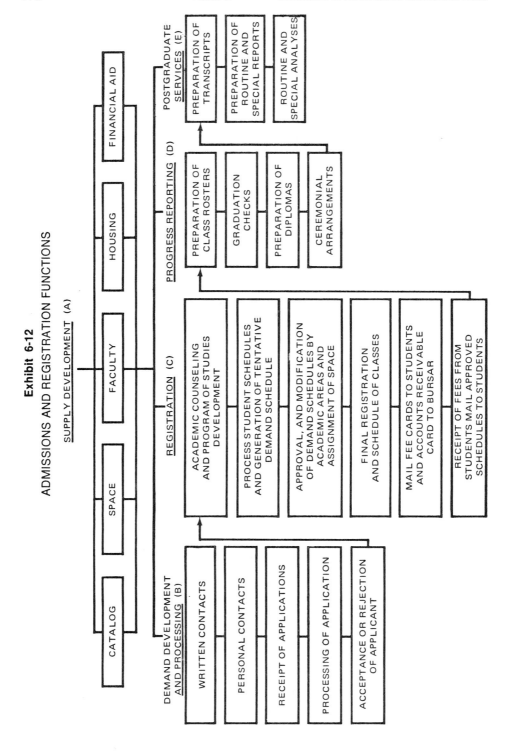

Classroom Space Inventory. A major constraint regarding the performance of the admissions and registration process is the availability of space for assignment of courses offered each quarter. Policies regarding space acquisition and allocation are the responsibility of the academic units and the university central administration. The admissions and registration office is responsible for implementation of these policies in the process of scheduling of courses and for coordination of space utilization throughout the university.

Faculty Availability. The effective performance of the admissions and registration process depends on the availability of faculty for assignment of courses offered each period. Policies regarding faculty acquisition and allocation and assignment to courses are the responsibility of the academic units and the university central administration. The admissions and registration office is responsible for implementation of these policies in the process of scheduling of courses and classes. The greater the number of changes in faculty assignments to courses, the more difficult is the registration process each quarter because many students change courses as instructors change.

Housing Availability. The availability of housing is a major constraint regarding the admissions process for those students required to live in university housing. Policies regarding mandatory residence in student housing are the responsibility of the academic units and the university central administration. The Director of Housing is responsible for implementation of these policies and for notifying the admissions office of the current availability of student housing. The admissions office uses this information to advise prospective students of the availability of housing.

Financial Aid. In some cases the availability of financial aid influences whether a student applies for admission to, or remains enrolled in, the university. Policies and procedures regarding granting of financial aid are the responsibility of the academic units and the university central administration. These policies and procedures are communicated to the admissions and registration office and the Director of Financial Aid for implementation and to attract students to the university.

Demand Development and Processing

The major types of effort involved in attracting students to the university are written and personal communications. The catalog provides the major information for both forms of communication. The admissions office has primary responsibility for initiating and responding to personal and written contacts with students and for coordination of these communications with the schools and colleges.

Demand processing, which is the responsibility of the admissions office, comprises two major activities: implementing admissions policies established in the university catalog, and processing applications received and maintaining information on admissions status for all categories of applicants until an accept or reject decision has been made.

Registration

The registration function comprises academic counseling; course demand analysis, scheduling, and assignment of space; enrollment; and collection of fees.

Academic Counseling. The academic units are responsible for counseling students, developing programs, and developing schedules. They submit approved class schedules and degree programs directly to the registrar.

Tentative scheduling and program development are accomplished for a period greater than one quarter, and ideally for entire program segments (for example, basic studies, upper division, majors, and schools). This permits a reduction of faculty time for counseling and permits a more thorough analysis of demand for courses prior to the beginning of the registration cycle.

Demand Analysis, Scheduling, and Assignment of Space. Based upon the above programs, the Registrar is responsible for developing a tentative demand schedule of sources. In addition to the tentative demand schedule, the tentative final examination schedule, course change procedures, and instructions are prepared and sent to the academic units for approval and for the assignment of classroom space and faculty.

Enrollment and Collection of Fees. The approved schedules from the academic areas are used for final enrollment of students by the Registrar. The Registrar mails a fee card to the students and provides the bursar with an accounts receivable card. Approved schedules are mailed to students by the Registrar after fees have been received by the bursar.

Status and Progress Reporting

Main categories of activity include: progressing class rosters and changes, grade and special status reports, graduation checks, and arrangements for graduation. Rigid controls are established for schedule changes.

Student Data Services

The admissions and registration units are responsible for maintaining student records and for providing routine and special reports and analyses pertaining to admissions and registration. The admissions and registration office also is responsible for developing continuing and special studies in work and data systems relating to admissions and registration activities.

RECOMMENDED STRUCTURE AND JOB DESCRIPTIONS

Exhibit 6-13 presents an organizational chart for the Admissions and Registration Division. Job descriptions for key personnel are as follows.

Exhibit 6-13

ORGANIZATIONAL ALIGNMENTS FOR ADMISSIONS AND REGISTRATION

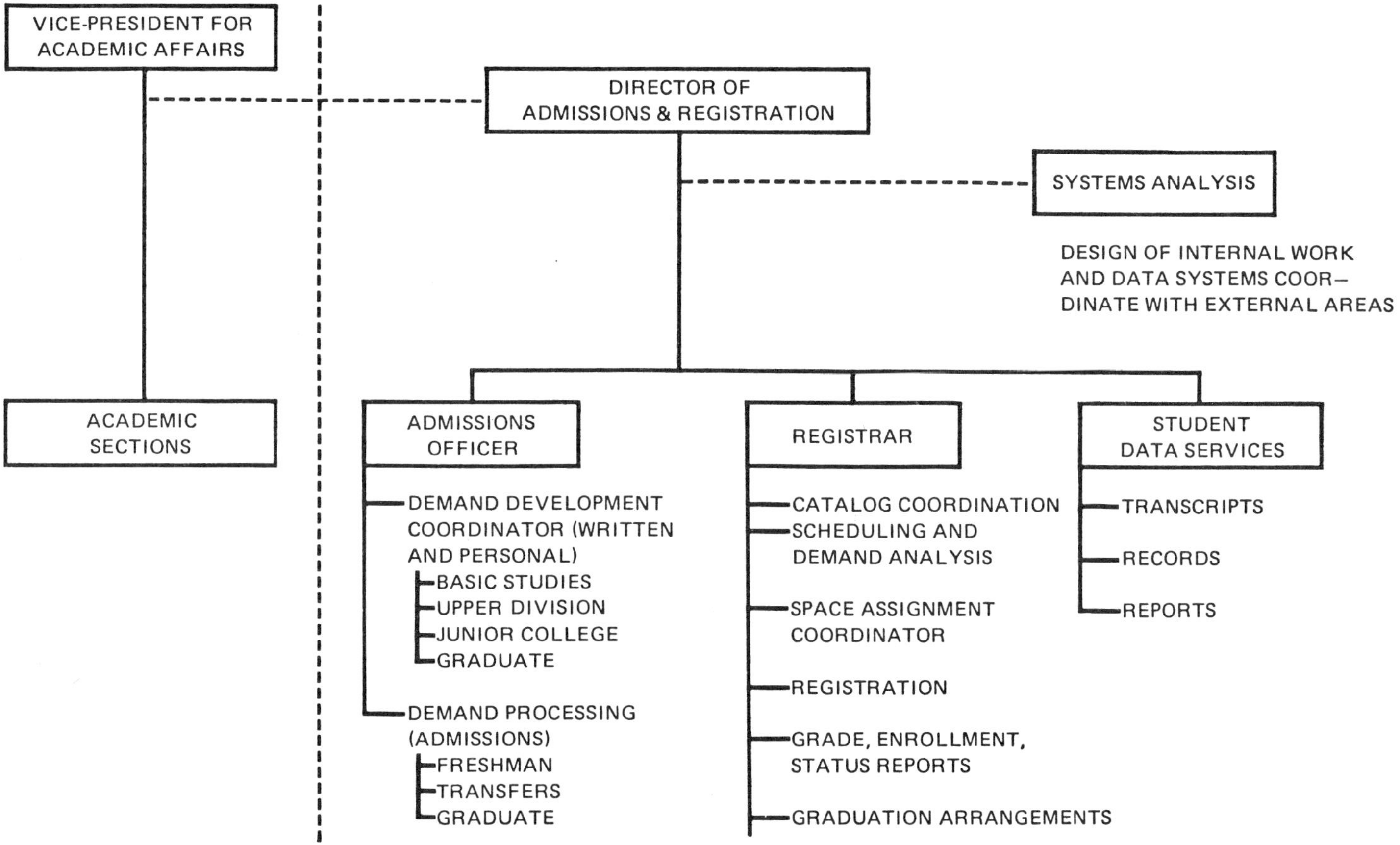

Director, Admissions and Registration

1. Responsible directly to the Vice-President for Academic Affairs for the planning, organization, and direction of the admissions, registration and record keeping of the University.
2. Implement University-wide policies and procedures relative to admissions and registration within the constraints of legislative statutes.
3. Direct and coordinate the preparation of operating budgets for the admissions and registration functions.
4. Participate in interpretation and implementation of University-wide policies with academic and student sectors and review policies recommended by subordinates in the admissions and registration area.
5. Provide information for use by external departments and organizations such as: academic deans, planning and research personnel, President and Vice-presidents, Board of Regents and staff, and U.S. Department of Education.

Admissions Officer

1. Report to and perform duties under the general direction of the Director, Admissions and Registration.
2. Implement the academic policies and regulations pertaining to the admission of students until an accept or reject decision has been made.
3. Provide for the supervision and processing of the admission of all students.
4. Provide for the evaluation of admissions of all undergraduate students.
5. Coordinate the evaluation for admission of all graduate students with the various schools and colleges.
6. Coordinate programs for giving advice and information to prospective students, parents, high school and junior college guidance counselors, and the general public concerning requirements, course offerings, and related matters.
7. Generate and send data on all activities, inquiries, and applications to Student Data Services.
8. Perform related duties as required or deemed appropriate to the accomplishment of the responsibilities and functions of the office.

Registrar

1. Report to and perform duties under the direction of the Director, Admissions and Registration.
2. Compile and maintain a master catalog for the University.
3. Administer the academic policies and regulations pertaining to registration and graduation.

4. Collect and process student schedules or programs as received directly from academic areas and generate tentative course demand schedules.
5. Coordinate tentative course demand schedules with academic units for approval, modification, and assignment of space (when appropriate), and develop final registration materials needed for scheduling classes.
6. Mail fee cards to students and accounts receivable cards to Bursar. (Bursar receives mail receipts of fees from students.) Mail approved class schedules to students after notification that fees have been received.
7. Supervise and process changes of schedules.
8. Coordinate the assignment and utilization of instructional space.
9. Prepare special status reports (class rosters, grades, graduation checks) and process and mail out final grades.
10. Coordinate graduation arrangements and requirements.
11. Perform related duties as required or deemed appropriate to the accomplishment of the responsibilities and function of the office.

Director, Student Data Services

1. Report to and perform duties under the general direction of the Director, Admissions and Registration.
2. Maintain official records of all present and former students.
3. Implement modifications or new systems for student data collection, storage, and display within the admissions and registration areas.
4. Prepare input data for processing by the Data Processing Department.
5. Provide coordination in the processing of student data among the: admissions and registration areas, Data Processing Department, and other departments such as Alumni Association, Student Affairs, and Financial Affairs.
6. Provide routine and special reports and analyses pertaining to admissions and registration.
7. Perform related duties as required or deemed appropriate to the accomplishment of the responsibilities and functions of the office.

Systems Analyst

1. A staff position reporting to and performing duties under the general direction of the Director, Admissions and Registration.
2. Responsible for performing continuing and special studies in work and data systems.
3. Responsible for coordinating special studies within the admissions and registration area, and among external organizational units having systems that interface with the admissions and registration activity.

Using the framework for analysis provided in Exhibits 5-1 and 6-1, perform the following:

1. Identify and discuss several constraints relating to the university environment, and specifically to students and faculty, that are important for the operation of the Admissions and Registration Division.

2. As the Director of Admissions and Registration, identify and describe the types of information that you feel you would need to minimize the types of problems that caused the formation of the study group. Identify the following types of information needs:

   a. Information needed for planning admissions and registration activities.

   b. Information needed for operational control of admissions, registration, and graduation activities.

3. Evaluate the proposed set of functions, organization, and responsibilities recommended by the study group in terms of their contribution for resolving the problems in the case.

7 INFORMATION FOR MANAGERIAL/FINANCIAL CONTROL

Managerial/financial control involves the evaluation of performance of the total operation and its responsibility centers on a periodic, postoperating basis. This means that the accomplishments of responsibility center managers, including the total organization as the major responsibility center, are measured, analyzed, and compared with the objectives and budgets formulated during the planning stage. Whereas operational control emphasizes the control of resource flows (inputs) and work performance (outputs) on a continuous basis, managerial/financial control emphasizes the control of entire processing systems as responsibility centers. This includes the evaluation of resources used and products/services produced by each responsibility center and the total organization, in addition to financial reporting for internal control and for satisfying external information requirements.

Much of the information developed and utilized in managerial/financial control is derived from planning and operational control reports and documents. Also, the decisions based on managerial/financial control information are in turn used for future planning of operational objectives, budgets, and policies. Thus, the preoperating (planning), operating (operational control), and postoperating (managerial/financial control) periods are intricately tied together by the information and reports produced in each period.

This chapter, which discusses the information needed for effective managerial/financial control, has these specific objectives:

1. To describe managerial/financial control and to provide examples of analyses involved in defining information needed for managerial/financial control.
2. To describe the structure, purpose, and use of managerial performance reports and provide examples of these reports.
3. To describe several types of financial control reports that are useful for evaluation of the financial performance of the organization and that are required by external agencies.

Before examining the information needs and the reports required for managerial/financial control, the meaning of managerial/financial control must be firmly established.

MANAGERIAL/FINANCIAL CONTROL

Managerial/financial control, as a major function of management, is concerned with the evaluation of performance of the total organization and its responsibility centers on a periodic basis. The evaluation relates this performance to the organization's objectives, plans, and budgets. The decisions made on the basis of this evaluation are linked with the operational control and planning functions of management since they concern future adjustments to objectives, plans, and operating budgets. A production cost overrun for office desks or an underprojection of net revenue per office desk will influence the company's next period operating cost and revenue budget, as well as the profit and cash flow projections. If costs become excessive or the price of desks decreases substantially, the company may be forced to alter its product lines or even drop a line of desks if it is very unprofitable.

The central emphasis of managerial/financial control is on the comparison and evaluation of actual versus projected performance of managers of responsibility centers and the financial performance of the total organization. The effective execution of the managerial/financial control function involves the evaluation of performance and corrective action. Exhibit 7-1 provides a conceptual framework for analyzing these activities for the purpose of defining the types of information needed to facilitate managerial/financial control. To support decisions relating to evaluation of performance and for taking corrective action, analyses are undertaken which should provide answers to the following two general questions:

1. What is the *actual versus projected performance of responsibility centers* (0810)?
2. What is the *actual versus projected financial performance of the total organization* (0820)?

Answers to these two general questions should produce information relating to the status of managerial performance (0811 to 0813) and organizational financial performance (0821 to 0832) so that adjustments to future objectives, plans, and operating budgets can be formulated (0911), or systems studies can be designed (0912).

The two general questions to be answered are not intended to be universal, yet they include the most important types of analyses which are needed for effective managerial/financial control. Without extensive analyses and information relating to the resources used and work produced by responsibility centers, managers of these responsibility centers can not be evaluated, nor can future resource needs be estimated effectively. This is also true for the total organization in that it is essentially a major responsibility center comprising a number of specialized functional responsibility centers. In addition, external agencies require information relating to the financial performance of the organization.

The following sections provide example answers to these two general questions for an office furniture manufacturer and a state university. These examples reflect the types of analyses and information involved in operational

Exhibit 7-1

THE MANAGERIAL/FINANCIAL CONTROL FUNCTION
(POSTOPERATING PERIOD ANALYSIS)

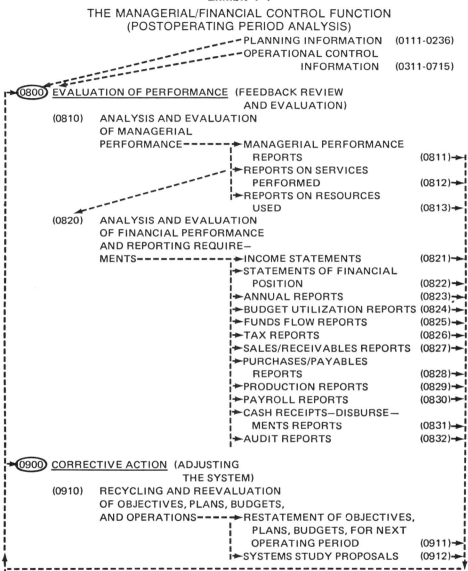

PLANNING INFORMATION   (0111-0236)
OPERATIONAL CONTROL
INFORMATION   (0311-0715)

(0800) EVALUATION OF PERFORMANCE (FEEDBACK REVIEW
AND EVALUATION)

(0810)   ANALYSIS AND EVALUATION
OF MANAGERIAL
PERFORMANCE————►MANAGERIAL PERFORMANCE
REPORTS   (0811)
►REPORTS ON SERVICES
PERFORMED   (0812)
►REPORTS ON RESOURCES
USED   (0813)

(0820)   ANALYSIS AND EVALUATION
OF FINANCIAL PERFORMANCE
AND REPORTING REQUIRE—
MENTS————————►INCOME STATEMENTS   (0821)
►STATEMENTS OF FINANCIAL
POSITION   (0822)
►ANNUAL REPORTS   (0823)
►BUDGET UTILIZATION REPORTS (0824)
►FUNDS FLOW REPORTS   (0825)
►TAX REPORTS   (0826)
►SALES/RECEIVABLES REPORTS   (0827)
►PURCHASES/PAYABLES
REPORTS   (0828)
►PRODUCTION REPORTS   (0829)
►PAYROLL REPORTS   (0830)
►CASH RECEIPTS—DISBURSE—
MENTS REPORTS   (0831)
►AUDIT REPORTS   (0832)

(0900) CORRECTIVE ACTION (ADJUSTING
THE SYSTEM)

(0910)   RECYCLING AND REEVALUATION
OF OBJECTIVES, PLANS, BUDGETS,
AND OPERATIONS————►RESTATEMENT OF OBJECTIVES,
PLANS, BUDGETS, FOR NEXT
OPERATING PERIOD   (0911)
►SYSTEMS STUDY PROPOSALS   (0912)

(0100) (0200) PLANNING FUNCTION

NOTES:

1. THE NUMBERING SYSTEM SHOWN IS AN EXTENSION OF THE ONE USED
   IN EXHIBIT 5-2.
2. SEE NOTES 2 AND 3 OF EXHIBIT 5-2 CONCERNING LIMITATIONS AND
   CHARACTERISTICS OF THE FLOWS, ACTIVITIES, AND DOCUMENTS DE—
   SCRIBED IN THIS EXHIBIT.

control for each type of organization, and they are patterned generally around the framework provided in Exhibit 7-1.

Evaluation of Managerial Performance

The evaluation of managerial performance involves periodic analysis and comparison of the products/services produced by organizational responsibility centers with the resources used to produce them. An office furniture company analyzes the unit costs of office desks and chairs fabricated by the fabrication department, assembled by the assembly department, and finished by the finishing department. In addition, the company needs information on the total resources used by each of these departments to perform analyses of future resource requirements for each of these production functions, as well as to evaluate the performances of their managers.

For a state university, the responsibility centers, such as schools or colleges, are service oriented. Information about services performed includes the number of credit hours produced, students advised, degrees granted, and research projects completed. Resources used include faculty salaries, classroom and research facilities and equipment, and materials and supplies. Performance of academic units is stated in terms such as cost per credit hour produced by each academic department, discipline, school, and college. Similar information is compiled for the total university in order to perform analyses of future resource requirements for its major functions such as instruction, research, and student advising.

The analyses and information relating to the evaluation of managerial performance are somewhat similar to those related to operational control in that they reflect actual versus projected performance in terms of resources used and products/services produced. The major features of managerial performance reports (versus operational control reports) are:

1. They emphasize evaluation of processing systems or responsibility centers, while operational control evaluates use of resources (inputs) or performance of work (outputs).
2. Their purpose is to evaluate the performance of specific people, namely managers of responsibility centers, rather than the flow of resources or production of work (as in the case of operational control). This evaluation process also develops a cost-benefit awareness on the part of managers, in that they are evaluated on the basis of resources used versus services performed.
3. They have periodic and somewhat regular reporting frequencies, unlike real-time or exception reports.
4. They relate formal organizational segments through managers (e.g., reports on the performance of the fabrication, assembly, and finishing departments can be combined to produce a production division performance report).

Because of the distinctive features of managerial performance reports, it is useful to treat these types of reports separately for the purpose of designing the MIS.

Evaluation of Financial Performance

The evaluation of financial performance is a natural extension of the evaluation of managerial performance in that the total organization is in itself a responsibility center. Thus, its performance is evaluated in terms of total resources used and total products/services produced. In addition, an extensive number of financial analyses are performed relating to six basic types of financial transactions: sales, accounts receivables, cash receipts, purchases, payroll, and cash disbursements, as shown in Exhibits 7-2 through 7-7, respectively. These six basic types of financial transactions are the core of the financial evaluation process, both for *internal control* and for *external financial reporting*. Financial transactions are the basic components of the organization's operations. They include exchanges of products/services with external parties and the transfer of resources and services within the organization. The primary activities involved in the flow of transactions, resources used, and work performed include authorization, execution, and recording of transactions and accountability for assets or resources.[1]

Authorization relates to any transaction that conforms to specified conditions. The establishment of sales prices for office furniture, setting of credit limits for furniture buyers, automatic reorder points for wood inventory, and manpower ceilings are examples of general authorizations. A specific authorization, on the other hand, includes conditions stipulated by both parties, such as purchase orders, employment contracts, materials specifications, and work orders.

Execution of transactions includes the steps necessary to complete the transaction. The execution of a sales transaction involves the acceptance of a sales order, shipment, billing, and collection of payment. A purchase transaction involves the requisition, procurement, receipt, inspection, and payment of purchase price.

Recording of transactions includes the records maintained with respect to all activities performed, resources used, and products/services produced relating to each transaction. The recording process includes the preparation and summarization of records and their posting to the general ledger and subsidiary ledgers.

Accountability for assets or resources requires the maintenance of records on their acquisition, use, and disposition, and a periodic comparison of information on these records with existing stocks of resources. The reconciliation of cash balances with bank statements and the reconciliation of perpetual inventory records with physical inventory counts are examples of the accountability process.

The evaluation of financial performance involves analyses of the six basic financial transactions described above. These analyses provide information to facilitate the evaluation of the organization's financial performance. For example, the furniture company analyzes its revenue transactions, resource acquisition transactions, and expense of its operations and its financial

---

[1] Based on Statement of Auditing Standards, AICPA, 1973.

Exhibit 7-2

SALES TRANSACTIONS

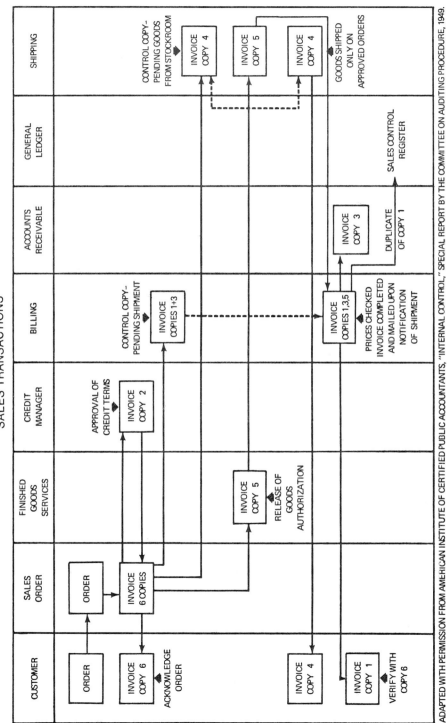

ADAPTED WITH PERMISSION FROM AMERICAN INSTITUTE OF CERTIFIED PUBLIC ACCOUNTANTS, "INTERNAL CONTROL," SPECIAL REPORT BY THE COMMITTEE ON AUDITING PROCEDURE, 1949.

Exhibit 7-3

ACCOUNTS RECEIVABLE TRANSACTIONS

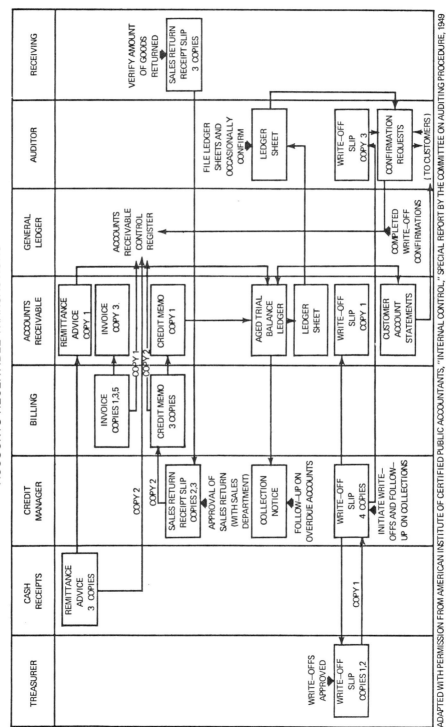

ADAPTED WITH PERMISSION FROM AMERICAN INSTITUTE OF CERTIFIED PUBLIC ACCOUNTANTS, "INTERNAL CONTROL," SPECIAL REPORT BY THE COMMITTEE ON AUDITING PROCEDURE, 1949

Exhibit 7-4

CASH RECEIPTS TRANSACTIONS

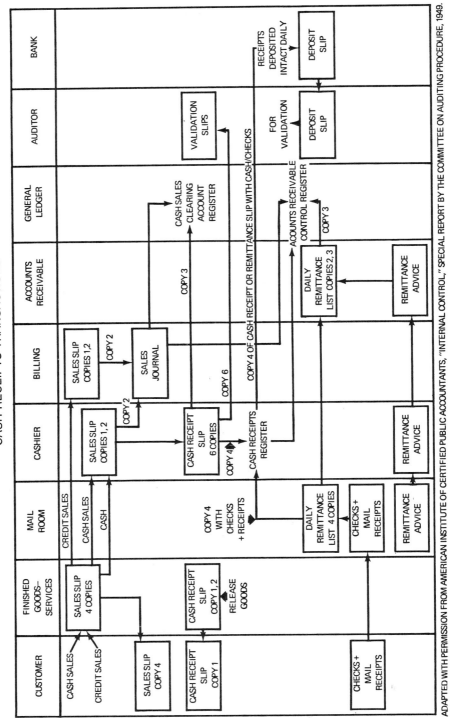

ADAPTED WITH PERMISSION FROM AMERICAN INSTITUTE OF CERTIFIED PUBLIC ACCOUNTANTS, "INTERNAL CONTROL," SPECIAL REPORT BY THE COMMITTEE ON AUDITING PROCEDURE, 1949.

Exhibit 7-5

PURCHASES TRANSACTIONS

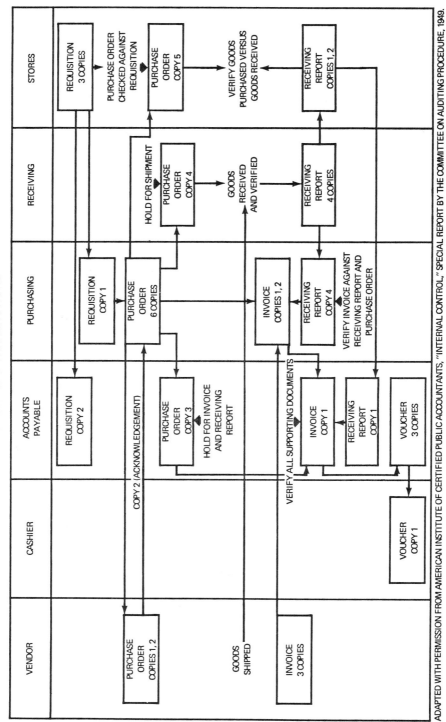

Exhibit 7-6
PAYROLL TRANSACTIONS

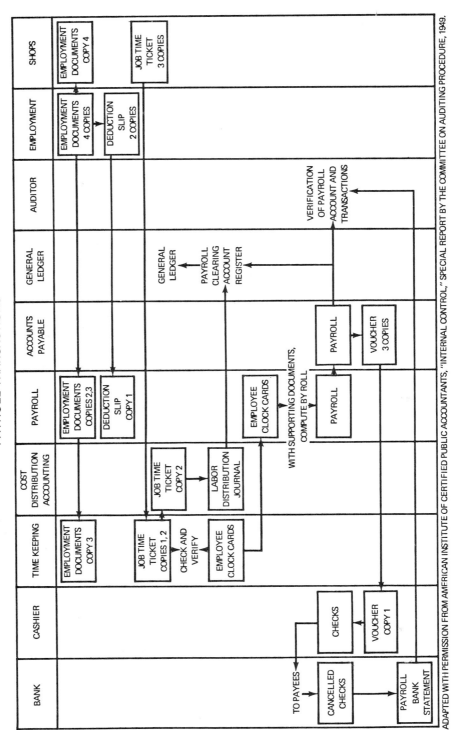

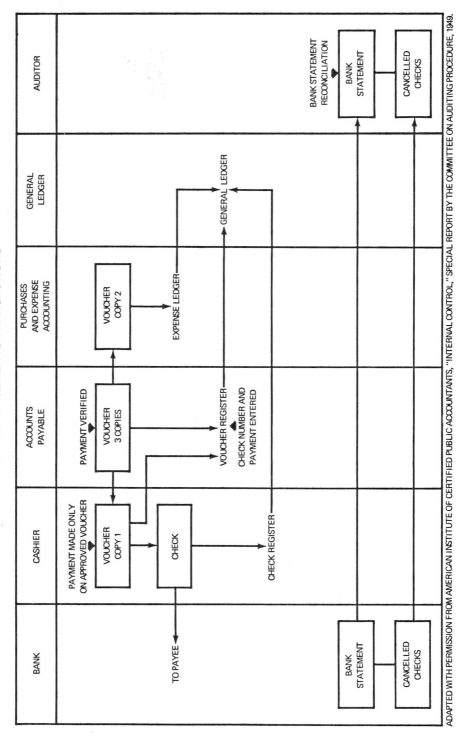

Exhibit 7-7
CASH DISBURSEMENTS TRANSACTIONS

ADAPTED WITH PERMISSION FROM AMERICAN INSTITUTE OF CERTIFIED PUBLIC ACCOUNTANTS, "INTERNAL CONTROL," SPECIAL REPORT BY THE COMMITTEE ON AUDITING PROCEDURE, 1949.

position, which are reflected in income statements, statements of financial position, and funds flow statements. In addition, the company performs analyses of transactions such as those relating to sales orders, sales returns, purchase orders, work orders, time slips, issue slips, and cash receipts and disbursements, in order to provide more detailed information on the financial performance of segments of its operations.

In a university, where no income statements or profits are involved, financial performance is evaluated in terms of budget utilization for the production of instructional, research, and student-related services. Except for the information relating to profits or sales, most of the financial information and related analyses are similar for a university and a business firm. The university is concerned with analyses of its purchases/payables, production (instruction and research), materials usage, schedules of work, and cash receipts and disbursements transactions or events, as is a business firm.

In both business firms and nonprofit organizations such as universities, a large amount of information is compiled for external agencies. The business firm must prepare information for stockholders, investors or creditors, and taxing agencies (federal, state, and local) in the form of compliance reports. The university prepares reports on its financial position for the Board of Regents, Department of Education, and the state legislature, plus national agencies such as the Department of Education or agencies that award contracts and grants to the university

Similarly to managerial performance information, financial performance information provides the basis for decisions which affect future objectives, plans and operating budgets. Thus, financial evaluation facilitates the linking of operational control and planning since periodic financial evaluations are timed to coincide with the budget cycle. The major features of financial evaluation are:

1. It includes information on revenues, costs, profits, and funds flow within the context of cost, profit, or investment responsibility centers.
2. Its purpose is to evaluate the financial performance of the total organization and its cost, profit, and investment centers and to report this performance to external agencies and to the management of the organization.
3. It has periodic reporting frequencies which coincide with the budget cycle.

The overall purpose of managerial/financial control is to insure that the operations of the organization are financially sound and that its managers are performing efficiently.

The evaluation of managerial/financial performance through transaction analyses interrelates the formal organizational components which have a vertical authority/responsibility emphasis and the flow of resources (through transactions), which tends to have a horizontal (or systems) organizational emphasis.

For example, a sales order for office desks originates in sales, its cost is estimated by a cost accountant, procurement acquires the materials for production to produce the desks which are delivered by the traffic department to the customer. The work involved and resource flows required to produce and deliver the desks on time and within the cost specified cuts across several organizational responsibility centers, and the control of these work and resource flows are facilitated by operational control information, such as schedules, cost, quantity, and quality variance reports related to the office desks produced. These reports do not reflect the performance of responsibility centers, such as the fabrication, assembly, and financing departments in production, or the sales, accounting, procurement, or traffic divisions. This does not mean that similar types of information are not included on both managerial performance and operational control reports, as will be shown in the discussion of managerial performance reports later in this chapter; however, the frequency, purpose, and arrangement of the information on managerial performance reports impose different requirements on the MIS.

The foregoing description and examples of managerial/financial control show that these evaluation processes are highly interrelated, and that they involve a large number of variables and types of information. Also, similar to planning and operational control, managerial/financial control analyses and decisions generate large amounts of important information (a number of examples are shown in Exhibit 7-1). Some of this information is a major input to the MIS, which processes it into reports for planning and corrective action. As such, it is a link between planning periods, since managerial performance and general financial performance information are used to develop demand analyses, resource capacity status reports, and budgets for the next operating period.

In many respects, managerial/financial control information is the primary segment of the MIS. Much of the information included in managerial performance and financial performance reports concerns planning and operational control. In addition, a large amount of managerial/financial control information is used by operating areas for evaluating the performance of managerial responsibility centers. Finally, external users and agencies utilize large amounts of financial performance information.

The foregoing discussion implies that management's information needs are highly interrelated. It is for simplicity and ease of analysis and design of the MIS that planning, operational control, and managerial/financial control functions are treated somewhat separately. The remainder of this chapter describes several types of managerial performance and financial performance reports.

MANAGERIAL PERFORMANCE REPORTS

The primary purpose of managerial performance reports is to facilitate the evaluation of each manager's performance. While the operational control reports described in Chapter 6 are also performance reports, they do not directly consider responsibility for performance. A managerial performance report provides information regarding what resources are used versus what products/services are produced by a specific responsibility center within the organization. This information is used by the next higher level manager to evaluate the performance of the lower level manager under his responsibility and to adjust operations within his responsibility center if unfavorable performance occurs. Thus, managerial performance reports provide information that interrelates the vertical chain of command explicit in the formal organization structure. On the other hand, operational control reports provide information on the interrelationship of decisions, work, and resource flows throughout the organization.

Within the basic framework of formal organization structure and the notion of relating resources used (inputs) to products/services performed (outputs), the following sections describe performance reports in the more detailed terms of reporting levels, measures of outputs, measures of inputs, and input-output performance measures. Some examples of managerial performance reports are also presented.

Reporting Levels

Since managerial performance reports focus on the formal vertical chain of command, the organization is viewed as a set of reporting levels as shown by the example in Exhibit 7-8. Exhibit 7-8 illustrates reporting levels, especially the relationship of the Production Superintendent to other organizational levels, of a hypothetical manufacturing company. There are six reporting levels that incorporate information on the operations of the Production Superintendent. At the first level, three foremen submit reports to the Production Superintendent, who in turn is required to report to the second level (General Manager of Production) on matters dealing with overall performance of the department. The General Manager of Production then submits information on overall performance of his operations to the Vice-President of Production. Pertinent information is compiled on overall operations for the President and Board of Directors.

Exhibit 7-9 shows a simplified example of the performance reporting system for the Production Superintendent, focusing on the interrelationship of the first two reporting levels that were identified in Exhibit 7-8. The interdependency of the two reporting levels is identified in Exhibit 7-9 by compiling cost and performance information at the foreman reporting level, and relating this information to cost and performance information for the next higher reporting level by production superintendent.

As reflected in the example report shown in Exhibit 7-9, each managerial performance report contains three major sections: measures of output, resources used, and measures of performance. The following sections describe these three parts of a managerial performance report in more detail.

Measures of Output

Measures of output should reflect the output produced by a responsibility center in terms of products/services produced. Measures of output may be stated in dollar or statistical terms (e.g., units or percentages), and they may be

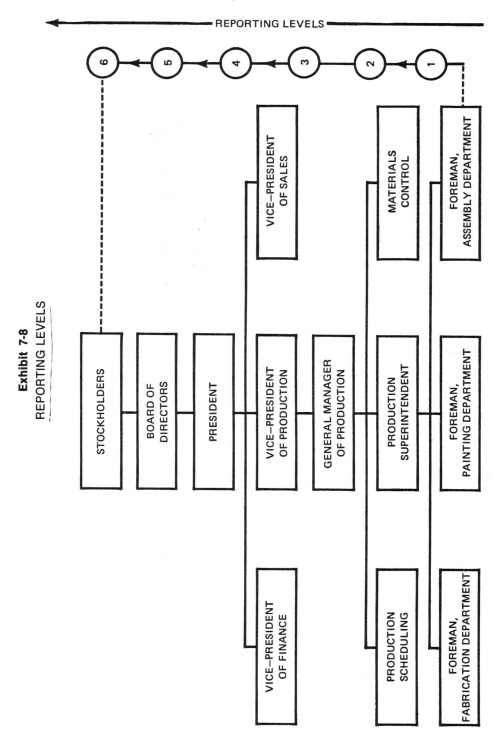

Exhibit 7-8
REPORTING LEVELS

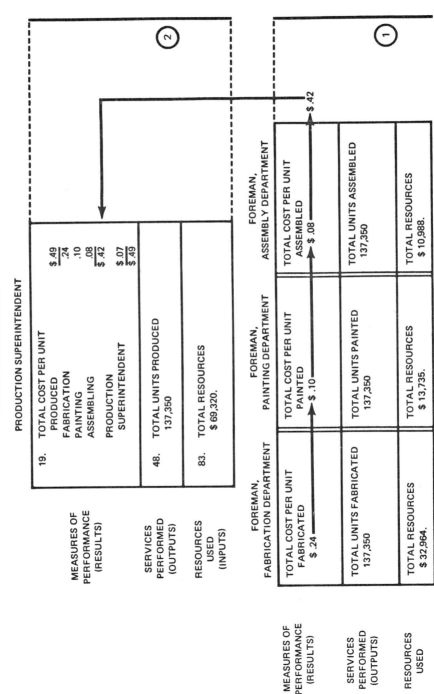

Exhibit 7-9
PERFORMANCE REPORTS

positive or negative in nature. The measures of output selected should reflect the nature of responsibilities assigned to the manager. Examples of measures of output are shown below.

For a Sales Responsibility Center

Dollars or units of sales generated
Percent or dollar share of sales market attained
Number of salesmen's calls completed
Number of customer complaints processed

For a Production Responsibility Center

Units of work completed or finished goods produced
Hours of production downtime
Units or dollars of materials wasted or lost
Number of quality rejects

For a Procurement Responsibility Center

Dollar value of purchase orders issued or processed
Number of purchase orders issued or processed
Number of late deliveries of materials
Number of material out-of-stock conditions

For a Personnel Responsibility Center

Number of employees served
Number of employee turnovers
Number of employee grievances handled
Number of job interviews completed

Defining valid output measures may be difficult, especially for a service activity where there is no physical product, such as personnel. To facilitate this procedure, it is useful to think in terms of the variables that can be used to justify a budget increase. Generally a manager can define a number of activity variables to support a budget request, and these should then be used as measures of output. A personnel manager may request additional personnel analysts because the number of job interviews or employee grievances is increasing. The evaluation of the performance of the personnel responsibility center should include these variables in order to evaluate changes in output (e.g., number of job interviews or employee grievances) that were projected in the budgeting process.

In this way, the budgeting process is related to the performance system. The controller may justify a budget increase of two additional accountants due to an increase in the volume of invoices to be processed. If the volume of invoices to be processed is a valid variable to justify a budget increase, then it also becomes a valid measure of output to be included in the controller's performance report.

Measures of Input

Resources used or costs incurred are the primary measures of input. As in the case of output measures, inputs may be stated in statistical (e.g., units or percentages) as well as dollar terms. Two major alternatives exist for deciding what costs should be included in the performance report of a manager. First, the costs included can be those that are controllable by the manager, or only variable costs which change in proportion to changes in activity might be included. Examples of these types of costs include materials and labor used in the production of finished goods, travel costs, and advertising costs.

A second major alternative for deciding which costs to include on a managerial performance report is total costs of the operation of the responsibility centers. This requires some allocation of costs for items such as occupancy and administration. Including total costs on his performance report will make the manager more aware of the impact of his decisions on total costs of his operation. For example, a manager generally does not have direct control over fringe benefits and occupancy costs, but his decisions regarding requests for additional space or personnel influence these costs. Justifications for these types of requests should include an evaluation of the total cost impact on the organization, rather than only direct salary or space acquisition costs.

If occupancy costs, fringe benefits, and other general administrative costs are placed in a general overhead account which is not allocated to specific responsibility centers, then the purpose and benefits of these overhead costs are not as clearly related to the performances of responsibility centers. Subsequently, managers are likely to develop the view that these overhead costs belong to, and should be controlled by, top management.

On the other hand, if top management allocates these overhead costs in the budgets of responsibility centers, and if they are included in the evaluation of managerial performance, managers will become more concerned with organization-wide financial problems and will examine the validity of the cost allocation to insure that it reflects their specific operations.

A special type of overhead cost allocation relates to the allocation of the costs of a computerized MIS. A responsibility center is charged for the direct costs of producing reports by data processing. Under the total cost allocation procedure, allocations for costs of managing the data processing facility, systems design and monitoring costs, and other supporting MIS costs are allocated to users of the MIS manpower and facilities. Users of the MIS outputs are more likely to examine the efficiency and effectiveness of the MIS than if total costs were not allocated.

In conclusion, measures of input should reflect the total costs of the responsibility center if its budget is to reflect meaningful projections of resources needed for future operations. In addition, more meaningful measures of performance (input-output measures) can be developed.

Measures of Performance

Measures of performance provide the means for relating the outputs produced by a responsibility center to its inputs. As input-output measures, they facilitate the evaluation of the cost-effectiveness of the activities of a responsibility center. Examples of measures of performance are shown below:

For a Sales Responsibility Center

Dollar or unit sales per salesman/sales region

Customer calls completed per salesman

Number of customer complaints processed per salesman/sales region

Advertising/distribution/salesman costs per dollar revenue

For A Production Responsibility Center

Labor/material/total costs per product or finished good

Dollar costs of material wasted per total dollar costs of materials used

Number of quality rejects per total number of units processed

Total production costs per total company revenues/budgets

For a Procurement Responsibility Center

Total procurement costs per total dollar purchases

Number of late deliveries per total number of purchases

Administrative costs of procurement per purchase order processed

Total procurement costs per total company revenues/budgets

For a Personnel Responsibility Center

Number of employee turnovers per total number of employees

Number of personnel employees per total number of employees

Number of grievances per total number of employees

Recruiting/training costs per employee hired/trained

A measure of performance as an input-output measure highlights favorable or unfavorable trends in the performance of a responsibility center. For example, an increase in the labor cost per finished good indicates a probable inefficiency in production. An increase in administrative costs of procurement per purchase order indicates a possible inefficient procurement procedure. Without relating inputs (e.g., labor cost or administrative procurement cost) to outputs (e.g., finished goods produced or purchase orders processed), the cost-effectiveness of the product or procurement activities can not be evaluated effectively. Looking at only inputs or outputs provides only partial explanation of the performance of the responsibility center.

Examples of Managerial Performance Reports

To extend the examples of the business firm and the university used throughout Chapters 4, 5, and 6, Exhibit 7-10 shows modified managerial performance reports for these two types of organizations. As shown in the foregoing examples, the types of information contained in managerial performance reports provide both good visibility concerning output and cost performance on a macro or total basis for each category of output or cost, and measures of performance which show unit cost/output information. For example, the increase in total resources used for the production of office desks in the fabricating department ($9,000) was due to an increase in the desk unit

Exhibit 7-10
MODIFIED MANAGERIAL PERFORMANCE REPORTS
FOR A BUSINESS FIRM AND A UNIVERSITY

Business Firm (Manager, Fabricating Department) *			
Services (Outputs) Performed:	Projected	Actual	Variance
* Office Desks Fabricated	200	250	+ 50
* Office Chairs Fabricated	400	500	+100
Resources (Inputs) Used:			

* *Direct Labor–*
  * Office Desks
  * Office Chairs
	$ 6,000
	3,200
		$ 7,750
		4,500
			+$ 1,750
			+ 1,300

* *Materials–*
  * Office Desks
  * Office Chairs
	$10,000
	6,000
		$13,750
		8,000
			+$ 3,750
			+ 2,000

* *Other Expenses–*
  * Offices Desks
  * Office Chairs
	$14,000
	8,800
		$17,500
		12,000
			+$ 3,500
			+ 3,200

*Total Resources
Used*
  • Office Desks
  • Office Chairs
	$48,000
	$30,000
	18,000
		$63,500
		$39,000
		24,500
			+$15,500
			+$ 9,000
			+ 6,500

Measures of Performance:			
Direct labor per desk Direct labor per chair Materials per desk Materials per chair	$ 30 8 50 15	$ 35 9 55 16	$ +5 +1 +5 +1

* Code numbers need to be assigned from coding system or chart of accounts. These will be developed for this example in Chapter 9.

cost of production as well as an increase in the number of desks produced (200 to 250). The fabricating department's unit cost of materials used has increased ($30 to $35), as well as its unit direct labor ($15 to $16). On the other hand, the faculty salary cost per credit hour taught has decreased for graduate instruction ($83 to $69), while the salary cost per undergraduate credit hour has increased ($56 to $67). These changes can be explained in terms of the increase in graduate enrollment (12,000 to 14,400 credit hours) and a comparable decrease in undergraduate enrollment, coupled with no change in the number of faculty (120) or faculty salaries ($1,000,000 and $800,000, respectively). The complete information for each of the examples (i.e., all outputs and resources used) would provide additional insights on the performance levels of each business manager or college dean.

In summary, managerial performance reports provide information which facilitates the evaluation of responsibility center managers in terms of the

Exhibit 7-10 (Continued)

University (Dean, School of Business) *			
Services (Outputs) Performed	Projected	Actual	Variance
* Credit Hours Taught- Undergraduate	14,400	12,000	−2,400
˙ Credit Hours Taught- Graduate	12,000	14,400	+2,400
Total Hours	26,400	26,400	..:....
* Students Graduated	600	500	− 100
Resources (Inputs) Used:			
* No. of Faculty	120	120	......
* Faculty Salaries- Undergraduate (000)	$ 800	$ 800	......
* Faculty Salaries Graduate (000)	$ 1,000	$ 1,000	......
* Other Expenses (000)	$ 300	$ 300	......
Total Resources Used (000)	$ 2,100	$ 2,100	......
Measures of Performance:			
Faculty salary cost per undergraduate credit hr.	$ 56	$ 67	+$ 11
Faculty salary cost per graduate credit hour	$ 83	$ 69	−$ 14
Total faculty salary cost per credit hour	$ 68	$ 68	......

efficiency of their input-output processing systems. This performance information provides insights on:

1. Which outputs are produced by the responsibility center.
2. Which resources or inputs are used to produce these outputs.
3. How effective the performance of the responsibility center is in terms of services performed (outputs) versus resources used (inputs).

These insights about responsibility center performance provide the basis for not only evaluating managerial performance, but also identifying favorable or unfavorable trends. The discovery of such trends enables the needed adjustments to operations to be made. Finally, managerial performance reports focus on performance of formal organizational components, while operational control reports focus on the flows of decisions, work, and resource use through formal organizational components. Financial control reports, which are discussed is the next section, focus on the financial condition of the organization for internal control and external reporting purposes.

FINANCIAL PERFORMANCE REPORTS

In many respects, the term financial reporting is misleading since all of the reports needed for operations and management include financial information. Demand analysis, resource capacity analysis, logistics management, and managerial performance reports include both financial and statistical information. The classification of part of the information needs for management as "financial performance reports" is used to emphasize the importance and extensiveness of the information involved to facilitate financial control.

Financial performance reports, as summaries of the financial condition of the organization, in many cases are compliance reports in that they reflect external demands for information by governmental agencies such as the Securities Exchange Commission and Internal Revenue Service, and by investor groups such as stockholders and creditors. In addition to the external compliance nature of financial performance reports, an extensive amount of financial information is used for internal control. These two broad types of financial performance information are described in the following sections. As in the case of other types of information needs of management, these two types of information overlap and are highly interrelated, and are separated here for illustrative purposes.

External Compliance Information

Three major types of financial information are related to external compliance reporting. One major type of information is related to the effectiveness or efficiency of operations and management over a period of time, which is reflected in income statements or statements of earnings and budget utilization reports. Exhibit 7-11 shows an income statement for a business firm. In actual practice, more detailed information is shown on the income statement or on subsidiary income statements relating to types of production costs (e.g., materials and labor), and operating expenses (e.g., advertising, salesmen's salaries, shipping, travel, and office salaries and wages).

Budget utilization reports are used in lieu of income statements by nonprofit organizations to summarize the operating expenses incurred relative to budget authorizations received during a specific period. A state university's budget utilization report shows the legislative appropriation received instead of gross revenues and funds from contracts, grants, and endowments as other income. The costs of instructional, research, and other services are itemized in place of production and selling expenses for a business firm. Finally, instead of net profits, the university shows budget overutilization or underutilization during the period.

A second major type of external compliance financial information is related to the financial condition of the organization at a point in time, which is reflected in statements of financial position. Exhibit 7-12 shows a statement of financial position for a business firm. In actual practice, more detailed information can be shown on the statement of financial position or on subsidiary statements relating to depreciation of fixed assets, types of investments, and details of debt incurred.

Exhibit 7-11

INCOME STATEMENT FOR A BUSINESS FIRM
FOR YEAR ENDED DECEMBER 31, 19x4

1. Gross Sales Revenues		$1,210,000
2. *Less*: Sales Returns		110,000
Net Sales Revenues		$1,100,000
3. Production Costs of Goods Sold		535,000
4. Gross Margin		$ 575,000
5. Operating Expenses:		
a. Selling Expenses	$110,000	
b. Administrative Expenses	55,000	
c. Miscellaneous Expenses	55,000	
Total Operating Expenses		$ 220,000
6. Net Profit From Operations		$ 355,000
7. Other Income		100,000
8. Total Net Profit Before Taxes		$ 455,000
9. Federal Income Tax		255,000
Net Profit		$ 200,000

NOTES: 1. The level can vary considerably on the income statement; however, the items shown in this exhibit should be considered minimum.
2. Figures used in this exhibit are for illustrative purposes only, and they are partially based on the profit budget shown in Exhibit 5-8 for the furniture company.

The statement of financial position is a summary of the organization's asset or resource status versus pending liabilities and claims against those assets or resources. As such, it is applicable to both profit and nonprofit organizations with differing types of assets, liabilities, and claims involved. For example, for a state university, similar types of information are shown on the statement of financial position with major emphasis on the condition and cost of instruction, research, and administrative facilities and equipment, and the status of bond financing, rather than on receivables, product inventories, and owners' equity.

The third major type of external compliance financial information is related to the changes in financial position of the organization in terms of sources and uses of funds over a period of time. The funds flow statement summarizes the changes in the statements of financial position for two different periods. Exhibit 7-13 shows a funds flow statement for a business firm using modified financial position statements for two periods (one period, December 31, 19x4, is based on Exhibit 7-12). Exhibit 7-13 shows that the firm has acquired funds from liquidation of some of its investments ($200,000), sale of common stock ($30,000), and increase in retained earnings ($200,000), which were used during the year to increase its current assets ($20,000) and fixed assets ($200,000) and to decrease its current liabilities ($10,000) and long-term liabilities ($200,000).

For a university, a similar summary of sources of funds from appropriations, endowments, grants, and investments, or from increase in liabilities or sale of assets can be developed versus uses of funds for payment of liabilities or increases in current and fixed assets. In practice, more detailed information is shown on the funds flow statement or on subsidiary statements relating to changes for types of current and fixed assets and investments, as well as for types of liabilities involved.

Exhibit 7-12   *Balance Sheet*

STATEMENT OF FINANCIAL POSITION
FOR A BUSINESS FIRM, DECEMBER 31, 19x4

ASSETS

Current Assets:			
Cash		$30,000	
Accounts Receivables		30,000	
Inventories:			
Finished Goods	$30,000		
Work in Process	10,000		
Raw Materials	20,000		
Total Inventories		$60,000	
Pre-Paid Expenses		10,000	
Total Current Assets			$ 130,000
Investments			600,000
Fixed Assets:			
Land	$100,000		
Facilities and Equipment	670,000		
Total Fixed Assets			770,000
Total Assets			$1,500,000

LIABILITIES AND OWNERS' EQUITY

Current Liabilities:			
Accounts Payable		40,000	
Taxes Payable		50,000	
Interest Payable		10,000	
Total Current Liabilities			$ 100,000
Long-Term Liabilities:			
Bank Loan			500,000
Total Liabilities			$ 600,000
Owners' Equity:			
Common Stock ($10 par value; au-			
thorized and issued			
10,000 shares)			100,000
Retained Earnings			800,000
Total Owners' Equity			$ 900,000
Total Liabilities and Owners' Equity			$1,500,000

NOTE: The level of detail can vary considerably on the income statements; however, the items shown in this exhibit should be considered minimum.

Other types of external compliance financial information generally are related to these three major types: income statements, statements of financial position, and funds flow statements. Annual reports to stockholders, reports to investors and creditors, tax reports, and securities reports include the types of information on these major types of reports. Often additional subsidiary information is developed which explains in more detail the financial performance of the organization. Much of this detailed information is derived from planning and operational control reports and from internal control information as described in the following section.

Exhibit 7-13

FUNDS FLOW STATEMENT FOR A BUSINESS FIRM
FOR THE YEAR ENDED DECEMBER 31, 19x4
(Based on Comparative Financial Position Information Shown Below)

Sources of Funds:	
Decrease in Investments	$ 200,000
Increase from Sales of Common Stock	30,000
Increase in Retained Earnings	200,000
	$ 430,000
Uses of Funds:	
Increase in Current Assets	$ 20,000
Increase in Fixed Assets	200,000
Decrease in Current Liabilities	10,000
Decrease in Long-Term Liabilities	200,000
	$430,000

MODIFIED COMPARATIVE STATEMENT OF FINANCIAL POSITION
AS OF DECEMBER 31, 19x3 AND DECEMBER 31, 19x4

	Dec 31, 19x3	Dec 31, 19x4
Current Assets	$ 110,000	$ 130,000
Investments	800,000	600,000
Fixed Assets	570,000	770,000
Total Assets	$1,480,000	$1,500,000
Current Liabilities	110,000	$ 100,000
Long-Term Liabilities	700,000	500,000
Common Stock	70,000	100,000
Retained Earnings	600,000	800,000
Total Liabilities and Owners' Equity	$1,480,000	$1,500,000

NOTES: 1. This exhibit includes changes in current assets and liabilities (as well as other assets, liabilities, and equity), for illustrative purposes; however, in actual practice working capital items may be excluded and only net changes in working capital (current assets minus current liabilities) are shown. See P.E. Fertig, D.F. Istvan, and H.J. Mottice, *Using Accounting Information* (2d ed.; New York: Harcourt Brace Jovanovich, 1971), Chapter 13, for an excellent discussion of the types of fund flow statements and their use.

2. The funds flow statement is also referred to as a statement of changes in financial position in accounting literature.

Internal Control Information

Internal control involves the development of procedures for controlling the authorization, execution, and recording of transactions, and the accounting for assets and resources used in these transactions. Exhibits 7-2 through 7-7 summarize the basic transaction subsystems within a firm: sales, receivables, cash receipts, payables, payroll, and cash disbursements. Effective internal control is vital for insuring that reliable financial data is acquired, classified, stored, retrieved, and processed into reports.

The major types of information required for effective internal control, as well as financial evaluation, are related to the six basic types of transactions. Sales summaries, receivables aging reports, cash reconciliation reports, asset reconciliation reports, purchase summaries, payroll summaries, and cash disbursement summaries contain information about transactions in each of these areas. These types of information are verified for accuracy before the transactions are classified and recorded in the following types of registers or ledgers:

Sales Control Register
Purchases Register
Payroll Clearing Account
General Ledger
Expense Ledger
Voucher Ledger
Check Ledger
Receivables Register
Cash Sales Clearing Account
Cash Receipts Register

These registers and ledgers serve as clearing points for verification of the accuracy of recorded transactions through reconciliation and auditing processes. Periodically, after transactions have been verified and reconciled, reports are produced which reflect transaction activity in the broad areas of sales-receivables, purchases-payables, production, payroll, and cash receipts-disbursements.

In general, information for financial control is used for external compliance as well as internal control. Financial evaluation reports are summaries of the financial performance and condition of the organization, and the financial reports of an organization make up the largest segment of the MIS. The examples listed in the preceding paragraph are only a few of the many interrelated reports that support financial evaluation and reporting. In fact, there are a great many subsidiary financial records that not only service general financial reporting requirements but also provide important inputs for generating reports such as logistics, demand analysis, managerial performance, and resource capacity status reports.

The *timing* of these reports is generally geared to an annual cycle with monthly supplements since they are tied to the budget cycle. The *quality* of information in these reports requires a high degree of accuracy and the verification of transactions because of the legal requirements of external agencies. The *quantity* or volume of information is generally a legal requirement, and for large organizations it is quite extensive.

SUMMARY

The overall purpose of managerial/financial control information is to facilitate activities involved in the evaluation of the performance of responsibility centers managers and the organization as the major responsibility center. Analyses are undertaken concerning financial transactions and events relating to sales-receivables, purchases-payables, production, payroll, and cash receipts-disbursements which provide information inputs for two major components of the MIS data base: managerial performance information and financial performance information.

Information relating to these two components of the MIS are merged, stored, analyzed, evaluated, and processed by the MIS to produce a series of reports such as those listed in Exhibit 7-14. The key features of these reports are: (1) the reports emphasize the *evaluation of past performance* of responsibility centers and their managers; (2) the reports provide the basis for taking *corrective action* and for making adjustments to future objectives, plans, and budgets; (3) the reports are *periodic* in that they are tied to the budget cycle and the reporting frequencies specified by external parties; and (4) the reports are oriented to *external compliance* and *internal control*.

The managerial/financial control information subsystem provides much of the information for planning and operational control, since a considerable amount of financial information is involved in the performance of these two functions. The MIS data base serves to interconnect the information subsystems described in Chapters 5, 6, and 7 so that multiple uses of inputs to the MIS can be achieved.

REVIEW QUESTIONS

1. What are the significant characteristics of managerial/financial control?
2. What types of analyses are involved in defining information needed for effective managerial/financial control?
3. What is the purpose of managerial performance information? What are several important effects of these reports on managers?
4. What types of information are included in managerial performance reports? Why?
5. What are the quality, timing, and volume requirements of these reports? What is the relationship between the timing of managerial performance reports to the budget cycle?
6. Give several examples of general financial reports. What functions do these reports perform for management?
7. Discuss the importance of internal control for the MIS.
8. How are financial reports related to planning and operational control reports?
9. Discuss the central role of financial performance information for the development of an MIS.
10. What are several constraints relating to general financial reports that may affect the development of an MIS?

Exhibit 7-14

MANAGERIAL/FINANCIAL CONTROL INFORMATION SUBSYSTEM

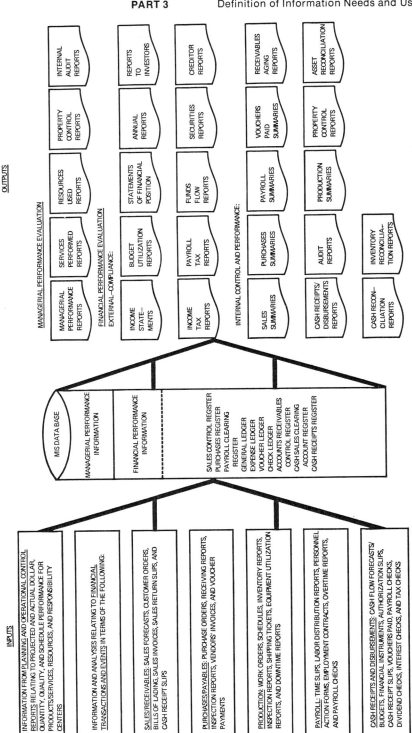

NOTE: THE EXAMPLES PROVIDED IN THIS EXHIBIT ARE INCLUDED TO SHOW THE MAJOR TYPES OF ANALYSES AND INFORMATION THAT ARE REQUIRED FOR EFFECTIVE MANAGERIAL/FINANCIAL CONTROL. THEY ARE NOT INTENDED TO BE A COMPLETE STATEMENT OF ALL INFORMATION INVOLVED IN MANAGERIAL/FINANCIAL CONTROL.

EXERCISE 7-1 Custom Machine Tool Company (Part C)

Refer to the description of the Custom Machine Tool Company in Exercises 5-1 and 6-1.

Using the framework for analysis provided in Exhibit 7-1, perform the following:

1. Identify and discuss the types of evaluation of managerial/financial performance that the company is currently using.

2. Design a managerial performance report that you feel would be useful for evaluating the company's major division managers (refer to Exhibit 7-10 for suggested format).

   a. How is this managerial performance report different from an operational control report (Chapter 6) or a financial performance report?

   b. How is the managerial performance information interdependent with planning and operational control information? Provide several examples of this interdependency.

3. Identify and describe several types of financial performance evaluation information that you feel would be useful to the company to facilitate internal financial control, and provide the basis for external-compliance reporting needs.

   a. Prepare a brief example of each type of financial performance report you feel is needed by the organization.

   b. How is the financial performance information interdependent with planning and operational control information? Provide several examples of this interdependency.

4. What are the quality, timing, and volume requirements of managerial performance and financial performance reports?

5. Summarize the managerial/financial control information subsystem of the organization in terms of:

   a. Major types of information input

   b. Major components of its data base

   c. Major types and purposes of reports produced

EXERCISE 7-2: Discount, Inc. (Part D)

Refer to the descriptions of Discount, Inc. in Exercises 4-1, 5-2, and 6-2. Using the framework for analysis provided in Exhibit 7-1 and the related discussion of information needs for managerial/financial control, perform the following:

1. Assume you are the President of the chain company to which Discount, Inc. Store Number 18 belongs. Identify the major types of financial control information you would require about Discount, Inc., and prepare brief examples of reports which would include this financial information.

2. As the manager of Discount, Inc. Store Number 18 what kinds of managerial/financial control information and reports would you require?
3. Summarize the managerial/financial control information subsystems of Discount, Inc. in terms of:
   a. Major types of information input
   b. Major components of its data base
   c. Major types and purposes of reports produced

EXERCISE 7-3: Admissions and Registration Division of State University (Part B)

Refer to the description of the Admissions and Registration Division presented in Exercise 6-3. Using the framework for analysis provided in Exhibit 7-1 and the related discussion of information needs for managerial/financial control, perform the following:

1. Assume you are the Vice President for Academic Affairs.
   a. What kinds of managerial performance information would you acquire, and why? Prepare a brief example of a managerial performance report that would provide you with the kinds of information you have identified.
   b. Indicate the kinds of financial control information you would require, and prepare brief examples of several basic financial control reports.
2. Assume you are the Director of Admissions and Registration.
   a. Prepare an example of a managerial performance report for the Admissions Officer, Registrar, and Student Data Services, respectively.
   b. What kinds of financial control information would you require for each of these areas?
3. Summarize the managerial/financial control information subsystems of the Admissions and Registration Division in terms of:
   a. Major types of information input.
   b. Major components of its data base.
   c. Major types and purposes of reports produced.

EXERCISE 7-4: Farm Products Corporation (Part E)

The objectives of this exercise are: to demonstrate the interrelationships between the operational decisions, activities, and information needed to perform them; and to provide practice in the identification of data elements which are contained in a typical transaction document and to show how these data elements can be combined to produce data inputs for subsequent management activities and decisions.

The organization chart of the Farm Products Corporation is shown in Exhibit 7-15. Assume that Exhibits 7-2 through 7-7 describe the transactions and documents for the company. Review the descriptions in Farm Products Corporation Parts A through D in Chapters 1 through 4.

1. Prepare a summary of the planning, operational control, and managerial/financial control functions of the company using the formats presented in Exhibits 5-2, 6-1, and 7-1.

2. Identify and discuss the major constraints and decision criteria that you feel are important for the operation of the company. Based on the information relating to the operation of the company, how would you describe the company image? The company objectives?

3. Identify the major demand determinants that impact the product potential of the company.
   a. Describe the types of demand analysis information that would be useful for developing sales forecasts.
   b. Prepare a simplified demand analysis report for the company.

4. Identify and describe several major types of resource capacity analyses and attendant information that would be useful to the company in commiting resources to products and organizational functions.
   a. Prepare a simplified resource capacity status report for the company.
   b. Describe the important interrelationships between demand information and the development of resource capacity reports.

5. Provide several examples of types of budget information that would be useful to the company, and explain why they would be useful.
   a. Identify dollar, quantity, time, and quality related budget information; provide an example of each type.
   b. Consider how demand, capacity, and budget information are interdependent, and provide several examples of this interdependency for this company.
   c. Contrast budgeting as a process for evaluating demand and capacity to perform and as a mechanism for communicating planning decisions to managers; provide an example of each.

6. Summarize the planning information subsystem for the company in terms of:
   a. Major types of information inputs.
   b. Major components of its data base.
   c. Major types and purposes of reports produced.

7. Identify and discuss the types of resource requisition and acquisition activities of the company and provide several examples of analyses and information that are involved in performing these activities.

8. Identify and discuss the types of production and distribution activities of the company and provide several examples of types of analyses and attendant information that are involved in performing these activities.

Exhibit 7-15
ORGANIZATION OF FARM PRODUCTS CORPORATION

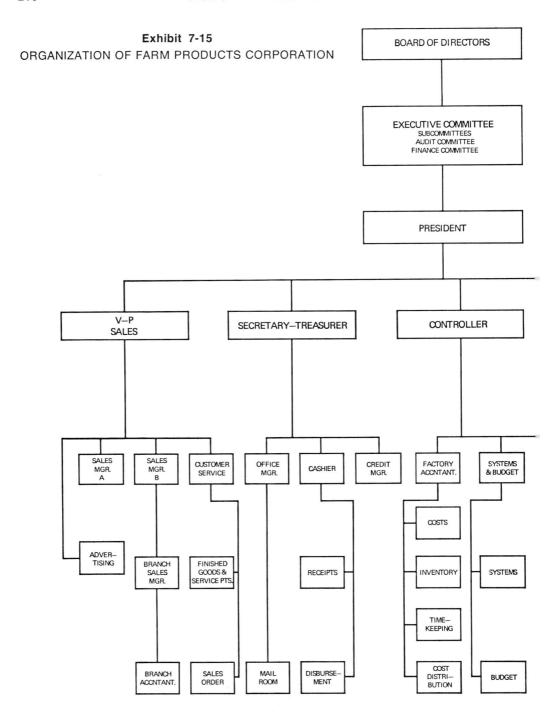

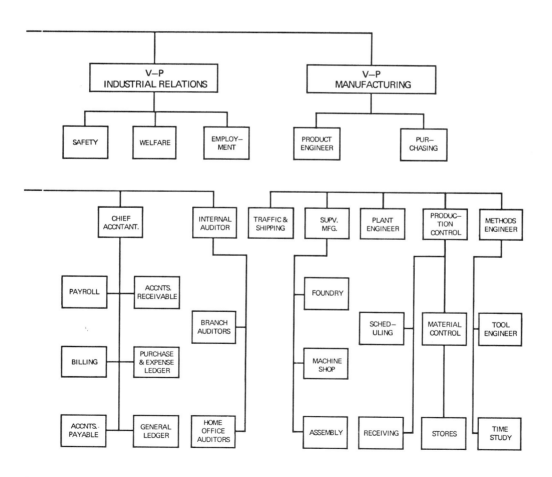

ADAPTED WITH PERMISSION FROM AMERICAN INSTITUTE OF CERTIFIED PUBLIC ACCOUNTANTS, "INTERNAL CONTROL," SPECIAL REPORT BY THE COMMITTEE ON AUDITING PROCEDURE, 1949.

9. Identify and describe several major types of general logistics information that would be useful to the organization to facilitate operational control.
   a. Identify cost, quality, quantity, and schedule performance information; and provide an example of each type of information.
   b. Identify several types of budget variance information which would be useful for operational control; and provide an example of each type of information.
   c. Describe how operational control information is dependent on planning information; and provide several examples of this dependency.

10. Identify and describe several major types of resource requisition/acquisition and production/distribution information that would be useful to the organization to facilitate operational control.
    a. Describe how resource requisition/acquisition activities are interdependent with production/distribution activities.
    b. Provide several examples of this interdependency for this company.

11. Summarize the operational control information subsystem of the company in terms of:
    a. Major types of information inputs.
    b. Major components of its data base.
    c. Major types and purposes of reports produced.

12. Identify and discuss the types of evaluation of managerial/financial performance that the company is currently using.

13. Design a managerial performance report that you feel would be useful for evaluating the performance of the company's major division managers (refer to Exhibit 7-10 for suggested format).
    a. How is this managerial performance report different from an operational control report (see Chapter 6) or a financial performance report?
    b. How is the managerial performance information interdependent with planning and operational control information? Provide several examples of this interdependency.

14. Identify and describe several types of financial performance evaluation information that you feel would be useful to the company for facilitating internal financial control, and provide the basis for external-compliance reporting needs.
    a. Prepare a brief example of each type of financial performance report you fell is needed by the organization.
    b. How is the financial performance information interdependent with planning and operational control information? Provide several examples of this interdependency.

15. What are the quality, timing, and volume requirements of managerial performance and financial performance reports?

16. Summarize the managerial/financial control information subsystem of the organization in terms of:

   a. Major types of information input.

   b. Major components of its data base.

   c. Major types and purposes of reports produced.

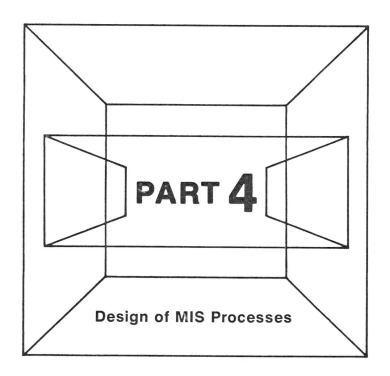

Design of MIS Processes

8 DESIGNING THE INFORMATION ELEMENTS AND DATA SOURCES

Detailed identification and classification of information elements is a prerequisite to the systematic determination of which data elements and related source documents will provide the needed information elements for all the reports to be included in an information system. Evaluation of these information elements using a set of quality, time, quantity, and cost criteria is necessary to determine which data elements will ultimately be included in the data base to permit preparation of the required reports.

Exhibit 8-1 gives an overview of the process of designing information elements and data sources. The exhibit indicates that this process involves several sequential steps, beginning with specification of the information elements to be contained in reports, identifying them, and classifying them into common categories. Each information element is then evaluated against a set of criteria drawn from the needs of operational and managerial personnel in the organization. These criteria include an assessment of the information against the quality, quantity, and timing requirements of the report users and against the cost limitations imposed by top management.

After the desired set of information elements has been evaluated, attention is given to specifying and classifying the data elements in existing source documents. Each data element is also evaluated against the same criteria used to evaluate information needs. It can then be determined whether existing source documents can provide the data necessary to produce the needed information within the quality, timing, quantity, and cost requirements. If the existing source documents cannot provide this, they must be revised or new source documents developed. As shown in Exhibit 8-1, design of information and data elements is a cyclical process involving reidentification, reclassification, and reevaluation of the needed elements as report needs change.

This chapter describes the procedures involved in designing the information elements and data source for the MIS. The objectives of the chapter are: to describe the procedures for identification and classification of information elements and data sources, and to describe the criteria and procedures which should be used for evaluating information and data sources.

SPECIFICATION OF INFORMATION ELEMENTS AND DATA SOURCES

Chapters 5, 6, and 7 define and describe a number of basic information needs common to most organizations. Now we must examine these needs in more

Exhibit 8-1

DESIGN OF INFORMATION ELEMENTS AND DATA SOURCES

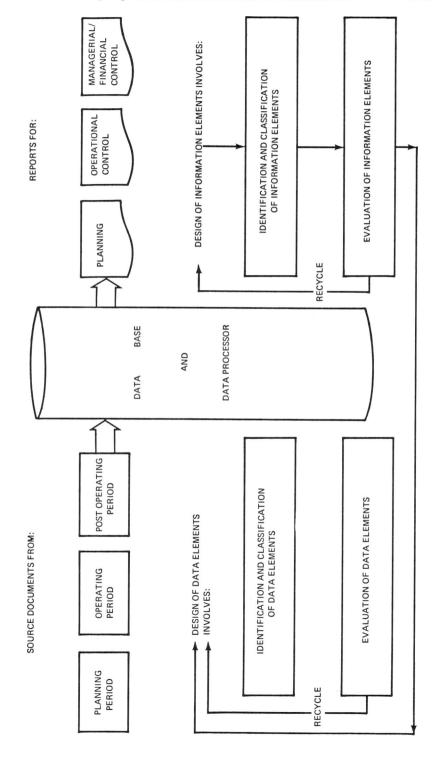

detail to design the final information content and capacity of the MIS. We must specify each information element to be included in the reports serving these basic information needs. After this set of information elements and reports has been evaluated and refined, it can then be used to guide the specification of source documents and data elements.

The tasks of identifying and classifying information elements and data sources are discussed in the following sections using sample reports developed in Chapters 5 through 7 for the business firm which manufactures office furniture (see Exhibits 5-3, 5-5, 6-2, and 7-10). The procedure for evaluating these information elements and source documents is covered later in the chapter.

Identification and Classification of Information Elements

Identification and classification of information elements involves screening each report and report request in order to prepare a complete listing of all information elements appearing on the proposed reports. This is a necessary preliminary step for specifying which information elements will eventually be included in the MIS and providing for their acquisition. For example, refer to Exhibit 5-3 on page 124. The screening of the report shown in this exhibit involves identification of the various information elements included on the report, such as output categories (column 1), units of measurement (column 2), user categories (column 3), and forecasts of demand (columns 4-12). Each of these information elements is then classified into one of two categories: (1) *measurement* elements which provide the actual measure of the events and transactions being reported, and (2) *identification* elements which properly identify and classify the events and transactions being reported. This classification is necessary to specify those elements which must be coded to facilitate their processing and subsequent evaluation as described later in this chapter.

Measurement elements are those items of information that quantify the reported events and transactions. For example, the numbers of desks, chairs, credit hours, and students in Exhibit 5-3 are examples of information elements which measure the potential demand for various types of outputs. In addition to units or numbers, measurements of events and transactions often are shown in dollars or percentages, such as costs incurred versus budgeted expenditures or the percentage of cost overrun. In some cases, qualitative explanations of measurements are also included, such as the reason for a cost variance.

Identification elements are those items of information which clarify the kinds of events and transactions being reported. For example, in Exhibit 5-3 the demand forecast is the event being reported and is characterized and classified by identification elements to answer the following questions:

> Forecast of demand for what? (types of output)
> In what terms are estimates of demand measured and reported? (types of units of measurement)
> Who are the expected customers or users? (types of users)

The answers to these kinds of questions help to clarify the event, forecast of demand, and permit more detailed analyses of demand.

Identification requirements normally do not change from one reporting period to another; therefore, they are typically predetermined and developed into a coding scheme, such as the traditional accounting chart of accounts. When changes occur, such as in the case of sales to new customers, additional code numbers must be assigned in order to properly identify these new sources of demand.

Additional examples of the distinction between identification and measurement elements are shown in Exhibit 8-2. The examples in Exhibit 8-2 refer to the reports shown in Exhibits 5-3, 5-6, 6-2, and 7-10. For each report shown in Exhibit 8-2, the information elements have been classified as identification or measurement elements.

The identification and classification of information elements within the framework presented in Exhibit 8-2 normally is done for every report to be utilized within the organization. A complete list of information elements classified into identification and measurement categories can then be compiled. This compilation facilitates the subsequent evaluation of information elements in each category, which in turn facilitates their inclusion into a final set of interrelated reports. This evaluation precedure is described later in the chapter.

Identification and Classification of Data Sources

The identification of sources of data involves analysis of operational decisions, activities, and work flows. You will recall that the analysis of operations served as the basis for determining information needs described in Chapters 5 through 7 and identified a number of process activators that were needed to perform work and make decisions. A *process activator* was described as a document that contains information about a decision made or activity that is used by others in the organization to make decisions or perform activities. An example of a process activator is a sales forecast. The forecast contains information assembled by the sales manager which reflects his estimate of future sales volume. This information is used by the production manager as a basis for scheduling his production. The production manager in turn prepares a purchase requisition containing information on materials needed for scheduled production. This requisition information is then used by the procurement manager to purchase the materials. Exhibits 5-2, 6-1, and 7-1 can be reviewed for other examples of process activators and how they are used to facilitate decision making and work performance.

The identification of process activators through the analysis of operations is important because process activators also contain data elements which are used as inputs to the MIS. Exhibit 8-3 shows a number of process activators (or source documents) which are common to most organizations, as described in Exhibits 5-2, 6-1, and 7-1. The types of source documents shown in Exhibit 8-3 are important for the design of the MIS because many of these source documents, such as budgets, purchase orders, employment contracts, cash receipt slips, and financial statements, must be created not only to facilitate decision making and the performance of work but also because of external reporting requirements of stockholders, creditors, and the Internal Revenue Service. Most organizations

Exhibit 8-2

IDENTIFICATION AND CLASSIFICATION OF INFORMATION ELEMENTS FOR SELECTED REPORTS OF A BUSINESS FIRM

DEMAND ANALYSIS REPORT (Exhibit 5-3)	RESOURCE CAPACITY STATUS REPORT (Exhibit 5-6)	LOGISTICS MANAGEMENT REPORT (Exhibit 6-2)	MANAGERIAL PERFORMANCE REPORT (Exhibit 7-10)
1. Identification Elements *Output Categories:* Office Desks, Office Chairs *User Categories:* Industry, Government *Units of Measurement*	**1. Identification Elements** *Input Categories:* Lumber, Carpentry Labor, Fabricating Equipment *Source Categories:* Lumber Company, Equipment Company *Output Category:* Office Desks *User Category:* Industry *Units of Measurement*	**1. Identification Elements** *Output Category:* Office Desks *Input Categories:* Labor, Lumber *Processor Categories:* Production Division, Fabrication Department, Procurement Division *User Categories:* ABC Company, Assembly Department, Fabrication Department, Production Division *Units of Measurement*	**1. Identification Elements** *Output Categories:* Office Desks, Office Chairs *Input Categories:* Direct Labor Costs, Materials Costs, Other Expenses *Processor Categories:* Fabrication Department *Units of Measurement*
2. Measurement Elements Forecasts of Demand Periods 1-*n* Probability variations (P, ML O)	**2. Measurement Elements** Capacity Information On Hand In Process Total Demand Information Current Future Reserve Total	**2. Measurement Elements** Normal/Projection Actual Variance Revised Projected	**2. Measurement Elements** Projected Actual Variance

generate these documents even though their specific titles or formats may vary from one organization to another. These documents represent a large source of data for the MIS. They reflect most of the important decisions and work performed in the organization.

Having identified existing sources of data through the analysis of operations, the source documents are classified into categories to facilitate their evaluation. This classification facilitates the compilation of data elements in

Exhibit 8-3

COMMON TYPES OF PROCESS ACTIVATOR DATA

Source documents

I. *PREOPERATING PERIOD* (Planning)

0231 and 0232	Statement of Objectives and Demand Forecasts
0233	Budgets
0234 to 0236	Work Statements and Schedules, Quality Specifications, and Resource Requisitions

II. *OPERATING PERIOD* (Operational Control)

A.*Source Analysis and Selection:*

0311	Purchase Orders
0312	Employment Contracts
0313	Financial Instruments

B.*Resource Input Processing:*

0411 to 0414	Receiving and Inspection Reports, Stock Receipts, and Purchase Invoices
0415	Personnel Action Forms
0416	Cash/Funds Receipt Slips

C.*Performance and Use of Resources:*

0511 to 0516	Work Completed, Inspection, Time, Materials Usage, Facilities Utilization, and Cost Reports
0611 to 0613	Stock Receipt Slips, Shipping/Issue Slips, and Sales Invoice/Charge or Transfer Slips
0711 to 0715	User Receiving Reports, Voucher Receivables, Credit Memos, Cash Receipt Slips, and Sales Return Slips

III. *POSTOPERATING PERIOD* (Managerial/Financial Control)

0811 to 0813	Manager Performance, Services Performed, and Resources Used Reports
0821 to 0832	Income Statements, Statements of Financial Position, Annual Reports, Budget Utilization Reports, Funds Flow Reports, Tax Reports, Sales/Receivables Reports, Purchases/Payables Reports, Production Reports, Payroll Reports, Cash Receipts/Disbursements Reports, and Audit Reports.

NOTE: The numbers refer to those used in Exhibits 5-2, 6-1, and 7-1.

source documents into major report categories defined through the analysis of operations. The need for information elements in reports can then be more readily matched with existing source documents.

EVALUATION OF INFORMATION ELEMENTS AND DATA SOURCES

Once a complete listing of all information elements and data sources has been compiled, each element and source must be carefully evaluated. This evaluation limits the final information capacity of the MIS to only those data elements and reports which are essential. Otherwise, the MIS will be unwieldy, overly expensive, and ineffective.

Criteria for Evaluation

In order for an objective evaluation to be made, we must have: (1) criteria for evaluation, and (2) a procedure for evaluation. The criteria are the basic MIS design criteria of quality, quantity, time, and cost which were introduced in Chapter 2. Use of these criteria forces consideration of the organization's capability to generate, collect, store, and process the needed information elements in a timely, effective, and economical manner. The following four sections describe these important criteria; the evaluation procedure is described later in the chapter.

Quality. Quality-related criteria involve the effectiveness of the information content in reducing the degree of uncertainty surrounding a particular decision. The effectiveness of information content can be increased by making improvements in relevancy, accuracy, and format.

The *relevancy* of information refers to its ability to satisfy the recipient's information need. More specifically, the degree of relevancy of information may be viewed as the extent to which the information can be utilized in a decision-making or problem-solving situation. Relevancy involves the validity of information used in decision making, as shown by the following examples:

Decision	Highly Relevant Information	Less Relevant Information
1. Forecast sales of desks in business market	Level of business employment	Level of government employment
2. Purchase materials needed for production of desks	Production schedules for desks	Sales forecasts for desks
3. Develop fall semester schedule of graduate course offerings	Previous fall semester enrollments in graduate courses	Previous spring semester enrollments in graduate courses
4. Purchase of a car which will be economical to operate	Gas mileage of cars	Prices of cars

Irrelevant information elements should not be included in reports, even though there is a temptation to include them just in case. The decision maker is thus not burdened with extraneous information. Unneeded information may actually perform a disservice by reducing the clarity of the relevant information.

The *accuracy* of information refers to its precision and exactness in defining the reported events or transactions. Accuracy is affected by errors or imprecision in the recording, computing, and reporting steps of the information gathering process.

In evaluating information needs, accuracy requirements must be carefully specified. The degree of information accuracy required is largely dependent upon the use to which the information will be put. For example, tax and stockholder reports are expected to contain extremely precise information on revenues, expenditures, assets, and liabilities. On the other hand, production scheduling or cost reports often require only estimates of schedule or cost variances because adjustments to operations must be made quickly and will be needlessly delayed if a high degree of information accuracy is sought.

Cost considerations may also require a lower degree of information accuracy. Sampling techniques are used in inspection procedures with the understanding that estimates, not true values, are determined at a cost which is only a fraction of that associated with the determination of the exact value.

Another important aspect of information quality relates to the *format* of the report. Format is important because it affects the ease with which the report can be read and assimilated. As the complexity of a report increases, its likelihood of extent of use falls. To increase the readability of reports, their formats should be consistent with the manner in which recipients use the information. For example, the information on an inventory status report is usually arranged according to major classes of inventory, showing description of material, code number, quantity on hand, and projected shortages. This is the normal sequence of review by a procurement manager who uses this type of report to determine which purchase orders must be placed.

Report formats are often not tailored precisely to users' needs. One reason for this is the programming costs associated with special arrangements of information, especially if several different users each request a unique format. A second reason for finding formats not tailored exactly to users' needs is that report designs are often based on the systems analysts' or programmers' preferences for programming ease. It is important for recipients of reports to participate in format design decisions, rather than to rely solely on systems analysts or programmers.

Information hierarchies also have direct implications for the format and cost of a report. Subsequent recomputations of the information on the basic report when preparing higher level reports is eliminated. The implication of the hierarchical structure is that standardized report formats will be used for all operations. If the reports are not standardized, then aggregating them for higher level reports is exceedingly complex.

✗**Time.** Time-related criteria involve the *frequency* of information dissemination. The use of information must be evaluated in order to determine how often reports should be prepared and distributed. For example, planning information generally is required at less frequent intervals than information for operational control because operational control is concerned with making continual adjustments to operations as unfavorable variances in output occur. Planning, on the other hand, is more of a periodic decision process, tied typically to the annual budgeting process. Because of this, information needs of lower level managers have a requirement for more frequent inputs than those of top managers.

The timeliness of information has a direct impact upon managerial performance. The exception principle enhances the timeliness of information and eliminates unneeded information which might contribute to processing delays. Traditionaly, the exception principle has been associated with the control function, and more specifically with the feedback element of control.

The frequency requirement has an obvious but important impact on information storage requirements. A continuing need for information requires that information be retained in a manner that enables continual retrieval flexibility. Because of the cost implications associated with such storage, a request for a recurring report should be evaluated carefully by both the managers using the report and the systems personnel designing the report. The full cost of updating data and retrieving information must be determined and evaluated as a part of the report approval.

Frequency requirements of reports directly affect the timing of data acquisition and processing. The analysis and evaluation of sources of data must take into account when and how often reports are produced so that data relating to events and transactions is recorded, classified, and processed in time.

Quantity. The quantity or volume of information influences the effectiveness of operations and management. Too many reports, too much information on a single report, or even too many copies of a single report may hamper the use of reports or even discourage their use entirely. Factors which contribute to excess information being generated include:

- Ease of duplication of reports.
- Desire to show considerable detail on a single report, such as a complete list of purchase transactions rather than a summary of inventory status.
- Use of multipurpose reports rather than several reports geared to specific uses.
- Simplicity with which massive and extremely complex computerized reports can be prepared.

The quantity of information generated and distributed by the MIS directly affects the cost of data acquisition, storage, retrieval, and processing. The exception principle is also applicable for resolving the problem of too much information.

Too little information can limit the effectiveness of reports. For example, a production cost report which shows only total cost variances for the combined production activities and products limits the corrective action to be taken by a production manager because the report does not include information about specific activities and products which have cost overruns. A problem of too little information may also occur because reports are not distributed to all personnel having need for the information.

The quantity of information specified in reports directly affects the analysis and evaluation of sources of data. If large amounts of information are required, it is likely that the amount of data acquired and processed will be extensive. The reduction of excessive information will directly reduce the quantity of data that must be recorded, classified, and processed. The resolution of the problem of too little information will increase the input data quantity requirement.

Cost. Each of the dimensions of quality, time, and quantity has an associated cost dimension. Variations in the content, frequency, and volume of reports have direct implications for the cost of providing information. Reports have value determined by their use and cost determined by their processing requirements. The relationship between the costs of MIS processing requirements and the benefits derived from the uses of information in operations and management is the cost-effectiveness of the MIS.

The direct costs of the information system, such as the costs of hardware and software utilized in MIS processes, can be determined. It is considerably more difficult, however, to determine the specific value derived from the use of information because of difficulty in measuring the degree of certainty provided by the information. Because of the inherent difficulty in measuring the value derived from the use of information, most decisions on the worth of an information element, report, or system are made on the basis of objective cost data and subjective (largely informal) value data. However, there are some useful general relationships between the subjective value derived from improving the quality, timing, and quantity of information and the resultant data acquisition and processing costs. These relationships are presented below as general guidelines for estimating the impact of changes in quality, timing, and quantity of information generated by the MIS on costs of data acquisition and processing. These guidelines summarize the points made in the foregoing sections of this chapter:

1. The greater the *relevancy* of information, the lower the information volume and subsequently the lower the processing costs.
2. The greater the *accuracy requirements* for information, the higher the processing costs.
3. The more tailored the *formats* for reports, the more effective is decision making, but generally the higher processing costs.
4. The more reports and the information they contain are designed into a well-defined *hierarchy of information needs,* the lower the costs of processing owing to less duplication of information processing and reporting.
5. The greater the *frequency of information flows,* the greater the difficulty for users to read and understand reports and the higher the costs of processing.
6. The greater the use of the *exception principle* in reporting, the greater the effectiveness of reports and the lower the costs of processing.
7. The greater the *volume* of information elements on a report, the number of different reports, or the number of copies of a single report, the higher the costs of processing.

Using the above guidelines, the quality, timing, and quantity of reports and the information they contain are identified within the cost limitations specified by top management. For example, a daily budget variance report showing budgeted versus actual costs by product line requires the daily submission and processing of completed work orders, timecards, and issue slips. If the costs of producing these reports daily are excessive or if the information on the reports is of poor quality (i.e., incomplete or inaccurate because of the difficulty in obtaining "good" data daily), then criteria for the timing of reports may be changed. Weekly or monthly budget variance reports may produce more accurate information within the cost limitations specified by top management.

The Evaluation Procedure

A definite *procedure* must be devised for employing the criteria objectively. This procedure consists of a combination of analytical questions and techniques for evaluating both the information elements and the data sources, as discussed in the following two sections.

Evaluation of Information Elements. A useful procedure for evaluating the information elements identified and classified consists of answering five basic questions using the analytical framework presented in Exhibit 8-4 as follows:

1. How is each information element being used? For example, in Exhibit 8-4, the purpose and distribution sections (columns C and D) reveal the nature of action taken (purpose) and the user of each information element shown in column A. The analyst may further investigate the need for the information element by various users if the purpose statement does not appear appropriate or if the purpose is known to be obsolete. A periodic review by the analyst and the users of information keep the information as meaningful as possible.

Evaluation of the purpose and distribution of information may reveal duplications of activities. For example, if it was found that several users required a certain type of information to expedite purchase orders (see column C, row 3), further investigation should determine more precisely the types of expediting actions performed and why this same function is apparently being undertaken by several people.

2. What duplications of information elements are sent to a manager? The information element "materials on order" in Exhibit 8-4 is received by the procurement manager in two reports (inventory status and purchase orders outstanding, rows 1 and 3). The analyst should investigate the feasibility of combining the reports or deleting the information element from one of the reports. However, because of multiple users or standardized formats, the duplication may be unavoidable.

3. What are the frequency and storage requirements? These requirements deal with the data base, data processor, and source documents. The required frequency of a report (column G) may differ from the periodicity of the transaction event. Normally, source documents are generated continuously within the operation as events, transactions, decisions, and activities occur. The data contained in the source documents may be fed into the data base as it is created or at regular intervals.

Exhibit 8-4
FRAMEWORK FOR EVALUATING INFORMATION ELEMENTS

	OUTPUT-USER ANALYSIS			SOURCE-INPUT IDENTIFICATION	PROCESSOR REQUIREMENTS	
(A) Information Element	(B) Report	(C) Purpose	(D) Distribution (User)	(E) Source Document	(F) Storage	(G) Frequency
(1) Materials (wood) on order	Resource (inventory) status report	Schedule production Purchasing	Production Procurement	Purchase order	Month Indefinite	Weekly Monthly
(2) Cash on hand	Cash flow report	Pay bills Financing	Treasurer Treasurer	Cash receipt disbursement slip	Indefinite	Daily
(3) Materials (wood) on order	Purchase orders outstanding report	Expedite purchase orders Expedite purchase requisition	Procurement Production	Purchase order	Year	Weekly
(4) Forecast of demand for desks	Demand analysis report	Budgeting Develop promotion program Schedule production	Controller Sales Manager Production	Sales forecast	Indefinite	Monthly
(5) Materials (wood) received	Resource (inventory) status report	Schedule production Purchasing	Production Procurement	Receiving report	Month Indefinite	Weekly Monthly

NOTE: This is usually prepared on a large-size spreadsheet within the format shown above. Variations to the form may be made according to the needs of the analyst.

The evaluation of storage requirements of a report (column F) must consider its reporting frequency requirements (column G) and the potential need for the information in future periods. Storage requirements for a particular report may vary, depending on whether the report is of a temporary nature, such as the logistics type (i.e., Purchase Orders Outstanding, column B, row 3) or more permanent, such as a financial report (i.e., Cash Flow Report, column B, row 2).

4. What source data is required? The format for evaluating information elements provided in Exhibit 8-4 also identifies the source documents that provide data elements. All of the information in every source document generally is not fed into the data base. This is especially true when any information element (e.g., materials on order) is generated by different source documents (e.g., purchase orders and receiving reports).

5. What value criteria should be applied? The analyst should determine in conjunction with users of reports the quality, quantity, and timing requirements of each information element. A number of important guidelines for evaluating each information element relative to these dimensions were described in the section dealing with criteria.

The evaluation procedure results in a final-design set of interrelated reports and information elements which are then used to guide the analysis of the necessary source documents and data elements. Evaluation of data sources is described in the following section.

Evaluation of Data Sources. The final task in this phase of the MIS design process involves an evaluation of how well the data elements from existing source documents match the information elements required on reports. This evaluation reveals the degree of compatibility between the need for an information element and the availability of existing data which can be acquired and processed to produce the information in the manner, volume, and time required.

Data-information matrix analysis is an analytical technique which can be used to facilitate the evaluation of data sources relative to information needs. As a framework for describing how data-information matrix analysis can be used, Exhibit 8-5 presents a partly completed data-information matrix analysis sheet. The data-information matrix analysis sheet has five major parts. *First,* the left center of the sheet lists the data elements that are identified in existing source documents. These data elements are also information elements which appear on reports, so they are designated as data-information elements. This part of the sheet simply has an identification function for the analysis that follows. *Second,* the top part of the sheet contains information about each existing source document which may contain data inputs for the MIS. In Exhibit 8-5 it can be seen that the time report source document is prepared weekly in two copies by all employees and is processed through the computer and stored indefinitely.

Third, the lower part of the sheet is similar to the top, except the information shown pertains to existing or planned reports of the MIS. Exhibit 8-5 shows that the payroll report is produced weekly in triplicate for the personnel department and is processed through the computer and stored indefinitely.

Exhibit 8-5

DATA-INFORMATION MATRIX ANALYSIS SHEET

	SOURCE DOCUMENTS	PURCHASE ORDER	TIME REPORT	CASH RECEIPT SLIP				
STORAGE	INDEF.	INDEF.	INDEF.					
COMPUTER APPLICATION	YES	YES	YES					
SOURCE	PROC.	ALL	CASH-IER					
COPIES	8	2	2					
FREQUENCY	AS RQ'D	WKLY.	DLY.					

DATA INFORMATION ELEMENT	SOURCE DOCUMENTS	PURCHASE ORDER	TIME REPORT	CASH RECEIPT SLIP				ANALYSIS/ COMMENTS
SOCIAL SECURITY NO.	✓	✓						
QUANTITY OF SUPPLIES ON ORDER	✓			✓				
CASH RECEIPTS			✓	✓				
NUMBER HOURS WORKED	✓	✓		✓				

	USER REPORTS	PAYROLL	CASH FLOW	INVENTORY STATUS	DAILY ATTENDANCE			
FRENQUENCY	WKLY.	DLY.	MO.	DLY.				
COPIES	3	2	1	2				
DESTINATION	PERS.	TREAS.	PROD.	EACH MGR.				
COMPUTER APPLICATION	YES	YES	YES	NO				
STORAGE	INDEF.	INDEF.	ONE YR.	ONE YR.				

NOTE: THIS IS USUALLY PREPARED ON A LARGE SPREADSHEET WITHIN THE FORMAT SHOWN ABOVE. VARIATIONS TO THE FORMAT ARE EASY TO ACCOMPLISH, DEPENDING ON THE NEEDS OF THE ANALYST.

Fourth, the matrix in the center indicates in which source documents and reports the data-information elements are contained. For example, "number of hours worked" shows a check in the upper portion of the rectangle under "time report" and a check in the lower portions of the rectangles above "payroll" and "daily attendance." Exhibit 8-5 also reveals that the frequency, storage, and computer processing dimensions of the time report and the payroll report are similar. Therefore, the time report is a suitable source document for producing the payroll report. On the other hand, the frequency of the time report is not consistent with the frequency required by the daily attendance report (weekly generation versus daily requirements). Thus if the daily attendance report is to be produced, the time report must be prepared daily or another source of data must be utilized.

Fifth, space is provided on the right center of the sheet for notations regarding the generation and use of the various data elements. Inconsistencies such as the frequency differences in the earlier example or inconsistencies in storage or computer processing features can be noted. Other factors, such as unused data elements included on source documents or excessive duplication of data elements on source documents would also be noted as observed.

Data-information matrix analysis facilitates the evaluation of sources of data relative to information needs. This evaluation technique insures that the information elements to be included on reports can be produced from source documents as they currently exist or as they are designed for the MIS. Through this evaluation technique official sources of data for specific documents are identified. This step is necessary to insure consistent data inputs, to provide a central point of verification of data inputs, and to assign responsibilities to insure proper categorization of data inputs. Unless specific responsibilities for providing source data are designated, inaccurate or conflicting data about various events, transactions, decisions, and information in reports will be difficult to resolve quickly, and adjustments to MIS processes will be difficult and costly.

RESPONSIBILITY FOR DESIGN OF INFORMATION ELEMENTS AND DATA SOURCES

The activities described as part of the specification and evaluation of information needs and source documents usually are performed by the MIS staff personnel. Chapter 3 described the MIS staff as having responsibility for the design, coordination, and monitoring of the MIS in an organization. This responsibility specifically includes the design and monitoring of an integrated set of data-information flows and reports, the review and evaluation of the effectiveness of MIS reports for operations and management, and the review and evaluation of data acquisition processes and sources of data.

In performing these activities the MIS staff serves as a liason group between the users of information, the providers of data, and top management. In this liason role the MIS staff suggests resolutions to problems which inevitably arise, such as requests for reports having excessive quality, quantity or time requirements. These excesses are reviewed and evaluated by the MIS staff using the general guidelines pertaining to the cost-related criteria and the evaluation procedure. Requests for new information or reports are analyzed in terms of possible duplication of existing reports, frequency requirements, report formats, and the cost impact on existing data acquisition, coding, storage, processing, and retrieval.

In this analysis, the intended uses of reports and the costs of producing them are evaluated. The MIS staff recommends changes in reports and coordinates these changes with the report users. Final report designs are then approved by the appropriate level of management, and the set of reports is approved by top management.

SUMMARY

The design of information needs and sources of data involves the specification of information elements and reports to be produced by the MIS and their evaluation based on the quality or accuracy, timing, quantity, and cost of information. The final-design set of reports and the information elements they contain provide the basis for identifying the source documents which can provide the data needed to produce the reports. A number of basic types of process activators or source documents common to most organizations are potential sources of data inputs to the MIS. Data-information matrix analysis is a technique for evaluating the compatibility between requested information and the data available to provide this information. There is a need to specify which source documents will serve as official sources of data for each information element in order to be able to trace and analyze errors in data acquisition and processing and to make adjustments to MIS processes quickly and effectively. The MIS staff personnel are responsible for performing the activities pertaining to specifying and evaluating information needs and sources of data. The MIS staff serves as a liaison between users of reports, providers of source data, and top management.

REVIEW QUESTIONS

1. Describe the important criteria for designing information needs and sources of data. What relationship do these criteria have to value-added dimensions?
2. What are several useful guidelines for evaluating the cost of information? Discuss several limitations relating to the use of these guidelines.
3. Outline the procedure for determining information need characteristics and for evaluating information elements.
4. What are two major classifications of information elements on reports? Why is it important to classify information elements?
5. Describe the parts of the data-information matrix analysis sheet and their use. Discuss the usefulness of the data-information matrix analysis sheet for evaluating sources of data.
6. Describe the procedure for specifying basic source documents needed for an information system.
7. Why should official sources of data be identified and classified?

8. Define a process activator and discuss its importance for the MIS.

9. What importance does the procedure for evaluating information elements and data sources have for the design of a data base?

10. Comment on the universality of the criteria and procedure for evaluating information elements and sources of data to business, governmental, and educational organizations. What limitations do you see?

EXERCISE 8-1: Identification and Classification of Information Elements

Exhibit 8-2 provides an example of a format for identifying and classifying information elements in selected reports for a business described in Chapters 5 through 7. Using this format, accomplish 1 or 2:

1. Using the reports shown in Exhibits 5-3, 5-6, 6-3, and 7-10 relating to the state university, prepare a summary of information elements in these reports.

2. Using the reports shown in Exhibits 5-7, 6-6, and 7-12, prepare a summary of information elements in these reports.

EXERCISE 8-2: Design of Information Elements and Sources of Data

Utilizing the sample reports and information related to the exercises at the end of Chapters 5 through 7, select one of the following organizations:

Custom Machine Tool Company (Exercises 5-1, 6-1, 7-1)
Discount, Inc. (Exercises 5-2, 6-2, 7-2)
Admissions and Registration Division of State University (Exercises 6-3, 7-3)
Farm Products Corporation (Exercise 7-4)
An organization with which you are familiar and for which you have access to some of its reports and source documents.

For the organization selected:

1. For several of the sample reports needed by the organization, identify and classify the information elements on the reports within the format in Exhibit 8-2.

2. Identify several major types of source documents that are described explicitly in the case materials or that you feel are needed by the organization based on the description of operational subsystems in Exhibits 5-2, 6-1, 7-1 through 7-7, and 8-3. For each source document list several major kinds of data that you feel would normally be included.

3. Using the format for evaluating information elements shown in Exhibit 8-4, prepare a summary of several information elements needed on the report you identified in question 1 and relate these information elements to appropriate source documents you identified in question 2. Extend your evaluation by developing a data-information matrix analysis sheet as shown in Exhibit 8-5 (assume or use hypothetical data as needed).

9

DESIGNING
THE DATA BASE

A data base is a collection of data inputs classified, stored, and arranged to facilitate precise and timely retrieval for production of the reports requested by operations and management. This chapter deals with the data base as an important facilitator for linking information outputs with data inputs. Actually, it may be more precise to refer to the data base as an information base, because the contents are selected pieces of relevant information rather than just raw data. However, the term data base is commonly used to designate all forms of stored data without regard to their type, and it will be used in this book.[1]

The purpose of this chapter is to describe the process involved in the design of a data base. The objectives of this chapter are to:

1. Describe the nature and purpose of a data base.
2. Define and discuss the basic requirements of a data base.
3. Describe the process for designing the structure of the data base.
4. Discuss a number of issues that are important for management of a large data base.

NATURE AND PURPOSE OF THE DATA BASE

As a broad concept, the data base includes all data regardless of form or type located in the organization. The data base then is actually segmented physically into parts consisting of manually or automatically stored data. Data stored and maintained manually typically consists of correspondence, memoranda, trip reports, and other infrequently used documents. Certainly, this type of data is a necessary part of an organization's entire base of data, and management of manually stored data is itself a specialized and important function. Management of this data is usually the responsibility of personnel trained in office and records management. In this book, the term data base refers to automated, especially computerized, storage of data specifically required for planning, operational control, and managerial/financial control. Other data of the type mentioned above (correspondence, memoranda, and the like) generally is not included in a computerized data base.

---

[1] The term data bank is sometimes used instead of data base; however, a strict definition is that a data bank is a facility where data is stored. Thus, the contents of a data bank comprise the data base.

The data base and the computerized data processor combine to create value or utility by converting data inputs into information needed for reports. For example, data elements on individual materials issue slips generally include units issued, receiver, reason for issue, unit cost, and date issued. If an organization generates many issue slips per month (for instance, 1,000), the data on a single slip has only limited utility. Unless data on all materials issue slips can be combined, classified, stored, and arranged for timely access in a data base using a computerized data processor, the data is of little use. The combining and processing of the data about material usage can be reflected on a monthly report showing for each type of material the number of units issued, their cost, the receiver, and why they were used during the month. In this report example, no real change of data form is involved; only a simple (although cumbersome if performed manually) tabulation of data is involved. On the other hand, the data elements on the issue slips can be used with the aid of specific processing instructions in the form of mathematical formulas or accounting procedures to produce new information forms, e.g., economic order quantities, comparative product material cost analyses, materials budgets and variances, and financial statements.

The data base also provides for the creation of other forms of utility. In the example of materials issue slips, the reports which can be produced from these kinds of data may have varying frequencies of use as well as different users. For example, the production manager is interested in more frequent reporting of material cost performance than are external users of company financial reports. The properly designed data base can satisfy variations in information requirements arising because of different uses.

The data base is a vital segment for the proper functioning of the MIS. The data it contains represents potential utility in the form of reports for operations and management. The next section considers a general procedure for defining the data if it is to produce the maximum utility for operations and management.

DEFINING THE BASIC REQUIREMENTS OF A DATA BASE

Data base design involves the definition, classification, selection, and coding of the data elements to be stored. This section describes a general procedure for defining data base requirements based on the quantity-, quality-, time-, and cost-related design criteria or value dimensions which were described in Chapter 8. A number of factors which influence the quantity, quality, time, and cost requirements of the data base are described.

Quantity Requirement

An unlimited amount of data cannot be stored in the data base indefinitely simply because of the limited resources of an organization. The storage capacities for several computerized storage devices are as follow:

Device	*Volume (Characters)*[2]
Magnetic core unit (bulk immediate access)	10 million
Magnetic disk (on-line direct access)	10 million to 1 billion
Magnetic tape (off-line)	More than 10 billion

Immediate or direct access of data refers to the ability to store and retrieve data from storage devices automatically, that is, without the need for human intervention. For immediate access of data, about 10 million characters or digits can be stored per device. To get a feeling for the size of this storage capacity, consider a firm that inputs and stores all data elements listed on its sales transaction records. A single sales transaction might require 100 data characters. If an average of 1,000 sales transactions are executed per day, recording sales would consume about one percent of the storage capacity of one magnetic core unit each day of operation. During one year three such units would be required to record only these transactions. When one considers that sales data may have to be stored for quite some time plus the fact that many other kinds of data are routinely stored by an organization, one can easily visualize how quickly storage capacity can be filled.

Since the purchase of storage capacity in the quantity suggested in the above example is extremely costly, considerable aggregation of data plus careful selection of data to be stored in the data base are necessary to make the MIS cost realistic. The major factors which are analyzed to determine the appropriate quantity of data to be stored are the acquisition requirement, the retrieval requirement, and the retention requirement.

Acquisition. The acquisition requirement refers to the manner and timing with which the data has been collected, recorded, coded, and processed into the data base. The acquisition requirement depends on the methods and location of data collecting, recording, coding, and processing, as well as the degree of detail desired. Data may be collected at its origin as it is generated, such as by using the sales slip prepared by a sales clerk as the source document. Data may also be collected from a summary listing of many pieces of original data. Such might be the use of a daily sales report prepared by a sales manager.

Collecting data at its origin eliminates the preparation of additional source documents. This procedure not only saves work and time but also reduces the possibility of data transcription errors. An additional advantage is that the document which was originally used to complete the transaction or event (for example, the sales slip) itself becomes a part of the data base. The information in a report can then be traced back to its original source documents. The capacity for this type of verification enables reporting errors to be located and necessary adjustments to be made quickly. If data is not collected at its origin,

---

[2] James C. Emery, *Organizational Planning and Control Systems: Theory and Technology* (New York: Macmillan Co., 1969), p. 47. Magnetic core units, disks, and tapes are different types of storage media for computers.

the verification process can proceed only to the point where the data was summarized for entry.

The use of documents which are produced during transactions or events as source documents requires a data coding system for classifying transactions and events. A sales slip is a basic source document which explains a sales transaction. The sales slip includes data on the type of product sold, its price, units sold, date of sale, method of payment, purchaser, store, salesman, and sales tax (if applicable). The product type, store, and salesman often are coded to simplify and speed recording. Other data such as price, number of units sold, date, and tax are typically not coded, but are entered into the data base as explanations of what transpired during the sales transaction.

As more detail is desired in the coding system, the number of data elements to be collected and stored is increased. For example, instead of a single code for identifying product type, there may be several levels of identification such as a number to indicate clothing, a second number to indicate men's, a third to indicate shoes, a fourth to indicate golf shoes, and so on.

Although the basic framework for coding data is similar for most organizations, the extent of classification depends on the nature and complexity of the organization. If the coding scheme is not extensive, data must usually be aggregated to fit into the data base structure, thereby reducing the volume and detail of stored data. For example, if the coding scheme does not provide for separate identification of regular and overtime hours worked, such data must be combined in one category as total hours worked. The number of stored data elements and the cost of storage are reduced; however, loss of detail also results. In the example about coding of data on the sales slip, as more factors relating to product type are coded, a greater quantity of data elements must be collected, processed, and stored. If less detail is coded (for example, simply men's clothing) there is considerably less opportunity to make detailed analyses of sales, but the amount and cost of data storage are decreased.

Source data can sometimes be recorded in a form directly readable by the computer. The use of optical, magnetic, or mark sense code which will be read by the computer greatly simplifies entry of data into the data base. This type of data entry is usually based on code numbers which identify transactions and events. Numbers are used because they can be machine processed with greater simplicity than nonnumeric characters.

Retrieval. The second factor to be analyzed in determining the appropriate volume of data to be stored is the retrieval requirement. Retrieval refers to the manner and timing of withdrawing data from the data base and processing this data into reports. The retrieval requirement depends on the desired degree of information detail and the distribution frequency of reports. Greater detail required on reports usually calls for greater volume of data to be collected, coded, and stored.

The preparation frequency of reports affects the retrieval requirement simply because more often used reports require more frequent data retrieval and processing. The purpose of reports often dictates or influences the frequency of their distribution. Reports may be prepared for several reasons—for taking immediate action, for control, or for information only. Reports on which immediate action is based are usually special-purpose reports, and the data requirements for these reports are specific and detailed. As a result, the volume of data to be stored is quite large. On the other hand, reports for control are usually exception reports containing summary data. In these cases, the volume of data to be stored is considerably smaller. Reports for information only are usually general in nature. The volume of data to be stored to support these reports is variable.

Retention. The retention requirement is the third major factor related to the volume of data to be stored in the data base. Retention refers to the length of time data should be held in the data base. The retention time of data is determined from analysis of information needs. Many needs for data are continuing, such as financial reports regarding expenditures, revenues, assets, liabilities, and general financial transactions. Data for these reports should be maintained indefinitely with regular updating. To many users, historical data has as much significance as current data. Other data needs are of a one-time or special purpose nature. Data gathered for these needs can eventually be discarded. For example, budget or schedule variance reports are used to adjust operations. Once the adjustments have been made, data can be discarded. Retention requirements also differ for operational versus strategic planning information needs. Operational requirements tend to be short-run, while strategic planning must rely on long-run predictions which require compiling and storing a greater amount of historical data over a long time. The implications of the retention requirement for data are that the greater the retention requirement, the larger the data base and subsequently the greater the cost of data storage.

Data base security is another aspect of the retention requirement which plays an important part in determining the size of the data base. It involves two important aspects: protection against loss or destruction of data and provision for maintaining data privacy. Backup protection against loss or destruction is provided by duplication and careful storage of essential data files. Controlled access to data files is usually accomplished through the coding system. Special coding designations are assigned to confidential data, and only those knowing the proper codes can secure this data. Typically, such a coding system requires partitioning of the storage area and a consequential increase in the total storage requirement.

Quality Requirement

Important factors to analyze related to determining the appropriate quality of data to be entered in the data base are the validity and accuracy of data inputs.

Validity. Validity refers to the ability of data to produce reports which satisfy a problem-solving or decision-making need. Confidence in information outputs depends on the validity of inputs and on data base security. The validity of data entered can be checked against the type, format, and range of values of similar data elements. For example, in collecting data to produce a payroll report on the number of hours worked by employees, a range of acceptable values can be predetermined. If an employee's timecard shows an unusually large number of hours worked for a day or week (for example 18 hours in a day or 80 hours in a week), this data input would not be entered without special checking because it is outside of an acceptable range of values, such as 10 hours a day or 50 hours a week.

This type of checking procedure is especially useful in discovering large errors that might destroy the validity of reports. Small errors often go undetected, but they ordinarily result in less disastrous consequences in reports. Provisions for purifying or validating data inputs are essential not only to insure that the information on reports is meaningful, but also to minimize the costs of data acquisition, storage, and retrieval. The concern over data validity is largely dependent on the user, his responsibilities, and the reward structure. Data checking becomes a significant problem when one segment of an organizational unit feels that it cannot rely upon the information generated by another segment. Thus, while the design analyst perceives that multiple use of a single data input is feasible and valid, individual users of reports containing this data element may feel more comfortable in generating their own data inputs. To overcome reluctance to share data inputs, the MIS staff must convince users that savings in data acquisition, storage, and retrieval can be reflected in users' budgets, and explain why the validity of information in their reports will not suffer. The data originator may have to upgrade the data validity to a point beyond his own needs to make it acceptable to others.

Accuracy. The accuracy of data contained in the data base refers to its precision in defining events or transactions. Accuracy depends on frequency of updating and on the method used to collect data. Historical data must be updated periodically if it is to represent accurately the current state of operations. For some data, such as expense data, weekly or monthly updating is sufficient to maintain accurate data files. For other types of data, such as that on inventory levels, it may be important to update the data file daily, hourly, or even instantaneously to maintain an accurate picture of current stocks.

Collecting data is usually expensive and is always subject to error. Consequently, any reduction in the volume of data collected can help to reduce the cost of collection and the number of measurement and recording errors. One effective way of reducing the amount of data collected is by the use of sampling. Collecting less than 100 percent of the data elements generated can reduce the volume of collected data to only a fraction of that generated. The sampling procedure is relatively simple: as source documents are prepared for processing, samples of the needed data can be extracted for storage in the data base. Except for those cases where every event or transaction must be recorded (such as time reports for payroll, cash receipts and disbursements, and other financial transactions), sampling can be effective in reducing the costs of data acquisition and storage without seriously reducing the usefulness of reports. The use of sampling is appropriate for data from repetitive types of activities, such as quality control inspection procedures or analysis of cost variances for products produced or work performed.

Time Requirement

The major factors to analyze related to determining the appropriate time requirement of data storage are the frequency of information retrieval and the access time, that is, the length of time required to retrieve information from the data base.

Frequency of Retrieval. The frequency of retrieval, or how often reports are produced, varies according to the uses of information. Operational control information, such as budget, quality, and schedule exception reports, are needed as soon as unfavorable variances occur. Information for strategic planning, such as capital budgeting and pricing decisions, is needed less frequently, normally on a monthly or yearly cycle. Information for financial control is produced at regular intervals and is normally coordinated with the budget cycle.

Access Time. Access time, or the time required to retrieve information from the data base, also has a bearing on the uses of data. Usually there is no urgency associated with planning data because planning decisions are rarely made hastily. On the contrary, operational control information is often needed immediately, especially when a critical problem is delaying operations. Information for financial control may be needed in varying time frames, such as for the quarterly and yearly production of financial statements. Information about operations that require continuous monitoring may be needed instantaneously, such as in continuous physical processes. Other types of exception reporting, such as that employed in cost control, do not call for instantaneous retrieval. Such information may be retrieved in batches at regular intervals, say weekly or bimonthly.

The required frequency and access times dictate the type of storage devices needed for the data base. Data that must be retrieved frequently must be stored in on-line random access storage devices, such as magnetic core or disk units, where no human intervention is necessary for retrieval. Other data needed less frequently and less rapidly can be stored in off-line devices, such as on magnetic tape. A complete description of these devices is included in Chapter 10.

Cost Requirement

Storing vast amounts of data in a manner that permits fast, efficient retrieval of the data is extremely expensive. This fact is indicated below by an example of cost estimates for computerized storage:

Device	Cost per Character[3]
Magnetic core unit (bulk immediate access)	More than 10 cents
Magnetic disk (on-line direct access)	About 1 cent
Magnetic tape (off-line)	About .001 cent

In the example presented in the discussion about quantity of a single transaction requiring storage of 100 characters, 1,000 transactions would involve about $1,000 in storage costs if stored on a magnetic disk and more than $10,000 if stored in magnetic core. Although these are rough estimates, they point out the necessity for being extremely selective about the data stored in a computerized data base and how it is maintained.

Any organization is limited financially in the amount of storage capacity it can purchase. Consequently, there is a tradeoff between the cost of storage and the value of integrated, on-line, directly accessible data files as opposed to segmented, off-line data files. Emery has suggested how this tradeoff might be resolved:[4]

> ... the allocation of storage should be such that the expected value of stored information is maximized. Expected value equals the probability of retrieval times the value of the information for a given response time. If the value drops sharply with increased response time, the information should be allocated to a storage medium with a short access time. In practice, it is difficult to estimate the relationship between value and response time, and so only the probability of retrieval is usually used (as estimated from the time interval since the last reference). In most systems, it is possible for the user to define maximum and minimum levels in the hierarchy for a given item of data in order to keep the response time within suitable limits.

Because of the difficulty in measuring the value of information, an organization must usually decide how much storage capacity to purchase based absolutely on what the organization can afford, that is, based on the cost rather than on cost savings. Fortunately, storage costs have declined as computer technology has advanced, and they should continue to do so in the future.

The management of an organization must treat information as a resource and attempt to develop methods for determining what this resource is worth to the organization. The value of information is difficult to measure because its measurement involves subjective estimates of the probability that a specific information element will reduce the level of uncertainty regarding a future event or transaction. Statistical probability techniques are useful for developing subjective probabilities of the value of an information element. The MIS staff is responsible for assisting users of reports in developing estimates of the value of information on their reports. It is often useful for users to place an estimate on

---

[3] James C. Emery, *Organizational Planning and Control Systems: Theory and Technology* (New York: Macmillan Co., 1969), p. 47. These storage costs were calculated by dividing the cost of the device by its storage capacity; storage time is not considered in these costs.

[4] *Ibid.*, p. 48.

the dollar value of reports so that a cost-effectiveness perspective can be developed throughout the organization.[5]

Another aspect of the cost requirement is efficient utilization of storage capacity. Considerable computer system expertise is necessary to avoid wasting storage and to insure proper utilization of storage. The propriety of utilization is dependent on the ability of the data coding system and data base to arrange and classify data efficiently and on the effectiveness of the procedure for reviewing and monitoring stored data. Data storage analysis must be based on an accurate assessment of data storage needs.

The cost requirement of data storage involves an analysis of the quantity, quality, and time requirements, as shown in Exhibit 9-1. The arrows between the quantity, quality, and time characteristics imply that these three categories of requirements are highly interdependent. The arrows between cost and each of the other three categories imply that each other requirement has an impact on cost.

STRUCTURE OF THE DATA BASE

Manual or automated data base design requires that the relationships between data elements be structured in a framework. The data base structure described in this section is applicable to both manual and computerized

Exhibit 9-1
THE COST REQUIREMENT OF DATA STORAGE

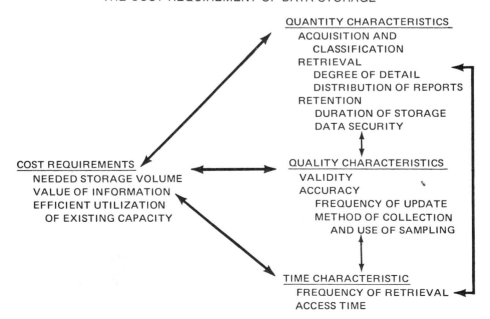

QUANTITY CHARACTERISTICS
ACQUISITION AND
    CLASSIFICATION
RETRIEVAL
    DEGREE OF DETAIL
    DISTRIBUTION OF REPORTS
RETENTION
    DURATION OF STORAGE
    DATA SECURITY

COST REQUIREMENTS
NEEDED STORAGE VOLUME
VALUE OF INFORMATION
EFFICIENT UTILIZATION
    OF EXISTING CAPACITY

QUALITY CHARACTERISTICS
VALIDITY
ACCURACY
    FREQUENCY OF UPDATE
    METHOD OF COLLECTION
    AND USE OF SAMPLING

TIME CHARACTERISTIC
FREQUENCY OF RETRIEVAL
ACCESS TIME

---

[5] Charles A. Gallagher, "Perceptions of the Value of a Management Information System," *Academy of Management Journal*, Vol. 17, No. 1 (March, 1974), pp. 46-55.

information systems. However, implementation of this data base structure is quite different for the computerized data base because of the differences in physical versus magnetic file storage devices (e.g., file cabinets versus magnetic disks). Therefore, the main focus here is on a conceptual framework for designing a computerized data base incorporating the characteristics of computerized data files.

The structure of the data base refers to the way in which data is aggregated, classified, and interrelated within the data base. The developer of the data base structure must consider a data classification scheme, the level of data detail to be employed, and the appropriate data coding system to use. These considerations are described in the following sections.

Classification of Data Elements

The terms *data base, data set, data file,* and *data list* are often used interchangeably to identify and classify stored data. These terms need not be confused, however, because they typically refer to different levels of aggregation of data. Data base, data set, data file, and data list constitute a hierarchical structure for data storage in descending levels of data aggregation. In other words, a data base comprises one or more data sets that comprise one or more data files that comprise one or more data lists. Exhibit 9-2 illustrates the structural hierarchy. Each level contains more detail than the preceding one. This hierarchical structure is extended further for computerized data

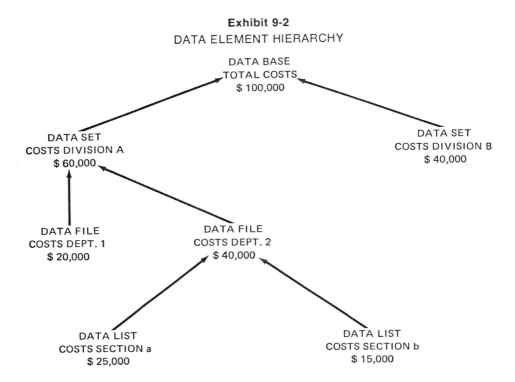

Exhibit 9-2
DATA ELEMENT HIERARCHY

storage. A data list is typically subdivided into data records, data fields, and data subfields.

This type of hierarchical data structure is somewhat analogous to the hierarchical structure of the organization itself. For example:

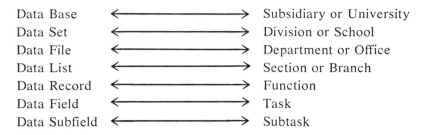

Data Base	⟷	Subsidiary or University
Data Set	⟷	Division or School
Data File	⟷	Department or Office
Data List	⟷	Section or Branch
Data Record	⟷	Function
Data Field	⟷	Task
Data Subfield	⟷	Subtask

This hierarchical data structure is a scheme for identifying and classifying data according to various levels of organization. This is by far the most common way of identifying and classifying data in organizations and is so because the reports produced from this arrangement of data are distributed to and used by the organizational units which are arranged in a structure paralleling the data. Also, the budgeting process, which is hierarchical in nature (i.e., budgets, sub-budgets, etc.), usually constitutes a significant portion of the information in the MIS.

The problem with this type of classification scheme is that, while it provides for classification vertically by organizational units, it does not provide a convenient way of classifying information horizontally by interrelated subsystems. In addition to information on total costs for budgeting and evaluation of financial performance, an organization usually needs information regarding costs of activities performed by various organizational units in producing a product or in performing a function or task. For example, the advertising, selling, procurement, production, shipping, and administrative costs of producing and selling a particular product must be compiled by cutting across or combining costs of several vertical organizational units such as those in marketing (sales, advertising), procurement (purchasing, receiving, and inspection), production (fabrication, assembly, and finishing), and administrative overhead (accounting and financing). Exhibit 9-3 demonstrates this horizontal compilation of data. Exhibit 9-3 shows that total direct costs ($37.00) per unit of product are generated throughout the organization by procurement, production, and marketing activities. Costs of this sort may need to be classified meaningfully and arranged in the data base so that product cost and pricing analyses can be accomplished. Other useful types of horizontal classification might be for categories of costs (e.g., material or labor for each product line) or for common types of functions performed (e.g., accounting, administrative, or data processing costs incurred in each organizational unit). Within this type of classification of data, vertical classification of costs is still possible (i.e., $40.00 total costs in Exhibit 9-3), in that the organization budgets by organizational unit and subunit as well as by product line.

Exhibit 9-3

HORIZONTAL COMPILATION OF DATA

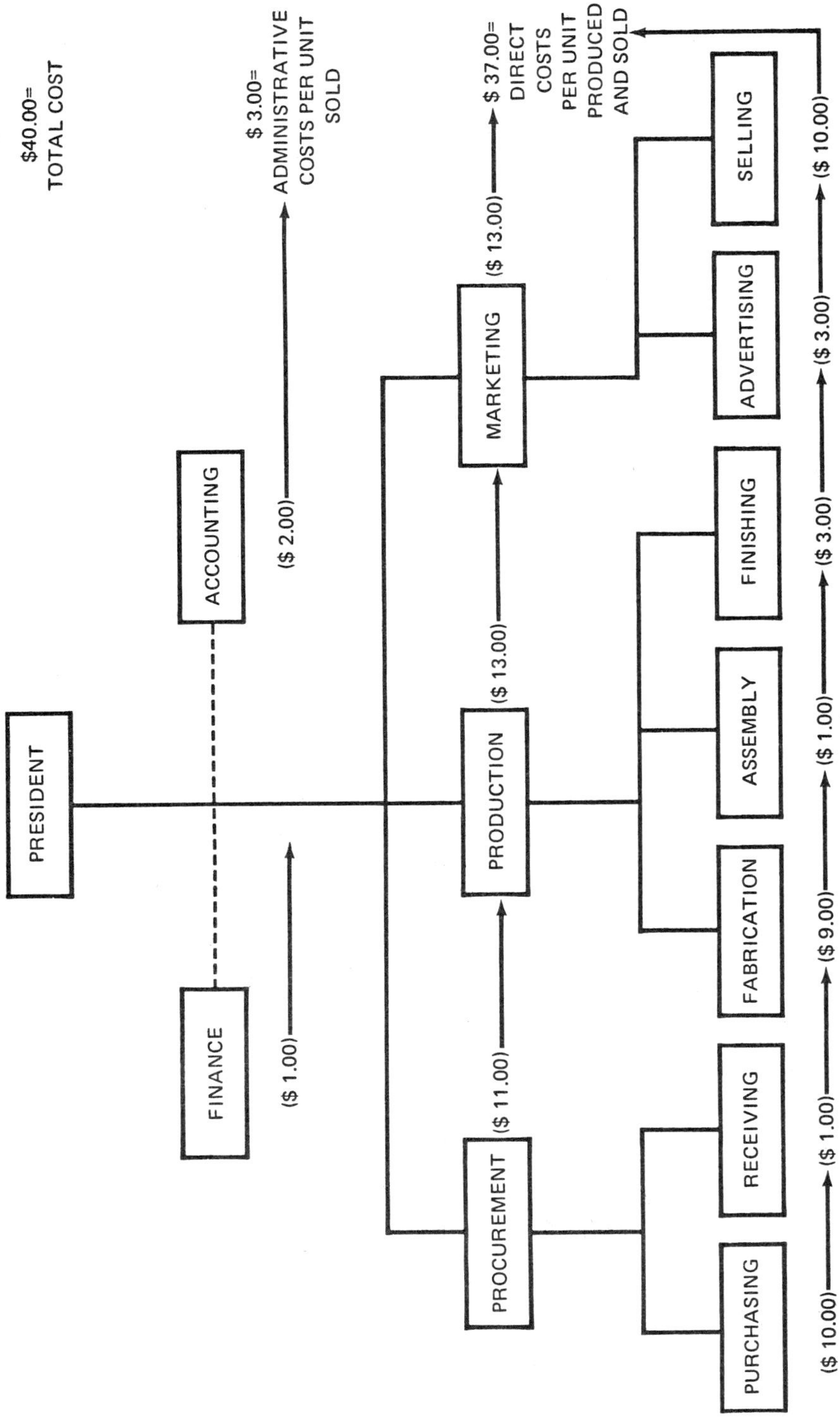

$40.00 = TOTAL COST

$3.00 = ADMINISTRATIVE COSTS PER UNIT SOLD

$37.00 = DIRECT COSTS PER UNIT PRODUCED AND SOLD

PRESIDENT

FINANCE

ACCOUNTING

($1.00)

($2.00)

PROCUREMENT ($11.00)

PRODUCTION ($13.00)

MARKETING ($13.00)

PURCHASING

RECEIVING

FABRICATION

ASSEMBLY

FINISHING

ADVERTISING

SELLING

($10.00)

($1.00)

($9.00)

($1.00)

($3.00)

($3.00)

($10.00)

Other ways of classifying stored data are not primarily hierarchical in nature. Blumenthal has classified data into working files, master files, and data base files according to the variety and permanence of the data each contains.[6] Working files are specific and temporary, such as a temporary trial balance used in financial accounting to verify transactions before the final financial statements are produced. Master files, such as equipment, accounts payable, and sales ledgers, persist throughout the life of a system. Data base files are more generalized in structure, are centralized, and serve a wide variety of user needs, for example, the total cost or product cost data bases.

Massey has classified data into three categories: operational or variable data, independent or internal data, and dependent or external data.[7] Data generated from day-to-day transactions, such as data from purchase orders, invoices, timecards, and work orders, is operational or variable data. Independent data is internal to the organization and includes payroll rates, standards, schedules, and budgets. Dependent data is externally derived and includes securities data, price data, and marketing research data.

All of these ways of classifying data provide considerable flexibility for retrieving information in a number of forms. Flexibility of retrieval is in essence a major reason why data needs to be classified, coded, and stored to permit easy, effective, and timely retrieval.

Regardless of the mix of classification schemes used, the essence of the data base is its content, that is, the data it contains. The fundamental unit of data in the data base is usually called a *data bit* or a *data element*. The term data element is preferred here because it is more general and because bit is a common computer term meaning binary digit. A data element as used here refers to a single item of data input that can be processed into an information output.

The structuring of the data base using this definition of a data element enables the identification and classification of data to permit both organizational (vertical) and systems-related (horizontal) activities, events, or transactions to be brought into the data base. The general taxonomy or classification scheme which can be used as the macro-structure for this type of data base is shown in Exhibit 9-4. In this exhibit, the data base structure has been developed using an input-output model. In all organizations, processing systems such as those shown in Exhibit 9-4 (for example, organizational responsibility centers, functions, and activities) form the vertical set of relationships. Since the entire organization is managed, budgeted, and evaluated through these vertical responsibility centers, data elements brought into the data base must be identified and classified according to the organizational units to which they relate.

Data that relates to organizational units, functions, and activities which must be identified and classified is of four major types, as shown in Exhibit 9-4. First, data is needed on the types of inputs or resources used by these various

---

[6] Sherman S. Blumenthal, *Management Information Systems: A Framework for Planning and Development* (Englewood Cliffs, N.J.: Prentice-Hall, 1969), pp. 43-45.

[7] L. Daniel Massey and John Heptonstall, *Management Information Systems* (Morristown, N.J.: D.H. Mark Publications, 1969), pp. 3-27.

Exhibit 9-4

GENERAL STRUCTURE OF THE DATA BASE

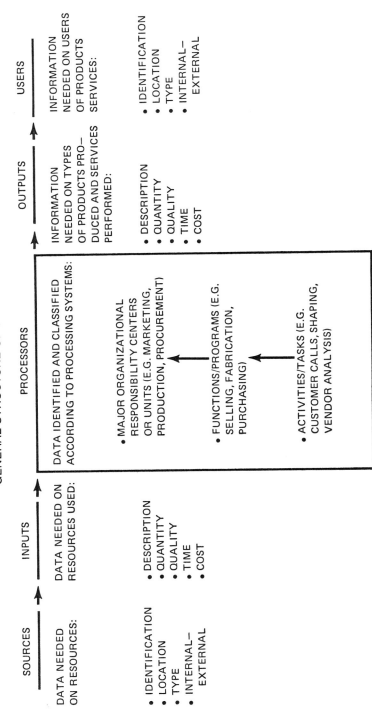

NOTES: 1. VERTICAL ARROWS INDICATE VERTICAL ORGANIZATIONAL RELATIONSHIPS.
2. HORIZONTAL ARROWS INDICATE SUBSYSTEM INTERACTIONS AND THE FLOWS OF RESOURCES THROUGH INTERRELATED
WORK, DECISION, AND ORGANIZATIONAL PROCESSING SYSTEMS.

processing systems. For example, reconstructing Exhibit 9-3 to reflect inputs would involve showing the kinds of descriptions of resources which were used, their quantity (units), quality (specifications), timing of use, and cost. Second, the sources of resources acquired by the organization must be identified and classified so that suppliers can be evaluated in terms of cost, quality, and delivery performance, as well as in relation to the effectiveness of use of resources by organizational units. Third, the data base must provide information on the types of products produced or services performed, including descriptions of these outputs, their quantity, quality, timing, and cost. This type of data, coupled with the resource data, is necessary so that cost and performance analyses can be performed by product lines. Fourth, to complete the analysis of product-service performance, information is needed relating to who uses the outputs of the organization, including descriptions and locations of customers or users.

The general structure of the data base shown in Exhibit 9-4 provides a flexible classification scheme to permit both vertical and horizontal identification of data elements to be brought into the data base. Input-output data can be related to vertical organizational units, functions, and activities with the assignment of code numbers for each type of data element included under the source-input-processor-output-user components of the data base structure. Before discussing the design of this type of coding system, it will be helpful to examine the level of detail of data disaggregation needed.

Level of Data Detail

The second major characteristic of data base structure is the level of detail or the extent to which the taxonomy is extended and the data disaggregated. The level of information detail required on reports determines the extent of data disaggregation and classification employed in the data base. One factor which determines the extent of data disaggregation and classification needed is the number of vertical units of analysis that are appropriate, that is, the number of classifications or layers of organizational responsibility centers, functions, and activities about which reports are required. If an organization needs cost information reports on every activity (shaping), function (fabrication), and organizational unit (production), the level of data disaggregation and classification must be much more extensive than if only total cost information is needed for major organizational units such as production, marketing, and procurement.

A second factor which determines the extent of data disaggregation and classification needed is the appropriate number of horizontal units of analysis, i.e., the number and types of classifications of inputs (resources) and outputs (products-services) or processing systems about which reports are required. Suppose the organization needs information for each product which identifies the types, locations, and sizes of customers who purchased the product and shows the quantity and cost of each kind of resource used to produce and sell the product. The level of data disaggregation and classification will be much more extensive than if only total cost per product is shown on reports.

The selection of the appropriate level of data detail depends on: (1) analysis of the quality-, quantity-, time-, and cost-related design criteria using the procedure for the evaluation of information needs described in Chapter 8, and (2) definition and analysis of the quality, quantity, time, and cost requirements of the data base using the procedure discussed at the beginning of this chapter. The central issues to be resolved relating to these analyses are "How much will it cost to obtain and retain each data element?" and "What is the value of the data element for operations and management?" The procedures for accomplishing this type of analysis require that all data elements to be included in the data base be identified. Their uses and needs must be determined, and their dollar value to operations and management estimated. The dollar estimate of the value of data elements can be compared with the estimated costs of data acquisition, classification, coding, storage, and retrieval, in order to determine an overall cost-benefit measure of a group of data elements.

In any organization there is usually a minimum level of data detail required. Exhibits 9-5 through 9-8 show examples of suggested minimum levels of detail for the basic financial accounting transactions identified and described in Chapter 7 (see Exhibits 7-2 through 7-7, pages 190 through 195). Exhibits 9-5 through 9-8 show transaction summaries and data base structures for sales-receivables, purchases-payables, cash receipts-disbursements, and personnel-payroll transactions. Each of these exhibits provides examples of the kinds of data and levels of detail that normally appear in the data base. For example, in Exhibit 9-5, customer name and address, account number, salesman's name, name of product, quantity ordered, and other related data would be included in the sales-receivables segment of the data base. Source documents that would normally be used to furnish this data include sales forecasts, customer orders, bills of lading, sales invoices, and cash receipt slips.

The data inputs in the sales-receivables data base produce two major transaction summaries, a sales control register and an accounts receivable register. These two registers are two major parts of the sales-receivables data base structure. Transaction summaries are used in the design of the data base to identify and classify data into meaningful aggregations. The data in the accounts receivable register can be retrieved to produce a report on outstanding accounts receivable. The data in a purchase control register (shown in Exhibit 9-6) can be used to produce a report on purchase orders outstanding, or data in the labor distribution journal (shown in Exhibit 9-8) can produce labor cost analysis reports for various product lines, functions, or activities.

The transaction summaries and data elements shown in Exhibits 9-5 through 9-8 make up the bulk of financial accounting transactions. These components of the data base provide most of the data for the generation of financial control reports, as well as much important data for demand analysis, resource capacity status, logistics, and managerial performance reports.

Exhibit 9-5

TRANSACTION SUMMARY AND DATA BASE STRUCTURE
FOR SALES-RECEIVABLES DATA
(Refer to Exhibits 7-2 and 7-3)

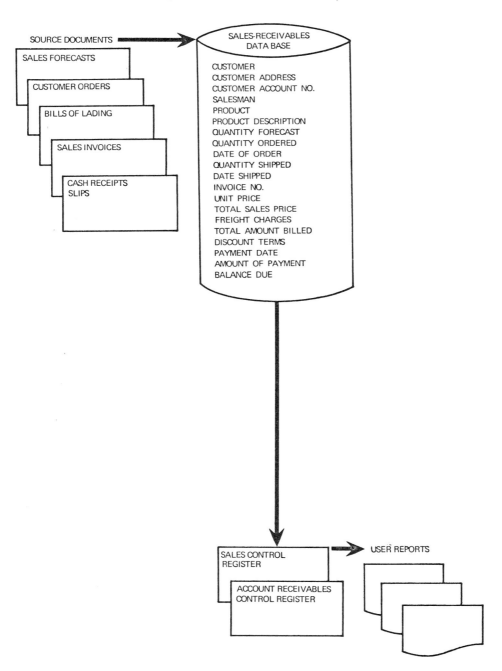

Exhibit 9-6

TRANSACTION SUMMARY AND DATA BASE STRUCTURE
FOR PURCHASES-PAYABLES DATA
(Refer to Exhibit 7-5)

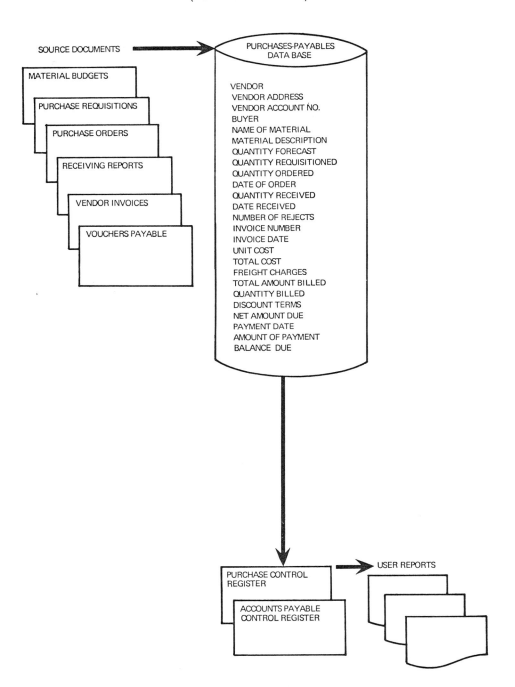

Exhibit 9-7

TRANSACTION SUMMARY AND DATA BASE STRUCTURE
FOR CASH RECEIPTS-DISBURSEMENTS DATA
(Refer to Exhibits 7-4 and 7-7)

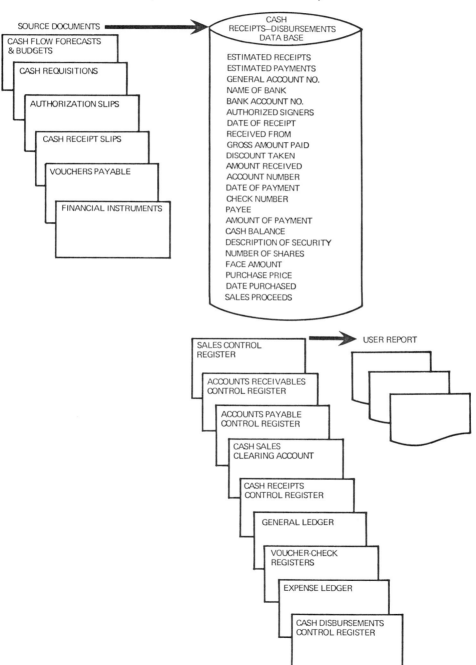

Exhibit 9-8

TRANSACTION SUMMARY AND DATA BASE STRUCTURE
FOR PERSONNEL-PAYROLL DATA
(Refer to Exhibit 7-6)

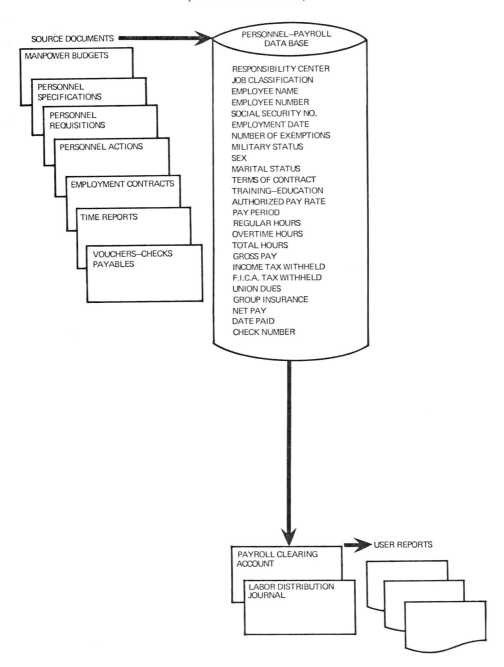

In addition to the kinds of transaction summaries and data base files shown in Exhibits 9-5 through 9-8, transactions can be summarized into separate data bases for planning, operational control, and managerial/financial control as shown in Exhibits 9-9, 9-10, and 9-11. These exhibits are patterned after the summaries of information needs presented in Chapters 5, 6, and 7 (refer to Exhibits 5-12 on page 140, 6-8 on page 169, and 7-14 on page 212). They present examples of the data elements that would be brought into the base, the source documents involved, and the data base summary files that would be needed. Exhibit 9-9 shows that source documents relating to demand and resource analysis, decision criteria, and constraints provide a variety of data inputs for the planning data base, e.g., name of responsibility center, name of product, sales price, units sold, units forecast, resource quantity forecast, shipping schedules, and sales orders received. These kinds of data are used to develop demand, resource capacity status, and budget summary files in the data base. These summary files are then used to produce user reports needed for defining objectives and committing resources during the preoperating or planning period. Exhibits 9-10 and 9-11 show how similar summary files are developed to provide information for reports which facilitate operational control and managerial/financial control.

Two other major types of transaction summaries not shown in Exhibits 9-5 through 9-8 which are important parts of the data base structure are resource (input) and service (output) files. Exhibit 9-12 shows the data elements that would be included in these files. For example, in the discussion relating to the general structure of the data base (refer to Exhibit 9-4), we stressed that for each major vertical organizational unit, function, and activity it was important to compile data about the resources used and products or services produced. Exhibit 9-12 shows that the description of the resource (what was used, where, and why), the quantity used, its quality specifications, the timing of its use, and the cost of the resource are minimum data to be identified, compiled, and classified in the data base. Similar kinds of data are important in the services file. Exhibit 9-12 also shows typical sources of resources and services data and kinds of reports normally generated from the resources and services transaction summaries.

Exhibit 9-13 shows a more detailed breakdown of a human resources file as an example of the level of detail normally employed. Other detailed files, such as those of current, fixed, and money resources, are similar in structure to the human resources file. They differ only in the type of data elements contained. The data elements contained in these files must be continuously collected, stored, and monitored in order to maintain relevancy to current reporting and decision-making needs.

In summary, determining the appropriate level of data detail in the data base structure requires an analysis of the need for information and the cost of data acquisition, classification, coding, storage, and retrieval. Based on this analysis, the level of data detail relating to vertical organizational units, functions, and activities, as well as resources used and services performed by these vertical processing systems, must be specified. The actual level of data

Exhibit 9-9

TRANSACTION SUMMARY AND DATA BASE STRUCTURE
FOR PLANNING DATA
(Refer to Exhibit 5-12)

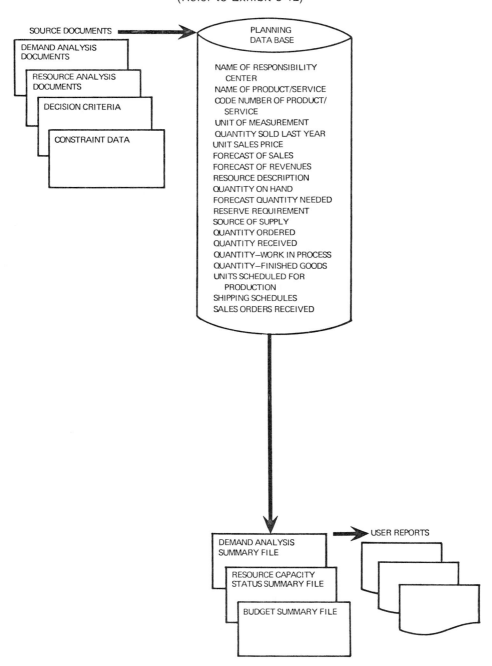

Exhibit 9-10
TRANSACTION SUMMARY AND DATA BASE STRUCTURE
FOR OPERATIONAL CONTROL DATA
(Refer to Exhibit 6-8)

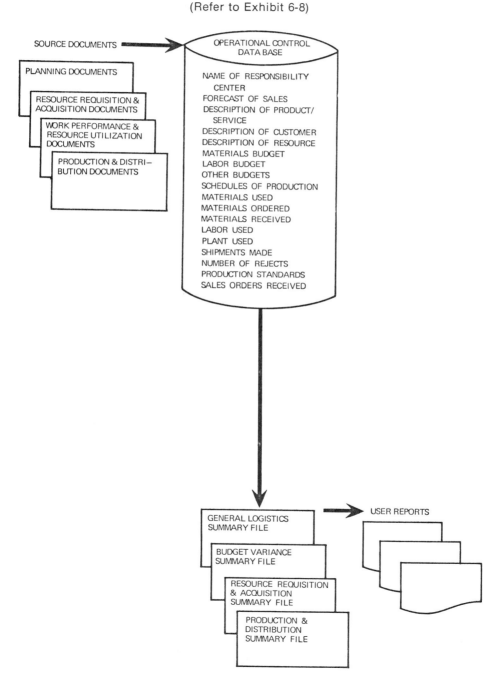

Exhibit 9-11

TRANSACTION SUMMARY AND DATA BASE STRUCTURE
FOR MANAGERIAL/FINANCIAL CONTROL DATA
(Refer to Exhibit 7-14)

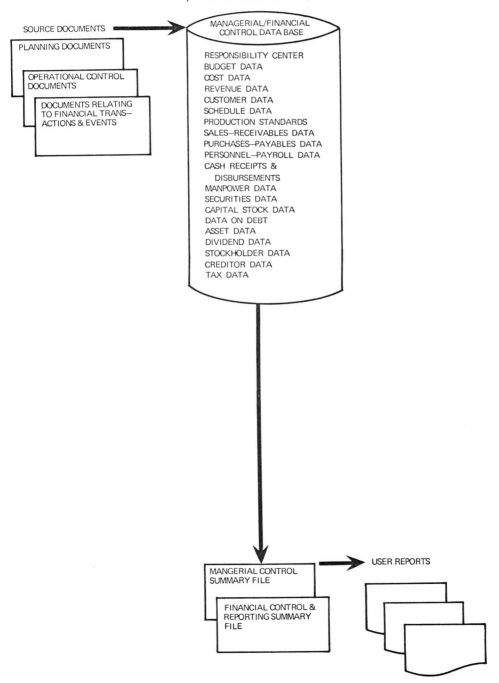

Exhibit 9-12

RESOURCES DATA FILE AND SERVICES DATA FILE

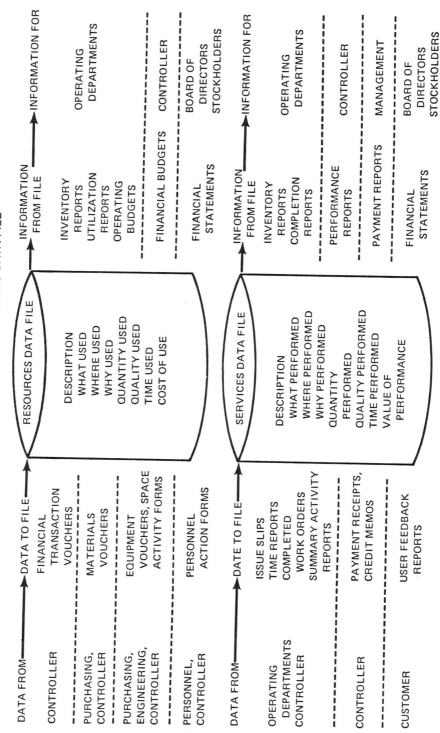

Exhibit 9-13

DETAILED STRUCTURE OF A HUMAN RESOURCES DATA FILE

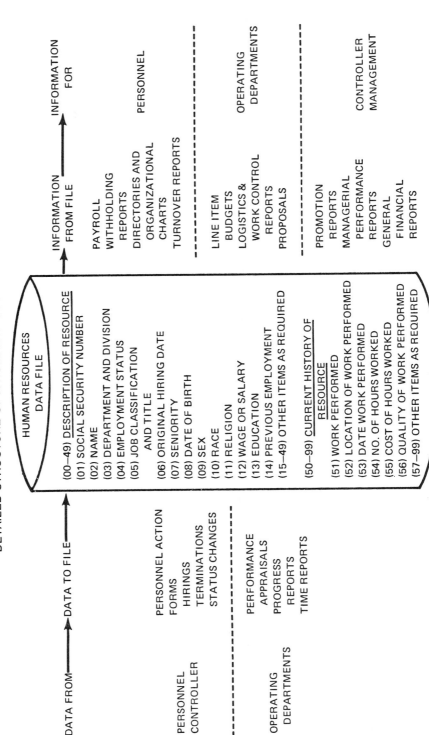

HUMAN RESOURCES DATA FILE

DATA FROM → DATA TO FILE

PERSONNEL CONTROLLER

PERSONNEL ACTION FORMS
HIRINGS
TERMINATIONS
STATUS CHANGES

OPERATING DEPARTMENTS

PERFORMANCE APPRAISALS
PROGRESS REPORTS
TIME REPORTS

(00–49) DESCRIPTION OF RESOURCE
(01) SOCIAL SECURITY NUMBER
(02) NAME
(03) DEPARTMENT AND DIVISION
(04) EMPLOYMENT STATUS
(05) JOB CLASSIFICATION AND TITLE
(06) ORIGINAL HIRING DATE
(07) SENIORITY
(08) DATE OF BIRTH
(09) SEX
(10) RACE
(11) RELIGION
(12) WAGE OR SALARY
(13) EDUCATION
(14) PREVIOUS EMPLOYMENT
(15–49) OTHER ITEMS AS REQUIRED

(50–99) CURRENT HISTORY OF RESOURCE
(51) WORK PERFORMED
(52) LOCATION OF WORK PERFORMED
(53) DATE WORK PERFORMED
(54) NO. OF HOURS WORKED
(55) COST OF HOURS WORKED
(56) QUALITY OF WORK PERFORMED
(57–99) OTHER ITEMS AS REQUIRED

INFORMATION FROM FILE → INFORMATION FOR

PAYROLL WITHHOLDING REPORTS
DIRECTORIES AND ORGANIZATIONAL CHARTS
TURNOVER REPORTS

PERSONNEL

LINE ITEM BUDGETS
LOGISTICS & WORK CONTROL REPORTS
PROPOSALS

OPERATING DEPARTMENTS

PROMOTION REPORTS
MANAGERIAL PERFORMANCE REPORTS
GENERAL FINANCIAL REPORTS

CONTROLLER
MANAGEMENT

detail depends on the objectives of the organization, its particular needs for information, and the resources the organization has available for the MIS. Once the structure of the data base, including its classification scheme and level of data detail, have been determined, the selection and design of a data coding system can proceed. The following section describes this procedure.

Data Coding System

A data coding system is a set of symbols, usually numbers, assigned to data elements. Use of a data coding system provides faster and more efficient identification, collection, storage, and retrieval of data elements in an information system. For example, a material used by an organization, such as wood for desks, may have a lengthy description, such as wood, walnut, grade A, medium grain. For ease of identification a code number, for example, 101, can be used to identify, record, store, and retrieve data on this material rather than using the total description.

The coding system chosen by an organization depends on its needs for aggregation of information. The discussion in this chapter relating to the classification of data according to varying levels of detail is relevant here. As more levels of data detail are employed, more extensive coding of data is required. If the total costs of a product must be identified for fabrication, assembly, finishing, advertising, selling, purchasing, receiving, and administrative functions, a code number for each of these functions must be developed. Costs of products produced and sold can then be identified and allocated to each function.

One coding system commonly used by organizations is the traditional chart of accounts, such as follows:

ASSETS

Current Assets
100 Cash in Bank
101 Savings
102 Investments in Securities
103 Accounts Receivable
110 Materials Inventory
111 Work in Process Inventory
112 Finished Goods Inventory

Fixed Assets
200 Production Equipment
201 Building
202 Vehicles
203 Land
204 Other

LIABILITIES

Short Term
300 Accounts Payable
301 Taxes Payable
302 Wages Payable
303 Other

Long Term
350 Notes Payable
351 Bonded Debt
352 Other

NET WORTH
400 Capital Stock
401 Retained Earnings
402 Surplus

INCOME
500 Sales Revenue
501 Investment Income
502 Other

OPERATING EXPENSES
600 Cost of Goods Sold
601 Direct Labor
602 Burden
603 Selling
604 Advertising
605 Fabricating
606 Assembly

607 Finishing
608 Procurement
609 Administrative
610 Salaries
611 Indirect Labor
612 Income Taxes
613 Travel
614 Depreciation
615 Other

MISCELLANEOUS

700 Dividends Paid
701 Profit Shares
702 Sale of Assets
703 Other

The code numbers in the chart of accounts can represent additional types of transaction summaries. Each item in the chart of accounts is a unit of analysis about which transactions and events occur and are recorded. At periodic intervals, the net effects of these transactions and events are reported on financial statements such as balance sheets and income statements.

The purpose of the chart of accounts is to facilitate the collection and classification of data relating to financial transactions in order to produce the organization's financial reports. Since it is somewhat limited in scope, it typically is not capable of producing all of the information needed for planning, operational control, and managerial/financial control. The following section describes a more comprehensive coding system that expands the chart of accounts concept. This system is capable of producing a large variety of information.

Designing the Coding System. The analysis of the operational subsystem of an organization described in Exhibits 5-2, 6-1, and 7-1 provides the basic activity framework for designing a comprehensive coding system to identify all data in the data base. The following is a summary of the operational subsystem and its nine phases (the numbers shown correspond with those used in Exhibits 5-2, 6-1, and 7-1):

0100   Definition of Objectives (Demand Analysis)
0200   Commitment of Resources (Resource Capacity Status Analysis)
0300   Requisition of Resources (Source Analysis)
0400   Acquisition of Resources (Resource Input Processing)
0500   Production (Resource Transformation)
0600   Distribution (Processing of Outputs)
0700   Utilization (Consumption of Outputs)
0800   Evaluation of Performance (Feedback Review and Evaluation)
0900   Corrective Action (Adjusting the System)

You will recall that phases 0100 and 0200 refer to planning; 0300 through 0700 to operational control, and 0800 through 0900 to managerial/financial control. Within each major phase, additional activities and their respective code numbers are identified in Exhibits 5-2, 6-1, and 7-1. For example, 0110 refers to analysis of constraints and decision criteria; 0210 to defining resource requirements; and 0510 to tasks related to resource utilization, work performance, and generation of products.

The examples of activities and tasks identified in Chapters 5 through 7 can be delineated as necessary to suit the level of data detail or disaggregation needed in each organization. Exhibit 9-14 shows a simplified yet complete coding scheme produced from the basic coding scheme. The coding scheme shown in Exhibit 9-14 consists of two digits for identification of inputs, six digits for identification of processors, and two digits for identification of outputs. The digits are combined into a ten-digit number for identification of input-processor-output combinations. The input code consists of four major categories of resources (current, fixed, human, and money) plus the data resource. Each major category is composed of various types of resources. For example, the human resource might include categories for engineers, technicians, accountants, machine operators, and inspectors. It may also be categorized into direct labor, indirect labor, and salaries. The processor is subdivided into organizational responsibility centers, activities, and tasks to identify completely what work is being performed by whom. The outputs consist of the categories of the different products and services produced. Depending on the size of the organization and the level of detail desired, field sizes may vary from those shown (for example, an organization may need more than 99 breakdowns of responsibility centers).

Some examples will aid in understanding how this ten-digit coding scheme is used. First, suppose that the complete numbering system for a particular organization is as follows:

INPUT

00-19 Current Resources
20-39 Fixed Resources
40-59 Human Resources
60-79 Money Resources
80-99 Data Resources

PROCESSOR

Responsibility Center	Activity-Task
00-09 Engineering	0100-0199 Definition of Objectives
10-19 Manufacturing	0200-0299 Commitment
20-29 Marketing	0300-0399 Requisition
30-39 Research	0400-0499 Acquisition
40-49 Procurement	0500-0599 Production
50-59 Accounting	0600-0699 Distribution
	0700-0799 Utilization
90-99 Special Staff Units	0800-0899 Evaluation
	0900-0999 Corrective Action

OUTPUT

00-49 Products Produced
50-99 Services Performed

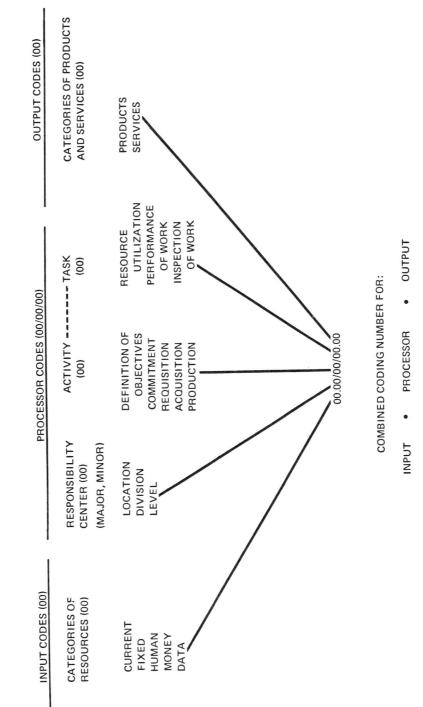

Exhibit 9-14
SIMPLIFIED STRUCTURE OF CODING SYSTEM

Consider a machine operator (input code 44) in a manufacturing department (responsibility center code 13) operating a machine in production (activity-task code 0517) to produce a particular product part (output code 35). These code numbers were obtained from the numbering system shown above for the categories of a human resource (input) in a manufacturing unit performing a production activity (processor) to produce a product (output). The ten-digit code for this example is:

44.130517.35
INPUT.PROCESSOR.OUTPUT

Another example might be an operations research specialist (input code 57) in a systems staff group (responsibility center code 91) performing a simulation study for planning purposes (activity task code 0235) to produce a capacity feasibility estimate (output code 72). The ten-digit code for this example is:

57.910235.72
INPUT.PROCESSOR.OUTPUT

In both examples, the resources used (input) and the product or service produced (output) are internal to the organization, i.e., the human resources are employees of the organization and the product (a manufactured part) or service produced (a capacity estimate) are used by other units within the organization. No provision has been made in this ten-digit coding system for separate designation of sources of inputs or users of outputs. If the sources and users are internal to the organization, no additional codes are needed, because the responsibility center codes for the processor constitute the appropriate internal sources and users of each input and output. When external sources and users exist, they must be identified separately. In this event, additional coding digits can be added onto the ends of the coding scheme to give a more complete coding system, as follows:

00.00.000000.00.00
SOURCE.INPUT.PROCESSOR.OUTPUT.USER

The general procedure for designing a complete coding system for an organization builds on the approach described in Chapter 8 for designing information needs and sources of data. You will recall in the discussion relating to identification and classification of information elements on reports, "identification" versus "measurement" elements were delineated. This approach involved the identification and classification of information elements and was demonstrated in Exhibit 8-2 by using selected reports of a business firm. The information classified as "identification requirements" in Exhibit 8-2 is shown on the top part of Exhibit 9-15. The identification requirements listed in Exhibit 9-15 are those items that have been previously identified as requiring code numbers. However, before code numbers can be assigned to these elements they must be classified within the source-input-processor-output-user framework. Also, duplicate information elements should be deleted, since each element to be coded must be assigned only one code number.

Exhibit 9-15

MODIFIED EXAMPLE OF DEVELOPMENT OF A CODING SYSTEM FOR A BUSINESS FIRM
(Refer to Exhibit 8-2)

DEMAND ANALYSIS REPORT (EXHIBIT 5-3)

1. OUTPUT CODES:
   A. OFFICE DESKS
   B. OFFICE CHAIRS
2. USER CODES:
   A. INDUSTRY
   B. GOVERNMENT

RESOURCE STATUS REPORT (EXHIBIT 5-6)

3. RESOURCE CODES:
   A. WOOD (SQUARE FEET)
   B. CARPENTRY LABOR (HOURS)
   C. FABRICATING EQUIPMENT
4. SOURCE CODES:
   A. ABC LUMBER COMPANY
   B. XYZ EQUIPMENT COMPANY
5. OUTPUT CODE:
   A. OFFICE DESKS
6. USER CODE:
   A. INDUSTRY

LOGISTICS REPORT (EXHIBIT 6-2)

7. OUTPUT CODE:
   A. OFFICE DESKS
8. INPUT CODES:
   A. CARPENTRY LABOR
   B. WOOD
9. PROCESSOR CODES:
   A. PRODUCTION DIVISION
   B. FABRICATION DEPARTMENT
   C. PROCUREMENT DIVISION
10. USER CODES:
   A. ABC COMPANY
   B. ASSEMBLY DEPARTMENT
   C. FABRICATION DEPARTMENT
   D. PRODUCTION DIVISION

MANGERIAL PERFORMANCE REPORT (EXHIBIT 7-10)

11. OFFICE CODES:
   A. OFFICE DESKS (FABRICATED)
   B. OFFICE CHAIRS (FABRICATED)
12. INPUT CODES:
   A. DIRECT LABOR COST (DESKS)
   B. DIRECT LABOR COST (CHAIRS)
   C. MATERIALS COST (DESKS)
   D. MATERIALS COST (CHAIRS)
   E. OTHER EXPENSE (DESKS)
   F. OTHER EXPENSE (CHAIRS)
13. PROCESSOR CODE:
   A. FABRICATION DEPARTMENT

SOURCE

4. A. ABC LUMBER COMPANY
4. B. XYZ EQUIPMENT COMPANY

INPUT

3. A. WOOD (SQUARE FEET)
3. B. CARPENTRY LABOR (HOURS)
3. C. FABRICATING EQUIPMENT
12. A. DIRECT LABOR COST (DESKS)
12. B. DIRECT LABOR COST (CHAIRS)
12. C. MATERIALS COST (DESKS)
12. D. MATERIALS COST (CHAIRS)
12. E. OTHER EXPENSE (DESKS)
12. F. OTHER EXPENSE (CHAIRS)

PROCESSOR

9. A. PRODUCTION DIVISION
9. B. FABRICATION DEPARTMENT
9. C. PROCUREMENT DIVISION

OUTPUT

1. A. OFFICE DESKS
1. B. OFFICE CHAIRS

USER

2. A. INDUSTRY
2. B. GOVERNMENT
10. A. ABC COMPANY
10. B. ASSEMBLY DEPARTMENT
10. C. FABRICATING DEPARTMENT
10. D. PRODUCTION DIVISION

NOTES:
1. THE UPPER PORTION OF THIS EXHIBIT REFLECTS THE GROSS CODING REQUIREMENTS TAKEN FROM THE "IDENTIFICATION AND CLASSIFICATION OF INFORMATION ELEMENTS" SHOWN IN EXHIBIT 8–2.
2. THE LOWER PORTION OF THIS EXHIBIT REFLECTS THE NET CODING REQUIREMENTS, THEREFORE DUPLICATE ELEMENTS ARE NOT REPEATED (E.G. 5A, 6A, 7A, 8A AND B, 11A AND B, AND 13) SINCE ONE CODE NUMBER WILL BE ASSIGNED TO EACH ELEMENT CLASSIFIED UNDER SOURCE, INPUT, PROCESSOR, OUTPUT, AND USER CATEGORIES.

The procedure for classifying information elements and for eliminating duplicate items is quite simple. Starting in the upper left-hand corner of Exhibit 9-15, each element to be coded is identified and listed as shown beginning with number 1a, office desks, through number 13a, fabrication department, shown on the right-hand side of the exhibit. In the lower half of Exhibit 9-15, the information elements shown on the upper portion have been classified and assigned to the appropriate source, input, processor, output, and user categories. For example, elements 1a and 1b (office desks and chairs) are listed under output on the lower portion of the exhibit, indicating two requirements for output code numbers. Similarly, elements 9a, 9b, and 9c (production division, fabrication department, and procurement division) are listed under processor, indicating three requirements for processor code numbers.

Note that duplicate information elements listed on the top of the exhibit are repeated in the process of listing coding requirements on the lower part. Such duplications are identified in note 2 of Exhibit 9-15. Also note that when information elements describing users are internal to the organization, such as 10b (assembly department), 10c (fabrication department), and 10d (production division), they should be listed and classified as coding requirements under processor, rather than under user. This procedure prevents duplication of code numbers for the same information element.

Based on the sample shown in Exhibit 9-15, the coding requirements for the four reports of this business firm are:

Source	*Input*	*Processor*	*Output*	*User*
2 items	9 items	4 items (including 10b, assembly department added from user category)	2 items	3 items (deleting 10b, c, d since they are listed under the processor)

Having identified the coding requirements in this manner, the next step is to define important categories to be coded within the classifications of source, input, processor, output, and user. For example, using the information in Exhibit 9-15 as summarized above together with the input-processor-output examples at the beginning of this discussion, the resource inputs may be categorized as follows:

> *00-19 Current Resources*
> > 01 Wood (square feet)
> > 10 Materials Costs (desks)
> > 11 Materials Cost (chairs)
> > 15 Other Expenses (desks)
> > 16 Other Expenses (chairs)
>
> *20-39 Fixed Resources*
> > 21 Fabricating Equipment

> *40-59 Human Resources*
>   40 Direct Labor (desks)
>   41 Direct Labor (chairs)
>   50 Carpentry Labor

and for the processor:

> *10-19 Manufacturing: 0500-0599 Production*
>   100500 Production Division
>   100510 Fabrication Department
>   100520 Assembly Department
>
> *40-49 Procurement: 0300-0399 Requisition*
>   400300 Procurement

and for outputs:

> *00-49 Products Produced*
>   10 Office Desks
>   20 Office Chairs

It is useful to categorize items to be coded within the major classifications of source-input-processor-output-user, so that series of numbers can easily be recognized as referring to specific categories of coded elements. For example, in the simplified categories shown in the foregoing paragraph, it can be seen that current resources numbers beginning with a zero (i.e. 01, wood) could be reserved for basic kinds of wood used for production of desks and chairs. The numbers 10-14 could be reserved for other materials, and 15-19 for miscellaneous unspecified current resources. As another example, code numbers 10510 to 10519 could be reserved for identifying tasks in the fabrication department (e.g. 100511 for shaping, 100512 for sanding, or 100513 for molding). Similarly code numbers 100520 to 100529 could be assigned to a task in the assembly department, such as 100521 for gluing. As a final example pertaining to human resources, code numbers 40 to 49 could be reserved for direct labor and 50 to 59 for labor related to functions such as carpentry (50), metalworking (51), or administration (59). In addition to facilitating the assignment of code numbers to transactions and events, categorization of code numbers can reduce the number of coding errors as employees become familiar with the range of code numbers assigned to each section of the code sequence.

Using the Coding System. To see how the coding system is used, it is necessary to examine the source documents in which coding of data elements is performed. Although coding can be accomplished when source documents are processed, it is usually more efficient to code transactions when data is initially generated or recorded. Data handling is then minimized and the possibility of errors is reduced.

Consider a timecard or time report source document of the general form shown in Exhibit 9-16. In this example, an employee has recorded his identification number (social security number), the ending date of the work period (week), the number (quantity) of hours worked (40), and the amount (quantity) of work produced (500). In addition, he has coded his resource type (44), the organizational unit for whom the work was performed (13), the type of activity and task (0517), and the type of product worked on (35). The code numbers used here are the same as those for the machine operator example on page 369. Exhibit 9-16 shows how the machine operator's timecard is prepared and coded. If coding of the timecard shown in Exhibit 9-16 is deferred until a labor utilization cost report is prepared (perhaps a month after the work is performed) and done by an administrative clerk rather than the machine operator, there is a greater chance for coding errors.

Exhibit 9-17 shows the flow of coded source data into the data base and out to reports. In this exhibit, source documents containing resource, processor, and product/service data comprise the inputs to the data base. *Resource data* should be coded by resource type (digit positions 1-2, input code) and by organizational unit, function, and activity-task (digit positions 3-8, processor code). The organizational unit, function, or activity for which the resource is used can then be identified for cost analysis. Some of the source documents that contain resource data are specification sheets, purchase orders, requisitions, and materials and equipment vouchers. *Processor data* should be coded by resource type (digit positions 1-2, input code), the using organizational unit, function, and activity-task (digit positions 3-8, processor code), and the type of product or service (digit positions 9-10, output code). This coding permits the development of cost data for each type of product or service produced as well as for organizational units, functions, and activities. If resources or products and services cannot be identified separately as they are used or produced, they must be allocated and coded by a formula. Examples of

Exhibit 9-16

CODED SOURCE DOCUMENT—TIMECARD

I.D. NUMBER:			FOR WORK PERIOD ENDING:		
205 34 7986			10 09 74		

CODE NUMBERS & QUANTITIES

RESOURCE TYPE	QUANTITY	ORGANIZATIONAL UNIT	ACTIVITY/ TASK	QUANTITY	WORK PERFORMED
4 4	4 0	1 3	0 5 1 7	5 0 0	3 5
— —	— — —	— —	— — — —	— — —	— —
— —	— — —	— —	— — — —	— — —	— —
— —	— — —	— —	— — — —	— — —	— —

Exhibit 9-17

FLOW OF CODED DATA INTO AND OUT OF THE DATA BASE

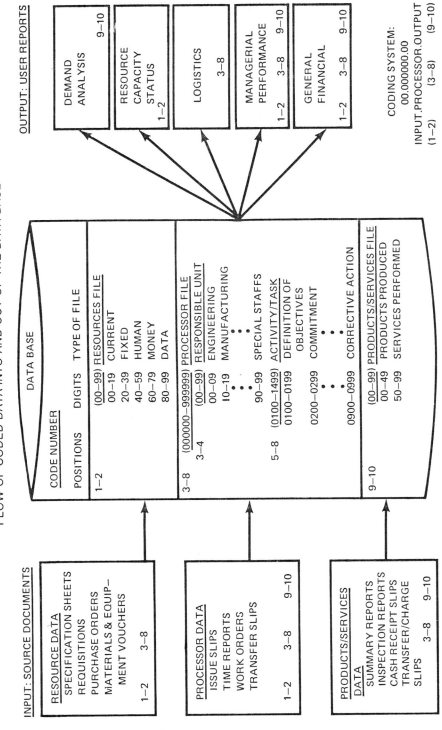

processor source documents are issue slips, time reports, work orders, inspection reports, and transfer slips. *Products and services data* should be coded for the producing organizational unit, function, and activity-task (digit positions 3-8, processor code), and by type of product or service produced (digit positions 9-10, output code). This coding is important so that information on products and services produced can be related to the organizations, functions, and activities responsible for producing them. Examples of these source documents are summary activity reports, inspection reports, utilization reports, checks, cash receipts, and credit slips.

As a more specific illustration, consider the example of the machine operator and his timecard shown in Exhibit 9-16. Data elements from the timecard (source document) are stored in the appropriate files in the data base. From these files they are retrieved for the managerial performance report (user report). Exhibit 9-18 demonstrates the flow of coded data, but it is not fully indicative of the complete multiplicity of uses of single data inputs into the data base. Actually, these data elements are also used in other reports, such as the human resource capacity status report and the manufacturing logistics and work control reports.

MANAGEMENT OF A LARGE INTEGRATED DATA BASE

An integrated information system implies centralized, coordinated information planning (design) and control (evaluation) activities and decentralized information processing activities. Decentralization is necessary because information processing involves not only data conversion, but also various other steps including collection and coding of data throughout the entire organization. For a large integrated data base, this data must serve a multiplicity of users, each having varying needs for information. Managers must become accustomed to sharing data if single data inputs are to serve multiple information needs. This is a basic premise of the integrated information syste : approach. Organizations cannot permit their managers to be so possessive about their data resource that others do not have access to it and, as a result, must generate duplicate data.

The concept of multiple use of a single data input suggests an expanded data classification scheme and coding system. In many respects, the problems associated with the management of an integrated data base often are influenced by the size and type of coding system. If the coding system involves using a 20-digit code instead of a 10-digit code, many more data elements must be coded, processed, stored, and manipulated to generate the needed reports and volume of detail. On the other hand, it may be justifiable economically to use the 20-digit code if the benefits to management from using more levels of details in reports are greater than the costs associated with this expanded classification scheme. These decisions are the responsibility of the systems design staff and top management.

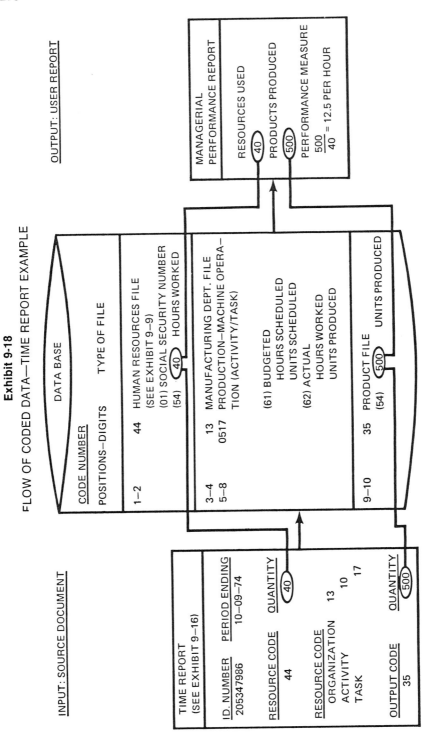

Exhibit 9-18

FLOW OF CODED DATA—TIME REPORT EXAMPLE

INPUT: SOURCE DOCUMENT

OUTPUT: USER REPORT

DATA BASE

CODE NUMBER

POSITIONS—DIGITS　　TYPE OF FILE

1–2　　　　44　　HUMAN RESOURCES FILE
　　　　　　　　　(SEE EXHIBIT 9–9)
　　　　　　　　　(01) SOCIAL SECURITY NUMBER
　　　　　　　　　(54)　HOURS WORKED

3–4　　　　13　　MANUFACTURING DEPT. FILE
5–8　　　0517　　PRODUCTION–MACHINE OPERA—
　　　　　　　　　TION (ACTIVITY/TASK)

　　　　　　　　　(61) BUDGETED
　　　　　　　　　　　　HOURS SCHEDULED
　　　　　　　　　　　　UNITS SCHEDULED
　　　　　　　　　(62) ACTUAL
　　　　　　　　　　　　HOURS WORKED
　　　　　　　　　　　　UNITS PRODUCED

9–10　　　35　　PRODUCT FILE
　　　　　　　　　(54)　UNITS PRODUCED

MANAGERIAL
PERFORMANCE REPORT

RESOURCES USED

40

PRODUCTS PRODUCED

500

PERFORMANCE MEASURE

$$\frac{500}{40} = 12.5 \text{ PER HOUR}$$

TIME REPORT
(SEE EXHIBIT 9–16)

ID. NUMBER　　PERIOD ENDING　　QUANTITY
205347986　　10–09–74

RESOURCE CODE　　QUANTITY
　　44　　　　　　　　40

RESOURCE CODE
ORGANIZATION　13
ACTIVITY　　　　10
TASK　　　　　　17

OUTPUT CODE　　QUANTITY
　　35　　　　　　　500

NOTE:
THE QUANTITIES OF RESOURCES USED AND PRODUCTS PRODUCED ARE ENTERED INTO THE MANUFACTURING DEPARTMENT FILE, SECTION 62, AS WELL AS THE RESOURCES AND PRODUCT FILES. THE DATA BASE SEGMENTS CONTAIN BOTH PERIOD AND CUMULA—TIVE DATA, BUDGETED AND ACTUAL. USER REPORTS ALSO SHOW BUDGETED AND ACTUAL QUANTITY DATA.

SUMMARY

This chapter describes the general procedure involved in designing the MIS data base. The data base is a facilitator of the creation of value or utility related to converting data into information for operations and management. The factors to consider in the definition of the quantity, quality, time, and cost requirements of the data base are identified within the general context of measuring the costs of data versus the benefits of information for operations and management.

The general structure of the data base is a way of identifying and classifying data about events and transactions so that meaningful information on reports can be produced. Both vertical organizational and horizontal subsystem classifications are important data classification schemes to be incorporated in the data base structure. Within this vertical-horizontal framework, the appropriate number of levels of data detail to include in the data base is dependent upon the nature of the organization and its information needs.

Data coding is a means of identifying, recording, storing, and retrieving data about events and transactions. The level of data detail required in the data base dictates the type of data coding system needed.

REVIEW QUESTIONS

1. Discuss the purpose of a data base. What value or utility does it provide?
2. Outline the general procedure for designing a data base. What orientation should the design effort take?
3. Discuss the acquisition, retrieval, and retention requirements related to the quantity or volume of data to be included in the data base.
4. The time requirement of data storage needs depends on frequency of retrieval and access time. What problems do you see in defining the time requirement?
5. Discuss the factors you would include in defining the quality requirement of data acquisition and storage. What problems do you see in this effort?
6. The classification of data elements into the data base must be flexible to provide for a number of retrieval needs. Identify several of these classifications or needs. How does this classification relate to the basic systems model?
7. Discuss the function of a data coding scheme or system.
8. Discuss the general approach or procedure for designing a data coding system. What problems do you see, and how would you alleviate these problems?
9. What problems do you see regarding the use of the data coding system? Why should responsibilities for coding be designated? Who is generally involved in the coding of data elements for the organization?
10. Comment on the universality of the data base concepts discussed in this chapter to business, governmental, and educational organizations. What limitations do you see?

EXERCISE 9-1:   Data Coding System Design

Select one of the following sets of reports that is included in or was developed for the student exercises for Chapter 8, using the format shown in Exhibit 8-2:

Custom Machine Tool Company (Exercise 8-2, question 1).
Discount, Inc. (Exercise 8-2, question 1).
Admissions and Registration Division (Exercise 8-2, question 1).
Farm Products Corporation (Exercise 8-2, question 1).
An organization with which you are familiar (Exercise 8-2).
State University (Exercise 8-1, question 1).
Other selected reports (Exercise 8-1, question 2).

For the set of reports selected as summarized in the format shown in Exhibit 8-2, accomplish the following:

1. Prepare a summary of the coding requirements for the information elements identified for the reports, and classify these coding requirements according to source, input, processor, output, and user categories within the format shown in Exhibit 9-15.
2. Based on the coding requirements identified and classified in question 1, develop a data coding scheme relating to Exhibit 9-15.

EXERCISE 9-2:   Chart of Accounts

Refer to the example of a chart of accounts shown on page 265. Based on the minimum or basic types of information needs required for planning, operational control, and managerial/financial control (as described in Chapters 5, 6, and 7):

1. What other coding requirements do you feel are needed to serve these basic information needs?
2. Evaluate the advantages and limitations of the data coding scheme utilized in the sample chart of accounts relative to a data coding scheme developed within the input-output model framework.
3. Show how you would revise the data coding scheme to accomodate the additional coding requirements you identified in question 1.

EXERCISE 9-3:   Literature Survey

Read and critique several articles on one or all of the following topics:

1. The nature, purpose, and structure of an integrated data base.
2. The nature, purpose, and structure of an integrated data coding scheme (including examples of data coding schemes).
3. Problems in designing an integrated data base or coding scheme.

In your readings, focus on larger and multifunctional data bases or data coding schemes, i.e., for a total organization or for several major parts of the organization's operations that are connected through one information system.

10 DESIGNING THE COMPUTERIZED DATA PROCESSOR

In Chapter 9, concepts and methodology relating to design of a data base for an MIS were presented. The primary focus was on providing an integrated structure and coding scheme for *linking* information outputs with data inputs throughout the entire organization. This chapter deals with the design of a computerized data processor to *transform* data inputs into information outputs. The data base and the data processor constitute the facilitator of MIS processes which provide the information needed for operations and management. For example, various data inputs about actual monthly sales volume classified by product, sales region, and salesman are retrieved from the data base and transformed by the computerized data processor into a sales forecast report for next month's sales meeting. Exhibit 10-1 presents an overview of the computerized data processor as the facilitator for transforming data inputs into information outputs.

This chapter describes the procedure for analysis and design of a computer system for an integrated management information system. In this context, "design" refers to selection of the desired computer model, configuration, components, and supplier based on a prescribed set of information processing needs. In other words, the task of designing a computerized data processor is in reality the task of analyzing alternative computer systems and selecting the best alternative.

Therefore the major objectives of this chapter are:

1. To describe the characteristics of a computerized data processor for an MIS.
2. To explain the feasibility study methodology used to select a computer system for the MIS, which involves:
   a. Analysis of computer use
   b. Analysis and design of computer system components
   c. Analysis of computer sources (suppliers), based on preimplementation and postimplementation economic feasibility.

CHARACTERISTICS OF A COMPUTERIZED DATA PROCESSOR FOR AN MIS

Computers have undergone extensive technological advancement since their introduction, and those which are now used in MIS applications have very complex configurations. In all, we have seen the introduction of four generations of computers. *First generation computers* (prior to 1959) were

Exhibit 10-1

THE COMPUTERIZED DATA PROCESSOR AS A FACILITATOR
FOR TRANSFORMING DATA INPUTS INTO INFORMATION OUTPUTS

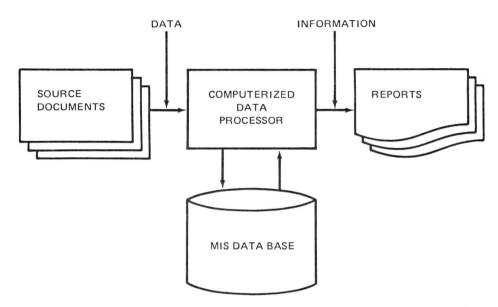

tube-type machines with relatively small storage capacity and relatively slow speed (in the millisecond range). *Second generation computers* (1959-1965) employed transitors in their circuitry, incorporated better input-output devices, had large modular-type or add-on core storage capacity, and were considerably faster (in the microsecond range). *Third generation computers* (since 1965) are characterized by integrated circuitry, interchangeable components, and extremely fast speeds (in the nanosecond range). In addition, they are oriented toward wide-area data communications and perform several operations simultaneously, thereby making possible remote, interactive use by many different users at the same time.

It is not yet entirely clear what *fourth generation computers* will be like. To date, marked changes in the technology over third generation machines have not occurred, although there continue to be advancements in circuit speed and in modularity, i.e., better unit standardization to facilitate assembly and enhance component flexibility. There is some consensus in the industry that fourth generation machines will be characterized by added compaction and miniaturization through large scale integration (LSI) of circuitry modules. This should increase computational speed and reduce hardware costs still further. In any event, these computers will undoubtedly be more sophisticated and better suited for use in integrated management information systems.

Third generation computers are now most widely used in MIS applications. A typical third generation computer system for an integrated MIS of the variety described in this book might have the following components and characteristics:

1. A *central processing unit (CPU)* which provides simultaneous information processing capability for many different users and has a moderate amount of storage capacity.
2. *On-line, direct-access magnetic disk devices*, each having a considerable amount of storage capacity.
3. *Off-line magnetic tape devices*, each having an almost unlimited magnetic tape storage capacity.
4. *Card reader, card punch, and high-speed printing devices* for routine batch processing.
5. *Remote typewriter terminals and visual display devices* for direct interactive information processing and decision making.

Although the configuration and characteristics listed above are typical of many third generation computer systems used for management information systems, many variations are possible The selectivity of characteristics makes possible further utilization of the computer as an information processor. Unfortunately, the large number of possible variations often makes the analysis and selection of a computer an exceedingly complex task. However, an understanding of the major differences in characteristics is usually helpful in this regard. Basic computer characteristics are described in the following sections. Examination of these characteristics also serves as an introduction to computer technology.

Random Versus Sequential Access

The method of access to stored data items is an important characteristic for a large data base. In *sequential access* devices, data elements must be accessed (i.e., stored or retrieved) in the order in which they were originally arranged. Punched cards are read and fed into the computer sequentially by a card reader, a sequential input device. Cards are punched in a sequential manner. Data read into the computer from a card reader may be stored on paper tape or magnetic tape. Consequently, tape devices are also sequential access devices. Data elements are not individually addressable (locatable) on the tape, and they must be retrieved by reading the tape sequentially from the beginning. This is time-consuming and requires handling a great quantity of data each time the tape is read to retrieve particular data elements.

In *random access* devices, individual data storage locations are addressable, so that data elements can be selectively stored and retrieved by the address at which they are located. Random access data files need not be read sequentially from the beginning. Internal CPU core storage is randomly accessible, since all storage locations are individually addressable. Magnetic drums and disks also have individually addressable storage locations; therefore, they have random access data storage and retrieval capability. In general, random access is a faster method of retrieval than sequential access, and much less data is read in each retrieval.

On-Line Versus Off-Line

The distinction between off-line and on-line input-output devices and storage devices is related to their method of operation rather than to their method of communication connection. All these devices are physically connected to the central processor when they are used. *Off-line devices* are those devices that require human intervention for operation and control, such as loading data cards into the card reader and card punch, and mounting paper or magnetic tapes that contain stored data or data to be stored. Therefore, the card reader, card punch, paper tape, and magnetic tape are off-line devices.

On-line devices do not require human intervention. Input data is generally transmitted from the point of event or transaction via a telephone line or other data channel directly to storage through the CPU. Output information is generally transmitted directly to the user from storage through the CPU. In addition to internal CPU core storage, magnetic drum and magnetic disk devices are on-line external devices requiring no operator intervention or control to access desired data. Consequently, on-line devices are less expensive to operate, primarily because they are fully automatic. They also provide immediate access to the CPU, since no operator delays are introduced.

Real Time Versus Lapsed Time

Real time is an often misunderstood concept, having two somewhat different connotations. If information can be received in sufficient time for a decision to be made without a penalty of any kind, then it is said to be received in real time. This receipt of information may include various steps, such as collection, storage, and retrieval. The time period can be quite variable, from a few seconds to several days of *lapsed time*. This aspect of real time versus lapsed time is perhaps confusing, because real time has no direct relationship to actual clock or calendar time. Real time pertains only to the actual time frame of the decision to be made.

There is a somewhat different connotation of real time which has developed as a result of modern, high-speed, third and fourth generation computer technology. In this case, real time is synonymous with *instantaneous* transfer of information. The concept of real time implies immediate updating of data in the data base as events or transactions occur, rather than only intermittent updates such as when the user requests information from the data base.

In this text, the latter concept of real time is most important for an integrated management information system. Because of the size and complexity of most organizations, rapid data storage and retrieval are necessary to expedite decision making and minimize delays. Moreover, if data is processed rapidly, it will be available for making most decisions regardless of their urgency.

Time Sharing Versus One-At-A-Time Usage

First and second generation computers were capable of running programs only one at a time. Some of the more sophisticated models of third generation computer systems are capable of simultaneous execution of two or more programs in a CPU. This is accomplished by partitioning the internal memory of the CPU to hold segments of several programs at once. The execution of these programs proceeds simultaneously according to a complex priority scheme which is aimed at keeping the CPU fully utilized. Scheduling the execution of program instructions is performed by a sophisticated set of control programs. With this capability, it is possible for several users located at different input-output devices to share the time of the central processor, balancing its load among several programs. This computer system feature, called *time sharing,* enables the CPU to be more fully utilized.

Time sharing is not restricted by organizational boundaries, and commercial time sharing services are widely available. Any organization, even the very small, can purchase computer time. Commercial time sharing services are sometimes called *computer utilities*, and it is predicted that in the future regional computer utility networks will be as common as other public utilities are today. This will result in more widespread use of computers in all types of organizations (and possibly in private residences as well).

Integrated Versus Batch Systems

In a *batch processing system,* an entire job or job batch is completely processed before another job is begun. The job batch may consist of a number of similar individual jobs, each requiring similar processing, that can be processed together efficiently in one processing sequence. In addition to the program to be executed, batch processing may involve handling both historical or permanent information and temporary information that is pertinent only to a single batch processing cycle. A conceptual view of a simple batch processing system is presented in Exhibit 10-2. Here, the program for execution (on magnetic tape) is input to the CPU, together with the data consisting of a master file (on tape) and detailed transactions (on punched cards or entered directly from a remote terminal). This batch is processed into reports (on a printer or a remote terminal), and the master file (on tape) is updated to include the detailed transactions just processed.

Payroll is a typical batch processing application. Usually a permanent master file contains name, department, salary rate, and detailed input consisting of regular hours worked and overtime hours that pertain only to one period worked and to one batch processing cycle. During processing, the permanent master file is updated to include current payroll data for the next batch processing cycle.

Exhibit 10-2
A SIMPLE BATCH PROCESSING SYSTEM

INPUT ⟶ PROCESSOR ⟶ OUTPUT

INPUT	PROCESSOR	OUTPUT
Program for Execution (tape)	CPU	Reports (printer, remote terminal)
Old Master File (tape)		Updated Master File (tape)
Detailed Transactions (cards, remote terminal)		

Batch processing is usually performed on jobs that can be scheduled in advance or run at regular intervals. Therefore, batch processing is normally conducted using off-line input-output and storage devices. These devices employ sequential access, thus their use is limited in real-time MIS applications where random access is essential.

Many recent data processing systems have employed indexed-sequential file organization as an alternative to simple sequential organization. In this scheme, file indexes, which can be assigned and changed during processing, are used to avoid processing entire files sequentially, thereby making batch processing more flexible and more applicable to real-time management information systems. Real-time applications are generally justified in terms of providing users with more timely information for making better decisions. They also may provide reduction in data processing costs and improved quality of processing if the volume of jobs is large and the size of jobs is small. This is because high volume decreases the marginal cost of processing and because small jobs are easier to process and to control. Therefore, the advantages of batch processing are dependent not only upon job regularity, but also upon the quantity and quality requirements of the job.

Integrated processing systems are on-line, real-time computer systems with time-sharing capability. The term integrated system means the combination of several on-line storage devices and input-output devices with a multiprocessing CPU for simultaneously performing many information processing tasks in real time. A conceptual view of an integrated system is given in Exhibit 10-3. In this system, data transmission channels link input and output devices to the CPU. Random-access storage for the data base is provided by magnetic core and disk devices. All the input-output devices are on-line to the CPU in an integrated system. Large amounts of data storage hold data and act as receivers for input-output operations which are slow compared with CPU processing speeds. This is a much more sophisticated technical system than the batch processing system described previously.

Some typical examples of integrated information systems are the Air Force SAGE Project, the American Airlines SABRE Project, and IBM's Project OMNI.[1] The SAGE System is a real-time, multiple input-output information processing network for U.S. air defense. The SABRE System maintains a complete, up-to-date inventory of airline passenger reservations and available seats and enables reservation agents anywhere to make, confirm, cancel, or change reservations and to determine seat availability in just a few seconds. The OMNI System is a totally integrated management information system for the IBM Office Products Division, which manufactures, markets, and services its entire product line. This system was designed to provide current information on all facets of manufacturing, orders, deliveries, and service. Although the full potential of computerized management information systems in business and industry has by no means been realized, these three systems are examples of what can be accomplished.

---

[1] These systems are described in Joseph F. Kelly, *Computerized Management Information Systems* (New York: Macmillan Co., 1970), pp. 213-221.

Exhibit 10-3
AN INTEGRATED DATA PROCESSING SYSTEM

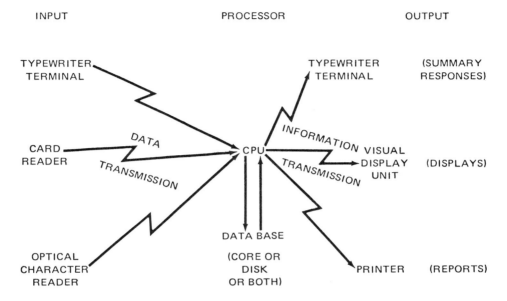

Other examples of the use of third and fourth generation computer systems in special-purpose information systems include: real-time monitoring of stock market transactions in brokerage firms; on-line control of inventory in catalog-order businesses (such as Sears Roebuck and Montgomery Ward); and recording and processing of financial transactions in savings and loan institutions. In each of these applications, real-time information is provided to many users at the same time using an integrated data processor with on-line data input and information output and with random access to a structured data base.

THE FEASIBILITY STUDY

The design of a computerized data processor for a comprehensive management information system involves analysis of computer use, specification of the computer system components, and economic analysis and identification of computer sources. The entire effort is commonly referred to as a *feasibility study*, and the ultimate objective is to select a computer system which will permit optimization of the cost-effectiveness of the entire MIS. In this context, the term "feasibility" is used to connote the idea of economic suitability of alternative computer system designs.

The feasibility study is ordinarily carried out by the systems design staff, discussed in Chapter 3. This staff has the responsibility for performing a comprehensive study, thus assuring that the selected computer configuration will fulfill the information processing needs of all organizational segments. Sometimes outside consultants and representatives of computer manufacturers are employed to assist in this effort, especially when the systems design staff is small or when it lacks the necessary computer expertise. However, representatives of computer manufacturers are quite likely biased toward selection of their own products. The feasibility study will be most successful if it is accomplished internally, with the assistance of outside consultants as needed.

The feasibility study normally consists of three major tasks: (1) the computer use analysis, (2) the analysis of computer system components, and (3) the computer source analysis. The first task, analysis of computer uses, is an extension of the analysis of information needs described in Chapters 5, 6, and 7. The second task usually involves two phases: analysis of input and output requirements, and central processing unit analysis. The third major task, computer source analysis, ordinarily consists of preimplementation and postimplementation evaluation of economic feasibility. The former is essential, and the latter is also important to ensure that anticipated benefits of the newly implemented system are actually achieved. Postimplementation evaluation is too often overlooked once the new system is in operation.

A comprehensive framework for the feasibility study is illustrated in Exhibit 10-4. Since a computer is a system, it is convenient to present this framework in a source-input-processor-output-use context. Beginning on the right side of the exhibit, computer use analysis is the first major task to be performed. The next task refers to computer system component analysis, namely input-output and CPU analysis. The last task is economic analysis having to do with selection of the source (supplier) of the computer. The function, type, and design criteria shown at the left side of the exhibit apply to each of the five system component headings. These will be discussed in detail in the following paragraphs.

Computer Use Analysis

There are two major uses of the computer: problem solving, and data processing. *Problem solving* is analytical in nature and involves the analysis of decision tradeoffs. For example, it may be necessary to decide between two different capital investment alternatives, such as expanding existing facilities or purchasing new facilities. Or it may be desirable to evaluate allocations of resources to different activities or programs. Because these comparisons are usually highly analytical and computationally complex, a high-speed computer processing capability is advisable. However, only relatively small amounts of data inputs and outputs may be involved. This is because the data inputs are often quite concise, and the computed results consist of specific solutions to problems rather than lengthy tables of results. Only a few items of data input may cause the computer to calculate for a long time to produce one single answer.

The objective of computer processing for problem solving is to improve the cost-effectiveness of operational subsystems and decisions by providing better information on a more timely basis. A greater quantity of data can be processed

Exhibit 10-4
FRAMEWORK FOR FEASIBILITY STUDY

← Computer System Component Analysis →

	COMPUTER SOURCE ANALYSIS	INPUT MEDIA/ DEVICES	CPU	OUTPUT MEDIA/ DEVICES	COMPUTER USE ANALYSIS
FUNCTION	Provide computer system	Conversion of user language to machine language Receive data inputs into processor and storage	Control Storage Arithmetic-logic Interface	Conversion of machine language to user language Distribute information outputs to users	Utilize computer system
TYPE	Third generation computer Configuration Manufacturer	Intermediate Punched cards Paper tape Magnetic tape Direct Teletypewriter Light probe	Batch Integrated	Intermediate Punched cards Paper tape Magnetic tape Direct Printer Teletypewriter Visual display	Problem solving Data processing
CRITERIA	Objectives Improve cost-effectiveness of operating system and information system Primary factors economic hardware software service	Capacity Error potential Speed Direct cost Equipment Operation Modularity	Size Storage Control Speed Internal transfer rate Arithmetic speed Cost Modularity	Capacity Error potential Speed Direct cost Equipment Operation Modularity	Decision making Reporting Quantity Quality Timliness Cost

by including more variables in the analysis and by extending the time horizon of the analysis. Increased information quality results from more relevant variables, more emphasis on analysis rather than data manipulation, and less human intervention in the analysis. More timely data processing is possible from faster collection, storage, calculation, and retrieval of data and from a larger storage capacity. These benefits increase operational cost-effectiveness to the extent that faster and more accurate decision making and problem solving are made possible.

Specific applications of computers for processing information in the problem solving mode include the various decision models developed by management scientists. *Simulation models* are symbolic representations of dynamic systems which when operated "in the computer" can be used to evaluate decision alternatives. Simulation models require extensive analytical computer processing in the form of repetitive, sequential computations. *Allocation models*, which are typified by linear programming models, are used to find solutions for allocation of scarce resources problems. Allocation models require extensive computational capability in order to perform the many iterative calculations needed to find the optimal allocation solutions. Other mathematical models used in operations research work, such as those for inventory replenishment, are also computationally rigorous and problem-oriented. The economic order quantity (EOQ) model is such a model.

The second major use of the computer is *data processing*, which involves producing reports or preparing documents. Data processing generally involves transforming data from one form into another, such as preparing time reports and paychecks from time cards or preparing purchase orders from materials requests. In this case, arithmetic operations are either relatively simple or virtually nonexistent, so only a very basic computational capability is required. On the other hand, large amounts of data are needed to prepare reports and documents. Often multiple documents must be processed and prepared for wide distribution throughout the organization. Consequently, the input-output handling requirement for data processing is extensive—just the reverse of the problem solving situation.

The objective of computerized data processing, contrasted with problem solving, is to improve the cost-effectiveness of the information system. This can be accomplished by reducing the amount of information generated, reducing the processing time, and increasing the quality of processing. First, computerizing the data base and the data processor permit variation in the amount and extent of reporting so that only summary information and exception situations are reported routinely. Second, reduced processing time is possible over manual methods because of computer processing rates and fast retrieval of data from a unified data base. Third, better quality of computerized data processing over manual methods results from standardized data management practices (to improve readability of reports), less human intervention (to reduce errors), and automated data processing procedures (to eliminate inconsistency). At present, use of computers in business for data processing heavily outweighs problem solving applications.

The criteria for analyzing computer use are quantity, quality, timeliness, and cost implications associated with problem solving and data processing. The quantity, quality, and timeliness criteria as applied to the two uses are summarized in Exhibit 10-5. Costs are interrelated with and dependent upon the other three criteria. Computational costs are relatively high for problem solving, and input-output processing costs are high for data processing due to the high speeds and volumes required in each. In either case, cost is dependent on the use of the processed information. Processing costs for problem solving must be weighed against the cost savings derived from a better, more accurate, more timely solution to a problem. For example, the use of the linear programming model must be justified in terms of providing a more profitable allocation of resources than without the model. Also, data processing costs for reporting must be weighed against the cost savings over other methods of processing or against the value derived from maintaining better operational control through more timely reporting. Frequent preparation and distribution of a report must be justified in terms of providing cost reduction through better control decisions.

Exhibit 10-5

CRITERIA FOR ANALYSIS OF COMPUTER USES

	Use	
CRITERIA	PROBLEM SOLVING	DATA PROCESSING
Quantity:		
Input-output volume	Small	Very large
Ratio of computations to input-output	Very large	Small
Storage volume	Small to medium	Large
Quality:		
Input-output	Moderately important	Very important
Timeliness:		
Input-output speed	Relatively unimportant	Very important
Computational speed	Very important	Relatively unimportant

Analysis of Computer System Components

Two system components must be analyzed: input-output media and devices and the central processing unit (CPU). Because output and input are very similar, they will be discussed together.

Input-Output Analysis. The functions of a computer *output* device are: to *convert* machine language from the processor into a user-oriented language such as FORTRAN or COBOL; and to *distribute* the processed information to users. Output devices make it possible for the user to receive information from the computer in an understandable, meaningful form.

Output media and devices can be classified into two general types, intermediate and direct. The intermediate type includes those media, such as punched cards, paper tape, and magnetic tape, that convert information or data into a user-oriented language in a form not easily readible by a (human) user. The major purposes of these output media are to move information and data out of the processor efficiently and to provide flexibility for preparing reports and documents in varying formats at different times, i.e., to provide temporary storage capacity.

Direct output media and devices include printers, typewriter terminals, and visual display devices. These devices convert the processing language of the machine into a language form directly readible by the user. When printed reports must be prepared or when information is needed for decision making, conversion to English letters and Arabic numerals is necessary so that they have meaning to the user, rather than only to the computer.

The functions of a computer *input* device are: to *convert* user-oriented languages into machine language, and to *receive* information and data inputs into the central processor for execution of storage. Another difference is that the activator of the input device may be either the central processing unit or a human operator, whereas the activator of the output device is ordinarily the central processing unit. For example, a user punches cards or operates a typewriter terminal to send data to the processor, but automated card punching or printing output devices are activated by the central processing unit.

Essentially the same criteria are used for analysis of the computer system components as were used for computer use analysis. For input-output media and devices, these criteria are quantity, quality, time, cost, and modularity. Quantity refers to the volume of information collected, converted, and distributed. Quality refers here to the degree of human intervention required and the potential for error. Timeliness refers to the transfer speed (i.e., the speed of reading data and writing information) of the various input-output devices. Cost is related to the complexity of the devices and to their information handling capacity and efficiency. Modularity refers to unit standardization to improve flexibility in combining devices. Modularity of components affects the potential for expansion or alteration of the system. These criteria are summarized in Exhibit 10-6.

The total cost of input-output devices involves indirect as well as direct costs. Direct costs include the cost of the devices themselves and their operation. For example, magnetic tape drives and visual display devices are expensive items, but the cost of operating these devices is relatively low compared with other devices that require more human attention. Indirect costs, on the other hand, refer to costs incurred in preparing to use these devices or in servicing them. Examples of indirect costs are:

Exhibit 10-6

CRITERIA FOR ANALYSIS OF INPUT OUTPUT COMPONENTS

CRITERIA	INTERMEDIATE TYPE			DIRECT TYPE		
	PUNCHED CARDS	PAPER TAPE	MAGNETIC TAPE	PRINTER	TYPEWRITER	VISUAL DISPLAY
Quantity	Medium	Medium to large	Very large	Large	Small	Medium
Quality	Moderate	Moderate	Low	Low	Moderate to high	Low
Timeliness	Slow	Slow	Very fast	Moderate	Very slow	Fast
Cost						
Equipment	Moderate	Moderate	High	High	Low	Moderate
Operation	Moderate to high	Moderate	Low	Low to moderate	Moderate	Low
Modularity	Good	Excellent	Excellent	Good	Fair	Fair

Learning operating procedures
Card punching
Assembling data for processing
Learning to interpret output
Card disposal (or retention)
Maintaining the devices

These indirect costs have not been included in Exhibit 10-6 because they cannot be meaningfully identified and separated as can direct costs.

Central Processor Unit Analysis. The central processing unit is the nucleus of the computer system. It is a combination of hardware (equipment) and software (programs) which perform four major functions: (1) control of processing, (2) arithmetic and logic operations, (3) storage of data and instructions, and (4) interface for all other components of the system.

In the *control function* of the CPU, sequencing, interpretation, and execution of program instructions take place in the electronic circuitry of the unit (hardware). Control programs (software) activate the circuitry and cause processing to occur. The user's program instructions to be processed are converted from user language (such as FORTRAN) to machine language by other programs called translators or compilers. Libraries of translators, as well as commonly-used application programs such as for statistical analyses, are maintained to facilitate all types of computer usage.

The second basic function of the central processor is performing *arithmetic and logic*. These operations take place in a set of special storage locations in the circuitry. In these locations, addition, subtraction, multiplication, division, and certain logical comparisons of data are performed. The computational capability of a computer is dependent upon the number and design of these special storage locations and the execution speed for each type of operation performed.

The third basic function of the central processor is *storage* or *memory*. The memory of the computer consists of numbered storage locations for data and program instructions. These numbers constitute addresses, so that the contents of each location can be identified.

There are two basic types of storage that pertain to the CPU: internal storage, which is actually part of the CPU, and external storage. *Internal storage* consists of magnetic core storage, and is composed of lattices or grids of tiny magnetic cores and wiring. In general, this type of storage is compact and durable, provides extremely fast access speeds, and has all addressable storage locations. *External storage* can be of two types: those that directly interface with the CPU so as to operate without human intervention (on-line), and those that do not (off-line). The former are typified by magnetic disk devices; the latter, by magnetic tape devices. These are both complex electromechanical devices, and storage of data is accomplished on magnetic disk or tape surfaces, rather than in a grid-type circuitry such as in the CPU.

A fourth function of the central processor is that of providing an *interface* for all other components of the system. For example, input and output devices must be interfaced (connected) with the CPU to get data into and information out of the CPU. This interface or connector function is carried out in conjunction with the control function of the CPU, utilizing the control circuitry (hardware) and the control programs (software). All sophisticated computer systems rely heavily on the control segment of the CPU to coordinate activities and to provide the necessary interfaces between its various components.

A conceptual view of the four functions of the CPU is presented in Exhibit 10-7. The storage function (unit) has several segments: one to accomodate inputs received from input devices; one to hold programs, both those being processed and those not currently being processed; and one to accomodate output until it is distributed to the output devices. Arithmetic and logical operations are performed by the arithmetic function (unit) on data and instructions from working storage. The control function (unit) regulates all the functions of the entire CPU operation.

The basic criteria for analysis of the central processing unit are quantity (capacity), quality (control), timeliness (speed), cost, and modularity, as shown in Exhibit 10-8. The size and speed requirements of the CPU are dependent upon computer use analysis. For problem solving and decision making requiring direct, rapid access to stored information, arithmetic speed, internal data transfer rate, and on-line storage capacity are important design characteristics. For data processing using mainly batch processing methods, external (input-output) data transfer rate, off-line storage capacity, and input-output volume are important characteristics. The former characteristics tend to increase computer equipment costs due to more sophisticated circuitry, while the latter characteristics tend to increase computer operating costs due to increased handling of data. The desired balance between these two costs depends upon the required mix of problem solving versus data processing needs of the organization. CPU modularity is a function of CPU design, and most third generation computers have modular, add-on storage units to facilitate enlarging total CPU storage capacity.

Computer Source (Supplier) Analysis

As emphasized in the section on analysis of computer use, the type of computer system that is required for an MIS is a function of the mix of user needs for problem solving versus data processing. Also, from input-output and central processor analysis, we know which criteria must be employed in selecting a particular computer system to meet these needs. The next step is to identify the one best computer system on the market (i.e. the model, configuration, and supplier which provide the desired information processing capabilities). This in the essence of computer source analysis, namely economic evaluation of the specific hardware and software components needed and the associated service provided by the computer supplier.

There are two phases of economic source analysis which must be performed: preimplementation and postimplementation assessment of economic feasibility. The former is the responsibility of the systems design

Exhibit 10-7
CONCEPTUAL VIEW OF THE CENTRAL PROCESSING UNIT

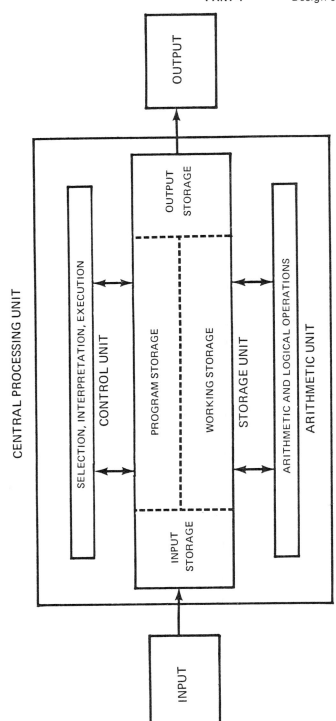

NOTE: THIS IS A SIMPLIFIED PRESENTATION OF THE COMPONENTS OF THE CPU, AS GENERALLY DESCRIBED IN COMPUTER TEXTS. FOR EXAMPLE, SEE DONALD H. SANDERS, *COMPUTERS IN BUSINESS* (2D ED.; NEW YORK: MCGRAW–HILL BOOK CO., 1972), P. 219.

Exhibit 10-8

CRITERIA FOR ANALYSIS OF THE CPU

	USE	
CRITERIA	PROBLEM SOLVING	DATA PROCESSING
Quantity		
Storage capacity		
Internal	Large	Small
External	Medium to small	Large
Storage efficiency	High	Medium
Quality		
Control capability	Extensive	Limited
Timeliness		
Arithmetic	Very fast	Relatively slow
Internal transfer	Fast	Slow
External transfer	Relatively slow	Fast
Cost		
Equipment	High	Moderate
Operation	Low	Moderate to high
Modularity	High	Low to moderate

staff, as indicated earlier in the chapter, whereas the latter is usually performed by the systems monitoring staff (assisted by the design staff as needed).

Preimplementation Economic Analysis. The major thrust of preimplementation economic analysis is on determining the anticipated cost-effectiveness of the entire information system and the computer system in particular. The key to this analysis is determining the value of the system and the value of information, as noted in Chapter 9. The value of a new system depends upon the costs and benefits of the new system. The costs include: hardware, software, and operating expense; development costs for hiring and training programmers and analysts; salaries; disruption of normal operations; and retraining of displaced personnel. System benefits include: decreased operating costs resulting from fewer people, less inventory, fewer penalties for late payments and deliveries, lower transportation and purchasing charges, fewer production shortages, and better scheduling, among other factors. Other system benefits are more intangible, such as those from obtaining information earlier, from increased accuracy of information, and from more accurate and more timely decisions as a result of the foregoing. These subjective factors are determinants of the values of information which are ordinarily difficult to quantify because there are no direct units of measure for them.

Two methods of cost-benefit analysis for assessing the economic feasibility of a new computer system prior to implementation are the payout method and the breakeven method. The anticipated *payout* of a new system can be determined from the estimated value of the system as follows:

$$\text{Payout (years)} = \frac{\begin{array}{l}\text{Cost of Feasibility Study} + \text{Cost of Computer} \\ + \text{ Cost of Installation} + \text{Cost of Implementation}\end{array}}{\begin{array}{l}\text{Value of System (annual basis, benefits minus} \\ \text{costs)}\end{array}}$$

The costs in the numerator of this equation are all one-time costs, whereas the value of the system in the denominator refers to yearly benefits and operating costs. For example, suppose we have the following:

Feasibility study cost	$ 50,000
Computer cost (hardware and software)	800,000
Installation cost (of hardware;	20,000
checkout of software)	
Implementation cost	40,000
(of hiring and training personnel, etc.)	
Total one-time cost	$910,000

If the annual costs (of operating labor, materials, utilities, etc.) are $100,000 and the annual benefits (from less inventory cost, fewer delivery penalties, better scheduling, and better decisions) are $300,000, then we will have:

$$\text{Payout} = \frac{\$910,000}{\$300,000 - 100,000} = 4.55 \text{ years}$$

The anticipated payout for a new computer system is ordinarily compared with the anticipated payouts from other capital budgeting projects, i.e., building a new plant which has a payout of eight years is not as attractive as the previous payout example for a new computer system. The estimate of the payout period will be inflated if the system benefits, based on determining the value of information, are underestimated. This is often the case when the benefits derived from making better decisions with a computer are intangible and therefore difficult to measure.

Break-even analysis is especially useful in relating the capacity of a new system to its anticipated costs and benefits. This method is illustrated in Exhibit 10-9. Here, nonrecurring development costs are those fixed costs specified in the numerator of the previous payout equation. The recurring operating costs and the benefits are variable in relation to the information processing capacity (i.e., the quantity criterion) of the computer. The benefits are primarily anticipated cost-savings derived from more effective, more efficient information processing with the new system. The intersection of benefits and total costs represents the break-even capacity, beyond which it will be profitable to procure the new computer system. Looking at it in another way, it is possible to determine what level of benefits (cost-savings) will be needed to break even for a given computer capacity prescribed by the problem solving and data processing usage mix.

In using either the payout or the break-even method to assess economic feasibility, hardware, software, and service factors must be considered.

Exhibit 10-9

PREIMPLEMENTATION FEASIBILITY ANALYSIS
USING THE BREAK-EVEN METHOD

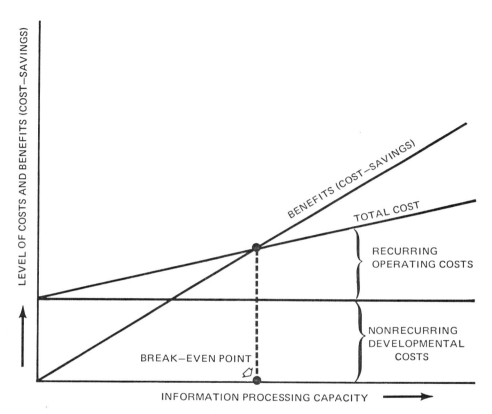

Hardware factors include performance, capacity, price, modularity, delivery date, and technological obsolescence. Factors concerning *software* are availability of programming languages, program efficiency, existence of program libraries and packaged programs, delivery dates, and planned software revisions. *Service factors* include programming assistance, conversion assistance, maintenance terms, and training of personnel. Each of these factors affects the cost of the new system for any given make and configuration of the computer components. This part of the analysis is performed by staff personnel who have technical expertise in the computer field.

The method of acquisition is also an important aspect of preimplementation economic feasibility analysis. Two methods of acquisition are usually available: leasing and purchase.[2] Most computer systems are leased, but there is a recent trend toward purchasing, probably because the rate of technological obsolescence is declining somewhat. There are advantages and

---

[2] Leasing here includes both renting and leasing. The primary difference between the two is that leasing generally requires a larger commitment in time, thereby making payments for computer use more predictable.

disadvantages to each of these acquisition methods. *Leasing* requires no large capital outlay, can have maintenance included in the lease, usually has declining charges after a specified period, and can be applied in part against the purchase price. On the negative side, leasing involves a sizeable monthly operating expense, constitutes a long-time obligation (up to several years), and often has a penalty clause for early cancellation which may offset the benefits of leasing.

Purchase of a computer is often less expensive over a long period of time and, as a capital investment, has certain tax advantages. However, it requires a large capital outlay, maintenance is not included in the purchase price, and there may be a high risk of technological obsolescence, especially when the data processing needs of the organization are changing rapidly.

For each of these methods of acquisition, the systems design staff must compare all of the foregoing factors in relation to leasing charges compared with purchase price, life of the equipment, maintenance costs, salvage value at the time of disposal, rate of return or cost of capital, future value of current dollars, and tax considerations. Ultimately, a recommendation to lease or buy must be based on a careful analysis of all the above factors, and the final decision is usually made by top management.

Postimplementation Evaluation of Feasibility. About one year after implementation of the new system, the second phase of feasibility analysis should be performed. This phase focuses on review and evaluation of four major areas: computer use; input-output components; the central processing unit; and cost-benefits. In this evaluation, the cost-benefit methodology described in the previous section is used as a guide or checklist to insure that a thorough postimplementation feasibility analysis is carried out.

Concerning computer use, the actual mix of problem solving versus data processing should be documented and compared with usage anticipated prior to implementation. This is done by surveying the users of the system regarding their satisfaction with the quantity, quality, and timeliness of reports and analyses. This survey should note the amount of manual manipulation by the users of computerized report information, which may indicate that the system was incorrectly designed, that implementation deviated from design, or that users' needs for information have changed.

Concerning input-output components and the CPU, users of information and providers of data should be surveyed to determine if they are satisfied with the input-output media available and with the capabilities of the CPU in storing and retrieving information, performing analyses, and preparing reports. Procedures for preventing data input errors should also be checked, and the format of reports should be reviewed to check their content, to assess their clarity, and to determine their effectiveness in facilitating planning, operational control, and managerial/financial control.

Actual cost data should be continuously collected after the new system is implemented as a basis for precise cost-benefit measurements. The expected level of cost-effectiveness is compared with the actual level to assess the actual real worth of the new system. The timing of this comparative analysis is important because the anticipated level of cost-effectiveness is not always achieved, especially during the early stages of implementation. There is often a downward-sloping (decreasing) effectiveness curve and an upward sloping (increasing) cost curve during the early stages of conversion to the new computer system. As indicated in Exhibit 10-10, there usually is a lag between: (1) the time at which cost savings actually occur (point B) versus the time predicted for cost savings to occur (point A); and (2) the time at which benefits from the new system are expected to be realized (point C) versus the time they are actually realized (point D). This can be due to a number of reasons, including unanticipated delays and problems with the new hardware and software, problems in training personnel to use the new equipment, or unrealistic estimates of costs and benefits. The break-even point occurs at point E, beyond which operation of the new system becomes increasingly cost effective.

The fundamental purpose of postimplementation evaluation of economic feasibility is to reduce the lags as much as possible, thereby achieving or surpassing the designed level of cost-effectiveness. Then the feasibility of the new system will have been assured.

Exhibit 10-10

A TYPICAL COST-EFFECTIVENESS PROFILE OF A NEW COMPUTER SYSTEM

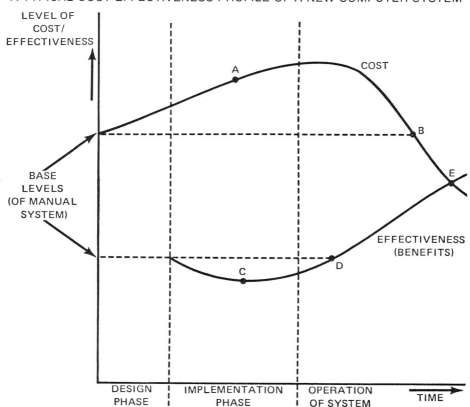

SUMMARY

This chapter has examined the computer as a facilitator for processing or transforming data inputs into the information outputs needed in an MIS for operations and management. The characteristics of a typical third generation computer system suitable for use in the sort of MIS being discussed here are: random access to stored information, on-line input-output devices, real-time operation with time sharing of the CPU, and integrated information processing.

The design procedure presented in this chapter is referred to as a feasibility study. The feasibility study has three major tasks: analysis of computer use, analysis and selection of computer components (i.e., the configuration), and analysis of computer sources (suppliers). Computer use analysis involves determining the desired mix of problem solving versus data processing needs for computer processing of data. This is an extension of the analysis of information needs described in Chapters 5, 6, and 7. Computer component analysis and selection involves analysis of input-output media and devices and analysis of the CPU and its functions.

Finally, computer source (supplier) analysis involves preimplementation and postimplementation evaluation of economic feasibility of the computer system. Two types of cost-benefit analyses, the payout method and the break-even method, are used to assess preimplementation economic feasibility. Costs of the new system consist of variable operating costs plus fixed, nonrecurring development costs, which are evaluated based on hardware, software, and service factors. Benefits of the new system are derived from various cost savings (fewer personnel, fewer errors, etc.), plus the intangible value of better decision making resulting from more accurate, more timely information. Postimplementation assessment of economic feasibility involves comparing actual cost-effectiveness of the new system with anticipated or projected cost-effectiveness as a basis for making operating adjustments and redesigning the system to satisfy users' needs for information in all segments of the organization.

REVIEW QUESTIONS

1. Discuss the nature of the data processor. What value or utility does it create? What is the role of the computer?

2. Discuss several of the variations in third generation computer systems that are available. Differentiate between: (1) sequential versus random access; (b) on-line versus off-line; (c) real time versus lapsed time; (d) one-at-a-time usage versus time sharing; (e) batch versus integrated processing.

3. Differentiate between problem solving and data processing uses of the computer. Why is it important to make this differentiation in designing and acquiring the data processor? How are these uses related to the operational and informational subsystems?

4. Outline the basic components of a computer. How are these basic components related to the basic systems model?

5. Identify the major types of input-output media and devices. What are several important factors to consider for each type in relation to organizational needs?

6. Concerning central processor analysis, what functions must be considered? How are they interrelated? What factors would you consider in your analysis of each function?

7. Discuss the economic, hardware, software, and service factors that are important in evaluating alternative computer sources and methods of acquisition.

8. Contrast and discuss the advantages and disadvantages of leasing versus purchase of computer hardware. What factors are important for your analysis?

9. "The feasibility study should consist of an evaluation at the time of implementation, as well as postimplementation, of the computerized data processor." Discuss the meaning and ramifications of this statement.

10. Comment on the universality of the computer and information processing concepts discussed in this chapter for an MIS in business, governmental, and educational organizations. What limitations do you see?

EXERCISE 10-1: A Computer Feasibility Study: Safeway Airlines, Inc. (Part B)[3]

On April 1, 1971, Safeway's Administrative Services Department published a system specification entitled Request for Proposal on Electronic Data Processing Equipment. The specification defined the data handling tasks to be performed, presented the system logic for the processing methods involved, and itemized the information to be contained in files, records, and input and output documents. The data volumes to be processed were projected from 1971 through 1977 at normal and peak levels, based upon forecasts supplied by Safeway's Research Department.

The specification was organized into two parts. Section I contained sixteen applications which were then being processed on unit record equipment plus three planned applications which were comparable in complexity to the other sixteen. Section II sets forth the structure of three additional applications: Inventory Control, Component and Aircraft Control, and Production Control. The applications in Section II required a departure from unit record concepts and necessitated the use of an electronic computer equipped with an auxiliary magnetic memory.

Exhibits 10-11 through 10-15 are samples taken from the systems specification. These examples are for illustrative purposes, and do not reflect the complete requirements. The specification was issued to six data processing equipment suppliers, all of whom responded with proposals.

---

[3] Part A of this case was presented as Exercise 3-1, page 63.

Exhibit 10-11

SAFEWAY AIRLINES, INC.
REQUEST FOR PROPOSAL ON ELECTRONIC DATA PROCESSING EQUIPMENT
TABLE OF CONTENTS

Exhibit 10-12

SAFEWAY AIRLINES, INC.
SYSTEM GROWTH PROJECTION CUMULATIVE ACTIVITY INDEX [1]

YEAR	INDEX CODE [2]							
	I	II	III	IV	V	VI	VII	VIII
1972	1.05	1.05	1.12	1.07	1.04	1.00	1.00	1.08
1973	1.08	1.05	1.23	1.05	.85	1.00	1.05	1.00
1974	1.58	1.49	1.84	1.64	1.20	1.20	1.20	1.37
1975	1.85	1.73	2.23	1.64	1.20	1.30	1.20	1.37
1976	1.85	1.73	2.30	1.64	1.20	1.30	1.25	1.37
1977	1.85	1.73	2.37	1.64	1.20	1.30	1.25	1.37

[1] Represents a cumulative growth factor over the base year 1971. It is not a statement of increase from one year to the next. For example, in Column I, 1972 is expected to be 105 percent of 1971; 1973, 108 percent of 1971; 1974, 158 percent of 1971; and so on.
[2] Index codes designate the following transaction or activity units:

I — Revenue plane miles	V — Number of stations
II — Revenue departures	VI — Inventory items
III — Revenue passengers	VII — Employees
IV — Number of flights	VIII — Number of aircraft

Exhibit 10-13
SAFEWAY AIRLINES, INC.
SYSTEM REQUIREMENTS

JOB NO. 6 — Flight Statistics

INPUT	— Daily Flight Data	Exhibit 6.1
INPUT	— On-Line Excess Baggage Data	Exhibit 6.2
INPUT	— Off-Line Excess Baggage Data	Exhibit 4.2
OUTPUT	— Daily Report of Passengers Boarded	Exhibit 6.3
OUTPUT	— Daily Load Factor Report	Exhibit 6.4
OUTPUT	— Flight and Station Load Factor Report	Exhibit 6.5
OUTPUT	— Flight and Day-of-Week Load Factor Report	Exhibit 6.6
OUTPUT	— Segment Load Factor Report	Exhibit 6.7
OUTPUT	— Origin-Destination Cargo Report	Exhibit 6.8
OUTPUT	— Flight Cargo Report	Exhibit 6.9
OUTPUT	— Monthly Average Traffic Report	Exhibit 6.10
OUTPUT	— Monthly Total Traffic Report	Exhibit 6.11
OUTPUT	— Transfer Passenger Report	Exhibit 6.12
OUTPUT	— Overflight Report	Exhibit 6.13
OUTPUT	— Nonrevenue Passenger Report	Exhibit 6.14
OUTPUT	— Minutes Delay Report	Exhibit 6.15
FILE	— Flight Statistics Master File	Exhibit 6.16
FILE	— Month-to-Date Statistics File	Exhibit 6.17

CYCLE: Daily

1.0 Processing the Daily Report of Passengers Boarded (Exhibit 6.3)

1.1 Input Processing (Exhibit 6.1)

1.1.1 Separate detail from total data. Sort data by flight and origin.

1.1.2 Look up miles, direction code, segment and day of the week in master file. (Exhibit 6.16)

1.1.3 Create exception output for missing flights.

1.1.4 Zero-balance detail data to total data for each flight:

1.1.4.1 Sort total data by origin.

1.1.4.2 Accumulate total passengers on board (+) by station.

1.1.4.3 Sort detail by origin.

1.1.4.4 Accumulate passengers boarded (+) by station.

1.1.4.5 Sort detail data by destination.

1.1.4.6 Accumulate passengers deplaned (−) by station.

1.1.4.7 Balance the flight data accumulated above as follows:

Plus passengers boarded first station
Minus passengers deplaned first station
Equals passengers on board first station

Exhibit 10-14

SAFEWAY AIRLINES, INC.
DAILY FLIGHT DATA

INPUT   Exhibit 6.1

JOB: Flight Statistics   NAME: Daily Flight Data (5-Channel Paper Tape)
SOURCE: Statistical Data Report
ACTIVITY FREQUENCY: Daily PEAK: 1,700 NORMAL: 1,400 INCREASE: II

ITEM NO.	DESCRIPTION	MAXIMUM CHARACTERS	PERCENTAGE OF USE
1	Report Code	2	100
2	Flight Number	3	100
3	Extra Section Code	1	100
4	Equipment Number	3	100
5	Date	2	100
6	Origin	3	100
7	Destination	3	100
8	Revenue Passengers	2	100
9	Nonrevenue Passengers	2	100
10	Transfer Passengers	2	100
11	Mail	4	100
12	Express	4	100
13	Freight	4	100
14	Minutes Delay	3	20
15	Delay Code	3	20
16	Block-to-Block Time	3	20
17	Off-To-On Time	3	20
18	Revenue Passengers Out	2	20
		Total 49	

Exhibit 10-15

SAFEWAY AIRLINES, INC.
DAILY LOAD FACTOR REPORT

OUTPUT   Exhibit 6.4

JOB: Flight Statistics   NAME: Daily Load Factor Report
ACTIVITY FREQUENCY: Daily   PEAK: 100 Lines   NORMAL: 90 Lines
INCREASE: IV

ITEM NO.	DESCRIPTION	MAXIMUM CHARACTERS	PERCENTAGE OF USE
1	Flight Number	3	100
2	Extra Section	1	100
3	Orgin	3	100
4	Destination	3	100
5	Daily Passengers Boarded	4	95
6	Daily Revenue Passenger Miles	6	95
7	Daily Seat Miles Available	7	98
8	Daily Load Factor	5	95
9	Month-To-Date Passengers Boarded	5	100
10	Month-To-Date Passenger Miles	7	100
11	Month-To-Date Seat Miles Available	7	100
12	Month-To-Date Load Factor	5	100

EVALUATING THE EDP EQUIPMENT SUPPLIERS' PROPOSALS

The suppliers' proposals were evaluated by consultants from a national accounting firm. They were assisted by their counterparts in the Safeway organization. The results of the evaluation were conclusive: a magnetic tape computer was justified; a transitional approach, utilizing an electronic card processor for the first 16 jobs, would not have been economical; and Firm VI's system provided the best balance of rental economy, processing capability, and expansion potential for Safeway's needs.

Although an electronic card processor would have permitted data handling and systems improvements beyond those which could have been achieved by upgrading the existing unit record machines, the acquisition of such equipment would have constituted only a temporary expedient. The potential at Safeway for clerical expense reduction and improved management control required a computer.

The evaluation also included the investigation of a transitional approach whereby Safeway first would have installed a card processor and then later reprogrammed for a large tape computer. With such an approach, the additional changeover expense would have more than offset the reduced equipment rental; and the full realization of potential savings would have been delayed. Therefore, the evaluation team rejected the transitional approach.

The team further recommended a slightly modified, minimum-cost alternative to Firm VI's proposal. By using existing personnel from Safeway's Administrative Services Department for the necessary programming, by minimizing leasehold improvements and environmental controls, and by slightly modifying Firm VI's proposed configuration, the team estimated that net direct tangible savings in excess of $170,000 would be realized during the projected system life. Exhibits 10-16 through 10-18 were taken from the accounting firm's recommendation concerning Firm VI's proposal. The exhibits were amended slightly in order to conceal the sources of the proposals.

In evaluating the proposals, the team considered five major criteria: (1) the systems approach which was taken by the supplier; (2) the supplier services to be provided; (3) the estimated equipment utilization; (4) the savings potential for each system; and (5) the capacity for future growth.

Exhibit 10-16 summarizes the team's assessment of the statements of systems approach made by each supplier. The team reviewed the proposed systems for adequacy of procedural descriptions, flowcharting, and record layouts. The team also appraised the auditability and general workability of the proposed systems.

The first point of comparison regarding supplier services was whether a full-time programmer was to be assigned to Safeway without additional charge and, if so, for what period of time. Next, consideration was given to the suppliers' software packages, that is, their library programs, programming languages, coding, and program assembly methods. These considerations, too, are summarized in Exhibit 10-16. As further indicated in Exhibit 10-16, program testing provisions in the six proposals varied widely. The amount of test time to

Exhibit 10-16

SAFEWAY AIRLINES, INC.
EVALUATION AND COMPARISON OF SIX PROPOSALS FOR
ELECTRONIC DATA PROCESSING EQUIPMENT

PROPOSAL ELEMENT	SUPPLIER					
	I	II	III	IV	V	VI
1. SYSTEMS APPROACH						
1.1 Description of Procedures	Not provided	Adequate	Not provided	Not provided	Very good	Very good
1.2 Flowcharts	Good	Not complete	Very good	Adequate	Very good	Very good
1.3 Auditability	Adequate	Indeterminable	Adequate	Good	Very good	Good
1.4 General Workability	Good	Indeterminable	Good	Indeterminable	Good	Good
2. SUPPLIER SERVICES						
2.1 On-Site Staffing	Not specified	Not specified	12 man-months	Not specified	12 man-months	12 man-months
2.2 Software	Indeterminable	Adequate	Good	Adequate	Adequate	Adequate
2.3 Programming Languages	Adequate	Adequate	Good	Adequate	Adequate	Good
2.4 Program Testing Provisions:						
2.4.1 Before Installation	40 hours	40 hours	Indefinite	22 hours	70 hours	35 hours
2.4.2 After Installation	First 90 days	Not specified	528 hours	First 30 days	First 180 days	Not specified
2.5 Back-up Equipment	Adequate	Adequate	Adequate	Adequate	Indeterminable	Very good
3. CAPACITY FOR FUTURE GROWTH						
3.1 With Original Equipment	Marginal	Inadequate	Very good	Inadequate	Good	Good
3.2 With Added Equipment	Good	Indeterminable	Very good	Marginal	Very good	Very good

Exhibit 10-17

SAFEWAY AIRLINES, INC.
ESTIMATE OF AVERAGE MONTHLY EQUIPMENT UTILIZATION
FOR SIX PROPOSED SYSTEMS [1]
(Run Times Only)

SUPPLIER	SECTION I HOURS	SECTION II HOURS	TOTAL HOURS
I	28	25	54[2]
II	Not comparable	Not comparable	Not comparable
III	21	35	56
IV	73	85	158
V	30	Not comparable	Not comparable
VI	37	46	83

[1] Run times for applications to be processed at daily, weekly, monthly, quarterly, and annual intervals were calculated, weighted, and added to arrive at the equivalent average monthly utilization.
[2] Subtotals for Sections I and II do not add to total hours because of rounding.

be provided by the manufacturer in advance of equipment delivery was of great importance because such testing permits a step-by-step check of the programs as they are completed and thus allows the progressive rework of any difficulties. By testing as each program is completed, it is possible to evaluate the competence and progress of the programmers and to preclude the basing of subsequent programming on unworkable first efforts. Postdelivery testing also is necessary for thorough program validation, although adequate arrangements for postdelivery testing ordinarily are made by equipment manufacturers.

The final major criterion for judging supplier services was the availability of backup equipment upon which Safeway could rely if its own equipment were to become inoperative at a critical time. Experience has shown electronic data processing equipment to be extremely reliable, normally on the order of 95 percent "up time." Malfunctions, when they occur, are most often in the peripheral devices, not in the central processor. Thus, it sometimes is possible to alter a program to bypass a trouble spot and accomplish a portion of the essential processing. Nevertheless, a major malfunction could occur at a critical period; therefore, a review of the availability of backup facilities was necessary.

Five of the systems were comparable on the basis of estimated run times for each of the applications. Those run times which showed significant variation were evaluated in terms of internal processing speeds and peripheral equipment speeds. Not all manufacturers included set-up times. As a result, a standard set-up of five minutes per run was assigned; and an allowance for unavoidable delays, schedule failures, and reruns was included.

Exhibit 10-18

SAFEWAY AIRLINES, INC.
COMPARISON OF INITIAL AND RECURRING COSTS
FOR SIX PROPOSED SYSTEMS

COST ELEMENT	SUPPLIER					
	I	II	III	IV	V	VI
Initial (Start Up) Costs						
Programming	$36,000	$27,000*	$48,000	$36,000	$36,000	$27,000
Free Access Floors	3,375*	3,375*	3,500*	2,800	6,500	3,375
Air Conditioning	5,000*	5,000*	4,840	5,000*	10,000	5,000
Magnetic Tapes	4,200*	3,140*	3,868	3,075	-0-	3,140
Disks or						
Magnetic Cards	-0-	-0-	-0-	9,800	10,335	-0-
Conversion	-0-	13,975*	-0-	13,975	-0-	-0-
Freight In	720	605	875	657	1,050	284
Return Freight	780*	780*	780*	780	780*	780*
Paralleling	3,200*	3,200*	3,200	3,083	3,200*	3,200*
Recorders	300*	300*	200	208	300*	300*
TOTAL	$53,575	$57,375	$65,263	$75,378	$68,165	$43,079
Recurring Costs [1]						
Minimum	$ 4,431 [2]	$ 3,863 [4]	$ 7,380	$ 4,723 [6]	$ 7,128	$ 5,088
Maximum	5,907 [3]	6,438 [5]	7,380	7,770 [7]	7,128	5,088

[1] Monthly rental and use tax   [5] Tape system
[2] First 12 months   [6] Model 1 (includes one sorter)
[3] After 24 months   [7] Model 2
[4] Card system

Two, and possibly three, of the proposed systems would have been unable to perform all the applications named in the specification. For example, one system would not have had sufficient capacity. That supplier proposed that at a future date the small system be upgraded to a more powerful one, which still would have been of marginal capacity. Another manufacturer proposed a system which would have required a fourth tape drive and a larger memory than was proposed. Yet another system would have required the addition of certain extra-cost features and also the extra expense of a multishift operation.

The value of the systems specification as an established common denominator for the proposals was dramatically apparent. At the time the specification was prepared, gross direct savings estimates also were developed. The savings were grouped into four categories:

1. The reductions in rentals for the existing unit record equipment (tabulators, summary punches, and calculator) which would be released in the event an electronic data processing system were installed, either a card processor or a magnetic tape computer.
2. The further reductions in rental for that existing unit record equipment (sorters and collator) which would be released only if a magnetic tape computer were installed.
3. Projections of the additional rental amounts which otherwise would have been necessary for expansion and upgrading of the existing unit

     record installation to accommodate anticipated company growth through 1977.
4. Clerical savings based upon staffing levels in force on April 1, 1971; however, no saving was included for the clerical additions which would be required to accommodate company growth through 1977 if procedures and methods remained unchanged.

    In addition to the direct savings, there were several potential indirect benefits or intangible savings which would accrue to the company. The first of these would be the ability to perform certain mathematical computations less expensively, e.g., aircraft weight and balance calculations and portions of airport analyses. Second, a more advanced inventory control system could be installed to yield a better balance between operating requirements, inventory possession, and acquisition cost. Third, there would be a considerably improved capability for processing and summarizing large amounts of data in connection with new or improved management reporting practices. Thus, a more adequate data processing system would considerably enhance Safeway's ability to make significant new procedural applications which could not be undertaken economically with only the existing unit record equipment.

    Exhibit 10-18 contains a summary of the initial and recurring costs of the systems which were proposed; for the most part, the figures are those supplied by the manufacturers. The evaluation team included any pertinent items which had been omitted by the manufacturers and adjusted certain items of the data as originally submitted in order to make the six proposals comparable. One element of start-up expense which was not included in the exhibit was the cost of electrical modifications or additions. Since the amount of that expense would depend on the location of electrical power lines in the building, none of the suppliers estimated it. In any event, the cost of such modifications would be approximately the same for all systems; therefore, it was not a critical factor in the selection of equipment.

    The costs as stated in Exhibit 10-18 are those which would have been incurred if installation of the electronic data processing equipment were approached as an entirely new activity. The evaluation team included as an element of initial cost the programming effort by Safeway to set up the applications in Section I on the computer. Those requirements, as estimated by each supplier, were priced by the team at $1,000 per man-month, an amount which also provided for the fringe benefits and travel expense incurred by the company programmers. In contrast, it should be noted that the alternative approach outlined below considered only the additional out-of-pocket expense which was essential to the installation and operation of the new equipment.

    The team recognized that it would be difficult for Safeway to absorb the initial costs listed in Exhibit 10-18. It was possible to reduce those expenditures by minimizing environmental controls. Moreover, Safeway was in the fortunate position of being able to eliminate most of the programming expense by using existing company personnel for this function, although certain evident restrictions were thereby imposed upon the systems analysts and the data processing staff in terms of their current workload. With Firm VI's system, it also was possible to reduce the monthly rentals by substituting the card punch from the system which was proposed.

Although such a modification also would have been possible with certain of the equipment proposed by other suppliers, the rental differential was not material except in the case of Firm VI. The team estimated that the initial out-of-pocket expense for this alternative would total approximately $10,000, unless additional programming staff had to be added. Thus, the required initial investment was reduced by $33,000; and Firm VI's system equipment rental, during the six-year system life, was reduced by another $14,000. Such an approach was expected to increase total net direct savings (conservatively estimated) with Firm VI's system to more than $170,000.

The cost recoveries, or cummulative cash flows, for each of the six proposed systems were tabulated and compared for a 6½ year period: one year for initial planning, programming, and site preparation prior to installation, plus the assumed operating life of the system, approximately 5½ years. The first year savings were prorated from the approximate delivery dates quoted in the proposals, and they varied with the delivery lead times of the suppliers.

Firm VI's proposed system, due to lower start-up costs and lower rental than the competitive equipment, would have been the first system to break even. It produced a positive cash flow after the first year of operation, and it would result in greater annual savings thereafter than would the competitive systems for the specified applications.

The systems approach taken by Firm VI was sound. Its on-site staffing, software, program testing, and back-up services were good. The projections showed that Firm VI's system would have the reserve capacity to absorb Safeway's anticipated growth, as well as new applications, through 1977. For those reasons, the evaluation team recommended that Firm VI be selected on the basis that it best met the needs of the company by providing a high performance, low cost, data processing system with good potential for expandability.

HOW IT TURNED OUT

Safeway Airlines, Inc., ordered Firm VI's computer system on January 9, 1972. The equipment arrived in August, 1972. The first application, flight statistics, was made September 1, 1972; and the company operated parallel systems for 105 days. Phase I was completed within a few days of the original schedule. The savings objectives have been exceeded, and the information system has developed according to plan. At the present time, July, 1974, Safeway is planning for a significantly more advanced computing system which will be placed in operation in about three years. Safeway has not found it necessary to retain consultants for any extensive technical role in the next computer project. One of the early objectives of the original project group was to build a suitable internal systems analysis and design capability. That objective was met. The next computer will be an on-line system to be used for controlling the reservations, seat inventory, and passenger name-records, in addition to Firm VI's existing applications.

1. For the time period covered in this case study, list the functions which were performed by personnel of Safeway Airlines and by the national accounting firm.
2. What is meant by the "total information systems concept"?
3. What are the major differences between tabulating equipment and electronic computers?
4. What purpose was served by the following activities referred to in the case?
   a. Flowcharting
   b. Forms control
   c. Determining reporting needs
   d. Preparation of Request for Proposal on Electronic Data Processing Equipment
5. What kind of education, training and experience background is required to perform the type of work described in the case?
6. What impact, if any, is the on-line system likely to have on the functional management activities at Safeway Airlines?
7. Based on the information presented in the case, what system would you have selected?
8. Based on the materials in chapter 10, what other types of information and analyses do you feel are needed before selecting one of the 6 firms?

EXERCISE 10-2: Literature Survey

Read and critique several articles on one or all of the following topics:
1. Emerging computer technology, its applications and limitations for management.
2. Status of development of integrated computerized information systems for management.
3. Feasibility analysis of computer applications; preinstallation and post-installation procedures and issues.

EXERCISE 10-3: Ongoing Computer Systems

Visit and study a computerized information system and perform the following:

1. Describe the purpose of the information system, including the major types of reports produced.
2. Identify the hardware components of the system, e.g., input-output devices, processor size and characteristics, and type of data storage facilities.
3. Describe the organization of the unit responsible for operating the computer facilities.
4. Based on your review of the system, as well as the views of persons who are responsible for operating and using the system, present a general evaluation of its strong and weak points.

11 BEHAVIORAL IMPLICATIONS OF MANAGEMENT INFORMATION SYSTEMS

The behavioral patterns which people bring into an organization are primary determinants of the effectiveness of information outputs and the availability of data inputs. If information is to serve as a vital mechanism for linking internal segments of operations and management and for linking the organization to its external environment, people in the organization must accept, interpret, and use the information as it is intended. Also, in the course of carrying out their organizational tasks, people must provide the input data needed by the MIS, which may involve them with information processing activities such as data classification, coding, summarizing, and reporting.

Because of this dual reliance on people, both for use of information output produced by the MIS and for the provision of input data to the MIS, the behavioral implications of designing and implementing a management information system are of great importance. Therefore, this chapter has the following objectives:

1. To describe some major behavioral science concepts and their importance to information systems design and implementation.
2. To provide an example of a typical behavioral climate related to an organization's information system.
3. To identify general behavioral and managerial concepts useful in developing a behavioral climate favorable to the MIS.

NATURE OF BEHAVIORAL SCIENCE

Behavioral science is concerned with understanding why people behave as they do, especially in relation to their interactions with others in the organization. A better understanding of behavior should lead to more effective ways of predicting, motivating, and coordinating behavior in order to induce performance which contributes to organizational as well as individual goals. For an information system this means that the attitudes and perceptions of managers, computer technicians, systems analysts, and other operating personnel must be defined and related to the purpose of the MIS, their respective roles in data processing activities, and the impact of the MIS on their formal and informal status in the organization. Once personnel behavior is understood, means can be devised to generate support of the MIS.

Since people have different needs and values, a basic understanding of the general reasons why people behave as they do in an organizational setting is necessary. This basic understanding serves as a point of departure for developing specific concepts for predicting and influencing behavior as it relates to MIS design and implementation. Important factors for understanding basic behavior are related to the nature of organizational goals and the heterogeneity and changing nature of people's values, needs, and wants.

Behavioral science views the organization as a social entity, and it assumes that the goals of the organization encompass the satisfaction of its members as individuals and groups. The motivation of members of the organization to support organizational goals is enhanced if their personal goals and values can be satisfied by the organization. For example, the design and implementation of an information system should involve managers who use MIS reports so that the potential contributions of the MIS to their managerial responsibilities and to their personal managerial styles will be considered.

The goals of the members of the organization vary among individuals depending on their individual value systems. Maslow's need hierarchy provides a general framework within which to analyze and evaluate the heterogeneity of man and his needs.[1] This need hierarchy consists of five basic levels of need: physiological, safety, love, esteem, and self-actualization (in ascending order).

Physiological needs are the most basic. They include those things necessary for survival such as food and water. Behavior is initially directed toward satisfying physiological needs. As physiological needs are met, individuals seek to satisfy higher level needs so that a hierarchy or an ascending ladder of needs exists. Safety needs include those physical and psychological factors that secure the individual from real or imagined dangers or threats. Love or belonging needs are concerned with the individual's desire to have social relations with others because he needs attention and acceptance from those persons with whom he associates. At the next level of the hierarchy, an individual seeks achievement, self-respect, prestige, and esteem from other people. The need for self-actualization or self-realization is the highest level of need in Maslow's hierarchy; it reflects the development of the individual to his fullest capability.

The importance of these needs varies for each individual depending on the level of need satisfaction he attains. This is especially true for the needs for esteem and self-actualization, because these needs are much more difficult to satisfy in large organizations. In addition, changes in individual value systems may motivate one to seek higher or lower level needs, depending on where the individual resides in the need hierarchy.

The factors of heterogeneity and changing nature of needs are important to consider when devising ways of encouraging support for the design and implementation of an information system. If the value systems and related needs of people who are affected by the MIS (managers, subordinates, staff specialists, computer technicians, and the like) are considered by top management and by the MIS systems analysts, a more effective level of support for the

---

[1] A. H. Maslow, *Motivation and Personality* (New York: Harper & Brothers, 1954), pp. 80-106.

MIS can be developed. Thus esteem and self-fulfillment needs of individuals, as well as economic needs of the organization, must influence the design and implementation of the MIS.

Coping with the heterogeneous and changing pattern of needs of people in the organization requires a range of alternatives and incentives for motivating people to support the MIS. Embodied in these alternatives is the use of an authority structure as a formal means of achieving a high degree of motivation. The selection of the optimum mix of incentives for influencing human behavior is based on the assumptions a manager makes about people in an organization. McGregor describes two polar views, which he has labeled Theory X and Theory Y.[2]

Several characteristics of McGregor's theory are shown in Exhibit 11-1 in relation to their impact on leadership style.

In an information system context, Theory X is based on satisfaction of lower level needs of Maslow's hierarchy, coupled with formal authority arrangements for motivating people. Under this view, managers affected by the MIS would tend primarily to emphasize their own functional information needs because they seek safety and security. Because of this, they typically resist organization-wide efforts to change the information system. Also, they are less innovative in resolving crises and problems relating to the information system because their personal goals are related more toward the lower levels of Maslow's need hierarchy rather than the upper levels. Under Theory Y, the

Exhibit 11-1

THEORY X AND THEORY Y RELATED TO LEADERSHIP STYLES

THEORY X	THEORY Y
(WORK–CENTERED VIEW)	(EMPLOYEE–CENTERED VIEW)
PEOPLE DISLIKE WORK.	WORK IS SATISFYING.
PEOPLE MUST BE DIRECTED.	PEOPLE SEEK RESPONSIBILITY.
PEOPLE MUST BE CONTROLLED.	SELF–CONTROL EMERGES.

RANGE OF ALTERNATIVES

AUTHORITARIAN LEADERSHIP	PARTICIPATION LEADERSHIP
STRONG RELIANCE ON FORMAL AUTHORITY	STRONG RELIANCE ON INITIATIVE OF PEOPLE
ECONOMIC AND JOB SECURITY AS INCENTIVES	SELF–ACTUALIZATION AS AN INCENTIVE
LITTLE INVOLVEMENT OF PEOPLE IN DECISION MAKING AND CHANGES IN THE INFORMATION SYTEM	WIDESPREAD PARTICIPATION AND INVOLVEMENT OF PEOPLE IN DECISION MAKING AND CHANGES IN THE INFORMATION SYSTEM
EXTENSIVE SPECIALIZATION	JOB ENLARGEMENT

---

[2] Douglas M. McGregor, *The Human Side of Enterprise* (New York: McGraw-Hill Book Co., 1960), Chapters 1-4.

opposite would tend to occur. For example, if top management and MIS systems analysts assume that managers are seeking higher levels of involvement, achievement, and self-actualization, greater opportunities emerge for their participation in the design and implementation of the MIS. More effective communication between managers concerning needs for information results, and they are likely more supportive of changes to the information system. This type of change-oriented attitude on the part of managers should also lead to the development of a more viable MIS, one that is attuned to their information needs.

Theory Y places more emphasis on the higher level needs of people, encouraging the use of a participative approach to management. The notion of participation involves the establishment of an organizational setting conducive to achievement of employees' personal goals through involvement in greater organizational responsibilities. This may involve consultation with people affected by the MIS on important design features, or even broadening the responsibilities of a manager. Job enlargement is aimed at making the job more interesting and challenging for managers affected by the MIS by providing them with more relevant and timely information.

Theory X and authoritarian leadership versus Theory Y and participative leadership represent two extremes on a continuum of alternatives for influencing behavior. Normally, a hybrid approach is utilized which takes into account the individual capabilities of managers to assume greater levels of responsibility. This suggests a situational or adaptive approach to leadership for development of a favorable behavioral climate.

Those organizations which have a favorable behavioral climate generally are characterized by a strong orientation of managers toward organizational goals. This means that each manager's departmental or functional, as well as personal goals, become more attuned to organizational goals. This is consistent with the idea of developing an objective-user orientation in designing the MIS.

Another characteristic of a favorable behavioral climate is the existence of effective communications between managers. As more effective communications and a stronger goal orientation are developed, resistance, fear, and conformity decline because managers perceive that they have more opportunities to become actively involved and influential in the overall management.

The next section describes a typical behavioral climate wherein these characteristics are lacking, and, as a result, an information system design project is falling short of the expectations of management. Following the example, the major behavioral limitations and a number of managerial concepts which are useful for alleviating the problems are discussed.

THE TYPICAL BEHAVIORAL CLIMATE: A CASE STUDY

The following sections describe a series of meetings and interviews conducted in an ongoing, real-life organization in an effort to design a comprehensive information system.[3] Previous to this meeting, the organization had a very

---

[3] The material presented is an adaptation of case materials developed by Harry Elwell and Dan Voich, Jr. The introductory portion of the dialogue appears in this text as Exercise 2-1. The material here, however, goes beyond the introductory level of Exercise 2-1.

limited investment in computerized data processing. Most of the information that was produced by the organization for its managers was developed by individual operating segments, such as production, personnel, procurement, and control. The president made a somewhat unilateral decision to invest in a large-scale computerized data processing facility. The data processing personnel that were acquired as of the result of this decision recommended the design of a comprehensive information system. Part of the rationale for investing in a larger-scale computerized facility and organization was based on the organization's extended history of severe problems relating to planning and controlling the receipt, production, and delivery of customer orders. Especially significant were problems relating to production downtime caused by late delivery of materials for production, inaccurate information as to customer specifications for products, and a substantial level of cost overruns on products produced.

The Monthly Staff Meeting: The Behavioral Setting

President: The next item on the agenda concerns the progress we are making with the new centralized, third generation, random-access, fully integrated, computer information system. We have made a substantial investment in equipment and personnel and I have not seen any appreciable improvement in operations. In fact, it appears we may have created another layer of problems and frictions. Where do we stand in terms of applications and problems?

Data Processing: We are currently testing the payroll and inventory control systems, and we are beginning the design of applications in other areas such as project control.

President: I certainly agree we should do something for project control. What are the problems in Data Processing and using areas?

Data Processing: Lack of agreement between users concerning types and frequency of information needs.

President: What is Data Processing's role in this effort?

Data Processing: Basically, we take the input and output flows as specified by the users and program them.

Controller: First let me say that the computer has great potential for accounting. Our basic problem is not one of knowing what information we need for accounting, but one of lack of technical knowledge in systems design and capabilities of equipment.

Production: Right now we do not have much on the computer, but what we have seems OK. To be frank with you, we have been so busy making a buck, we haven't been interested in another system. Our two big operating problems stem from two

	areas: continual demands for expediting production and configuration changes; and unavailability of materials when required. Both of these problem areas, I might add, are not directly under our control.
Procurement:	There is no question in my mind that there are computer applications for Procurement. The basic question is can my budget afford it?
Controller and Production:	We have the same question.
Data Processing:	I admit costs are high, but right now we are operating at considerably less than full capacity; therefore, higher rates are charged to present users. It is important to generate more applications, so a lower rate will be used and fixed costs can be spread over greater output levels.
President:	What has been the general reaction of managers to computer applications?
All Using Areas:	Initially, skepticism and fear, or apprehensions. Now, skepticism plus an ''I told you so'' attitude.
President:	How do we stand concerning our original estimates of applications, schedules, and costs?
Data Processing:	We are four to six months behind, but much of this is because we have changed our original applications. Naturally, as our applications increase, cost estimates must be revised.
President:	In other words, the feasibility study isn't feasible anymore. Does anyone have a clear conception of what our information needs are now and in the future; or do we even have a framework that can be used to analyze our requirements? I think we need to reevaluate what we are now doing in the whole area of information systems, and develop a feasible set of objectives and plans for the future. I am going to ask the Corporate Systems Staff to conduct a thorough study of these problems.

Perceptions of Top Management

The President contemplated the period of rapid growth of the company and the large number of problems needing his immediate decision. During the last several years, there appeared to be an increasing number of malfunctions in the administration of projects and contracts at every level of the organization. Yet, in spite of these problems, the company has been quite successful and continued to grow. However, efficiency in management must eventually be attained. The great variety of problems brought to the President for decisions ranged from conceptual objectives of the firm to operating level problems such as job scheduling. The latter instances came about because of the President's first-hand knowledge of production techniques and familiarity with many of the production personnel. A high degree of centralization of decision making characterized the management structure.

Although taking part of the blame for this extreme centralization of decision making, the President also blamed subordinate managers. The President had provided them with up-to-date data processing facilities and capabilities which were supposed to provide for analysis of problems and for control systems. In talking with the Corporate Systems Staff, the President expressed concern over the ineffectiveness of the automatic data processing systems developed thus far in accounting. Also, problems in project planning and control as they related to the accounting area did not seem to decrease. The following is a summary of the President's discussions with the Corporate Systems Staff:

President: We have made a substantial dollar investment in data processing equipment and personnel over the last few years, but I haven't seen any appreciable improvement in our operations. In fact, we have created another layer of problems in data management, besides creating some interdivisional frictions in designing and implementing the system. The controller's staff has additional problems with the automatic system because it is cumbersome and expensive. The budget has increased tremendously, and the elimination of clerks has not occurred to the extent expected.

Systems Staff: We haven't been real close to this development. What seem to be the major problems?

President: Basically, we can classify them into two categories, technical and human. I think our systems design approach needs improvement, as well as selling potential users on the advantages of data processing.

Systems Staff: Do we have any completed adaptations besides accounting?

President: Only partial, and these are by-products of the accounting system. I want your staff to make a complete study of our problems relating to project planning and control, and take a good look at our present manual and automatic systems. Then come up with a recommendation of an integrated total data management system including the proper interfaces between manual and automatic capabilities.

Systems Staff: Can we get some help on this from the systems analysts in Data Processing on technical matters?

President: Yes, I will ask the head of Data Processing to work with you. Also, at our next staff meeting I will bring this topic up.

Perceptions of the Head of Data Processing: The Computer Specialist

Later that day, the head of the Corporate Systems Staff met with the head of Data Processing.

Data Processing:	We have developed an automated accounting system, and are moving toward development and applications in other areas such as project control in terms of materials, costs, and schedules. In fact, we have completed some of these programs and systems; however, we are confronted with great reluctance to change to automatic systems.
Systems Staff:	What are the primary objections?
Data Processing:	Well, nothing very concrete. We hear comments such as "it costs too much" or "loss of control and management prerogatives will result."
Systems Staff:	In terms of costs, are these objections valid?
Data Processing:	Well, partly. Right now we are operating at considerably less than full data processing capacity; therefore, users of automatic systems are charged at a higher rate than would be applicable if full utilization of our hardware was achieved. It is important to expand the usage of automatic systems in order to spread fixed costs over greater output. Right now users have a valid claim to some extent that automatic systems are costly, but looking at the long run, especially if our growth rate continues, costs will decrease.
Systems Staff:	How about loss of control? Is there any merit in this complaint? If the systems are sound I do not understand why the operating divisions do not take advantage of these modern developments.
Data Processing:	You run into this whenever you recommend a change. Of course, the systems are sound. We have had our best analysts design and program them. I am certain that once undertaken, the operating personnel will agree. Perhaps a word from the President at our next staff meeting will provide the final impetus we need to really move into a complete integrated automatic data processing system. I know we have the necessary capabilities in terms of hardware and systems men, and it is foolish not to utilize them.
Systems Staff:	If we went into this thing completely, then our present investment in systems hardware and personnel would be sufficient.
Data Processing:	Well, at least for a while, but in order to effect an immediate changeover from manual to automatic data processing in all possible areas, I believe it is more feasible to expand our systems staff now rather than later. In this way the additional staff can be used to monitor the ongoing systems.
Systems Staff:	Just how big a department do you visualize you will need?
Data Processing:	Taking into consideration our commercial systems work, probably in the neighborhood of 50 percent increase in personnel. This is hard to estimate on the spur of the moment,

especially since we need more experience data on the time required for monitoring the system.

Systems Staff: I do not understand this need for heavy and continual monitoring of the system. I thought the systems designs were adequate. I am beginning to sympathize with the operating personnel. Will the automatic systems provide the efficiency in project management we need, or are we creating another layer of problems?

Data Processing: Perhaps I have misstated this concept of monitoring. Let me put it this way. As we move forward toward a completely automatic system for project control, we are basically interested in controlling costs, schedules, and quality of performance. In addition, various operating divisions will require additional planning and scheduling of activities and increased control data. For example, the accounting system requires information on operating expenses of materials, direct labor, and overhead for accounts payable and receivable. Contract administration needs cost information for pricing, bidding, and negotiation. Purchasing needs material usage, prices paid, and vendor appraisal information. Production needs information on schedules, costs, and performance. We need job control, project control, and general accounting reporting. In many cases the information needs of users overlap. As additional applications are found for automatic systems, perhaps existing outputs and reports, with slight modifications, may be used. This precludes the development of an entirely separate system. It is this refinement or interfacing of various automatic subsystems, along with manual systems, that we refer to as monitoring.

Systems Staff: As I understand it we have completed the transition toward a completely automatic accounting system, haven't we?

Data Processing: Well, not exactly. We received an understatement of the volume of activity we could expect from the Controller. Also, after we devised the initial system, there were changes in report formats and types of reports required by accounting. As a result, the Controller is somewhat dissatisfied with the present system in terms of costs and outputs. We have instituted changes which I am certain will satisfy him in both areas. I am not criticizing the Controller, since these things are difficult to estimate, but if we had gotten a correct or reasonable statement of expected volume and required outputs, the transition would be complete. In moving toward the development of further automatic systems, it is important that potential users clearly specify their needs and volume. Once we have this, our analysts can devise the necessary system.

Systems Staff:	When will Accounting's system be completed?
Data Processing:	If we do not get any other changes from the Controller, within the next few months.
Systems Staff:	About three months then?
Data Processing:	Well, we'd better be conservative and figure on six to preclude handling of unforeseen problems and testing of the programs.
Systems Staff:	This seems like a long period in view of the fact we have already been working on it for about six months. What is involved?
Data Processing:	Well, after we get a statement of needs from the user in terms of volume and outputs, our systems analysts develop a general program indicating major milestones. This is then coordinated with the user to insure validity of the various types, frequencies, and formats of inputs and outputs. Then we have to design various data onto cards, and these must be coordinated with the users. A manager and the Accounting personnel cannot devote full time on this because of other duties.
Systems Staff:	Why don't you do it for them? Isn't this your job?
Data Processing:	Essentially yes; however, our analysts do not have a high degree of familiarity with accounting needs. Therefore, we have to rely on the Controller's suggestions.
Systems Staff:	What essentially is your contribution then?
Data Processing:	Basically, we take the input and output flows as specified by the user and design a computer program which will satisfy the user.
Systems Staff:	In other words, the nature of your work is technically oriented.
Data Processing:	Yes.
Systems Staff:	Is this also true of our commercial systems design work?
Data Processing:	Yes, but this does not mean our analysts do not make suggestions in those areas where they feel qualified.
Systems Staff:	How long would it take to get on a completely automatic system in all possible areas?
Data Processing:	I think we would need concrete information on the volume of inputs and outputs, as well as nature of data and information flows, before I could make a guess. Roughly, in the neighborhood of one year.
Systems Staff:	Will we need additional equipment?
Data Processing:	Yes, we will. Presently we do not have any on-line and real-time capabilities. I visualize that as we move further toward a complete automatic system some real-time capabilities will be justified.

Systems Staff:	In what areas?
Data Processing:	Well, for example, in project control, data regarding costs and schedules for the total project or contract, as well as jobs pertaining to the contract, can be fed in to the computer master files as the project progresses. Also, this will permit random information retrieved as needs arise merely by dialing directly into the computer by operating personnel. This obviates the need for some batch processing and periodic reports, since information is only received as it is needed. I think the Contract Administrator, Purchasing, Production, and Accounting would all benefit from this flexibility. Also, our field divisions could capitalize more fully from our investment in data processing since the location of terminal stations is not restricted by distance.
Systems Staff:	This sounds like you are moving toward a very sophisticated total data management system, and although some of the technical aspects are not completely clear to me, I feel that it may have worthwhile applications in the areas of project planning and control. I do feel, however, we should look at our present data systems, both manual and automatic, and identify the problem areas more clearly. Then I feel you should come up with an estimate of cost of the automatic system which can be used as a basis for determining whether we can afford it. Justifying a large investment in data processing may pose a problem unless we can furnish concrete evidence of dollar savings, and not qualitative justifications such as "improved control." In this respect, the President has given me the job of conducting a feasibility study of the applications of data processing in our operations. Reactions of the Controller, operating division heads, Treasurer, and Director of Procurement will be included in the study. I want you and your people to help me with the technical aspects of the study.
Data Processing:	Fine. When do you plan to complete the study?
Systems Staff:	In view of the problems we have now, speed is of the essence. Let's see, this is July 15, I think we ought to plan on a presentation on September 1. In the next staff meeting I will announce our plans.

Perceptions of the Controller: The Major User

After the discussion with Data Processing, the head of the Systems Staff talked with the Controller.

Systems Staff:	As you have probably heard, I have been given the job of doing a complete systems study, both manual and automatic, for planning and controlling the various contracts or

projects from the request for quote stage through the delivery of the finished product and receipt of payment from the customer. This study will focus on the various resource flows and the dimensions of cost, time, and quality of performance for the total project as well as the jobs making up each project.

Controller:

I can honestly say we really need it. The volume of variables and types of accounting data to be processed has increased with the growth of the company so that timely accounting and reporting is a real problem. Coupled with this is the constant demand by the auditors for information on present project status, as well as completed projects.

Systems Staff:

As I understand it, your accounting system has been mechanized to a great extent, primarily in the areas of accounts payable and receivable, cost accounting for labor, materials, and overhead by cost centers and jobs, including general wage and salary records and payments. In addition, aren't the financial accounting functions such as balance sheet and income statement reporting included in this mechanization?

Controller.

We have completed the initial phase of this transition in these areas, but the systems need considerably more refinement. They are still cumbersome and the processing of raw data inputs is still a bottleneck. Also, many of the reports that are generated are very difficult to digest and use, partly because the formats are not exactly what we need and partly because they are in a form difficult for the layman to comprehend. However, we are making headway.

Systems Staff:

In talking with Data Processing, I get the impression that some of these problems came about because your people did not give them a clear statement of expected volume and types of inputs, as well as the types and formats of reports you need. I am trying to determine where we missed on this transition, so that designing systems for other operating divisions can proceed more efficiently.

Controller:

I think that impression is correct, but you must keep in mind that we are basically accounting oriented, and not data processing specialists. Much of the problem has been one of not so much knowing what we need in accounting, but what we do not know concerning format requirements and capabilities of the equipment. For example, I can tell you that we need a report on items stocked in inventory, including the types of information required on each item such as quantity on hand, or order, unit price, and so forth. I can't tell you, however, what the best method of getting this data on cards is and what type of master files in data processing we need in order to give us this information. These decisions, I feel, should be made by the data processing people. In summary, then, I do not feel the advice from the data processing people in these technical areas has been adequate.

Systems Staff: In your opinion, why haven't the hoped for savings and efficiency in the accounting system come about?

Controller: Again, I feel it is because of this lack of advice in systems design from the data processing people. They want us to devise the system and they will program it, without questioning whether some of our data flows are relevant, or whether better methods can be used. As a result we are undertaking a large number of changes which should have been foreseen in the initial phase of system design. I don't feel our people have this technical capability in systems design.

Systems Staff: As a whole, what has been your personnel's reaction to data processing?

Controller: Initially, skepticism and for a large number of employees fear, or perhaps apprehension of potential change and loss of job, or at least change of duties.

Systems Staff: How about now after a great part of the transition has been completed, although refinements are still needed?

Controller: Skepticism still prevails, and perhaps an "I told you so" attitude.

Systems Staff: How about your managers or supervisors?

Controller: Initially, similar attitudes, and now they question whether the results thus far, or for that matter ever, are worth the cost. The time devoted to assisting the data processing people has greatly diluted the efforts they are able to give in keeping the work flows moving. They haven't seen any real tangible benefits thus far.

Systems Staff: If you had to do it all over again, and if you had a choice, what would you do differently?

Controller: Essentially, I believe in automatic data processing and what it can do for accounting. I also believe that eventually we will get an efficient system. I think most of my managers and supervisors feel this way, although they don't advise it. In terms of hindsight, I think at least three changes should have been made. First, I feel the data processing people could have contributed more innovations in design and carried most of the load in the technical development. Second, I think that I should have designated several full-time Accounting people to assist Data Processing in the design.

Third, I believe the transition should have proceeded at a slower pace and perhaps in a more piecemeal fashion. In otherwords, convert one manual phase at a time and completely define it, before moving on to the next. In this way, we have less of an overlap of problems, and we can build confidence and sell the idea of data processing to other users. For example, if accounts receivable were automated successfully, the accounts payable people would begin to realize the potential.

Systems Staff: Doesn't doing it on a piecemeal fashion pose problems of interfacing the subsystems later?

Controller: Yes, but this is a cost you incur for the benefits of achieving support of the people concerned and the smaller degree of disruption of work flows. I think this human problem in many cases is a more difficult problem than the technical problem.

Perceptions of Production, Procurement, and Other Users

That evening, the head of the Systems Staff contemplated the discussions with the Controller and the head of Data Processing. The Systems Staff head came to the conclusion that this study was going to be difficult to accomplish because of the staff's limited technical background in data processing. Also, behavioral problems were emerging. A sound technical program was only the beginning; a good data management system included both design proficiency and implementation capabilities. The Systems Staff head planned to talk to the Production Division heads in Electronics and Manufacturing. Each of these areas only had small segments of their data flows on mechanized systems, and these were primarily offshoots of the accounting adaptations.

Systems Staff: As you both already know, I am working on a study to make recommendations concerning automatic data processing applications and the development of an integrated data management system. I want to get your views concerning the feasibility of putting some of your data flows on the computer. I guess the best place to begin is to ask you if you are satisfied with that portion already automated, and secondly, how do you feel about future adaptations?

Manufacturing: Well, right now we do not have much on the computer, but what we do have seems OK. We have been so busy that I haven't really been too interested in another system. I don't think we have any serious problems in our data flows here in Manufacturing. We have a good procedures manual and most of our problems stem from two major sources: the customers' unreasonable demands for expediting and requests for configuration changes; and our inability to get the

	materials when we need them. Both of these problems are not directly under our control. When we had authority and responsibility to obtain our own materials and handle our own contract negotiations we did a much better job. Now with centralized purchasing and contract administration we have lost some of our control and flexibility.
Electronics:	I agree. We need more authority in the materials and negotiations areas, rather than another data system.
Systems Staff:	Then, you don't feel that automatic data processing has any application in your areas?
Electronics:	Basically, no. The nature of our material requirements precludes any adaptation in that area, and our production control techniques are pretty sound.
Systems Staff:	What do you mean?
Electronics:	I don't see any application of data processing where orders and usage volume are in terms of quantities generally less than ten. It is not the same as if you had large inventories and automatic reorder systems.
Systems Staff:	But can't the computer produce analyses of item price history, vendor appraisal, and purchase order status?
Manufacturing:	We don't have any significant control over these areas. Perhaps the Purchasing Department has some need for these analyses. At least it appears they have need for something new since we don't seem to be getting the service from them that we need to do our job.
Systems Staff:	But don't you need cost data and schedule data for specific jobs and contracts?
Electronics:	Yes, but we get these from Accounting. Actually, Accounting needs this data for billing and budgeting.
Manufacturing:	I don't want to seem anti-data processing, but I am not technically competent in data processing. And I would not be opposed to any new data system if it can be shown how I can solve some of my planning and control problems. But the impression I get from our efforts to date in data processing is that they have created administrative problems greater than the benefits received.
Electronics:	I agree. You can look at Accounting's problems as examples. If a system could be devised that I can be sure will work and benefit us, I will have no objections.
Systems Staff:	In other words, you really don't feel the computer can assist you in your operations?
Manufacturing:	At least not from my present situation in terms of my present problems, and my limited knowledge of the technical

| | capabilities of data processing. I will listen to any suggestions, and of course, give you any assistance I can in your study. |
| Electronics: | I agree. I think our problems are different and do not fit into the automatic systems concepts. You can count on my cooperation, however. |

The head of the Systems Staff then visited the Director of Procurement. Purchasing was a vital area which must be included in the study, and the Systems Staff head felt that it would be an area which could have major possibilities for automatic data processing. On several previous occasions, the Director of Procurement has mentioned his interest in the computer as a possible means for providing better service by his department.

Procurement:	I sure need a break from talking with the production people. They have been in here frequently recently.
Systems Staff:	What seem to be their problems?
Procurement:	Well, generally they come in here to lodge complaints against my buyers for not giving them good service, or they ask us to work overtime in expediting their material needs.
Systems Staff:	I just finished talking to the Production heads and they did indicate they had some problems. It seems that they would prefer to handle their own purchasing as in the past. I detected the traditional arguments for decentralization of purchasing in their comments, but I think we should look at this problem again to determine where the purchasing function should be performed, and once this is decided, how to implement the decision and to satisfy all parties. We do have company objectives to consider.
Procurement:	I agree with you, and I can sincerely say that centralization of purchasing is the answer. If we assume equal efficiency of procedures and personnel, I cannot see any other alternative than at least partial centralization. For example, the benefits of volume discounts, specialized buying effort, and flexibility of utilization of buying personnel cannot be achieved to as great an extent with decentralization. In addition, Accounting requires centralized development and administration, and I think the production people would tend to let this area slip when production crises arise. I think these administrative requirements are misunderstood in many cases until it is too late, for example when audits are made.
Systems Staff:	What are Production's complaints with purchasing?
Procurement:	One complaint is the administrative documentation required. They feel that this slows up delivery of the material

needs, and it does. However, this is a constraint, and we must develop data systems which can alleviate these problems. Production people also feel that we do not give them the expediting service they need.

Systems Staff: Is this true?

Procurement: Of course not. Upon investigating complaints we generally find that requisitions were not received by Purchasing until the materials were ready to be used. In other words, Production has not given us enough advance planning time. Granted, true emergencies arise, but in many cases if we would get a bill of materials as soon as the contract was received, much of this expediting would be eliminated.

Systems Staff: Why don't they do this?

Procurement: I don't know. They normally wait until a few days before the materials are scheduled for production. They feel that the certainty of the configuration design is greater the longer they wait; therefore, this obviates the need for cancellations. However, the trade-off is in terms of large costs of expediting materials and delays in production.

Systems Staff: How do you feel about the use of the computer to alleviate some of these problems?

Procurement: There is no question in my mind that there are applications in material acquisition, utilization, and control, and I have asked the data processing people to come up with recommendations. However, the costs of automatic systems suggested are too great.

Systems Staff: Are you satisfied with the technical aspects of the systems design?

Procurement: Generally yes; however, the systems suggested thus far seem cumbersome. I feel the reports and analyses provided by the systems are very good and would result in better service by our people, but the processing of data inputs could be improved.

Systems Staff: What is the current status of moving some of your data flows into the computer?

Procurement: Only to the extent of offshoots from the accounting system, and except for our stock items the reports we receive are not very useful.

Systems Staff: What is wrong with them?

Procurement: They are generally too lengthy, and do not focus on problem areas. What we need, basically, are reports which will give us a basis to take action on system or human failure. Employ the exception principle.

Systems Staff: Weren't these provisions included in the previous systems design?

Procurement: To some extent, but they were too costly. I feel that a system could be devised that would give us the information we need on a timely and discriminatory basis, but I am not technically qualified to suggest one that would be economical. To me, investment in data processing must provide a reasonable return, just like any other investment.

Upon later discussions with the Quality Control Personnel, the head of the Systems Staff received similar reactions to data processing. Problems of cost and human reservations were expressed, coupled with emphasis on a data flow problem and the possibility that the computer might be the answer.

SUMMARY OF BEHAVIORAL LIMITATIONS

The example presented in the preceeding sections reflects a number of behavioral limitations that are especially important for designing and implementing a computerized management information system. These limitations are described in the following sections and a number of alternatives for resolving these behavioral problems are then presented.

Lack of Objective-User Orientation

An objective-user orientation implies a high level of understanding and support by managers, staff specialists, and operating personnel for the information system. Throughout the example, it is apparent that none of the personnel, including top management, clearly understand the purpose of a management information system. In fact, there is also strong evidence that key managers are not effectively coordinating their project planning and control activities.

The lack of objective-user orientation often occurs in a new information system. Each user perceives a different set of values to be derived from the new system. These may range from no value, as may be the case of users in Production; to potential value in mechanizing clerical functions, as is typical with users in the Controller's area; to a potential value nearing panacea, as perceived by specialists in Data Processing.

Lack of objective-user orientation can become a critical problem if top management support and direction are not provided. For example, in the example described, top management has given only general support for a large-scale data processing capability with the necessary hardware and manpower. However, this support has dysfunctional ramifications because top management did not involve all potential large users of the computer, such as Production, Procurement, and the Controller, in the decision to acquire a large-scale data processing system. Instead, the data processing group had to convince operating managers of the benefits of the computer system after it had been installed. Quite often, as was the case in this example, data processing specialists sell the system directly to top management, rather than involving the operating managers who are the potential users of the information. This generally leads to inadequate support by operating managers for the computerized data processing system and its purpose. Undesirable reactions such as resistance, fear, and failure to support the organization and the MIS often result from this kind of development, and they are usually difficult to overcome.

Vertical-Functional Overemphasis

Managers and operating personnel may adopt many different perspectives regarding the kinds of information the organization needs. Individual line segments, staff segments, and information specialists all feel they have peculiar needs, even though the decisions, activities, and work they perform are somewhat similar. In the example, the planning and control of projects cuts across a number of functional areas such as procurement, production, controller, and personnel. Thus, each of these organizational segments, as well as top management, has a varied set of perceptions about the value of information and its related costs. Top management must be concerned with providing each operating segment or manager with information to satisfy his particular information needs. However, top management also requires different kinds of information that are basically integrative in nature, i.e., they emphasize horizontal as well as vertical interrelationships of decisions, activities, and work flows.

A natural by-product of the lack of objective-user orientation is overemphasis on vertical-functional relationships. In the example, Production is almost exclusively concerned with production matters, the Controller with accounting matters, and Procurement with purchasing matters. This is a natural by-product of a formal organization arrangement with specialization of labor. The organization is having difficulty in establishing a clear picture of how decisions, activities, and work are interrelated. The organization's proposed information system, as recommended by Data Processing, is supposed to provide better information to more effectively control the flow of decisions, resources, and work. However, each segment of the organization perceives its activity or responsibility as being most important and is reluctant to become involved in larger organizational matters, such as design of an integrated information system.

The behavioral climate in this organization is now one where forced involvement by managers and forced suboptimization of their operating segments is likely to occur because the actions of top management up to this time have not been directed toward designing an integrated system. The President has assumed that the computerized information system would be designed and implemented effectively without his active involvement. Since it was not, and since the behavioral climate that has evolved is one which is not supportive, a strong decentralized emphasis is likely to develop in the design of the information system. There likely will be competition between Production, the Controller, and Data Processing to influence the President's future MIS decisions. This competition could result in Production's exerting the greatest influence because this has been the President's primary area of interest in the past. Thus, the loyalty of the President to a single function (production), rather than to his current role (top management), may lead to a less than optimum information system for the organization.

Stress, Conflict, Fear, and Resistance

The organization described in the example is one characterized by stress and potential conflict, such as that which exists between Production and other organizational segments and between Data Processing and potential users of the information system. Any attempts to change operating policies and procedures, as well as information flows, will be met with fear and resistance. This is common when a large information system design and implementation effort is undertaken. Specific points where stress occurs are the interfaces between Production and Procurement concerning the availability of materials, Production and staff units such as Data Processing and the Controller relating to information flows; and Data Processing and users of potential information concerning needs for computerized data processing. In most organizations, stress tends to occur between specialists and operating managers. When such stress occurs, resistance to change generally follows. The situation is further aggravated when top management does not provide effective leadership and communication of objectives.

An integrated MIS implies greater visibility of performance by all operating segments of the organization through better and different kinds of information. This typically leads to fear of intervention by top management in operating matters, resulting in loss of middle and lower management prerogatives because more information is provided to higher levels of management. In the example, managers in the Production, Procurement, and Controller areas are apprehensive of a centralized or integrated information system because it will provide greater visibility of their operations to top management. This apprehension is often expressed in criticisms of the system, such as the system costs too much, or there is no need for new types of information, without a thorough analysis of costs versus benefits of the system. In the example, shifting of blame is evident, such as between Data Processing and the Controller. Even though the organization described in the example has serious problems in operational matters such as materials acquisition and utilization and in project planning and control, the operating managers and key staff personnel do not admit to any personal shortcomings in reference to these problems. Yet it is evident that someone must be responsible. A frequent outlet is to blame top management, and in this case there is strong support for this view. On the other hand, the more influential managers have not exerted leadership to resolve problems before they reach a critical stage. For example, the Controller is a key source of information for the organization, while the Production and Procurement managers are major users of information. Yet they appear to be waiting for a better information system to evolve. Instead, as key managers in the organization, they should come together voluntarily to define specific operating problems and suggest an approach for designing and implementing an MIS that is directly attuned to resolving these problems.

Unless this kind of leadership is forthcoming on the part of these managers, an outside staff unit often attempts to do this, as described in the example. If this occurs, resistance to change develops, and at least in the short run operating managers oppose the development of a comprehensive management information system.

DEVELOPING A FAVORABLE BEHAVIORAL CLIMATE

The remainder of this chapter deals with a number of important concepts for alleviating behavioral problems associated with designing and implementing an integrated information system. People are the most significant single ingredient for achieving an effective MIS. As described at the beginning of this chapter, individuals have values that must be satisfied if the information system is to be truly supported and integrated. Satisfying individual needs and personal interests are important ways of motivating people. This is especially true in developing a favorable behavioral climate for an information system. People view new information flows in terms of how the flows affect their professional specialties in the organization or how the information system will contribute to satisfying individual needs.

When a computerized information system is introduced as a means for achieving integration of information flows, the potential for dysfunctional results is often great. As a rule, people simply do not understand and are often reluctant to learn how a computerized information system can satisfy individual needs as well as organizational objectives. This attitude generally persists as an end, rather than as a means to an end. The acquisition of a computer often becomes the primary reason for making changes in information flows, rather than the needs for information by operating managers and organizational staff groups. In the example presented in this chapter, the decision to commit the organization to a large-scale data processing effort was made without considering in depth the operational or managerial needs for computerized information. As a result, the major impetus for making changes in information flows was to utilize computer facilities and manpower more fully rather than to serve operations and management. A number of managerial concepts are important for minimizing the behavioral problems inherent in designing and implementing an MIS.

Management by Objectives

First, the concept of management by objectives provides a unifying mechanism within which the design, implementation, and monitoring of information systems should be considered.[4] Simply stated, this concept begins with a statement of organizational objectives which serve as the basis for identifying

---

[4] For a detailed discussion of management by objectives, see Peter F. Drucker, *The Practice of Management* (New York: Harper & Brothers, 1954), pp. 135-136; John W. Humble, *Management By Objectives in Action* (New York: McGraw-Hill Book Co., 1970); and George S. Odiorne, *Management by Objectives: A System of Managerial Leadership* (New York: Pitman Publishing Corporation, 1965).

objectives throughout all segments of the organization. For the MIS, this means that the definition of information needs and the design of MIS processes must be evaluated in terms of their contribution to managerial decision making and operating activities. When agreement is reached on the objectives of the information system, its design and implementation are facilitated. Thus, any contemplated changes related to the information system should be reviewed and evaluated in terms of their contribution to organizational objectives and the costs associated with the design and operation of the information system. The notion of cost-benefit analysis was discussed in Chapter 10.

Top Management Support

Top management support and involvement are vital to developing a management information system. If for no other reason, this is important because of the potentially large cost involved. Aside from cost, success in getting a good economic payout and in developing a favorable behavioral climate depend upon top management involvement. This has been clearly brought out in numerous studies of information systems. As early as 1963, a McKinsey survey of 300 computer installations showed that the most successful ones were those that had effective top management direction, rather than merely good technical skills and adequate computer hardware.[5] These findings were supported and reinforced in a study by Booz, Allen, and Hamilton. Here, the need for top management involvement was critical for effective design and implementation of a management information system.[6] A more recent study of three large complex organizations (government, aerospace, and business) emphasized the desirability of top management support of the design, implementation, and operation of the MIS.[7]

Large Investment Alternative

A computerized information system is a large investment alternative that must compete with other operational investment opportunities. The Booz, Allen, and Hamilton study emphasized that the successful computer operation is managed in a manner similar to other company operations; that is, its design and operation are evaluated similarly to other types of capital investment decisions of the organization.[8] Evaluating the MIS in this way will result in more effective involvement and support by top management and by operating managers and in more effective communications between operating managers and staff specialists.

---

[5] John T. Garrity, "Getting the Most Out of Your Computer," in Joseph Orlicky, *The Successful Computer: A Management Guide* (New York: McGraw-Hill Book Co., 1969), pp. 207-208.

[6] See James W. Taylor and N. J. Dean, "Managing to Manage the Computer," *Harvard Business Review* (September-October, 1966), p. 28.

[7] See Winford E. Holland, "Socio-Technical Aspects of MIS," *Journal of Systems Management* (February, 1974), p. 16.

[8] Taylor and Dean, *op. cit.*, p. 27.

Participation

A fourth concept is the provision for participation and involvement of people affected by changes in the information system. The need for participation by major users in the analysis and design of the information system was discussed in detail in Chapter 4. The active involvement and commitment of people at the beginning of the change process is essential for minimizing resistance and conflict, and facilitates the implementation of new or modified systems. The Booz, Allen, and Hamilton study emphasized the need to provide managers the opportunity to share responsibility for planning computer applications instead of relying solely on computer specialists.[9] Also, the study by Holland emphasized that users of information felt they should be involved in the design of the MIS.[10] These views are reinforced by a study by Gallagher which indicated that managers who were actively involved in the design of the MIS placed a considerably higher value on the information it produced.[11]

Education

A fifth concept that is also important for design and implementation of the MIS relates to education about computerized information systems. The education of key operating managers and top management personnel in computerized systems concepts is essential if they are to be meaningfully involved in the planning, implementation, and review of the system's performance. Education of information and computer specialists in operational and managerial activities is just as essential. The Booz, Allen, and Hamilton study showed that criteria for selection of key computer management personnel place heavy emphasis on knowledge of the organization's operations as well as knowledge of computer and information technology.[12] An obvious result is a favorable behavioral climate in which managers and specialists are able to interface more effectively.

SUMMARY

Behavioral science provides concepts that are important for explaining, predicting, and influencing human behavior in an organizational setting. Individuals have a hierarchy of needs that must be considered in the design and implementation of the MIS, ranging from basic physiological needs to needs for involvement, growth, and self-actualization. Because man is heterogeneous, multiple approaches for inducing performance must be considered.

The lack of objective orientation, vertical-functional overemphasis, and the existence of stress, conflict, fear and resistance are examples of a number of typical behavioral limitations for the design and implementation of the MIS.

In developing a favorable behavioral climate, it must be recognized that people not only have heterogeneous needs, but that they also have varying

---

[9] Taylor and Dean, *op. cit.*, p. 28.
[10] Holland, *op. cit.*, p. 15.
[11] Charles A. Gallagher, "Perceptions of the Value of a Management Information System," *Academy of Management Journal* (March, 1974), p. 54.
[12] Taylor and Dean, *op. cit.*, p. 28.

capabilities. Important managerial concepts for achieving a favorable behavioral climate include management by objectives, top management involvement and support of the MIS, treatment of the MIS as an investment alternative, provision for active participation and involvement of people in the design and implementation of the MIS, and the continuous education of personnel about advantages and limitations of computerized information systems.

REVIEW QUESTIONS

1. Explain how the lack of objective-goal orientation among various information systems users can lead to a nonsupportive behavioral climate in a large organization.
2. Contrast horizontal (system) with vertical (functional) orientation, and discuss how overemphasis on the vertical-functional dimension can lead to behavioral problems related to information needs.
3. Discuss several important characteristics of people in an organizational setting related to their needs for information. How are these characteristics interrelated?
4. Identify some specific examples of the behavioral problems of stress, conflict, fear, and resistance in an organizational context. Discuss the nature of these problems, why they tend to emerge, and how they are related to information system implementation.
5. Discuss the importance of leadership, communication, and authority in designing and implementing an information system.
6. What is management by objectives? What contribution does it make in an information system?
7. How might involvement of top management contribute to a more effective information system? What evidence do you see to support this?
8. Since a computerized information system involves a large investment in both human and money resources, how should it be justified? What part does cost-benefit analysis play in the evaluation?
9. Why should managers and key operating personnel be educated in information system design concepts? Why should computer specialists be knowledgeable about managerial needs for information?
10. Discuss the need for participation of users of information in MIS design.

EXERCISE 11-1: Behavioral Implications of MIS

Consider the case study presented in this chapter. For this behavioral setting, perform the following:

1. Summarize and contrast the perceptions of top management, the head of Data Processing, the Controller, and other users, including Production and Procurement.
2. Identify the specific behavioral problems which exist in this example, and explain what managerial concepts might be used to resolve these problems.

3. Using the materials relating to MIS design described in Chapter 4, develop a detailed methodology which you feel would be appropriate for resolving the information-related problems described in the example.

EXERCISE 11-2: Literature Survey

Read and critique several articles on one or more of the major behavioral problems which have implications for large computerized organizational information systems:

a. Lack of objective orientation.
b. Vertical-functional overemphasis.
c. Creation of stress, conflict, fear, or resistance.

In your critiques of the articles you read, comment on the nature of the approaches for dealing with these problems related to designing and implementing a computerized information sytem.

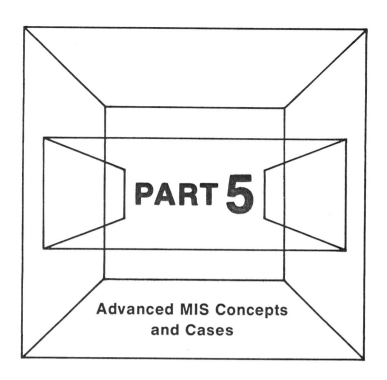

PART 5

**Advanced MIS Concepts
and Cases**

12 ADVANCED INFORMATIONAL CONCEPTS FOR PLANNING

As organizations increase in size and become more complex, planning becomes much more complicated and there is mounting pressure for more extensive, more intricate types of planning information. Developments in information processing technology and other theoretical and applied informational developments have made it possible to obtain the information needed for use in advanced planning models and techniques.

This chapter examines two informational developments which have had a significant impact upon planning and upon the design of information systems for planning activities. These developments, industrial dynamics and planning-programming-budgeting systems, provide a theoretical basis upon which advanced information systems for planning can be developed. In addition, these two developments, coupled with others presented in Chapter 13, have provided the impetus for the development of integrated information systems for management.

SYSTEM SIMULATION

System simulation is an experimental computerized approach for studying the dynamic behavior of entire systems or of large subsystems. Simulation means the process of representing or giving the appearance or effect of something, in this case of a system. In operations research and systems analysis, system simulation connotes the process of mathematically modeling a complex system, such as a university or its registration activity, and performing experiments on a computerized version of the system model. These experiments involve projecting the system model through time in order to solve problems in the structure or policies of the real system or to decide on and plan for an optimal course of action. The justification for system simulation is that it is usually easier and less costly to experiment with the system model than with the system it represents.[1]

Industrial Dynamics

One system simulation approach, industrial dynamics (ID), is described here in some detail.[2] It was selected for presentation because: it is especially

---

[1] For a more thorough discussion of system simulation, see Julius S. Aronofsky (ed.), *Progress in Operations Research: Relationship Between Operations Research and the Computer* (New York: John Wiley & Sons, 1969), III, Chapters 2 and 3.

[2] Industrial dynamics has recently been renamed system dynamics to reflect broader application of its methodology; the original name is used here for consistency with cited references.

appropriate for simulating entire large complex systems; it is based on simpler, more aggregated, and less detailed definitions of system flows than other approaches and therefore it is easier to understand; it incorporates an operational and an informational subsystem similar to that depicted in the organizational systems model used in this text; and it is representative of the time-oriented or period-to-period (for example, month-to-month or year-to-year) technique employed in most simulation approaches.

Industrial dynamics was developed in the late 1950's by Jay W. Forrester and his associates to study the information-feedback characteristics and time-varying behavior of business and industrial systems and other types of organizations.[3] Forrester characterized his development as "enterprise engineering" to emphasize its utility in constructing effective organizational systems. In this respect, ID has broad application in developing objectives and committing resources in organizational systems. It permits the design of an optimal system structure and optimal policies for attaining organizational objectives by means of an experimental modeling approach using computer simulation for investigating alternative structures and policies.

The major feature of the ID approach is that it shows how organizational structure, amplification in policies, and time delays in decisions and actions interact to influence the success or failure of the enterprise. ID defines the operational and informational subsystems of the organization. It focuses on period-to-period sequences of interrelated activities linked together by information, and it emphasizes the erratic impact of delays in resource and information flows at one period upon decisions and activities in subsequent periods. This feature is discussed in more detail later.

Industrial dynamics studies have been successfully conducted on a variety of topics, including production-distribution systems, market dynamics, growth, commodities, research and development, and recently on urban and world dynamics.[4] Forrester believes that industrial dynamics also will have broad applications in areas such as the psychology of group behavior, dynamics of conflict, epidemics, and internal medicine, because it can provide a complete, precise, analytical description of a system in any field of study. The extent to which these applications are developed will depend upon the ingenuity of researchers in stating the interrelationships mathematically and in refining the methodology used to quantify them. Quantification and simulation of the interrelationships in social systems has been extremely limited because of the difficulty in modeling human interactions and the cost involved in modeling large-scale systems. More applied research utilizing industrial dynamics and similar experimental approaches is needed to help remove these limitations.

ID Methodology. The methodology for conducting an industrial dynamics study involves the following steps:[5]

1. Identification of a problem.

---

[3] Jay W. Forrester, *Industrial Dynamics* (Cambridge: M.I.T. Press, 1961).
[4] Jay W. Forrester, *Urban Dynamics* (Cambridge: M.I.T. Press, 1969); and Jay W. Forrester, *World Dynamics* (Cambridge: Wright-Allen Press, 1971).
[5] Adapted from Forrester, *Industrial Dynamics*, p. 13.

2. Isolation of the factors that appear to interact to create the observed symptoms.
3. Tracing of the cause-and-effect information feedback loops that link decisions to action and to resulting information changes and new decisions.
4. Formulation of acceptable formal decision policies that describe how decisions result from the information streams.
5. Construction of a mathematical model of the decision policies, information sources, and interactions of the system components.
6. Generation of the behavior through time of the system's variables using a digital computer.
7. Comparison of results against all pertinent available knowledge about the real system.
8. Revision of the model until it is acceptable as a representation of the real system.
9. Redesign within the model of the organizational relationships and policies which can be altered in the real system to find the changes which improve system behavior.
10. Alteration of the real system in the directions that model experimentation has shown will lead to improved system performance.

As an illustration of the use of ID methodology, consider the case of a manufacturing firm which is experiencing large, cyclical fluctuations in profits. The problem (step 1) is to identify the underlying cause of the firm's fluctuating profits so that policies can be established for stabilizing revenue behavior. (Large fluctuations in profits are assumed to be undesirable because they complicate planning and cause overall organizational inefficiency.)

Six factors (or variables) can be isolated (step 2) which together appear to cause the fluctuations in profits. These factors are promotional effort, demand, order backlog, delivery time, production, and revenue. Certain other factors might have minor effects. Fluctuations in gross revenue are assumed to have a direct effect upon profits.

Two cause-and-effect feedback loops (step 3) interrelate the six major factors, as shown in Exhibit 12-1. In one loop, promotional effort affects the market (demand) for the firm's product, generating orders (with a backlog) to the factory for production of the product. The finished product is shipped and sold, generating revenue for use in promotional effort. This loop (loop 1) is a *positive feedback loop* in which a change in a variable will cause a chain of events which reinforces the change in that same variable. In other words, an increase in promotional effort results in an increase in demand, generating more orders to production, followed by a subsequent increase in shipments and revenue, which in turn increases promotional effort still further.

Loop 2 is a *negative feedback loop* in which the opposite effect occurs. An increase in demand results in increasing order rates, a larger order backlog, and an increase in delivery time, which tends to decrease demand. This is a nonreinforcing effect. This entire system involves a negative feedback loop imbedded in a larger positive feedback loop, one nonreinforcing and the other reinforcing, which together produce fluctuations in demand, revenue, and profits.

Exhibit 12-1

SIMPLIFIED ID MODEL OF MANUFACTURING FIRM

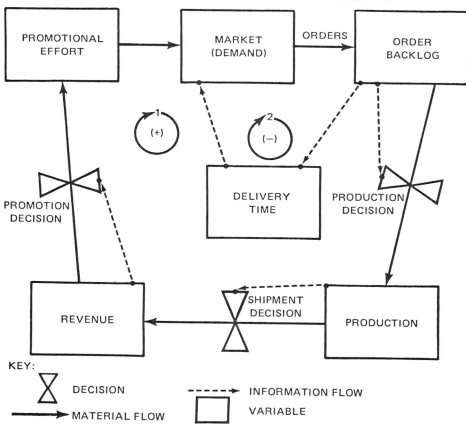

Three decision policies (step 4) which describe how decisions result from the available information are also identified in Exhibit 12-1, namely the production decision, the shipment decision, and the promotion decision. These decisions are based on information flows concerning the amounts of the order backlog, product produced, and revenue, respectively. The information flows are shown as dotted lines connecting each decision with the corresponding factor (variable) on which it is based.

Next, a mathematical model (step 5) of the firm is constructed, using a computer language called DYNAMO. The model is quantified using data from the firm's actual operations, and the firm's behavior through time (step 6) is simulated in test runs on the digital computer. The results of initial tests are then compared (step 7) against all pertinent knowledge about the real system so that the model can be revised (step 8) to represent the real system accurately. Additional tests are performed and the model is redesigned (step 9) as necessary to identify how delays in the flow of resources and information and the decision policies interact to create fluctuating profits. The results of this experimentation ordinarily provide a better understanding of the dynamic behavior of the system, which enables subsequent alteration of the real system (step 10) in the direction that the model tests have shown will lead to reducing profit fluctuation and to stablization of system performance. For example, experimentation of this nature has shown that the production decision should be based on not only information about the order backlog but about potential demand as well.

The foregoing example of the use of ID methodology is oversimplified for clarity. Using this methodology to solve a problem in a real organization is quite complex, especially steps 5 through 9 which require expertise in computer simulation techniques and in the DYNAMO language. However, the potential benefits are substantial, and industrial dynamics has proven to be a useful approach for improving organizational planning and design processes.

Implications for MIS. In addition to being a general planning and design technique, ID has certain direct implications for the development of management information systems. Some of the theoretical foundations of ID pertain directly to information needs and flows and to organizational decision making. These foundations are the experimental modeling of complex systems, the decision-making process, and information-feedback systems. They are concerned with the structure, delays, and amplification which interact to create the dynamic behavior of the system.

Experimental Modeling of System Structure. The *experimental modeling* technique for defining system structure consists of four elements, as shown in Exhibit 12-2:

1. Multiple levels of variables, such as the level of material inventory and work-in-process.
2. Flows that transport the contents of one level to another, such as the flow of material from inventory to work-in-process.
3. Decisions that control the rates of flow between levels, such as the production decision between material inventory and work-in-process.
4. Information channels that connect the decisions to the levels, such as the information linkages connecting the shipment decision to material inventory and to work-in-process.

The levels are the accumulation of stocks within the system, such as inventories, bank balances, and number of employees. The rates of flow correspond to activity, while the levels represent the state to which the system has been brought by the activity. The decisions are statements of policy that prescribe the rates of flows between levels, and they are dependent upon information about the levels.

The previous example shows only one type of operational subsystem network, a materials flow network. Other operational subsystem networks can be defined, such as an orders network, a money network, a personnel network, and an equipment network. A complete model of a manufacturing firm would ordinarily consist of all of these and perhaps others. The connecting network among all these operational subsystem networks is the information network, or information subsystem. Information is also the facilitator of decision making

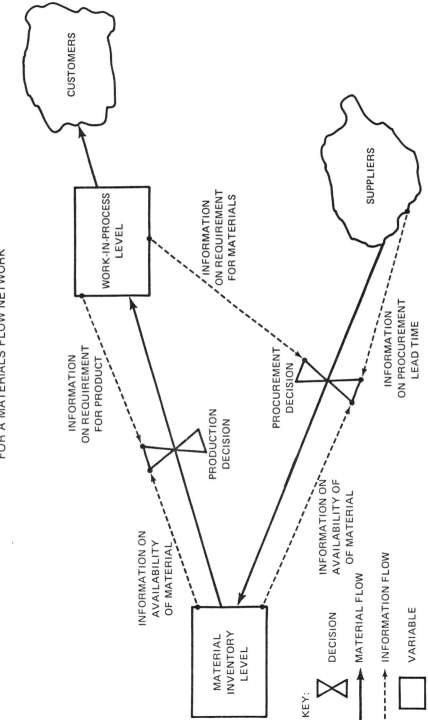

Exhibit 12-2

INDUSTRIAL DYNAMICS MODEL STRUCTURE
FOR A MATERIALS FLOW NETWORK

throughout the entire structure, since all decisions are dependent upon information about the levels of the variables.

Concerning the MIS, the foregoing ID model structure is conceptually useful in defining information needs for the decisions and activities of the operational subsystem. Construction of an ID model is a schematic or flowcharting technique for identifying basic information needed for decisions about the levels of the variables. Also, simulation experiments with the model can be used to evaluate and redesign basic information needs throughout the organizational system. Although this approach has not as yet been widely employed, it does offer an alternative for defining information needs rather than simply asking decision makers what information they want. It is important to satisfy individual users' needs for information, but as organizations become more complex it is also increasingly necessary to define information needs from a wholistic perspective, that is for all users. In this respect, industrial dynamics can be an efficient approach for defining information needs for an integrated MIS for the entire organization.

The Decision-Making Process and Information Delays. The conceptual treatment of the decision-making process in ID is also useful in understanding and minimizing the effects of information delays in the MIS. In general, the decision-making process consists of three parts:

1. Formation of a set of concepts indicating the goals or results of the system that are desired.
2. Observation of what appear to be the actual results.
3. Generation of corrective action to bring apparent results toward desired results.

As illustrated in Exhibit 12-3, distorted and delayed information about actual results forms the basis for establishing the desired results and for recognizing the apparent results. Corrective action will in turn be delayed and distorted by the system subsequent to its effect on actual, and then apparent, results. In this information-decision-action model, decisions are transformed into actions which produce real results. Information about the real results is subject to delay, distortion, and inaccuracy so that the feedback of information to the decision-making process represents only apparent results. For example, if information about actual material inventory level in Exhibit 12-2 is inaccurate or delayed, then the actual level of inventory will not be known when the procurement decision must be made. In this event, the decision must be made based on outdated information which does not reflect the actual current inventory level. Therefore, the decision-making and decision transformation processes produce results that tend to oscillate around these desired, apparent, and real conditions, making system behavior generally unstable.

Decision making is governed by various explicit and implicit policies of behavior. Here, a policy is a rule that states how operating decisions are made or in other words, a formal statement of a decision giving the relationship between information sources and the resulting operational flows. Two types of decisions are identified in industrial dynamics methodology:

Exhibit 12-3

INFORMATION-DECISION-ACTION MODEL
OF THE DECISION-MAKING PROCESS

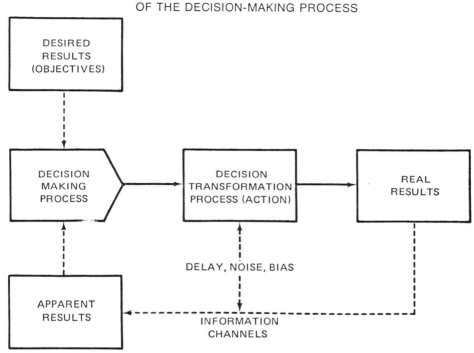

SOURCE: ADAPTED FROM EDWARD B. ROBERTS, "INDUSTRIAL DYNAMICS AND THE
DESIGN OF MANAGEMENT CONTROL SYSTEMS," *MANAGEMENT SYSTEMS,* EDITED BY
PETER P. SCHODERBEK (NEW YORK: JOHN WILEY & SONS, 1967), pp. 24–255.

1. The overt or explicit decision, which involves conscious effort to take action, for example intentionally increasing production to meet an expected increase in sales.
2. The implicit decision, which results from an unavoidable state of the system, for example automatic reordering of materials to meet increases in production requirements.

   Inclusion of both types of decisions in the ID approach makes it possible to deal with desire as well as actuality in decision making. Conditions may lead to a desire for action, coupled with the need for action, which together determine what actually happens. For example, a desired reduction of inventory in response to anticipated decreasing sales may be offset by a needed increase in inventory to maintain the minimum optimum level. The actual result is no net change in inventory.

   The foregoing decision-making concepts have implications for MIS design in two respects. First, they enable a better understanding of the effect of information delays upon the decision making process, emphasizing the importance of timely or real-time information. Second, both explicit and implicit types of decisions must be considered in analyzing operational decisions as a prelude to identifying information needs. The MIS must contain both nonroutine information to make explicit decisions as desired by operating managers and routine information for implicit (predetermined) decisions when necessary. Consideration of these concepts aids the MIS designer in providing for all organizational information needs.

Information Feedback and Amplification of Decisions. The information-feedback concept prevalent in ID has to do with the amplification effect of information in decision making. An information-feedback system exists "whenever the environment leads to a decision that results in action which affects the environment and thereby influences future decisions."[6] According to Forrester, information-feedback systems are basic to all forms of life and human endeavor, and virtually everything done in our society is carried out in the context of an information-feedback operation. There are numerous examples common to everyone:

> A person taking a shower feels the water get colder, adjusts the faucets, and obtains the desired water temperature.
> A person realizes that he is slow in performing a task, speeds up his motion, and completes the task on time.
> A firm projects demand for its products, adjusts its production schedules, and thereby avoids an out-of-stock condition.

All these examples involve information feedback, whereby results of a process lead to decisions and actions that keep the system in continuous motion. As shown in Exhibit 12-1, feedback may be positive or negative. Positive feedback increases the action the system is taking. Negative feedback decreases the magnitude or direction of what the system is already doing. Negative feedback is predominant in most information feedback situations, and it is the mechanism which tends to keep the system under control. Amplification of system behavior is caused by either reinforcement of desired conditions or overreaction to undesired conditions. For example, amplification of an increase in production occurs when this increase leads to more shipments of product, more sales, and further increases in production to meet the higher demand. The reverse can also occur, such as when an increase in orders for production leads to longer delivery times and a subsequent decrease in demand and orders. Feedback occurs in a closed-loop structure, as shown below:

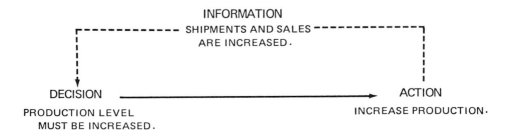

INFORMATION
SHIPMENTS AND SALES ARE INCREASED.

DECISION — ACTION

PRODUCTION LEVEL MUST BE INCREASED.

INCREASE PRODUCTION.

---

[6] Forrester, *Industrial Dynamics*, p. 14.

Information is the input to a decision that produces actions yielding new information. In an industrial system or social organization in which many interrelated activities and decisions are occurring, this simple loop becomes a complex, multiple-loop, interconnected system, as exemplified below:

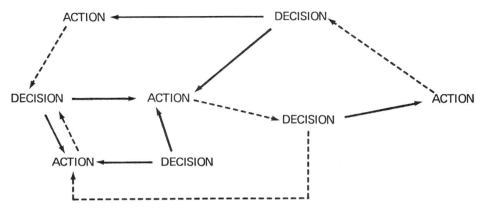

This structure of interconnected information-feedback loops, containing the information linkages (the dotted lines) taken all together, actually describes the entire informational subsystem of an organization. An example of this type of structure related to the level-of-financing decision in a manufacturing firm is illustrated in Exhibit 12-4. This example shows three feedback loops with eight information linkages between actions and decisions. The combined effect of the various decisions and actions shown in this example is to increase or decrease the level of the firm's financing based upon information feedback about increases in cash receipts (loop a), payments (loop b), and money requirements (loop c).

The conceptualization of an organization as an information-feedback system is important for MIS design. It calls attention to the interrelatedness of decisions throughout the organization, thereby focusing on the multiplicity of information needs which have common origins. Thus the ID modeling approach can be useful in identifying common needs for information in different segments of the organization, which is essential for integrating MIS processes.

Other Simulation Approaches

There are a number of other approaches for simulating operational and information systems. One of the more widely used approaches is General Purpose Simulation System (GPSS), which was developed by IBM from efforts to solve the design of communication and data-handling systems.[7] GPSS is an event- or transaction-oriented simulation technique. The occurrence of events or transactions is the basis for timing the simulation sequence, rather than a fixed time as in the period-oriented technique. Models are constructed in a specialized computer language using a flowchart, and the modeling elements used in the

---

[7] For a presentation of GPSS and other simulation techniques, see J. W. Schmidt *et. al., Simulation and Analysis of Industrial Systems* (Homewood, Ill.: Richard D. Irwin, 1970).

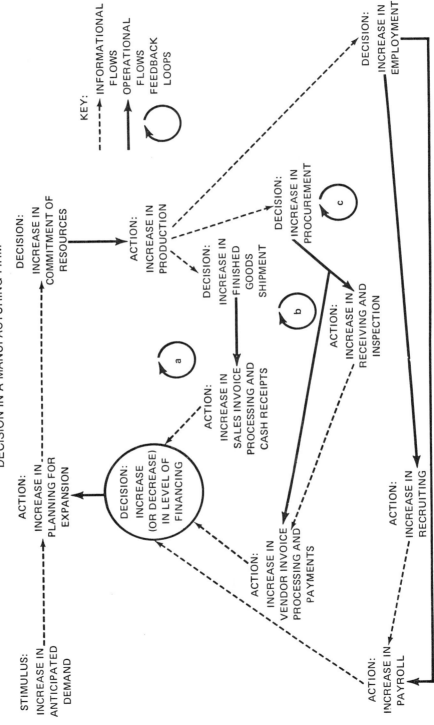

Exhibit 12-4

INTERRELATED FEEDBACK LOOPS DESCRIBING THE LEVEL-OF-FINANCING DECISION IN A MANUFACTURING FIRM flowchart constitute the basic programming statements which represent the logic of the real system. Systems are described in GPSS in terms of facilities, storage, and queues which are manipulated through time to study the effects of interactions of transactions upon the system flows.

GPSS is primarily designed to simulate transaction-flow systems in which stocks pile up and queues develop. An example of the GPSS technique is shown in Exhibit 12-5 for a simple queuing system.

The GPSS reporting scheme for the simulation shown in Exhibit 12-5 includes compilation of statistics on the time spent in the queue and in the entire system for each simulated transaction plus average times and other statistics. These results are useful in problem solving and in designing transaction-flow systems which are too complex to be analyzed or structured mathematically.

Other approaches and computer languages for system simulation are SIMSCRIPT, developed at the Rand Corporation; GASP, developed at U.S.

Exhibit 12-5
GPSS SIMULATED QUEUING SYSTEM

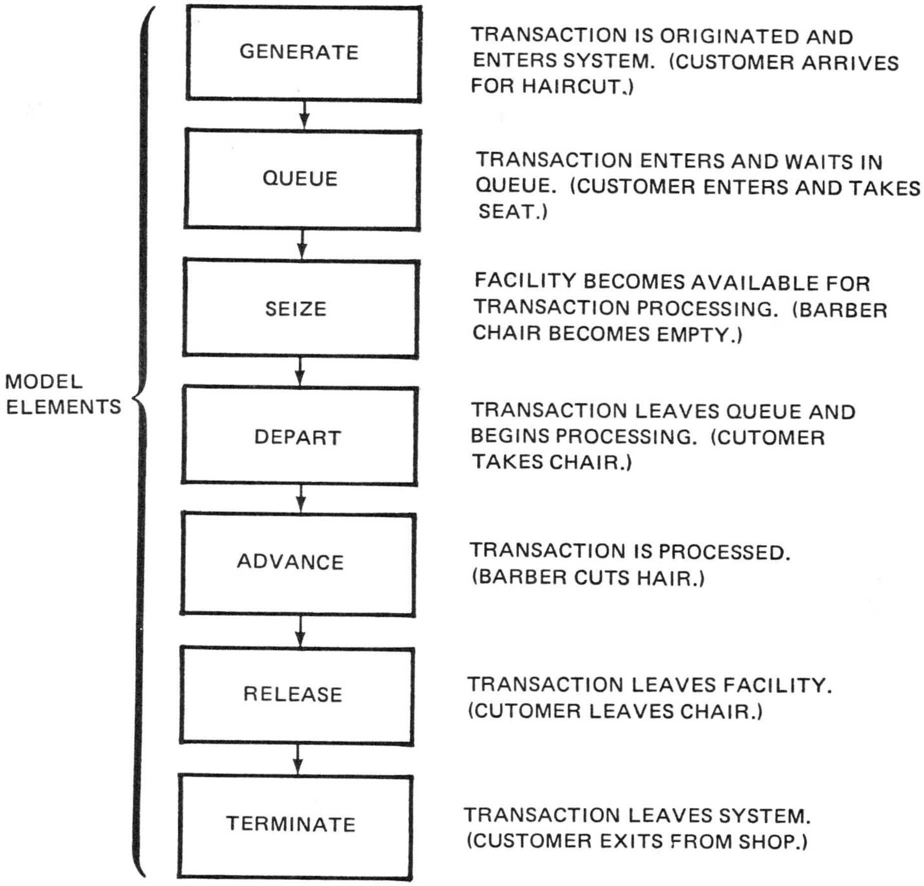

MODEL ELEMENTS

GENERATE	TRANSACTION IS ORIGINATED AND ENTERS SYSTEM. (CUSTOMER ARRIVES FOR HAIRCUT.)
QUEUE	TRANSACTION ENTERS AND WAITS IN QUEUE. (CUSTOMER ENTERS AND TAKES SEAT.)
SEIZE	FACILITY BECOMES AVAILABLE FOR TRANSACTION PROCESSING. (BARBER CHAIR BECOMES EMPTY.)
DEPART	TRANSACTION LEAVES QUEUE AND BEGINS PROCESSING. (CUTOMER TAKES CHAIR.)
ADVANCE	TRANSACTION IS PROCESSED. (BARBER CUTS HAIR.)
RELEASE	TRANSACTION LEAVES FACILITY. (CUTOMER LEAVES CHAIR.)
TERMINATE	TRANSACTION LEAVES SYSTEM. (CUSTOMER EXITS FROM SHOP.)

Steel; SIMPAC, developed at Systems Development Corporation; and numerous lesser known ones, such as JOSS, SIMULA, and CSL. All of these are digital computer techniques for simulating dynamic systems; however, each represents a different approach to the design of a simulation language and focuses on different levels of detail in system flows. In other words, particular features of the languages are better suited for different applications.

PLANNING-PROGRAMMING-BUDGETING SYSTEM

For some time, traditional functional planning and budgeting have been used for decision making by both government and industry. But in 1965, the federal government instituted a particularly new system of planning and budgeting. This was a significant step since:

> . . . It denoted the formal recognition by our nation's leaders that formal long-range planning and objective analysis were reasonable and necessary complements to subjective analysis and informal short-run planning in determining the actions and future course of a huge organization whose actions affect the daily life of virtually every human being.[8]

This new system was called a *planning-programming-budgeting system (PPBS)*.

PPBS is an output-oriented approach for financial planning and simultaneous evaluation of alternative means (programs) for achieving stated objectives. Cost-benefit analysis is the basic analytical technique used in PPBS and involves comparing the benefits of outputs with the costs of inputs for alternative programs and courses of action. Although PPBS was devised as a financial planning device, it relies upon evaluation of past performance as a basis for planning and projecting future performance of alternative programs. This is the basic nature of the planning-budgeting-evaluating-planning sequence for any organization.

There are numerous applications of PPBS in business, education, and government, the best known of which are those involving the federal government. These applications have been developed from work by the Rand Corporation and others in the 1950's on new governmental budgeting, accounting, and planning procedures. Now applications of PPBS can be found in many areas of the federal government, including the Postal Service, VISTA, the Forest Service, the Veterans' Administration, and the Defense Department. The applications involve a variety of topic areas, ranging from disease control to control of airport congestion. The basic structure of PPBS has been refined in some instances to suit particular applications. For example, in 1969 the Department of Defense introduced a feature in PPBS called Project PRIME, which focuses on achieving consistency between program budgets and reporting systems to provide a capability of progress reporting specifically related to the program objectives.[9]

---

[8] David I. Cleland and William R. King, *Systems Analysis and Project Management* (New York: McGraw-Hill Book Co., 1968), p. 113.

[9] Allen Schick, "Multipurpose Budget Systems," *Program Budgeting and Benefit Cost Analysis: Cases, Text & Readings,* edited by Harley Hinrichs and Graeme M. Taylor (Pacific Palisades, Calif.: Goodyear Publishing Co., 1969), pp. 358-372.

In business and industry, firms such as General Motors and DuPont have been using similar budgeting and financial procedures to attain major objectives for some time. The procedures used by General Motors involve program definition and estimation of potential profits and losses under various conditions.

PPBS Methodology

PPBS methodology involves the following general steps:

1. Identification of alternative programs for achieving stated objectives.
2. Specification of a future time horizon.
3. Determination of the costs of resource inputs and benefits of value-added outputs for each program, i.e., development of a program budget.
4. Use of quantitative methodology to obtain meaningful cost-benefit ratios for evaluating each program.
5. Recognition of the existence of uncertainty of future events.
6. Realization that the program environment is highly complex, involving highly interrelated key variables.

Basic to the entire PPBS methodology and to the first step in particular is the concept of a *program*. Literally, a program is "a plan or schedule to be followed." In the federal government, the term program is used interchangeably with "function," "activity," and "performance." In a PPBS context, precisely what constitutes a program is most nearly similar to the objectives of an organization. Therefore, one of the major characteristics of a program is that it is output-oriented. Programs are defined based on what the organization is trying to achieve, that is, the value of the outputs it produces. Generally, the output categories are classified into program categories, program subcategories, and program elements. Some examples of program categories for a university are:

Professional Programs
  Business Subprograms
    Management Sub-sub-programs
      Behavioral Science Sub-sub-sub-program
      Management Science Sub-sub-sub-program

Each is a breakdown of the previous category into activities with narrowing objectives and more specific uses of resources.

The major difficulty involved in defining and categorizing programs in this manner is related to the poorly defined objectives of many organizations, especially in educational and governmental organizations where objectives are not profit-related. For example the objectives of an educational institution could be "quality education" or "significant research." Such objectives are difficult to define and evaluate because no one agrees on their precise value. Obviously, there are no set rules which can be rigidly applied to define a program structure. However, it is essential for the application of PPBS methodology that the program structure enable comparison of alternative methods of attaining objectives.

Programs serve as instruments for long-range planning by focusing on planning conducted over an extended five- to ten-year time horizon. In general, planning involves defining broad objectives, policies, and resources required for programs and their elements. In PPBS, planning is carried out within an input-output framework. Various objectives (outputs) are defined which provide the basis for designing and developing programs which in turn require a variety of resources (inputs).

The long-run time horizon of planning is also a central feature of PPBS. The planning period should be based on that period of time needed to fulfill the commitments involved in a particular program. As an example, consider the case of a PPBS for developing an energy conservation program over a six-year time horizon, as illustrated in Exhibit 12-6. This PPBS can be viewed as a three-dimensional structure in which the inputs and outputs of alternative programs are defined and compared over time rather than at just one point in time.

The next step in PPBS methodology is the development of a *program budget*. A budget is a financial plan for future expenditure, and a program budget is merely a financial expression or statement of the program plan. Cost determinations are necessary in comparing and evaluating alternative programs. The use of a program budget, as contrasted with the traditional budget by organizational unit, provides a basis for determining the cost of program inputs and services, as shown in Exhibit 12-7. Functional budgets are traditionally those which define the costs of inputs to the functional segments of the organization, such as finance, procurement, engineering, and production. These are compiled upward through the formal organization. Program budgets cut across organizational lines to reflect the costs of inputs and services provided by each functional segment for each program.

The program and the program budget form the basis for objective analysis of alternative programs by focusing on the goals and objectives of one program contrasted with another. Thus alternative means of attaining any given set of objectives can be directly evaluated. Duplication is eliminated and more exact determination of the requirements for attaining objectives is possible. In addition, the program budget defines the nature, quantity, quality, and timing of services provided, and the cost, both total and by item, of these services. Preparation of the program budget is not just a superficial exercise in revising functional budgets. On the contrary, it reflects the real objectives of the entire organization.

Two basic types of budget documents are used in the federal government's PPBS: the multiyear program and financial plan and the program memorandum. The program and financial plan (PFP) is a transformation of specific organizational objectives into combinations of activities and tasks to attain those objectives within specified time periods. It is usually stated in terms of the program structure and covers a year-by-year time period consistent with the objectives and operations of the organization. An example of this type of document for a welfare program is shown in Exhibit 12-8.

In the exhibit, Task 1 in Activity A is budgeted to increase in dollar effort, while Task 1 in Activity B is budgeted to decrease. Tables like Exhibit 12-8 are

Exhibit 12-6
THREE-DIMENSIONAL DIAGRAM OF PPBS FOR DEVELOPING
AN ENERGY CONSERVATION PROGRAM

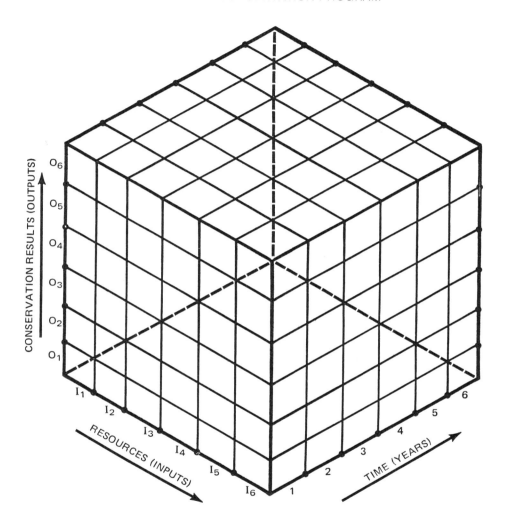

prepared for the costs and the benefits associated with the various program, activity, and task categories for each organization. Benefits might be shown in the form of dollar cost savings, or they might be expressed in more qualitative terms, such as number of people served, quality of service, satisfaction of users, or reduction in delays.

A program memorandum (PM) is prepared regularly for each program category in the PFP, and it is used to support the findings and recommendations of the PFP. A PM presents the results of and a summary of the methodology used

Exhibit 12-7

PROGRAM MANAGEMENT ORGANIZATION

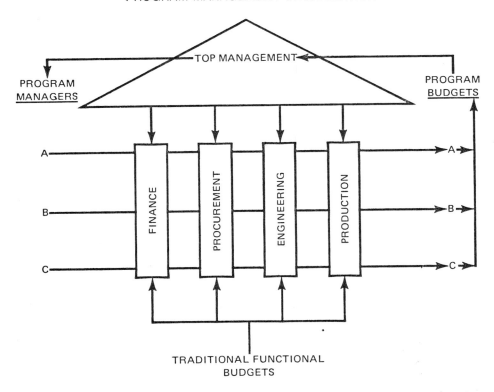

TRADITIONAL FUNCTIONAL
BUDGETS

Exhibit 12-8

TYPICAL PROGRAM AND FINANCIAL PLAN FORMAT
(Costs in Thousands of Dollars)

	Last Year	This Year	Next Year	2d Year	3d Year	4th Year
I. Rehabilitation Program						
A. Activity: Locate Jobs						
1. Task: Survey job market	100	120	130	150	180	200
2. Task: Interview employers	300	350	400	425	450	475
B. Activity: Counsel Clients						
1. Task: Individual therapy	500	400	400	350	300	200
2. Task: Group therapy	150	200	275	325	350	375

in analyzing and contrasting alternative programs. The PM is a basic program budget document to justify the organization's current objectives and programs.

The next and most crucial step in PPBS methodology is the use of cost-benefit analysis, which is an analytical technique for relating the benefits of program outputs to the costs of its inputs. An example of the application of cost-benefit analysis in the PPBS methodology is shown in Exhibit 12-9. A company with the objective of maximizing sales revenues is evaluating the alternatives of advertising versus personal selling. Based on the first-year estimates of cost-benefits (dollar revenues generated per dollar of cost incurred), advertising is the most favorable alternative. Considering the impact on the future (a three-year impact of the $100,000 investment), advertising is still the best alternative to pursue ($2.50 versus $2.30 dollar revenues per dollar cost of programs), other things remaining equal.

The final two steps in PPBS methodology involve recognizing the existence of *uncertainty* and *complexity* in the future program environment. These steps often complicate the analysis of alternative programs so that clear-cut distinctions between programs are difficult without using probability estimates of future events and additional program alternatives. The application of probability theory to the cost-benefit analysis in Exhibit 12-9 shows that the expected value from personal selling ($179,000 or $1.79 per dollar cost) is greater than the expected value from advertising ($172,000 or $1.72 per dollar cost), making personal selling the best alternative. However, if other program

Exhibit 12-9

APPLICATION OF COST-BENEFIT ANALYSIS

OBJECTIVE: Maximize Sales Revenues

1. *Program Alternatives:* Advertising vs. Personal Selling

2. *Determine Costs and Benefits of Programs:*
   Advertising: Costs, $100,000. Benefits, $120,000.
   Personal Selling: Costs, $100,000. Benefits, $110,000.

3. *Cost-Benefit Measures: Dollar revenue generated per dollar cost incurred*
   Advertising: $150,000 ÷ $100,000 = $1.50 (1st year)
   Personal Selling: $110,000 ÷ $100,000 = $1.10 (1st year)

4. *Impact on Future:*   1st year   2d year   3d year   Total
   Advertising: $150,000 + $80,000 + $20,000 = $250,000 ($2.50)
   Personal Selling: $110,000 + $80,000 + $40,000 = $230,000 ($2.30)

5. *Probability Estimates and Expected Values:*
                          1st year   2d year   3d year   Total
   Advertising: .80($150,000) + .60($80,000) + .20($20,000) = $172,000 ($1.72)
   Personal Selling: .90($110,000) + .80($80,000) + .40($40,000) = $179,000 ($1.79)

6. *Environmental Impact Variables:*
   Competitors' actions regarding advertising and personal selling
   New competing product lines
   Changing users' demands and needs

environmental variables are considered, adjustment of the estimates of future benefits and probabilities may result in other alternatives for maximizing sales revenues (for example, investing all or part of the $100,000 in product development, improvement of quality, or providing services or guarantees). In any event, the general framework of PPBS methodology based on cost-benefit analysis is applicable for considering additional alternatives and a range of estimates of future benefits.

Implications for MIS

PPBS has direct application to the preoperating period of the operational subsystem in which planning and budgeting activities are performed. Since PPBS is an output-oriented technique, it can be useful to supplement traditional input-oriented planning and budgeting practices. Use of both of these approaches to planning and budgeting enables definition of a more comprehensive set of information needs for carrying out these activities.

Three basic concepts of PPBS, namely output or objective orientation, the relationship of outputs to inputs of programs, and cost-benefit analysis are directly analogous to the three major characteristics of the MIS presented in Chapter 2: objective-user orientation, integration of information processes, and effective management (of information). Both PPBS and MIS are directly objective-oriented, focusing on identification of program needs and information needs respectively. Integration of information processes involves defining, analyzing, and integrating information outputs (needs) relative to data inputs (sources). This procedure is also an important part of program budget development in PPBS. Finally, cost-benefit analysis from PPBS can also be applied in managing the MIS so as to attain a cost-effective information system.

SUMMARY

This chapter has described two advanced information concepts, system simulation and planning-programming-budgeting systems (PPBS), within the context of facilitating the planning function of management. System simulation, and specifically industrial dynamics, is a time-period-oriented, computerized, experimental approach which utilizes information-feedback and modeling concepts to facilitate decision making. The major objective of industrial dynamics is to show how organizational structure, policies, and time delays interact to influence the behavior of the organization.

Four central features of the industrial dynamics model structure are multiple levels, rates of flow, decisions, and information linkages. The operational subsystem of the model is comprised of several networks such as materials, orders, money, personnel, and capital equipment. The informational subsystem is the connecting network between the operational networks. Decisions which determine the rates of flow are dependent upon information about levels of materials, orders, money, personnel, and capital equipment.

Event-oriented simulation approaches were also described, such as the General Purpose Simulation System (GPPS), which has been used to design communication and data-handling systems. Descriptions of facilities, storage, and queues are formulated and manipulated through time to study the effects of interactions of events upon the flows of the system being analyzed.

The planning-programming-budgeting system (PPBS) is an output-oriented planning and budgeting system for developing goals and allocating resources to programs. The structural aspects of PPBS include time, outputs (program services), and inputs (resources) which are used to prepare program budgets for program evaluation. Two basic types of program budget documents are used in PPBS: the multiyear program and financial plan and the program memorandum. The primary analytical technique used in PPBS is cost-benefit analysis, which involves determining the cost versus the value of alternative programs and objectives within a multiyear framework. The application of PPBS has been primarily in governmental and educational organizations because of the need to evaluate the service-oriented outputs of their programs as compared with product planning and budgeting in business firms.

REVIEW QUESTIONS

1. What are the characteristics and application of industrial dynamics? What do you see as major limitations?

2. Discuss the foundations and methodology of industrial dynamics. How is industrial dynamics related to the scientific method?

3. Distinguish between positive and negative feedback loops, and give examples of each. Which is more important to management?

4. How are the networks in industrial dynamics similar to the operational and informational subsystems? How are the networks interrelated? What is the significance of using a system of networks?

5. Contrast some of the other approaches for simulating systems with the industrial dynamics approach. Comment on the universality of these system simulation concepts for business, education, and government.

6. What is the importance of PPBS? Contrast the traditional functional budgeting approach with PPBS.

7. Discuss the key concepts underlying PPBS methodology.

8. What role does cost-benefit analysis play in PPBS? Is PPBS a technique for defining the best objectives to pursue or the best means of achieving objectives?

9. Upon which basic features of the MIS concept does PPBS focus? How does this emphasis differ from that of the other informational developments described in this chapter?

10. Discuss the similarities and differences between industrial dynamics and PPBS.

EXERCISE 12-1: City Hospital

City Hospital is in the process of developing more effective information for planning and budgeting and for the analysis of various medical activities. The basic input-output systems model is used as a conceptual framework for identifying types of information relating costs of resources (inputs) to services performed (outputs). Exhibit 12-10 shows the hospital as an input-output system. The components of the input-output model are as follows:

Sources of Resources. Internal sources of resources include materials, personnel, and supplies that may be moved from one department to another. External sources of resources include medical schools, nursing schools, and pharmaceutical companies.

Resources. Resources include personnel, materials, equipment, drugs, and facilities.

Processors. Hospital departments and activities are the transformation units that produce the services or outputs required by patients. These include surgery, nursing, x-ray, administration, and purchasing.

Services Performed. The services performed are the outputs, for example surgical, medical, obstetrical, and administrative.

Users. The user of the hospital output is the patient. The basic element of usage is the patient's hospital visit.

Exhibits 12-11, 12-12, and 12-13 contain more detailed examples of how the input-output model can be used to describe activities of City Hospital. Three departments, nursing, surgery, and pharmacy, are shown in these exhibits which describe how activities in the three departments are involved in providing services for a patient experiencing an appendectomy. These exhibits are examples and therefore do not show all the activities and services performed by each department for the patient.

In the appendectomy example, the Nursing Department (Exhibit 12-11) is involved in assisting in surgery, providing general care, and administering medication. Quantitative measures of service performed for these major activities include such items as the number of days of care, the number of medications administered, and the number of reports handled, as shown under services performed. The primary measure of resource use for conducting these activities is cost. Budgeted operating costs for these activities can be determined

Exhibit 12-10

HOSPITAL PROCESSING SYSTEM

SOURCES OF RESOURCES	RESOURCES USED	PROCESSORS	SERVICES PERFORMED	USERS
Internal	Materials	Departments	Surgical	Patients
External	Personnel	Activities	Medical	
	Equipment		Obstetrical	
	Facilities		Administrative	
	Services			

Exhibit 12-11

DEPARTMENTAL PROCESSING SYSTEM—NURSING

SOURCES	RESOURCES USED		PROCESSING ACTIVITIES	NUMBER OF SERVICES PERFORMED ANNUALLY	USERS
Internal and External	Nursing Salaries				
	Surgery	$ 7,000*	Surgery Assistance	Operations: 300 Reports/Documents Processed: 600	Appendectomy Patients
	Medication	4,500	Providing Medication	Dosages Given: 2,700 Reports/Documents Processed: 600	
	General Care	36,000	General Care	Days of Care Provided: 900 Patients Cared for: 300 Reports/Documents Processed: 900	
	Subtotal	$47,500			
	Administrative/Clerical Salaries				
	Surgery	$ 1,500*			
	Medication	1,500			
	General Care	2,250			
	Subtotal	$ 5,250			
	Total Salaries	$52,750			
	Supplies				
	Drugs for Medication	$ 5,400			
	Drugs for General Care	1,800			
	Subtotal	$ 7,200			
	Administrative/Clerical	1,200			
	Total Supplies	$ 8,400			
	Total	$61,150			

* Also shown on Surgery Department budget (Exhibit 12-12).

Exhibit 12-12

DEPARTMENTAL PROCESSING SYSTEM—SURGERY

SOURCES	RESOURCES USED		PROCESSING ACTIVITIES	NUMBER OF SERVICES PERFORMED ANNUALLY	USERS
Internal	Salaries		Surgery	Operations: 300	Appendectomy Patients
	Doctors' Fees	$45,000	Administrative/	Reports/Documents	
	Nursing	7,000*	Clerical	Processed: 600	
	Administrative/				
	Clerical	1,500*			
	Subtotal	$53,500			
	Supplies				
	Drugs, etc.	$15,000			
	Administrative/				
	Clerical	500			
	Subtotal	$15,500			
	Total	$69,000			

* Performed by Nursing personnel (see Exhibit 12-11).

Exhibit 12-13

DEPARTMENTAL PROCESSING SYSTEM—PHARMACY

SOURCES	RESOURCES USED		PROCESSING ACTIVITIES	NUMBER OF SERVICES PERFORMED ANNUALLY	USERS
Internal and External	Salaries		Prescription Processing	Prescriptions Filled: 100	Appendectomy Patients
	Pharmacists	$ 4,000	Inventory Management	Purchase Orders Processed: 100	
	Inventory Mgr.	2,000	Administrative/ Clerical	Items Stocked: 1,000	
	Admin./Clerical, Pharmacy	1,000		Reports/Documents Processed: 200	
	Admin./Clerical, Inventory	2,000			
	Subtotal	$ 9,000			
	Supplies				
	Admin., Pharmacy	$ 1,000			
	Admin., Inventory	1,000			
	Admin., Stock	1,700*			
	Drugs for Stock	22,200*			
	Subtotal	$25,900			
	Total	$34,900			

* Administrative supplies and drugs budgeted by Surgery and Nursing Departments.

using an allocation formula based on the percentage of time spent on each activity as a percentage of the total time spent in each department. Patient costs, such as those for drugs and supplies, can be compiled on an actual usage basis and recorded.

The Surgery and Pharmacy Departments (Exhibits 12-12 and 12-13) also are involved in appendectomies. The services performed in these departments can be similarly measured and costs allocated using an activity allocation formula or an actual usage basis.

Exhibit 12-14 shows a modified budget for the hospital dealing with only one type of service, the appendectomy. The budget data presented is taken from the examples in Exhibits 12-11, 12-12, and 12-13. The budget data reflects only those costs associated with appendectomies; that is, the salaries, supplies, and other costs are prorated according to the amount used in support of appendectomies. The figures do not show total costs incurred by the hospital.

1. Review and comment on the general framework for developing budgets at City Hospital. Consider the following:

   a. Other types of input-output measures that might be useful to the Hospital Director or to each department.
   b. The applicability of the framework to other types of patient care.
   c Other types of information needs of the departments and the Hospital Director for planning and control of operations.

'. What problems do you forsee in developing cross-functional/departmental information in the hospital presented?

3. Comment on the usefulness of the input-output framework for program budgeting and for planning in general; for the simulation of hospital cost-benefits; for traditional budgeting; for an integrated information system.

4. Consider the information in Exhibit 12-14. Which of the input-output measures would be most useful for planning and budgeting?

5. Assume that the budget for City Hospital contains the following additional information:

Appendectomy	*Next Year*	*5th Year*
Direct Cost	$262.33	$300.00
Medical Support Cost	140.00	250.00
Administrative Cost	39.83	100.00
Total Cost	$442.16	$650.00
Pregnancy		
Direct Cost	$205.00	$260.00
Medical Support Cost	200.00	250.00
Administrative Cost	95.00	70.00
Total Cost	$500.00	$580.00

   a. Comment on the meaning of the above information.
   b. Comment on the usefulness of this type of information for comparative program analysis.
   c. What other types of information are needed before any generalizations can be made about the appendectomy and pregnancy budgets?

Exhibit 12-14
PROGRAM BUDGET FOR APPENDECTOMIES

RESOURCES USED (INPUTS)			SURGERY DEPARTMENT		NURSING DEPARTMENT		PHARMACY DEPARTMENT	SERVICES PERFORMED (OUTPUTS)
Direct Appendectomy Costs								300 appendectomies per year
Doctors' Fees	$45,000		$45,000		- -			
Nursing-Surgery	7,000		- -		$ 7,000			Direct cost per year = $262.33
Nursing-Medication	4,500		- -		4,500			
Drugs	22,200		15,000		7,200			
Subtotal	$78,700	=	$60,000	+	$18,700			
Medical Support Costs								
Nursing-General Care	$36,000				$36,000		- -	
Pharmacist	4,000				- -		$ 4,000	Medical support costs per patient
Inventory Manager	2,000				- -		2,000	
Subtotal	$42,000	=			$36,000	+	$ 6,000	visit = $140.00
Admin./Clerical Support Costs								
Salaries	$ 8,250		$ 1,500		$ 3,750		$ 3,000	Administrative
Supplies	3,700		500		1,200		2,000	costs per patient
Subtotal	$11,950	=	$ 2,000	+	$ 4,950	+	$ 5,000	visit = $39.83
Total	$132,650	=	$62,000	+	$59,650	+	$11,000	Total cost per patient visit = $140.00

EXERCISE 12-2: Using ID Methodology

Study carefully the interrelated feedback loops describing the level-of-financing decision of a manufacturing firm, as shown in Exhibit 12-4. Using ID methodology, perform the following:

1. Outline an ID study of a firm which is experiencing undesirable fluctuations in its level of financing.
2. Construct an ID model of this firm using the model elements and structure illustrated in Exhibit 12-2. Your model should include decisions, operational flows, information flows, and key variables (factors).
3. Explain how your model might be used to show how the organizational structure of the firm, time delays (in operational and information flows), and amplification in policies might interact to cause the fluctuations in the firm's financial level.

EXERCISE 12-3: Research Project

Review and critique several articles concerning simulation, industrial dynamics, or planning-programming-budgeting systems. In your reading, focus on examples of how these concepts facilitate planning and the integration of information for planning. Indicate the problems encountered as well as emerging developments related to these concepts.

13 ADVANCED INFORMATIONAL CONCEPTS FOR CONTROL

From Chapters 6 and 7, we know that operational control and managerial/financial control consist of acquiring and utilizing resources for the production and distribution of goods and services and evaluating the entire operation of the organization. We also know that certain basic types of information are needed to facilitate operational and managerial/financial control. As organizations have increased in size and their operations have become more diffused and decentralized, control has become much more complicated. More extensive and more intricate types of information are needed.

This chapter examines three informational developments which have had a significant impact upon control and upon the design of information systems to facilitate control activities. The objectives of the chapter are to define communication and information theory, cybernetics, and Program Evaluation and Review Technique, and to explain how they are used in evaluating the performance of programs and projects and how they are related to information system design. These three developments provide a useful theoretical basis upon which advanced information systems for operational and managerial/financial control can be developed.

COMMUNICATION AND INFORMATION THEORY

Chapter 1 defined information as both a process and the output of that process. In this section, we will examine certain of the theoretical aspects of this concept and its implications for MIS. First, we will discuss the nature and purpose of communication and information theory (CIT).

Nature and Purpose of CIT

Communication and information theory is generally considered to be a single field; however, it is useful to consider its two components separately. Communication theory refers to the theoretical aspects of communicating, that is, making something known, or imparting or transmitting knowledge or information. Information theory refers to the theoretical aspects of information as a process and information as the output of the process. There is little distinction between the two terms, but they do have a somewhat different orientation and scope.

Communication theory originated in the telephone and telegraph industry, and much of the pioneering work is credited to Claude E. Shannon of the Bell Telephone Laboratories. Communication theory originally focused upon the design of a communication system and equipment to achieve technically accurate transmission of a message, excluding problems with semantics and effectiveness of the communication itself. According to Shannon:[1]

> The fundamental problem of communication is that of reproducing at one point either exactly or approximately a message selected at another point. . . .The significant aspect is that the actual message is one selected from a set of possible messages. The system must be designed to operate for each possible selection, not just the one which will actually be chosen, since this is unknown at the time of design.

Shannon's basic model of a communication system appears as Exhibit 13-1. Here the channel merely acts as a conductor between the transmitter and the receiver; it has no memory. The encoder transforms the input signal from the transmitter into electronic pulses that are acceptable to the channel. The decoder is a device at the receiving end of the system that converts those electronic pulses into human-sensible symbols (the message). Distortion in the channel such as static is the noise in the system. This model is primarily technical as it focuses on the syntactic content (that is, the technical accuracy) of a message. In Shannon's model, the information output should accurately reproduce the data input.

Other pioneers in this area, including Warren Weaver and Colin Cherry, tried to broaden Shannon's work by concerning themselves with mathematical aspects of communication circuits and networks and their implications for human communications.[2] As a result of their efforts, *information theory* is

Exhibit 13-1

COMMUNICATION SYSTEM MODEL

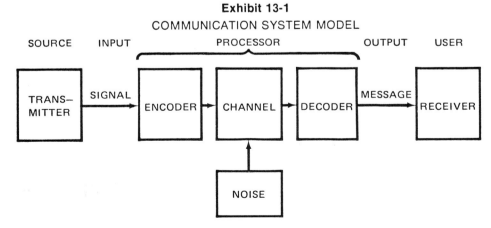

---

[1] Claude E. Shannon, "The Mathematical Theory of Communication," *Bell System Technical Journal* (July and October, 1948), p. 3.

[2] Warren Weaver, "Recent Contributions to the Mathematical Theory of Communications," *The Mathematical Theory of Communication,* edited by Claude E. Shannon and Warren Weaver (Urbana: University of Illinois Press, 1949); and Colin Cherry, *On Human Communication* (Cambridge: M.I.T. Press, 1957).

sometimes referred to by communications engineers as the mathematical theory of communication. It also has a much broader context than communication theory, as expounded by Weaver in his extension of Shannon's original work. There are three basic aspects of information theory: the syntactic level, the semantic level, and the effectiveness or influence level. The *syntactic level* focuses upon the technical accuracy of communication in respect to the transmission and receiving of symbols from Shannon's basic model. But even though information is transmitted and received correctly, it may not be understood by the receiver. This is the *semantic aspect* of information theory. Semantic difficulties often arise in organizational information systems, for example when a manager and a specialist interpret the same information symbols differently. The third level of information theory, the *effectiveness or influence level,* involves the suitability of a message as a motivator of human action. If the receiver responds to the message as intended, then communication has been accomplished effectively at all three levels of the theory. If the manager receives, interprets, and responds meaningfully to the information supplied to him by the specialist, communication between them has been effected.

Some examples of the application of communication and information theoretic concepts for the informational subsystem of an organization are presented in Exhibit 13-2.

All three levels of information from CIT are illustrated in this exhibit. In the last example, the data on course and instructor quality should be accurately reflected in the instructional evaluation report (the syntactic level); this report should be understandable to the dean and university administration (the semantic level); and the report should influence the dean and other administrators to evaluate and control the quality of the course and the instructor's performance (the effectiveness level).

CIT Methodology

Various methodological approaches have been devised to employ communication and information theory in the analysis of organizational information. Most of these approaches have originated from Shannon's model and consist of rigorous mathematical and statistical procedures and nonquantitative techniques. Two mathematical approaches and one nonquantitative approach which have contributed to the enrichment of CIT and its application in an organizational environment are examined in the following paragraphs.

Mathematical Approaches. One of the more commonly known and widely used mathematical technique is Shannon's entropy model for measuring the amount of information generated by a communication process. This model is:

$$H = -K \sum_{i=1}^{n} p_i \log p_i$$

Exhibit 13-2

APPLICATION OF CIT FOR INFORMATIONAL SUBSYSTEMS

SOURCE (Transmitter) →	INPUT (Signal) →	PROCESSOR (Encoder, Channel, Decoder) →	OUTPUT (Message) →	USER (Receiver)
Acquisition & production phases	Resource level & usage data	Informational subsystem	Inventory status	Operating personnel
Production phase	Hours worked Work-in-process data	Informational subsystem	Logistics information	Operating personnel
Preoperating & operating periods	Data on products or services	Informational subsystem	Managerial performance	Management
Preoperating & operating periods	Costs, sales, other financial data	Informational subsystem	General financial status	Management Government Public
Some specific examples of the above are:				
Receiving & production clerks	Data on receipt, transfer, and current level of supplies	Data processing	Report on usage rate, projected levels of supplies	Production supervisor
Payroll clerk	Data on hours worked & deductions	Data processing	Paycheck	Employee
Students	Data on course and instructor quality	Data processing	Instructional evaluation report	Academic dean, university administration

where K = a positive constant
          p_i = probabilities of occurrences of a set of events
          H = entropy (a measure of the uncertainty about the situation)

This model gives a measure, called entropy (H), of the degree of uncertainty or the lack of information resulting from a particular communication event.

As an example of the use of this model, consider the first item from Exhibit 13-2. Suppose the warehouse manager (the user) wishes to know how much uncertainty exists in the projected inventory status report. Assume that he knows the probabilities of occurrence of projected resource usage (p_i = .7, .8, .9) for the next three months (i = 3). These qualities are substituted in the model with a constant (K = 1) peculiar to this information transformation process, to give the following:[3]

$$H = -1\,[.7(\log .7) + .8(\log .8) + .9(\log .9)]$$
$$= -1\,[.7(-.155) + .8(-.097) + .9(-.046)]$$
$$= -1\,(-.11 -.08 -.04)$$
$$0.23$$

This result means that the projected inventory status report contains 23 percent uncertainty or that its content is 77 percent certain. This calculation is useful in assessing the utility of this report for operational control decisions.

Another much more complex mathematical approach is that of Gregory and Van Horn, who devised a mathematical model for determining the value of information for multiperiod recurrent decision making.[4] In the inventory status report example, this model might be used to determine the value of the report based upon its success in making monthly inventory decisions. The major factors in the Gregory and Van Horn model that affect the value of information are the accuracy of the information, the precision of the information, the time interval covered, and the delay in obtaining the information. Their model is:

$$V = K\left[\frac{1}{F}\sum_{n=1}^{F} f(A,T,Y,n) - g(P,Y)\right] - h(A,F,T)$$

where V = Value per time period from using a given set of information
          K = Profit in dollars for making a correct decision
          A = Accuracy of information (ratio of correct decisions to
                total decisions over several time periods)
          T = Processing delay time to obtain information (in time periods)
          Y = The number of decisions made each time period
          P = Probability of making a correct decision without information
          F = Interval over which information is used (time period per
                report)
          f,g,h are mathematical functions

---

[3] The value of H computed from this equation ranges from 0 to 1.
[4] Robert H. Gregory and Richard L. Van Horn, *Automated Data Processing Systems: Principles and Procedures* (Belmont, Calif.: Wadsworth Publishing Co., 1960), pp. 365-372.

This model computes the expected value of a set of information based on the usefulness of the information in enabling satisfactory decisions to be made in a sequential decision situation and on the economic return from these satisfactory decisions. In practice, this is obviously a much-needed type of assessment of any information transformation and reporting process.

Theoretically the model seems valid, but because of the difficulty in estimating values of certain of the parameters it has not been widely accepted in actual practice. For example, estimates for such parameters as the probability of making a correct decision without information are not easily or precisely determined. This problem has been studied by Shrode, who found that lower-level managers were not easily able to quantify their own particular estimates of these probabilities in their routine decisions.[5] However limited this particular model may be in its application, it does represent the type of effort needed in extending communication and information theory to useful proportions in modern organizational information systems.

Administrative Communications. Nonmathematical approaches for extending CIT to organizational information systems have focused on the study of communications networks and the analysis of communication flows between groups and subsystems within the organization. This effort is generally referred to as the study of *administrative communications*, which means communication between individuals in an organizational setting, particularly administrative in nature, such as between a superior and subordinate.

Research in the area of administrative communications includes among others the work of Haveland on man-to-man communications;[6] of Bales on small group interaction;[7] of Cherry on multiple communication networks;[8] of Cohen on hierarchical information flow;[9] and of Guetzkow and Simon on communication nets in small groups.[10] These researchers have used Shannon's basic model and other models to study communication processes in an organizational environment. Much of this work is behaviorally oriented and has as its main objective the improvement of all facets of organizational communication through better understanding of the nature of communication and the transmission process. Although this work originated in the human relations movement of the 1940's and 50's from the concern over efficiency and accuracy of transmission of messages from one person to another (the syntactic aspect of communication theory), it now has much broader and more pragmatic

---

[5] William A. Shrode, "An Analysis of Lower-Level Managerial Decision Making in an Industrial Firm," *American Institute of Industrial Engineers Transactions*, Vol. III, No. 3 (1970), pp. 214-220.

[6] C.J. Haveland, "Social Communication," *Proceedings of American Philosophical Society*, Vol. 92 (1948), pp. 371-375.

[7] R.F. Bales, *et al.*, "Channels of Communication in Small Groups," *American Sociological Review*, Vol. 16 (1951), pp. 461-468.

[8] Cherry, *op. cit.*

[9] A. R. Cohen, "Upward Communication in Experimentally-Greater Hierarchies," *Human Relations*, Vol. 11 (1958), pp. 41-53.

[10] Harold Guetzkow and Herbert A. Simon, "The Impact of Certain Communication Nets Upon Organization and Performance in Task-Oriented Groups," *Management Science*, Vol. 1 (1955), pp. 233-250.

emphasis relating to the purposes of communication and the needs for information in organizations.

The basic elements of human communication as perceived by proponents of administrative communication are: symbols for communicating (words), rules for using the symbols (language), and mutually perceived role relationships between the communicators (sender and receiver). These three elements are analogous to the syntactic, the semantic, and the effectiveness levels in information theory. The sequence that occurs in an administrative communication has been described as: who says (or does not say) . . . what . . . to whom . . . when . . . in what way . . . under what circumstances . . . with what intended effect.[11] This sequence generally conveys the basic idea of Shannon's model.

The specific methods employed in administrative communication involve: (1) the tools and techniques of effective communication, such as observing, reading, and listening skills and the mechanics of oral and written communication; (2) preparation, presentation, and adaptation of communication instruments; and (3) forms, media, and channels of administrative communication. These three methods are usually supported with formal emphasis on administrative writing and reporting.

The dynamics of administrative communication involve an understanding of the nature of people, communication, administration, and their interrelationship in organizational behavior. Although this field of interest resulted from the now-declining emphasis of the human relationists some 20 to 30 years ago, it still has important applications to modern information systems in facilitating operational and managerial/financial control.

Some applications of administrative communication concepts are design of procedures and instructions for data identification; design of clearer, more readable, easier to understand report formats; and design of better forms and channels of report dissemination.

CIT Implications for MIS

The implications of communication and information theory derive from Shannon's basic communications model and from CIT methodology. Shannon's model has been widely used or referenced in information systems research for almost 30 years. This book is no exception, since the basic source-input-processor-output-user model (a variation of Shannon's model) has also been incorporated in our methodology for MIS design.

From CIT have also come various mathematical approaches, such as the entropy model. As yet, these and other quantitative models have not been widely applied, but their limited success suggests that it is feasible to develop quantitative techniques for more accurately evaluating information needs and uses. Determining the value of information produced by the MIS in precise terms is necessary so that MIS cost-effectiveness can be computed objectively and compared meaningfully with other capital expenditures.

---

[11] Lee O. Thayer, *Administrative Communication* (Homewood, Ill.: Richard D. Irwin, 1964), Chapter 3.

Although the field of administrative communications has not provided any quantitative techniques to aid in determining MIS cost-effectiveness, its methodology for facilitating human-human communication has proven useful in a qualitative way in defining information needs relative to individual and group tasks and in designing clear, concise reports for MIS users. In this respect, CIT has contributed to a better understanding of communication and information processes which in turn has aided in the design of these processes in organizational information systems.

CYBERNETICS

The idea of control dates back to the time of Plato, who, in his *Republic*, used the term *kybernetike* (a Greek word meaning the art of steersmanship), both literally for piloting a vessel and figuratively for piloting the ship of state, i.e., for governing. During this century, Norbert Weiner and his associates at M.I.T. began investigating the relationships and analogies between control mechanisms in animals, especially the actions of the nervous system, and feedback control in machines, such as governors on steam engines. At the same time, electronic computing machines were being developed, with particular emphasis on the design of sensing, memory, and control devices. This research on animal-machine interrelationships during the 1940's and 50's became a science. Weiner named his new science "cybernetics," which is derived from the Greek word *kybernetes,* meaning to pilot or govern.

Nature and Purpose of Cybernetics

Cybernetics is defined as "the science of control and communication processes" in both animals and machines. The field of cybernetics is very broad, dealing with the theory of systems such as the nerve and muscle networks in animals, mechanisms for the automatic control of machinery, and information processing systems. Consequently, it overlaps the fields of neurophysiology, computer science, information theory, and automation. In the broadest sense, the application of cybernetics to any system involves the use of control to minimize the uncertainty of the environment. Therefore, the term cybernetics is sometimes used to refer to the study of all information-feedback control systems. However, it is more appropriately applied to exceedingly complex, probabilistic control systems, such as the human brain, an organization, or the economy, where self-regulation and adaptation to the environment are vital. These two concepts, self-regulation and adaptation, are the essence of cybernetic theory.

Self-regulation, or *homeostasis*, refers to the ability of a system to control itself between desired limits while the environment around it is varying. The most common example of a system with this property is the simple thermostat for temperature control, as shown in Exhibit 13-3.

The thermostat, consisting of a receptor for sensing the temperature level and a detector for comparing the sensed level against the desired level, actuates the furnace to raise the temperature to the desired level. This type of device is

Exhibit 13-3
THE THERMOSTAT AS A SELF-REGULATING SYSTEM

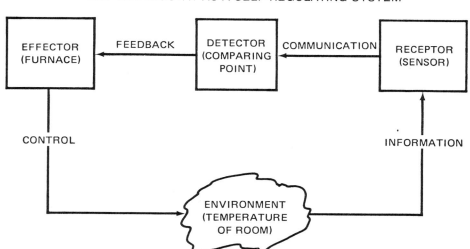

often referred to as a *closed-loop, information-feedback control system*, whereby information about the environment is communicated by the receptor to the detector, actuating feedback of information to the effector which results in control of temperature in the environment. This is analogous to the human hand touching something hot (information), whereby a signal is sent via nerves to the brain (feedback) which results in withdrawal of the hand from the heat (control).

Adaptation is a somewhat broader concept than self-regulation in that it refers to the ability of a system to control itself in a changing environment irrespective of desired limits. This implies that self-regulation and adaptation represent different degrees of control relative to the environment. In fact, Porter has identified four degrees or levels of control for which communication and feedback are necessary: protection, automatic regulation, optimal control, and multivariable automatic control.[12] *Protection* is the lowest level of information feedback control systems, and it is vital to the existence of any living organismic system (for example, an animal has an instinct for survival and uses its senses for this purpose). In *automatic regulator systems*, measurement is performed continuously or at regular intervals, and control is activated by the difference between the controlled variable and a preset desired value. This is the level typified by the thermostat.

At the third level, *optimal control* involves not only regulation of selected control variables in accordance with their desired values but also continual adjustment of desired values to satisfy predetermined goals. For example, a person may adjust his geographical preferences for a higher paying job. Optimal control requires a memory, something the simple thermostat does not have. At the fourth level, *multivariable automatic control* systems are capable of

[12] Arthur Porter, *Cybernetics Simplified* (London: English Universities Press, 1969), pp. 5-18.

changing their internal structure, circuitry, or memory to achieve optimal behavior in spite of continuous changes in the environment. This capability is generally recognized as learning. A computer may someday be designed to reprogram itself to perform computations different from those for which it was originally programmed (such as the computer HAL in the film *2001: A Space Odyssey*).

In an organizational context, cybernetics has its primary application in facilitating the performance of the control function of management. The control function implies adjustment or corrective action based on organizational objectives and predetermined standards of performance. Feedback about performance provides the means for achieving organizational objectives in a dynamic situation. In these respects, the organization (through its management) is cybernetic in nature, constantly regulating itself to carry out or revise its objectives in a dynamic environment. Emphasis on the feedback of information for evaluation, control, and change is basic to the study of all organizational systems.

There are numerous current examples of automated processes and operations. Petrochemical and oil refining operations are continuously controlled in automated plants with only cursory monitoring of processing equipment by human operators. Automated rubber tire making processes with machines that require human intervention only for introducing raw materials and collecting the finished product have been developed by major tire manufacturers. Some baking processes are almost fully computerized and automated, from the mixing of ingredients to the packaging of baked products. One producer advertises that the only nonautomated part of its process is the application of the icing on the cakes. These are present-day examples of man-machine cybernetic systems having varying degrees of complexity. The major difference is that the interface between man and machine is at a higher level of control in some systems than in others, depending upon the nature of the operations performed. For example, an airplane can be flown on full automatic pilot, but an automobile cannot be fully operated automatically. In each of these examples, the man-machine interface is generally found at that level where learning and adaptation to the environment become necessary, such as the situation of an automobile operating on a busy street or highway. The man must be capable of learning good driving habits and adapting to changing conditions, because the machine does not have this capability.

Models of Cybernetic Systems

The application of cybernetic theory to organizational systems is best illustrated through the use of a conceptual model. As is generally the case for any model, the purpose of a cybernetic model is to aid in relating the underlying concepts of the theory to those characteristics of the organizational system with which we are familiar, such as objective orientation, input/output transformation, and feedback for control. Specifically, we want to understand how and to what extent an organizational system can be treated as a cybernetic system, and what implications this has for information systems design. These implications are discussed later in the chapter.

A basic conceptual model of a cybernetic system is shown in Exhibit 13-4. This model is generally applicable to any biological system, mechanical system, or to a biomechanical system such as a human being operating a piece of mechanical equipment. In addition to the basic effector, receptor, and detector elements contained in the thermostat, this model also contains a memory bank and a more sophisticated central control unit to provide a learning capability. Specifically, the system functions in the following manner.

Beginning at the bottom of Exhibit 13-4, the operating conditions of the system are affected by inputs from its environment, and operation of the system results in outputs which in turn act upon the environment. Information

Exhibit 13-4

MODEL OF A CYBERNETIC SYSTEM

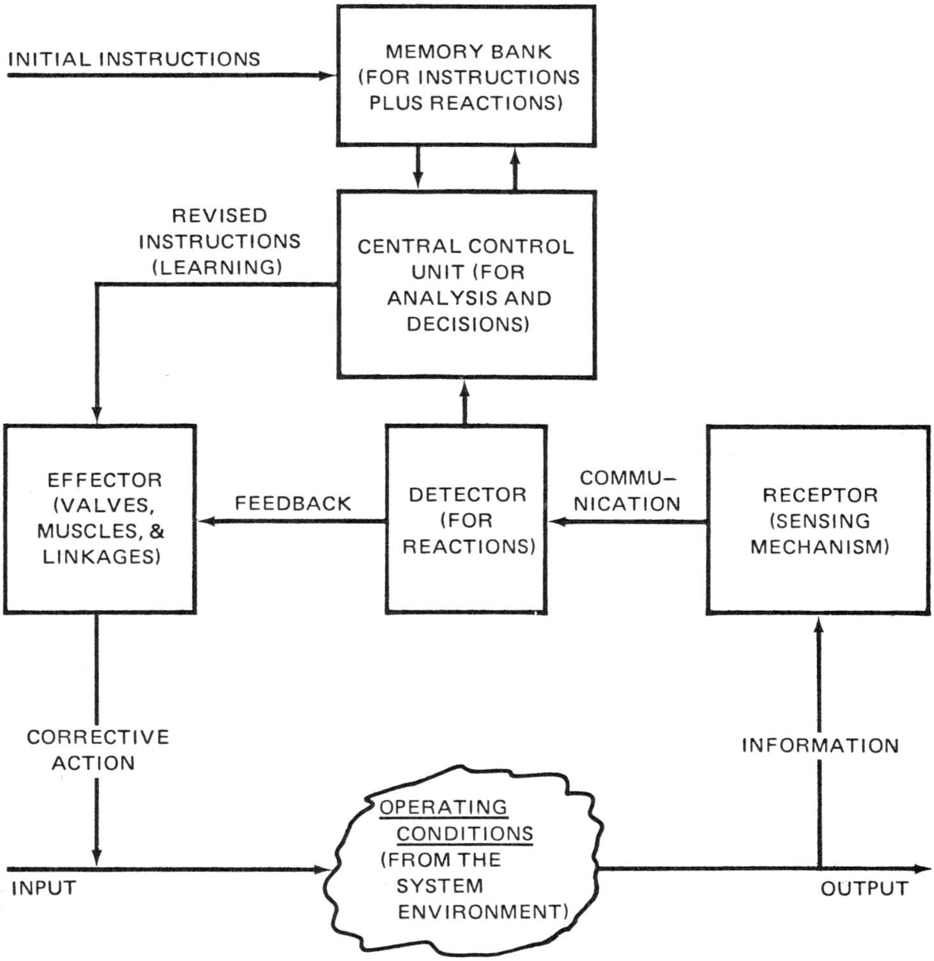

about the outputs is sensed by a receptor and communicated to a detector for comparison with system standards. Through feedback to the effector, corrective action is exerted whenever necessary upon the inputs to maintain control. This sequence of events constitutes self-regulation of the system within prescribed limits.

When communication received by the detector is unusual (i.e., outside normal limits), the central control unit must analyze the situation, make decisions, and issue revised instructions to the effector. The memory is updated to reflect the new conditions and reactions of the system. Naturally, the memory of a new system must be provided with a set of initial instructions and standards for beginning its operation. This sequence of events constitutes adaptation of the system to environmental changes.

To make the foregoing discussion less abstract, an example model of the production function of a typical manufacturing organization as a cybernetic system is presented in Exhibit 13-5. In the cybernetic production model, information about procurement operations is sensed by automated input devices and operating personnel and communicated by an information system to automatically controlled machines, machine operators, and supervisors, who take corrective action to keep the system under control. When environmental changes require that production operations be revised, analyses are performed and decisions are made by the production manager and his staff with the help of the computer and the production data base.

The cybernetic view of an entire organizational system and its subsystems is analogous to that of a living organism interacting with its environment. Like the living organism, an organization is exceedingly complex, and it is humanly impossible to comprehend all the interactions taking place at once in such a system. However, cyberneticians suggest that it is theoretically possible to amplify man's intellect so as to understand and control an exceedingly complex system such as an entire organization using a cybernetic machine or machines.[13] Certainly, much more research is needed before this can be accomplished

Cybernetics Implications for MIS

It is apparent that an information system is the heart of a cybernetic system. It serves as the detector for all actions and reactions of the system, and it facilitates necessary analysis and decision making. As yet the complete cybernetic system has not been perfected, since mechanization or computerization of the central control unit must be augmented by the human brain at some point in the operation to supplement the limited capability of machines and computers. Brown has noted that the following elements are needed for a nonhuman system to function cybernetically:[14]

---

[13] For example, see the model of a cybernetic factory in Stafford Beer, *Cybernetics and Management* (New York: John Wiley & Sons, 1959), p. 150.

[14] Robert Kevin Brown, "City Cybernetics," *Land Economics*, Vol. 45 (November 1969), pp. 406-412.

Exhibit 13-5

CYBERNETIC PRODUCTION SYSTEM

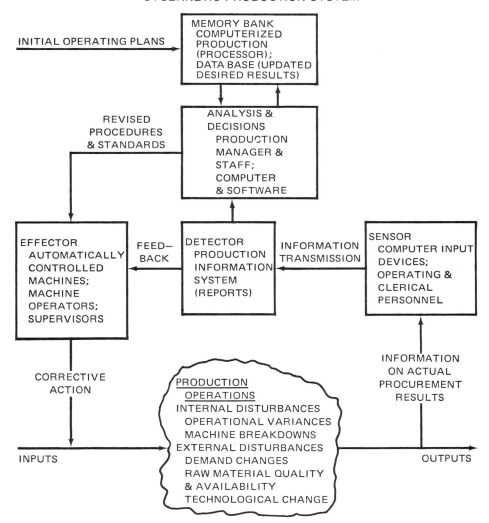

1. A system capable of self-regulation through closed-loop information and feedback.
2. Machines capable of storing information necessary for decision making (computers with large memories).
3. Software (computer programs) to analyze information and provide revised feedback concerning quantifiable elements (e.g., availability of resources, quality standards, and schedules) and nonquantifiable elements (e.g., values, attitudes, and their associated behavior).
4. The information itself, with self-updating provisions (a historical data base having real-time storage and retrieval capability).

These four elements which Brown says are crucial for the existence of a completely cybernetic system are actually the components of an MIS as described in this book, namely, procedures for acquiring and using information, computer hardware and software, and a data base containing the information needed to manage the system. A fully automated MIS would be a cybernetic system; therefore, cybernetics and MIS have common theoretical foundations.

As a final note, the major barrier to perfection of the cybernetic feedback control loop in automated machines is in the memory area and the machine's ability to learn. In very limited types of problem solving, such as chess games, machines have proven their ability to learn from experience when initial instructions include quantifiable standards of success and provision for weighing the degree of success or failure as actions are compared to their reactions. Machines have also learned to "talk," that is, to give semirational responses when reinforcement is given to correct ·answers by a human participant. Also, through heuristic self-programming, machines may be capable of eliminating inconsistency in decision-making from day-to-day variability in human value judgments. However, Weiner has cautioned that the development of learning machines might progress too far. Machines that can win at chess might also win or overrule in the decisions of a war game. The fast reaction time of machines far outweighs man's capability to analyze a situation from a human point of view.

On the positive side, cybernetics has two major virtues, according to Ashby.[15] First, it offers a single vocabulary and set of concepts for representing the most diverse types of systems. Second, it offers a method for the scientific treatment of the system in which complexity is too great and too important to be ignored. Cybernetics offers the hope of providing effective methods for the study and control of exceedingly complex systems, such as an MIS. Although these methods are unperfected, cybernetics provides a foundation on which these methods can be built with only human capabilities as the limiting factor.

PROGRAM EVALUATION AND REVIEW TECHNIQUE

The developments in cybernetics and the need to facilitate operational and managerial/financial control of complex projects consisting of many highly interrelated activities have led to the development of a repertoire of applied project planning and control techniques. One of the best known of these techniques, *Program Evaluation and Review Technique (PERT)*, was developed by the Navy Special Projects Office in conjunction with Booz, Allen, & Hamilton, a management consulting firm, for the Polaris missile program.[16] PERT is a general method of planning and controlling unique and complex projects which are comprised of a set of highly interrelated activities to be performed over a fixed time horizon. PERT is a method of eliminating or

---

[15] W. Ross Ashby, *An Introduction to Cybernetics* (New York: John Wiley & Sons, 1963), pp. 4-6.

[16] Due to the inseparability of planning and control, PERT is both a planning and a control system. The emphasis here is on PERT as a control system to illustrate application of information and control theories.

reducing production delays, conflicts, and interruptions in order to coordinate and control the various activities comprising the overall project and to assure its completion as scheduled. PERT is also an information system in that it provides status reports on developments as they occur.

PERT methodology involves two concepts: an event and an activity.[17] An event is an accomplishment occurring at a specific time. An activity is a distinct task or segment of work which requires time and other resources for its completion. Complex projects or systems involve an interrelated network of activities and events, such that various activities are carried out simultaneously and sequentially. For example, consider the relatively simple PERT network for the project of the opening of a new store shown in Exhibit 13-6. This project consists of nine activities and six events spanning from the start of the project to the opening of the store. Events 1 through 5 serve a dual role; they are ending events for one or more activities and beginning events for others. Some activities must precede others, such as hiring of clerks before training them. Also, some activities are carried out concurrently, such as preparation of the building concurrent with acquiring personnel and merchandise.

The PERT network can be used to identify the sequence of activities which takes the longest time so that these activities can be accelerated if necessary to avoid delaying completion of the project. This sequence is designated as the *critical path* (the longest time sequence of activities), which in this example is 16 weeks. The acquisition of merchandise, which requires 12 weeks, is the most critical single activity in this sequence. There is slack or extra time in all the other sequences of activities.

More complex projects consist of many more highly interrelated activities and events that the foregoing example, thereby making coordination and control of the entire project much more difficult. For example, the Polaris project for which PERT was developed involved coordination and control of the interrelated activities performed by several hundred prime contractors and several thousand subcontractors. Without the use of a project planning and control system such as PERT, it is highly unlikely that the Polaris project could have proceeded at the remarkable rate at which it did, considering that hundreds of thousands of interrelated activities had to be performed successfully and on time.

There are numerous uses of PERT in industry. Manufacturing firms have used PERT in research and development projects; builders and contractors have used it in large construction projects; and advertising agencies have employed PERT to control various marketing activities. In all these applications, the use of PERT involves two cycles, one for planning and the other for control, as shown in Exhibit 13-7. Although we have focused on the control aspects of PERT, both dimensions should be recognized as important.

As shown in Exhibit 13-7, PERT forces the manager and his staff to plan a project in its entirety, beginning with establishment of objectives and ending with review and revision of plans based on defining tasks and preparing time

---

[17] For a detailed treatment of PERT methodology, see Richard I. Levin and Charles A. Kirkpatrick, *Planning and Control with PERT-CPM* (New York: McGraw-Hill Book Co., 1966).

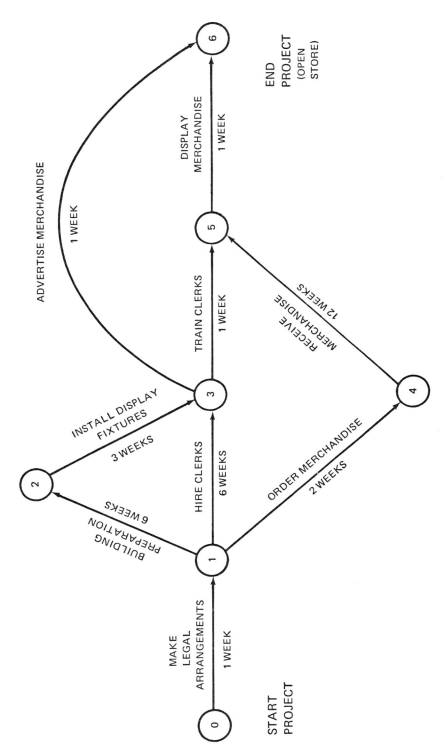

Exhibit 13-6

PERT NETWORK FOR OPENING A NEW STORE

Exhibit 13-7
PERT PLANNING AND CONTROL CYCLES

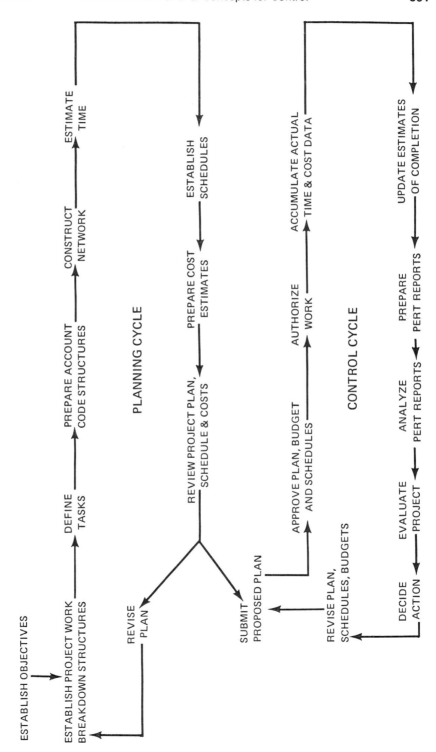

and cost estimates. PERT also enables the manager to control the entire project, from submission and approval of the proposed plan to evaluation of results and revision of plans, schedules, and budgets as needed. PERT helps meet project deadlines because it provides continuous review and control, thereby contributing to better utilization of time, capital, and personnel.

There are several variations of the PERT methodology, such as PERT/Cost and the PERT milestone systems.[18] In addition, there are numerous similar techniques, including Critical-Path Method (CPM), Line of Balance (LOB), Least Cost Estimating and Scheduling (LESS), Integrated Control (ICON), Program Evaluation Procedure (PEP), and Scheduling and Control by Automated Network Systems (SCANS). PERT/Cost is a technique for examining project cost related to project time to determine added costs resulting from accelerating or "crashing" certain activities to insure completion of the overall project on time. The other techniques listed have been devised by various firms or agencies for specialized applications related to planning and control of project time and cost.

PERT has direct implications for MIS in two respects. First, it is itself a specialized type of information system for supplying specific information needed in fixed-length projects and programs. Therefore, it is useful in defining information needs in project-oriented activities. Second, it is an extremely useful planning and controlling technique for an information system development project. This is a highly complex type of project consisting of various interrelated tasks for which PERT was specifically designed. PERT can significantly enhance planning and control of an MIS project (see an example of the use of PERT in Exercise 4-5, page 104).

SUMMARY

This chapter describes the informational concepts of communication and information theory, cybernetics, and PERT in the context of facilitating the control function of management. Communication and information theory focuses on the effectiveness of information in instituting action. Modern information theory focuses on quantifying the value of information produced by the information system. Administrative communications methodology involves the study of communications networks and the analysis of communications flows between groups and subsystems within the organization.

Cybernetics is the science of communication and control, focusing on self-regulation and adaptation to environmental changes. Protection, automatic regulation, optimal control, and multivariable automatic control are four degrees or levels of control which are essential ingredients of a cybernetic control system. The cybernetic concept is primarily applicable for facilitating control through a closed loop of information, communication, feedback, and corrective action. Cybernetics provides a single vocabulary and a set of concepts for representing diverse types of systems, and it offers a method for

---

[18] See Levin and Kirkpatrick, *op. cit.,* pp. 147-157, for a comprehensive description of variations of PERT.

the scientific treatment of the system in which complexity is too great and too important to be ignored.

Program Evaluation and Review Technique (PERT) is a method of planning and controlling unique and complex projects which are comprised of highly interrelated activities to be performed over a fixed time period. PERT is a method for eliminating or reducing delays, conflicts, and interruptions in completion of a project. PERT involves estimating, coordinating, and sequencing activities to determine the critical path for completing the project on time and within cost constraints.

REVIEW QUESTIONS

1. Compare and contrast communication theory and information theory.
2. Discuss the syntactic, semantic, and effectiveness levels of information theory and their applicability to operational control.
3. How does cybernetics differ from communication and information theory? What do you see as its applications to management versus physical resource flow systems?
4. Discuss the significance of self-regulation or homeostasis for the management process. How is this concept related to the management of change?
5. Differentiate between the various degrees or levels of control. What is the significance of each for management?
6. Compare and contrast administrative communications with mathematical approaches to communication and information theory.
7. What limitations do you see in developing a completely cybernetic control system for an organization?
8. Relate communication and information theory and cybernetics to the operational subsystem of the organizational system.
9. Compare and contrast PERT, cybernetics, and communication and information theory in terms of their purposes and applications.
10. Discuss the interrelationships of the informational concepts discussed in this chapter with those discussed in Chapter 12.

EXERCISE 13-1: The Total Firm as a Cybernetic System

An enterprise is a system with activities which can be considered as subsystems or responsibility centers. The concept of cybernetics for control and communication can be applied to this system in its entirety or to the individual subsystems. We can identify responsibility centers and schematically describe each as a closed-loop self-regulating unit. Exhibit 13-8 is an illustration of the total firm as a cybernetic system.

At the top management level, the manager is concerned with integrating three major subsystems: procurement, production, and sales, each comprising a cybernetic system in itself. The manager must understand the interactions

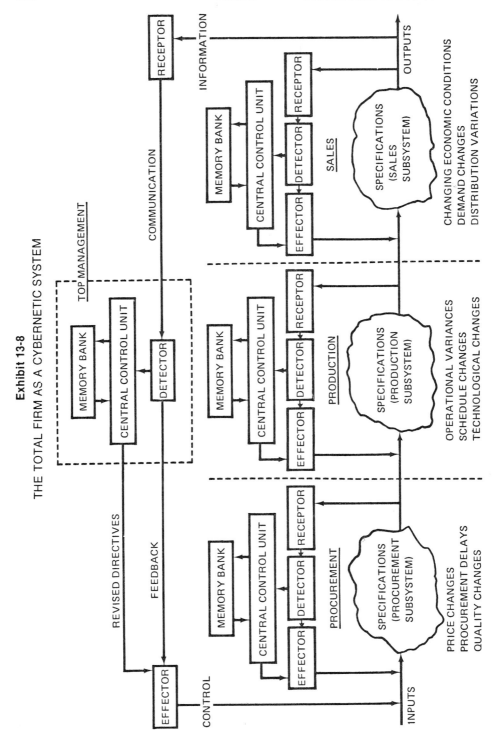

Exhibit 13-8

THE TOTAL FIRM AS A CYBERNETIC SYSTEM

involved in the flows of work, resources, and information between these subsystems in terms of quality, quantity, timing, and cost of performance. He also needs to become skilled in making decisions based on existing information in his memory (reference file or data base) and newly received information, such as schedule or cost variances. Assuming he had determined the overall unit goals, made a plan, established policies, and determined critical decision points, what feedback does he need to complete the system? He probably would want answers to the following questions:

From Sales: Are sales exceeding or lagging goals? Why? Are customers dissatisfied with products? If so, why? What new items or changes are being asked for? Are finished goods keeping up with orders? What's being done to correct the unsatisfactory conditions?

From Production: Is operation above or below normal capacity? Why? Is finished goods output ahead or behind schedule? Why? What's being done? Are finished goods piling up in the warehouse? Why? Is finished goods inventory depleted? Why? What's being done about it? Are large numbers of finished goods being rejected for being below standard? Why? What's being done about it?

From Procurement: Are inventories piling up or depleted? Why? What's being done? Are deliveries ahead or behind schedule? Why? Are supplies below standard? Why? What's being done?

Feedback of this type of information from various sources to top management will provide necessary additional data for required decisions and actions. Often the top manager's action consists of concurring in the action taken by subordinates in procurement, production, and sales to correct undesirable situations. However, when their actions do not correct the situation, he may step in himself with specific orders for further actions. He may decide to change supervisors, product emphasis, overall personnel policies, or whatever else may appear to be the cause of the variance. In any event, in a cybernetic system the necessary information is available to the top manager to act if he sees that this intervention is necessary.

At the lower decision levels (procurement, production and sales), the managers will need more detailed information than the top manager. For example, if sales are lagging, the sales manager will want to know how many calls his salesmen are making, or how much radio, TV, and periodical exposure his products are getting. If these are below normal, he has them increased. If they are normal, he may increase them, but he looks further for why there is a drop or lag in sales. The market may be glutted by a cheaper competitor or an import. If it is a fad item, the fad may be waning. Perhaps a newer, better item is being marketed by a competitor. For these more serious causes, he may recommend a product change to top management.

In Exhibit 13-8, there are two levels (i.e. top management versus procurement, production, and sales). Each manager at these two levels determines the overall inputs, outputs, policies, and standards for his system or subsystem. He selects the critical indicators he has to watch to be sure of reaching his goals. He sees that each subsystem manager under his control is provided with the information he needs to keep his activity at the planned level.

A manager is presumed to have already within his memory a considerable amount of information with respect to the system or subsystem he is managing. Consequently, for purposes of control, he does not need to have the entire information output from the system returned to him as feedback. However, he does need information on any new development which may affect his output, and he does need occasional summary reports on the status of his operation to keep up to date. This can be accomplished through the exception reporting technique. As long as he gets no report indicating trouble in his system, he assumes everything is proceeding toward the system's goals as planned. When he does get a report about trouble in his system, he either has to make a decision or accept the decision of a subordinate. When an exception occurs and the manager must make a decision, he usually follows up his decision by observing and evaluating the results. Thus, he prepares himself for any further corrective action and also adds to his knowledge about the system.

1. For each system or subsystem described (top management, procurement, production, and sales) perform the following:
   a. Describe the nature of decisions for each.
   b. Identify the types of information needed for each decision, and for each memory bank.
   c. Specify standards of performance which would be useful for each.
2. Identify the kinds of information that would be conducive for developing a cybernetic control system for the firm, i.e., what kinds of decisions are recurring in nature.

EXERCISE 13-2: Literature Review

Review and critique several articles related to one or more of the following concepts presented in this chapter: communication and information theory, cybernetics, and Program Evaluation and Review Technique. In your review and critique, focus on the applicability of the concept in practical versus theoretical situations (i.e., look for examples of applications to real life problems). Also, describe the problems associated with the application of each concept. Finally, comment on the contributions of these concepts to the development of integrated information systems for management.

14 COMPARATIVE ORGANIZATIONAL ENVIRONMENTS FOR INFORMATION SYSTEMS DESIGN

Educational, governmental, and business institutions are three of the predominant influences in our society. This chapter describes and compares the characteristics of these sectors of our society in a systems and information framework. The objectives of this chapter are to examine the nature and systemic characteristics of comparative organizational systems and to discuss how these characteristics affect the analysis and design of educational, governmental, and business information systems.

This chapter provides the background for three comprehensive cases which appear at the end of the chapter. One case relates to an educational organization, one to government, and one to business. These cases involve detailed descriptions of organizations and provide opportunities to analyze each area in greater detail and apply information systems concepts and methodology in comprehensive situations.

Educational institutions pervade our society. Education affects man's life from an early age for a considerable period of time. Indirectly as taxpayers or directly as users of educational services, most people interact with some type of educational institution, its operations, or its information system. The educational institution, as an important part of our society, utilizes large amounts of resources, but more importantly it generates value for a large segment of society.

The *governmental institution* serves as a facilitator for various other institutions in our society in providing a variety of services. All individuals, groups, and organizations are influenced in some way by governmental agencies or programs. The widespread impact of governmental institutions on business and educational operations is reflected at local, state, and federal levels through a combination of approval, compliance, and informational systems and regulations. The governmental institution is also an interactive sociopolitical mechanism for individuals and social groups.

The *business organization* provides economic goods and services and also makes significant contributions in the areas of organizational or institutional research, managerial techniques, and information systems. The business organization is the mechanism through which our society's resources are channeled to generate economic value in the form of goods and services. Specific business organizations vary according to such characteristics as size, industry, markets, and products. In spite of these variations and others, the business organization has a number of characteristics that distinguish it from governmental and educational institutions.

The nature of these various systems are shown in Exhibits 14-1, 14-2, and 14-3 in the context of the organizational systems model presented in Chapter 5. The systemic characteristics of these three types of systems are compared in the following sections.

PURPOSE AND OBJECTIVES

Educational System

The general purpose of the educational system is to generate and disseminate knowledge. This is a service objective with several important dimensions in the contexts of time, quantity, quality, and cost. The time dimension of educational service tends to be long run in that the learning process extends over long periods of time. The usefulness of the knowledge gained also extends indefinitely into the future. Since the value of knowledge gained from the learning process is difficult to quantify, significant limitations exist in developing estimates of the cost-benefits of educational programs.

The quantity of value added also is difficult to measure; thus short-run proxy variables, such as credit hours generated and number of students graduated, are used to reflect the volume of educational service provided. The pervasive and indefinite nature of the educational process and the utilization of knowledge in the long run also severely limit the definition and measurement of the quality of knowledge generated. This service-type output environment, with the limitations associated with measurement and definition of timing, quantity, and quality dimensions of value added, makes it difficult to define cost versus value relationships related to the educational system's outputs.

Potential users of an educational institution's services include business, governmental, and educational institutions, as well as the students themselves. The measurement problem is further complicated since the student is both a user of educational services and the raw material being transformed by the educational system. A student's perception of value added may change appreciatively as he proceeds through a series of learning situations.

The service objective of the educational system involves a research output for higher-level educational systems. Also, services to the community such as symposiums, training programs, and consultation are important value-added objectives of educational institutions. Thus, an important characteristic of the educational system is that it is heterogeneous. The lack of a clear-cut objective for the educational system (in lieu of the profit motive) presents an important constraint for the design and analysis of an educational information system.

Governmental System

The governmental institution provides a service output in the form of regulatory programs with approval or compliance dimensions. Approval dimensions relate to licensing and permission to operate a business or agency, while the compliance function concerns the review and evaluation of various business, educational, and governmental operations in order to insure

Exhibit 14-1
THE EDUCATIONAL SYSTEM

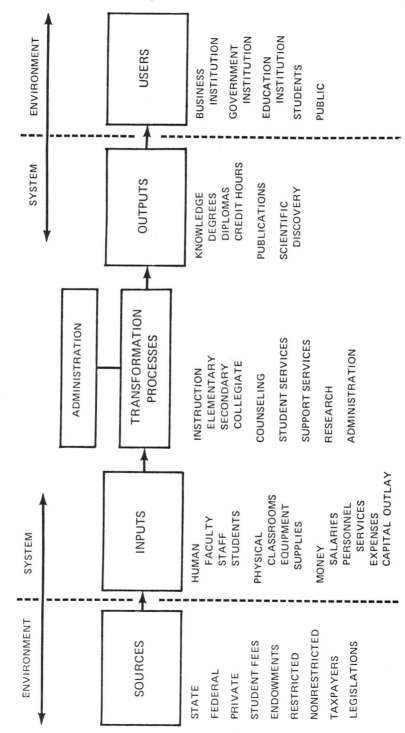

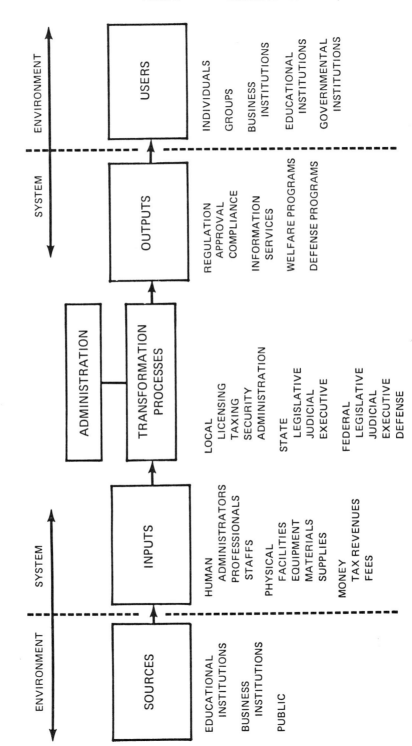

Exhibit 14-2
THE GOVERNMENTAL SYSTEM

Exhibit 14-3
THE BUSINESS SYSTEM

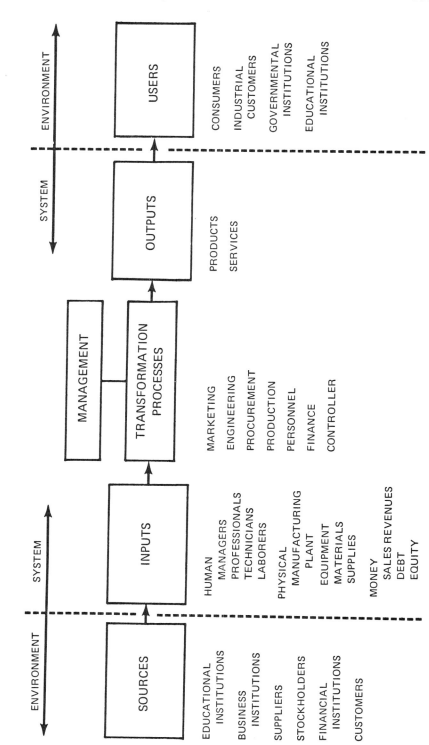

compliance with laws. Other important outputs and objectives of governmental institutions range from defense to welfare services.

The service nature of the outputs poses a significant challenge to information system design for a governmental agency. The benefits of governmental outputs are difficult to define and measure, and quite often subjective, relative measures must be employed. Also, value criteria for evaluating competing governmental programs and services are not generally agreed upon because of the lack of a clear-cut single objective, such as the profit motive for a business institution. Users of governmental services are often difficult to identify except in terms of broad categories, for example, the public, minority groups, and industries. Even within each of these broad categories, all users do not have similar perceptions of the objectives or value of governmental services.

Business System

The general purpose of the business system is to generate economic goods and services. Potential users of these economic goods and services include consumers, other industrial and commercial organizations, governmental institutions, and educational institutions. The value-added objectives of the business organization relate to producing goods and services for satisfying specific quality, quantity, and timing requirements of users at an acceptable price level. Compared with those of educational and governmental institutions, the economic objectives of the business organization are more easily defined and measured. There is a monetary exchange based on clearly defined units at the time goods and services are accepted by users.

The characteristics relating to specific output definition, measurement, and accounting have important implications for information systems. Since the business organization has a revenue function, most of its operations and organizations tend to be related to their impact on revenues or profits. Thus, the generally agreed-upon profit objective provides a convenient mechanism for facilitating decision tradeoff analysis within the business organization. The business information system also incorporates these more easily identified variables relating to revenues, profits, and market share within its reporting structure.

TRANSFORMATION PROCESS

Educational System

The transformation process in educational systems generally includes the following subsystems, programs, and activities: instruction, counseling, support services, student services, administration, research, and community services. A distinguishing characteristic of the general transformation process, explicitly related to instruction, counseling, and student services and implicitly to support services and administration, is that the primary input is a human resource, the student. This human input is not merely a passive recipient of the learning processes but in fact is quite active and often influential in determining the effectiveness of transformation (learning) processes. The student's motivation to learn, as well as his aptitude or capacity, affect the quality, quantity, timing, and cost of the transformation processes.

The transformation processes of educational systems are service-oriented, aimed at providing social and cultural knowledge as well as specific educational or training concepts and techniques. Support services for the educational processes include physical plant maintenance and student services, such as food, housing, and financial aid.

Governmental System

The governmental system's major transformation processes can be viewed as legislative, executive, and judicial. Each of these can be broken down further to reflect levels of governmental agencies (local, state, and federal) or the specific programs involved in each category (for example, licensing, taxing, security, and administrative). For the most part, these transformation subsystems use resources for the generation and provision of services, rather than physical products or outputs.

This service processing function makes it difficult to define small units of analysis for design of information systems. Instead, information flows must be developed for larger program or agency units. In developing an information system for a governmental agency, resource information may not vary significantly from the types of resources utilized by a business organization. The problem is the allocation of those resources to specific, small-scale transformation processes and their related outputs.

Business System

The transformation processes within business systems commonly include the following subsystems: marketing, engineering, procurement, production, personnel, finance, and controller. The distinguishing characteristic of the transformation process of the business organization is the creation of economic value or utility. The design and evaluation of transformation processes are based on their contribution to efficiency or stimulation of demand (that is, increases in goods and services sold). The resources used by the business organization are often quite similar to those of the educational or governmental institutions. However, the transformation process of the business organization usually involves a physical conversion of materials into products. The development of information needs for a physical flow process is generally easier to accomplish than for a service flow process because units of work, inputs, and outputs are more visible.

The business organization also differs significantly in its sources of funds. Stockholders, financial institutions, and customers, as primary sources of financing, deal directly with each individual business organization. Governmental and educational institutions rely on legislation for most of their funds. The business organization must negotiate for funds based on expected financial returns to equity and debt sources, and its information system must include appropriate revenue-profit-cost variables. These variables tend to be more objective for planning and control decisions.

INTERFACES

Educational System

The primary interface in any organization is the man-man interaction. In an educational institution, this man-man interface is a sensitive one because the basic purpose of the organization and its transformation processes is to develop man's capabilities and personality. The faculty-student interface is the primary man-man interface wherein this development occurs. Another important type of interface that exists in the educational systems is the program-program or discipline-discipline interface. The educational institution is an interdisciplinary system which integrates various disciplines into programs which themselves must be integrated. The faculty-faculty interface is an important linking mechanism for achieving program integration.

Superimposed on the faculty-student and faculty-faculty interactions are the administrative and support or service interactions that facilitate the educational transformation processes. Thus, the faculty-student-administration triad represents a dynamic and sensitive interactive setting within the educational system. The educational system's interaction with its environment makes the nature of interface an extremely sensitive one. The infusion of value criteria of parents, contributors of funds, citizens as taxpayers, governmental regulatory agencies, and potential users of educational services all work to provide a complex interactive environment.

Governmental System

Important man-man interfaces for the governmental institution include the users of services and the sources of funding. For a governmental institution, the large variety of interest groups often makes it difficult to define what interfaces actually exist. Often these interest groups have conflicting value criteria. Thus, the governmental institution tends to react to those groups that are the most influential for continuance of their programs.

Complexity of interfaces presents important challenges to designing an information system for the government institution. Legal requirements for information make up only a part of the important information needs. The information system also must provide insights into changing value criteria for a constantly changing set of interest groups competing for tax dollars or for a favorable mix of governmental services.

Business System

In the business organization, the man-man interface tends to be complicated by perceptions about how it influences revenues or costs. This is true externally as well as internally. Internally, key interfaces include those that occur between professionals, technicians, management and labor, and staff and line. Externally, consumer interactions with sales representatives, suppliers with buyers, and financial sources with controller/finance personnel are typical interfaces.

Superimposed on these interfaces are a number of indirect or implicit influences. These include social considerations relating to such issues as ethics, business practices, and concern for the environment. Within these indirect or implicit interfaces, value systems emerge and interact to modify objectives and decisions based solely on the profit motive. Thus, the modern business information system must be broadened to take into account these social interfaces and the value criteria emerging from them.

REGULATION AND ADJUSTMENT

Educational System

The foregoing description of interfaces truly reflects the openness of the educational system. Within this multidimensional interactive environment, regulation and adjustment must cope with the rapidly changing value criteria of all those associated with the educational system. Program obsolescence and innovation occur continuously and at an accelerating pace. The educational information system must be flexible and viable in providing insights to faculty, students, and administrators concerning future objectives, alternatives, and directions for the educational system.

Internal regulation and adjustment are often constrained because of the open nature of the educational system. Creativity and innovation by faculty and students are vital to the educational system's purpose, yet economic constraints require effective evaluation mechanisms for internal adjustment. Traditional financial, accounting, and organizational concepts are not sufficiently flexible for coping with modern educational systems. Improved viability of and accountability for the educational system's objectives and performance are required. The notion of cost effectiveness within a program budgeting framework has become an essential characteristic of educational information systems.

Governmental System

The internal regulation of a governmental organization is often influenced by legislative approval of a program. This provides a set of legal, regulatory and evaluative procedures and policies to be used by the administrator of a governmental institution. Some flexibility for innovation in developing information for evaluation of program performance may be lost, and the regulatory effort becomes one of compliance to bureaucratic procedures.

There is opportunity, however, for innovation during periods of refunding or expansion of programs or when new programs are being proposed. The information system can have a more significant impact in the adjustment or adaptation of the governmental institution to changing needs of users. This is especially true in long-range planning with the use of planning-programming-budgeting techniques.

Business System

The regulation and adjustment requirements of the business organization are tied to the profit objective. Regulatory standards, specifications, schedules, and budget guidelines are developed in the context of projected volume-cost-profit relationships. Adjustments to changing demands of users or new opportunities for demand are justified in terms of their impact on short-run or long-run profits. The evaluation of existing product lines is made within a similar analytical framework.

With the growing concern for social issues and changing information processing technology, the information system of the business organization must be flexible in providing insights for its managers concerning objectives, alternatives, and directions for the firm. The business organization is continually required by local, state, and federal regulatory agencies to provide information about its operations and the effects of those operations on social and environmental issues.

INTEGRATION

Educational System

The environmental constraints and changing value criteria of users of educational services and providers of resources to the educational system represent important challenges. Obtaining general agreement on the objectives of the programs and methodology of the system is essential for effective system integration. This is no easy task because of the diverse interests, needs, and value criteria of users of educational services. To complicate matters, the growth in knowledge and the increasing specialization among educational personnel often leads to internal disagreement on priorities for resource utilization. These factors represent important challenges to the viability of the educational information system.

Governmental System

Integration of programs within a governmental organization is essential to formulating funding requests. Comparative evaluation of cost-benefits of internal programs is often difficult, yet this is a requirement of agencies reviewing funding requests. The problem is often increased for interorganization analyses and evaluations to support legislation. The challenge to information systems is extremely great at this time due to qualitative rather than quantitative criteria being used in most cases. Those programs which can show more objective measures of cost-benefits generally have more success with funding requests.

Business System

The increasing complexity of environmental constraints and changing social value criteria represent important challenges to the business organization. Developing broader objectives which include both economic and social dimensions is essential for survival and growth. This is often difficult because of the heterogeneity of value criteria impacting the business organization. Growth in knowledge and increasing specialization among personnel often lead to disagreement on objectives and priorities for resources utilization. These factors represent important challenges to the business information system.

SUMMARY

This chapter describes and compares the characteristics of educational, governmental, and business systems as they relate to design of information systems. The basic issues described are the systemic characteristics of educational, governmental, and business systems and the impact of their systemic characteristics on the design of information systems.

The issues are described and analyzed on a comparative basis and serve as a background for application of integrated information systems concepts and methodology to the three comprehensive cases which follow. An introduction to each case identifies the pertinent informational, systems, and organizational concepts.

REVIEW QUESTIONS

1. Contrast the purpose and objectives of education, government, and business, and identify types of information that would be useful for planning in these institutions or organizations.

2. Identify and compare several major constraints upon education, government, and business as they relate to designing an information system.

3. Discuss the usefulness of the systems approach to designing an information system for an educational, government, or business organization.

4. Compare the nature of transformation processes in education, government, and business.

5. Compare the nature of interfaces in education, government, and business. Which do you feel are likely to provide the most difficulty in designing an information system?

6. Describe the open characteristics of education, government, and business systems. Which do you feel are likely to provide the greatest problems or uncertainty in designing an information system?

7. What are the primary problems of achieving integrated attitudes in education, government, and business organizations?

8. Discuss the applications and limitations of the systems and information concepts described in Chapters 4 and 5 for education, government, and business organizations.

9. Compare the regulation and adjustment characteristics of education, government, and business organizations. Which do you feel are likely to provide the greatest difficulties in designing an information system? Why?

10. Discuss the applications and limitations of the integrated information system concept for education, government, and business organizations.

EXERCISE 14-1: Comprehensive Study

Select an organization in education, government, or business with which your are familiar and:

1. Prepare a summary of its purpose, transformation processes, interfaces, regulation and adjustment mechanisms, and integration problems.

2. Describe its information system and contrast it with the essential features of the integrated information system concept.

EXERCISE 14-2: Research Report

Prepare a research report about the development and status of the integrated information system approach in the educational, governmental, or business sector on a national, regional, state, or local level.

CONTRACT ADMINISTRATION DEPARTMENT

The Contract Administration Department (CAD) is responsible for providing administrative and technical support to state governmental offices and industry contractors in a southeastern state. These services facilitate the analysis and evaluation of the administration and performance of governmental contracts for a variety of goods and services purchased by the procurement agency of the state Purchasing Division. In this respect, CAD serves as liaison between industry suppliers or contractors and state agencies as users of goods and services.

CAD was established in response to the need to develop greater uniformity of field procurement and subcontracting procedures and contract performance. The idea behind the CAD organization is that it is practical and proper that the administration of state procurement contracts should be performed in a uniform manner by a single contract administration organization. This organization would monitor contract performance from the time of issuance through performance by subcontractors and payment by the state. This type of centralized responsibility for contract administration would constantly maintain direct communication with the buying offices in the state procurement agency and regional procurement agencies of the state on procurement problems.

ORGANIZATION AND FUNCTIONS

Exhibits 1-A and 1-B summarize the organization and functions of CAD. The organization is designed to be flexible and responsive with maximum delegation of authority to its field elements. The organization includes a hierarchy of regional offices with substantial numbers of employees where concentrations of industry suppliers exist. The organization provides maximum administrative decision-making authority in proximity to contractors' locations.

CAD is responsible for monitoring and administering the performance of contracts for the State Purchasing Division. A standard pattern of contract administration services provided by CAD are described in the following sections.

Quality Control

Quality control responsibility includes periodic inspections and evaluations of contractor performance and the goods and services they

Exhibit 1-A

ORGANIZATION CHART OF CONTRACT ADMINISTRATION DEPARTMENT

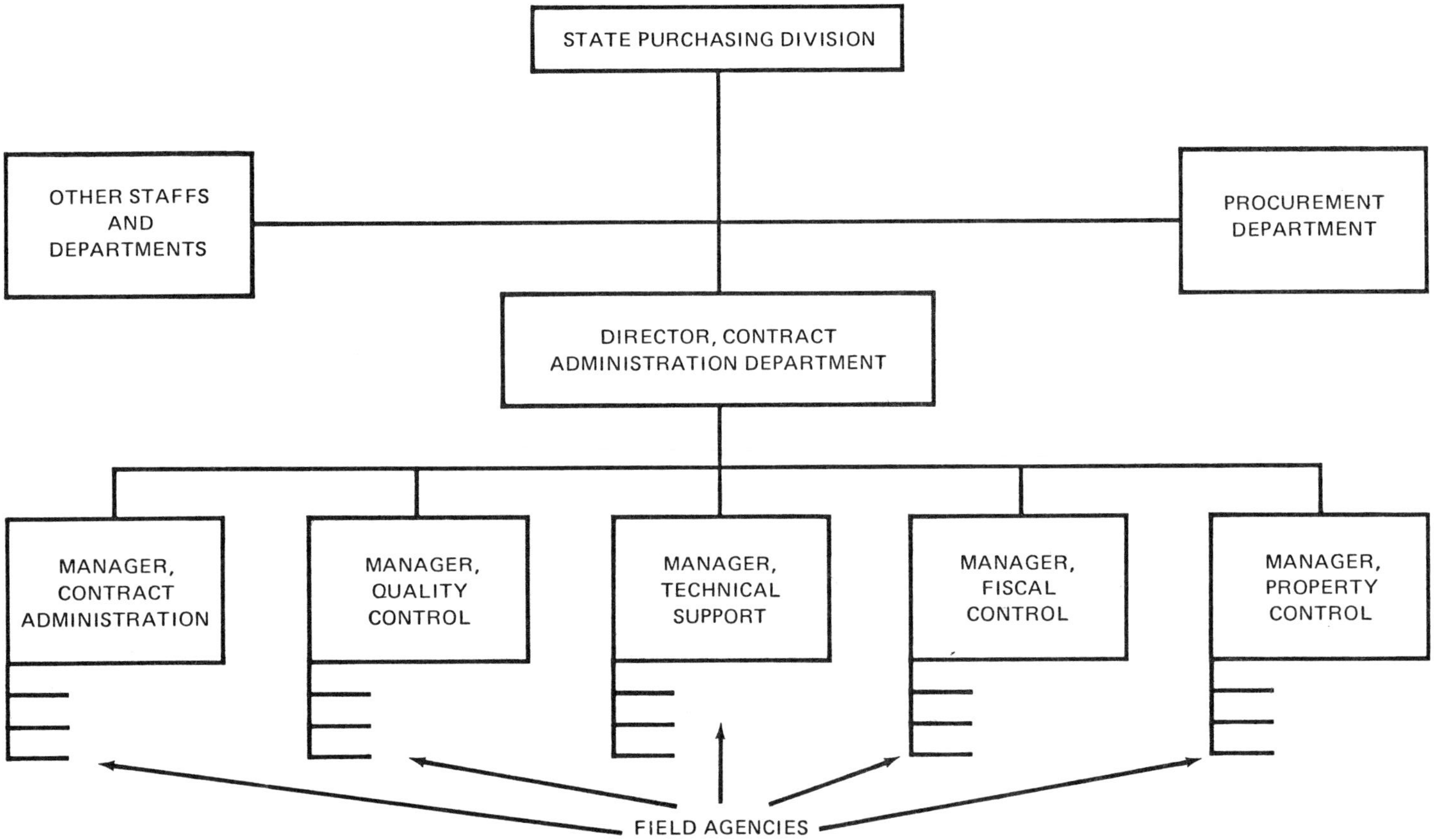

Exhibit 1-B

ORGANIZATIONAL SYSTEMS MODEL OF CONTRACT
ADMINISTRATION DEPARTMENT

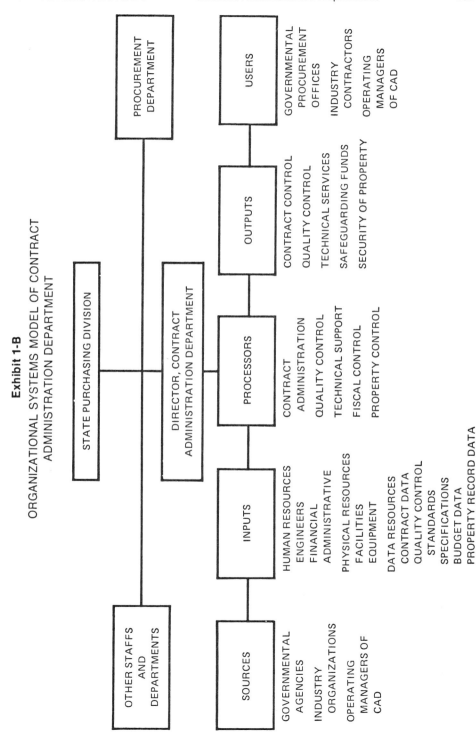

PROCUREMENT
DEPARTMENT

STATE PURCHASING DIVISION

OTHER STAFFS
AND
DEPARTMENTS

DIRECTOR, CONTRACT
ADMINISTRATION DEPARTMENT

SOURCES

GOVERNMENTAL
AGENCIES

INDUSTRY
ORGANIZATIONS

OPERATING
MANAGERS OF
CAD

INPUTS

HUMAN RESOURCES
ENGINEERS
FINANCIAL
ADMINISTRATIVE

PHYSICAL RESOURCES
FACILITIES
EQUIPMENT

DATA RESOURCES
CONTRACT DATA
QUALITY CONTROL
STANDARDS
SPECIFICATIONS
BUDGET DATA
PROPERTY RECORD DATA

PROCESSORS

CONTRACT
ADMINISTRATION
QUALITY CONTROL
TECHNICAL SUPPORT
FISCAL CONTROL
PROPERTY CONTROL

OUTPUTS

CONTRACT CONTROL
QUALITY CONTROL
TECHNICAL SERVICES
SAFEGUARDING FUNDS
SECURITY OF PROPERTY

USERS

GOVERNMENTAL
PROCUREMENT
OFFICES

INDUSTRY
CONTRACTORS

OPERATING
MANAGERS
OF CAD

provide. CAD makes decisions relating to the acceptance or rejection of materials or services. CAD also insures that contractors have acceptable quality control and inspection procedures which can provide a high degree of probability that they have the capability to produce and deliver the required products and services on time, in the quantity and quality desired, and within budget limits. Finally, CAD maintains an up-to-date set of state government quality assurance procedures.

Technical Support

Technical support generally takes the form of offering expert advice to governmental agencies and industry suppliers on specialized requirements, such as data processing, engineering specifications, and other technical matters. CAD maintains delivery surveillance to insure products and services procured are received on schedule. Procurement priorities are evaluated to facilitate the allocation of time and resources of procurement offices. Contractors' production facilities and labor are evaluated as a part of pre-award surveys relating to new contracts with new suppliers. Finally, CAD monitors and gives on-the-spot support to the buying office concerning contractors' engineering efforts, expenditures, value engineering programs, and engineering change proposals.

Fiscal Control

Fiscal control is primarily a cost reporting and accounting responsibility, but it also includes the final review and authorization for disbursement of funds. CAD monitors progress payments, the allowability of costs on cost-plus contracts, advance payments to contractors, disputes between contractors and state procurement offices, and cost over- or underruns. Also CAD negotiates overhead rates as on-the-spot support for its procurement offices.

Administration of Government Property Used by Contractors

Property control responsibility involves accounting for governmental property and facilities utilized by industry suppliers as specified in the contract. CAD accounts for, reviews, and controls state property and facilities utilized by contractors. In addition, CAD develops projections of future needs for state property and facilities.

Contract Administration

CAD is responsible for processing and maintaining records relating to contract performance and to the general planning and control of contract performance. Other contract administration functions which may be delegated from time to time by buying offices to CAD include: settling and formalizing contract changes under contract change provisions and policies; finding new sources of supply; and conducting pre-award negotiations. Generally these types of contract administration services are requested and performed because of CAD's proximity to and familiarity with industry contractors.

FUTURE PLANS OF CAD

CAD plans to develop reporting systems which will include computerized data banks with up-to-date information processing and performance evaluation systems. Management reports are to provide timely management information in the desired degree of detail to all management levels and within all regional agencies. A system of management by exception and special reports will keep managers at all levels aware of problems. The decentralized nature of the CAD organization and its decision-making process, together with the use of the latest data processing equipment and information carrying devices, will maximize the efficiency of procurement activities.

The CAD headquarters organization will provide a concentration of highly skilled experts in all fields of contract administration. The field organization will. deal with and respond directly to the buying offices and using agencies. The headquarters organization will normally be bypassed except on major problems, projects, and policy matters.

ADVANTAGES AND LIMITATIONS OF CAD

One major advantage of the CAD organization within the State Purchasing Division is that state procurement planners are provided with an opportunity to utilize experts and modern management practices to develop better and more standardized techniques. With the new organization, CAD management can more effectively plan procurement needs and monitor contract negotiations, performance, and payments.

A second major advantage of the CAD organization is its decentralized field activities located near the industry suppliers and governmental users.

Third, the centralization of contract administration and payment functions makes CAD more responsive to contractor needs. A contractor has only one office to look to if he is suffering a critical delay in receiving a payment.

Fourth, greater opportunities are available for developing better and more timely information regarding the performance of buying offices and contractors.

Fifth, CAD can administer state contracts in a more uniform manner than in the past. Now it is possible for a contractor to deal with only one agency, have one group of government people in his plant, and deal in a uniform manner in resolving problems.

A major limitation of the CAD organization is that both the governmental agencies which use the projects and services procured and the state procurement offices view CAD as an administrative agency which exerts a potentially high degree of control over their operations. Therefore, although CAD functions primarily as a service activity which is not directly responsible for procurement functions, it may in fact infringe on the authority and responsibility assigned to procurement offices.

In performing its service responsibilities, CAD may also be subject to influences of other state agencies in the area of allocation of resources to the State Purchasing Division. Less funds are likely to be devoted to procurement activities because of state funding priorities. The state legislature will tend to evaluate the total cost of state purchasing; if a substantial amount of the State Purchasing Division budget is devoted to CAD, less will be devoted to actual procurement activities.

INFORMATION NEEDS OF CAD

In order to facilitate the operations of CAD, its management listed a number of basic types of information needs relating to the performance of procurement activities. Some samples from the list appear below.

1. Procurement Effectiveness

Number of delinquent deliveries
Delays in governmental operations due to lack of materials, supplies, and contract services
Frequency and number of schedule revisions
Success of procurement offices in minimizing the effects of changes to schedules of delivery
Number of procurement contracts that needed to be expedited because of poor planning for procurement needs
Number of contract revisions
Cost of administering procurement contracts
Number of deliveries rejected
Number of overdue orders in open purchase order file

2. Price Performance

Number of price changes
Number of purchase orders utilizing competitive bidding
Number of purchase orders placed through negotiation with suppliers
Number of orders covered by long-term purchase contracts
Actual prices paid compared with published market prices
Inventory valuation; actual cost versus replacement cost
Variances from standard costs of products/services purchased

3. Cost Savings From:

Change of source of supply
Change in method of buying
Substitution of products/services
Standardization of materials and supplies
Type of transportation
Delivery provisions and terms
Quantity discounts earned through timely payment

4. Inventory Performance

Ratio of dollar inventory to sales volume
Inventory increase or decrease during month
Inventory turnover
Number of items under maximum-minimum stock control
Quantity discounts earned through revision of stock limits

5. Efficiency of Operations

Total cost of purchasing related to dollar volume of products/services procured
Number of buyers used
Number of nonbuying personnel by functional activity performed

Number of unprocessed purchase requisitions
Number of small orders processed
Cash discounts earned and forefeited
Average waiting time for salesmen

The foregoing types of information would facilitate the accomplishment of the following objectives:

1. To provide products/services at the lowest possible cost.
2. To keep investment in inventories at the lowest level consistent with the needs of state agencies.
3 To maintain the lowest possible storage and inventory carrying costs and develop optimum turnover rates.
4. To improve communication between organizational divisions and departments, and thereby reduce administrative costs.
5. To develop and maintain continuity in delivery.
6. To develop and maintain favorable relations with sources of supply.
7. To reduce acquisition, maintenance, obsolescence, and deterioration costs of inventories.
8. To improve purchasing management and inventory control.
9. To obtain the highest possible quality of products/services in relation to minimum costs of products/services.
10. To minimize the costs of administering and processing invoice and payment documents.
11. To minimize the costs of government property used by contractors and to insure that it is used properly.

QUESTIONS

1. Analyze the operational aspects of CAD, the objectives, environmental constraints, functions, activities, and organizational relationships of its headquarters and field components. From this analysis:

   a. Identify the major kinds of information that CAD will need to achieve its objectives.

   b. Develop sample reports which you feel would facilitate the performance of CAD's operations.

   c. Design a data base and data coding system that you feel would provide the types of information and reports needed by CAD.

2. What major information subsystems do you feel will be useful to CAD and to its functional organizational units?

   a. Using the materials in Chapters 5 through 7 relating to operational subsystem flows, identify the major types of source documents that would be available to CAD.

   b. Identify additional types of information and reports that CAD should or must generate besides the types specified in the case.

3. Using the systems methodology for MIS design presented in Chapter 4, outline and describe how you would design the kind of MIS that CAD needs to accomplish its objectives.

STATE UNIVERSITY[1]

State University has experienced rapid and large growth in enrollment. (The organization of State University is shown in Exhibit 2-A.) Along with this growth, greater pressures for involvement of students and faculty in decisions relating to programs, budgets, and policies have developed. The new president of the university is young and energetic and has moved up from the position of Dean of the School of Social Welfare. At his first Council of Deans meeting in which he served as president, he expressed a desire that a more effective information system be developed, and he asked each dean to submit ideas on how this might be accomplished. At the next meeting, in August, these ideas were discussed and preparations were made to begin development of the information system in the fall. The following are excerpts from the August Council of Deans meeting.

President: I appreciate your interest and efforts in developing a more effective information system at State University. I have reviewed your ideas and have provided each of you with copies of summaries of the comments of the other deans. I would like to give you an overview of what I think the information system will accomplish. First, it will permit greater participation of colleges and departments in goal setting and resource allocation decisions. Second, better communication about the university's constraints, priorities, programs, and budgets can be achieved since deans and department heads will be brought into the process earlier than in the past. Third, a more rational approach to planning and resource allocation should develop through the process of joint review of goals, programs, and budgets. Since we operate under a state program budgeting system, it is important to tie the information system directly into the university planning and budgeting system. Exhibit 2-B shows how I see this being accomplished. What are your views?

---

[1] This case is an extension of the Admissions and Registration Division case presented as Exercise 6-3, page 176, which provides general background about State University. The portion of this case relating to the Council of Deans meeting is adapted with permission from William A. Shrode and Dan Voich, Jr., *Organization and Management: Basic Systems Concepts* (Homewood, Ill.: Richard D. Irwin, 1974).

Exhibit 2-A

ORGANIZATION OF STATE UNIVERSITY

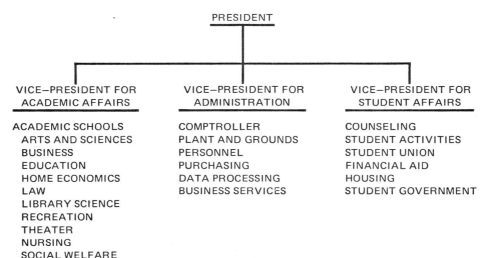

PRESIDENT		
VICE–PRESIDENT FOR ACADEMIC AFFAIRS	**VICE–PRESIDENT FOR ADMINISTRATION**	**VICE–PRESIDENT FOR STUDENT AFFAIRS**
ACADEMIC SCHOOLS	COMPTROLLER	COUNSELING
ARTS AND SCIENCES	PLANT AND GROUNDS	STUDENT ACTIVITIES
BUSINESS	PERSONNEL	STUDENT UNION
EDUCATION	PURCHASING	FINANCIAL AID
HOME ECONOMICS	DATA PROCESSING	HOUSING
LAW	BUSINESS SERVICES	STUDENT GOVERNMENT
LIBRARY SCIENCE		
RECREATION		
THEATER		
NURSING		
SOCIAL WELFARE		
ACADEMIC RESEARCH		
ADMISSIONS AND		
REGISTRATION		
CONTINUING EDUCATION		

Dean, College of Business: I see that you visualize involvement of the department or program heads in the planning and budgeting. Is this the extent of decentralization you expect or do the colleges decide the extent of decentralization?

President: I encourage considerable faculty involvement; however, I realize that the extent of decentralization may vary among colleges.

Dean, College of Education: My faculty are not interested or qualified in planning and budgeting.

President: That may be true, but don't your faculty know what their priorities, programs, and resource needs are better than anyone else?

Dean, College of Education: Yes, but they are not interested in assuming a large responsibility for completion of paperwork and attending administrative meetings.

President: But don't you feel that your faculty should be given the opportunity to decide for themselves what sort of involvement they wish?

Dean, College of Arts & Sciences: I'm not sure what you mean by involvement. Exactly what authority will the deans have concerning goals, priorities, and budgets for their colleges?

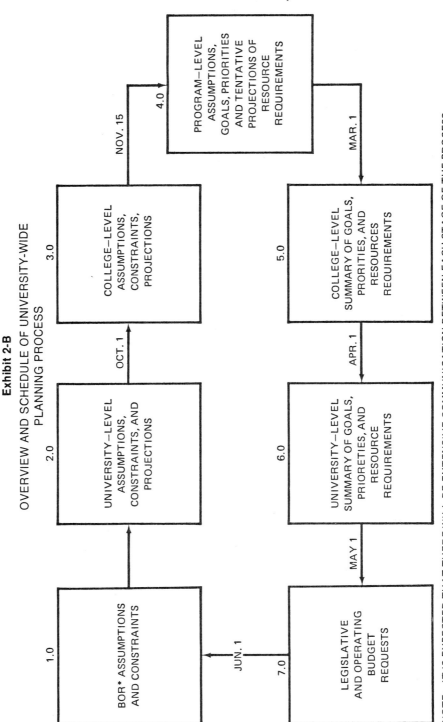

Exhibit 2-B

OVERVIEW AND SCHEDULE OF UNIVERSITY-WIDE PLANNING PROCESS

1.0 BOR* ASSUMPTIONS AND CONSTRAINTS

JUN. 1

2.0 UNIVERSITY–LEVEL ASSUMPTIONS, CONSTRAINTS, AND PROJECTIONS

OCT. 1

3.0 COLLEGE–LEVEL ASSUMPTIONS, CONSTRAINTS, PROJECTIONS

NOV. 15

4.0 PROGRAM–LEVEL ASSUMPTIONS, GOALS, PRIORITIES AND TENTATIVE PROJECTIONS OF RESOURCE REQUIREMENTS

MAR. 1

5.0 COLLEGE–LEVEL SUMMARY OF GOALS, PRORITIES, AND RESOURCES REQUIREMENTS

APR. 1

6.0 UNIVERSITY–LEVEL SUMMARY OF GOALS, PRIORETIES, AND RESOURCE REQUIREMENTS

MAY 1

7.0 LEGISLATIVE AND OPERATING BUDGET REQUESTS

NOTE: IT IS EXPECTED THAT THERE WILL BE EXTENSIVE COMMUNICATION BETWEEN EACH STAGE OF THE PROCESS.
*BOR=BOARD OF REGENTS

President:	This has not been finalized, but in general each college will set its own priorities and develop programs to implement them. However, since funds are limited by the legislature and the Board of Regents, colleges will compete for resources based on contribution of their goals and programs to the university's and the state's goals and priorities.
Dean, College of Arts & Sciences:	That sounds like how we do it now in that all important decisions are not made at the college level, but at the university central administration level.
President:	It seems to me that there will be a number of decisions that will and should be made at each level—department, college, and central administration. After all, that is why you have administration at each level. The resolution of conflicting priorities or competition for scarce resources will be brought into the open and discussed and debated at the college level. If consensus cannot be reached at that level, the central administration must decide. Also, the central administration must insure that the priorities and constraints of the legislature and the Board of Regents are taken into account.
Dean, College of Law:	I tend to agree with the Dean of the College of Education in respect to not involving faculty and departments too extensively in the decision-making process. It seems to me the administration at the college level should be the lowest point of decentralization; otherwise you will involve faculty in too much administrative detail which is not their job. I certainly agree the deans should be involved earlier and more extensively in the decision-making process, and be given considerably more authority for the allocation of resources.
Dean, College of Education:	I agree, and I don't see why the Council of Deans can't be the primary decision-making body of the university regarding the allocation of resources to each college. A majority vote of the deans would resolve any problems regarding priorities. Each dean would have a number of votes determined by enrollment in his college.
President:	What would be the responsibility of the university central administration under that arrangement?
Dean, College of Education:	Primarily one of liaison between the colleges and the Board of Regents.
Dean, College of Business:	I see two problems relating to that type of arrangement. First, I do not agree that our faculty do not wish to become involved at the departmental and even the individual level relating to planning and budgeting. In fact,

we have been operating in a highly decentralized way for some time. I also feel that given the opportunity to participate, our faculty can provide valuable insights on program needs since they are closer to developments in their disciplines. Second, I don't see how you can exclude the central administration level or any higher level of administration from having a voice in the decisions that are made which affect the university. We live in a time when we feel that involvement is a key for generating success, and decentralization of decision making is a necessary feature of involvement. But this does not mean the subordination of higher level authority to lower levels of authority, since responsibility for performance cannot be delegated to lower organizational levels. In plainer words, the president will be held responsible for the operation of the university, and not the deans, so he must retain some veto power over the decisions of the Council of Deans.

Dean, College of Arts & Sciences: I agree with the first point the dean of the College of Business made concerning involvement of faculty in the decision-making process. Our faculty have been polled, and a substantial majority have indicated not only a strong desire, but also a serious need, to become involved. However, they feel that if they devote time and effort to the decision-making process, considerable weight should be given to their views in the final decision. I think a major reason why you have conflict and disruption in any organization is that the organization expects its members to adapt to organizational goals, but the organization does not adapt to goals of its members. This develops an environment of we versus them, where we as organizational members are expected to become conditioned to comply with the demands of them, the bureaucratic organization.

President: The situations you have described relate to a lack of integrative attitudes and a conflict of goals. These often arise because of a highly bureaucratic and highly centralized decision-making, organizational structure. And these are the kinds of problems which I think we can overcome with a more effective information system.

But on the other hand, if we go to the other extreme that has been implied, all decisions will be made by individual faculty members, their programs, departments, colleges, central administration, and the Board of Regents, in that order. In other words, we have simply inverted the bureaucratic organization. In this case the bottom, or the individual faculty member, would decide what he wants to do and what resources he needs. He would present these decisions to his program or department head, who must comply and who will add other needs for his program and department and forward them to the dean of the college for compliance. So, in the inverted case, instead of true involvement and participation, we have simply changed the we's—the slaves, or organizational members—and the thems—the oppressors, or the bureaucratic organization. In my mind, that does not accomplish anything, and in fact it makes the problems more severe.

I think that maybe we expect too much out of formal structure, policies, and procedures as vehicles of resolving problems relating to goal conflict, communications breakdown, and fear, resistance, and compliance. In fact, overreliance on formal structure and authority may aggravate these kinds of problems. Then, if formal structure and authority have limitations, even though they are useful and must exist for certain reasons, how can we as a highly professional organization develop an environment of goal congruence, provide opportunities for involvement, and ensure the growth and development of the individual, discipline, college, and university without destroying important and needed segments of its operations? The point I'm trying to emphasize is that the development of this type of integrative environment can be accomplished only with the development of proper attitudes by organizational members, especially its key managers and professionals, which in our case are the deans, department heads, and faculty. And in order to achieve this integrative environment, we need a more effective information system.

SETTING UP A PROJECT TEAM TO DESIGN THE INFORMATION SYSTEM

Several days after the meeting, the president set up a project team of faculty and administrators to analyze and evaluate the university's need for information and to recommend a conceptual design of an information system.

The project team identified a number of problems relating to current data processing activities at State University, as outlined below:

Various forms collecting duplicate information.
Lack of rigid edit-check routines for computer input.
Lack of procedure to update data once it is collected.
Duplicate responsibility for collecting, utilizing, and distributing data.
Little or no documentation of work flow system.

Inefficient work flow systems.

Serious time lags in work flow system.

Same function being performed by various departments.

Lack of a formal communications channel to resolve systems problems between departments.

Inefficient utilization of current computer facilities.

Almost a one-to-one correspondence between data files maintained and reports generated.

Poor or no communication of available information.

In order to resolve these problems and to design and implement the proposed information system, the project team recommended a comprehensive design and implementation program. The objectives of the program were defined as follows:

A. Improve the cost-effectiveness of university operations and programs.
  1. Better quality of information for resource allocation, evaluation, and control relating to operations and programs.
    a. Greater accuracy of data inputs because of designating official sources of data and providing for verification of data before processing.
    b. Greater flexibility in the manipulation of data inputs dealing with facilities, personnel, and other resources and expenditures by areas of responsibility, programs, functions, and personnel through the development of an extensive chart of accounts.
  2. Greater volume of relevant information concerning historical data and budget standards through the development of a comprehensive data bank.
  3. More timely information due to the reduction in duplication of data inputs and storage of data.

B. Improve the cost-effectiveness of the university information function.
  1. Central authority over the data management function.
    a. Control, coordinate, and integrate the generation and design of reports, forms, and records.
    b. Provide for more efficient utilization of university computer equipment and personnel.
    c. Designate official sources of information dealing with university operations, programs, personnel, and facilities.
    d. Provide for verification of data inputs.
  2. Development of centralized and flexible data bank.
    a. Provide for maximum information outputs per data input (reduction of duplication of inputs and storage).
    b. Maintain a high degree of flexibility for manipulation of data inputs by various budget locations, programs, and time periods according to needs.

The project team recommended that resources be devoted to the design and implementation program as shown at the top of page 413.

Resource Requirements [2]		YEARS		
		1	2	3
1. *Personnel*				
1 Project Director	1 FTE [3]	$14,000	$14,000	$14,000
1 Asst. Director	1 FTE	12,500	12,500	12,500
3 Graduate Assts.	1½ FTE	14,400	14,400	14,400
1 Administrative Assistant	1 FTE	5,200	5,200	5,200
Outside consulting services		2,000	2,000	2,000
Total personnel costs		$48,100	$48,100	$48,100
2. *Expenses*				
Travel		$ 2,000	$ 1,500	$ 1,000
Materials		800	800	800
Miscellaneous		600	600	600
Total expenses		$ 3,400	$ 2,900	$ 2,400
Grand total		$51,500	$51,000	$50,500
Three-year program costs				$153,000

The project team also outlined several organizational requirements if the program was to proceed with maximum effectiveness. The project team must be afforded the ability to cut across organizational lines in order to develop an integrated system. The project team must also be organized as an independent staff unit reporting to the vice-presidential level. Thus top level support of the design and implementation phases of the project is assured. It would seem logical that this unit report to the Vice-President for Administration since the majority of systems design would occur in departments under his control. In addition, each major department head must support the project. To gain this support, the administration must explicitly define the purpose of the project team and communicate this to the major department heads.

The following general phases of design and implementation were followed:

Identification of major information users.

Survey of each major user's information requirements.

Detailed documentation of work flows and information flows of each major user.

Interviews with major users to verify documentation and define additional requirements.

Design or redesign of necessary forms, procedures, work flows, master files, and report formats to meet all requirements.

PROPOSED INFORMATION SYSTEM

About four months later the project team presented a recommended information system for the university as outlined in the following sections.

---

[2] Consulting services from university personnel will be utilized (released time). In addition, outside services may be required to support the current programming function, and there probably will be some additional hardware requirements.

[3] FTE = Full Time Equivalent.

Summary of Information System

The following functional areas represent the major segments of the information system, which were identified during the study:

a. **Personnel-Payroll System.** This system integrates the information requirements of personnel administration, payroll, line-item budgeting, and miscellaneous functions relating to personnel information.

b. **Student Information System.** This system integrates the student information requirements of the offices of admissions and registration, housing, continuing education, academic departments, comptroller, financial aid, and other miscellaneous users.

c. **Financial Information System.** This system integrates the financial information requirements of the comptroller, university operating departments, and the university administration.

d. **PPBS Reporting System.** This phase of the project integrates the resources used with the services performed by the university in a comprehensive reporting system.

Exhibits 2-C through 2-J summarize the reports, master files, and sources of data that the project team believed were needed to produce the kinds of information encompassed in the four broad information subsystems.

Exhibit 2-C

SAMPLE MASTER BUDGET FILE [1]

1. Personal services
2. Contractual services
3. Materials & supplies
4. Current charges & obligations
5. Capital outlay
6. Debt service
7. Grants & aids

[1] The categories of expenditures will be broken down by geographical location, major organizational unit, minor organizational unit, discipline or function, and responsible unit.

Exhibit 2-D
SAMPLE SPACE INVENTORY FILE [1]

Buildings and Number

A. Number of classrooms and room number
   Number of student stations
   Net assignable square feet

B. Number of auditoriums and room number
   Number of student stations
   Net assignable square feet

C. Number of conference rooms and room number
   Number of stations
   Net assignable square feet

D. Number of office areas and room numbers
   1. Instructional Staff
      Number of rooms
      Net assignable square feet

   2. Research staff
      Number of rooms
      Net assignable square feet

   3. Administrative Staff
      Number of rooms
      Net assignable square feet

   4. Graduate Assistants
      Number of rooms
      Net assignable square feet

   5. Other
      Number of rooms
      Net assignable square feet

E. Number of laboratories and room numbers
   Number of rooms
   Number of student stations
   Net assignable square feet

[1] Each category would be shown by assignment to each geographic location, major organizational unit, minor organizational unit, discipline or function, and responsible unit.

Exhibit 2-E

SAMPLE PERSONNEL INVENTORY FILE

1. Name
2. Social security number
3. Alphabetic department code
4. Division
5. Budget paid from
6. FTE
7. University appointment type
8. Rank
9. Original appointment date
10. Tenure
11. Graduate faculty
12. Sex
13. Monthly salary
14. Responsibility for teaching
    On campus
    Off campus
15. Space requirements
16. Interests—subject area
17. Degree
    Major
    Minor
18. Month and year of birth
19. Religion
20. Race
21. State of previous employment
22. Type of employment
23. Previous institution
24. Years service
25. Highest degree
26. Year of highest degree
27. Begin leave of absence
28. End leave of absence
29. OPS assistant costs [1]
30. Equivalent time teaching
31. Equivalent time academic administration
32. Equivalent time research
33. Equivalent time other
34. Current activities
    Research
    Teaching
    Outside services
    Administration
35. Graduate assistant
36. Teaching contact hours

[1] OPS = Other Personal Service.
NOTE: Items 1 through 26 will be gathered from the original appointment papers. Items 30 through 36 will be gathered from a quarterly report from each dean.

Exhibit 2-F

SAMPLE FIXED EQUIPMENT
INVENTORY FILE

1. Type of equipment
2. Equipment number (Tag No.)
3. Serial number
4. Date acquired
5. Purchase cost
6. Book value
7. Charge—to location
            school
            department
8. Last inventory location
        School
        Department
        Building
        Room

Exhibit 2-G

SAMPLE STUDENT
INFORMATION FILE

1. Personal Data
        Social security number
        Name
        Sex
        Residence address
        Mailing address
        Phone
        Birthplace
        Permanent home address
        Religious preference
        Military status
        Marital status
2. Academic Data
        Major field of study
        Minor field of study
        Total academic load
        Cumulative hours earned
        Cumulative grade point average
        Current schedule of classes
3. Test Statistics
        12th Grade Test score
        SAT score
        SCAT score
        GRE score
        Law School score

Exhibit 2-H

SAMPLE CURRICULUM CATALOG
AND SCHEDULE FILE

1. Courses Cataloged
    Division
    Department
    Course number
    Descriptive title
    Credit hours
    Contact hours
2. Courses Offered
    Division
    Department
    Course number
    Location number
    Student enrollment
    Credit hours produced
    Quarter offered
    Building course taught
    Room course taught
    Social security number of instructor
    Day and time course meets
    Location taught (on campus, off campus)

Exhibit 2-I

SAMPLE ALUMNI FILE

1. Name
2. Address
3. Telephone number
4. Social security number
5. Year graduated
6. Degree
7. Major
8. Employer
9. Position
10. Salary
11. Last year's contribution

Exhibit 2-J

SUMMARY OF INFORMATION SYSTEM

SOURCES	INPUTS	PROCESSOR	OUTPUTS	USERS
Comptroller	Financial Transaction Vouchers, Revenue, Salaries & Wages, Expenses, Debt, Capital Outlay	Master Budget File (See Exhibit 2-C)	Departmental Ledger, Financial Budgets, Financial Statements	Board of Regents, Administration
Plant & Grounds and Comptroller	Building Activity Forms, Additions, Renovations, Retirements	Space Inventory File (See Exhibit 2-D)	Space Utilization Reports, Capital Budgeting Forecasts	Academic Schools
Personnel & Comptroller	Personnel Action Forms, Appointments, Terminations, Changes In Status	Personnel Inventory File (See Exhibit 2-E)	Payroll, Deduction Reports, Directories, Turnover Reports, Line Item Budgets	Operating Departments
Plant & Grounds and Comptroller	Equipment Vouchers, Purchase Order, Salvage Order, Transfer Order	Fixed Equipment Inventory File (See Exhibit 2-F)	Equipment Inventory Report, Depreciation Report	Comptroller
Admissions & Registrar	Student Data, Acceptance Forms, Registration Forms	Student Information File (See Exhibit 2-G)	Student Personal Data	Registrar
Registrar	Curriculum Data, Curriculum Change Form, Class Schedule Cards, Enrollment Forms, Grade Reports	Curriculum Catalog and Schedule File (See Exhibit 2-H)	Class Schedules, Curriculum Analysis, Board Reports	Students, Academic Schools, Board of Regents
Alumni Office and Registrar	Graduate Data, Degree Application, Sample Surveys	Alumni File (See Exhibit 2-I)	Graduate Analysis, Solicitation Reports, Alumni Reports	Personnel Department, Miscellaneous Users

Sample PPBS Reports

This section presents sample PPBS reports as conceptualized by the project team. These reports relate resource usage and services performed within a program structure for various organizational and program levels in the university. For example, Exhibits 2-K, 2-L, and 2-M present sample reports for an individual as a responsibility center, John Smith, an associate professor. In Exhibit 2-K, information is presented relating to the individual's responsibilities during a particular quarter or semester in the areas of instruction, research, and administration. Smith taught two courses and spent half of his time in research. Exhibit 2-L converts these responsibilities to percentage of time spent on research and instruction and the dollar salary equivalents ($2,000 for each responsibility). The report format shown in Exhibit 2-L provides opportunities for further classification of Smith's efforts within the categories of instruction, research, and administration and within the expenditures categories of OPS, expense, and capital outlay. The Program Analysis Report shown in Exhibit 2-M presents a number of productivity measures using some of the information shown in Exhibits 2-K and 2-L and adding information regarding enrollments, sections taught, and credit hours produced. From these kinds of information the cost per credit hour or FTE student can be developed.

Exhibit 2-K
PERSONNEL ACTIVITY REPORT

John J. Smith	Assoc. Prof.	316-24-7362
NAME	RANK/TITLE	SOCIAL SECURITY NO.

NATURE OF WORK

1. Instruction: (Courses Taught)

LOCATION	DISCIPLINE	SCHOOL	DEPART-MENT	LEVEL	COURSE NO.	SECTION NO.
Main Campus	Systems	Business	MGMT	GRAD.	BSA 554	01
Main Campus	Org. Theory	Business	MGMT	GRAD.	BSA 551	01

2. Research: (Supported)

GEOGRAPHIC LOCATION	DISCIPLINE	DEPARTMENT	PROJECT NAME & PROJECT NUMBER	FTE %	
				RESEARCH	ADMINIS-TRATIVE
Main Campus	Systems	Academic Research	Univ. Info. Syst. 001	50%	0%

3. Administration:

CATEGORY	FTE %	DEPARTMENT NO.	DEPT. NAME

Exhibit 2-L

PROGRAM ANALYSIS REPORT

RESPONSIBLE UNIT: John J. Smith

PERIOD: Spring Quarter

SECTION I—PROGRAM ELEMENT COSTS

EXPENDITURES	INSTRUCTION						RESEARCH				ADMIN.		SUPPORT		TOTAL	
	LOWER		UPPER		GRADUATE		SUPPORTED		NONSUPPORTED							
	FTE'S	COST	FTE'S	COST	FTE'S	COST	FTE'S	COST	FTE'S	COST	FTE'S	COST	FTE'S	COST	FTE'S	COST
Salaries					½	$2,000			½	$2,000					1	$4,000
OPS																
Expenses																
Capital Outlay																
Other Costs																
TOTAL					½	$2,000			½	$2,000					1	$4,000

Exhibit 2-M

PROGRAM ANALYSIS REPORT

RESPONSIBILITY UNIT: John J. Smith   PERIOD: Spring Quarter

SECTION II—INSTRUCTIONAL ACTIVITIES AND COSTS

CRITERIA	LOWER LEVEL	UPPER LEVEL	GRADUATE LEVEL
FTE Students Enrolled			30
Class Sections Taught			2
Credit Hours Produced			150
Number of Graduates			—
Average Class Section Size			15
Average Teaching Load Per Instructor			10 Hrs.
Total Cost of Instruction			$2,000.00
Average Cost Per Credit Hour Produced			$ 13.33
Average Cost Per FTE Student			$ 66.66
Average Cost Per Class Section			$1,000.00

SECTION III—RESEARCH ACTIVITIES AND COST

CRITERIA	MEASUREMENT
Total Cost of Research as a Percent of Total Costs	50%
Total Cost of Research as a Percent of Total Costs of Instruction	100%
Salary Costs of Research as a Percent of Total Salary Costs	50%
Salary Costs of Research as a Percent of Total Salary Costs of Instruction	100%

SECTION IV—ADMINISTRATIVE COSTS

CRITERIA	MEASUREMENT
Total Cost of Administration as a Percent of Total Costs	
Total Cost of Administration as a Percent of Total Costs of Instruction	
Salary Costs of Administration as a Percent of Total Salary Costs	
Salary Costs of Administration as a Percent of Salary Costs of Instruction	

SECTION V—SUPPORT ACTIVITIES COSTS

CRITERIA	MEASUREMENT
Total Cost of Support as a Percent of Total Costs	
Total Cost of Support as a Percent of Total Costs of Instruction	
Salary Costs of Support as a Percent of Total Salary Costs	
Salary Costs of Support as a Percent of Total Salary Costs of Instruction	

In Exhibits 2-N and 2-O similar kinds of information which are included in Exhibits 2-L and 2-M are reported for the program element Systems Discipline, rather than for an individual member.

The cost information shown in Exhibit 2-N includes salaries of others teaching systems courses and other research related to systems.

The productivity measures shown in Exhibit 2-O indicate that upper division cost per credit hour or student was considerably less than for the graduate level.

Exhibit 2-N

PROGRAM ANALYSIS REPORT
(Refer to Exhibit 2-L)

ELEMENT: SYSTEMS   PERIOD: Spring Quarter

SECTION I—PROGRAM ELEMENT COSTS

EXPENDITURES	INSTRUCTION						RESEARCH				ADMIN.		SUPPORT		TOTAL	
	LOWER		UPPER		GRADUATE		SUPPORTED		NONSUPPORTED							
	FTE'S	COST	FTE'S	COST	FTE'S	COST	FTE'S	COST	FTE'S	COST	FTE'S	COST	FTE'S	COST	FTE'S	COST
Salaries			½	$2,000	½	$2,000	½	$2,000	½	$2,000					2	$8,000
OPS																
Expenses																
Capital Outlay																
Other Costs																
TOTAL			½	$2,000	½	$2,000	½	$2,000	½	$2,000					2	$8,000

Exhibit 2-O

PROGRAM ANALYSIS REPORT
(Refer to Exhibit 2-M)

ELEMENT: <u>SYSTEMS</u>　　　　　　　　　　　　PERIOD: Spring Quarter

SECTION II—INSTRUCTIONAL ACTIVITIES AND COSTS

CRITERIA	LOWER LEVEL	UPPER LEVEL	GRADUATE LEVEL
FTE Students Enrolled		60	30
Class Sections Taught		2	2
Credit Hours Produced		240	150
Number of Graduates		—	—
Average Class Section Size		30	15
Average Teaching Load Per Instructor		8 Hrs.	10 Hrs.
Total Cost of Instruction		$2000.00	$2000.00
Average Cost Per Credit Hour Produced		$ 8.33	$ 13.33
Average Cost Per FTE Student		$ 33.33	$ 66.66
Average Cost Per Class Section		$1000.00	$1000.00

SECTION III—RESEARCH ACTIVITIES AND COST

CRITERIA	MEASUREMENT
Total Cost of Research as a Percent of Total Costs	50%
Total Cost of Research as a Percent of Total Costs of Instruction	100%
Salary Costs of Research as a Percent of Total Salary Costs	50%
Salary Costs of Research as a Percent of Total Salary Costs of Instruction	100%

SECTION IV—ADMINISTRATIVE COSTS

CRITERIA	MEASUREMENT
Total Cost of Administration as a Percent of Total Costs	
Total Cost of Administration as a Percent of Total Costs of Instruction	
Salary Costs of Administration as a Percent of Total Salary Costs	
Salary Costs of Administration as a Percent of Salary Costs of Instruction	

SECTION V—SUPPORT ACTIVITIES COSTS

CRITERIA	MEASUREMENT
Total Cost of Support as a Percent of Total Costs	
Total Cost of Support as a Percent of Total Costs of Instruction	
Salary Costs of Support as a Percent of Total Salary Costs	
Salary Costs of Support as a Percent of Total Salary Costs of Instruction	

Building up to larger program elements, Exhibits 2-P and 2-Q (Management Department), 2-R and 2-S (School of Business), and 2-T and 2-U (Total University) show similar kinds of information. In this way a larger scope of analysis can be developed, and the integrity of lower level information and reports is maintained. As larger elements are summarized, larger costs and numbers of personnel and different kinds of costs and activities are involved.

Exhibit 2-P

PROGRAM ANALYSIS REPORT

(Refer to Exhibit 2-N)

ELEMENT: Management Department   PERIOD: Spring Quarter

SECTION I—PROGRAM ELEMENT COSTS

EXPENDITURES	INSTRUCTION						RESEARCH				ADMIN.		SUPPORT		TOTAL	
	LOWER		UPPER		GRADUATE		SUPPORTED		NONSUPPORTED							
	FTE'S	COST	FTE'S	COST	FTE'S	COST	FTE'S	COST	FTE'S	COST	FTE'S	COST	FTE'S	COST	FTE'S	COST
Salaries			15	$40,000	10	$20,000	2	$4,000	4	$8,000	1	$4,000			32	$76,000
OPS			5	$ 1,500	10	$ 6,000	1	$ 900							16	$ 8,400
Expenses				$ 2,000		$ 4,000										$ 6,000
Capital Outlay						$ 250										$ 250
Other Costs																
TOTAL			20	$43,500	20	$30,250	3	$ 4,900	4	$8,000	1	$4,000			48	$90,650

Exhibit 2-Q

PROGRAM ANALYSIS REPORT
(Refer to Exhibit 2-O)

ELEMENT: Management Department   PERIOD: Spring Quarter

SECTION II—INSTRUCTIONAL ACTIVITIES AND COSTS

CRITERIA	LOWER LEVEL	UPPER LEVEL	GRADUATE LEVEL
FTE Students Enrolled		600	200
Class Sections Taught		20	10
Credit Hours Produced		2400	1000
Number of Graduates		20	10
Average Class Section Size		30	20
Average Teaching Load Per Instructor		12	10
Total Cost of Instruction		$43,500.00	$30,250.00
Average Cost Per Credit Hour Produced		$ 18.13	$ 30.25
Average Cost Per FTE Student		$ 72.50	$ 151.25
Average Cost Per Class Section		$ 2,175.00	$ 3,025.00

SECTION III—RESEARCH ACTIVITIES AND COST

CRITERIA	MEASUREMENT
Total Cost of Research as a Percent of Total Costs	14%
Total Cost of Research as a Percent of Total Costs of Instruction	17%
Salary Costs of Research as a Percent of Total Salary Costs	16%
Salary Costs of Research as a Percent of Total Salary Costs of Instruction	20%

SECTION IV—ADMINISTRATIVE COSTS

CRITERIA	MEASUREMENT
Total Cost of Administration as a Percent of Total Costs	4%
Total Cost of Administration as a Percent of Total Costs of Instruction	5%
Salary Costs of Administration as a Percent of Total Salary Costs	5%
Salary Costs of Administration as a Percent of Salary Costs of Instruction	7%

SECTION V—SUPPORT ACTIVITIES COSTS

CRITERIA	MEASUREMENT
Total Cost of Support as a Percent of Total Costs	
Total Cost of Support as a Percent of Total Costs of Instruction	
Salary Costs of Support as a Percent of Total Salary Costs	
Salary Costs of Support as a Percent of Total Salary Costs of Instruction	

Exhibit 2-R

PROGRAM ANALYSIS REPORT

(Refer to Exhibit 2-P)

ELEMENT: School of Business   PERIOD: Spring Quarter

SECTION I—PROGRAM ELEMENT COSTS

EXPENDITURES	INSTRUCTION						RESEARCH				ADMIN.		SUPPORT		TOTAL	
	LOWER		UPPER		GRADUATE		SUPPORTED		NONSUPPORTED							
	FTE'S	COST	FTE'S	COST	FTE'S	COST	FTE'S	COST	FTE'S	COST	FTE'S	COST	FTE'S	COST	FTE'S	COST
Salaries			100	300,000	50	100,000	25	50,000	25	50,000	15	45,000	5	10,000	220	555,000
OPS			20	3,000	30	6,000	5	1,000	5	2,000	5	1,000			65	13,000
Expenses				10,000		15,000		5,000		10,000		20,000				60,000
Capital Outlay				5,000		5,000		2,000		2,000		3,000				17,000
Other Costs																
TOTAL			120	318,000	80	126,000	30	58,000	30	64,000	20	69,000	5	10,000	285	645,000

Exhibit 2-S

PROGRAM ANALYSIS REPORT
(Refer to Exhibit 2-Q)

ELEMENT: School of Business   PERIOD: Spring Quarter

SECTION II—INSTRUCTIONAL ACTIVITIES AND COSTS

CRITERIA	LOWER LEVEL	UPPER LEVEL	GRADUATE LEVEL
FTE Students Enrolled		2,000	1,000
Class Sections Taught		100	60
Credit Hours Produced		8,000	5,000
Number of Graduates		100	30
Average Class Section Size		20	17
Average Teaching Load Per Instructor		12	10
Total Cost of Instruction		$318,000.00	$126,000.00
Average Cost Per Credit Hour Produced		$ 39.75	$ 25.20
Average Cost Per FTE Student		$ 159.00	$ 126.00
Average Cost Per Class Section		$ 3,180.00	$ 2,100.00

SECTION III—RESEARCH ACTIVITIES AND COST

CRITERIA	MEASUREMENT
Total Cost of Research as a Percent of Total Costs	19%
Total Cost of Research as a Percent of Total Costs of Instruction	28%
Salary Costs of Research as a Percent of Total Salary Costs	18%
Salary Costs of Research as a Percent of Total Salary Costs of Instruction	25%

SECTION IV—ADMINISTRATIVE COSTS

CRITERIA	MEASUREMENT
Total Cost of Administration as a Percent of Total Costs	11%
Total Cost of Administration as a Percent of Total Costs of Instruction	16%
Salary Costs of Administration as a Percent of Total Salary Costs	8%
Salary Costs of Administration as a Percent of Salary Costs of Instruction	11%

SECTION V—SUPPORT ACTIVITIES COSTS

CRITERIA	MEASUREMENT
Total Cost of Support as a Percent of Total Costs	2%
Total Cost of Support as a Percent of Total Costs of Instruction	2%
Salary Costs of Support as a Percent of Total Salary Costs	2%
Salary Costs of Support as a Percent of Total Salary Costs of Instruction	3%

Exhibit 2-T

PROGRAM ANALYSIS REPORT
(Refer to Exhibit 2-R)

ELEMENT: Total University   PERIOD: Spring Quarter

SECTION I—PROGRAM ELEMENT COSTS

EXPENDITURES	INSTRUCTION						RESEARCH				ADMIN.		SUPPORT		TOTAL	
	LOWER		UPPER		GRADUATE		SUPPORTED		NONSUPPORTED							
	FTE'S	COST	FTE'S	COST	FTE'S	COST	FTE'S	COST	FTE'S	COST	FTE'S	COST	FTE'S	COST	FTE'S	COST
Salaries	500	1,000,-000	1,000	2,000,-000	500	1,000,-000	50	100,-000	100	200,000	50	300,-000	75	200,-000	2,275	4,800,-000
OPS	20	5,000	100	20,000	75	22,500	50	15,000	50	15,000	10	3,000	10	3,000	315	84,500
Expenses		20,000		30,000		40,000		10,000		10,000		10,000		30,000		150,000
Capital Outlay		5,000		6,000		6,000		2,000		3,000		2,000		5,000		29,000
Other Costs																
TOTAL	520	1,031,-000	1,100	2,056,-000	575	1,068,-500	100	127,-000	150	228,000	60	315,-000	85	238,-000	2,590	5,063,-500

Exhibit 2-U

PROGRAM ANALYSIS REPORT
(Refer to Exhibit 2-S)

ELEMENT: Total University   PERIOD: Spring Quarter

CRITERIA	LOWER LEVEL	UPPER LEVEL	GRADUATE LEVEL
FTE Students Enrolled	4,000	6,000	3,000
Class Sections Taught	100	200	200
Credit Hours Produced	60,000	100,000	36,000
Number of Graduates	—	500	300
Average Class Section Size	30	20	15
Average Teaching Load Per Instructor	15	12	10
Total Cost of Instruction	$1,031,000.00	$2,056,000.00	$1,068,500.00
Average Cost Per Credit Hour Produced	$ 17.18	$ 76.15	$ 29.68
Average Cost Per FTE Student	$ 257.75	$ 342.66	$ 356.16
Average Cost Per Class Section	$ 10,310.00	$ 10,280.00	$ 5,342.50

SECTION III—RESEARCH ACTIVITIES AND COST

CRITERIA	MEASUREMENT
Total Cost of Research as a Percent of Total Costs	7%
Total Cost of Research as a Percent of Total Costs of Instruction	9%
Salary Costs of Research as a Percent of Total Salary Costs	6%
Salary Costs of Research as a Percent of Total Salary Costs of Instruction	8%

SECTION IV—ADMINISTRATIVE COSTS

CRITERIA	MEASUREMENT
Total Cost of Administration as a Percent of Total Costs	6%
Total Cost of Administration as a Percent of Total Costs of Instruction	8%
Salary Costs of Administration as a Percent of Total Salary Costs	6%
Salary Costs of Administration as a Percent of Salary Costs of Instruction	8%

SECTION V—SUPPORT ACTIVITIES COSTS

CRITERIA	MEASUREMENT
Total Cost of Support as a Percent of Total Costs	5%
Total Cost of Support as a Percent of Total Costs of Instruction	6%
Salary Costs of Support as a Percent of Total Salary Costs	4%
Salary Costs of Support as a Percent of Total Salary Costs of Instruction	5%

Exhibit 2-V shows a sample program analysis report for a nonacademic unit, Buildings and Grounds, with sample measures of performance. The expenditure breakdown is the same in this report.

Exhibit 2-V

PROGRAM ANALYSIS REPORT
SUPPORTING PROGRAMS

ELEMENT: Buildings & Grounds   PERIOD: Spring Quarter

SECTION I—SUPPORT ACTIVITIES COST

EXPENDITURES	FTE'S	COST	TOTAL
Salaries:			
Administration	20	40,000	
Other	80	120,000	160,000
O.P.S.	10	3,000	3,000
Expenses		10,000	10,000
Capital Outlay		2,000	2,000
Other Costs		—	—
TOTAL	110		$175,000

SECTION II—SUPPORT ACTIVITIES ANALYSIS

CRITERIA	MEASUREMENT
Total Cost of Support as a Percent of Total Costs	0.5%
Total Cost of Support as a Percent of Total Costs of Instruction	4.0%*
Salary Costs of Support as a Percent of Total Salary Costs	1.0%
Salary Costs of Support as a Percent of Total Salary Costs of Instruction	4.0%*

* Refers to Exhibit 2-T.

QUESTIONS

1. Identify the major problems you see in this case relating to:
   a. The way the change process was implemented by the president.
   b. The purpose and features of the information system.
   c. The attitudes and value systems of the individuals in the case, as they relate to a favorable climate for change.
   d. The environment of the university, e.g., state controlled, professional personnel, type of services produced, and related factors.
2. Do you feel that the problems you have identified in question 1 are universal to most large organizations?
3. Assume you are the (a) president, and then (b) one of the deans, and respond to the following: What would you do now to successfully develop supportive attitudes toward the proposed information system?
4. Evaluate the proposed integrated university information system in relation to needs of the university. Consider in your evaluation:

   a. Academic needs for information.

   b. Administrative needs for information.

   c. Information needs relating to students.

   d. Other information needs.

5. Evaluate the structural aspects of the proposed system. Consider in your evaluation:

   a. Conceptual framework of the system.

   b. Report types, formats, and purposes related to the major segments of the university.

   c. Proposed master files.

   d. Hierarchy and interrelatedness of the proposed reports.

   e. Degree of flexibility provided by the system.

   f. The extent of integration achieved by the proposed information system.

6. Develop a set of criteria for evaluating relative information needs throughout the university. Relate these criteria to the objectives of the study. (Refer to Chapter 8.)

7. Develop a preliminary coding scheme for the proposed integrated information system. (Refer to Chapter 9.)

8. What impact will the proposed information system have on organizational structure?

9. Formulate a set of policies, procedures, and materials you feel would be useful for implementing the system and for orienting personnel as to its purpose and operating characteristics.

10. Do you feel the behavioral environment, especially the man-man interface, is generally supportive or disruptive to the type of information system proposed? (Refer to Chapter 11.)

ELVO CORPORATION (Part A)[1]

The Elvo Corporation is a provider of research and development services and products to firms in the aerospace industry and to NASA. This case focuses upon the interaction between business and governmental systems with emphasis on the constraints imposed by the government contracting mechanism.

In working with this case, the student will become familiar with the operational complexities of a larger organizational system and the impact of these complexities on the design of its information needs. Organizational, behavioral, informational, and economic issues are raised. A comprehensive description of the organization, its operations, work flows, and information characteristics is included.

Conceptual issues included in the case are:

Examples of organizational conflicts which arise because of the emphasis on specialization and on a vertical-functional orientation.

The influences of the systemic characteristics of objective orientation, input-output framework, interface, regulation, and wholism for centralizing and designing an integrated information system for a business organization.

Examples of how government restrictions and conditions impact the management of an organization and the design of its information system.

The applications and limitations of the systems and information concepts described in Chapters 12 and 13 in a project-oriented, business-government interactive setting.

Examples of the interrelationships between the operational and informational subsystems and the potential of the integrated information system concept for improving operational and informational subsystem performance.

A number of questions relating to information system design are presented at the end of the case. These questions provide opportunities for reviewing important concepts and applying them in a complex organizational setting.

GENERAL COMPANY BACKGROUND

The overall objective of the Elvo Corporation is to serve the aerospace industry with the highest quality of custom-made products and services. Its

---

[1] The Elvo Corporation cases are based on case materials developed by Harry Elwell and Dan Voich, Jr. The dialog presented in Chapter 11 is also part of these materials.

specialties are research and development engineering, electronic component/system design and manufacture, and custom machine shop products. Production is limited to small-volume jobs. Elvo's prime customers are NASA and contractors providing services to NASA. The company desires to decrease its dependence on NASA by developing commercial product lines and offering data processing and system design services to other companies.

The company growth has increased sharply and at a greater than linear rate since 1962. The total dollars of sales per employee ratio rose sharply from $4,000 to $20,000 in the eight years ending in 1970, with sales revenues increasing from $1,000,000 to $80,000,000 during the same period. With increased sales and a larger base to carry plant overhead, research, and management fixed costs, the profitability based on sales dollars increased from 4.5 percent in 1962 to 7 percent or higher in recent years. Problems became apparent in 1969, with a worsening of the situation in 1970. Profit figures dropped to 6 percent in 1970, and are projected at 5 percent in 1971. Sales leveled out at $80,000,000 in 1970 and are expected to drop to $60,000,000 in 1971. At the same time, employment figures in 1971 are expected to remain at about 4,000 with a corresponding drop in sales-per-employee to $15,000.

Exhibit 3-A presents the general organization of the Elvo Corporation. A high degree of centralization exists. The six divisions report directly to the executive vice-president who in turn reports to the president. Manufacturing (the machine-shop operation) and electronics (two divisions) are the production segments. Each has somewhat complete authority over the product from the request for quote and contract negotiation stage to final shipment. Contract administration includes the negotiation, legal, financial, and configuration management phases of the project. When a new contract is negotiated, the contract administrator is responsible for the control of costs, schedules, and performance. The contract normally consists of several broad phases, such as development of the prototype, testing of the prototype, and production of the finished product. These broad phases are broken down into perhaps several hundred jobs, each requiring cost, time, and performance controls. The performance of the contract often includes manufacturing and electronics contributions, plus subcontracting of certain jobs because of schedule restrictions or lack of capabilities in-house.

Integrating the various phases for each project in terms of costs, schedules, and performance requires continued effort by the contract administrator's personnel. Most contracts are written on the basis of cost plus fixed fee or cost plus incentive fee. Because of the nature of the contracts, the intense competition in the aerospace industry, and the efforts of government auditors, cost control is an important activity.

Labor makes up the larger portion of expenses (about 40 percent of sales) because of the highly paid engineering and technical personnel. Materials account for about 20 percent of sales.

The following sections describe in detail several of Elvo's divisions, including material relevant to both operational and informational flows.

Exhibit 3-A
ELVO CORPORATION ORGANIZATION

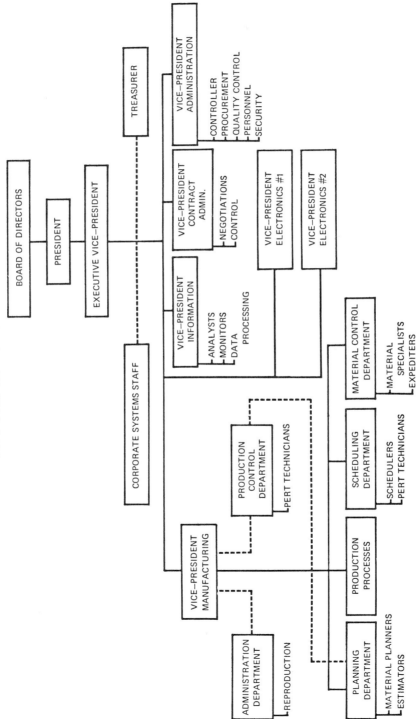

NOTE: THE ORGANIZATIONS OF ELECTRONICS # 1 AND ELECTRONICS # 2 ARE IDENTICAL TO THE ORGANIZATION OF THE MANUFACTURING DIVISION .

PRODUCTION DIVISIONS (ELECTRONICS AND MANUFACTURING)

Each production division (Electronics #1 and #2 and Manufacturing) is organized as outlined in Exhibit 3-A. The Production Control Department is a staff group responsible for overall planning, coordination, and control of the projects of a specific production division from the request-for-quote stage to the delivery of the finished product. Primary emphasis is given to the control of schedules, materials, and costs. The project control officer has functional authority on matters pertaining to projects assigned to his department. He has a final voice on matters such as authorization of overtime, changes in product configuration, and changes in schedules. From 10 to 50 projects are in progress at one time (usually 2 to 6 major projects), and the number of jobs per project averages about 25 (about 6 major milestones for each project).

When a request for quote is received by a production division, it is assigned to a production control officer. A production control folder is set up to collect documents related to the project. A request for quote summary sheet and the specifications are forwarded to the Planning Department where a material planner prepares a detailed bill of materials. Depending on the size of the job and the current workload, from one to seven days are required to prepare the bill of materials. The average time is three to four days. The bill of materials is given to an estimator who prepares a job control sheet which includes estimates of labor hours and costs for each job in the project as well as totals for the entire project.

The bill of materials and job control sheet are typed on duplicating masters and the labor hours and costs estimates are entered on the request for quote summary sheet. This completes the initial responsibilities of the Planning Department. The request for quote summary sheet, bill of materials, and job control sheet are forwarded to the Material Control Department and the Production Control Department is notified. This notification is normally given by phone or by telling the secretary in the production control manager's office (which is physically located across the hall at the main plant). The bill of materials and the job control sheet are given to a material specialist in the Material Control Department who reviews the material requirements for each job of a project. He compiles cost and availability information for all materials, including component parts and subcontract items. For those items which are carried in company stock, he obtains cost information from the stock catalog (published weekly by the Data Processing Department and updated by computer). If insufficient quantities are available in stock, the material specialist phones the responsible buyer in the Procurement Department of the Administration Division to get an estimate on delivery. For items not listed in the stock catalog (including items to be subcontracted), the material specialist requests the Procurement Department to obtain cost and delivery information. This is done by phone; however, two copies of a follow-up purchase requisition (marked "quote only") are sent to Procurement. One copy is returned to the material specialist when the necessary information has been obtained and the other is held by the buyer.

When complete cost and delivery data are acquired and recorded on the request for quote summary sheet, bill of materials (cost data), and job control sheet (delivery data), the material specialist forwards these documents for the Scheduling Department and notifies the production control officer, usually by phone. It takes the material specialist about five days to process these documents, but this time may vary considerably if procurement must locate a subcontractor. The documents are normally not forwarded to the Scheduling Department until all data on materials is obtained.

The Scheduling Department reviews the documents and estimates when each job within the project can be completed. Current and planned workloads, production capacity, and priorities are considered, and second and third level PERT analyses are accomplished. Estimated completion dates are recorded on the request for quote summary sheet. All documents are then forwarded to the production control officer, who combines the information with estimates of fixed costs and desired profits (obtained from the controller's office) and submits a formal bid. All documents are filed in the project folder pending notification of acceptance of the bid. When a bid has been accepted, the production control officer records on the bill of materials and job control sheet the contract number, priority designation, desired delivery date, account classification (assigned by the Accounts Receivable Section of the Controller's office by phone or in writing), and job numbers for each part of the project (assigned by the Cost Accounting Section of the controller's office). The bill of materials and job control sheet are reproduced by the Administration Department. Copies of each are distributed as follows:

1—Production Control Department (with masters)
1—Planning Department for information and file
1—Material Control Department for preparation of stockroom requisitions (stock items), or purchase requisition (nonstock items or subcontract items)
1—Scheduling Department to finalize manufacturing schedules and commit production facilities and time
3—Controller
    1—Accounts Receivable Section
    1—Accounts Payable Section
    1—Cost Accounting Section

In the event a contract is awarded without bidding, the procedure is essentially the same. The production control officer sets up a project folder and a contract summary sheet (instead of a request for quote summary sheet) and forwards the contract summary sheet with specifications to the Planning Department where the bill of materials and job control sheet are compiled. The contract summary sheet includes data pertaining to the contract number, priority, account classifications, job numbers, and desired delivery date. All of this data is entered by the production control officer on the contract summary sheet and transferred to the bill of materials and job control sheet by the Planning Department. The Material Control and Scheduling Departments then perform as previously stated. At this point, however, the manufacturing schedule is a firm commitment, rather than tentative proposal as is the case in a request for quote. The documents are forwarded to the Administration Department for reproduction and distribution as outlined previously.

The material specialist, upon receipt of the copies of the bill of materials from the Administration Department, screens the bill of materials for those items which are kept in stock. A stockroom requisition is prepared for all items of a similar category or all items pertaining to a single job number (two different forms are used). The Cost Accounting Section receives a copy of this stockroom requisition. As materials are used, a material usage report which also includes the job and contract number is prepared by the work station. A copy of the material usage report is also furnished to the Cost Accounting Section. For items to be procured, a purchase requisition is prepared for items pertaining to a single job number (average of 2 or 3 items per purchase requisition). Requisitions (stockroom and purchase) are normally completed and forwarded to the Stockroom in Procurement on a piecemeal basis. The material specialist tries to screen out and requisition the most critical items first. Identification data (the contract number, priority, account classification, and job number) is included on the stockroom requisition and the purchase requisition. These forms also show the customer's name, delivery date, shipping instructions, and the quality and reliability requirements. Another important job of the material specialist is that of being an expediter for constant liaison and follow-up the Procurement Department to insure timely delivery of materials.

At the end of each day the Material Specialist updates his bill of materials control sheet, and sends the Production Control Department the following:

1. A list of items requisitioned that day from the Stockroom or from Procurement
2. A list of items for which a purchase order has been issued by Procurement
3. A list of items received by the Receiving Section and satisfactorily inspected by the Inspection Section (both in Procurement Department)
4. A list of items that have been received but rejected by the Inspection Section
5. A list of items which are overdue in terms of production schedules

The production control officer updates his bill of materials, job control sheets, and PERT charts accordingly. For those items overdue he contacts the Director of Procurement to expedite delivery. In a few cases, the production control officer has referred late deliveries to the president's office on high priority contracts.

Upon receipt of the bill of materials and job control sheet from the Reproduction Section of the Administration Department, the Scheduling Department prepares a master manufacturing schedule, according to each work station, for each project. The job number, project or control number, priority, date work is to begin and end, and total hours scheduled are included on the master manufacturing schedule, which is distributed as follows:

1—Each foreman responsible for work stations involved (up to six)
1—Production control officer
1—Scheduling Department (for control of total scheduling)

As the work progresses, employee timecards are maintained showing daily entries by job number for time spent on the job. Timecards are authenticated by the foremen and submitted to the Cost Accounting Section of the controller's office daily at the end of each work shift. Timecards include the employee's identification number, wage rate, and related personal data.

As changes in the manufacturing schedule occur due to breakdowns, late delivery of materials, absence of workers, incorrect estimates, or other reasons, a manufacturing schedule change form is prepared by the Scheduling Department. Copies of the manufacturing schedule change form are distributed similarly to the master manufacturing schedule in order that work station schedules may be prepared for dissemination of information on work to be done to the manufacturing areas.

PROCUREMENT DEPARTMENT

An organization chart of the Procurement Department is shown in Exhibit 3-B. As a purchase requisition is received (two copies) from the Production Division, it is logged in by the administration clerk. The date and time it was received are stamped on the back of the requisition. Each job number specified on current purchase requisitions is checked against those recorded in the open work authorization report. This step insures that the job is still open and that the original material cost estimates and allocations have not been exceeded. If the job is closed or if costs as estimated have been exceeded, the requisition is returned to the requisitioner for authorization. All requisitions are forwarded to the Quality Control Section. Quality and reliability terms are checked by Quality Control, and the requisitions are returned to the administrative clerk, who then delivers them to the chief purchasing agent or the subcontracting officer, as applicable.

The chief purchasing agent reviews the requisitions and forwards them to one of the specialist buying groups: Electronics, Office Supplies, Commodities, or Hardware. The buyer or subcontracting officer then searches for sources of supply. If a request for quote had been previously handled, he begins with this information. If the item has been procured previously, the item price history card is analyzed to determine previous sources used, prices paid, dates purchased, and quantities purchased. Vendor rating cards are reviewed to determine delivery and quality performance of the vendors being considered. For purchase orders of $250 or more, formal request for bids are required, unless the item is a sole-source item or a customer-specified-brand item or is acquired for emergency reasons. Emergency reasons occur when a production foreman requests stock items on a special requisition form after a bill of materials has been filed.

Purchases of the company are characterized by many small-volume, low dollar-value purchase orders, with a small percentage of items kept in stock (many of these are office supplies). About 35 percent of the purchase orders are for less than $25.00, 50 percent are for less than $50.00, and 85 percent are for less than $250. For example, total value of items procured during 1966 was

Exhibit 3-B
PROCUREMENT DEPARTMENT ORGANIZATION

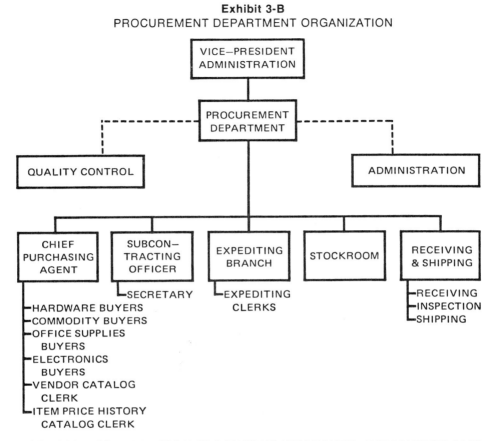

NOTE: STOCKROOM AND RECEIVING & SHIPPING ARE LOCATED IN PRODUCTION AREA.

about $16 million. This value covered about 60,000 line items on 25,000 purchase orders. Of the 10,000 different line items used over a period of time, about 2,000 items are in stock.

About 300 of the high-volume items are purchased through long-term agreements with quantity discounts based on the volume purchased. There are ten major sources of supply which account for about 50 percent of the total dollar volume of purchases and the total number of purchase orders. Twenty sources of supply account for 75 percent of the total dollar volume of purchases and total number of purchase orders.

Orders are usually placed by phone, but confirmation purchase orders are sent if required. For items purchased locally under $25.00 per order, a special local purchase form is prepared by the buyer, and the Receiving Section dispatches a vehicle to the vendor to pick up the items. The vendor records cost information on the local purchase order form, but bills the company only once a month. The driver delivers the items to the Receiving Section where quantities are verified and recorded on the local purchase order form. The items are forwarded to the Inspection area, then delivered to the Stockroom or to the user as specified on the original requisition.

Copies of the local purchase order form are distributed as follows:

2—Procurement
    1—filed by job number
    1—filed by purchase order number
2—Controller
    1—Accounts Payable Section (after items are processed through Receiving and Inspection)
    2—Cost Accounting Section
1—Receiving Section file (by purchase order number)
1—Inspection Section file (by purchase order number)
2—Requisitioner (after receipt and inspection)
    1—Material specialist
    1—Production control officer
1—Stockroom (with items)

At the time a vendor is selected, the buyer or subcontracting officer completes the sections of the regular purchase requisition dealing with vendor name, vendor number, location of vendor, purchase order number, quantity ordered, delivery date, unit price, tax, terms, FOB, shipment instructions, and related data. If the vendor is new, the buyer contacts the Accounts Payable Section of the controller's office to obtain a new vendor number. The duplicate copy of the purchase requisition is then returned to the material specialist in the Production Division and the original is given to the Procurement Administration Section for typing of the purchase order.

The typed purchase order is checked by Quality Control to insure correct quality and reliability terms. These terms are spelled out on the reverse side of the form and are coded numerically. The applicable numerical codes are typed on the front of the purchase order. The purchase orders are then signed: by the buyer for orders less than $5,000; by the chief purchasing agent for orders less than $10,000; and by the director of procurement for orders over $10,000. The subcontracting officer also signs orders for less than $10,000. Distribution of copies of the purchase order is as follows:

2—Vendor
2—Controller
    1—Accounts Payable Section
    1—Cost Accounting Section
2—Requisitioner
    1—Material specialist
    1—Production control officer
3—Procurement
    1—Numerical file (purchase order number)
    1—Buyer file (by vendor, alphabetically)
    1—Expediting Section follow-up copy (by date due)
1—(Master)—Receiving Section (filed by purchase order number in open file)

As shipments are received, the receiving clerk pulls the master purchase order copy (which has space provided to record quantities, dates delivered, and inspection data). A record is made of the quantity received of each line item and the date it is received. Copies of the purchase order (which now serves as a receiving and inspection report) are made and distributed as follows:

> 2—Controller
>> 1—Accounts Payable Section
>> 1—Cost Accounting Section
> 2—Requisitioner
>> 1—Material specialist
>> 1—Production control officer
> 1—Procurement (Expediting Section)
> 8—Inspection (with materials)
> 1—(Master)—Receiving Section (filed by purchase order number in pending or completed file, depending on whether shipment is a partial or total order)

The Procurement Expediting Section pulls the follow-up copy and the receiving data is entered. If the order is complete, the follow-up copy is placed in a completed purchase order file (numerically by purchase order number). If the shipment is a partial one, the updated follow-up copy is returned to the pending file (by date due).

When materials are inspected, the results of the inspection are recorded on the seven copies of the purchase order (receiving and inspection formats). If there are no defects in quality, distribution of the eight copies is as follows:

> 1—Stockroom (with materials)
> 1—Inspection file (by purchase order number)
> 2—Requisitioner
>> 1—Material specialist
>> 1—Production control officer
> 4—Destroyed by Inspection area

If a partial or total reject occurs, distribution is as the foregoing except the four copies which were destroyed in the case of acceptable materials are distributed as follows:

> 2—Controller
>> 1—Accounts Payable Section
>> 1—Cost Accounting Section
> 1—Procurement Expediting Section (to correct follow-up copy and determine disposition of defects)
> 1—Receiving Section with defective items to await disposition instructions (accepted items are forwarded to Stockroom)

The procurement expediter coordinates disposition of defects with the material specialist and the vendor. He notifies the Receiving Section and the disposition is effected.

CONTROLLER

The Cost Accounting Section of the controller's office compiles the estimates of materials required (copy of bill of materials), labor hours and costs (copy of job control sheet), and fixed costs (allocated by the Cost Accounting

Section). These estimates are made up by job number and contract number and are used as standards of performance. The Cost Accounting Section forwards the estimates to the Data Processing Department for keypunching and preparation of the open work authorization master file. The open work authorization report is made up from the outstanding or open work orders. As daily timecards are received by Cost Accounting, they are forwarded to Data Processing and the open work authorization master file is updated. Similarly, material usage reports are received by Cost Accounting and forwarded to Data Processing for updating of the work authorization report. Actual fixed-cost allocation data is forwarded to Data Processing for updating the open work authorization report.

Receiving report data, as it is received by Cost Accounting, is forwarded to Data Processing for updating the raw materials master file. As materials are requisitioned from the Stockroom by the work stations (by means of stockroom requisitions), Cost Accounting furnishes the stockroom requisition data to the Data Processing Department to transfer material data from the raw materials master file to the work-in-process master file. Finally, as a job is completed, a copy of the shipping report is furnished the Cost Accounting Section, material data is transferred from the work-in-process to the finished goods inventory master file, and the account receivable master file is decreased accordingly.

The Accounts Payable Section receives copies of purchase orders, receiving reports, and rejection reports. Data Processing is furnished data pertaining to purchase commitments (in terms of purchase orders issued for stock items only) and increases in raw materials inventories (receiving reports for all items). A weekly purchase order commitment report is prepared by Data Processing for stock items by purchase order numbers. A weekly stock catalog is prepared for stock items. Data Processing also prepares a monthly report on usage of stock items which is used by Procurement to determine maximum and minimum levels and to screen out slow-moving items.

DATA PROCESSING

The executives of Elvo are proud of their firm's data processing equipment. The company has two IBM System/360 computers. One is a Model 50 that replaced an IBM 7094 and the other is a Model 30 that replaced an IBM 1401. The company has an extensive library of programs as well as a system for allocations of costs to users.

The IBM 360/50 is a high-speed (one million cycles per second), third generation, digital computer which uses integrated circuits to perform its primary functions. The computer has over 256,000 positions of core storage capacity, each consisting of eight binary digits of data capacity. On-line equipment includes a card reader/punch, a printer (1,100 lines per minute), five 9-track/800 characters-per-inch tape drives, and four 2311 disk drives. These devices are on one multiplexor and two selector channels to provide for optimum use of high-speed and low-speed input/output generations. The Model 50 has the capacity for multiprogramming and can accomodate up to 14 problem programs in memory at one time. Input/output, channel to channel operations, and internal data manipulations and calculations can occur simultaneously. This computer is especially suited to problem solving operations involving extensive calculations and large arrays of numbers. Supporting software for the computer includes many programs developed at Elvo and a large number of program routines and applications available from IBM's SHARE library.

The IBM System/360 Model 30 is designed for rapid calculations and input/output flexibility and speed. It has a cycle time of 3.2 microseconds (.0000032 second/cycle) and is equipped to run programs prepared for the previous IBM 1401 for as long as is necessary. The 360/30 is used primarily for file update and business report processing. It has 16,000 positions of memory. The system includes a 1403 printer, four tape drives (and has access to one drive shared by the Model 50) and two 2311 disk drives. It has a card reader that operates at 800 cards per minute and a punch with a speed of 250 cards per minute. The paper tape unit reads at 500 characters per second and can write at 150 characters per second. The IBM 360/30 has one selector and one multiplexor channel on which its input/output devices are located.

All of Elvo's tape drives are high-density 9-track tapes with the exception of one multiple-density 7-track drive to handle historical data prepared on previous second generation equipment. A large number of 1316 disk packs are retained in the library. Each 1316 disk pack can store over seven million characters of data and is demountable for convenient storage. These are used on the 2311 disk drives.

It is standard practice to prepare programs to run on either computer whenever possible. This allows one machine to replace the other in the event of equipment failure. Under normal conditions, most programs are run on the 360/50 since it is anticipated that the data files relating to these programs will also be used in other programs which run on that machine.

Standard costs have been developed for the Data Processing Department. These charges are applied for work which the department performs for the other divisions of the company. Charges are based on a 52-week, 250-working-day year. These charges are:

IBM 360/30 CPU time: $60.00 per hour
IBM 360/50 CPU time: $180.00 per hour
IBM 029 time (Keypunch): $6.50 per hour (100 cards per hour)
Programming: $5.00 per hour
Testing: $60.00 per hour
Printout: 5¢ per 10 lines or $60.00/hour (depending on type of job)
IBM 047 paper tape to card conversion: $4.00 per hour

By way of comparison, a local processing firm had quoted the following charges relating to a purchase order system:

Keypunch purchase orders and receiving reports @$2.50/hour: $80.00 per month or $960.00 per year
Keypunch receipts and rejections of shipments @$2.50/hour: $80.00 per month or $960.00 per year
Frieden Computyper and Flexowriter: $768.00 programming charge and $768.00 per month use charge

IBM 632 (Model 3): $95.00 programming charge and $380.00 per month use charge

Paper tape to card conversion @$4.00/hour: $120.00 per month or $1,440.00 per year

Additional data about Elvo's data processing operations follows:

1. Procurement Related:

Purchase orders: 25,000 per year
Line items: 2,000 stock and 8,000 nonstock
Vendors (listed in catalog): 300
Receiving reports: 50,000 per year
Purchasing costs:
    1. $12.00 preparation cost per purchase order.
    2. 2 catalog clerks @$2.00/hour or $4160.00 per year each.
    3. 3 expediters @$7,000.00 salary per year each.
    4. 8 buyers @$9,000.00 salary per year each.
    5. 3 administrative clerks @$2.50/hour or $5,200.00 per year each.
    6. 5 receiving clerks @$2.00/hour or $4,160.00 per year each.
    7. 2 purchase order typists @$2.50/hour or $5,200.00 per year each.
    8. Director of purchasing salary—$13,000.00 per year.
    9. Materials and supplies—$18,880.00 per year.
   10. Overhead—$120,000.00 per year.

2. Production Related:

    1. 3 planners @$9,000.00 salary per year each.
    2. 3 schedulers @$9,000.00 salary per year each.
    3. 3 material specialists @$9,000.00 salary per year each.
    4. 2 expediters @$8,000.00 salary per year each.
    5. 3 administrative clerks @$2.50/hour or $5,200.00 per year each.

QUESTIONS

1. Document the operational and information flows in the Elvo Corporation within the general framework described in Chapters 5, 6, and 7, showing:

  a. Major types of decisions made within each activity of the operational subsystems.

  b. Major categories of information needed for each decision.

  c. Sources of information needed for each decision (process activators, i.e., documents and organizational segments furnishing the information).

  d. Major types of information created or generated from each decision (i.e., new process activators).

  e. Uses of new information generated.

2. Based on question 1, summarize the problem areas regarding operational and information flows that you feel are the most serious ones confronting the company. In this summary, consider the following:

  a. The volume and timing of documentation generated.

  b. The impact of the information generated on the operational subsystem's performance.

    c. Organizational characteristics as they impact the operational and infor-
mational subsystems.

    d. The effectiveness of material planning and control as it relates to produc-
tion planning and control.

    e. The effectiveness of data processing as a facilitator of management.

3. Utilizing the information systems design methodology described in Chapter
4, prepare an outline of a systems study for one or more of the problems
identified in question 2.

4. Comment on the usefulness of systems theory concepts described in this
book for resolving some of the problems in this case. For example:

    a. Is Elvo a viable organization reflecting the systemic characteristics de-
scribed in Chapter 14?

    b. Are there potential applications of the systems and information concepts
described in Chapters 12 and 13?

    c. Does the integrated information system concept offer a favorable poten-
tial for Elvo?

4

ELVO
CORPORATION
(Part B)

Elvo Corporation (Part B) can be used independently of Part A as a feasibility analysis exercise; however, the general company background information of Part A should be reviewed. Part B can also be used to supplement Part A as an exercise in designing a materials planning, control, and procurement system, as well as for evaluating the feasibility of alternatives. The general format of Part B includes three alternatives for designing a materials planning and control system, which incorporates procedural descriptions and extensive cost data for each alternative. It is an example of a piecemeal approach (i.e., it focuses on the production and procurement areas, rather than broader types of information needs of Elvo).

The purpose of the case is to become familiar with the types of information required in analyzing and designing a system and in performing a feasibility analysis of alternatives. Examples of formats for developing and presenting operating and financial data concerning design alternatives are presented. Nonrecurring and recurring cost categories involved in information system design are identified and analyzed. This case is useful in familiarizing the student with the more technical features of information systems design and with feasibility analysis of alternative designs. The questions and assignments at the end of the case provide opportunities for reviewing important concepts described in this book and applying them in a comprehensive setting.

ALTERNATIVE A

Alternative A is a system for converting purchase requisitions to punched cards which are processed by Data Processing to print purchase orders and receiving reports daily. Weekly, monthly, and yearly reports are optional. Three master files are created and maintained in Data Processing: the purchase order file (open and closed), the vendor catalog, and the stock item catalog. From these master files a large variety of information could be generated. Each evening all purchase requisitions are forwarded to Data Processing for keypunching in purchase order format. Each night, Data Processing prints sets of carbonized purchase orders and receiving reports which are forwarded to Procurement each morning with a printout of purchase orders (by number) processed that night. Distribution of purchase orders and receiving reports is made by Procurement. As shipments are received, Data Processing is notified. When invoices are received, Procurement does the necessary matching and authorizes payment, then notifies Accounts Payable. For partial shipments, Data Processing automatically prints another set of updated receiving reports for Procurement. Copies of stockroom requisitions are forwarded to Data Processing daily to account for material usage on a continuing basis.

Procedure for Alternative A

Purchase Orders and Receiving Reports Processed and Printed by Data Processing Daily.

Step 1: Production Division

Receives request for quotation on job with specifications and drawings. Forwards drawings to planner and records date.

Step 2: Planner (Production)

Converts drawings into a bill of materials and requisition, listing:

1. *For Job*
    (1) Estimate number
    (2) Contract number
    (3) Priority rating
    (4) Cost center
    (5) Job number
    (6) Description of job
    (7) Drawing number
    (8) Delivery to—
    (9) Customer delivery date
    (10) Planner
    (11) Dates request for quote is received, and forwarded to Scheduler.

2. *For Each Item*
    (1) Quantities desired
    (2) Description of item
    (3) Quality requirements
    (4) Single source justification
    (5) Codes for like items

Step 3: Scheduler (Production)

1. Determines production time and completion date of job.
2. Enters on bill of materials and requisition:
    a. Date bill of materials received from planner.
    b. Desired delivery date for each item.
    c. Date bill of materials forwarded to Production Control.

Step 4: Production Control or Authorized Individual

Checks, signs, dates, and releases bill of materials and requisition to the Procurement Department.

Step 5: Procurement Administration

1. Records date and time bill of materials received in log.
2. Reproduces bill of materials as required; forwards bill of materials to Quality Control.

Step 6: Quality Control Representative

Checks quality requirements and forwards bill of materials to Procurement Administration.

Step 7: Procurement Administration

Distributes copies of bill of materials to appropriate Buyers.

Step 8: Buyer

1. Analyzes history data on price, delivery, vendors used, and performance of vendors from items price history catalog.
2. Selects sources of supply, completing sections of bill of materials and requisition dealing with vendor, small business classification, location of vendor, purchase order number, quantity ordered, delivery date, unit price, tax, terms, FOB, shipment instructions, and related data.
3. For new vendors, obtains a vendor number from Accounting.
4. Forwards bill of materials and requisition to Procurement Administration.

Step 9: Procurement Administration

1. Keypunches purchase order from bill of materials and requisition. (See sample of card format.)
2. As order is punched, records date of order on bill of materials. At the end of each day, forwards punched cards to Data Processing.
3. Bill of materials and requisition are held pending printing of purchase orders by Data Processing.

Step 10: Data Processing (Each Night)

1. Processes purchase order cards.
2. Prints sets of carbonized purchase orders and receiving reports for each purchase order card (includes more than one line item per order in some cases).
3. Each morning furnishes to the Procurement Department:
   a. Purchase orders issued.
   b. Receiving reports for purchase orders issued the previous day.
   c. A list of purchase order numbers processed.

Step 11: Procurement Administration

1. Checks purchase orders against bill of materials and requisition.
2. Checks and hand carries receiving reports to Receiving Department after purchase orders are signed.
3. Distributes copies of purchase orders as follows:

    2—Vendor
    3—Accounting
    2—Requisitioner
    3—Procurement—
        1—Follow-up file
        1—Numerical file
        1—Buyer file
4. Files copy of completed bill of materials and requisition by job number, and forwards one copy to the requisitioner.

Step 12: Receiving Department

1. Files sets of receiving reports in open file by purchase order number.
2. As shipments are received, pulls receiving reports and enters quantities and dates received.
3. Distributes copies of receiving report as follows:
    1—Requisitioner
    1—Receiving Department file
    2—Procurement Administration
        1—Accounting's copy held until
            order is complete
        1—Action copy
    2—Material cards
    1—Receiving Inspection (master)
4. If shipment is complete, files copy of receiving report in completed file. If shipment is partially complete, files in open file.

Step 13: Procurement Administration

1. Upon receipt of two copies of receiving report:
    a. Files one copy temporarily in Accounting folder.
    b. Keypunches receiving card (see sample card for format). Forwards cards to Data Processing daily.
2. If shipment is complete, files copy of receiving report in completed purchase order file.
3. If shipment is partially complete, files copy of receiving report in open purchase order file (used for expediting and follow-up).
4. When invoices are received, matches and verifies invoice, receiving report, and purchase order, and forwards to Accounting authorizing payment.

Step 14: Data Processing

1. Each night processes receiving cards and updates master purchase order file.
2. If shipment is partially complete, prints a new set of receiving reports for entire purchase order, indicating partial shipments completed to date in appropriate spaces (See sample of receiving report format).
3. Forwards receiving reports to Procurement each morning.

Step 15: Procurement Administration

Checks and forwards new receiving reports to the Receiving Department.

Step 16: Receiving Department

The new receiving report is filed in the open file, removing the copy of the past partially received report (complete information on receipts is duplicated on the new set of receiving reports). As additional shipments are received on the same purchase order, the process is repeated until the purchase order is complete.

Step 17: Inspection Department

If a reject occurs, rejection report master is completed and copies of rejection report are run off and distributed as follows:
   1—Quality Control
   2—Procurement Administration
      1 copy to Accounting
   1—Requisitioner
   1—Vendor

Step 18: Procurement Administration

1. One copy of rejection report is forwarded to the buyer to determine disposition instructions.
2. One copy of rejection report is filed in the Accounting folder.

Step 19: Buyer

Determines disposition instructions and forwards copy of completed rejection report to Procurement Administration.

Step 20: Procurement Administration

1. Notes disposition instructions on Accounting's copy of rejection report.
2. Key punches rejection report data, and forwards the card to Data Processing daily (See attached sample of card format).
3. Informs Receiving Department of disposition instructions.

Step 21: Data Processing

1. Processes rejection card and updates purchase order master file.
2. If Vendor is to replace items, prints another set of receiving reports (and the process is repeated).

Receiving and Rejection Reports—Card Formats

Receiving Report Card Format

Columns	Characters	Data
1—6	6	Purchase order number
7—12	6	Purchase order date

13—14	2	Item number
15—20	6	Quantities received
21—26	6	Dates received
27—80	54	Blank

Rejection Report Card Format

Columns	Characters	Data
1—6	6	Purchase order number
7—12	6	Purchase order date
13—14	2	Item number
15—20	6	Quantities received
21—26	6	Quantities rejected
27—32	6	Dates rejected
33—80	48	Reason for rejection

Purchase Order Card Format

Card 1:

Columns	Characters	Data
1—2	2	Card number code (not to appear on purchase order)
3—9	7	Purchase order number (seventh digit for amendments)
10—11	2	Blank
12—15	4	Agreement number
16	1	Purchase order code (not to appear on purchase order)
		1—purchase order—materials & supplies
		2—subcontracts
		3—long-term agreements
		4—miscellaneous orders
17—22	6	Purchase order date
23	1	Confirmation of purchase order code
		1—phone
		2—wire
24—29	6	Date order placed
30—44	15	Contract number
45—52	8	Priority
53—57	5	Cost center
58—65	8	Account classification
66—74	9	Name of requisitioner
75—80	6	Blank

Card 2:

Columns	Characters	Data
1—11	11	Same as Card 1
12	1	Tax code
		1—Yes
		2—No
13—22	10	Terms
23	1	"Ship To" code (preprinted choices on purchase order)
24—25	2	Buyer code (79—buyers name code, 80—commodity code)
26—31	6	Vendor number
32	1	Small business code (not to appear on purchase order)
		1—Small
		2—Large
33	1	Vendor location code (not to appear on purchase order)
		1—Local
		2—Other
34—35	2	Vendor location code (not to appear on purchase order)
		01—50 (state identification)
36	1	F.O.B. code (preprinted choices on purchase order)
		1—Shipment destination
		2—Vendor plant
		3—Other
37	1	"Ship Via" code (preprinted choices on purchase order)
		1—Air
		2—Special delivery
		3—Freight
		4—Railway Express
		5—Other
38—42	5	Vendor quote number
43—48	6	Vendor quote date
49	1	Certification of quality
		1—Yes
		2—No
50—69	20	Quality terms
		01—30 (Up to ten quality terms)
70—80	11	Blank

Card 3:

Columns	Characters	Data
1—9	9	Same as card 1
10—11	2	Item number on purchase order
12—17	6	Quantity ordered
18—26	9	Unit price
27—30	4	W/O number
31—36	6	Date to be delivered
37—46	10	Stock number (stock items)
47—80	34	Begin description of item

Card 4:

Columns	Characters	Data
1—9	9	Same as card 1
10—11	2	Item number on purchase order
12—80	69	End description of item (103 letters total)

NOTE: For each succeeding item on the purchase order, two cards are added with the format indicated in cards 3 and 4.

ALTERNATIVE B

Alternative B is a system for typing purchase orders in the Procurement Department and generating purchase order cards and receiving reports on paper tape (using a Frieden Computyper). Purchase order cards are forwarded to Data Processing each evening to update the three master files weekly, and to generate the necessary weekly, monthly, and yearly reports. The paper tape is used to prepare receiving report sets by Procurement for new purchase orders (using a Frieden Flexowriter). When shipments are received, a copy of the receiving report is forwarded to Data Processing. If the shipment is a partial shipment, Procurement pulls the paper tape from the purchase order file and produces another set of receiving reports for the remaining shipment and the process is repeated. Alternative B primarily differs from Alternative A in that printing of purchase orders and receiving reports is not accomplished by Data Processing, thereby not requiring daily updating of master files and daily print-out costs.

Procedure for Alternative B

Purchase orders and receiving reports are prepared in the Procurement Department.

Steps 1-8: Same as Alternative A

Step 9: Procurement Administration

1. Types purchase order from bill of materials and requisition.

2. Punches order on a card (purchase order data) and produces a paper tape (receiving report data). At the end of each day, forwards cards to Data Processing. Data Processing updates master purchase order files weekly.
3. From paper tape, produces sets of carbonized receiving reports and forwards them to Receiving Department the following morning.
4. Files paper tape with copy of purchase order in Procurement Administration. Distributes copies of purchase orders as follows:
   2—Vendor
   3—Accounting
   2—Requisitioner
   3—Procurement
       1—Follow-up file
       1—Numerical file
       1—Buyer file

Step 10: Receiving Department

1. Files sets of receiving reports in open file by purchase order number.
2. As shipments are received, pulls receiving reports and enters quantities and dates received.
3. Distributes copies of receiving report as follows:
   1—Requisitioner
   1—Receiving Department file
   2—Procurement Administration
       1—Accounting's copy held until order is complete
       1—Action copy
   2—Material Cards
   1—Receiving Inspection (Master)
4. If shipment is complete, files copy of receiving report in completed file. If shipment is partially complete, returns to open file.

Step 11: Procurement Administration

1. Upon receipt of two copies of receiving report, files one copy temporarily in the Accounting folder pending receipt of invoice and completion of shipment if the current receiving report is a partial shipment.
2. From Procurement's copy of receiving report, locates paper tape and produces card for Data Processing to update master purchase order file. Cards are forwarded to Data Processing each evening. If shipment is a partial shipment, produces another set of receiving reports, entering quantities and dates received. Receiving reports are forwarded to the Receiving Department, and the process is repeated.

Step 12: Receiving Inspection

If a reject occurs, rejection report (master) is completed and copies of rejection report are run off and distributed as follows:

    1—Quality Control
    2—Procurement Administration
        1—copy to Accounting
    1—Requisitioner
    1—Vendor

Step 13: Procurement Administration

1. One copy of rejection report forwarded to the buyer to determine disposition instructions.
2. One copy of rejection report filed in the Accounting folder.

Step 14: Buyer

1. Determines disposition instructions and forwards copy of completed rejection report to Procurement Administration.

Step 15: Procurement Administration

1. Notes disposition instructions on Accounting's copy of rejection report.
2. With paper tape, reproduces receiving report, entering rejection and disposition data. Card is punched and forwarded to Data Processing daily to update the master purchase order file.
3. Informs the Receiving Department of disposition instructions. If vendor is to replace shipment, forwards another set of receiving reports to the Receiving Department.

Purchase Order Card Format

Card 1

Columns	Characters	Data
1—2	2	Card number code
3—9	7	Purchase order number
10—11	2	Blank
12—15	4	Agreement number
16	1	Purchase order code
17—22	6	Purchase order date
23—37	15	Contract number
38—42	5	Cost center
43—50	8	Account classification
51—56	6	Vendor number
57	1	Small business code
58	1	Vendor location code (local or other)
59	1	Vendor location code (by state)
60	1	Approved vendor code
61—80	20	Blank

Card 2:

1—9	9	Same as Card 1
10—11	2	Item number on purchase order
12—17	6	Quantity ordered
18—26	9	Unit price
27—32	6	Date to be Delivered
33—42	10	Stock number (stock items)
43—80	38	Begin description of item

Card 3:

1—9	9	Same as Card 1
10—11	2	Item number on purchase order
12—80	69	End description of item (107 letters total)

NOTE: For each succeeding item on the purchase order, two cards are added with the format indicated in cards 2 and 3.

Paper Tape Format

Spaces	Characters	Data
1—7	7	Purchase order number
8—13	6	Purchase order date
14—28	15	Contract number
29—33	5	Cost center
34—41	8	Account classification
42—50	9	Name of requisitioner
51—53	3	Certification of quality (yes-no)
54—73	20	Quality terms
74—88	15	"Ship To" (destination)
89—94	6	Vendor number
95—154	60	Vendor name
155—156	2	Item number
157—162	6	Quantity ordered
163—171	9	Unit price
172—175	4	W/O number (work order)
176—181	6	Date to be delivered
182—191	10	Stock number (stock items)
192—300	109	Description of item (109 letters)

NOTE: For each additional item, 146 spaces are required, in the format indicated by spaces 155-300.

Alternative C

Alternative C is a system for typing of purchase orders in the Procurement Department on an IBM 632, Model 3. An order format is generated which is forwarded to Data Processing for daily printing of receiving reports, updating of the three master files, and preparation of weekly, monthly, and yearly reports. Handling of receipts of shipments and other procedures are similar to Alternative A.

The basic differences of the three alternatives are the extent of daily outputs required from Data Processing, the location of the printing of purchase orders and receiving reports, and differences in types of equipment required. All three systems provide similar capabilities for generation of reports from Data Processing. One Computyper and one Flexowriter are required for alternative B; one IBM 632, Model 3 for alternative C; and a keypunch lease arrangement is required for alternatives A and C (since Procurement and not Data Processing does the work).

Procedure for Alternative C

Receiving reports are processed and printed by Data Processing daily.

Steps 1-8: Same as Alternative A

Step 9: Procurement Administration

1. Types purchase order from bill of materials and requisition.
2. As order is typed, punches a card (see sample of card format). Forwards cards to Data Processing at the end of each day.
3. Distributes copies of purchase orders as follows:
    2—Vendor
    3—Accounting
    2—Requisitioner
    3—Procurement
        1—Follow-up file
        1—Numerical file
        1—Buyer file
4. Files copy of completed bill of materials and requisition by job number, and forwards one copy to the requisitioner.

Step 10: Data Processing (Each Night)

1. Processes purchase order cards.
2. Prints sets of carbonized receiving reports for each purchase order card (includes more than one line item per order in some cards). See format of receiving report data.
3. Each morning furnishes the Procurement Department with:
    a. Receiving reports for purchase orders issued the previous day.
    b. A list of purchase orders processed.

Step 11: Procurement Administration

Checks and hand carries receiving report to the Receiving Department each morning.

Step 12: Receiving Department

1. Files sets of receiving reports in open file by purchase order number.
2. As shipments are received, pulls receiving reports and enters quantities and dates received.
3. Distributes copies of receiving reports as follows:
    1—Requisitioner
    1—Receiving department file
    2—Procurement Administration
        1—Accounting's copy held until order is complete
        1—Action copy
    2—Material cards
    1—Inspection (Master)
4. If shipment is complete, files copy of receiving report in completed file. If shipment is partially complete, returns to open file.

Steps 13-21: Same as Alternative A

Purchase Order Card Format

Card 1:

Columns	Characters	Data
1—2	2	Card number code (not to appear on purchase order)
3—9	7	Purchase order number
10—11	2	(Blank)
12—15	4	Agreement number
16	1	Purchase order code
17—22	6	Purchase order date
23—37	15	Contract number
38—42	5	Cost center
43—50	8	Account classification
51—59	9	Name of requisitioner
60	1	Certification of quality code
		1—yes
		2—no
61—80	20	Quality terms (up to ten terms)
		(01—30)

Card 2:

Columns	Characters	Data
1—11	11	(Same as Card 1)
12	1	Ship to code
13—18	6	Vendor number
19	1	Small business code
20	1	Vendor location code (local or other)

| 21—22 | 2 | Vendor location code (by state) |
| 23—80 | 58 | Vendor name |

Card 3:

Columns	Characters	Data
1—9	9	(Same as Card 1)
10—11	2	Item number on purchase order
12—17	6	Quantity ordered
18—26	9	Unit price
27—30	4	W/O number
31—36	6	Date to be delivered
37—46	10	Stock number (stock items)
47—80	34	Begin description of item

Card 4:

Columns	Characters	Data
1—9	9	(Same as Card 1)
10—11	2	Item number on purchase order
12—80	69	End description of item (103 letters)

NOTE: For each succeeding item on the purchase order, two cards are added with the format indicated in cards 3 and 4.

PROPOSED REPORTS AND MASTER FILES

Each of the three alternatives are designed to generate a number of reports relating to materials acquisition and utilization. Descriptions of these reports, along with descriptions of the required master files, are included in the following sections. These descriptions of reports and master files pertain to all three alternatives.

Reports Generated by Data Processing

Present Reports

Inventory Stock Status Report of Shelf Balance (Weekly to Procurement)

1. Stock item
2. Unit of Purchase
3. Description of item
4. Receipts
5. Issues
6. Quantity on hand
7. Maximum level
8. Minimum level
9. Opening balance (quantity)

10. Reserved
11. On order

Inventory Stock Status of Invoiced Items (Weekly to Accounting)

1. Stock item
2. Unit of purchase
3. Description of item
4. Receipts
5. Issues
6. Quantity on hand
7. Maximum level
8. Minimum level
9. Opening balance (quantity)
10. Reserved
11. On order

Weekly Purchase Order Status of Stock Items (Weekly to Accounting and Procurement)

1. Stock number
2. Unit of purchase
3. Quantity
4. Dollar value
5. Purchase order date
6. Delivery date
7. Buyer
8. Purchase order number
9. Agreement number
10. Define transaction
11. Transaction code

Open Work Authorization Log (Weekly to Accounting, Divisions, and Procurement)

1. Cost center
2. Job number
3. Account number
4. Effective date
5. Delivery date
6. Allotted costs
   a. Total
   b. Labor
   c. Materials
   d. Hours
7. Project Management office
8. Activity date

Inventory Usage Report of Stock Items (Monthly to Procurement and Accounting)

1. Stock number
2. Unit of purchase
3. Quantity used for last 12 months, total 12 months, and monthly average

Purchase Order, Purchase Order Receipt, Vouchered Receipt, Accrual Errors, and Correction Manifest (Monthly to Accounting)

1. Date of transaction (purchase order)
2. Unit of issue
3. Stock number
4. Purchase order number
5. Vendor number
6. Quantity
7. Value
8. Delivery date voucher number
9. Buyer-manifest purchase order number
10. Master unit of issue
11. Kickout
12. Unit price
13. Voucher received flag
14. Purchase order flag
15. Procurement flag
16. Direct
17. Correct
18. Transaction code

Vendor Catalog (Semiannually to Accounting and Procurement)

1. Vendor number
2. Vendor number and address
3. ZIP code
4. Type of company (small or large)

Accounts Payable Register (Yearly to Accounting)

New Reports

Purchase Orders Overdue Report, By Vendor (Weekly to Procurement)

1. Vendor name and address
2. Purchase order number
3. Description of items
4. Job number
5. Cost center
6. Date due
7. Quantities received to date for each item

Small Business Report (Monthly to Procurement)

1. Total dollar volume to small businesses (local, other, state)
2. Total dollar volume to large businesses (local, other, state)
3. Total dollar volume of business (local, other, state)
4. Percent of procurement to small businesses (local, other, state)
5. List of vendors receiving orders of $1,000 or more (include vendor name and amount of each order).
6. Nonprocurement dollar volume of small and large businesses (local, other, state)

Vendor Catalog (Monthly and Yearly to Procurement and Quality Control)

1. Vendor number
2. Vendor name and address
3. Vendor location (local, other, state)
4. Small business classification
5. Quantities shipped
6. Quantities accepted (quality)
7. Vendor rating (quality)
8. Number of purchase orders
9. Number of late deliveries
10. Vendor rating (delivery)
11. Total dollar volume of orders
12. Average purchase order size (dollars)
13. Number of agreements
14. Total dollar volume of agreements

Item Catalog of Nonstock Items Alphabetically and Stock Items by Number (Monthly and Yearly to Procurement, Divisions (Items 1-3 and 6-13), and Accounting (Items 1-3 and 6-13).

1. Stock number
2. Description of item
3. Unit of purchase
4. Yearly usage
5. For each vendor used during last year:
   a. Vendor
   b. Quantities purchased
   c. Unit price
   d. Vendor quality rating
   e. Vendor delivery rating
   f. Dates purchased
   g. Purchase order number
   h. Agreement numbers
   i. Job numbers
   j. Cost centers
   k. Average lead times

6. Total receipts
7. Quantity on hand
8. Maximum level
9. Minimum level
10. Reserved for jobs
11. On order
12. Balance available
13. Invoice data

Monthly Completed Purchase Order Report (Monthly to Procurement and Accounting)

1. Purchase order number
2. Purchase order date
3. Agreement number
4. Contract number
5. Cost center
6. Account classification
7. Vendor number
8. Vendor name

Future Reports

Agreement Report (Monthly to Procurement)

1. Agreement number
2. Vendor name
3. Dollar amount of agreement
4. Stock item numbers
5. Agreement date
6. Expiration date
7. Quantity purchased
8. Quantity delivered
9. Unit price

Material Status by Job Number (Weekly to Divisions)

1. Job number
2. Estimate number
3. Contract number
4. Cost center
5. Date of bill of materials
6. For each item:
   a. Stock number
   b. Description of item
   c. Quality requirements
   d. Quantity required
   e. Desired delivery date
   f. Purchase order number
   g. Agreement number

  h. Subcontract number
  i. Quantity on hand
  j. Quantity available
  k. Quantity purchased
  l. Vendor used
  m. Unit price
  n. Expected delivery date
  o. Date received

Master Files in Data Processing

Purchase Order File (Open and Completed)

1. Purchase order number
2. Purchase order code
3. Purchase order date
4. Agreement number
5. Contract number
6. Cost center
7. Account classification
8. Vendor number
9. Small business code
10. Vendor location code
11. Item number on purchase order
  a. Quantity ordered
  b. Unit price
  c. Delivery date promised
  d. Stock number (stock items)
  e. Description of item
  f. Quantity received
  g. Quantity rejected
  h. Date received

Vendor Catalog (Alphabetical and numerical)

1. Vendor number
2. Vendor name and address
3. Vendor location (local, other, state)
4. Small business classification
5. Quantities shipped
6. Quantities accepted (quality)
7. Vendor rating (quality)
8. Number of purchase orders
9. Number of late deliveries
10. Vendor rating (delivery)
11. Total dollar volume of orders
12. Average purchase order size (dollars)

13. Number of agreements
14. Total dollar value of agreements

Stock Item Catalog (Stock Items by Stock Number, Others Alphabetically)

1. Stock number
2. Description of item
3. Unit of purchase
4. Yearly usage
5. For each vendor used during last year:
   a. Vendor
   b. Quantities purchased
   c. Unit price
   d. Vendor quality rating
   e. Vendor Delivery rating
   f. Dates purchased
   g. Purchase order numbers
   h. Agreement numbers
   i. Job numbers
   j. Cost centers
   k. Average lead times
6. Total receipts
7. Quantity on hand
8. Maximum level
9. Minimum level
10. Reserved for jobs
11. On order
12. Balance available
13. Invoice data

ESTIMATED DATA PROCESSING AND RELATED COSTS

The following sections include comparative cost figures for the three alternatives. The data is categorized by: comparative summary of total costs, comparative summary of data processing costs (Exhibit 4-A), and summary of data processing costs. Following this cost data are flowcharts (Exhibits 4-B through 4-E) showing how data will be processed through the computer.

Comparative Summary of Total Costs

I. Set-up Costs:	A	B	C
a. Data Processing Programming and testing	$2,976	$2,496	$2,668
b. Frieden Programming Costs		768	
c. IBM Programming Costs (IBM 632)			95
	$2,976	$3,264	$2,763

NOTE: Figures do not include costs for part-time systems analyst (quarter time), about 6 months.

Exhibit 4-A
COMPARATIVE SUMMARY OF DATA PROCESSING COSTS
(250-work-day year; 52-week year)

Job Activity	Frequency			Programming & Testing			Processing & Printing		
	A	B	C	A	B	C	A	B	C
1. Card to tape processing and editing (Purchase order and receiving report cards)	D	W	D	$ 196	$ 196	$ 196	$ 2,250 yr.	$ 1,384 yr.	$ 2,250 yr.
2. Maintain Vendor Master File	D	W	M	220	220	220	1,500	936	216
3. Processing of purchase orders, receiving reports, transaction list	D	W	D	1,060	580	752	21,750	4,680	14,250
(Daily Subtotal)				1,476	996	1,168	25,500 yr.	7,000 yr.	16,716 yr.
4. Processing of weekly purchase order overdue reports (weekly subtotal)	W	W	W	380	380	380	3,744 yr.	3,744 yr.	3,744 yr.
5. Processing of Vendor Catalog	M	M	M	110	110	110	108 yr.	108 yr.	108 yr.
6. Processing of Stock Catalog	M	M	M	130	130	130	216 yr.	216 yr.	216 yr.
7. Processing of Small Business Report	M	M	M	280	280	280	864 yr.	864 yr.	864 yr.
8. Processing of Completed Purchase Order Report	M	M	M	340	340	340	540 yr.	540 yr.	540 yr.
(Monthly Subtotal)				860	860	860	1,728 yr.	1,728 yr.	1,728 yr.
9. Reorganization of Vendor Master File (Semiannual Subtotal)	S	S	S	260	260	260	180 yr.	180 yr.	180 yr.
TOTAL				$2,976	$2,496	$2,668	$31,152 yr.	$12,652 yr.	$22,368 yr.

D—Daily
W—Weekly
M—Monthly
S—Semiannually

II. Recurring Annual Costs:

a. Data Processing Costs	$31,152	$12,652	$22,368
b. IBM Lease Payments ($81 per month for Keypunch)	972[a]		
c. Frieden Lease Payments ($848 per month for Computyper and Flexowriter)		10,176	
d. IBM Lease Payments ($283 per month for IBM 632, Model 3)			3,396
e. IBM Lease Payments ($81 per month for Key punch)			972[b]
f. Paper tape to card conversion (By Data Processing)			1,440[c]
Subtotals	$32,124	$22,828	$28,176

Less:	*A*	*B*	*C*
g. IBM Lease Payments ($380 per month for IBM 632, Model 1)	$ 4,560	$ 4,560	$ 4,560
h. Elimination of 3 positions ($1,000 per month)	12,000	12,000	12,000
Subtotals	$16,560	$16,560	$16,560
Net Recurring Costs	$15,564	$ 6,268	$11,616

[a] Option to keypunch purchase orders and receiving reports ($972) or furnish copies of requisitions or receiving reports to Data Processing for keypunching, $9,750 year ($6.50 hour × 6 hours per day).

[b] Option to keypunch receipts and rejections of shipments ($972 year) or furnish copies to Data Processing for keypunching, $4,000 ($6.50 hour × 4 hours per day).

[c] $4.00 hour × 30 hours month.

Summary of Data Processing Costs

Daily Processing

1. Card to tape processing and editing input cards (purchase orders and receiving reports)
   a. Programming and program testing

(1) Programming labor. 32 hours × $5 per hour	$160.00
(2) Test and assemble (IBM 360-30). .6 hour × $60 per hour	36.00
Total, Alternatives A, B, and C	$196.00

   b. Job run costs

(1) Daily run (IBM 360-30). .15 hour × $60 per hour (Alternatives A and C)	$ 9.00 day
(2) Weekly run (IBM 360-30) (Alternative B)	$ 27.00 week

2. Update vendor master file
   a. Programming and program testing
      (1) Programming labor. 32 hours × $5 per hour $160.00
      (2) Test and assemble (IBM 360-30). 1 hour ×
            $60 per hour   60.00
      Total, Alternatives A, B, and C $220.00
   b. Job run costs
      (1) Daily run, 20 cards per day. .1 hour × $60
            per hour (Alternative A) $ 6.00 day
      (2) Weekly run (Alternative B)   18.00 week
      (2) Weekly run (Alternative C)   18.88 month

3. File maintenance and program generation
   a Programming and program testing
      (1) Programming labor. 140 hours × $5 per
            hour (Alternative A) $700.00
      (2) Programming labor. 80 hours × $5 per
            hour (Alternative B)   400.00
      (3) Programming labor. 100 hours × $5 per
            hour (Alternative C)   500.00
      (4) Test and assemble (IBM 360-50). 2 hours ×
            $180 per hour (Alternative A)   360.00
      (5) Test and assemble. 1 hour × $180.00 per
            hour (Alternative B)   ₁80.00
      (6) Test and assemble. 1.4 hours × $180 per
            hour (Alternative C)   252.00
   b. Job run costs
      (1) Daily run (IBM 360-50). .3 hour × $180 per
            hour (Alternative A) $ 54.00 day
      (2) Weekly run (Alternative B)   90.00 week
      (3) Daily run. .2 hour × $180.00 per hour
            (Alternative C)   36.00 day
   c. Printing costs of receiving reports
      (1) Print 100 receiving reports daily. .2 hour ×
            $60 per hour (Alternatives A and C)   12.00 day
      (2) Alternative B   0
   d. Printing costs of purchase orders
      (1) Print 100 purchase orders daily. .2 hour ×
            $60 per hour (Alternative A)   12.00 day
      (2) Alternatives B and C   0
   e. Printing costs of transaction list
      (1) Print daily transaction list. .15 hour ×
$60 per hour (Alternatives A and C)   9.00 day
      (2) Alternative B   0

4. Summary of daily processing costs
   a. Setup or one-time costs

	A	B	C
	$ 1,020.00	$ 720.00	$ 820.00
	456.00	276.00	348.00
	$ 1,476.00	$ 996.00	$ 1,168.00

   b. Recurring costs

	A	B	C
	$25,500.00 yr.	$7,000.00 yr.	$16,716.00 yr.

Weekly Processing

1. Generate weekly reports
   a. Programming and program testing
      (1) Programming labor. 40 hours × $5 per hour .... $ 200.00
      (2) Test and assemble (IBM 360-50). 1 hour × $180 per hour 180.00
      Total, Alternatives A, B, and C ...... $ 380.00
   b. Job run costs (Alternatives A, B, and C)
      (1) Weekly run. .2 hour × $180 per hour ...... $ 36.00 week
      (2) Print weekly purchase order status report. .2 hour × $60 per hour ...... 12.00 week
      (3) Sort and print weekly purchase orders overdue report
         (a) Sort costs. .1 hour × $180 per hour ...... 18.00 week
         (b) Print costs. .1 hour × $60 per hour ...... 6.00 week
         ...... $ 24.00 week

2. Summary of weekly processing costs
   a. Setup and one-time costs
      (1) Programming labor ...... $ 200.00
      (2) Test and assemble 180.00
      Total, Alternatives A, B, and C ...... $ 380.00
   b. Recurring costs, Alternatives A, B, and C ...... $ 72.00 week

Monthly Processing

1. Vendor Catalog
   a. Programming and program testing
      (1) Programming labor. 16 hours × $5 per hour ...... $ 80.00
      (2) Test and assemble (IBM 360-30). .5 hour × $60 per hour 30.00
      Total, Alternatives A, B, and C ...... $ 110.00
   b. Job run costs, 40 cards. .15 hour × $60 per hour ...... $ 9.00
2. Stock catalog
   a. Programming and program testing

      (1) Programming labor. 20 hours × $5 per
          hour $ 100.00
      (2) Test and assemble (IBM 360-30). .5 hour ×
          $60 per hour   30.00
      Total, Alternatives A, B, and C $ 130.00
  b. Job run costs, 200 cards. .3 hour × $60 per
      hour $ 18.00 month

3. Small business report
  a. Programming and program testing
      (1) Programming. 20 hours × $5 per hour $ 100.00
      (2) Test and assemble (IBM 360-50). 1 hour ×
          $180 per hour)   180.00
      Total, Alternatives A, B, and C $ 280.00
  b. Job run costs
      (1) Short time. .15 hour × $180 per hour $ 27.00
      (2) Run time. .2 hour × $180 per hour   36.00
      (3) Print time. .15 hour × $60 per hour   9.00
      Total, Alternatives A, B, and C $ 72.00

4. Monthly completed purchase order report
  a. Programming and program testing
      (1) Programming. 32 hours × $5 per hour $ 160.00
      (2) Test and assemble (IBM 360-50). 1 hour ×
          180 per hour   180.00
      Total, Alternatives A, B, and C $ 340.00
  b. Job run costs
      (1) Monthly run. .2 hour × $180 per hour $ 36.00
      (2) Print time. .15 hour × $60 per hour   9.00
      Total, Alternatives A, B, and C $ 45.00 month

5. Summary of monthly processing costs
  a. Setup or one-time costs
      (1) Programming labor $ 440.00
      (2) Test and assemble   420.00
      Total, Alternatives A, B, and C $ 860.00
  b. Recurring costs $1,728.00 year

Semiannual Processing
  Reorganize vendor file
    a. Programming and program testing
      (1) Programming labor. 16 hours × $5 per
          hour $ 80.00
      (2) Test and assemble (IBM 360-50). 1 hour ×
          $180 per hour   180.00
    Total, Alternatives A, B, and C $ 260.00
    b. Job run costs
      (1) Semiannual run. .5 hour × $180 per hour $ 90.00
      (2) Print time. .15 hour × $60 per hour   9.00
    Total $ 99.00

Exhibit 4-B

FLOWCHART OF DAILY PURCHASE ORDER DATA PROCESSING

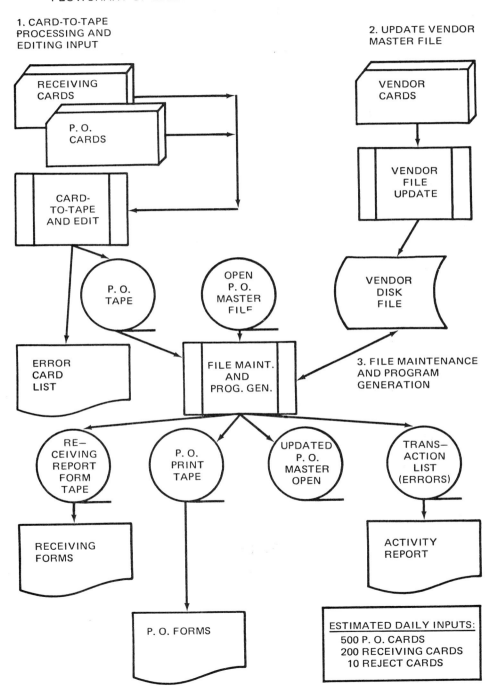

1. CARD-TO-TAPE PROCESSING AND EDITING INPUT

2. UPDATE VENDOR MASTER FILE

RECEIVING CARDS

P. O. CARDS

VENDOR CARDS

CARD-TO-TAPE AND EDIT

VENDOR FILE UPDATE

P. O. TAPE

OPEN P. O. MASTER FILE

VENDOR DISK FILE

ERROR CARD LIST

FILE MAINT. AND PROG. GEN.

3. FILE MAINTENANCE AND PROGRAM GENERATION

RE—CEIVING REPORT FORM TAPE

P. O. PRINT TAPE

UPDATED P. O. MASTER OPEN

TRANS—ACTION LIST (ERRORS)

RECEIVING FORMS

ACTIVITY REPORT

P. O. FORMS

ESTIMATED DAILY INPUTS:
500 P. O. CARDS
200 RECEIVING CARDS
10 REJECT CARDS

Exhibit 4-C
FLOWCHART OF WEEKLY PURCHASE ORDER DATA PROCESSING

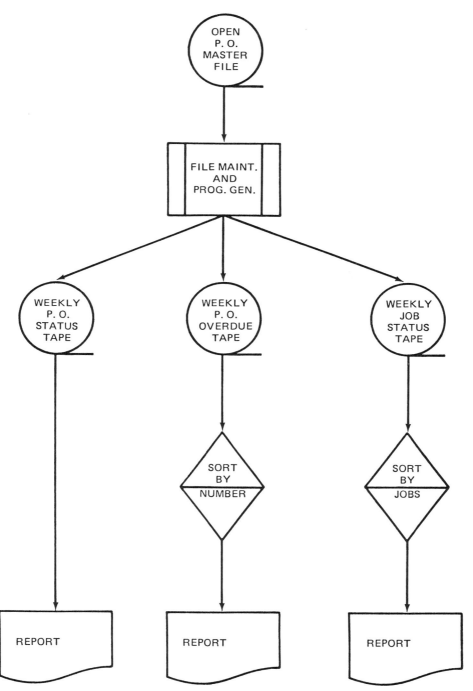

Exhibit 4-D

FLOWCHART OF MONTHLY PURCHASE ORDER DATA PROCESSING

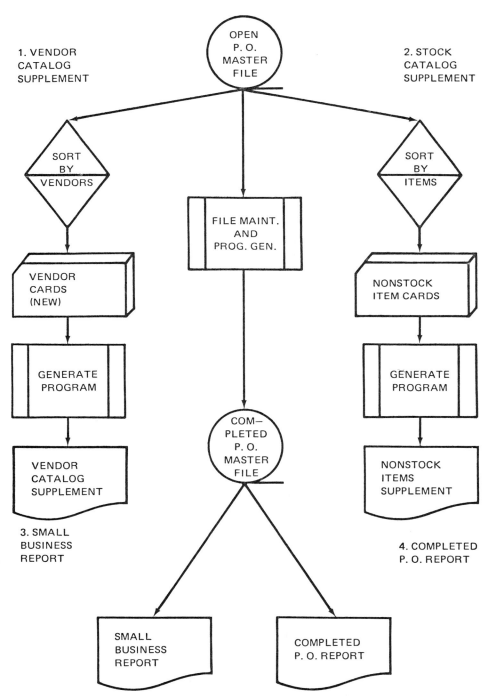

1. VENDOR
CATALOG
SUPPLEMENT

2. STOCK
CATALOG
SUPPLEMENT

OPEN P. O. MASTER FILE

SORT BY VENDORS

SORT BY ITEMS

FILE MAINT. AND PROG. GEN.

VENDOR CARDS (NEW)

NONSTOCK ITEM CARDS

GENERATE PROGRAM

GENERATE PROGRAM

VENDOR CATALOG SUPPLEMENT

COM—PLETED P. O. MASTER FILE

NONSTOCK ITEMS SUPPLEMENT

3. SMALL
BUSINESS
REPORT

4. COMPLETED
P. O. REPORT

SMALL BUSINESS REPORT

COMPLETED P. O. REPORT

Exhibit 4-E
FLOWCHART OF SEMIANNUAL PURCHASE ORDER DATA PROCESSING

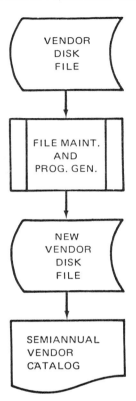

QUESTIONS

1. Comment on the effectiveness of each of the three alternatives relating to the materials planning and control system. Consider the following:
   a. The adequacy of procedures for insuring optimum materials flow.
   b. The adequacy of the proposed reports for effective planning and control of materials acquisition and utilization.
   c. The manner of presentation of the alternatives, i.e., procedures, reports, and file descriptions.
   d. Other types of information you feel would be useful for understanding and evaluating these alternatives.
2. Comment on the usefulness and limitations of the cost breakdowns, formats of presentation, and level of detail provided relating to presentation of cost data. What other types of data do you feel would be useful for performing a feasibility analysis?

3. Based on the procedural and cost data presented for each alternative, which of the alternatives do you feel is the most optimum? In performing this feasibility analysis, consider at least the following:

   a. Costs of each alternative.

   b. Cost savings and other benefits derived from each alternative.

   c. Cost-benefit measure for each alternative.

ELVO
CORPORATION
(Part C)

Elvo Corporation (Part C) is a follow-up case to Elvo Corporation (Part A). It utilizes the materials and information provided in Part A to describe a more comprehensive and integrated management information system for improving the Elvo Corporation's operations.

The purpose of the case is to become familiar with the complexities involved in designing an integrated MIS for a large business organization. Conceptual issues developed in the case include:

An example of an information system aimed at making the organization a more viable system.

Examples of applications of several systems and information concepts described in Chapters 12 and 13 to an ongoing organization.

The use of computer technology for problem solving as well as data processing.

The questions and assignments at the end of the case provide opportunities for reviewing important concepts presented in the text and evaluating their applications and limitations in a large and complex organizational setting.

This case describes a proposed management information system, submitted by a consulting firm to Elvo Corporation. The primary goal of the information system is to assist in the management of the entire company effort. A formal, automated management information system can be applied effectively to the planning function and the control function. The following paragraphs discuss use of the information system to aid in the planning function, both long range and short range. The development of a computerized simulator to aid in this process is of particular importance. Later paragraphs will describe the information system as applied to the control function. The use of analysis reports to improve management effectiveness in the long run will be emphasized as a desirable complement to control in real time.

THE PLANNING FUNCTION

The planning needs of Elvo are determined by the unique character and problems of the organization. Elvo is characterized by a large number of small jobs. Each of these jobs requires a combined effort from the many responsibility centers. To further complicate the process, the efforts of the individual centers must be phased and coordinated in time. The basic nature of this workload indicates a complex but necessary job of planning on a day-to-day (short-range) basis. The past performance of the company has resulted in tremendous growth. Management desires to continue this rate of growth. This being the case, considerable effort will have to be applied to the orderly planning of facility expansion and personnel training (long-range). The information system to be described in the remainder of this section can be applied effectively to both of these planning problems.

Short-Range Planning

The short-range planning process can be viewed in two phases: analysis and planning required when each job is viewed as an independent entity, and planning required to integrate many jobs simultaneously into the Elvo system. Exhibit 5-A shows the relationship between the two. The role of the information system is quite different in each phase.

The job analysis phase requires considerable creative thinking and interpretation. The function of the information system in this phase is to provide the information required by the planners in support of their creative work. The figure shows the maintenance of supply catalogs and information on standard jobs. The supply catalog enables the material planners to know which parts are being stocked and their costs. Information on standard job lengths is supplied to assist the planners in costing the various manpower tasks.

Exhibit 5-A

SHORT-RANGE PLANNING PROCESS

PHASE	ACTION ITEMS		MIS INPUT
I	SPECIFICATIONS		
Job Analysis	Planned Approach	Materials Requirements	* Stock Catalog Price and Availability * Standard Job Lengths
II Job Integration	Facility Commitment & Scheduling	Materials Ordering & Supply	* Facility Scheduling * Inventory Control

A computer can provide more meaningful support during the job integration phase. The purpose of this phase is to take the plans developed in the analysis phase and assign Elvo's manpower and material resources to insure the job's successful completion. These assignments must be made in view of prior commitments, priorities, available resources and flexibility in schedules. It can be seen that the emphasis here is on memory as to prior resource commitments. Decision rules would be based on the priority system, leading to a relatively uncomplicated process once this priority has been assigned. In a procedure requiring the application of straight-forward decision rules and memory, the computer is of greatest value. The management information system will perform the task of facility scheduling and the control of inventory levels.

The overall flow of information in this planning process is illustrated in Exhibit 5-B. The following paragraphs describe two key aspects of the information system—the facility commitment program and the material control program.

The *facility commitment program* is designed to take the job plans which are developed under the assumption of infinite resources (assuming that all materials and facilities will be available as required) and integrate the job into a system which has already been committed to processing a number of other jobs. Exhibit 5-C shows the basic logic upon which this program is based. The input data must describe for each job the facility required, the length of time estimated, and delivery dates of nonstock parts (A Class). This input data will

Exhibit 5-B

MIS FOR SHORT-RANGE PLANNING

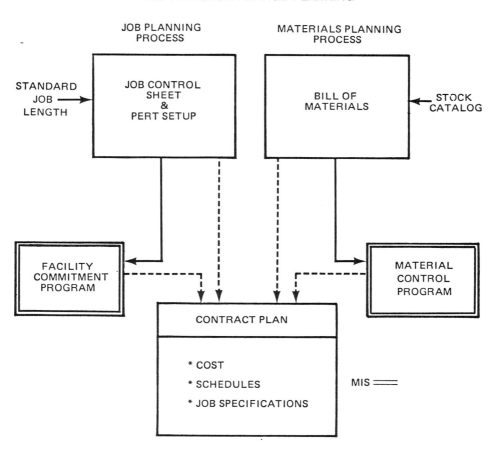

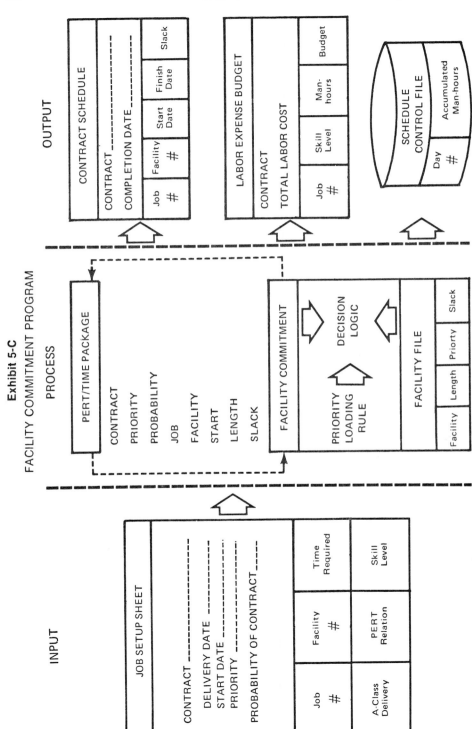

Exhibit 5-C
FACILITY COMMITMENT PROGRAM

constrain job start dates and the sequential relation of a given job to other jobs (PERT relationship). The program itself works in two phases. An initial PERT analysis is performed on the input data to determine the best plan for completing the job on schedule. The results of this analysis are fed into the facility subroutine where the availability of the facilities at the desired time in view of prior commitments is determined. When a conflict arises, a decision must be made as to which job will be performed in the contested time period. Since a PERT analysis has been performed on each job entering the facility subroutine, the amount of slack is known. Therefore, a test is conducted to see if either one of the conflicting jobs can be delayed without effecting the overall contract. If not, the job with the higher priority will take precedence. When a job cannot be fit into the desired time period after its slack has been used, a new critical path will be created and a new PERT analysis must be conducted based upon the new constraints. This cycling procedure continues until a workable schedule is developed. This schedule becomes a key input to the overall project plan. The output is shown in Exhibit 5-C.

The *priority loading rule* bears discussion at this point. In most cases a company has a multilevel priority system developed in coordination with the customer. Such classifications as ROUTINE, RUSH, or URGENT are descriptive of these levels. A need for further classification within each of these levels is still apparent. Generally for jobs of the same priority, a first-in first-out (FIFO) system of scheduling is used. Recent research indicates that such a system is probably the least desirable from a standpoint of overall customer satisfaction. In a study conducted to determine optimum scheduling policies in a job shop, the following results were obtained:

PRIORITY RULE	MEAN TARDINESS
FIFO	36.6 time units
Earliest Scheduled Start Date	24.7 time units
Minimum Slack in Remaining Operations	16.2 time units
Shortest Job First	11.3 time units
Minimum Ratio (Cost of Late/Length of Late)	2.6 time units

A decision by Elvo management to use minimum mean tardiness as a policy for optimizing overall customer satisfaction is recommended. In addition to the schedule, man-hour estimates are multiplied by standard wage rates to develop a project labor budget. This becomes part of the project plan, in addition to serving as future standards for cost accounting. A file is also set up at this point (schedule control file) to store the accumulated authorized man-hours for each day of the job's duration. The use of this information for schedule control will be discussed in a later paragraph.

The *material control program* insures that a specified group of materials (B Class) are available as required so that job delays will be minimized. All items of recurring usage requiring a moderate investment are included in this class.

The intent is to isolate the problem of materials expediting to those items which are special (nonrecurring) or expensive. The expediting of routine items will be eliminated by using the computer to anticipate and plan the need for these materials. Exhibits 5-D and 5-E show the basic logic of the material control program and the policy programs required to feed it. The input comes from the bill of materials which is made up by the materials planners during the RFQ response stage. In this way information concerning potential material usage is captured and used at the earliest possible time. By weighting the RFQ requirements by the probability that the contract will be obtained, a measure of expected requirements over future time periods can be developed. This process is carried out in the material control program where the expected requirements are subtracted from the on-hand levels to anticipate levels in future weeks. These levels are then compared with the corresponding reorder points. When an anticipated level falls below a reorder point, an instruction to initiate a purchase order for this item and the recommended quantity are printed out. The reorder points are updated monthly, reflecting changes in usage rates as well as changes in costs or lead times which would affect the inventory policy.

Long-Range Planning

The need for long-range planning is especially important in an expanding business environment such as Elvo's. This is particularly true when planning the acquisition of resources which require long lead times to develop and install. Expansion must be phased properly with expanding business to forestall either excess or under capacity. An adaptation of the MIS used as a tool in operational planning can assist management in long-range planning. The key element in the information system described thus far is the facility commitment program. In effect, this program acts as a simulator of the various engineering and production units, accepting work up to the limit of the facility and manpower capacity while delaying additional input until in-process work is complete. When used as a scheduling tool for operational planning, the simulator operates upon an actual in-house workload. To serve as a long-range planning tool, the simulator can operate similarly upon a forecasted workload. As shown in Exhibit 5-F this forecast would be supplied quarterly for each product group by Marketing. The facilities and manpower requirements associated with the manufacture of each major product are then added to determine the requirements in each work center in future time periods. (Since Elvo does not produce a standard product, it will be necessary to use probabilistic descriptions of the requirements for similar products types). The simulator could show projections of future facility and manpower requirements compared to capacity, as well as customer waiting times and other similar measures. These analyses enable management to foresee the need for increases in capacity to meet customer demands and reduce delays. The simulator provides an adequate planning horizon for the construction of facilities requiring long lead times.

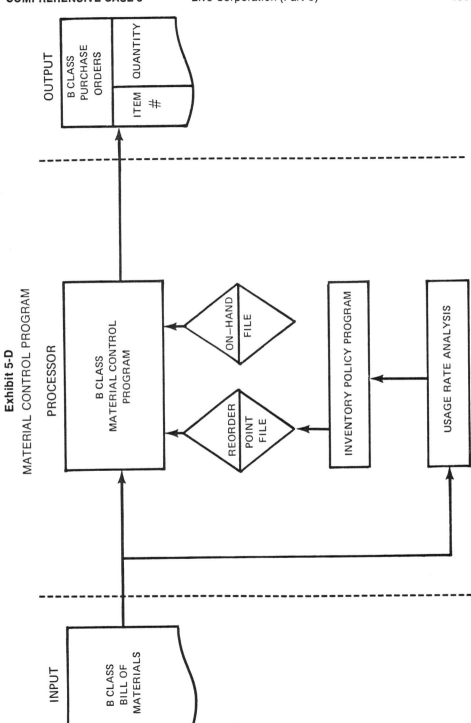

Exhibit 5-D
MATERIAL CONTROL PROGRAM

Exhibit 5-E
INVENTORY PLANNING AND CONTROL SYSTEM

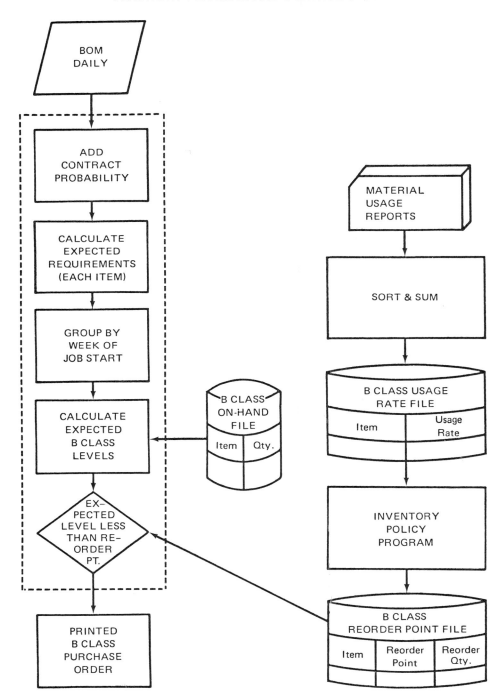

Exhibit 5-F
MIS FOR LONG-RANGE PLANNING

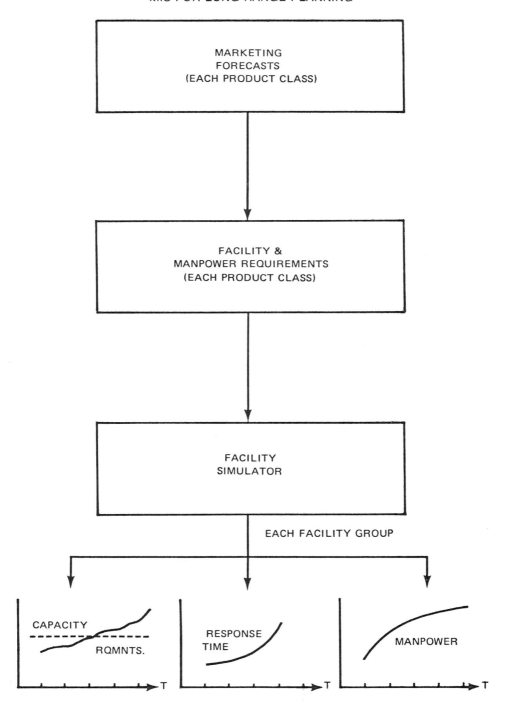

THE CONTROL FUNCTION

The control function uses the guidelines established in the planning phase as standards for each contract. It can be assumed that a job performed to the specifications of this initial plan (allowing for minor changes) will be to the satisfaction of both customer and management alike. The MIS uses these time and cost specifications as standards to which actual performance is controlled in real time. A longer range element of control stems from periodic management analysis reports. Based upon the contents of these reports, management at all levels is expected to analyze its performance over a longer time frame and apply corrective measures for improvement.

Control in real time is taken to mean control in a time frame which is sufficiently short to permit satisfactory corrective action. The length of this time varies with the parameters being controlled. The three parameters which the MIS can aid in controlling are project schedules, project labor cost, and project material cost. Exhibit 5-G shows the source of the standards which will serve as reference points for control of the above. The conventional method of maintaining project control, cost accounting, is felt to be too slow for the Elvo environment. In Exhibit 5-G, two additional devices are introduced to permit control to be exercised over labor and material consumption. The cost accounting system is then delegated the task of bookkeeping at a later date.

The control of labor consumption is based upon the schedule control file. This file is set up by the facility commitment program when the initial schedule is developed. An assumption is made that once a job has begun, time will be expended at a uniform rate over the interval of performance. This is generally a valid assumption when small jobs are defined at the third level in a PERT structure. This being the case, management's prime concern is only with jobs where the rate of labor consumption deviates from the budgeted rate by more than some acceptable amount. Exhibit 5-H illustrates this point. The solid line represents the accumulated authorized man-hours at each day of the job's duration. The bracketed lines on either side enclose an acceptable range of deviation from this standard. As long as consumption stays within this range, labor expenditure can be assumed under control. Deviations outside the limits are signals for management concern. A deviation on the high side indicated a possible overrun on cost. A deviation on the low side indicated possible schedule slips. Exhibit 5-I shows the information flow which enables this control to be exercised.

The control of *material consumption* in real-time is accomplished through the use of a Stockroom Material Control Log. This log, as shown in Exhibit 5-G, lists all items and quantities which are authorized for consumption on a given job through that stockroom. The use of unauthorized materials or excessive use of authorized materials must be coordinated with production control. A material usage form and a material return form are used to make charges through cost accounting as well as to make adjustments to records in inventory levels (on-hand files).

Exhibit 5-G
REAL-TIME CONTROL STANDARDS

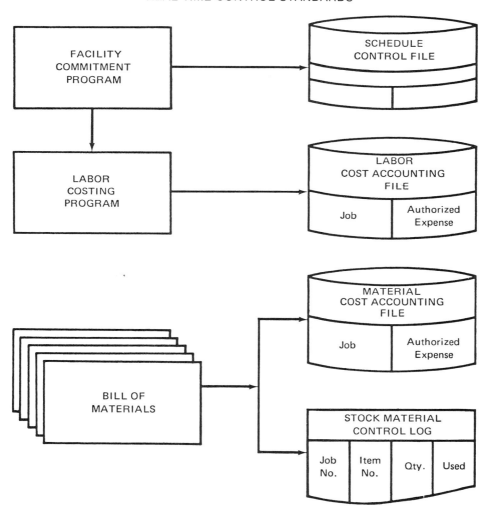

MANAGEMENT ANALYSIS

Management analysis relates to day-to-day routine of individual project planning and control to the larger framework in which a multitude of projects are being simultaneously integrated and processed. Failure to do so gives rise to the common problem of "not seeing the forest for the trees." To help prevent this, periodic management analysis reports portray the overall effectiveness of management in carrying out their responsibilities. These reports view the total product of a responsibility center as a summation of the many projects processed in a time period. The intent is to identify and monitor

Exhibit 5-H

CONTROL OF LABOR CONSUMPTION

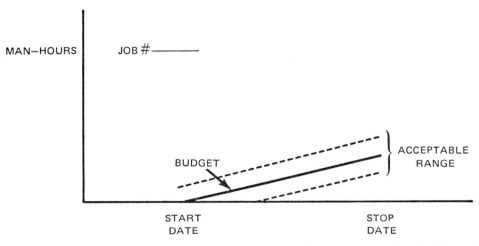

the responses of various parameters which will lead to self-analysis and long-run improvement. Typical examples of these reports are:

Logistics management

Vendor Performance Analysis

Quantitative evaluation of the past performance of each vendor in the areas of timeliness, quality, and cost.

Thru-Time Analysis

Analysis of the processing time and delay time incurred in each logistics unit while processing purchase orders.

Reorder Point Analysis

Periodic review of changing parameters which give rise to changes in inventory policies.

Inventory Status and Transaction Analysis

Periodic review of actual inventory performance versus planned, including stockouts and usage rates.

Production

Machine Load Levels

Analysis of machine utilization rates to evaluate management planning as well as changing equipment requirements.

Thru-Time Analysis

Evaluation of processing time and delay times in all production facilities.

Labor Performance Analysis

Comparison of actual labor expenses to budgeted in each production facility over sufficiently long time spans.

Material Usage Analysis

Comparison of actual material usage to budgeted in each production facility over sufficiently long time spans.

Exhibit 5-I

SCHEDULE AND LABOR CONTROL

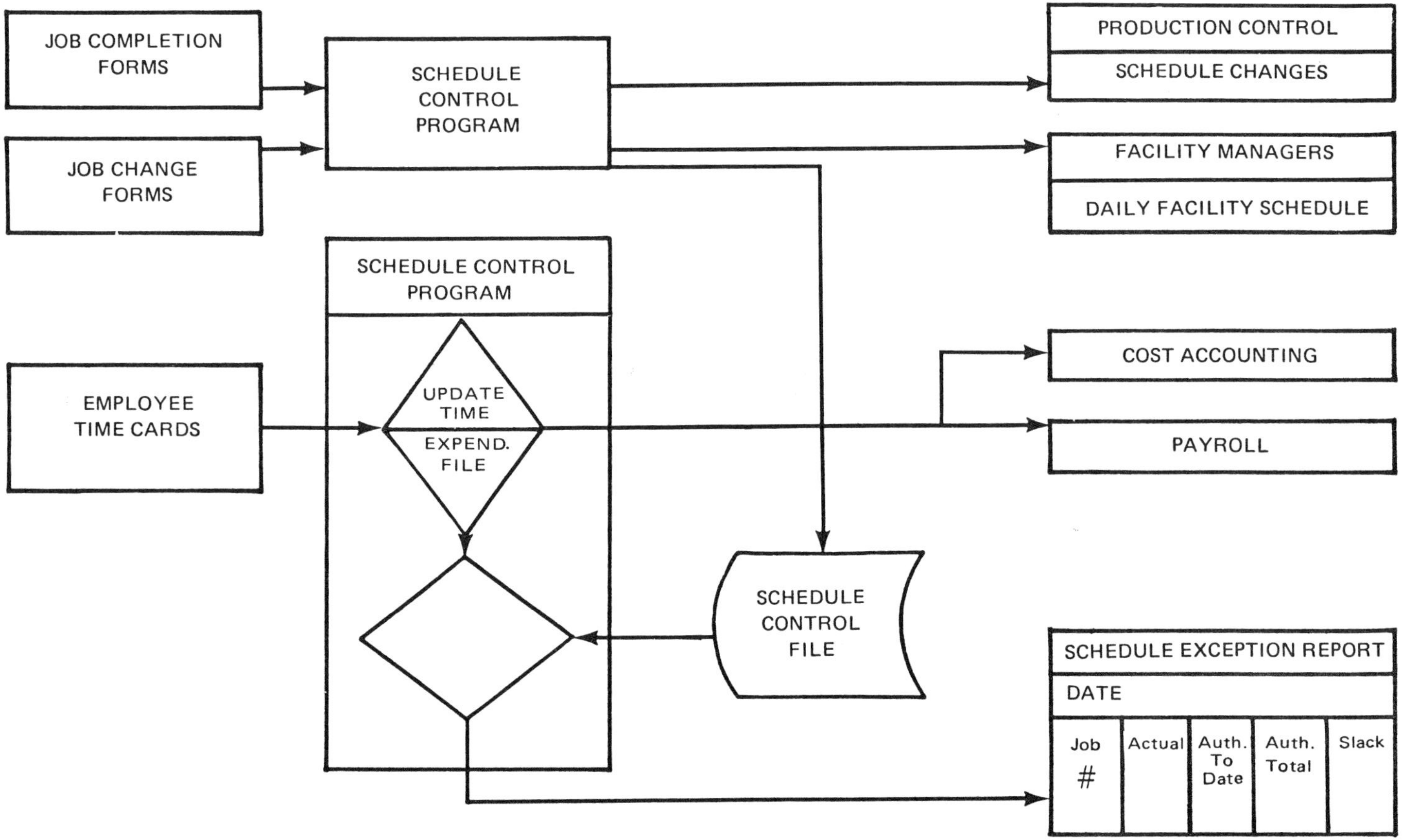

Scheduling Effectiveness
Comparison of actual to scheduled completion dates in production facility.

SUMMARY

The proposed MIS will provide Elvo with an information system that will optimize the planning and control processes and will provide the needed information for effective management analysis. The major characteristics of the MIS are objective-user orientation, integrative design, and viability. Elvo is encouraged to review its potential for resolving its information systems problems.

QUESTIONS

1. Review and evaluate the proposed management information system and comment on:
    a. Its conceptual design and objectives.
    b. Its potential for alleviating the problem of Elvo's existing system.
2. What impact will the management information system have on the organizational structure, and the authority/responsibility assignments of the company.
3. What bearing will the behavioral climate described in Chapter 11 have on the implementation of the proposed MIS (or a similar type of integrated information system) in Elvo Corporation? How would you propose to gain acceptance and support for the MIS?
4. Comment on the use and limitations of concepts from cybernetics, simulation, and PERT as they are included in the proposed MIS.
5. Evaluate the proposed types of management analysis reports identified, and discuss their purpose and usefulness. Relate your discussion to the types of basic information requirements described in Chapters 5, 6, and 7.
6. Comment on and give examples of the use of the computer in the MIS as facilitator of problem solving and as a facilitator of data processing.

Appendix   FLOWCHARTING TECHNIQUES AND EXAMPLES

A central part of systems design methodology is definition and analysis of information needs. A common technique for analyzing the activities and information flows in a work system is flowcharting. Flowcharting has the following characteristics and benefits:

Graphic presentation of the system.
Identification and differentiation of activities, devices, and information.
A clear picture of the sequence of activities and events.
An understanding of the interrelationships between information uses and data sources.
A blueprint for designing information processes.

This appendix is intended to serve as a guide to the types and uses of flowcharting symbols for information system analysis and design. A comprehensive example of flowcharting a personnel information system at a university is presented to illustrate flowcharting techniques and their advantages for defining information flows and designing information processes.

PROGRAM FLOWCHART SYMBOLS

PROCESSING

A GROUP OF PROGRAM INSTRUCTIONS WHICH PERFORM A PROCESSING FUNCTION OF THE PROGRAM.

INPUT/OUTPUT

ANY FUNCTION OF AN INPUT/OUTPUT DEVICE.

CONNECTOR

AN ENTRY FROM OR AN EXIT TO ANOTHER PART OF THE PROGRAM FLOWCHART.

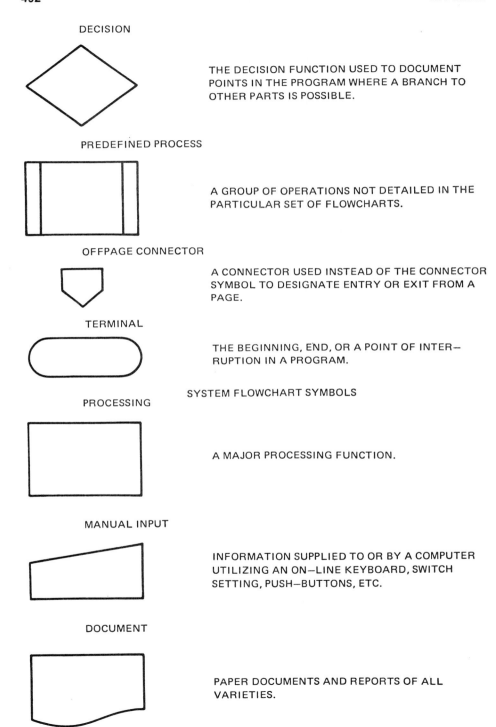

DECISION

THE DECISION FUNCTION USED TO DOCUMENT POINTS IN THE PROGRAM WHERE A BRANCH TO OTHER PARTS IS POSSIBLE.

PREDEFINED PROCESS

A GROUP OF OPERATIONS NOT DETAILED IN THE PARTICULAR SET OF FLOWCHARTS.

OFFPAGE CONNECTOR

A CONNECTOR USED INSTEAD OF THE CONNECTOR SYMBOL TO DESIGNATE ENTRY OR EXIT FROM A PAGE.

TERMINAL

THE BEGINNING, END, OR A POINT OF INTER— RUPTION IN A PROGRAM.

SYSTEM FLOWCHART SYMBOLS

PROCESSING

A MAJOR PROCESSING FUNCTION.

MANUAL INPUT

INFORMATION SUPPLIED TO OR BY A COMPUTER UTILIZING AN ON—LINE KEYBOARD, SWITCH SETTING, PUSH—BUTTONS, ETC.

DOCUMENT

PAPER DOCUMENTS AND REPORTS OF ALL VARIETIES.

ON—LINE STORAGE

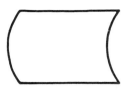

A MAGNETIC DISK OR DRUM DEVICE.

MAGNETIC TAPE

A MAGNETIC TAPE SPOOL OR DEVICE.

PUNCHED TAPE

PAPER OR PLASTIC TAPE.

SORTING

AN OPERATION ON SORTING OR COLLATING
EQUIPMENT.

INPUT/OUTPUT

ANY TYPE OF MEDIUM OR DATA.

PUNCHED CARD

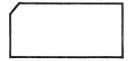

ALL VARIETIES OF PUNCHED CARDS.

AUXILIARY OPERATION

A MECHANICAL OPERATION SUPPLEMENTING THE
MAIN PROCESSING FUNCTION.

MANUAL OPERATION

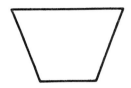

A MANUAL OFF—LINE OPERATION NOT REQUIRING
MECHANICAL AID.

DISPLAY

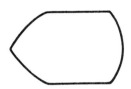

INFORMATION DISPLAY BY PLOTTERS OR VIDEO
DEVICES.

OFF—LINE STORAGE

OFF—LINE STORAGE OF CARDS, MAGNETIC TAPE,
OR PERFORATED TAPE.

COMMUNICATION LINK

THE AUTOMATIC TRANSMISSION OF INFORMATION
FROM ONE LOCATION TO ANOTHER VIA COMMUNI—
CATION LINES.

SUPPLEMENTARY SYMBOL FOR PROGRAM AND SYSTEM FLOWCHARTS

ANNOTATION

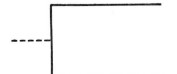

THE ADDITION OF DESCRIPTIVE COMMENTS OR
EXPLANATORY NOTES AS CLARIFICATION.

FLOWCHART OF PERSONNEL INFORMATION SYSTEM

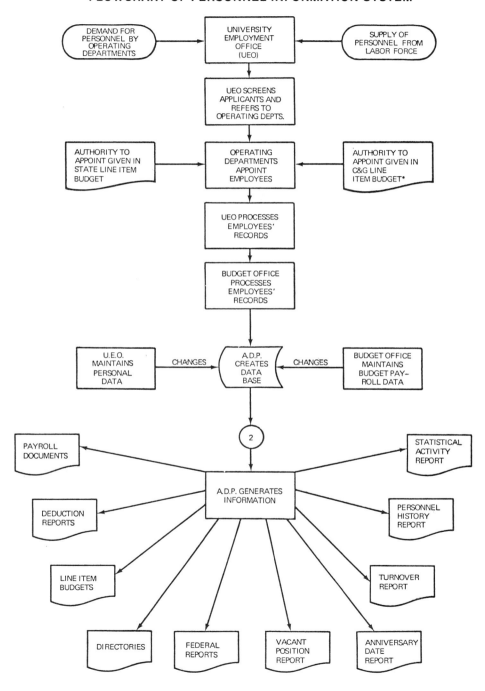

* C&G · CONTRACT AND GRANT

1. APPLICANT SEEKING STAFF POSITION AT F.S.U.

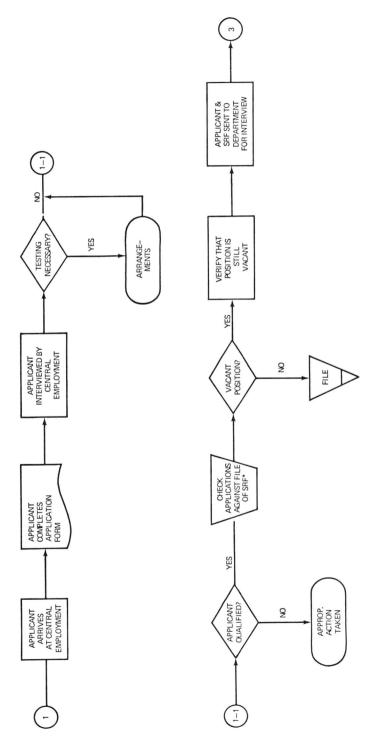

* SRF — STAFF REQUIREMENT FORM

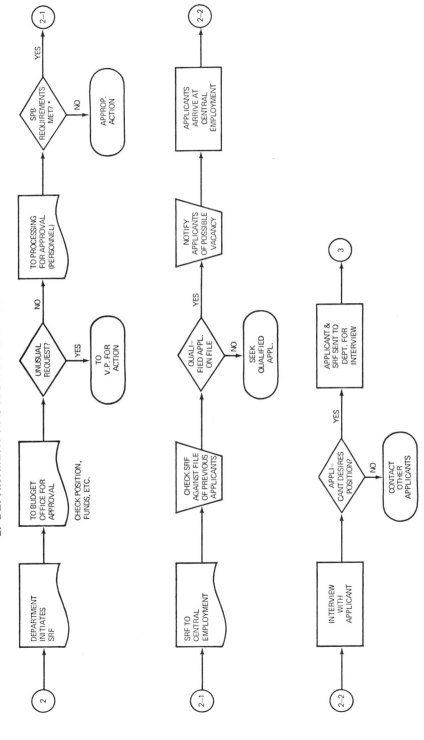

2. DEPARTMENT HAS A STAFF MANPOWER REQUIREMENT

* SPB – STATE PERSONNEL BOARD

3. DEPARTMENT INTERVIEWS STAFF APPLICANTS

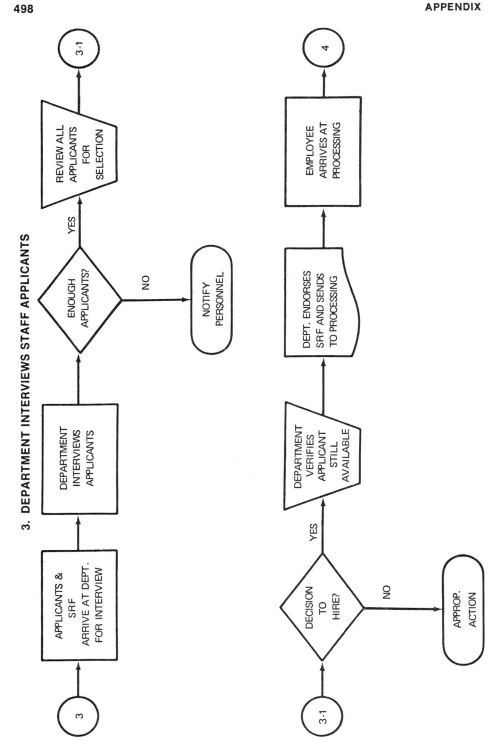

4. EMPLOYMENT PROCEDURES FOR STAFF PERSONNEL

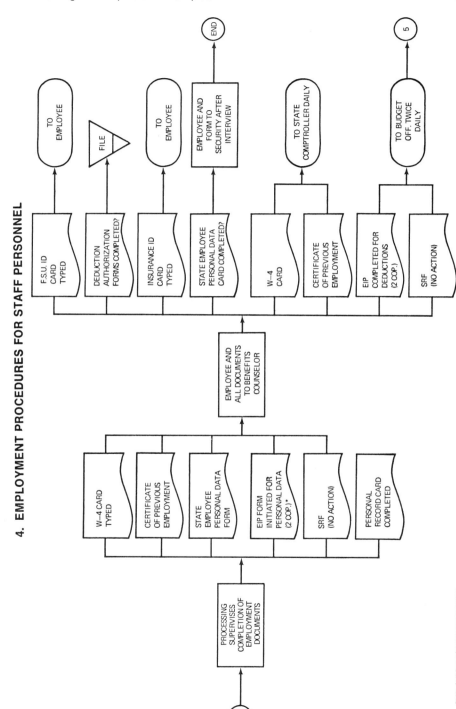

* EIP – EMPLOYEE INFORMATION PROFILE

5. BUDGET EMPLOYMENT PROCEDURE FOR STAFF

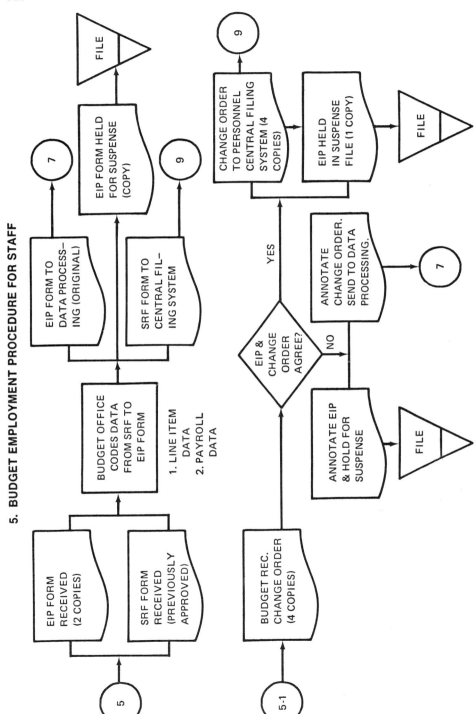

6. BUDGET EMPLOYMENT PROCEDURE

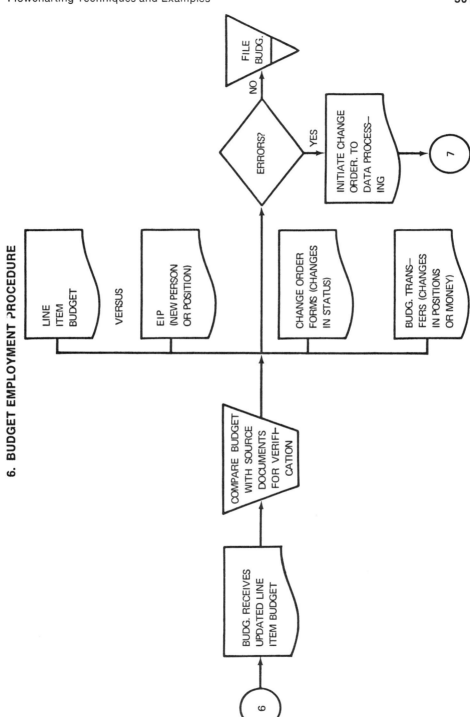

6. BUDGET EMPLOYMENT PROCEDURE (CONTINUED)

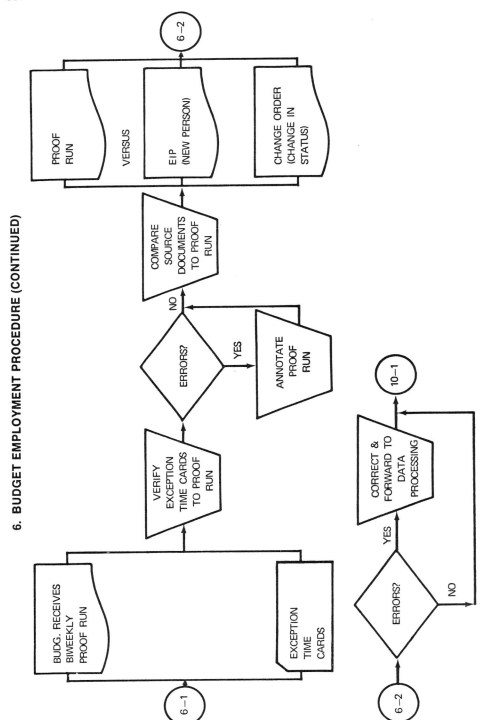

7. CREATION OF DATA BASE

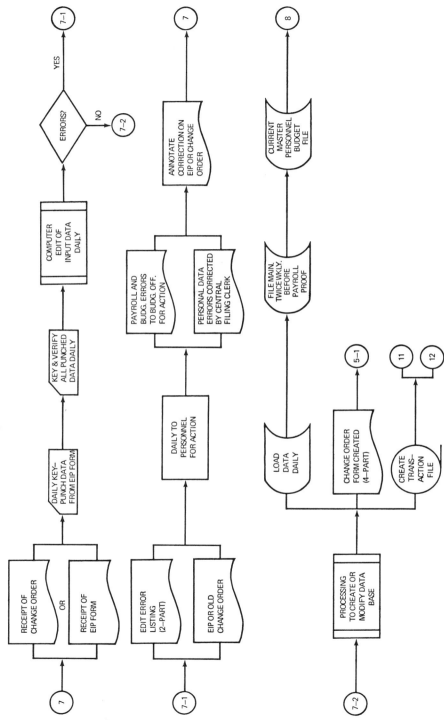

8. MAINTENANCE OF DATA BASE

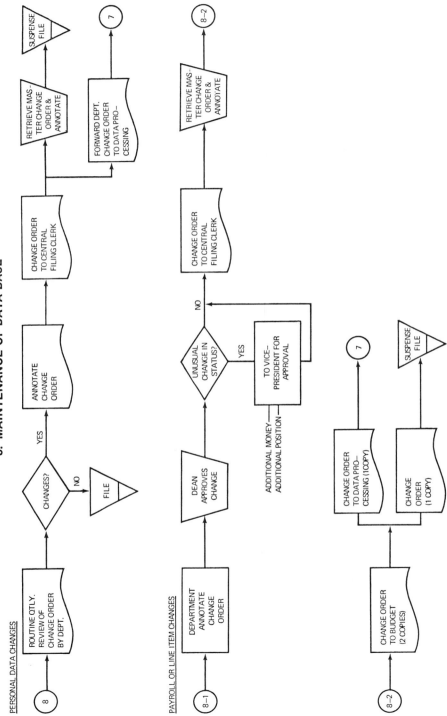

9. CENTRAL FILING SYSTEM

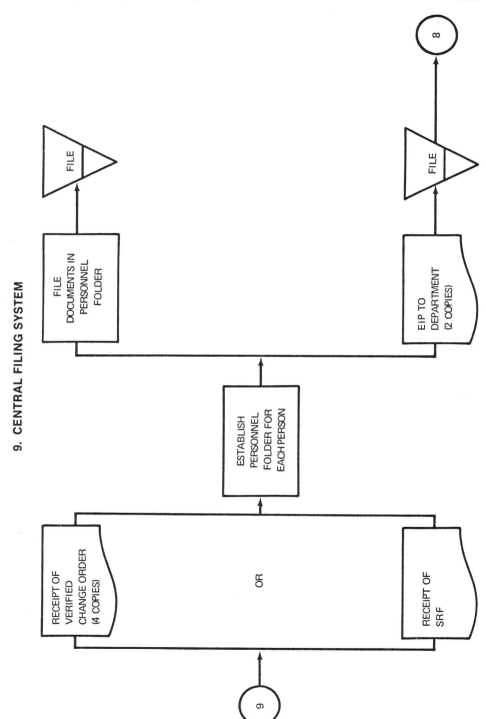

10. OUTPUTS GENERATED BY DATA PROCESSING (BIWEEKLY PAYROLL)

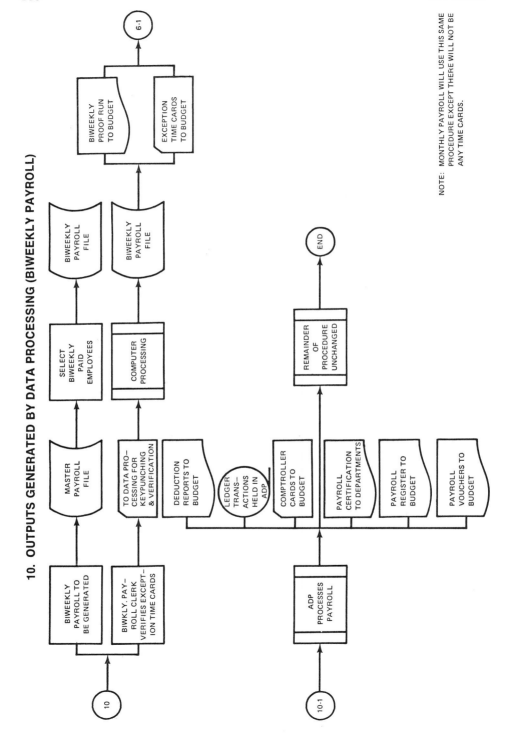

NOTE: MONTHLY PAYROLL WILL USE THIS SAME PROCEDURE EXCEPT THERE WILL NOT BE ANY TIME CARDS.

11. OUTPUTS GENERATED BY DATA PROCESSING

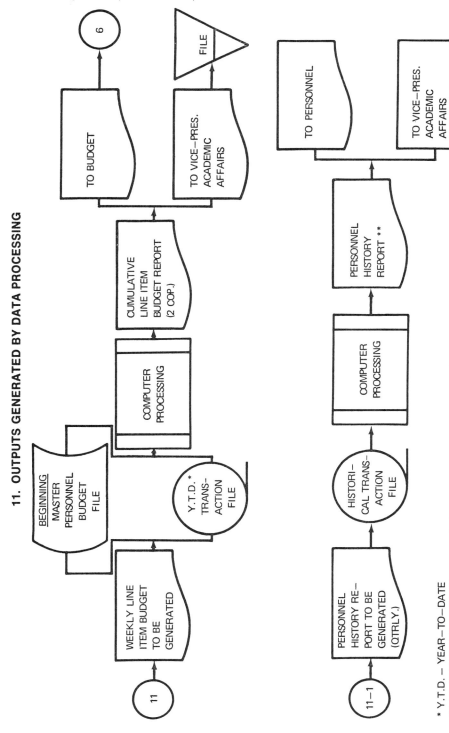

* Y.T.D. – YEAR–TO–DATE
** PRODUCED FOR EACH INDIVIDUAL EXPERIENCING A CHANGE IN STATUS
   DURING THE PREVIOUS QUARTER.

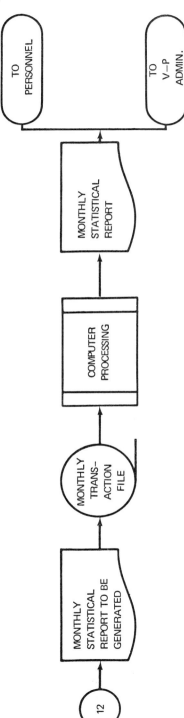

12. OUTPUTS GENERATED BY DATA PROCESSING

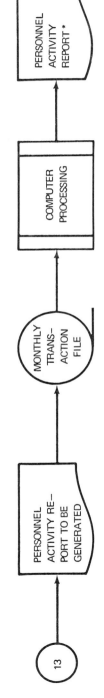

13. OUTPUTS GENERATED BY DATA PROCESSING

* REPORT REVEALS INDIVIDUAL CHANGES IN STATUS FOR UNIVERSITY PERSONNEL.

DISTRIBUTION:

LIBRARY	POSTMASTER
V–P ACADEMIC AFFAIRS	SWITCHBOARD
ADDRESSOGRAPH	INFORMATION SERVICES
GRADUATE SCHOOL	STUDENT GOVERNMENT
INFORMATION DESK	

14. OUTPUTS GENERATED BY DATA PROCESSING

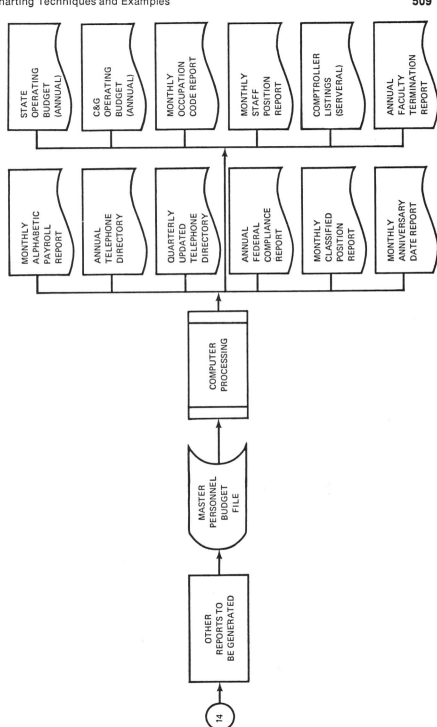

BIBLIOGRAPHY

Part 1

Beckett, John A. *Management Dynamics: The New Synthesis.* New York: McGraw-Hill Book Co., 1971. Illustrates how the systems approach has changed management thinking and practice and provides a framework for understanding systems concepts applied to the management process.

Boore, William F., and G. Murphy. *The Computer Sampler.* New York: McGraw-Hill Book Co., 1968. A readings book concerning management perspectives of the computer in the organization. Problems and issues dealing with the introduction of computers and their applications for operations management.

Buckley, Walter (ed.). *Modern Systems Research for the Behavioral Scientist: A Sourcebook.* Chicago: Aldine Publishing Co., 1968. Contains articles on major developments and recent research applications of systems theory to behavioral science.

Cleland, David I., and William R. King. *Systems, Organizations, Analysis, Management.* New York: McGraw-Hill Book Co., 1969. Readings about the four major areas named in the title. Intended to complement texts in the topical areas which do not emphasize systems concepts.

Drucker, Peter F. *The Age of Discontinuity: Guidelines to Our Changing Society.* New York: Harper & Row, Publishers, 1969. Describes the discontinuities between technology, economics, organizations, and knowledge. Useful for studying information systems relative to changing environment and greater information needs.

Greenwood, William T. *Decision Theory and Information Systems: An Introduction to Management Decision Making.* Cincinnati: South-Western Publishing Co., 1969. Readings merging information systems concepts and decision theory. Covers quantitative model building, computers, and organizational diagnostic techniques.

Litterer, Joseph A. *Organizations.* 2 vols. New York: John Wiley & Sons, 1969. Presents a series of important writings on organizations. Volume 1 deals with two levels of abstraction: structure and the simple steady state. Volume 2 deals with higher levels of abstraction: systems, cybernetics, and open and closed systems.

Schoderbek, Peter P. (ed.). *Management Systems,* 2d ed. New York: John Wiley & Sons, 1971. Readings related to systems theory and related topics: information technology, human problems of systems, cybernetics, computers, models, simulation.

Shrode, William A., and Dan Voich, Jr. *Organization and Management: Basic Systems Concepts.* Homewood, Ill.: Richard D. Irwin, 1974. Presents basic concepts of organization and management in a framework of systems theory. Recent research in management science and behavioral science.

Von Bertalanffy, Ludwig. "General Systems Theory—A Critical Review," *General Systems: The Yearbook of the Society for General Systems Research.* Vol. VII, 1962, pp. 1-20. Reassessment of general systems theory, its foundations, achievements, criticisms, prospects.

Whisler, Thomas L. *Information Technology and Organizational Change.* Belmont, Calif.: Brooks/Cole Publishing Co., 1970. Summarizes the evolution and impact of computer technology on the organization. Describes the problems of transition and change and previews future technological developments.

Part 2

Blumenthal, Sherman S. *Management Information Systems: A Framework for Planning and Development.* Englewood Cliffs, N.J.: Prentice-Hall, 1969. Presents the operational subsystem of an organization and a hierarchy of planning and control responsibilities.

Boguslaw, Robert. *The New Utopians: A Study of System Design and Social Change.* Englewood Cliffs, N.J.: Prentice-Hall, 1968. Examines the systems approach and the methodology of system design by comparing computerized systems design with classical utopian attempts to create perfect systems.

Boutell, Wayne S. *Computer-Oriented Business Systems,* 2d ed. Englewood Cliffs, N.J.: Prentice-Hall, 1973. Presents tools useful for information system analysis and design, including system and program flowcharts and decision tables.

Churchman, C. West. *The Systems Approach.* New York: Dell Publishing Co., 1968. Discusses applications of systems thinking, including program budgeting and management information systems.

Hare, Van Court, Jr. *Systems Analysis: A Diagnostic Approach.* New York: Harcourt, Brace & World, 1967 An introductory systems analysis text. Covers systems definitions, defining and describing systems, systems classifications, control, and simulation.

Hodge, Bartow, and Robert N. Hodgson. *Management and the Computer in Information and Control Systems.* New York: McGraw-Hill Book Co., 1969. The use of the computer in the management control hierarchy.

Johnson, Richard A., F.E. Kast, and J.E. Rosenweig. *The Theory and Management of Systems,* 3d ed. New York: McGraw-Hill Book Co., 1973. Systems concepts relative to management functions. Presents techniques such as network analysis, numerical control, and rhochrematics.

Kepner, Charles H., and Benjamin B. Tregoe. *The Rational Manager.* New York: McGraw-Hill Book Co., 1965. Describes a systematic approach to problem solving and decision making.

Optner, Stanford L. *Systems Analysis for Business Management,* 2d ed. Englewood Cliffs, N.J.: Prentice-Hall, 1968. A concise text which describes the systems approach to business problems, systems concepts, characteristics of computers, and management science techniques.

Seiler, John A. *Systems Analysis in Organizational Behavior.* Homewood, Ill.: Richard D. Irwin, 1967. Analysis of organizational behavior in a system of interdependent forces using the input-output model.

Systems and Procedures Association. *Business Systems.* Cleveland: Systems and Procedures Association, 1966. A methodological presentation of procedures for systems study and analysis. Covers systems function and concepts, fact gathering, flowcharting, work measurement, forms analysis and design, documentation, records management, and office tools.

Van Gigch, John P. *Applied General Systems Theory.* New York: Harper & Row, Publishers, 1974. A methodological treatment of general systems concepts.

Part 3

Albrecht, Leon K. *Organization and Management of Information Processing Systems.* New York: Macmillan Co., 1973. A common sense approach to systems concepts and design.

Alexander, M.J. *Information Systems Analysis.* Chicago: Science Research Associates, 1974. Provides a conceptual framework for applying computer technology to the functional areas of business.

Beishon, John, and Geoff Peters (eds.). *Systems Behavior.* New York: Harper & Row, Publishers, 1972. A collection of papers and articles on the nature and behavior of systems.

Bocchino, William A. *Management Information Systems: Tools and Techniques.* Englewood Cliffs, N.J.: Prentice-Hall, 1972. An introductory text focusing on use of MIS tools and techniques for creating a viable MIS.

Bower, James B., Robert E. Schlosser, and Charles T. Zlatkovich. *Financial Information Systems: Theory and Practice.* Boston: Allyn & Bacon, 1969. Deals with systems theory and practice and reconciles traditional theories of accounting, management, and other business areas with the real business world.

Coleman, Raymond J., and M.J. Riley (eds.). *MIS: Management Dimensions.* San Francisco: Holden-Day, 1973. A collection of recent nontechnical articles about the design and use of management information systems.

Davis, Gordon B. *Management Information Systems: Conceptual Foundations, Structure, and Development.* New York: McGraw-Hill Book Co., 1974. A comprehensive text focusing on MIS development from user and designer perspectives.

Eliason, Alan L., and Kent D. Kitts. *Business Computer Systems and Applications.* Chicago: Science Research Associates, 1974. Describes common computer applications in business, the process of computer system design and components of computer applications.

Kelly, Joseph F. *Computerized Management Information Systems.* New York: Macmillan Co., 1970. Stresses the use of third-generation computers to facilitate improvements in operations, planning, and control.

Lucas, Henry C., Jr. *Computer-Based Information Systems in Organizations.* Chicago: Science Research Associates, 1973. An introductory text about computer applications in information systems.

Mader, Chris, and Rober Hagin. *Information Systems: Technology, Economics, Applications.* Chicago: Science Research Associates, 1974. An introductory book concerning information system technology and applications in an economic and organizational environment.

Mockler, Robert J. *Information Systems for Management.* Columbus: Charles E. Merrill Publishing Co., 1974. Intended to help practioners and managers to work effectively with systems technicians in MIS development.

Part 4

Carrithers, Wallace M., and Ernest H. Weinwurm. *Business Information and Accounting Systems.* Columbus: Charles E. Merrill Publishing Co., 1967. Discusses the use of coding techniques to facilitate communication, classification, and recording of data and information.

Elliott, C. Orville, and Robert S. Wasley. *Business Information Processing Systems,* 3d ed. Homewood, Ill.: Richard D. Irwin, 1971. An introduction to the use of information processing systems in business, with emphasis on computer hardware and software.

Emery, James C. *Organizational Planning and Control Systems: Theory and Technology.* New York: Macmillan Co., 1969. Discusses activities and problems associated with data collection, classification, indexing, compression, and storage. Presents guidelines for developing the data base and for storing and retrieving data.

Flores, Ivan. *Data Structure and Management.* Englewood Cliffs, N.J.: Prentice-Hall, 1970. An analytical book examining ways data can be organized, relationships among data segments, and input-output devices and software.

Joslin, Edward O. (ed.). *An Introduction to Computer Systems.* Arlington: College Readings, 1969.

_____. *Management and Computer Systems.* Arlington: College Readings, 1970.

_____. *Software for Computer Systems.* Arlington: College Readings, 1970. A three-part readings series with current articles on background, applications, and technology of computers; planning for computer use; control, organization and staffing; benefits of computers; and computer software.

Kindred, Alton R. *Data Systems and Management.* Englewood Cliffs, N.J.: Prentice-Hall, 1973. An intermediate information systems book focusing on the nature, organization, and application of computer systems.

Li, David H. *Design and Management of Information Systems.* Chicago: Science Research Associates, 1972. An introductory book on information systems analysis and design, which focuses on the systems function.

Massey, L. Daniel, and John Heptonstall. *EDP Feasibility Analysis.* Morristown, N.J.: D. H. Mark Publications, 1968. Concerned with evaluating how computers process data to support storing and analyzing functions of information in business.

_____. *Management Information Systems.* Morristown, N.J.: D.H. Mark Publications, 1969. A condensed description of the MIS concept with detailed description of routine and demand reports.

_____. *Managing the Human Element in EDP.* Morristown, N.J.: D.H. Mark Publications, 1969. Discusses the internal management of the EDP facility, the relationship of the EDP facility to other areas, and the role of management as users of output from the EDP facility.

Orlicky, Joseph A. *The Successful Computer System.* New York: McGraw-Hill Book Co., 1969. Describes the planning, development, and management of a computer system in a business.

Prince, Thomas R. *Information Systems for Management Planning and Control,* rev. ed. Homewood, Ill.: Richard D. Irwin, 1970. Contains material dealing with the analysis and design of management information systems. Primary emphasis on financial information systems.

Randall, Clarence B., and Sally Weimer Burgly. *Systems and Procedures for Business Data Processing,* 2d ed. Cincinnati: South-Western Publishing Co., 1968. Describes methods of coding and condensing data for the development of the data bank. Includes guidelines for constructing a coding scheme and a detailed example of a coding scheme.

Sanders, Donald H. *Computers in Business,* 2d ed. New York: McGraw-Hill Book Co.,
  1972. An introduction to the fuctions and characteristics of the stored computer
  program and the impact of computers on management.

Part 5

Beer, Stafford. *Cybernetics and Management.* New York: John Wiley & Sons, 1959.
  An introduction to cybernetics for the student of management. Includes material on
  the black box, feedback, and purposiveness.

Cherry, Colin. *On Human Communication: A Review, A Survey, and A Criticism,* 2d
  ed. Cambridge: M.I.T. Press, 1968. A series of essays on topics related to
  communication. Includes an extensive bibliography.

Forrester, Jay W. *Industrial Dynamics.* Cambridge: M.I.T. Press, 1961. Discusses the
  nature of dynamic information-feedback systems and describes the methodology of
  industrial dynamics for modeling and experimenting.

_____. *Urban Dynamics.* Cambridge: M.I.T. Press, 1969. Presents an
  application of industrial dynamics in modeling an urban system.

_____. *World Dynamics.* Cambridge: Wright-Allen Press, 1971. Presents a
  simulation model of the world. Results of experiments with the model show that
  there are real limits to growth of the world system.

Gallager, Rober G. *Information Theory and Reliable Communication.* New York: John
  Wiley & Sons, 1968. A text in information theory which treats information theory
  as a mathematical-statistical branch of communication theory.

Gordon, Geoffrey. *System Simulation.* Englewood Cliffs, N.J.: Prentice-Hall, 1969.
  Written by the originator of GPSS, this book is a highly functional treatment of
  system simulation and its applications to management, engineering, and the sciences.

Hinrichs, Harley, and Graeme M. Taylor. *Program Budgeting and Benefit Cost
  Analysis: Cases, Text, and Readings.* Pacific Palisades, Calif.: Goodyear
  Publishing Co., 1969. Contains a number of interdisciplinary articles and cases
  about applications of PPBS and cost-benefit analysis in various areas of the federal
  government.

Levin, Richard I., and Charles A. Kirkpatrick. *Planning and Control With
  PERT/CPM.* New York: McGraw-Hill Book Co., 1966. An introduction to the
  methodology and application of PERT and CPM for project planning and control.

Novick, David (ed.), *Program Budgeting: Program Analysis and the Federal Budget,*
  2d ed. Cambridge: Harvard University Press, 1967. Readings concerning the principles and applications of program budgeting. Describes the decision-making process in government and the role of budgeting in governmental activity.

Shannon, Claude E., and Warren Weaver (eds.). *The Mathematical Theory of
  Communication.* Urbana: University of Illinois Press, 1949. Readings pertaining
  to the mathematical and statistical theory of communication. Describes
  communication models and communication networks.

Thayer, Lee O. *Administrative Communication.* Homewood, Ill.: Richard D. Irwin,
  1964. An introductory text focusing primarily on the meaning and effectiveness of
  communication in organizations.

Wiener, Norbert. *Cybernetics.* New York: John Wiley & Sons, 1949. Describes
  Wiener's original, now classic, work in cybernetics pertaining to communication
  and control in animals and machines.

INDEX